D1285271

McGraw-Hill Higher Education

A Division of The **McGraw-Hill** *Companies*

HARMONY IN CONTEXT
Published by McGraw-Hill, an imprint of The McGraw-Hill Companies, Inc. 1221 Avenue of the Americas, New York, NY, 10020. Copyright © 2003, by The McGraw-Hill Companies, Inc. All rights reserved. No part of this publication may be reproduced or distributed in any form or by any means, or stored in a database or retrieval system, without the prior written consent of The McGraw-Hill Companies, Inc., including, but not limited to, in any network or other electronic storage or transmission, or broadcast for distance learning. Some ancillaries, including electronic and print components, may not be available to customers outside the United States.

This book is printed on acid-free paper.

2 3 4 5 6 7 8 9 0 DOC/DOC 0 9 8 7 6 5 4 3 2

ISBN 0-69-735487-3

Editorial director: *Phillip A. Butcher*
Executive sponsoring editor: *Christopher Freitag*
Developmental editor: *Nadia Bidwell*
Project manager: *Scott Scheidt*
Lead production supervisor: *Heather D. Burbridge*
Media producer: *Todd Vaccaro*
Coordinator of freelance design: *Mary Kazak*
Supplement associate: *Kate Boylan*
Cover design: *VP Graphic Design*
Cover artwork: *Vicente Pascual.* Circles/Cycles LIX, *mixed media on paper 2000*
Interior design: *Jamie O'Neil*
Typeface: *10/12 Times Roman*
Compositor: *UG / GGS Information Services, Inc.*
Printer: *R. R. Donnelley & Sons Company*

Library of Congress Cataloging-in-Publication Data

Roig-Francolí, Miguel A., 1953-
      Harmony in context / Miguel A. Roig-Francolí.
         p. cm.
      Includes index.
      ISBN 0-697-35487-3 (alk. paper)
      1. Harmony. 2. Music theory.
   MT50 .R689 2003
      781.2'5—dc21   2001044135

www.mhhe.com

Miguel A. Roig-F.

College-Conservatory oj

University of Cinc.

Harmony *harmony* in Context

Boston   Burr Ridge, IL   Dubuque, IA   Madison, WI   New York   San Francisco   St. Louis
Bangkok   Bogotá   Caracas   Kuala Lumpur   Lisbon   London   Madrid   Mexico City
Milan   Montreal   New Delhi   Santiago   Seoul   Singapore   Sydney   Taipei   Toronto

Dedication

To my wife, Jennifer, and my sons,
Gabriel and Rafael.
And to the memory of my father.

*"Tell me, and I may forget.
Show me, and I may remember.
Involve me, and I will learn."*
Anonymous Pedagogue

Contents

Preface

This textbook strives to strike a balance between a variety of pedagogical and theoretical approaches to teaching music theory. The following are the basic principles that govern its style:

1. This is an essentially complete harmony and analysis textbook. It is meant to be used by undergraduate music majors, and it covers all of the tonal harmony usually studied in undergraduate theory core curricula over a period of three or four semesters in the freshman and sophomore years. Music fundamentals are summarized and reviewed in the introductory chapters. Because harmony exists only in the context of musical form, form and formal processes are studied throughout the book, both in discussions of specific pieces within chapters dealing with harmonic topics and in chapters devoted to the main formal types and genres in part 2. Twentieth-century post-tonal art music, on the other hand, is not covered in this text, and it is assumed that it will be studied in one or more different courses at the end of the harmony sequence, using appropriate materials.

2. The "context" to which the title refers is not only the formal context of harmony. The book also includes frequent references to the metric and rhythmic contexts of harmony, as well as to its historical and stylistic contexts, and to the relationships between drama, text, and harmony in vocal music. Also taken into consideration is the *professional context of the music student.* Students are encouraged and guided throughout the book to understand the relevance of what they are studying here (harmony, musical processes, form) to the better understanding of the music they listen to and perform daily. And they are constantly encouraged to translate this better understanding of processes, tonal direction, harmonic and formal function, and so on, into *better performances and better listening,* thus providing a true context for "theoretical" work.

3. Good, logical organization, clarity of exposition, and easy-to-use format are primary considerations. The style of presentation is concise and efficient, although in general the outline format has been avoided: Explanations are necessary and pedagogically desirable, and so are analytical discussions of pieces.

   Teaching the student how to think analytically about music and how to make connections between analytical thought and performance decisions has been a major concern in this book. A "Socratic" pedagogical approach has often been used for this purpose. By asking questions on examples, rather than providing answers, I have tried to involve the reader in an active process of inquiry and discovery as a learning tool.

4. The contents are thorough, with equal attention devoted to all significant areas and concepts of tonal harmony, including a detailed coverage of late-Romantic chromatic harmony. The book is aimed at providing both craft in written harmony and the techniques of voice leading, and good understanding of harmonic processes as found in actual music. Chords throughout the book are not presented as isolated vertical units, but rather as *functional* components within larger musical segments, which at the same time also result from horizontal or *linear* processes. These

functional and linear processes are themselves studied in their role as form-generating structures within the context of long-range tonal designs. Besides numerous examples from the literature included in each chapter, a musical anthology is also provided in the second part of the accompanying workbook. Recordings for most of the musical examples from the literature included in the book, workbook, and anthology are provided on a separate compact disc set.

5. Women and minority composers are broadly represented in both the book's musical examples and the anthology. The jazz, musical theater, pop, and rock repertoires are also amply represented by approximately fifty examples of either actual music or, in a few cases, cited titles.

6. Ignoring the pedagogical musical value of such basic Schenkerian concepts as harmonic prolongation, passing and neighbor chords, or long-range harmonic direction, leads to a vision of harmony in no way up-to-date with our understanding of musical structure and harmonic processes. Although extensive reductive graphs or any full-scale exposition of Schenkerian theory will not be found in this book, I have incorporated a number of Schenkerian concepts and techniques in a pedagogical way. Theory teachers who have not had extensive training in Schenker will not have any difficulty understanding or applying these concepts, even though they may choose not to stress them. Here again, I have strived to find a balance between an approach that requires full commitment to Schenker on the part of the instructor, and one that ignores the major contribution of Schenkerian theory to our understanding of tonal harmony.

The introductory chapters provide a review of fundamentals and introductions to both musical style and species counterpoint (acknowledging the fact that many instructors like to teach pedagogical counterpoint either during or at the beginning of harmony curricula). After that, the book is structured in two parts: part 1, "Diatonic Harmony," and part 2, "Chromatic Harmony and Form." Part 1 begins with elementary definitions and voice-leading guidelines, and covers each of the diatonic triads and seventh chords separately and progressively. Other major topics studied in this first part are harmonic function (including prolongation as a function), texture, cadences, phrase structure and melodic organization, nonchord tones, harmonic rhythm, and hypermeter. Part 1 closes with an appendix in which the essential concepts of diatonic harmony are summarized and placed in musical context.

Part 2 includes secondary dominants, modulation to closely related keys, borrowed chords, the Neapolitan sixth, augmented sixth chords, altered triads, extended tertian chords, and a thorough study of modulation to distant keys. Binary and ternary forms are fully discussed in the context of modulation to closely related keys, with emphasis on long-range harmonic design. Two more chapters on contrapuntal genres and larger formal types cover the study of chorale preludes, inventions, fugues, sonata form, and rondo. In chapter 28, the essential concepts of chromatic harmony are summarized and reviewed, now in the context of the German Romantic *Lied*. Chapters 29 and 30 are devoted to the study of late nineteenth-century chromatic and linear harmony, as well as to early twentieth-century music featuring nonfunctional pitch centricity.

Chapters include clear expositions of harmonic function, voice-leading guidelines, and study of standard progressions for the specific chord or technique discussed. The pedagogical stress regarding chord progressions is on standard, normative *harmonic and voice-leading patterns.* To emphasize this approach further, chapters include a section of *melodic pitch patterns* (in which harmonies and chord connections are linearized as an aural exercise) and a section of *keyboard progressions* (located in the corresponding workbook chapters). Students are encouraged to discover and discuss the practical application of the harmonic concepts studied in each chapter in sections entitled "Practical Application and Discussion." The importance of these sections, which will help students make the connection between what they study in theory class and their performance experience, cannot be sufficiently emphasized. More detailed and in-depth analytical applications of the topic under study can be found in sections entitled "Further Analysis." A list of "Terms for Review" at the end of each chapter provides a taxonomical summary of the chapter's contents.

Exercises and musical examples for analysis are included in a worksheet following each chapter, which instructors may wish to use for in-class practice. The accompanying workbook provides a second set of exercises to be used as assignments, plus the anthology. Students are required to realize a variety of tasks, including analysis, four-voice chorale-style exercises, melody harmonization (beginning in chapter 4), writing their own progressions, and writing keyboard harmonizations (both beginning in chapter 11). It should be noted that, up to chapter 10, exercise types in the workbook parallel those in the worksheets. Beginning with chapter 11, however, the types of exercise found in the corresponding worksheet and workbook sets will not necessarily be exactly parallel. This allows for greater exercise variety (if a type of exercise appears in a particular worksheet, a different type is occasionally requested in the corresponding workbook set, rather than repeating all the same types already featured in the worksheet), given the diversity of exercise types that have been introduced by chapter 11. Answers to the analytical questions in both the worksheets and workbook, as well as sample realizations for most of the harmony exercises, can be found in a separate instructor's manual.

Finally, in sections entitled "Composers and Their Music," students are requested to write short biographies of newly introduced composers and to listen to well-known, representative compositions by composers mentioned in each chapter. This serves to familiarize them with the historical and musical context of the appropriate period, as well as to build knowledge and appreciation not only of frequently performed repertoire, but also of less broadly known music by numerous composers, including minority and women composers. An added advantage of the biographical assignments is that they will give students a chance to practice and improve their essay-writing skills, and to apply them to a musical topic.

Far from adopting any kind of dogmatic stance with respect to music theory instruction, this book results from a flexible and eclectic acceptance of different pedagogical and theoretical approaches. Moreover, the author has sought to provide the richest possible musical context for the study of harmony. A result of this broad and inclusive vision of "music theory" and "harmony" is that some of the components in this book may be covered elsewhere in a particular institution's curriculum. When that is the case, and if time is a factor (as it often is), particular instructors or theory programs may choose not to use some of the pedagogical tools provided in the book, and by doing so they will not cause any detriment to its other pedagogical aspects. The following are some of the book components that fall into this category:

1. *The introduction to species counterpoint.* Some programs include the study of counterpoint after harmony, as an upper-level course.

2. *Musical styles, and the biographies/listening assignments.* Some instructors may feel confident that these topics are amply covered in music history courses.

3. *Pitch patterns and keyboard progressions.* These components could just as well be covered in aural skills courses running parallel to the corresponding theory courses.

4. *Schenkerian graphs.* Although a number of Schenkerian concepts are ingrained in the pedagogy developed in this book, reductive graphs constitute only a small portion of discussions and assignments, and can very easily be omitted should an instructor choose to do so.

5. *Form.* Basic formal concepts such as phrase and period structure are central to the study of harmony. The study of small forms in association with modulation (chapter 20) is also highly recommended. Chapters 21, the second part of 22, and 26, on the other hand, are mostly meant for programs that integrate the study of large forms within the study of harmony. In some theory programs, however, large forms and contrapuntal genres are studied in a separate course toward the end of the theory sequence (perhaps using one of the available textbooks focusing exclusively on form). Instructors who follow the latter type of curriculum may simply wish to skip chapters 21, second half of 22, and 26 fully or partially. Doing so will cause no detriment to the study of harmony as found in adjacent chapters.

Miguel A. Roig-Francolí

College-Conservatory of Music
University of Cincinnati

A Message to the Student

WHY DO WE STUDY MUSIC THEORY?

When we perform or listen to music, we are dealing with an artistic expression that unquestionably reaches us emotionally. Musical composition and performance (as well as listening), however, are not only emotional—no more than we, as humans, are made up *only* of emotions. There is also an intellectual, rational aspect to music. Music is a means of expression, a language (albeit an abstract one), that functions according to a system and a set of principles and conventions. We can immediately tell a Mozart sonata from an Indian rāga or a piece for Japanese shakuhachi because the languages they use are different.

We all would agree that, when actors recite, say, Shakespeare, their knowledge of English vocabulary, grammar, and syntax is a great asset to their understanding and rendition of the structure, rhythm, and form of what they are reciting. Similarly, our knowledge of normative English allows us to enjoy the beauty and idiosyncrasies of Shakespeare's expression.

Musical performance is made up of at least three essential components. The technical component is achieved by hours of practice. The instinctive, emotional aspect (which we usually call "musicality") is part of what we know as "talent," and is partially innate, and partially acquired by listening to good music, having a good teacher, or playing with good musicians. Finally, many musical decisions are intellectual or rational. Such decisions require information and understanding. Our study of the musical language provides this understanding, as well as many criteria to evaluate or appreciate more fully the beauty of specific works. The better we understand the normative, conventional syntax of musical discourse, the better we can enjoy, both as performers or listeners, the styles of specific composers, or the richness of their particular musical idioms.

This understanding of the musical system is provided by the study of music theory in its many branches (such as harmony, counterpoint, form, and analytical techniques). Many of the things we will learn in the book have a direct bearing on both performance and listening. We will learn that a chord or set of chords creates a tension, and why it does so; that this tension may or may not be resolved, that the resolution may be delayed, avoided, prolonged; that some chords do not have a structural entity, but rather act as "harmonic ornaments," or simply prolong other chords that do have a structural role; and that these, and many other harmonic forces, generate larger expressive units such as phrases, periods, sections, and whole compositions.

A good composer knows the musical language, and composition is as rational as it is emotional; besides following their instinct and "inspiration," composers plan and realize the shape and structure of their musical works by means of intellectual processes. All of it is directly relevant to performance and to listening, at least if their full potential is to be achieved. The beauty of understanding, provided by music theory, is a rewarding complement to the emotional experiences afforded by music making.

Acknowledgments

Among the many individuals whose direct or indirect contributions have been instrumental to the completion of this book, I would first like to acknowledge two groups of persons: my teachers and my students. Some of my teachers who deserve special recognition are Miguel A. Coria (with whom I first studied harmony and counterpoint in my native Spain); my counterpoint teachers at Indiana University, Lewis Rowell and the late Douglass Green (to whom I am especially indebted for many of the ideas behind the design of chapter D); and Mary Wennerstrom, with whom I studied (and from whom I learned a great deal about) music theory pedagogy. A special token of recognition goes to David Neumeyer and Marianne Kielian–Gilbert, under whose supervision I first taught written theory, as a graduate assistant, at Indiana University. Many of their ideas, methodologies, and musical examples are still reflected in my own teaching and certainly in this book.

The book has grown out of years of teaching undergraduate theory at Indiana, Ithaca College, and Northern Illinois University. I am grateful to my students at these institutions, as well as to my counterpoint and music theory pedagogy students at the Eastman School of Music. I have learned a lot from all of them, and without them this book would never have been written. (Although I moved to the University of Cincinnati when the book was in its very final stages, my numerous students at this institution's College-Conservatory of Music should not go unacknowledged).

The musical examples were copied on Finale by Patrick Long (and, in the early chapters, by Rufus Brown). I am grateful to both of them, and also to the three institutions that provided generous grants to defray copying costs: Northern Illinois University, the College-Conservatory of Music at the University of Cincinnati, and, very especially, the Eastman School of Music (I particularly thank two Eastman directors, Robert Freeman and James Undercofler, for their support in this important matter). Five University of Cincinnati graduate students helped me proofread the voluminous collection of musical examples and exercises: Deborah Calvano, James DeFiglia, Joseph Hupchick, Erin Lafferty, and Carl Serpa.

Walter Everett made a substantial contribution to the book by providing all the musical examples from the jazz, musical theater, popular song, and rock repertoires. My colleagues Roger Freitas, Ralph Locke, and Gretchen Wheelock, members of the Eastman musicology faculty, provided many useful suggestions for chapter G. Many good ideas and suggestions offered by the reviewers of earlier drafts were incorporated into the final version of the text. These reviewers include Claire Boge, Miami University; Richard Brooks, Nassau Community College; Walter Everett, University of Michigan; Joseph Kraus, University of Nebraska; Eric McKee, Pennsylvania State University; Paul Paccione, Western Illinois University; Edward Pearsall, The University of Texas at Austin; Penelope Peters, Oberlin Conservatory; Gary Potter, Indiana University; Elizabeth Sayrs, Kenyon College; and Judith Solomon, Texas Christian University.

I am grateful to my editors Chris Freitag, JoElaine Retzler, and Nadia Bidwell from McGraw-Hill, as well as to the book's project manager (Scott Scheidt) and copy editor (Gretlyn Cline), for their encouragement and support and for their numerous

ideas and suggestions. Encouragement, support, and patience are also gifts I have received in abundance from my wife, Jennifer. I thank her not only for these intangible gifts, but also for the many hours she has invested word processing and editing large parts of the manuscript. Moreover, many ideas she has offered, as an experienced performer, on ways to make connections between theory and performance have been incorporated into the book.

To all of them go my acknowledgments and sincere gratitude.

Harmony

harmony in Context

INTRODUCTION

*The Fundamentals
of Music*

Chapter A

Pitch: Notation and Intervals

Unlike music in other cultures, the Western tonal music tradition has been built largely on notated sound, at least before the advent of such twentieth-century styles as jazz and rock. The notational system we use, developed throughout the Middle Ages and the Renaissance, is based on a variety of symbols and conventions that regulate the notation of pitch and rhythm. These symbols allow us to write on paper, and then to read, any musical sounds or combinations of sounds, as well as their relative durations, and the groupings that result from these durations. In this chapter we will review the basic principles for the notation of pitch in Western music.

THE NOTATION OF PITCH

The Notes

The fundamental, standard Western collection of notes is made up of seven pitches. When ordered from lowest to highest or highest to lowest, such a collection is called a **scale**. If a scale contains only the seven basic, unaltered pitches, we call it a **diatonic scale**. In English, we use seven letters (**letter names**) to refer to the seven pitches of a diatonic scale: C–D–E–F–G–A–B–C. Notice that after the seventh pitch, B, the first pitch, C, appears again. Because this C is eight notes away from the original C, we say that it is (or it sounds) an *octave higher*. The same seven notes recur in the form of different octaves, as you can easily see in example A.1.

The upper part of this example shows the location of the notes on a keyboard. Note that the same seven notes appear in several different octaves. Although the letters used in each octave are the same, we also use numbers to indicate which octave a pitch belongs to. In this system, the pitch we usually call **middle C** is C4. All the pitches in this octave, from C to B, may carry the suffix 4, as in F4, A4, or B4. The octaves above this **middle octave** are indicated by the **numerical suffixes** 5 to 8, whereas the octaves below it carry the suffixes 3, 2, and 1, respectively.

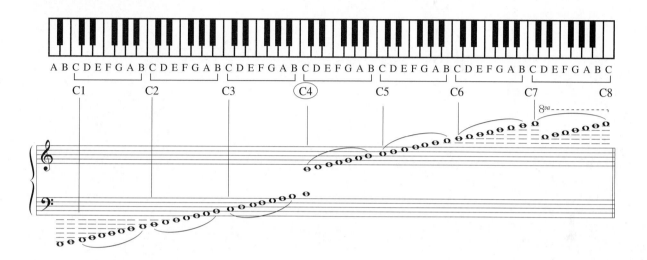

🎵🎵🎵Example A.1

The Staff

We notate pitches by means of note heads on a **staff**. A staff consists of five **lines**. For the time being, our note heads will be white notes. We can write a note on each of the five lines, or in each of the four **spaces** between the lines. We can also extend the staff by adding additional lines, which we call **ledger lines**. Example A.2 shows pitches notated on lines, in spaces, and with ledger lines.

Clefs are used to indicate which letter names correspond with each of the lines and spaces in the staff. Although there are many possible clefs, we will illustrate here only the four clefs most commonly found in modern scores: the **treble**, **bass**, **alto**, and **tenor clefs**. The treble clef is a **G clef**; that is, it shows where the pitch G is notated. The bass clef is an **F clef**, and both the alto and tenor clefs are **C clefs**. Example A.3a shows each of these clefs and the pitch each of them indicates. Example A.3b shows the notation of middle C with each of these clefs. By using clefs, we can avoid writing too many ledger lines (which make for cumbersome notation). This is illustrated in example A.3c, where the same scale is notated first with a single clef and then with

🎵🎵🎵Example A.2

Example A.3

several clefs. In modern scores, the viola is mostly written in alto clef, and the cello, bassoon, and trombone use mostly bass and tenor clefs. Clefs, moreover, are useful for transposition, as we will discuss in chapter C. For these reasons, and to help you become familiar with at least the four basic clefs, we will use all of them in worksheet and workbook exercises for the introductory chapters on music fundamentals.

In the lower part of example A.1 you can see what we call a **grand staff**, in which two staves are connected by a brace. The bass clef is used in the lower staff, and the treble clef is used in the upper staff. The grand staff allows us to notate the complete range of the keyboard, with the help, of course, of ledger lines above and below it.

EXERCISE

To practice identifying and notating pitches in various clefs, refer to exercise A.1 in worksheet A at the end of this chapter.

INTERVALS

Half Steps, Whole Steps, and Accidentals

Look at the keyboard in example A.1 and observe the following points:

1. Although the diatonic scale contains only seven different notes (the white keys of the keyboard), there are twelve different keys if you also count black keys.

2. The modern Western tuning system **(equal temperament)** divides the octave into twelve equal parts. The resulting twelve-note scale is called the **chromatic scale**.

3. The distance between two adjacent pitches in the chromatic scale is called a **half step** or **semitone**. The half step is the smallest distance between two different pitches in the standard Western tuning system.

4. Going back to the diatonic scale (the white keys), you can see that some adjacent pitches are related by half step (E–F and B–C), while the rest of them are at the distance of two half steps (C–D, D–E, F–G, G–A, and A–B). In each of the latter, there is a black key between each of the dyads (a **dyad** is a pair of pitches). The distance of two half steps between two pitches is called a **whole step** or a **whole tone**.

Although there are twelve different pitches in the chromatic scale, we use only seven different letters to designate notes. In order to notate the remaining five pitches (the black keys) we use symbols known as **accidentals**. Accidentals (which always *precede* the affected note) raise or lower a note in the following ways:

1. A **sharp** symbol (♯) raises a note by a half step.

2. A **flat** symbol (♭) lowers a note by a half step.

3. A **natural** symbol (♮) cancels out any previous accidental.

4. A **double sharp** symbol (𝄪) raises a note by a whole step.

5. A **double flat** symbol (♭♭) lowers a note by a whole step.

We can easily observe that any of the twelve pitches can be notated in different ways using accidentals. To begin with the most obvious, each of the notes represented by black keys can be spelled as a sharp or as a flat note. The pitch between C and D, for instance, is both C♯ and D♭. White-key notes, however, can also be notated by means of accidentals: D is the same pitch as C𝄪, C is the same as D♭♭, F is the same as E♯, and so forth. Notes that are spelled differently but sound the same, such as C♯ and D♭, are said to be *enharmonic*. Example A.4a shows the two possible spellings (the **enharmonic spellings**) for each of the black-key notes in the chromatic scale. In practice, however, we use only one of the spellings at a time.

♪♪♪ Example A.4

Which one we use is determined by the harmonic and musical context, as we will study throughout this book. As a general melodic principle, however, sharps are used in ascending passages and flats in descending passages. Examples A.4b and c illustrate an ascending chromatic scale using sharps, and a descending chromatic scale using flats.

A result of enharmonic spellings is that we can notate a half step in different ways. A half step spelled using different letter names, as in C–D♭, is called a **diatonic half step**, whereas the same half step, spelled using the same letter name, C–C♯, is a **chromatic half step**.

Types of Intervals

An **interval** is the distance between two pitches. If the two pitches sound simultaneously, the interval is **harmonic**. If the pitches sound successively, the interval is **melodic**. The right hand (upper staff) in measures (mm.) 5–7 of example A.5 is eminently melodic, and its intervals are heard horizontally, or melodically. The left hand (lower staff), on the other hand, presents a succession of vertical, or harmonic, intervals. Are the intervals in each hand in mm. 8–10 harmonic or melodic?

To label intervals we use two terms. The second term denotes the **size of the interval**: second, third, fourth, and so on. (2nd, 3rd, 4th, etc., will be used to indicate the interval size.) The first term describes the **quality of the interval** (perfect, major or minor, and augmented or diminished). Thus, we speak of a minor 2nd, a perfect 4th, a major 6th, and so forth.

Intervals can be **ascending** or **descending**. The same note names, C and F for example, may be used to denote two different intervals: the ascending distance between C and F (C–D–E–F) is not the same as the descending distance between C and F (C–B–A–G–F).

To determine the size of an interval, count the number of notes between the two pitches, including both pitches in your count. Thus, an ascending C–F is a 4th (four notes, C–D–E–F); an ascending E–C is a 6th (E–F–G–A–B–C); a descending C–F is a 5th (C–B–A–G–F); and a descending A–G is a 2nd (A–G).

♪♪♪ Example A.5   Paul Hindemith, Interlude, from *Ludus Tonalis*, mm. 5–10

Example A.6

Perfect Intervals

The modifier **perfect**, used to indicate the quality of certain intervals, refers to the pure and essential sound of these intervals. The only perfect intervals are the perfect unison (abbreviated PU), the perfect 4th (P4), the perfect 5th (P5), and the perfect 8ve (P8). Examples of each of these intervals, starting from C, appear in example A.6.

1. The *perfect unison* or perfect prime (PU) is the interval formed by any pitch and itself (C–C, D–D, E♭–E♭, F♯–F♯, etc.). The *P8,* on the other hand, is formed between a pitch and its octave projection, as in C4–C5, D2–D3, and so forth.

2. The *P4* is made up of five half steps. You should learn *by memory* all the possible P4s built from diatonic (white-key) pitches. In ascending form, these are C–F, D–G, E–A, F–B♭, G–C, A–D, B–E. You can see that the only "glitch" in the system is the P4 from F, which requires an accidental (B♭). The interval F–B♮ is not a P4, because it contains six, and not five, half steps. If we want a P4 with B♮ as the upper pitch, then we need an F♯: F♯–B♮.

3. The *P5* is made up of seven half steps. The ascending P5s from white keys are C–G, D–A, E–B, F–C, G–D, A–E, and B–F♯. Here again, the only "glitch" also involves the notes B and F. Seven half steps up from B take us to F♯. If we want a P5 with F♮ as the upper pitch, we need a B♭: B♭–F♮.

4. How about spelling P4s and P5s from pitches other than white keys? Leaving aside the P4s and P5s involving the notes B and F, an accidental applied to any of the pitches in the P4s and P5s listed above automatically requires the same accidental for the other pitch. For instance, in the P4 category, you will have C♯–F♯, D♭–G♭, E♭–A♭, and so on. And in the P5s, you will end up with C♯–G♯, D♯–A♯, E♭–B♭, and so on. Examples A.6b and c illustrate the application of accidentals to P4s and P5s; example A.6d shows the P4s and P5s involving the notes B and F.

Measures 1–6 of example A.7 are exclusively made up of perfect intervals. Identify and label all of them. Then, identify and label the perfect intervals in mm. 7–12.

EXERCISE

To practice writing perfect intervals, refer to Exercise A.2 in worksheet A at the end of this chapter.

♪♪♪ Example A.7   Fritz Kreisler, "Praeludium and Allegro," for Violin and Piano, mm. 1–12

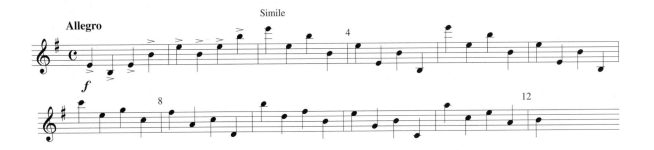

Major and Minor Intervals

Refer to the chromatic scale in example A.4a. If you try to build a 3rd up from C, you will probably think first of the pitches C–E. That is indeed a 3rd. The pitches C–E♭, however, also form a 3rd. There are several intervals that allow for two possible standard forms, one smaller and one larger in size. These intervals are the 2nd, 3rd, 6th, and 7th. In each of these cases, the larger interval is called **major** (abbreviated M), and the smaller interval is called **minor** (abbreviated m). In all cases, the difference between major and minor is a half step (major is a half step larger than minor). Examples of each of these intervals presented in ascending form from C appear in example A.8.

1. *M and m 2nds.* We have already discussed these intervals as the whole tone and the semitone (whole step and half step). The M2 contains two semitones, and the m2, the smallest possible interval in our system other than the unison, is made up of a single semitone.

2. *M and m 3rds.* The m3 contains three semitones, and the M3 four. As we will study in chapter E, these intervals are the basic building blocks for triads (three-note chords). The lower interval in a major triad (C–E–G) is a M3 (C–E), whereas the lower interval in a minor triad (C–E♭–G) is a m3 (C–E♭).

♪♪♪ Example A.8

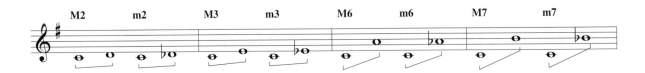

3. *M and m 6ths*. The easiest way to figure out these intervals is by referring them to a P5. A M6 (C–A) is a whole step larger than a P5 (C–G), and a m6 (C–A♭) is only a half step larger than a P5.

4. *M and m 7ths*. Here again, it is easier to figure out these intervals with reference to the P8. The M7 (C–B) is only a half step smaller than the P8 (C–C), whereas the m7 (C–B♭) is a whole step smaller than the P8.

The following passages will allow you to practice the recognition and labeling of 3rds (example A.9a), 3rds and 6ths (example A.9b), and 2nds and 7ths (example A.9c). For further practice, identify and label all the nonperfect intervals in example A.7.

| ♪♪♪Example A.9a | Johann Sebastian Bach, Prelude no. 6 in Dm, from *The Well-Tempered Clavier,* I, mm. 1–6 |

♪♪♪ Example A.9b   Frédéric Chopin, Étude in CM, op. 10, no. 7, mm. 2–5

♪♪♪ Example A.9c   Richard Wagner, Prelude to *Tristan und Isolde*, mm. 18–28

EXERCISE

To practice writing M and m intervals, refer to exercise A.3 in worksheet A at the end of this chapter.

Augmented and Diminished Intervals

In example A.9b you may have noticed some intervals that do not fit our perfect/major/minor definitions. In measure 4, for instance, the fifth dyad in the right hand, E♭–A, is a 4th (from E to A there are four notes), but it contains six half steps. It is one half step larger than the P4. The ninth dyad, E♭–F♯, is a 2nd (two notes from E to F), but its three half steps make it one half step larger than the M2. In measure 2, on the other hand, the eleventh dyad (D–A♭) is a 5th, but its size is only six half

♪♪♪ Example A.10

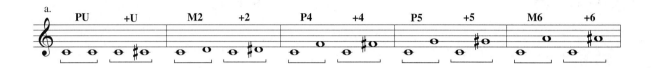

steps, one half step smaller than the P5. These are all **augmented** or **diminished** intervals.

1. An augmented interval (abbreviated +) is a half step larger than the corresponding P or M interval. Although any interval can be augmented, the most frequent among these intervals are the +2 (three half steps) and the +4 (six half steps). The +6 is also a prominent interval in chromatic harmony, and so is the +5. Example A.10a shows some augmented intervals, along with the P or M intervals from which each of them is derived.

2. A diminished interval (abbreviated °) is a half step smaller than the corresponding P or m interval. The diminished intervals most frequently found in music are the °5 and the °7. Some diminished intervals, along with the P or m intervals they are derived from, appear in example A.10b.

Because the +4 consists of three whole tones (C–D–E–F♯), it is often called a **tritone** (a term which is sometimes also used, inaccurately, to refer to the °5). The tritone appears in the diatonic scale between F and B (see example A.9b, m. 3, third dyad). We have already discussed that in order to spell a P4 or a P5 involving the pitches F and B we need some accidental. The reason is that, with no accidental, F–B is an +4, and B–F a °5.

Notice also that, although sometimes augmented or diminished intervals can be spelled enharmonically as perfect, major, or minor intervals, the two groups of intervals have very different musical functions. In isolation, for instance, an +2 (A♭–B) may sound like a m3 (G♯–B), but in a musical context these are two very different intervals. Sing or play, as an example, the two interesting non-Western scales in example A.11, both of which feature +2s, and you will appreciate the characteristic melodic color of the +2 as opposed to the m3. In Western music, however, the +2 is considered awkward melodically, an interval usually to be avoided.

♪♪♪Example A.11

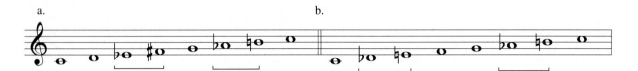

 EXERCISES

To practice writing augmented and diminished intervals, refer to exercise A.4 in worksheet A at the end of this chapter. To practice enharmonic spellings of intervals, refer to exercise A.7 in worksheet A at the end of this chapter. To practice writing and identifying all intervals, refer to exercises A.5, A.6, A.11, and A.12 in worksheet A at the end of this chapter.

Compound Intervals

All the intervals we have seen so far are no larger than an octave (**simple intervals**). Intervals larger than an octave are called **compound intervals**. Musically, a compound interval results from the addition of a simple interval plus an octave. Numerically, however, the size of a compound interval results from the formula: simple interval + 8 − 1 (or simple interval + 7). In other words, a compound second will be a 9th (2 + 8 − 1 = 9), a compound third will be a 10th (3 + 8 − 1 = 10). Very often we reduce compound intervals to their simple equivalents mentally, and we speak of "a minor 3rd" when what is written is really "a minor 10th." Jazz musicians, however, are very familiar with a type of chord that uses compound interval terminology, and which we will study later in this book (see chapter 27): ninth, eleventh, and thirteenth chords. The simple/compound equivalences are as follows:

2nd → 9th

3rd → 10th

4th → 11th

5th → 12th

6th → 13th

7th → 14th

8ve → 15th

 EXERCISE

To practice identifying compound intervals, refer to exercise A.8 in worksheet A at the end of this chapter.

Interval Inversion

You may already have observed that two different intervals are possible with any two pitches: C–F is a 4th and F–C is a 5th (both ascending). A 4th plus a 5th equals an octave (C–F–C, ascending). These intervals are the **inversion** of each other.

1. To invert an interval, place the lower pitch an octave above, over the higher pitch. Or place the higher pitch an octave below, under the lower pitch.

2. Two intervals related by inversion add up to an octave. Numerically, they add up to nine. All the intervallic inversions by size are presented in the following table:

   U   → 8ve (8 + 1 = 9)   8ve → U

   2nd → 7th (2 + 7 = 9)   7th → 2nd

   3rd → 6th (3 + 6 = 9)   6th → 3rd

   4th → 5th (4 + 5 = 9)   5th → 4th

3. When you invert an interval, the intervallic quality also inverts in the following way:

   P inverts into P

   M inverts into m

   m inverts into M

   + inverts into °

   ° inverts into +

Example A.12 presents a summary of intervallic inversions as explained above.

Example A.12

EXERCISE

To practice writing intervallic inversions, refer to exercise A.9 in worksheet A at the end of this chapter.

THE OVERTONE SERIES

Sound is produced by mechanical vibration of an object or sounding body (such as a string, a metal bar, a reed, the vocal chords or the lips, a piece of wood, a drum head, or an air column). Moreover, sound is transmitted by vibrational motion (sound waves)

♪♪♪ Example A.13

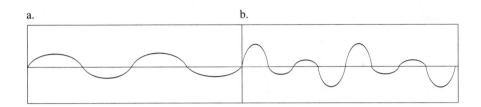

a.   b.

through a medium such as air, water, or a solid material. Wave shapes may be simple, as in Example A.13a, and then they produce what we know as a **pure tone** or also **sine tone**. Pure tones, such as the sound produced by a tuning fork, are unusual in a musical setting. Most often musical sounds are **complex tones**, and their wave forms are more complicated than the simple sine wave represented in example A.13a. An example of a more complex wave shape appears in example A.13b.

Complex tones are actually made up of several pure tones that are combined. The different components that make up a complex tone are known as **partials**, **harmonics**, or **overtones**. When we strike a key on a piano, for instance, we hear a complex tone made up of the actual pitch we played plus a variety of partials or harmonics that sound above it and simultaneously with it. The pitch we actually played is known as **fundamental** because it is the lowest tone in the complex of partials. The rest of the tones that make up the complex (the overtones) sound above the fundamental. Although the fundamental is the pitch we really perceive clearly, a complex tone actually consists of a blend of a fundamental and overtones. The complete set of overtones produced by a given pitch is known as the **overtone series**. Example A.14 shows the overtone series for the pitch C2 (the fundamental in this case), up to the sixteenth partial (the series continues, but the higher the partial, the weaker its acoustical effect). Notice that

♪♪♪ Example A.14

Fundamental

partials are numbered beginning with the fundamental (partial no. 1). Partials nos. 7, 11, 13, and 14 are only represented by an approximate notated pitch (their actual sound is "out of tune" with the notated pitch).

From a musical point of view, the overtone series is significant in various ways. In the first place, the sound produced by different instruments stresses different combinations of partials within the overtone series. These different combinations produce the different timbres of instruments. **Timbre** is the tone quality or tone color that distinguishes one instrument from another. From a different perspective, the order of intervals as they appear in the overtone series is also significant in several ways, as we will discuss in the following section.

CONSONANT AND DISSONANT INTERVALS

The concepts of intervallic consonance and dissonance are largely determined by cultural and historical contexts and will vary depending not only on the world culture under consideration, but also within Western music on such factors as geographic location or historical period. Our present discussion of these intervallic categories will be based on criteria that apply, at least in a general way, to Western music roughly from the fifteenth century to the late nineteenth century.

Intervals are **consonant** if they produce a sense of stability. **Dissonant** intervals, on the other hand, create a sense of tension or instability, which we normally perceive as a clash that requires resolution to a consonance. The consonant intervals are the unison, the 8ve, and all the intervals found in major and minor triads, along with their inversions: P5, M3, m3, m6, M6, and P4 (see example A.15). All other intervals are dissonant: m2, M2, m7, M7, and all augmented and diminished intervals.

The most stable consonances are the U, 8ve, and P5. These are called **perfect consonances**. The 8ve and 5th are represented by the first three partials in the overtone series. These partials thus define the most stable intervallic relationships in tonal music and, as we will see in chapters C, 1, and 2, the strongest tonal relationships in Western music, defined by pitches a 5th apart.

3rds and 6ths are called **imperfect consonances**. The **P4** (perfect 4th) is sometimes consonant and sometimes dissonant, depending on its context, as we will discuss in chapters D, E, and 9. Notice that all perfect intervals, including the P4, appear

♪♪♪ Example A.15

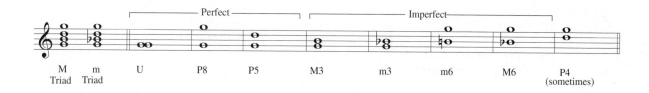

Example A.16

a.   b.   c.   d.

m2 → m3   M2 → 3   m7 → 6   m7 → P5   m7 → 3   M7 → P5   °7 → P5   °5 → 3   +4 → 6   +6 → P8

among partials 1–4 in the overtone series, and also that all imperfect consonances appear among partials 4–8. In other words, all the consonant intervals (including perfect and imperfect consonances, as well as the P4) can be found among the first eight partials in the series.

As we mentioned above, dissonant intervals produce an effect of instability or unrest which, in a tonal context, usually resolves to a consonance. Example A.16 illustrates several dissonant intervals, followed by possible resolutions to consonant intervals. First, play each of the dissonant intervals alone, and notice the impression of instability they produce. Then play each dissonant interval followed by the provided resolution. Playing them together you will appreciate how dissonance creates a sense of motion toward a resolution. Notice that the consonant intervals that appear in this example are not necessarily the required resolutions for each of the dissonant intervals. They show, however, some possible (and common) resolutions in a tonal-harmonic context, such as the one we will study in this book. When only the interval size has been indicated (and not its quality), as in M2→3 or m7→6, the resolution can be to either a M or m 3rd or 6th, as indicated also by the flat sign in parentheses.

How do the resolutions in example A.16 represent standard motions from dissonant to consonant intervals? In a harmonic context, for instance, the lower pitch in a 2nd usually resolves down by step (example A.16a). Similarly, the upper pitch in a 7th (the inversion of a 2nd) also resolves down by step, regardless of whether the interval as a whole moves to a 6th, a 5th, or a 3rd, as in example A.16b. This principle of resolution of a 7th by step applies equally to a M7, a m7, or a °7. Both pitches in a °5, on the other hand, usually move "inwardly" by step to a 3rd, and similarly, an +4 usually resolves "outwardly" by step to a 6th (example A.16c). Finally, the +6, an interval with great harmonic significance, usually resolves "outwardly" to a P8 (example A.16d).

EXERCISE

To practice identifying consonant and dissonant intervals, and to practice resolving dissonant intervals to consonant intervals, refer to exercise A.10 in worksheet A at the end of this chapter.

ASSIGNMENT

For an assignment based on the materials learned in this chapter, refer to chapter A in the workbook.

Terms for Review

Scale
Diatonic scale
Letter names
Middle C
Middle octave
Numerical suffixes for octaves
The staff
Lines, spaces, ledger lines
The clefs
Treble, bass, alto, tenor clefs
G, F, C clefs
Grand staff
Equal temperament
Chromatic scale
Half step, semitone
Dyad
Whole step, whole tone
Accidentals
Sharp, flat, natural, double sharp, double
    flat
Enharmonic spellings
Diatonic half step

Chromatic half step
Interval
Melodic and harmonic intervals
Interval size, interval quality
Ascending and descending intervals
Perfect intervals
Major and minor intervals
Augmented and diminished intervals
The tritone
Simple and compound intervals
Interval inversion
Pure tone, sine tone
Complex tones
Partials, harmonics, or overtones
Fundamental
Overtone series
Timbre
Consonant and dissonant intervals
Perfect consonances
Imperfect consonances
The perfect 4th (P4)

Worksheet A

Knowing the intervals and their relationships is an essential component of musician-ship. The following exercises will help you verify your knowledge and will show you possible ways to learn and practice intervals. You should, however, work on your own at memorizing as much as possible all the intervals from any given pitch. Knowing and memorizing the keyboard will help you in this task. For instance, you should know, without having to think about it, all M and m 3rds up and down from any pitch. Having a clear picture of the keyboard in your mind can facilitate your memorization of intervals.

EXERCISE A.1

1. Name the notes in exercise A.1a, and provide the octave suffix for each of them.
2. Notate the notes in exercise A.1b in the correct octave.

F4 B♭5 A3 D6 E♭5   D4 G♯2 F♯3 E2 A3   G3 D♭4 E3 F♯4 A3   B3 C3 E♭4 A4 F♯3

EXERCISE A.2

1. In exercise A.2a write the perfect intervals above the given notes.
2. In exercise A.2b write the perfect intervals below the given notes.

a. Above   b. Below

P8 P4 P5 P4 P5   P5 P4 P5 P5 P4   P8 P5 P4 P5 P4   P5 P4 P8 P5 P5

18

NOTE

In this exercise and the ones that follow, do not write enharmonic equivalents unless specifically requested to do so. In other words, F–B♭ (a P4) is not the same as F–A♯ (What interval is this?), although the two intervals sound the same.

EXERCISE A.3

1. In exercise A.3a write the following M or m intervals above the given notes.
2. In exercise A.3b write the M or m intervals below the given notes.

a. Above   b. Below

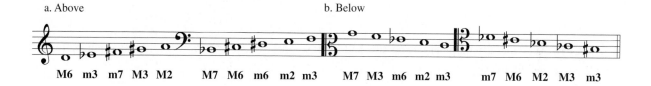

M6   m3   m7   M3   M2   M7   M6   m6   m2   m3   M7   M3   m6   m2   m3   m7   M6   M2   M3   m3

EXERCISE A.4

1. In exercise A.4a write the + or ° intervals above the given notes.
2. In exercise A.4b write the + or ° intervals below the given notes.

a. Above   b. Below

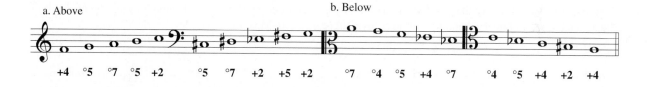

+4   °5   °7   °5   +2   °5   °7   +2   +5   +2   °7   °4   °5   +4   °7   °4   °5   +4   +2   +4

EXERCISE A.5   Write the intervals above and below the given notes as requested.

Above   M7   °5   P4   m2   M3   M6   +5   m3   +4   M2

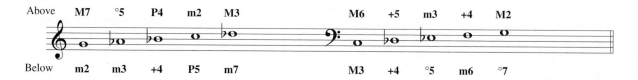

Below   m2   m3   +4   P5   m7   M3   +4   °5   m6   °7

EXERCISE A.6   Identify the intervals by size and quality.

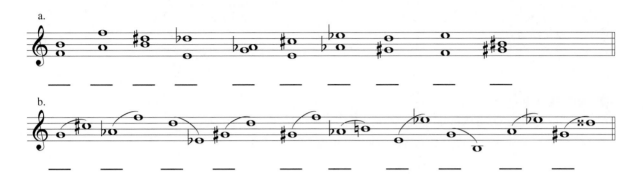

EXERCISE A.7   Identify the intervals by size and quality. Then, renotate the lower note enharmonically, and identify the resulting interval.

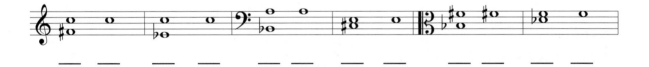

EXERCISE A.8   Identify the compound intervals by size and quality. For each of them, provide labels for both the actual compound interval and its simple equivalent (e.g., M10–M3).

EXERCISE A.9   Write the intervallic inversion for each of the following intervals. Identify both the given interval and its inversion.

EXERCISE A.10

1. Refer back to exercises A.6a and b. Under each of the intervals in these exercises, write a C or D depending on whether the interval is consonant (C) or dissonant (D).

2. These are all dissonant intervals. Identify the intervals, and resolve each of them to a consonance, following the models and criteria of resolution provided in example A.16.

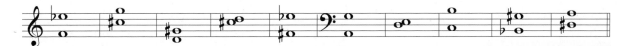

EXERCISE A.11 In the melodic examples from the literature in example A.17, identify each of the numbered intervals by size and quality.

| ♪♪♪ Example A.17a | Béla Bartók, *Music for String Instruments, Percussion, and Celesta,* I, mm. 4–6 |

| ♪♪♪ Example A.17b | B. Bartók, *Music for String Instruments, Percussion, and Celesta,* I, mm. 69–71 |

| ♪♪♪ Example A.17c | J. S. Bach, Fugue 24 in Bm, from *The Well-Tempered Clavier,* I, mm. 1–4 |

♪♪♪Example A.17d   J. S. Bach, Canon no. 2, from *A Musical Offering*

♪♪♪Example A.17e   J. S. Bach, "Kyrie," from Mass in Bm, mm. 10–15

EXERCISE A.12   Identify the numbered intervals in example A.18. What characteristic can you recognize in this succession of intervals? (How may intervals are there, and of what type?)

♪♪♪Example A.18   Luigi Dallapiccola, "Fregi," from *Quaderno musicale di Annalibera*, mm. 2–4

Chapter B

Rhythm and Meter

Sing or play the tune "London Bridge." The following observations will be immediately clear to you:

1. Not all notes have the same *duration*.

2. Notes are *grouped* in various ways. The melody can be *partitioned* into these groups, and some of the groups form durational *patterns* which are repeated (such as, for instance, the pattern to the words "falling down" in our tune).

3. Regardless of the note durations or patterns, you can easily tap what we usually call the "beat," that is, you can "keep time" to the music by establishing a regular "pulse." Your pulses, however, will not all be equally stressed. Some of them will naturally come out more *accented* than others. If we notate pulses (accented or not) as syllables in italics, and accented beats as syllables in boldface, we will come up with the following interpretation of the "London Bridge" words:

> ***Lon****don bridge is **fall**ing down, **fall**ing down, **fall**ing down,*
>
> ***Lon****don bridge is **fall**ing down, **my** fair **la**dy.*

These are temporal aspects of the "London Bridge" tune, having to do specifically with rhythm and meter. This chapter will focus on the rudiments and notation of rhythm and meter. The term **rhythm** refers to the *grouping, patterning, and partitioning of musical events* (such as notes), whereas **meter** refers to the *measurement of the number of pulses between regularly recurring accents*. We will now study the notation of these two temporal aspects of music separately.

DURATIONAL SYMBOLS

In order to notate rhythm we need **durational symbols**, that is, symbols that express the relative duration of notes. The elements of rhythmic notation needed to express duration are represented in example B.1a. Durational symbols are made up of **note**

♪♪♪ Example B.1a   The Elements of Rhythmic Notation

Stem → ♪ ← Flag
Note head →

← Beam

♪♪♪ Example B.1b   Basic Durational Symbols

VALUE	NOTE	REST
Breve (double whole)	‖○‖ = ○ + ○	▮ = ▬ + ▬
Whole	○ = 𝅝 + 𝅝	▬ = ▬ + ▬
Half	𝅗𝅥 = ♩ + ♩	▬ = 𝄽 + 𝄽
Quarter	♩ = ♪ + ♪	𝄽 = 𝄾 + 𝄾
Eighth	♪ = ♪ + ♪	𝄾 = 𝄾 + 𝄾
Sixteenth	𝅘𝅥𝅯 = 𝅘𝅥𝅯 + 𝅘𝅥𝅯	𝄿 = 𝄿 𝄿
Thirty-second	𝅘𝅥𝅰 = 𝅘𝅥𝅰 + 𝅘𝅥𝅰	𝅀 = 𝅀 𝅀
Sixty-fourth	𝅘𝅥𝅱	𝅁

heads, **stems**, and **flags** or **beams**. The chart in example B.1b presents all the basic durational symbols, their equivalence in terms of the next shorter duration, and the notation of the **rest** equivalent to each of the durations.

EXERCISE

To practice equivalences among various durational symbols, refer to exercise B.1 in worksheet B at the end of this chapter.

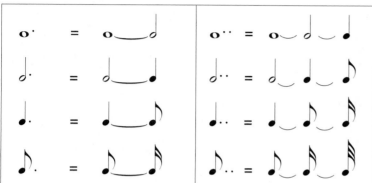

a.   b.

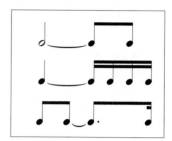

The possible durations that can be notated increase enormously when we use dots and ties. A **dot** added *after* a note or rest increases the duration of that note or rest by half its value. A **double dot** increases the duration of a note or rest by three-quarters its original value (half the original duration, plus half the first dot). **Ties** are used to connect two values of any kind. Of course, we can express dotted notes by means of ties (this is how they have to be notated over a bar line) but, on the other hand, we can write many durations by means of ties that cannot be expressed with dots. Example B.2a shows some dotted notes and their equivalent notation with ties; example B.2b presents some tied values that cannot be expressed in any other way.

EXERCISE

To practice durational values that require the use of dots and ties, refer to exercises B.2 and B.3 in worksheet B at the end of this chapter.

PULSE, BEAT, AND METER

Consider the undifferentiated stream of time points that appears in example B.3a. These are regularly recurring time points, which we call **pulses**. Now tap or say (on "tah") the line in example B.3b. We have added an accent every other pulse. Accents are points of emphasis, and through them we create groupings in the stream of pulses. The grouping in example B.3b is "in two." In example B.3c, the accents appear every three pulses, and they create a grouping "in three." Similarly, the grouping in example B.3d is "in four." These examples illustrate meter, as defined on page 23. For a musical context to be metric we need pulses and recurring accents. We will refer to pulses in a metric context as **beats**. In other words, the time points in example B.3a are pulses, whereas in the other three examples the same time points become beats because the regularly recurring accents provide a metric frame.

♪♪♪ Example B.3

TEMPO

Because the exact meaning of some meter signatures depends on how fast the music moves, we need to review the concept of **tempo** at this point. The term *tempo* (Italian for "time") refers to the speed of the beat. Most frequently, Italian terms (**tempo markings**) are also used to describe the tempo of a movement or composition. These terms are relative and have meant different things in different historical periods. In general, tempos (or tempi) were faster in the Baroque and Classical periods than in the Romantic period. A Baroque *adagio*, for instance, would be performed faster than a late-Romantic *adagio*. Having said this, however, the slow tempos (listed from slower to faster) are *grave*, *largo*, *lento*, and *adagio*; the moderate tempos are *andante*, *moderato*, and *allegretto*; and the fast tempos are *allegro*, *vivace*, and *presto*.

A more "objective" measurement of tempo is provided by metronome markings. In scores from the last two centuries one often finds a metronome marking accompanying, or replacing, the tempo marking. The letters M.M., which stand for "Maelzel's metronome," often precede the metronome marking. The metronome setting (a number) indicates fractions of a minute. Thus, M.M. "♩ = 60" means a quarter note per second (60 quarter notes per minute, or fairly *adagio*); "♩ = 80" means 80 quarter notes per minute (*moderato*), and "♩ = 120" means a quarter note every half second, or 120 quarter notes per minute (a fast tempo).

SIMPLE AND COMPOUND METERS

Sing the tunes "Camptown Races" and "Greensleeves," while you tap or conduct the beat in each case. (If you don't know these tunes, you can also try "Mary Had a Little Lamb" and "Row, Row, Row Your Boat.") Then sing them again, and now *divide* the beat. That is, tap more than once per beat, following the beat division appropriate to each song. If you are doing this right, you will have come up with two divisions per beat in "Camptown Races" and "Mary Had a Little Lamb," and three divisions per beat in "Greensleeves" and "Row, Row, Row Your Boat." Meters with a duple division of the beat are called **simple meters**, while meters with a triple division are **compound meters**. Now sing "Pop Goes the Weasel," "Star Spangled Banner" ("O Say Can you See"), "Old MacDonald," and "My Bonnie," and determine whether each of them is in simple or compound meter.

THE NOTATION OF METER

A complete metric unit is called a **measure**, and measures are indicated by **bar lines**. Meters are indicated by means of **meter signatures** or **time signatures**. A meter signature consists of two numbers written one over the other. The exact meaning of meter signatures changes between simple and compound meters, as we will discuss next.

Meter Signatures in Simple Meters

The most common simple meters are $\frac{2}{4}$, $\frac{3}{4}$, and $\frac{4}{4}$. The upper number in meter signatures for simple meters is 2, 3, or 4. In simple meter, the upper number indicates the *number of beats per measure*. Thus, in $\frac{2}{4}$ there are two beats per measure, in $\frac{3}{4}$ there are three, and in $\frac{4}{4}$ there are four. The lower number indicates the **value of the beat**. By convention, "4" means "quarter note." The beat value in each of the three meters we have just mentioned ($\frac{2}{4}$, $\frac{3}{4}$, and $\frac{4}{4}$) is, then, a quarter note. The lower number 2 means a half note per beat, and 1 means a whole note. Similarly, 8 means an eighth note, and 16 means sixteenth note. Examples B.3b, c, and d show how each of the metric phrases, which we first notated by means of accents, can be notated using a meter signature and bar lines.

Any meter with two beats (such as $\frac{2}{4}$, $\frac{2}{2}$, or $\frac{2}{8}$) is called a **duple meter**. Meters with three beats (such as $\frac{3}{4}$, $\frac{3}{2}$ or $\frac{3}{8}$) are **triple meters**, and meters with four beats ($\frac{4}{4}$, $\frac{4}{2}$, or $\frac{4}{8}$) are **quadruple meters**. Notice that $\frac{4}{4}$ can also be referred to as **common time** (symbol **c**), and $\frac{2}{2}$ as **cut time** (symbol **¢**).

Meter Signatures in Compound Meters

The most common compound meters are $\frac{6}{8}$, $\frac{9}{8}$, and $\frac{12}{8}$. The upper number in meter signatures for compound meters is 6, 9, or 12. Compound meter signatures, however, lend themselves to some confusion if we think of them in the same terms we defined above for simple meters. The beat in such compound meters as $\frac{6}{8}$, $\frac{9}{8}$, and $\frac{12}{8}$ is the dotted quarter, not the eighth note. The eighth note is the beat *division*. In other words, the top number in these signatures does not indicate the number of beats per measure, but rather the number of divisions. And the bottom number does not indicate the value of the beat, but rather the value of the division. $\frac{6}{8}$ will normally be conducted *in two* because it has two beats (compound duple); $\frac{9}{8}$ is normally conducted *in three* because it has three beats (compound triple), and $\frac{12}{8}$ *in four* because it has four beats (compound quadruple). Each

Example B.4   Simple Meters

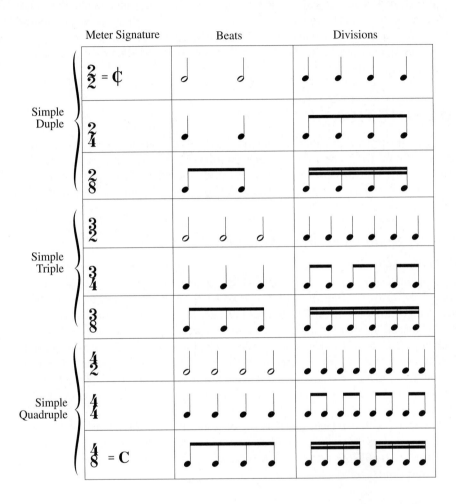

of these meters, however, is often subdivided in slower tempos. Thus, a $\frac{6}{8}$ with a *largo* indication will be conducted or felt *in six*. The following charts present a summary of the most common simple and compound meters and their characteristics.

EXERCISES

To practice identifying simple and compound meter signatures and counting beats in a variety of simple and compound meters, refer to exercise B.4 in worksheet B at the end of this chapter. To practice providing meter signatures for given rhythmic passages, and identifying rhythmic errors in given meters, refer to exercises B.5a and B.6 in worksheet B at the end of this chapter.

Example B.5   Compound Meters

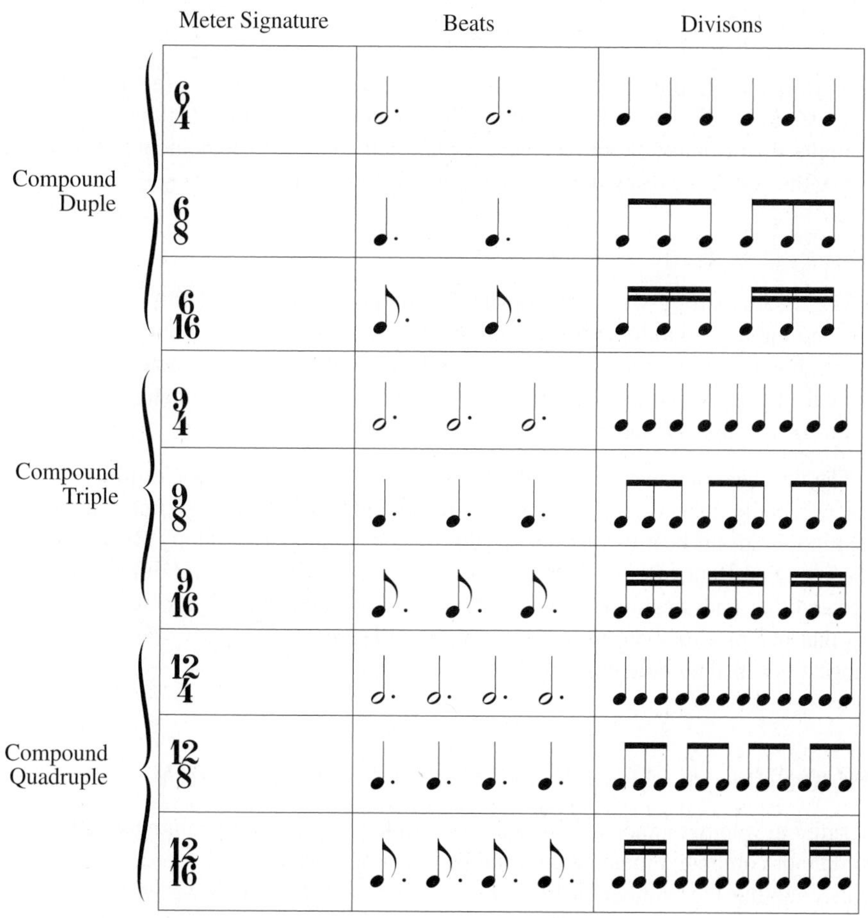

Meter Signature	Beats	Divisons

METRIC ACCENT

We have already seen that beats in a metric context are not all equally stressed. That is, some beats are naturally more accented than others as a result of the grouping of pulses into regularly recurring patterns. We call these accents, which result from metric organization, **metric accents. Strong and weak beats in all meters** are illustrated below.

1. In duple meter beat 1 is strong and beat 2 is weak. We will use the symbols – for strong and ⌣ for weak.

$\frac{2}{4}$ 1 2 | 1 2 ‖

2. In quadruple meter the odd-numbered beats are strong (1 and 3), whereas even-numbered beats are weak (2 and 4). Beat 3, however, is weaker than beat 1.

$$\frac{4}{4} \; 1 \quad 2 \quad 3 \quad 4 \quad | \quad 1 \quad 2 \quad 3 \quad 4 \; \|$$

3. In triple meters, only beat 1 is strong. In principle, beats 2 and 3 are weak. Beat 2, however, is often stressed by a variety of means, one of which is illustrated in example B.11a. Thus, although beat 2 is metrically weak, we may indeed perceive it as either weak or strong depending on the musical context.

$$\frac{3}{4} \; 1 \quad 2 \quad 3 \quad | \quad 1 \quad 2 \quad 3 \; \|$$

4. These same strong-weak relationships also apply to beat divisions. In a beat divided into two eighth notes, the first one is strong, the second one weak. If the division is into four sixteenth notes, notes 1 and 3 are strong, and notes 2 and 4 are weak. In beats divided into 3 notes (in triplets or compound meters), note 1 is strong, and notes 2 and 3 are weak.

The first beat in a measure is called a **downbeat**; the last beat is an **upbeat**. Weak beats, especially upbeats, create a metric tension that usually calls for continuation to a resolution, a strong beat or downbeat. Sing the beginnings of "Happy Birthday" and "Star Spangled Banner" ("O Say Can you See"). You will find that both are in triple meter and that both begin on upbeats (on beat 3). An **anacrusis** is a note or group of notes that begins a melodic phrase on an upbeat. The type of melody which begins on an upbeat is called an **anacrusic melody**.

CHOOSING A METER TO NOTATE A MELODY

Determining whether a melody is in duple or triple meter and determining whether it is in simple or compound meter should not be much of a problem. This process basically entails counting the number of beats between downbeats (which we will easily perceive as metrically accented beats), and checking whether the beat division is in two or three. Once we have decided on these points, however, several possibilities arise. Take, for instance, the tune "Oh! Susanna." There seems to be no question that its meter is simple quadruple, as notated in example B.6a. It is difficult, however, to distinguish between quadruple ($\frac{4}{4}$ or $\mathbf{c}$) and duple ($\frac{2}{4}$ or $\frac{2}{2}$) meters and, as a matter of fact, that is often an arbitrary decision of the composer. Examples B.6b and c show two alternative notations for "Oh! Susanna," each of which is perfectly plausible. What is at issue in each of these versions is what value gets the beat and how long the measure is. Notice that we could also assign example B.6c a $\frac{4}{8}$ meter signature without changing the notation in any other way.

The same notational ambiguities apply to compound meters. In example B.7a we have chosen to notate "Pop Goes the Weasel" in $\frac{6}{8}$, that is, with a dotted quarter beat. The notation in example B.7b, in $\frac{6}{4}$ (we have doubled the value of the beat, which now

Example B.6   Stephen Foster, "Oh! Susanna"

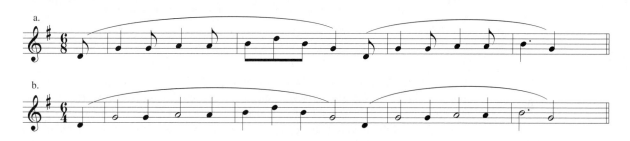

Example B.7   "Pop Goes the Weasel"

is a dotted half note), is also perfectly correct. These examples show the relativity of exact meter signatures. What matters mostly is to identify and represent correctly the fundamental metric parameters (duple or triple, simple or compound).

EXERCISE

To practice various possible metric notations for a melody, refer to exercise B.7 in worksheet B at the end of this chapter.

ASYMMETRICAL METERS

All the meters we have discussed so far are **symmetrical** or **divisive**. We think of them in terms of their divisions, and the divisions form symmetrical patterns. A different type of meter, however, is **asymmetrical** or **additive**. When we think of $\frac{5}{8}$, for instance,

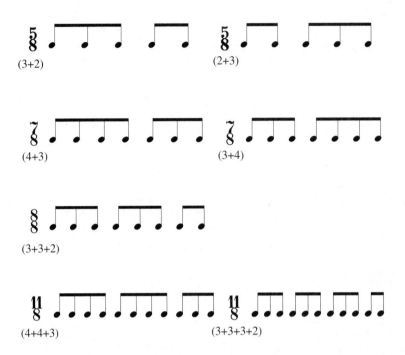

♪♪♪Example B.8

we usually think of two combined metric units (3 + 2 or 2 + 3) which form an asymmetrical metric structure. Similarly, $\frac{7}{8}$ and $\frac{11}{8}$ are asymmetrical meters. All of these meters are conducted in unequal beats. $\frac{5}{8}$ is usually conducted in two (subdivided as 3 + 2 or 2 + 3). How would you conduct $\frac{7}{8}$ and $\frac{11}{8}$? Notice that $\frac{8}{8}$ (very much unlike $\frac{4}{4}$) is often an asymmetrical meter to be conducted in three: 3 + 3 + 2. Example B.8 shows some possible patterns with asymmetrical meters.

EXERCISE

To practice providing meter signatures for given passages in asymmetrical meters, refer to exercise B.5b in worksheet B at the end of this chapter.

IRREGULAR DIVISIONS OF THE BEAT

Although the normal division of the beat in simple meters is into two or four parts, and the normal division of compound beats is into three or six parts, beats (or any note values) can also be divided irregularly. Thus, beats or notes which would normally be divided in multiples of two can also be divided into three parts (triplets), five parts (quintuplets), six parts (sextuplets), seven parts (septuplets), and so forth. Beats or

♩♪♪Example B.9

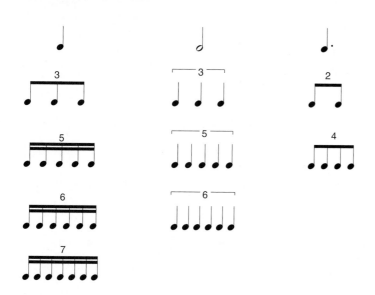

notes which would normally be divided in multiples of three can also be divided into two parts (duplets), four parts (quadruplets), and so on. The notation of the most frequent irregular divisions of notes is shown in example B.9.

IRREGULAR RHYTHMIC AND METRIC RELATIONSHIPS

Meter and rhythm allow for numerous irregular relationships, which have often been used by composers in order to break the regularity of notated meter, metric divisions, and metric accents. We will now mention some of these possible irregularities.

1. **Syncopation** is the rhythmic contradiction of a metrical pattern of strong and weak beats. This occurs when a metrically weak beat or beat division is emphasized by a rhythmic and/or dynamic accent (example B.10a).

2. **Hemiola** consists in the juxtaposition of, or interplay between, three and two beats at the metric level. A usual hemiola pattern is based on the alternation of $\frac{6}{8}$ and $\frac{3}{4}$ (that is, alternating two and three beats, as in Leonard Bernstein's song "America," from *West Side Story*). In another type of hemiola, a sense of three $\frac{2}{4}$ measures (or of one $\frac{3}{2}$ measure) is created in the place of two $\frac{3}{4}$ measures. Both of these types of hemiola are illustrated in examples B.10b and B.10c. In the Robert Schumann example, the notated meter suggests beats grouped in three, whereas the beat grouping we actually hear is in two.

Example B.10a

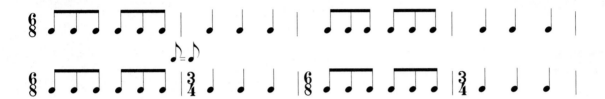

Example B.10b

Example B.10c   Robert Schumann, Symphony no. 3 in E♭M, I, mm. 1–7

3. Whereas metric accents create a recurring pattern of strong-weak beats, other types of accent may generate patterns that conflict with the underlying metric patterns. Accents that result from grouping, note length, a sense of harmonic or tonal arrival, and other nonmetrical factors, are **rhythmic accents**. In the phrase from Bach's "Chaconne" reproduced in example B.11a we hear a rhythmic accent on beat 2 of a $\frac{3}{4}$ meter, produced by the longer note and the dotted rhythm pattern, both of which begin on beat 2. A rhythmic accent produced by the duration of a

Example B.11a   J. S. Bach, "Chaconne," from Partita no. 2 in Dm for Violin Solo, mm. 1–5

Example B.11b   Johannes Brahms, Intermezzo in CM, op. 119, no. 3, mm. 23–25

note (that is, by a note of longer duration) is called an **agogic accent.** As we saw on page 30, beat 2 in triple meter may be weak or strong, depending on the context. This example illustrates a case of a strong beat 2 in a $\frac{3}{4}$ meter, and the stress is produced by agogic accent.

4. In example B.11b, on the other hand, Johannes Brahms explicitly requires an accent on the last eighth note of every beat by writing a *sforzando* mark (*sf*). An accent created by a dynamic mark is called a **dynamic accent.** Notice that syncopations are usually heard as accented notes. What kind of grouping does this syncopation/dynamic accent generate in the right hand, and how does it conflict with the metric grouping?

5. A sure way to break the sense of metric regularity is to write constant **meter changes,** as Igor Stravinsky does in example B.12a.

6. In example B.12b we see that, besides the constant changing meters, Stravinsky also builds in a **rhythmic/metric displacement:** the double bass plays a four-note **ostinato** (a repeated figure), which constantly creates a conflict and a displacement between the rhythmic grouping (four eighth notes) and the metric accents produced by the notated changing meter, preserved in the violin part. This simultaneity of contrasting rhythmic groupings is also called **polyrhythm.**

Example B.12a   Igor Stravinsky, *The Soldier's Tale,* "The Royal March," mm. 85–91

Example B.12b   I. Stravinsky, *The Soldier's Tale,* "Music to Scene I," mm. 86–95

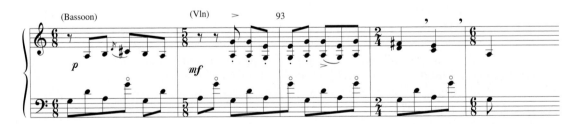

EXERCISE

To practice identifying syncopations and hemiolas, refer to exercise B.8 in worksheet B at the end of this chapter.

SOME NOTES ON THE CORRECT NOTATION OF RHYTHM

The following are some points that should be observed when copying rhythmic notation by hand.

1. If you are writing a single melodic line, stems should go up if the note is below the middle line and down if the note is above the middle line. If the note is on the middle line, the stem may go up or down, depending on the stems of adjacent notes (example B.13a).

2. If you are writing two voices on the same staff, the stems for the upper voice will go up, and the stems for the lower voice will go down (example B.13b).

3. Beams that connect groups of notes should reflect the standard metric grouping (the beats) for the meter of the passage, rather than obscuring it (example B.13c).

 Example B.13

4. In dotted notes that are on a line, dots are usually placed above the line (not *on* the line).

5. Meter signatures are written only at the beginning of a piece (unless there are meter changes). They should not be written again at the beginning of each staff.

6. The whole-note rest can be used to indicate a full measure of rest in any meter, even if the measure does not add up to four beats (for instance, in a $\frac{3}{4}$ measure).

 EXERCISE

To practice renotating rhythms providing appropriate beamings, refer to exercise B.9 in worksheet B at the end of this chapter.

ASSIGNMENT

For an assignment based on the materials learned in this chapter, refer to chapter B in the workbook.

Terms for Review

Rhythm
Meter
Durational symbols: breve, whole, half, quarter, eighth, sixteenth, thirty-second, sixty-fourth notes
Note head, stem, flag, beam
Rest
Dot
Double dot
Tie
Pulse
Beat
Tempo
Tempo markings
Simple meters
Compound meters
Measure
Bar line
Meter signatures (Time signatures)
Beat values
Duple meter
Triple meter
Quadruple meter
Common time

Cut time
Beats in compound meters
Metric accents
Strong and weak beats in all meters
Downbeat
Upbeat
Anacrusis
Anacrusic melodies
Symmetrical (divisive) meters
Asymmetrical (additive) meters
Irregular divisions of the beat
Irregular groups in simple meters: triplet, quintuplet, etc.
Irregular groups in compound meters: duplet, quadruplet, etc.
Syncopation
Hemiola
Rhythmic accent
Agogic accent
Dynamic accent
Meter changes
Rhythmic/metric displacement
Ostinato
Polyrhythm

Worksheet B

EXERCISE B.1 Supply the information required in the blanks.

A 𝅝 note = _____ 𝅘𝅥 notes   _____ 𝄾 rests = 1 𝄻 rest

A 𝅗𝅥 note = _____ 𝅘𝅥𝅮 notes   _____ 𝄻 rests = 4 𝄼 rests

A 𝅘𝅥 note = _____ 𝅘𝅥𝅯 notes   _____ 𝄿 rests = 1 𝄻 rest

A 𝅘𝅥𝅮 note = _____ 𝅘𝅥𝅯 notes   _____ 𝅘𝅥𝅯 rests = 2 𝄿 rests

EXERCISE B.2 For each of the following patterns, write the equivalent duration with only one note value. (You will need dots in some cases.)

𝅘𝅥 𝅘𝅥 =   𝅘𝅥 𝅘𝅥𝅮 𝅘𝅥𝅮 =

𝅘𝅥𝅮 𝅘𝅥𝅮 𝅘𝅥 =   𝅗𝅥 𝅘𝅥 𝅘𝅥 =

𝅘𝅥𝅮 𝅘𝅥𝅮 𝅘𝅥𝅮 𝅘𝅥𝅮 𝅘𝅥𝅮 𝅘𝅥𝅮 =   𝅘𝅥 𝅘𝅥 𝅘𝅥 𝅘𝅥 𝅘𝅥 =

𝅘𝅥 𝅘𝅥 𝅘𝅥 =   𝅘𝅥. 𝅘𝅥𝅮 =

EXERCISE B.3 Show, by means of tied notes (as few as possible in each case), the value of each dotted or doubly dotted note.

𝅘𝅥𝅮. =   𝅗𝅥.. =   𝅘𝅥.. =   𝅘𝅥𝅮. =

EXERCISE B.4   Using the fewest possible notes, along with ties where needed, write a single duration lasting the number of beats specified in each of the following cases. Include bar lines if more than one measure is needed. In a parenthesis after the required number of beats, write whether this meter is simple or compound, and what the beat value is (see the provided example).

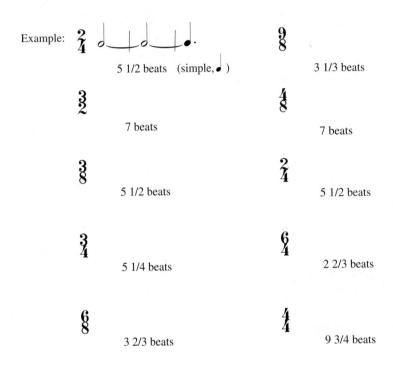

Example:

5 1/2 beats   (simple, ♩)

3 1/3 beats

7 beats

7 beats

5 1/2 beats

5 1/2 beats

5 1/4 beats

2 2/3 beats

3 2/3 beats

9 3/4 beats

EXERCISE B.5   Write an appropriate meter signature for each of the following examples.

a.

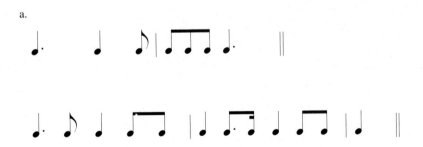

b.

EXERCISE B.6   Locate and correct a total of eight mistakes in the following examples.

EXERCISE B.7   Transcribe the following melody from $\frac{6}{8}$ to $\frac{6}{16}$ and $\frac{6}{4}$.

EXERCISE B.8   In the following examples, mark every syncopation with an *x*, and draw a bracket over every hemiola.

EXERCISE B.9   Correct the notation of the following examples so that the beaming clarifies the meter and rhythm.

a.

b.

Chapter C

Tonality: Scales, Keys, and Transposition

Sing or play the tune "The First Noël" (example C.1). There is no doubt that the pitches in this melody are organized according to some system. What intuitive observations can we make about this system, at least as it applies to this melody?

1. One pitch seems to be the most important of all, the **tonal center** around which other pitches are organized. We call this pitch the **tonic**. If you sing the tunes "Twinkle, Twinkle" and "Oh! Susanna," you will notice that both begin and end on a pitch which provides a sense of stability, repose, and, at the end, closure. These are characteristics of the tonic pitch.

2. What is the tonic in "The First Noël"? Sing the tune, and then sing the tonic. You should come up with the pitch C. In this case, the melody does not begin and end on the tonic, but the tonic feeling of C is nonetheless evident. Notice that the lowest and highest pitches are C4 and C5, respectively. The span between the lowest and highest pitches of a melody is called the **range**. In this case, the range is an octave, from tonic to tonic.

3. The space between C4 and C5 in mm. 1–3 of "The First Noël" is covered by means of an ascending succession of pitches moving by steps. As we saw in chapter A, the organization of a collection of pitches by successive ascending or descending steps is called a **scale**.

4. Another pitch that has a very prominent role in our tune is G (the pitch a 5th above C). G in emphasized as a "long pitch" (that is, by agogic accent) in mm. 2 and 4, where it splits the octave into two segments (C4–G4–C5). In mm. 4 and 6, moreover, the melody changes direction every time it touches on G. Measures 4–7 are built around the melodic segment G4–C5. The pitch a 5th above the tonic is called the *dominant*, and it is indeed a very important pitch (second only to the tonic) in the system we are discussing.

5. Other than C and G, we see that E (a 3rd above the tonic) is a prominent pitch in "The First Noël," because the melody begins and ends on it. The 3rd above the tonic is called *mediant*, because it is halfway between the tonic and the dominant.

♪♪♪ Example C.1   "The First Noël," mm. 1–8

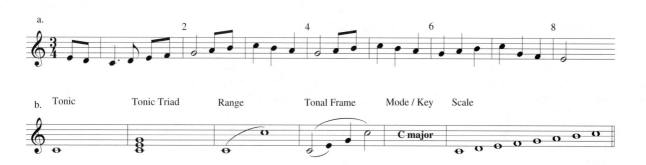

The three pitches, C– E–G, form what we call a **triad**, that is, a collection of three pitches which we call the **root**, the **third** (a 3rd above the root), and the **fifth** (a 5th above the root). Because C–E–G in this case is the triad built on the tonic, we call it the **tonic triad** (we will study triads in detail in chapter E).

6. All of the above information is summarized in example C.1b. In this example we also see what we will call the melody's **tonal frame**. The tonal frame is the basic pitch structure on which a melody is built. Most often, it will involve the members of the tonic triad, or at least the tonic and the dominant. To show the hierarchy among these pitches, we will represent the tonic as a stemmed white note, the dominant as a stemmed black note, and the mediant or any other prominent pitch as an unstemmed black note. What is the tonal frame for "Twinkle, Twinkle"?

We have discussed the basics of a system in which *pitches are organized hierarchically*. This type of system is called a **tonal system**. In principle, there are many different tonal systems in the world. The musics of India, Indonesia, medieval Christianity, and Mozart, to name just four different styles, are all based on different tonal systems. We have come to know the specific system on which Western music is based from about the mid-seventeenth to the late nineteenth centuries (the "common practice" period) as **tonality**, or also (somewhat abusively) as "*the* tonal system." Although other tonal systems are constructed mostly around melodic relationships (the Indian *rāga* system for instance), the Western tonal system is built on both *melodic* and *harmonic* relationships. Whereas in this book as a whole we will study in detail the harmonic relationships that define Western tonality, in this chapter we will review some of the basic principles of tonal melodic organization.

MODES AND SCALES

Western tonality is also known as **major-minor tonality** and as **functional tonality**. We call it major-minor tonality because it is based almost exclusively on two *types of scales*, or *modes*: the major mode and the minor mode. We call it functional tonality because each of the steps (or *degrees*) in these scales has a *tonal or harmonic function* with respect to the tonic, as we will study in chapters F and 3.

The Major Mode and the Scale Degrees

You will remember from chapter A that the standard Western collection of notes is made up of *seven pitches*. If a scale contains only the basic, unaltered pitches, we call it a *diatonic scale*. Example C.2a shows the diatonic **major scale** which begins on C, that is, which has C as the tonic. This is the C major (abbreviated CM) scale, which uses only the white keys of the keyboard (that is, it contains no accidentals). "The First Noël" is built on this scale, and as a matter of fact a passage of this song is based on the statement of the complete scale in ascending form (mm. 1–3). A composition based on this scale is said to be "in CM."

The pitch members of a scale, or its steps, are called **degrees**. In example C.2a we see that scale degrees are labeled in two ways. First, each degree is assigned a number with a little caret on it, such as $\hat{1}$, $\hat{2}$, and so forth. These symbols are read "scale degree 1," "scale degree 2," and so on, and they tell us the degree function of a specific pitch within a specific scale (that is, with respect to a specific tonic). Thus, D is $\hat{2}$ with respect to the tonic C, and F is $\hat{4}$. But, of course, D is also $\hat{4}$ with respect to the tonic A, and F is $\hat{6}$ with respect to A.

The other label for scale degrees is a **scale degree name**. We already know the names **tonic** ($\hat{1}$), **dominant** ($\hat{5}$), and **mediant** ($\hat{3}$). Now we add **supertonic** (the degree above the tonic, $\hat{2}$), **subdominant** ($\hat{4}$, the degree a 5th *below* the tonic, as opposed to the dominant, a 5th above the tonic), **submediant** ($\hat{6}$, a 3rd below the tonic, as opposed to the mediant, a 3rd above the tonic), and **leading tone** ($\hat{7}$, a half step below the tonic).

♪♪♪ Example C.2

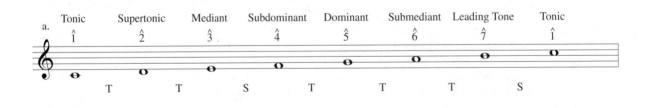

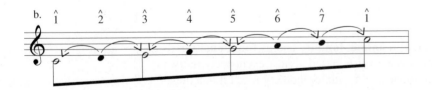

The **melodic tendencies of scale degrees** are an important component in the Western tonal system. Thus, although $\hat{1}$ is a stable degree and $\hat{5}$ and $\hat{3}$ are also relatively stable, the remaining degrees are all characterized by instability because of their melodic tendency to move to a different degree, in all cases to one of the adjacent, or neighbor, degrees. Thus, $\hat{2}$ tends to resolve down to $\hat{1}$ (or up to $\hat{3}$). Sing or play "Oh! Susanna," and verify what happens with each of the $\hat{2}$s in the tune. $\hat{4}$ tends to move up to $\hat{5}$ or down to $\hat{3}$. Can you think of any tune in which you can verify the motions from $\hat{4}$? $\hat{6}$ often functions as a melodic upper neighbor to $\hat{5}$, but also as a passing step in the motion $\hat{5}$–$\hat{6}$–$\hat{7}$–$\hat{1}$. How does $\hat{6}$ function in "Twinkle, Twinkle" and "Oh! Susanna"? And how does it function in "The First Noël"? Finally, $\hat{7}$ usually creates a strong pull towards $\hat{1}$, except when it is part of a descending scale from $\hat{1}$. Verify the role of all the $\hat{7}$s in "The First Noël," and then try hearing the motions from $\hat{7}$ in the opening phrase of both "Joy to the World" and "My Country 'Tis of Thee." The most common melodic tendencies for each of the degrees are represented in example C.2b. The stable pitches of the tonic triad are shown as white notes linked by a beam, the "active" degrees appear as black notes, and their melodic tendencies are shown by arrows.

An essential aspect of the major scale, which defines what we know as the **major mode**, is the major 3rd between the tonic and the mediant (C–E). Otherwise, all intervallic relationships between adjacent pitches are also characteristic of the major mode. There are only two half steps in the diatonic major scale, marked S (for "semitone") in example C.2a, and they are always placed between $\hat{3}$–$\hat{4}$ and $\hat{7}$–$\hat{1}$, respectively. All other steps between degrees are whole steps, marked T (for "tone") in example C.2a.

The Minor Mode

Unlike the major mode, which features a single scale, the **minor mode** can be represented by several scale forms. The essential interval that defines the minor mode as opposed to the major mode is a lowered $\hat{3}$. The interval between the tonic and the minor mediant is thus a minor 3rd (C–E♭). There are, however, two other degrees that are also lowered in what we know as the **natural minor scale**. These are $\hat{6}$ and $\hat{7}$. The lowered 7th degree is called the **subtonic**. The natural minor scale on C, or the C minor scale (abbreviated Cm) is shown in example C.3a. The two half-step motions in this scale are found between $\hat{2}$–$\hat{3}$ and $\hat{5}$–♭$\hat{6}$ respectively.

In a harmonic context, that is, in chord progressions, $\hat{7}$ in minor is raised to become the leading tone. The minor scale with a lowered $\hat{6}$ and a raised $\hat{7}$ is called **harmonic minor scale**, and it is represented in example C.3b. Notice that the interval between $\hat{6}$ and raised $\hat{7}$ is a +2, which is usually avoided as a melodic interval.

NOTE

In general, we will refer to the diatonic $\hat{6}$ and $\hat{7}$ in minor (that is, lowered and with respect to the major mode) simply as $\hat{6}$ and $\hat{7}$. If we need to be specific, however, and are referring to the lowered $\hat{6}$ or $\hat{7}$, we may use the terms "♭$\hat{6}$" and "♭$\hat{7}$" for clarity. Similarly, we will at times refer to "♯$\hat{6}$" or "♯$\hat{7}$" to refer to raised $\hat{6}$ or $\hat{7}$.

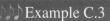Example C.3

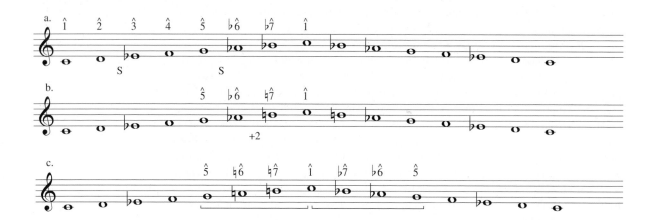

In a melodic context, a way of avoiding the +2 is to raise $\hat{6}$ when it ascends to $\hat{7}$. The resulting scale is called a **melodic minor scale**, and it features an ascending $\hat{5}$–#$\hat{6}$ –#$\hat{7}$–$\hat{1}$ segment (example C.3c). Because in descending melodic passages $\hat{7}$ does not function as the leading tone (it does not move up to $\hat{1}$), it does not need to be raised. Descending melodic segments from $\hat{1}$ are often $\hat{1}$–♭$\hat{7}$–♭$\hat{6}$–$\hat{5}$. The melodic minor scale, then, features raised $\hat{6}$ and $\hat{7}$ in its ascending form, and lowered $\hat{6}$ and $\hat{7}$ in its descending form.

A fun and useful exercise is to turn major tunes into minor. Try singing "Twinkle, Twinkle" and "Oh! Susanna" in minor. Try also with any other major-mode song you wish. Singing "The First Noël" in minor will provide you with some good chances to practice the melodic minor scale. What is the character of the minor mode, as opposed to the major mode? What does the minor mode do to the character of all these songs? Try, for instance, singing "Happy Birthday" in minor. Does it convey the type of mood you would expect in the circumstances in which that song is usually sung?

EXERCISE

To practice writing major and minor scales, refer to exercise C.4 in worksheet C at the end of this chapter.

KEY SIGNATURES

Transposition

Compare examples C.4a and b with example C.1a. In example C.4a, we have written the beginning measures of "The First Noël" one step higher than in example C.1a. The tonic or tonal center is now D rather than C, and we are "in DM" rather than "in CM."

♪♪♪ Example C.4

These are different keys. A **key** is a set of pitch relationships that establish a note as a tonal center. In our discussion of the major mode, we defined a set of scale degrees and intervallic relationships which we illustrated using the key of CM. That is, we applied these relationships to establish the note C as the tonic. In example C.4a we have **transposed** the tune one step up. This transposition has shifted the tonal center to D. In order to preserve the intervallic characteristics of the major scale, we need to add two sharps to the scale D–D (F♯ and C♯). This will allow us to establish the key of DM using the same scale degree and intervallic relationships which we previously applied to CM. In other words, we are transposing not only the tune, but also the key, from CM to DM. As a matter of fact, we can transpose the major scale to turn any of the twelve notes of the chromatic scale into a tonic. We can speak of twelve major keys, all of which have a different tonic, but all of which preserve exactly the same inner tonal relationships. In example C.4b the transposition is down a step, and the new scale requires two flats in order to preserve the intervals of the major scale. The new key is now B♭M.

The Major Key Signatures

Because the accidentals needed to define a key are an essential part of the key and its scale, we can write them at the beginning of the piece in the form of a **key signature**. Because there are twelve major keys, there will also be twelve major key signatures, without counting possible enharmonic spellings of the same key, such as D♭M and C♯ M. (Notice that, unlike meter signatures, key signatures are also notated along with clefs at the beginning of each staff.) You should learn all the key signatures by memory, and there are several ways to help you do so. In the first place, look at example C.5. This is the **circle of 5ths**. Pitches (or keys) are here organized by 5ths: if you move clockwise along the circle, you will see that keys move up by 5ths (C–G–D–A, etc.); counterclockwise motion will take you down by 5ths (C–F–B♭–E♭, etc.).

The outer circle in example C.5 shows the twelve major keys. Beginning with CM (no accidentals in the key signature), every step we move clockwise (up by 5ths) will add one sharp: GM (1♯)–DM (2♯)–AM (3♯), and so forth. Every step we move counterclockwise will add one flat: FM (1♭)–B♭M (2♭)–E♭M (3♭), and so on. Example C.6a

♪♪♪ Example C.5

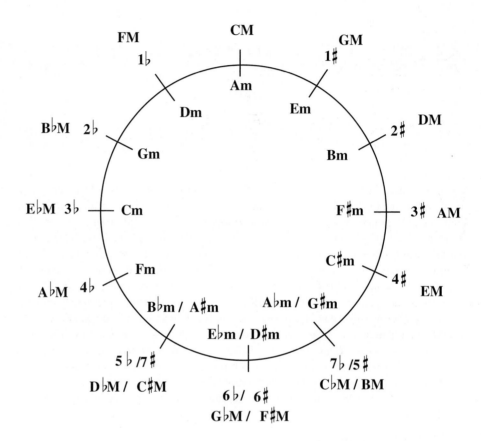

shows all the possible major key signatures. You will see a total of fifteen different key signatures, although there are only twelve major keys. What are the three keys that are duplicated enharmonically in this listing? Example C.6c shows the correct placement of sharps and flats in key signatures in C clefs.

Although the quickest way to identify key signatures is memory, another quick way to identify major key signatures is the following. First, you need to memorize the order of sharps and flats in key signatures.

- The **order of sharps** is: F–C–G–D–A–E–B (an ascending circle of 5ths).

- The **order of flats** is: B–E–A–D–G–C–F (a descending circle of 5ths).

Once you have memorized these orderings, you can identify a key signature by the following rules:

- *Major keys with sharps in the signature:* The last sharp is the leading tone in our key. For instance, if the signature has four sharps (F♯–C♯–G♯–D♯), then D♯ is the

♪♪♪ Example C.6

a. Sharps

b. Flats

c.

leading tone in our key. The key is then EM. What is the key if the signature has five sharps?

- *Major keys with flats in the signature:* The next to last flat is the actual key. For instance, if the signature has four flats (B♭–E♭–A♭–D♭), then the next to last flat, A♭, provides the name of the key, A♭M. What is the key if the signature has six flats?

EXERCISE

To practice writing and identifying major key signatures, refer to exercises C.2.1 and C.3.1 in worksheet C at the end of this chapter.

The Minor Key Signatures; Parallel and Relative Keys

In example C.3 the key of Cm is used to illustrate the minor mode. This permits us to see the parallelism between CM (example C.2) and Cm, the major and minor keys with the same tonic. These pairs of keys, which share a tonic, are indeed called **parallel keys**. We thus say, for instance, that the parallel minor of DM is Dm. Another possibility in example C.3 would have been to use the minor key with no accidentals in the key signature, Am, which is also closely related to CM. In their diatonic forms (that is, considering the natural minor scale), both use the same set of pitches, the white keys of the piano. Pairs of major-minor keys that use the same set of pitches in their scales, or, in other words, whose key signatures are identical, are called **relative keys**. We thus say that Bm is the relative minor of DM (they both feature two sharps in their key signatures). In all cases, the tonic of a relative minor is a minor 3rd below the tonic of its relative major (as in B–D). In summary,

1. *Parallel M/m keys*: Same tonic, different set of pitches in their scales, for example, CM–Cm.

2. *Relative M/m keys*: Different tonic, same set of pitches in their scales, same key signatures. Relative minor tonic: a m3 below corresponding relative major, for example, CM–Am.

EXERCISE

To practice determining relative major and minor keys, refer to exercise C.1 in worksheet C at the end of this chapter.

The easiest way to determine the **key signature for a minor key** (other than memory) is to refer the key to its relative major, that is, to think of the major key whose tonic is a m3 above our minor key. For instance, the key signature for F♯m will be the same as the key signature for the major key a m3 above, AM, or three sharps. Conversely, what is the minor key whose signature has four flats? The major key with four flats is A♭M. The minor key a m3 below A♭ is Fm, which will then have four flats.

The inner circle of keys in example C.5 shows the circle of 5ths for minor keys. You can also see, in the correspondence between the outer and inner circles, all the relative M/m relationships among all 24 keys (12 major and 12 minor, without counting enharmonic spellings of keys).

EXERCISE

To practice writing and identifying minor key signatures, refer to exercises C.2.2 and C.3.2 in worksheet C at the end of this chapter.

OTHER MODES AND SCALES

Although the major or minor scales are the ones most often found in common practice Western music, other scales are at times also used. Among these, the medieval and Renaissance Church modes (often used in jazz) are especially important.

The Church Modes

In essence, the **medieval Church modal system** was based on four basic modes, to which two more were added in the Renaissance. The four original modes are **Dorian**, **Phrygian**, **Lydian**, and **Mixolydian**. The two added modes are **Aeolian** and **Ionian**.

♪♪♪Example C.7

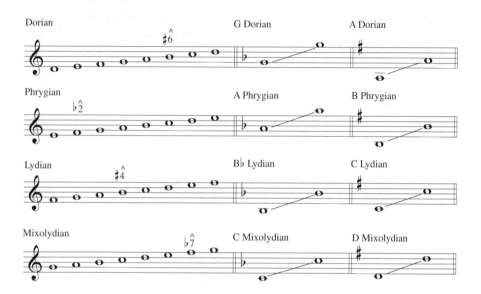

We can first think of these modes as using different white-key scales. Example C.7 first shows the white-key (no key signature) scale for each of the modes. Moreover, we can think of the modes in relation to the familiar major and natural minor scales, and remember which scale degree is different in each of the modes:

1. *Dorian (scale D–D)*: a natural minor scale with a raised $\hat{6}$ (♯$\hat{6}$, or B♮).
2. *Phrygian (E–E)*: a natural minor scale with a lowered $\hat{2}$ (♭$\hat{2}$, or F♮).
3. *Lydian (F–F)*: a major scale with a raised $\hat{4}$ (♯$\hat{4}$, or B♮).
4. *Mixolydian (G–G)*: a major scale with a lowered $\hat{7}$ (♭$\hat{7}$, or F♮).
5. *Aeolian (A–A)* is like natural minor (not included in example C.7).
6. *Ionian (C–C)* is like major (not included in example C.7).

To these modes we can add the modern mode **Locrian**, made up of the octave B–B (a minor scale with a lowered $\hat{2}$ and a lowered $\hat{5}$).

Transposing the Modes

After the white-key scales in example C.7, we first see the most common transposition of these modes in the Middle Ages and the Renaissance: up a 4th. A transposition up a 4th adds a flat to the signature. If we go down a 4th, on the other hand, we add a sharp. In modern times, the modes can be transposed to begin on any tonic. What is the relationship between M/m key signatures and transposed modal signatures? Comparing each of the transposed modes in example C.7 with the M or m key which has the same tonic, we come up with the following set of equivalences:

1. *Transposed Dorian*: one fewer ♭ or one more ♯ than the minor key with the same tonic. For example, Dorian on G has one ♭, whereas Gm has two ♭s (−1♭); Dorian on A has one ♯, and Am has no ♯s (+1♯).

2. *Transposed Phrygian*: one more ♭ or one fewer ♯ than the minor key with the same tonic. For example, Phrygian on A has one ♭, whereas Am has no ♭s (+1♭); Phrygian on B has one ♯, and Bm has two ♯s (−1♯).

3. *Transposed Lydian*: one fewer ♭ or one more ♯ than the major key with the same tonic. For example, Lydian on B♭ has one ♭, and B♭M has two ♭s (−1♭); Lydian on C has one ♯, and CM has no ♯s (+1♯).

4. *Transposed Mixolydian*: one more ♭ or one fewer ♯ than the major key with the same tonic. For example, Mixolydian on C has one ♭, whereas CM has no ♭s (+1♭); Mixolydian on D has one ♯, and DM has two ♯s (−1♯).

EXERCISES

To practice identifying modal key signatures, refer to exercise C.5 in worksheet C at the end of this chapter.

To practice writing modal scales, refer to exercise C.6 in worksheet C at the end of this chapter.

Other Scales

The number of different scales one could build with different combinations of twelve pitches is obviously enormous. Some tonal systems, like the Indian *rāga* system, use a truly astounding wealth of scales. South Indian, or Karnatic, music, for instance, is based on 72 reference scales (*mēlakartā rāgas*), from each of which one can further generate various other derived scales. We will show here a few scales commonly found in the Western tradition, along with a few other "exotic" scales. Although you should memorize the first group (example C.8), you need not memorize the second group (example C.9) unless you wish to do so. It is only given as a tiny sample of interesting and unusual scales of the type found in non-Western traditions.

1. The **chromatic scale** contains all twelve pitches, and all motion is by half steps (example C.8a).

2. The **whole-tone scale** is made up only of whole tones and contains only six different pitches (example C.8b).

3. A **pentatonic scale** consists of only five different pitches. There are numerous types of pentatonic scales. Example C.8c shows the most usual type found in Western music. It is called "anhemiotic" because it lacks semitones.

4. The **blues scale** (example C.8d) is a major scale with two added chromatic inflections: scale degree $\hat{3}$ can appear as either ♭$\hat{3}$ or ♮$\hat{3}$, and scale degree $\hat{7}$ can appear as either ♭$\hat{7}$ or ♮$\hat{7}$.

♪♪♪ Example C.8

a.

b.

c.

d.

♪♪♪ Example C.9

5. Two other types of pentatonic scales are among those frequently used in Asian music. Both contain semitones and appear in examples C.9a and b. Both are frequently used in Asian music. The first one is a characteristic scale of Indonesia's *pelog* tuning system, also found in South India as the *Gambhīranāta rāga.* The second scale is found in South Indian music as the *Śuddha Sāvēri rāga,* and also in Indonesian and Japanese repertoires.

6. Two beautiful and more complex scales which were already mentioned in chapter A (see example A.11) appear again in examples C.9c and d. The first one, known as "the Gypsy scale," plays a prominent role in Hungarian Gypsy music. The second one is a characteristic scale of Arabic and Middle Eastern music, also found in South India as the *Mayāmālavagaula rāga.*[1]

EXERCISE

To practice identifying tonal characteristics and scale types for melodies from a variety of repertoires, refer to exercise C.9 in worksheet C at the end of this chapter.

TRANSPOSITION: RELATED ISSUES

Using Clefs for Transposition

Examine example C.10a. You will recognize again the opening measures of "The First Noël," notated in CM and treble clef. Imagine that you need to perform or notate this same tune in DM (that is, up a M 2nd) and all you have is this CM/treble clef score available. There are several things you could do. You could just read pitch by pitch and think "a M 2nd up" for each pitch (a fairly inefficient process). Or you could read the tune as it is notated in our CM/treble version as if it were notated in alto clef, adding the corresponding DM key signature. You would then be reading the opening notes as F♯–E–D instead of E–D–C, as shown in example C.10b. In other words, by reading the tune as if it were in alto clef, we are transposing it a 2nd up. It you read it in tenor clef, as shown in example C.10c, you will transpose it a 2nd down. Whether these transpositions are a M2 or a m2 up or down depends only on the accidentals or key signatures you assign to them. Compare, for instance, examples C.10c and d. In both cases, you read the same letter names: D–C–B. If you read them with a BM key signature, then they become D♯–C♯–B, and we are transposing a m2 down. If the key signature we assign is B♭M, then we read D–C–B♭, and we transpose a M2 down. Finally, example C.10e shows that by reading the tune in bass clef we can transpose it a 3rd up. By means of other clefs, one can also realize a variety of other transpositions.

Example C.11 shows a similar process in transposing a melody notated in the bass clef, using the clefs we have learned so far. The alto clef transposes the bass clef notation down a 2nd. The tenor clef transposes bass clef notation up a 5th, and the treble

---

[1]Students interested in the fascinating world of South Indian *rāgas* and scales can consult Ludwig Pesch's *The Illustrated Companion to South Indian Classical Music* (Delhi: Oxford U. Press, 1999).

♪♪♪ Example C.10

a.

CM: E D   C

b. 2nd up

Think: Write or play:

DM: F♯ E   D

c. 2nd down

Think: Write or play:

BM: D♯ C♯   B

d. 2nd down

Think: Write or play:

B♭M: D C   B♭

e. 3rd up

Think: Write or play:

EM: G♯ F♯   E

clef transposes it down a 3rd. The following chart summarizes all the transpositions we
have just discussed.

To transpose a melody written in treble clef:

- *Up a 2nd*: read in alto clef.

- *Down a 2nd*: read in tenor clef.

- *Up a 3rd*: read in bass clef.

To transpose a melody written in bass clef:

- *Down a 2nd*: read in alto clef.

- *Up a 5th*: read in tenor clef.

- *Down a 3rd*: read in treble clef.

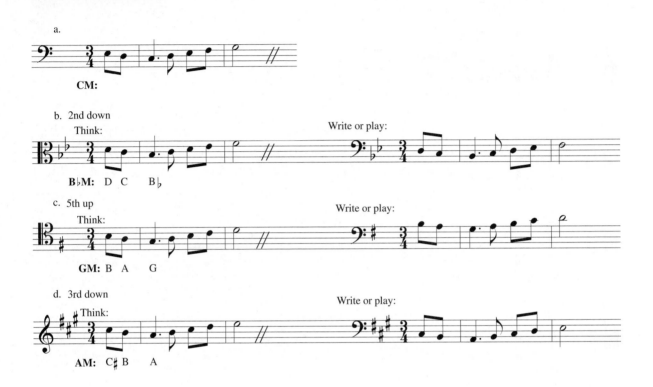

Example C.11

a.

CM:

b. 2nd down
Think: Write or play:

B♭M: D C   B♭

c. 5th up
Think: Write or play:

GM: B A   G

d. 3rd down
Think: Write or play:

AM: C♯ B   A

EXERCISE

To practice various transpositions of a melody, refer to exercise C.7 in worksheet C at the end of this chapter.

Transposing Instruments

If you play a scale notated as CM on a flute, an oboe, a bassoon, a trombone, a violin, or a variety of other instruments, what you will hear will actually be a CM scale. This statement would be trivially obvious if it were not that you do *not* hear a CM scale in many other instruments when you play what is notated like one. A scale notated as CM will sound a M2 lower (sounding like a B♭M scale) when played on a clarinet in B♭. Or it will sound a P5 lower (sounding like an FM scale) when played on a horn in F. These are what we call **transposing instruments**. In all these instruments, the actual sounding pitches are not the same as those notated. Example C.12 shows how some common transposing instruments would sound if they all read the same opening of our

♪♪♪ Example C.12

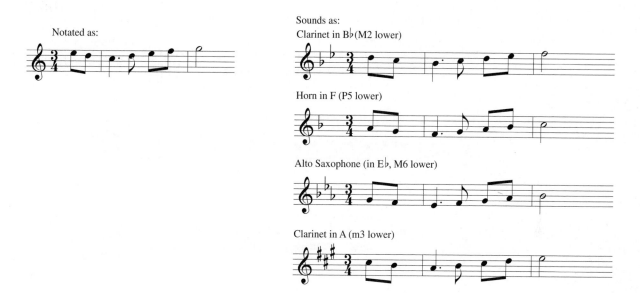

familiar "The First Noël" notated in CM. As you will see, if they all played together from the same score in C, the resulting sound would be quite interesting indeed! The following comments refer to this example.

1. When we say that an instrument is "in B♭" we mean that if that instrument plays a notated C the actual sound (or "concert pitch") will be B♭. A clarinet in B♭ sounds a M2 lower than notated. We hear both the pitches and, therefore, the key, transposed down a M2.

2. When we say that an instrument is "in F" we mean that if that instrument plays a notated C the actual sound will be F. A horn in F sounds a P5 lower than notated. We hear both the pitches and, therefore, the key, transposed down a P5.

3. Based on these two examples, explain what we mean when we say that an instrument is in E♭ or in A, and what we hear exactly when an alto saxophone (in E♭) or a clarinet in A plays our tune notated in CM.

Example C.12 shows how you should read transposing instruments when you find them notated on a score. Writing for these instruments, however, presents the opposite problem. Example C.13 shows how we should notate a melodic fragment from Maurice Ravel's *Bolero* if we want it to sound "in C" on the same transposing instruments

♪♪♪ Example C.13

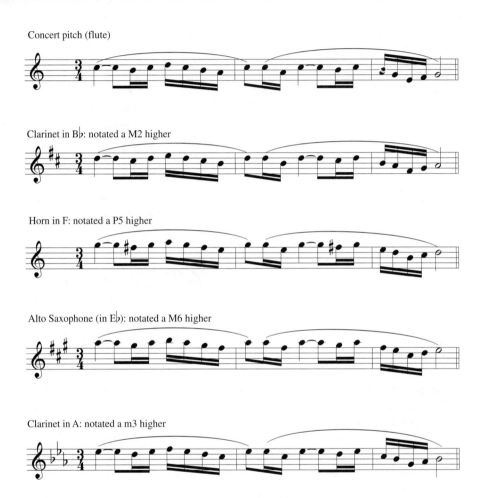

Concert pitch (flute)

Clarinet in B♭: notated a M2 higher

Horn in F: notated a P5 higher

Alto Saxophone (in E♭): notated a M6 higher

Clarinet in A: notated a m3 higher

we discussed above. If these instruments now played this fragment as notated for each of them, the resulting sound would be a unison line in CM. The comments below refer to this example.

1. If you want a clarinet in B♭ to sound a B♭, you need to write a C. To notate a line for clarinet in B♭, you should then transpose it a M2 higher. The same applies to the key signature: if the resulting key is CM, you should notate the clarinet's key signature transposed a M2 higher, in DM.

2. If you want a horn in F to sound an F, you need to write a C. To notate a line for horn in F, you should then transpose it a P5 higher. Of course, the key will also be transposed a P5 higher, but, by an old notational convention, we do not write a key signature in French horn parts. Instead we write the accidentals before each note.

In example C.13, you will see that the horn has been indeed transposed to GM, but we write the necessary sharp signs before each F, rather than in the key signature. This convention applies only to the French horn and does not affect any other transposing instrument.

3. Now comment on how (and why) we should notate the same line for an alto saxophone in E♭ and a clarinet in A, based on example C.13.

The following table provides a summary of transpositions in the transposing instruments most commonly found in orchestras and bands (other transpositions are possible for instruments such as the horn and the trumpet). The following instruments are in C, and hence are written in concert pitch: flute and piccolo (notated an octave lower than it sounds), oboe, bassoon, contrabassoon (notated an octave higher than it sounds), trumpet in C, trombone, tuba, and all string instruments (the double bass is notated an octave higher than it sounds).

Transposing Instruments

Instrument	Sound with Respect to Notation	Transposition Needed to Notate
English horn (in F)	P5 lower	P5 up
Clarinet in B♭	M2 lower	M2 up
in A	m3 lower	m3 up
in E♭	m3 higher	m3 down
Bass clarinet in B♭	M9 lower (M2 + 8ve)	M2 + 8ve up
Soprano saxophone in B♭	M2 lower	M2 up
Alto saxophone in E♭	M6 lower	M6 up
Tenor saxophone in B♭	M9 lower (M2 + 8ve)	M2 + 8ve up
Baritone saxophone in E♭	M13 lower (M6 + 8ve)	M6 + 8ve up
Horn in F	P5 lower	P5 up
in E♭	M6 lower	M6 up
in E	m6 lower	m6 up
in D	m7 lower	m7 up
Trumpet in B♭	M2 lower	M2 up
in D	M2 higher	M2 down

EXERCISE

To practice reading and notating melodies for transposing instruments, refer to exercise C.8 in worksheet C at the end of this chapter.

ASSIGNMENT

For an assignment based on the materials learned in this chapter, refer to Chapter C in the Workbook.

Terms for Review

Tonal center
Tonic
Range
Scale
Triad
Root, third, fifth
Tonic triad
Tonal frame
Tonal system
Tonality
Major-minor tonality
Functional tonality
Major scale
Scale degrees
Scale degree names: tonic, supertonic,
    mediant, subdominant, dominant,
    submediant, leading tone
Melodic tendencies of scale degree
Major mode
Minor mode
Natural minor scale
Subtonic

Harmonic minor scale
Melodic minor scale
Key
Transposition
Major key signatures
Circle of 5ths
Order of sharps and flats
Parallel M/m keys
Relative M/m keys
Minor key signatures
Medieval Church modes: Dorian,
    Phrygian, Lydian, Mixolydian,
    Aeolian, Ionian
Locrian
Transposing the modes
Chromatic scale
Whole-tone scale
Pentatonic scale (anhemiotic)
Blues scale
Using clefs for transposition
Transposing instruments

Worseet C

EXERCISE C.1

1. Write the relative minor for the following major keys:

    E♭M: A♭M: AM: EM: F♯M:

    DM: FM: GM: BM: D♭M:

2. Write the relative major for the following minor keys:

    Gm: Dm: Bm: C♯m: Em:

    Fm: E♭m: Cm: B♭m: F♯m:

EXERCISE C.2

1. Identify the *major* key signatures in exercise C.2a.

2. Identify the *minor* key signatures in exercise C.2b.

3. Identify the *major or minor* key signatures in exercise C.2c.

a.

b.

c.

EXERCISE C.3

1. Write the *major* key signatures in exercise C.3a. Make sure to write sharps and flats in the correct order and to place them in the correct location on the staff.

2. Write the *minor* key signatures in exercise C.3b.

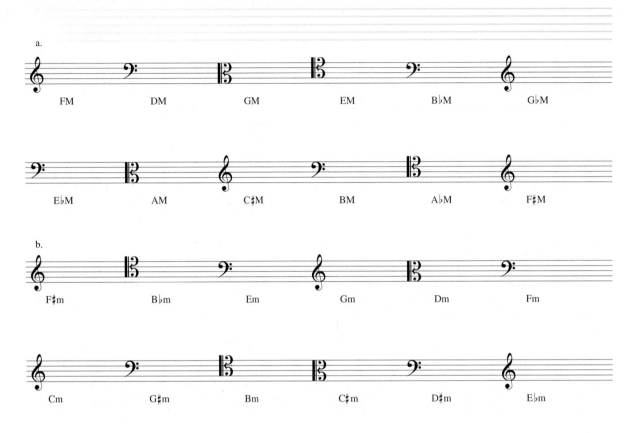

EXERCISE C.4   Write the following *major and minor* scales without using key signatures (use accidentals before each note as needed). The tonic for each scale is given.

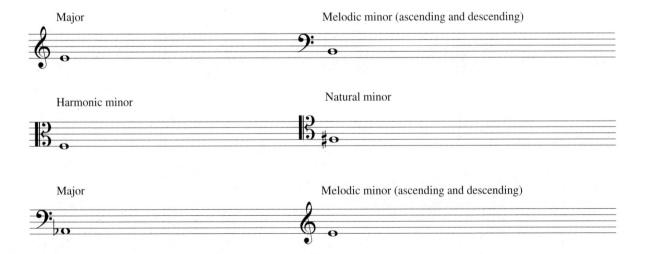

EXERCISE C.5   Identify the following *modal* signatures, given the signature and the tonic. In all cases, these are transposed Church mode signatures.

EXERCISE C.6   Write the following transposed modal scales without using signatures (write accidentals before each note as needed).

EXERCISE C.7   Transpose the melody in exercise C.7 to the required intervals. In each case, first determine what the transposed key will be. Then, write the transposed key signature, and finally transpose the pitches to the required interval. Can you use any of the clefs you have learned so far to help you realize any of these transpositions?

1. Up a P4 in exercise C.7a.

2. Down a M2 in exercise C.7b.

3. Up a M3 in exercise C.7c.

EXERCISE C.8

1. Suppose that the melody in exercise C.8a, from Felix Mendelssohn's Violin Concerto, II, is to be performed as notated by a clarinet in B♭, an English horn, and an alto saxophone. Write, in the spaces provided, what the melody would sound like as played by each of these instruments.

2. Suppose that you need to write the Polish folk tune in exercise C.8b to be performed in unison by a soprano saxophone, a horn in F, and a clarinet in A. In the spaces provided, write the correct part for each of these instruments as they would have to perform it in order for the melody to sound in FM as notated in the given version. Notice the accidentals in this melody, and make sure you transpose them correctly.

EXERCISE C.9   Sing or play each of the following melodies. Then, analyze the melody to determine the following items: Tonic pitch (or tonal center), tonic triad, range, tonal frame, mode or key, and scale. Write each of the items in the spaces provided under each melody. The answers for the first melody are provided as an example. This same process is also illustrated in example C.1.

For mode or key, the following options are possible: Any major or minor key, any of the Church modes (Dorian, Phrygian, etc.), pentatonic, or whole tone. Among the scales, the chromatic scale is also a possibility (in the context of any major or minor key). Because some of these melodies are not really based on the principles of major-minor tonality as we have presented them in this chapter, some of the items do not apply to them. You will find these items marked with the sign N/A.

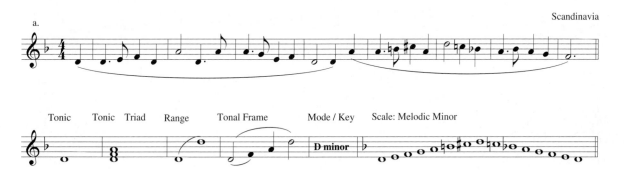

b.   Bartók

Tonic   Tonic Triad   Range   Tonal Frame   Mode / Key   Scale:

c.   Fine   France
                                                                                         D.C.

Tonic   Tonic Triad   Range   Tonal Frame   Mode / Key   Scale:

d.   Mozart

Tonic   Tonic Triad   Range   Tonal Frame   Mode / Key   Scale:

e.   Plainchant

As - per - ges   me Do - mi - ne   hys - so - po   et   mun - da - bor

Tonic   Tonic Triad   Range   Tonal Frame   Mode / Key   Scale:

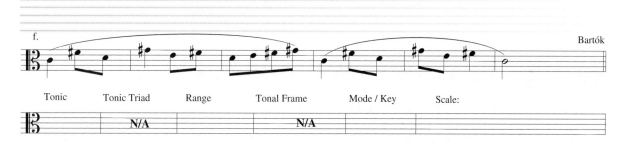

f.   Bartók

Tonic   Tonic Triad   Range   Tonal Frame   Mode / Key   Scale:

                        N/A   N/A

g.   Mussorgsky

Tonic   Tonic Triad   Range   Tonal Frame   Mode / Key   Scale:

h.   Scotland

Tonic   Tonic Triad   Range   Tonal Frame   Mode / Key   Scale:

i.

                                                                                      Hassler

Tonic   Tonic Triad   Range   Tonal Frame   Mode / Key   Scale:

Adam de la Hale

j.

Tonic   Tonic Triad   Range   Tonal Frame   Mode / Key   Scale:

King Frederick the Great / Bach

k.

Tonic   Tonic Triad   Range   Tonal Frame   Mode / Key   Scale:

Chapter D

Introduction to Species Counterpoint

Music made up of several different melodic lines or voices is known as **polyphony**. The term **counterpoint** refers to both the art of combining two or more melodic lines and to the set of technical principles that regulates such combination of voices. All music in which different independent voices are presented together is contrapuntal. Composers in some musical periods, however, have been particularly inclined to writing in contrapuntal style. It is usually considered that the two high points of contrapuntal art were reached in the late Renaissance (second half of the sixteenth century, by composers such as Giovanni Pierluigi da Palestrina, Tomás Luis de Victoria, and Orlande de Lassus) and the late baroque (first half of the eighteenth century, notably by J. S. Bach). Of these, modal Renaissance counterpoint presents one of the most strict and rigorous sets of principles and technical regulations of any style in the whole history of music. For this reason it has been used throughout the centuries, to this day, as an excellent pedagogical tool to teach the craft of voice leading.

In 1725, Austrian composer and theorist Johann Joseph Fux published a treatise on counterpoint, *Gradus ad Parnassum* ("Steps to Parnassus") in which he presented a gradual, pedagogical approach to teaching counterpoint based on the principles of sixteenth-century contrapuntal style.[1] Fux's method is usually known as **species counterpoint**. Because it teaches strict control of the musical material, and because it provides the foundation for all tonal voice leading, species counterpoint has been a staple component of a composer's craft-building education since it was first used by Fux. As a valuable example, Beethoven's studies of species counterpoint with his teacher, Haydn, are reproduced in 54 pages of the book *The Great Composer as Teacher and*

---

[1]For a modern edition of Fux's *Gradus ad Parnassum,* refer to Johann Joseph Fux, *The Study of Counterpoint,* by Alfred Mann (New York: Norton, 1971). More specifically stylistic approaches to the study of sixteenth-century counterpoint (including the study of melody, rhythm, and text setting) can also be found in any of the following books: Knud Jeppesen, *Counterpoint* (New York: Dover, 1992); Robert Gauldin, *A Practical Approach to Sixteenth-Century Counterpoint* (Prospect Heights, IL: Waveland Press, 1995); and Peter Schubert, *Modal Counterpoint, Renaissance Style* (New York: Oxford University Press, 1999).

Student by Alfred Mann (New York: Dover, 1994). Although the study of species counterpoint is not indispensable to the study of harmony and voice leading, it provides a very strong musical and technical foundation on which to begin the studies of harmony. We will study, throughout this book, a variety of harmonic and linear concepts and techniques that can be referred back to species counterpoint, such as the good shape of melodic lines, the relationship between outer voices in a four-voice harmonic setting, the theory of nonchord tones, and especially the theory of suspensions.

In this chapter we will provide an introduction to species counterpoint. A full coverage of all five species in two, three, and four voices would require several chapters. We will limit our introductory study to three species (first, second, and fourth) in only two voices. Besides providing a foundation for your studies of harmony, going through the discipline of writing two-voice counterpoint will also give you some appreciation of the complexity of a good Renaissance composer's (or any good composer's) craft. For a glimpse into the style of Renaissance music which was composed following these principles of counterpoint, you may listen to Victoria's *Kyrie* from the Mass *O magnum mysterium* (anthology, no. 1), and read the discussion of this style in chapter G.

THE MELODIC LINE IN SPECIES COUNTERPOINT

In the Middle Ages and the Renaissance, polyphony was often built on preexistent melodies, usually borrowed from plainchant or other sources. A preexistent melody used as the basis for polyphonic composition is known as **cantus firmus.** Species counterpoint is usually also written on *cantus firmi.* We will then write our counterpoint on given melodies.

Because one of the functions of counterpoint is to preserve the independence and quality of individual lines, we will first practice writing single good lines. We will write for one of the four usual voice types: soprano, alto, tenor, or bass. You should keep your melodies within the acceptable range for each of these voices. You will find the vocal ranges in chapter 1, example 1.6.

In our counterpoint exercises we will write modal melodies using the modal scales we learned in chapter C. We will avoid, at this stage, the complexities of the medieval and Renaissance modal system. In its simplified form, sufficient for our purposes, the system is made up of the six basic modes we know from chapter C. The melodies in example D.1 are Fux's examples of modal melodies for each of these six modes. Examine and sing each of them. Then notice the following characteristics common to all of these melodies.

1. Fux's melodies are diatonic. Most of the melodic motion is by steps or small leaps. There are no repeated notes.

2. Each of Fux's single leaps is preceded or followed by motion in the opposite direction (the only exception to this observation is the opening leap in the Ionian melody; it is acceptable to begin a melody with a leap of a 3rd followed by stepwise motion in the same direction). Leaps larger than a 5th are rare, but if they occur (as in the 8ve leap in the Phrygian melody), they are both preceded and followed by motion in the opposite direction.

♪♪♪ Example D.1   Johann Joseph Fux's Modal *cantus firmi*

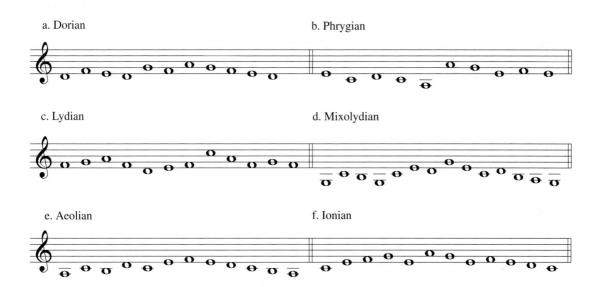

a. Dorian

b. Phrygian

c. Lydian

d. Mixolydian

e. Aeolian

f. Ionian

3. Two successive leaps in the same direction (or double leaps) outline the pitches of a major or minor triad, and in all cases they are both preceded and followed by motion in the opposite direction. You will find double leaps in the Lydian and Mixolydian melodies.

4. Each of Fux's melodies has a single focal point (a high or a low point). Verify the single focal point in each of the melodies. Do the melodic lines build up toward their focal points?

5. Each of Fux's melodies begins and ends on the tonic pitch. Final tonic pitches are approached by step from above or below. These are musical points of arrival or **cadences**, in this case articulated melodically by step ($\hat{2}$–$\hat{1}$ or $\hat{7}$–$\hat{1}$).

We can organize these observations in the form of the following guidelines, which you should carefully follow when you write your melodies. These principles are based on the melodic style of sixteenth-century sacred polyphony. To begin with, we will write melodies in whole notes, without bar lines.

Melodic Guidelines in Species Counterpoint

1. Your melodies should be *diatonic* (except for the leading tone at cadences in minor modes and G modes, and in the ascending fragment $\hat{5}$–$\sharp\hat{6}$–$\sharp\hat{7}$–$\hat{1}$ in minor). Always raise $\hat{7}$ at cadences (not within phrases) in minor modes and Mixolydian, but *not* in Phrygian.

2. Notes are *rarely repeated.*

3. Melodic motion will be mostly *by steps*.

4. Leaps are acceptable, with the following limitations:

   a) No *augmented or diminished* intervals are allowed.

   b) In general, leaps should not be *larger than a P5* (except for P8).

   c) Occasionally you may write an *ascending m6* (not descending, not a M6).

   d) All leaps should be *preceded or followed* by motion in the opposite direction.

   e) The ascending m6 and all P8s should be *both preceded and followed* by motion in the opposite direction.

   f) Occasionally you may write *two successive leaps in the same direction*. In this case:

     1) Both leaps should be preceded and followed by motion in the opposite direction.

     2) Both leaps may outline only a major or minor triad (not a diminished triad, that is, a triad whose fifth is diminished, as in B–D–F), or an 8ve (divided, from the bottom, as 5th + 4th, not 4th + 5th: D–A–D, not D–G–D).

5. Your melody should have a *single climax* or *focal point*. A high point is called a **zenith**, and a low point a **nadir**. A focal point should not be an isolated pitch. Rather, you should build up (or down) toward it progressively.

6. The last three or four notes of a passage in a single direction should not stress a tritone (although a diminished 5th is acceptable).

7. Your melodies should end on suitable *melodic cadences*. All of your melodies should end on Î. Approach the final Î by step from above or from below.

Verify that all the melodies in example D.1 follow the above guidelines. Example D.2, on the other hand, shows several faulty melodic segments. Identify the problem or problems in each of the melodies.

♫♪ Example D.2   Melodies for Error Detection

To practice writing melodies in each of the modes, refer to exercise D.1 in worksheet D at the end of this chapter.

GENERAL GUIDELINES FOR TWO-PART COUNTERPOINT

Before we begin studying the species one by one, consider the following guidelines, which apply equally to all species in two voices.

1. Counterpoint is made up of *equally good independent voices* in opposition: There should be no static voices. Do not "sit on a pitch."

2. Climaxes in both voices should be at different times, or of different types.

3. Begin the counterpoint with a PU (unison), P5, or P8.

4. End on a PU or a P8 only.

5. You will write counterpoint on a given *cantus firmus*.

   a) If the counterpoint (CTP) is above the *cantus firmus* (CF), then CF begins on $\hat{1}$, and CTP on $\hat{1}$ or $\hat{5}$.

   b) If CTP is below CF, then CTP begins on $\hat{1}$ (and so does CF).

You may verify each of the above points in the two-voice examples in example D.4. In example D.4a, moreover, we can see all four possible **types of motion** between two voices (*dyads,* or pairs of simultaneous pitches, are numbered in example D.4 for easy reference) as discussed below:

1. **Oblique motion**: A voice moves (up or down), the other voice stays on the same pitch. The motion between dyads 1 and 2 is oblique.

2. **Parallel motion**: Voices move in the same direction preserving the harmonic interval between them. See dyads 2 and 3.

3. **Contrary motion**: Voices move in opposite directions, as between dyads 3 and 4.

4. **Similar motion**: Voices move in the same direction, but the harmonic interval between them is not preserved. See dyads 4 and 5.

FIRST SPECIES (1:1)

In **first-species** counterpoint we write a note of counterpoint against each *cantus firmus* note. For this species we will use the same notation of whole notes with no bar lines. Keep in mind the general principles of both melodic writing and two-voice counterpoint which we outlined in the previous sections. Otherwise, the following criteria apply to first species in particular.

1. In first species we use *only consonances* as harmonic intervals: P5, P8, m3, M3, m6, M6.

2. *The* **harmonic P4** *is a dissonance in two-voice counterpoint.* It should be avoided, along with all other dissonances.

3. The PU is used *only to begin or to end* a phrase in first species, not within the phrase.

4. Perfect intervals (PU, P5, and P8) should be approached only by *contrary* or *oblique* motion, not by parallel or similar motion (examples D.3a and b).

5. **Parallel perfect unisons**, **5ths**, **or 8ves** *are always incorrect,* even if they are approached by *contrary motion* (as in P5–P12 or PU–P8). See example D.3b.

6. The only exception to rule no. 4 is what we know as **horn 5ths** (similar motion descending from a 3rd to a P5, or ascending from a 6th to a P5) if the top voice moves by steps (example D.3c). Similar motion into a perfect interval with the top voice leaping produces the incorrect motion known as **direct** or **hidden unison**, **5th, or 8ve**, as we indicated in example D.3b.

7. *Voices should not overlap.* **Voice overlap** takes place when the higher voice is on a lower pitch than the lower voice's immediately preceding note, or vice versa. Overlap results, for instance, from a faulty direct unison (see example D.3b).

Example D.3   Motions into Perfect Intervals

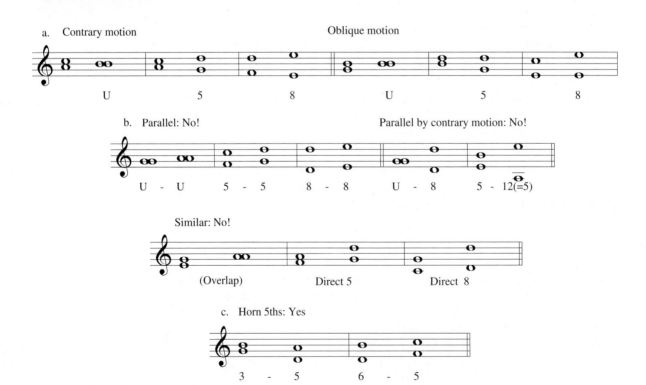

♪♪♪Example D.4

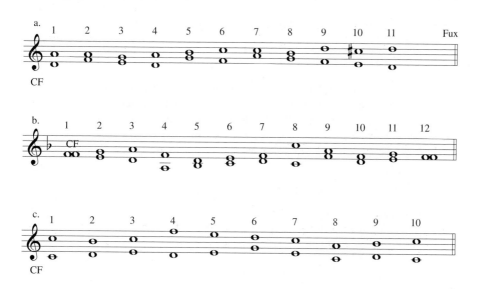

8. *Voices should not cross.* In **voice crossing** the upper voice moves below the lower voice, or vice versa.

9. You should not write more than *three parallel 3rds or parallel 6ths* in succession.

Three examples of correct first-species counterpoint appear in example D.4. Sing through them in class or with a friend. Then, analyze and verify the consonances, the motion between dyads, the quality of the individual voices, and their contour and independence. After you do this, analyze the two phrases in example D.5, which include several melodic or contrapuntal errors. Mark and identify all the errors in these two examples.

♪♪♪Example D.5

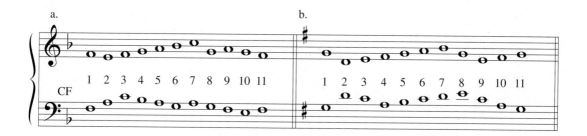

EXERCISE

To practice writing first-species counterpoint, refer to exercise D.2 in worksheet D at the end of this chapter.

SECOND SPECIES (2:1)

In **second-species** counterpoint we write two notes of counterpoint against each *cantus firmus* note. We will notate second species in cut time, with bar lines. In this meter, the counterpoint consists of a metrically stressed half note (beat 1) and a metrically unstressed half note (beat 2) per measure. Second species allows for the first type of dissonance in our studies of counterpoint, as we explain in the following guidelines.

1. The *stressed half note* may only be consonant.

2. The *unstressed half note* may be consonant or dissonant (examples D.6a–b).

3. The only possible dissonance in second species is the **passing tone** (PT). A PT fills in a melodic gap of a 3rd by steps (examples D.6b–c).

♪♪♪ Example D.6

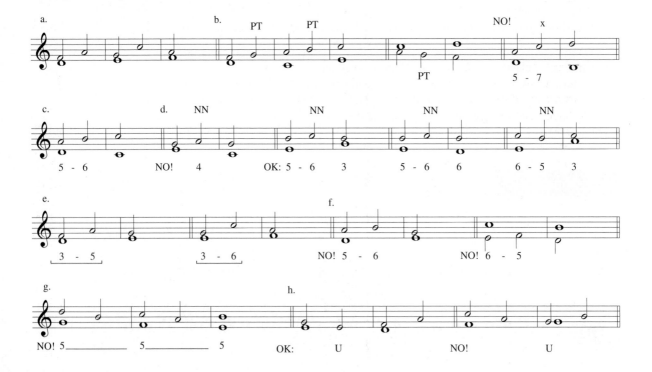

4. A PT may be *consonant* or *dissonant.* A consonant PT is, for instance, a 5–6 figure (example D.6c).

5. The unstressed half note should not be a *dissonant* **neighbor note** (NN), although it may be a *consonant neighbor note.* A neighbor note moves up (upper NN) or down (lower NN) one step from a given pitch, and returns also by step to the same pitch. A dissonant NN as well as consonant NN figures involving 5–6 or 6–5 motions are illustrated in example D.6d.

6. If the second half note is consonant, it should stay *within the same triad* which was implied by the first half note. In other words, you should not write a 5–6 or 6–5 figure unless the second half note is a PT or a NN. In example D.6e, all three notes in the 3–5 figure belong to the same triad (D–F–A), and so do the three notes in the 3–6 figure (C–E–G). In Example D.6f, on the other hand, both the 5–6 and the 6–5 figures imply two different triads per measure.

7. Avoid parallel 5ths or 8ves *between strong beats* (example D.6g).

8. A *unison on a weak beat* is acceptable. But a unison on a strong beat (in 2 voices) is not (example D.6h).

9. Avoid repeated notes in the voice in half notes (the counterpoint).

10. You may begin the counterpoint with a half-note rest.

11. The last two notes (the cadence) may be in whole notes.

Sing, in class or with a friend, the two examples of second species in example D.7. Verify the consonances and dissonances in these phrases, and the quality of the individual lines. Notice that in example D.7b the zenith in the counterpoint is reached

♪♪♪Example D.7

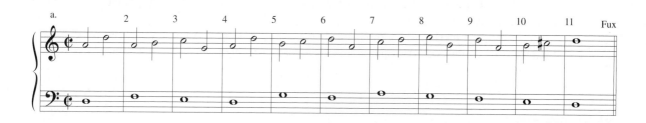

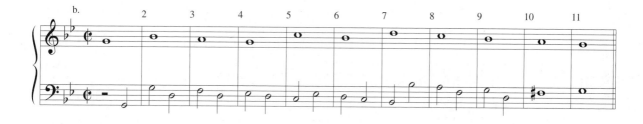

in the same measure as the zenith in the *cantus firmus*. But because the zeniths are not actually simultaneous (they take place in different beats), the phrase is perfectly acceptable.

EXERCISE

To practice writing second-species counterpoint, refer to exercise D.3 in worksheet D at the end of this chapter.

FOURTH SPECIES (SYNCOPATED)

In **fourth species** the counterpoint is a *syncopated voice*. Fourth-species syncopes are written across the bar line, so they span beat 2 of a measure (weak) and beat 1 of the next measure (strong). The syncopes may be *consonant* or *dissonant*. If a syncope is *consonant,* both beats are consonant with the CF. If the syncope is *dissonant,* its weak half is consonant, but its strong half is dissonant. In other words, *the weak beat of a syncope must always be consonant.*

Suspensions

The only possible dissonance on the strong beat of a syncope is a **suspension**. Refer to example D.8. First, you will see two thirds in first-species counterpoint (example D.8a). Then, the upper voice is delayed by one beat, in such a way that the motion from A to G does not come until beat 2 (example D.8b). Instead of a 3–3 counterpoint, we now have a 3–4–3 counterpoint, which includes a dissonance (the 4th) on the strong beat, resolving to a consonance (the 3rd) on the weak beat. Then, the lower voice is delayed by one beat (example D.8c). Instead of a 3–3 counterpoint we now have a 3–2–3 figure, in which the dissonance on the strong beat (a 2nd) resolves to a consonance on the weak beat.

A suspension thus creates a dissonance on a strong beat by delaying the motion between two consonances. A suspension figure actually has three parts: a **preparation**

Example D.8

♪♪♪ Example D.9

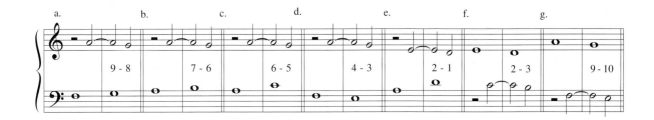

(P), always consonant and on a weak beat; the **suspension** (S), dissonant and on a strong beat; and the **resolution** (R), consonant and on a weak beat. *The resolution of a suspension is always by step and always descending.*

Suspension labels state the dissonant interval followed by the interval of resolution, both always counted from the bass upward. The suspension in example D.8b is, then, a 4–3 suspension, and in example D.8c we have a 2–3 suspension. There are three types of dissonant suspension when the syncopation is in the upper voice, as you can see in example D.9. These are the **9–8, 7–6, and 4–3 suspensions**. The **6–5 suspension** is not considered a real suspension by some authors, because it is not dissonant. We have nevertheless listed it in example D.9, because it functions as a suspension, albeit consonant. The **2–1 suspension** is similar to the 9–8 suspension, but instead of a 9th resolving to an 8ve, we have a 2nd resolving to a unison. *There is only one possible suspension when the syncopated voice is in the bass.* This is the **2–3 suspension**, or its compound version, the **9–10 suspension**. Beware that 4–3 and 7–8 bass suspensions are not possible or correct.

EXERCISE

To practice writing suspensions, refer to exercise D.4 in worksheet D at the end of this chapter.

Syncopated Counterpoint

Example D.10 shows two fragments of fourth-species counterpoint by Fux. In the first fragment, only consonant syncopes are used. The second fragment uses a string of dissonant syncopes, all 7–6 suspensions. To write a consonant syncope, one must find a note that is consonant with two adjacent notes of the CF. To write a dissonant syncope, one must be able to resolve the dissonant note to a consonance by means of a descending second. Study now examples D.11a and b, and write in the intervals between voices for every beat. Verify that all dissonances are treated as correct suspensions, and that all suspensions in example D.11b are of the 2–3 type or its compound.

In example D.12a we see that, because a suspension is a retardation of note-against-note counterpoint, a string of 4–3 suspensions (4–3–4–3–4–3) can be reduced

Example D.10

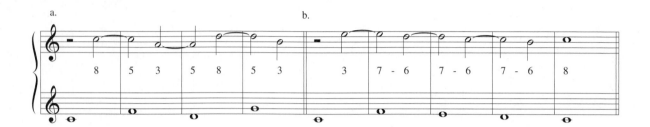

to a series of parallel 3rds (3–3–3). Similarly, a string of 9–8 suspensions (9–8–9–8–9–8) amounts to a series of parallel 8ves (8–8–8), and thus should be avoided (example D.12b). A string of 6–5 suspensions, on the other hand, is perfectly acceptable, because the 5ths are separated by consonant intervals (the 6ths), and so they do not amount to a series of parallel 5ths (example D.12c). Parallel 5ths between strong beats are correct in fourth species as long as they are separated by consonances, as in example D.12d. The same is true for 8ves, but you should not write more than two in a row (more would weaken the sonority of the passage).

The *best suspensions* are 7–6 and 4–3, because both resolve to imperfect consonances. 9–8 is acceptable, although weaker in two voices (it resolves to an octave), and

Example D.11

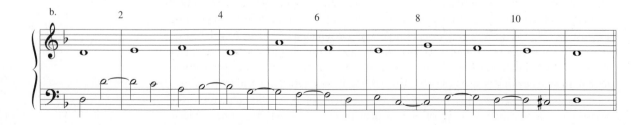

♪♪♪Example D.12

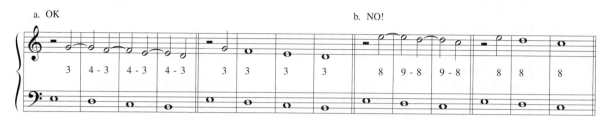

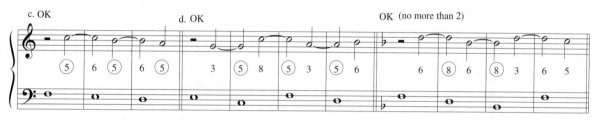

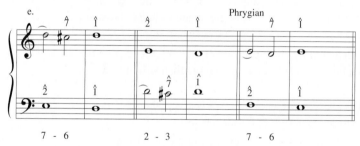

2–1 is tolerable, although it is the weakest of all (the unison within the phrase, however, is acceptable in fourth species).

Cadences should feature what is known as a ***clausula vera***, "true cadence." In a *clausula vera,* a M6 formed by degrees $\hat{2}$–$\hat{7}$ (with $\hat{2}$ in the bass, and a leading-tone $\hat{7}$ in all modes except for Phrygian) resolves to the octave $\hat{1}$–$\hat{1}$, or the inversion of the M6, a m3 ($\hat{7}$–$\hat{2}$, with $\hat{7}$ in the bass) resolves to a unison $\hat{1}$–$\hat{1}$ (or an octave if the m3 is compound).

If the cadence is of the M6 type, it will be approached with a 7–6 suspension. The m3 type will include a 2–3 suspension. These two standard cadential types appear in example D.12e. In this example you will also find another standard cadential type, the **Phrygian cadence**. In this type of cadence, $\hat{2}$–$\hat{1}$ is usually in the bass, and we do not raise $\hat{7}$ to make it a leading tone. The half-step motion in this cadence takes place as the "Phrygian $\hat{2}$–$\hat{1}$" in the bass, and not as an upper-voice leading tone.

Finally, you will have noticed that in example D.11 the chains of syncopations are occasionally broken. It is acceptable to do so, only occasionally, and if no better solution can be found. Do not break the chain, however, more than once or twice in an exercise of this length.

EXERCISE

To practice writing fourth-species cadences, refer to exercise D.5 in worksheet D at the end of this chapter.

The following points summarize what we have discussed regarding fourth species:

1. Syncopes: Consonant or dissonant.

2. Dissonant syncopes: suspensions.

3. Suspension: preparation (consonant, weak beat); suspension (dissonant, strong beat); resolution down by step (weak beat).

4. Suspensions: 9–8, 7–6, 4–3, and their compounds; only suspension in the bass: 2–3; consonant suspension: 6–5.

5. A suspension is a retardation of 1:1 counterpoint. 3–3–3–3 thus becomes 4–3–4–3–4–3 (example D.12a). Then, 9–8–9–8 is wrong; it amounts to //8–8 (example D.12b). But 6–5–6–5 is correct (both intervals are consonant, example D.12c).

6. Parallel 5ths on strong beat separated by consonances are fine: 3 | 5 8 | 5 3 | 5 6 | (example D.12d). The same applies to octaves, but to no more than two in a row: 6 | 8 6 | 8 3 | 6.

7. Best suspensions: 7–6 and 4–3 (and 2–3 in the bass); 9–8 is acceptable; 2–1 is tolerable (unison may be used within the phrase in fourth species).

8. Cadences: only 7–6 or 2–3, with both voices resolving to $\hat{1}$ (example D.12e).

9. It is possible to break the chain of syncopes, only occasionally and if no better solution is available.

Example D.13 contains *numerous* errors. Analyze this example carefully, mark all the errors, and identify the type of problem each of them represents.

♪♪♪ Example D.13

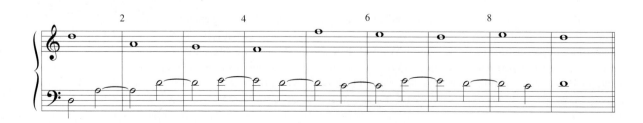

EXERCISES

To practice writing fourth-species counterpoint, refer to exercise D.6 in worksheet D at the end of this chapter.

For further practice in any of the species, use any of Fux's cantus firmi *in example D.1.*

ASSIGNMENT

For an assignment based on the materials learned in this chapter, refer to chapter D in the workbook.

Terms for Review

Polyphony
Counterpoint
Species counterpoint
Cantus firmus
Cadence
Zenith, nadir
Types of motion: oblique, parallel,
    contrary, similar
First species
Harmonic P4
Parallel perfect intervals
Horn 5ths
Direct or hidden unison, 5th or 8ve

Voice overlap
Voice crossing
Second species
Passing tone
Neighbor note
Fourth species
Suspensions
Preparation, suspension, resolution
4–3, 7–6, and 9–8 (or 2–1) suspensions
6–5 suspension
2–3 (or 9–10) suspension
Clausula vera
Phrygian cadence

Worksheet D

EXERCISE D.1 Write six melodies, one in each of the modes, following the guidelines discussed in the section, "The Melodic Line in Species Counterpoint," and the models provided in example D.1.

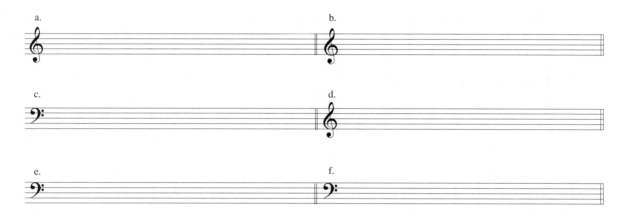

EXERCISE D.2 Write first-species counterpoints above and below the following *cantus firmus*. As a suggestion, you may find it helpful to first write the opening pitches, then the cadence, and then plot a curve for your melody before you realize the rest of the counterpoint.

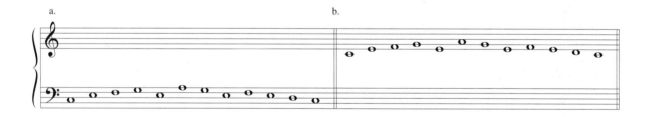

EXERCISE D.3 Write second-species counterpoints above and below the following *cantus firmus*.

b.

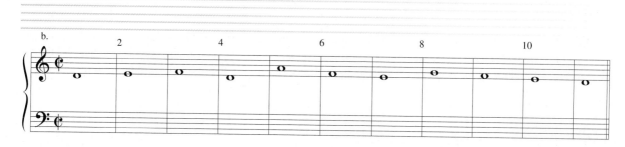

EXERCISE D.4   Complete the suspensions in this exercise in two voices. Some of the given notes are marked P for "preparation" or R for "resolution."

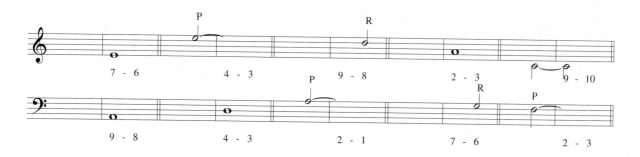

EXERCISE D.5   Complete these cadences in two voices, following the *clausula vera* and Phrygian cadential models in example D.12e.

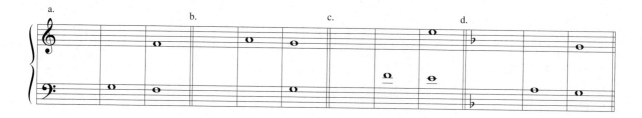

EXERCISE D.6   Write fourth-species counterpoints above and below the following *cantus firmus*. As a suggestion, you may find it helpful to work from both ends toward the middle. First write the opening pitches and the cadence, and then plan a tentative curve for your melody before you realize the rest of the counterpoint.

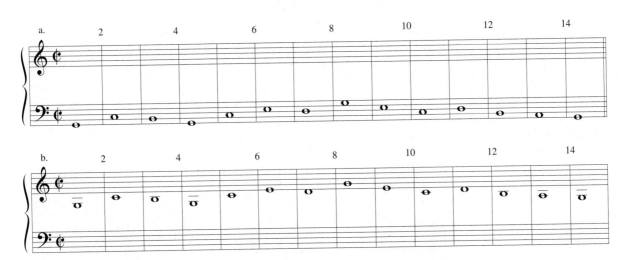

Chapter E

The Rudiments of Harmony I: Triads and Seventh Chords

When we listen to music, we hear two dimensions of sound. On the one hand, music moves forward in time. This is the horizontal dimension. On the other hand, we hear simultaneous sounds, musical "moments" in which several pitches sound at the same time. This is the vertical dimension. Horizontally, music is made up of melodies or lines; vertically, of chords or harmonies. Melodies and harmonies are totally interdependent. Harmonies result from several horizontal lines sounding together. Example E.1a demonstrates how four independent melodic lines create vertical harmonies. Melodies, in turn, are an elaborate linear or horizontal presentation of their underlying harmonies, as you can see in example E.1b. Notice that the melody in the upper staff is constructed mostly with the same pitches that constitute the harmonic accompaniment in the lower staff, along with some other ornamental pitches. The brackets in mm. 24–25, for instance, indicate the melodic and harmonic use of the pitches F–A–C, and the brackets in mm. 27–28 mark a similar use of the pitches C–E–G–B♭.

As a preparation for the study of tonal harmony (which we will begin in chapter 1), in this chapter we will focus on its vertical building blocks (triads and seventh chords), and in chapter F we will learn to label chords in a tonal context.

CHORDS

A group of three or more pitches sounded simultaneously is known as a **chord**. Example E.2a includes several chords in which all the pitches sound literally at the same time (**block chords**). The pitches in a chord, however, may also be sounded in close succession as in examples E.2b, c, and d. In this case we speak of **broken** or **arpeggiated chords**. The tonal system which we will study in this book is based almost exclusively on **tertian chords** (chords built of 3rds), and especially on triads and seventh chords.

♪♪♪ **Example E.1a**   J. S. Bach, Chorale 21, "Herzlich thut mich verlangen," mm. 1–4

♪♪♪ **Example E.1b**   Wolfgang Amadeus Mozart, Piano Concerto in CM, K. 467, II, mm. 23–29

In chapter A we discussed consonant and dissonant intervals. We can also speak of **consonant and dissonant chords**. A chord is consonant if each of the intervals formed by any two of its pitches are consonant. The first chord in example E.2a is consonant because, taking any two of its pitches, the possible intervals are a M3, a m3, and a P5. Chords 2 and 3, on the other hand, contain at least one dissonance each; hence, they are both dissonant. Identify all the possible dissonant intervals in these chords.

Example E.2

TRIADS

A **triad** is a chord made up of three pitches, which we call the **root** (the lowest pitch), the **third** (a M3 or m3 above the root), and the **fifth** (a P5, °5, or +5 above the root). The root is also called the **fundamental**. To differentiate triad members from intervals, in this book triad members will be fully spelled out (as in third and fifth), whereas intervals will be abbreviated (as in 3rd and 5th). Depending on the quality of the intervals involved, there may be four **triad types**, as illustrated by example E.3.

1. In a **major** triad (**M**) the third is a M3 above the root, whereas the fifth is a P5 above the root. If you think of the triad as a 5th divided into two 3rds, a major triad consists of a M3 at the bottom and a m3 at the top.

2. In a **minor** triad (**m**) the third is a m3 above the root, and the fifth is a P5 above the root. A minor triad consists of a m3 at the bottom and a M3 at the top.

3. In a **diminished** triad (°) the third is a m3 above the root, and the fifth is a °5 above the root. A diminished triad consists of two minor 3rds.

4. In an **augmented** triad ($^+$) the third is a M3 above the root, whereas the fifth is an +5 above the root. An *augmented* triad ($^+$) consists of two major 3rds.

All the triads in example E.3 are in *root position*, which means that the root is the lowest pitch (that is, the root is in the bass). *A triad is named after its root.* The major triad built on G (G–B–D), for instance, is the G major (GM) triad, and the minor triad built on D is the D minor (Dm) triad. We can similarly speak of the B diminished triad (B°) or the C augmented (C$^+$) triad.

Major and minor triads in root position are consonant and form the basic harmonic material in Western music since the Renaissance. Both diminished and augmented triads in root position, on the other hand, are dissonant because of the dissonant fifth.

Example E.3

Play each of these triad types, and hear the stable character of M and m triads (for instance, you can end a piece on one of these triads) as opposed to the unstable character of ° and ⁺ triads.

EXERCISE

To practice identifying and writing triads in root position, refer to exercises E.1 and E.2 in worksheet E at the end of this chapter.

Diatonic Triads in the Major and Minor Keys

Triads can be built on each degree of a major or minor scale. The triads most frequently used in diatonic harmony, as well as their quality, are indicated in example E.4. Example E.4a shows the triads on each degree of the major scale. In chapter C we learned the scale degree names (tonic, supertonic, mediant, etc.). The same terms are used to refer to the triads built on each of these degrees. Thus, the triad built on $\hat{1}$ is the tonic triad, the triad built on $\hat{2}$ is the supertonic triad, and so forth, as indicated in example E.4a.

The minor scale normally used in harmony is the harmonic minor scale (that is, the scale with $\flat\hat{6}$ and $\natural\hat{7}$). The chords in example E.4b, the most usual in minor-mode harmony, result from this scale (with the only exception of the chord on $\hat{3}$, which is most often major, and thus does not result from the harmonic minor scale because it includes a $\flat\hat{7}$). The occasional use of melodic or natural scales, however, may also produce other triads in the minor mode, as we will see in later chapters.

EXERCISE

To practice identifying the quality of triads built on each of the scale degrees, refer to exercise E.3 in worksheet E at the end of this chapter.

♪♪♪ Example E.4

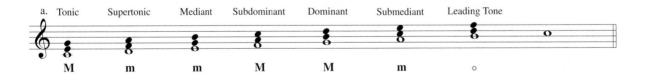

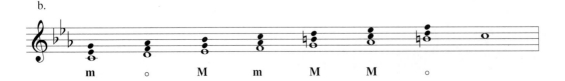

♪♪♪Example E.5

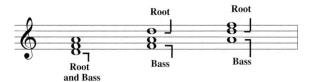

Bass and Root

Notice how the first two chords in example E.2b are different. In the first chord, C–E–G, the root (C) is in the bass. The **bass** is the lowest pitch in a sonority or texture, and it must not be confused with the **root** of a chord (the generating pitch on which a tertian chord is built). *The bass is not necessarily the root of a chord.* The second chord in example E.2b, ordered in 3rds, would be G–B–D. However, in example E.2b the root is not in the bass. Rather, the third (B) is in the bass. The diagram in example E.5 will help clarify the difference between root and bass: whereas the root of all three chords in this example is the same (the chord is always D–F–A, with D as its root), the bass in each case changes (D in the first chord, F in the second, and A in the third).

Chord Position: The Inversion of Triads

The **position** of a chord is determined by the chord member that is in the bass. The three positions of a triad are illustrated in example E.6a. Triad members in this example are indicated by the labels R (root), 3 (third), and 5 (fifth). Notice that what matters here is what triad member is in the bass. The pitches above the bass can appear in any order or register, regardless of the triad position:

1. A triad with the root in the bass is said to be in **root position**.

2. In the second triad we have moved the root up an octave, and the third is now in the bass. A triad with the third in the bass is in **first inversion**.

3. Finally, in the third chord in example E.6a we have also moved the third of the triad up an octave, and the fifth is now in the bass. This triad is in **second inversion**.

♪♪♪Example E.6

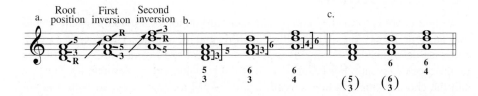

The following table summarizes all triad positions.

Triad Positions   Root is in the bass: triad in *root position*

Third in the bass: triad in *first inversion*

Fifth in the bass: triad in *second inversion*

The figures under the chords in example E.6b represent *intervals above the bass.* We can use this type of figure (which we call **figured-bass symbols**) to analyze or refer to chords and chordal positions (here again, pitches above the bass can be realized in any order or register).

1. A triad in $\frac{5}{3}$ position is a root-position triad, because the intervals above the bass are a 3rd and a 5th.

2. A $\frac{6}{3}$ indicates a 3rd and a 6th above the bass, or a first-inversion triad.

3. A $\frac{6}{4}$, a 4th and a 6th above the bass, represents a second-inversion triad.

In practice, some of these figures are usually abbreviated. Thus, no figures under a triad mean that the triad is in root position, and a 6 indicates a triad in first inversion. The figures under the chords in example E.6c represent both the symbols most frequently used in practice (without parentheses) and complete figured bass symbols (in parentheses).

NOTE

We have seen that major and minor triads in root position are consonant. Both types of triads in first inversion are also consonant. In second inversion, on the other hand, M and m triads feature a P4 which involves the bass. Whereas harmonic P4s in upper voices are consonant, P4s involving the bass are sometimes dissonant. (In chapter D, for instance, we studied that all P4s in two-voice counterpoint are considered dissonant.) $\frac{6}{4}$ chords often result from melodic motion, rather than from triadic inversion, and they may be consonant or dissonant depending on their context. *We will study the melodic processes that shape $\frac{6}{4}$ chords, as well as their treatment as dissonant chords, in chapter 9.*

EXERCISE

To practice writing and identifying triads in first and second inversions, refer to exercises E.4 to E.6 in worksheet E at the end of this chapter.

SEVENTH CHORDS

A seventh chord is formed by adding one more 3rd on top of a triad. A seventh chord thus has four pitches: the root, the third, the fifth, and the seventh. The types of seventh chord are determined by the quality of the triad formed by the root, third, and fifth, and by the type of seventh. For instance, if the triad is major and the seventh is minor, we call the chord a "major-minor seventh chord," or Mm_7. A minor triad with a minor

♪♪♪ Example E.7

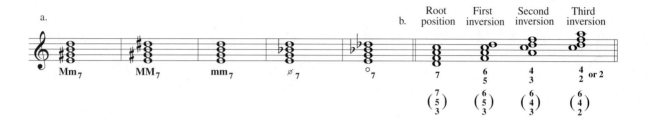

seventh is a "minor-minor seventh chord" (mm$_7$), and so on. The most frequent **types of seventh chords** used in tonal harmony (and shown in example E.7a) are as follows:

1. **Major-minor** (Mm$_7$): major triad–minor 7th
2. **Major-major** (MM$_7$): major triad–major 7th
3. **Minor-minor** (mm$_7$): minor triad–minor 7th
4. **Half diminished** ($^{\varnothing}_7$): diminished triad–minor 7th
5. **Fully diminished** ($^{\circ}_7$): diminished triad–diminished 7th

Because seventh chords are made up of four pitches, they allow for three inversions. The four possible positions of a seventh chord are shown in example E.7b, with indication of both the complete figures for each (in parentheses), and the abbreviated figures more commonly used to indicate seventh chords in root position or inversion. The following table summarizes all **seventh chord positions** and their corresponding **figured-bass symbols**.

Seventh-Chord Positions   Root in the bass: seventh chord in *root position* ($_7$)

Third in the bass: seventh chord in *first inversion* ($^6_5$)

Fifth in the bass: seventh chord in *second inversion* ($^4_3$)

Seventh in the bass: seventh chord in *third inversion* ($^4_2$)

Because in all cases the 7th is a dissonant interval (and so is its inversion, the 2nd), seventh chords are dissonant. Moreover, *the seventh of the chord usually results from linear (melodic) motion*. In chapters 12 and 15 we will study seventh chords in a harmonic context, and we will discuss both their linear nature and their role as dissonant sonorities.

Diatonic Seventh Chords in the Major and Minor Keys

Example E.8 shows the **diatonic seventh chords** which result on each of the scale degrees of major and minor scales. The seventh chords on the minor scale shown in this example are the most commonly used in minor keys, and, as in the case of triads, result from the harmonic minor scale, with the only exception of the seventh chord on $\hat{3}$. Scale degree $\hat{7}$ in this chord is not raised to become the leading tone.

Example E.8

EXERCISES

To practice writing and identifying seventh chords in root position and inversions, refer to exercises E.7 to E.8 in worksheet E at the end of this chapter.

To practice identifying both triads and seventh chords in all positions, refer to exercises E.9 to E.10

ASSIGNMENT

For an assignment based on the materials learned in this chapter, refer to chapter E in the workbook.

Terms for Review

Chord
Block chord
Broken chord
Arpeggiated chord
Tertian chords
Consonant and dissonant chords
Triad
Root, third, fifth, fundamental
Triad types: M, m, °, +
Diatonic triads on each scale degree
Bass and root

Chord position
Root position
First inversion
Second inversion
Figured-bass symbols for triad positions
Seventh chord
Types: Mm, MM, mm, °, °
Figured-bass symbols for seventh-chord positions
Diatonic seventh chords on each scale degree

Worksheet E

EXERCISE E.1 Identify and label the following triads by root and type (M, m, °, $^+$), and label each triad as shown in the example.

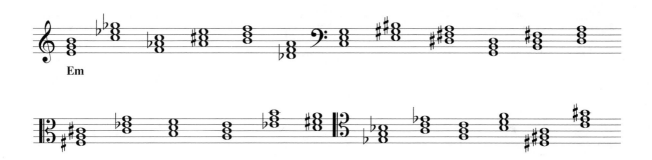

EXERCISE E.2 Write the indicated triads in root position. A triad member (root, third, or fifth) is given. Identify the root for each triad, and notate it under the triad type, as indicated in the given examples.

> **Procedure**: If the root is given, first write the third (a M3 or m3 depending on the triad type), and then the fifth (a P5, °5, or +5 depending on the triad type). If the third is given, first write the root (a M3 or m3 below the third depending on the triad type), and then the 5th above the root. If the fifth is given, first write the root (a P5, °5, or +5 below the fifth), and then the third.

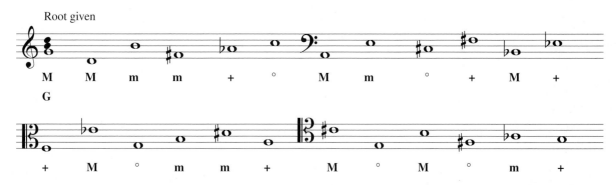

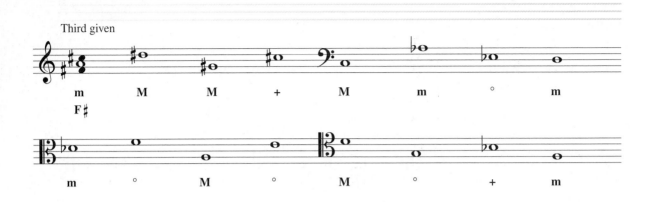

Third given

m   M   M   +   M   m   °   m

F#

m   °   M   °   M   °   +   m

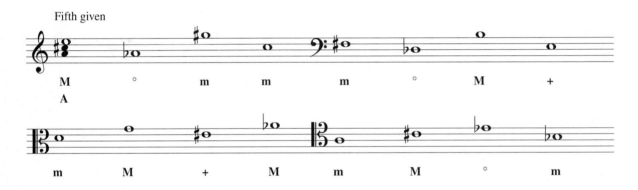

Fifth given

M   °   m   m   m   °   M   +

A

m   M   +   M   m   M   °   m

EXERCISE E.3 In a major key, the diatonic triad on scale degree

$\hat{2}$ is: M / m / ° / $^+$ (*circle one*)

$\hat{7}$ is: M / m / ° / $^+$

$\hat{3}$ is: M / m / ° / $^+$

$\hat{1}$ is: M / m / ° / $^+$

$\hat{6}$ is: M / m / ° / $^+$

$\hat{5}$ is: M / m / ° / $^+$

$\hat{4}$ is: M / m / ° / $^+$

In a minor key, the following are the most usual diatonic triads, which result from the harmonic-minor scale (with the only exception of the chord on $\hat{3}$, which includes $\flat\hat{7}$):

The triad on

$\hat{2}$ is: M / m / ° / $^+$

$\hat{7}$ is: M / m / ° / $^+$

$\hat{3}$ is: M / m / ° / $^+$

$\hat{1}$ is: M / m / ° / $^+$

$\hat{6}$ is: M / m / ° / $^+$

$\hat{5}$ is: M / m / ° / $^+$

$\hat{4}$ is: M / m / ° / $^+$

EXERCISE E.4   Write the following M, m, or ° triads in *first inversion* on the given bass (the third of the chord). Identify the root for each triad, and notate it under the triad type, as indicated in the given example.

Procedure: First determine the root of the triad (a M3 or m3 below the third depending on the triad type). Then, determine the fifth (a P5 or °5 above the root depending on the triad type). Write both pitches *above* the given bass.

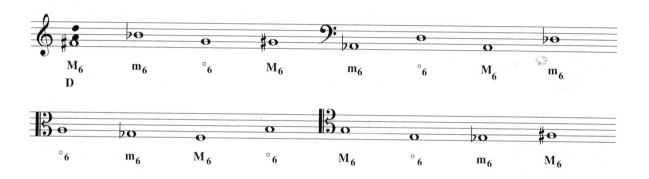

EXERCISE E.5   Write the following M or m triads in *second inversion* on the given bass (the fifth of the chord). Identify the root for each triad, and notate it under the triad type, as indicated in the given example.

Procedure: First determine the root of the triad (a P5 below the fifth in both M and m triads), and then the third. Write both pitches *above* the given bass.

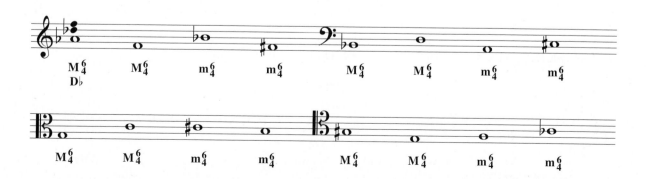

EXERCISE E.6   The following triads are in first or second inversion. Identify the root, the type, and the inversion for each of them, and label each triad as shown in the example. Your labels should be of the following type: Dm_6, GM_4^6, $E°_6$, F^{+6}_4, etc.

Procedure: First determine the triad position: Are the intervals above the bass a 6th and a 3rd (first inversion), or a 6th and a 4th (second inversion)? Then determine the root. In $^6_3$ position, the root is the 6th. In $^6_4$ position, the root is the 4th. Once you have the root, you can determine the triad type by imagining mentally the three pitches organized by 3rds above the root and checking the quality of the third and the fifth.

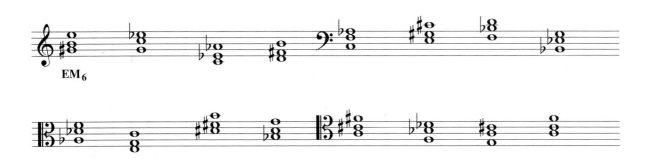

EXERCISE E.7   Identify and label these seventh chords by type (Mm, MM, mm, ^{ø}, $^°$).

EXERCISE E.8   Write the indicated seventh chords in root position. The root is given.

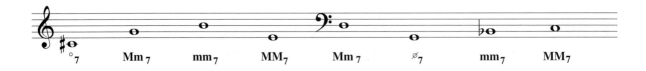

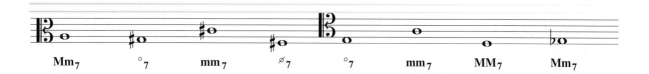

Mm₇   °₇   mm₇   ⌀₇   °₇   mm₇   MM₇   Mm₇

EXERCISE E.9   Identify the following chord types and inversions. Notice that both triads and seventh chords are included in this exercise. Label each chord with the usual chord-type symbols and with figures to indicate inversion, and also write down its root (e.g., M_4^6/A, Mm_3^4/G, mm_5^6/D, m_6/F, etc.).

> **Procedure to identify a chord**: The key to recognizing a chord is to organize its members in thirds. If the chord is in root position, its structure by thirds is likely to be evident (although an arrangement such as, from the bottom up, C–G–E, still requires some reorganization to become C–E–G, evidently organized by thirds). If the chord is in inversion, find the arrangement of pitches that reveals the chord's structure by thirds, determine the pitch on which the chord is built (the root), identify the chord member in the bass, and determine the chord position.
>
> For instance, the pitches G♯–B–E (always reading from the bottom up), when organized in thirds as E–G♯–B, reveal a M triad on E. Because the third, G♯, was in the bass, the original chord was in first inversion. The chord F–B♭–D becomes B♭–D–F, a M triad; with the fifth, F, in the bass, the chord was in second inversion. Finally, the pitches A–C–D–F♯ can be organized in thirds as D–F♯–A–C, a Mm₇ chord; because the fifth, A, was in the bass, this is a seventh chord in second inversion ($\frac{4}{3}$). Now practice by identifying the following chords (identify type and inversion, and notate it, for instance, as M_4^6, Mm_5^6, m_6, etc.):
>
> D♯–F♯–B: E–G–A–C:
>
> B–E–G: B♭–G–E♭:
>
> C♯–E–G–A: G–E–B:
>
> B–D–G♯:   B♭–E–C–G:

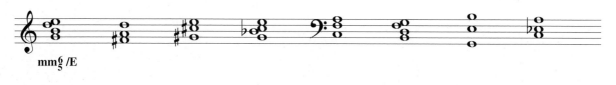

mm⁶₅ /E

EXERCISE E.10   Refer to the passage by J. S. Bach reproduced in example E.9. Eighteen chords are numbered. Study each of the chords, and determine whether it is consonant or dissonant, a triad or a seventh chord, the root and type of chord (DM, Cm, EMm$_7$, Fmm$_7$, etc.), and the appropriate figures to indicate the chord's position ($\frac{5}{3}$, $\frac{6}{3}$, $\frac{6}{4}$, 7, $\frac{6}{5}$, $\frac{4}{3}$, etc.). You may provide all the above information in the following table (the information for chord 1 has been provided as an example).

Example E.9   J. S. Bach, Chorale 298, "Weg, mein Herz, mit den Gedanken," mm. 1–9

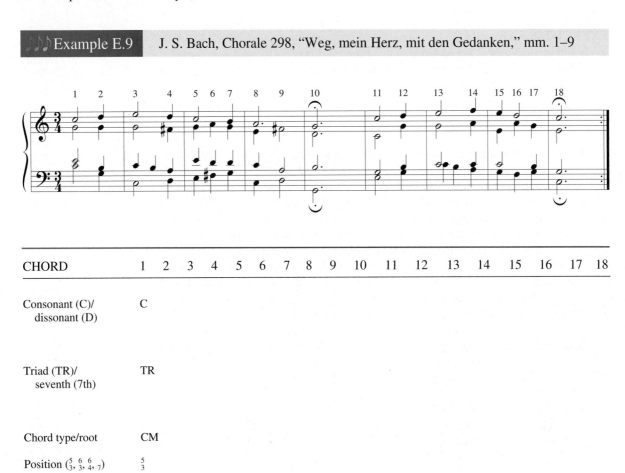

CHORD	1	2	3	4	5	6	7	8	9	10	11	12	13	14	15	16	17	18
Consonant (C)/ dissonant (D)	C																	
Triad (TR)/ seventh (7th)	TR																	
Chord type/root	CM																	
Position ($\frac{5}{3}$, $\frac{6}{3}$, $\frac{6}{4}$, 7)	$\frac{5}{3}$																	

Chapter F

The Rudiments of Harmony II: Labeling Chords

In chapter E we studied the fundamental material of harmony: triads and seventh chords. We should now learn how to refer to these chords in a tonal context. This means understanding the tonal hierarchy of chords, how they relate to the tonic, and how they relate to one another. In this chapter we will study two systems of chord reference and labeling that have been used by musicians and theorists in the last few centuries, and are still widely used in harmonic instruction: Roman numerals and figured bass.

HARMONIC FUNCTION, ROMAN NUMERALS

The term **harmonic function** refers to the relationship of a chord with the other chords in the same key, and specifically to its relationship with the tonic, the chord on $\hat{1}$. We already learned in chapter C that tonality is a hierarchical system based on a center (the tonic pitch and, harmonically, the tonic triad). Harmonic function determines the behavior of chords in relation to other chords, according to this hierarchy around the tonic. **Roman numerals** are used precisely to indicate the function of a chord with respect to tonic. Thus, no matter what the major key, the symbol I indicates the tonic triad (the triad built on $\hat{1}$); the symbol V indicates the dominant triad (the triad built on $\hat{5}$); IV indicates the subdominant triad (the triad built on $\hat{4}$), and so forth. The standard behavior and role of each of these chords within the system will be our focus of study throughout part 1 of this book.

Example F.1 shows the **Roman numerals for each of the diatonic triads in major and minor keys. Capital-letter Roman numerals** indicate a major triad; **lowercase Roman numerals** are used for minor triads (you can review the quality of triads on each degree in example E.4). The symbol ° next to a lowercase Roman numeral means diminished triad. Scale degree numbers in this example show the correspondence between Roman numerals and bass scale degrees. As we discussed in chapter E, *scale degree $\hat{7}$ will usually be raised in the minor mode, to become the leading tone,* when the pitch is part of the V chord (the third) or of the vii° chord (the root). As part

Example F.1

of the III chord in minor keys (the fifth), however, $\hat{7}$ is usually not raised, thus allowing for a major (rather than an augmented) chord on $\hat{3}$.

We will most often use a combination of Roman numerals and figures to refer to chords in a tonal context. In this system, a root position tonic triad in a major key is represented as I, and its inversions become I_6 and I_4^6, respectively. Similarly, the three positions for, say, the subdominant triad in a minor key are iv, iv_6, and iv_4^6. Example F.2 illustrates the use of some of these symbols, which provide us information about the quality, the inversion, and the function of a triad.

EXERCISE

To practice writing triads from given Roman numerals and labeling given triads with Roman numerals, refer to exercises F.1 to F.4 in worksheet F at the end of this chapter.

In example F.3 you can see the **Roman numerals for each of the diatonic seventh chords** in major and minor keys. Here again, we use a combination of Roman numeral labels and figures to indicate both function and position. Thus, ii_7 is a mm_7 chord built on the supertonic, whereas the three inversions of this supertonic seventh chord will be notated as ii_5^6 (first inversion), ii_3^4 (second inversion), and ii_2^4 (third inversion). Notice that, in Roman numerals for seventh chords, capital or lowercase symbols refer to the lower triad of the seventh chord, not to the seventh itself. Because both MM_7 (for instance, IV_7 in major) and Mm_7 (V_7) are built on major triads, they are represented with capital Roman numerals. Conversely, seventh chords built on minor or diminished triads are represented by lowercase Roman numerals.

Example F.2

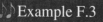

EXERCISE

To practice writing seventh chords from given Roman numerals, refer to exercise F.5 in worksheet F at the end of this chapter.

FIGURED BASS

The system of numerical symbols used in the baroque period (approximately 1600–1750) to indicate harmonies above a bass is known as **figured bass** or **thoroughbass**. The system provides a notational shorthand, allowing a performer of a keyboard instrument to play complete harmonies from only a notated bass with added Arabic numerals (figures). The same system is still used in harmonic instruction to indicate harmonies that the student must fully realize in four voices from a given bass line with added figures.

The figures, which are notated below (or above) bass notes, represent *intervals above the bass*. In chapter E you were already introduced to figured bass in the discussion of triad and seventh chord positions. You learned that a $\frac{5}{3}$ means that the chord consists of a 3rd and a 5th above the bass, hence it is a root-position triad. A $\frac{6}{3}$ (a 3rd and a 6th above the bass) represents a first-inversion triad, and $\frac{6}{4}$ (a 4th and a 6th above the bass) represents a second-inversion triad. You also studied the abbreviated figures for both triads and seventh chords in root position or inversion, as summarized in the following tables.

Figured-Bass Symbols for Diatonic Triads

Triad in root position: $\frac{5}{3}$ or no figures
Triad in first inversion: $\frac{6}{3}$ or 6
Triad in second inversion (or linear $\frac{6}{4}$ chord): $\frac{6}{4}$

Figured-Bass Symbols for Diatonic Seventh Chords

Seventh chord in root position: $\frac{7}{5}{}_{3}$ or 7

Seventh chord in first inversion: $\frac{6}{5}{}_{3}$ or $\frac{6}{5}$

Seventh chord in second inversion: $\frac{6}{4}{}_{3}$ or $\frac{4}{3}$

Seventh chord in third inversion: $\frac{6}{4}{}_{2}$, $\frac{4}{2}$, or 2

♪♪♪ Example F.4

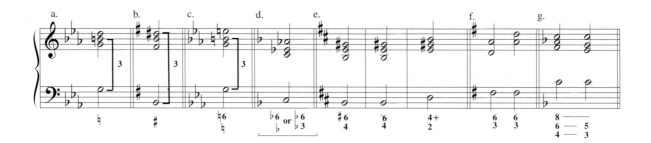

Accidentals are also indicated in figured basses.

1. An accidental alone applies to the 3rd above the bass (examples F.4a and b).

2. Other accidentals precede or follow the numeral that represents the affected note (examples F.4c and d).

3. A slash across a number or a + sign after it have the same meaning as a ♯ next to that number—the note must be raised a half step (example F.4e).

NOTES

Figures do not determine the specific arrangement of upper voices. Although, for instance, in a $^6_3$ chord there must be a 6th and a 3rd somewhere above the bass, it does not matter whether the 6th is above the 3rd, or vice versa (see example F.4f).

Notice also that 8ve doublings are usually not indicated by figures, although they may be if the composer wishes a particular pitch to be doubled. In example F.4g the 8 means that the bass of the first chord (the C) must be doubled; the line after the 8 indicates that the C must be sustained in the same voice into the next chord. Otherwise, in a $^{6-5}_{4-3}$ figure the 6th and 5th above C should be in the same voice, as indicated by the dash between the 6th and the 5th (6–5, or A–G), and the same for the 4th and 3rd above C (4–3, or F–E).

Example F.5 reproduces two fragments of a composition by George F. Handel, a sonata for flute and continuo. Handel wrote only the flute part and the figured bass. This type of texture or technique is called **continuo** or **basso continuo**. Example F.5 shows a possible realization of the figured bass for a keyboard instrument. A different realization might feature different arrangements of the right-hand chords, different 8ve doublings, or different ornamental pitches or *nonchord tones* (pitches, such as passing tones or neighbor notes, that are not part of the chord with which they sound). Examine the realization, and verify the interpretation of the figures provided in the keyboard's upper staff.

1. $\frac{5}{3}$ or no figures indicate a root-position triad.

2. $\frac{6}{3}$ or 6 indicate a first-inversion triad.

3. $\frac{6}{4}$ indicates a second-inversion triad or a linear $\frac{6}{4}$ chord.

4. A single accidental applies to the 3rd above the bass.

5. Other accidentals precede or follow the numeral that represents the affected note (as in ♯4 and ♭6, or 4♯ and 6♭).

6. A ♯ before or after a number, a slash across a number, or a + sign after the number all mean that the note should be raised by a half step.

7. The figures 7, $\frac{6}{5}$, $\frac{4}{3}$, and $\frac{4}{2}$ indicate seventh chords in root position and each of the three inversions, respectively.

♪♪♪ Example F.5　　George Frideric Handel, Sonata for Flute and Continuo, op. 1, no. 7

Example F.5a features only triads in root position or first inversion, and a seventh chord. The following comments will help you in your study of the realization.

1. Taking m. 13 as an example, you will see that a C with a 6 means an Am triad in first inversion, an E with a ♯ means a root position chord on E with a raised 3rd, and an A with no figure means a root position Am triad.

2. Notice also that the first two measures of the keyboard's left hand imitate the flute melody. Because of this melodic nature of the initial eighth notes in the bass, not all notes need to be harmonized (the B and the D are *passing tones* between the members of the Am triad, A–C–E).

3. The 7th in m. 14 (A) is prepared (by the same pitch in the same voice in the previous chord) and resolved down by step (to G♯). The 6–5 in the same measure indicates a melodic motion (in the flute) of a 6th and a 5th over the bass. The flute figure is accompanied in 3rds by the keyboard's upper voice (the eighth-note D in the keyboard is also a passing tone).

The figures in example F.5b are more complex. Try to understand their meaning, and then read the following comments.

1. The slash across the 6 in m. 27 means that the 6th over the A needs to be raised (F♯).

2. The symbol 5+ in m. 28 also means a raised 5th over B, hence the F♯. Why is the D also raised?

3. In mm. 28–29 you will see two $\frac{6}{5}$ labels. Verify that both cases indicate seventh chords in first inversion. Identify the complete seventh chord in each case, as well as the 6th and the 5th above the bass. What does the slash across the 6 in the second $\frac{6}{5}$ chord refer to?

4. Explain the 5+ symbol in m. 29, beat 3. The 4–♯ figures also represent a suspension which you studied in Chapter D, a 4–3 suspension. Find the suspension in the music, and verify its preparation and resolution.

 EXERCISES

To practice figured-bass realization and analysis, refer to exercises F.6 to F.7 in worksheet F at the end of this chapter.
To practice chord and Roman numeral analysis, refer to exercise F.8.

ASSIGNMENT

For an assignment based on the materials learned in this chapter, refer to chapter F in the workbook.

Terms for Review

Harmonic function
Roman numerals
Roman numerals for each diatonic triad
    in M and m keys
Capital and lowercase Roman numerals
Roman numerals for each diatonic
    seventh chord in M and m keys

Figured bass
Thoroughbass
Continuo
Basso continuo
Figured-bass symbols for triads and
    seventh chords in all positions

Worksheet F

EXERCISE F.1   Write the triads represented by Roman numerals in the given keys.

> **Procedure:** First write the root of the triad (the correct scale degree in the given key, as given by the Roman numeral). Then, determine the remaining two pitches, making sure that the triad type is correctly spelled (in some cases, you will need to use accidentals for this purpose).

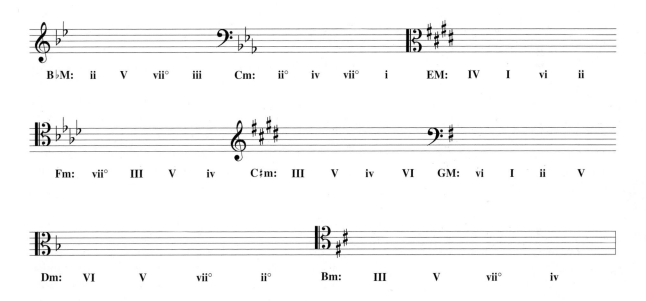

B♭M: ii   V   vii°   iii   Cm: ii°   iv   vii°   i   EM: IV   I   vi   ii

Fm: vii°   III   V   iv   C♯m: III   V   iv   VI   GM: vi   I   ii   V

Dm: VI   V   vii°   ii°   Bm: III   V   vii°   iv

EXERCISE F.2   Write the following diatonic triads above the given bass notes. Triads are here represented by a Roman numeral (and a figure to indicate an inversion) in a given key. Identify the root for each triad, and notate it under the triad type, as indicated in the given example.

GM: V₆   I⁶₄   vii°₆   IV   FM: ii₆   V⁶₄   vi   vii°₆

109

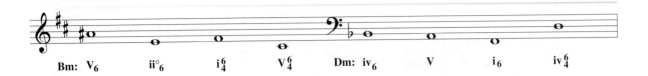

Bm: V₆   ii°₆   i⁶₄   V⁶₄   Dm: iv₆   V   i₆   iv⁶₄

EXERCISE F.3   Write the following diatonic triads, indicated by Roman numerals, in the given key.

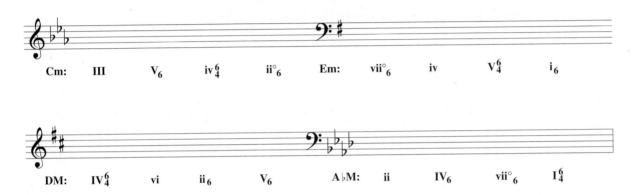

Cm: III   V₆   iv⁶₄   ii°₆   Em: vii°₆   iv   V⁶₄   i₆

DM: IV⁶₄   vi   ii₆   V₆   A♭M: ii   IV₆   vii°₆   I⁶₄

EXERCISE F.4   Provide the Roman numeral and position for the triads in this exercise in the given keys. Triads may appear in root position or inversion. Your labels should be of the following types, as shown in the example: V⁶₄, ii₆, IV, vii°₆, etc.

Procedure: Once you have determined the root of the triad, you can figure out what scale degree that root represents in the given key, and that will tell you the Roman numeral, including the triad type (which, however, you can confirm by checking the triad intervals). The triad member in the bass will, of course, determine the position.

FM: I₆   Bm:

GM: Am:

EXERCISE F.5   Write the seventh chords represented by Roman numerals in the given keys.

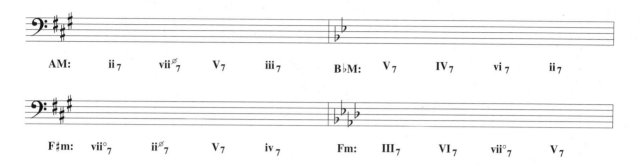

AM: ii₇   vii^ø₇   V₇   iii₇   B♭M: V₇   IV₇   vi₇   ii₇

F♯m: vii°₇   ii^ø₇   V₇   iv₇   Fm: III₇   VI₇   vii°₇   V₇

EXERCISE F.6   Realize the following isolated figured-bass chords. Exercises F.6a and b are all triads, and you will need only two upper voices, as in the example, to notate a complete chord. Items c and d are all seventh chords, and you will need three upper voices for complete sonorities.

Procedure: One could notate these chords intervallically by simply realizing in the upper voices the intervals indicated in the figures. Thus, a $^6_5$ below an A in Em requires a 5th and a 6th in the upper voices (E and F♯) plus, of course, a 3rd which is omitted from the figures (C). At this stage, however, it is better to think of the chord type and position represented by the figures. Thus, $^6_5$ below A means a seventh chord in first inversion, in which A is the third. The complete chord is thus F♯–A–C–E, and my upper-voice pitches will then be F♯–C–E. After you determine the pitches, be sure to add whatever accidentals are required in the figured bass. Accidentals are best calculated intervallically: a ♮4 affects the 4th above the bass, a ♭6 affects the 6th, etc.

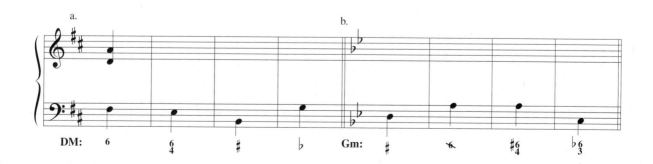

a.   b.

DM: 6 $^6_4$ ♯   ♭   Gm: ♯   6   ♯$^6_4$ ♭$^6_3$

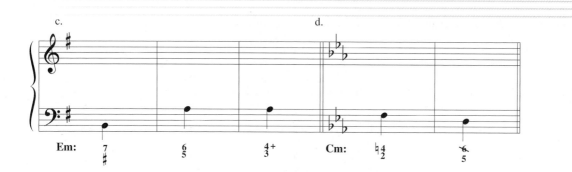

EXERCISE F.7   Analyze the chorale by J. S. Bach with figured-bass symbols (example F.6). That is, imagine that you want to write a figured-bass reduction of this chorale for a keyboard player, using exactly Bach's harmonies. Under the chorale, notate the exact figures you would need to have in your figured bass.

Procedure: First determine the type of chord you are labeling. Is it a triad or a seventh chord? In what position is it? That will give you the basic figures you need to write under the chord. Then, make sure that all upper-voice accidentals are incorporated into your figures. preceding the figure which represents the note with the accidental. Of course, accidentals in the bass will not be notated in the figures.

♪♪♪ Example F.6   J. S. Bach, Chorale 217, "Ach Gott, wie manches Herzeleid"

EXERCISE F.8   Refer to the passage by Mozart reproduced in example F.7. Fifteen chords are boxed and numbered. Although some chords are complete in the left hand, others need to include some pitches from the upper staff to be complete. Not all right-hand pitches, however, are chord members. Some of them are nonchord tones, with a melodic, ornamental function. When a pitch of this type falls within one of the circled chords, it has been marked with an X, and you should ignore it for purposes of identi-fying the chord.

Study each chord, and determine whether it is consonant or dissonant, a triad or a seventh chord, its position, and, for chords 1–7, provide the complete Roman numerals (with figures indicating position, e.g. ii$_6$) in the key of DM. You may provide all the above information in the following table (the information for chord 1 has been pro-vided as an example).

♩♪♪ Example F.7   W. A. Mozart, Piano Sonata in DM, K. 284, III, mm.1–8

♪♪♪ Example F.7   Continued

CHORD	1	2	3	4	5	6	7	/	8	9	10	11	12	13	14	15
Consonant (C)/ dissonant (D)	C															
Triad (TR)/ seventh (7th)	TR															
Chord type	M															
Position ($\frac{5}{3}$, $\frac{6}{3}$, $\frac{6}{4}$, 7)	$\frac{5}{3}$															

CHORD	1	2	3	4	5	6	7	/	8	9	10	11	12	13	14	15
Roman numeral in DM (chords 1–7)	I							/	X	X	X	X	X	X	X	X

Chapter G

Musical Style

When we listen to a composition without knowing who its composer was or when it was composed, we can often identify characteristic musical elements that allow us to make an "educated guess" of composer and compositional period. The set of distinguishing musical traits that allow us to make such a guess is usually known as **musical style**. Style traits can be characteristic of a particular composer, a musical period, or both. They can also define musical features limited to a specific period of a composer's life (such as, say, "late Beethoven"), or to a group of composers or compositions within a historical period (such as, for instance, seventeenth-century German Lutheran music or nineteenth-century Italian opera).

In this book we will often refer to style traits of a composer or a period. At the end of each chapter you will find suggested listening assignments; you will be asked to place each composition you listen to into one of the style periods, and to comment on why you think the composition is (or is not) representative of the period's style. In this chapter we will provide basic guidelines for the study of style in Western music, and we will review briefly some of the defining aspects of style in each of the main musical periods.

Not all of the terms used in the following discussion will be defined at present. Most of them, however, will appear (or have already appeared) in chapters devoted to specific stylistic elements (such as rhythm, texture, or form), and in those chapters they will generally receive much more thorough coverage. Although you may not be able to answer fully all the questions posed below until you study some of the later chapters, these stylistic guidelines will help you both in your listening assignments and as you perform or listen to music outside this course.

THE ELEMENTS OF STYLE

In order to determine the style of a composition, we need to ask a number of questions regarding different aspects of the piece. The following are some of the main musical elements we need to examine and some of the questions we can ask about each of them. Notice that, although the following list may appear to break up musical style into seemingly separate or independent components (only for the purpose of pedagogical clarity), some of these features are very closely intertwined in actual music (for instance, rhythm and melody, melody and harmony, or melody, harmony, and tonality).

Rhythm, Meter, and Tempo

These are "temporal" components of music, and they are interrelated. As we studied in chapter B, the term **rhythm** refers to the grouping of pitches (or other musical events) into patterns. **Meter**, on the other hand, is the grouping of musical time into patterns of strong (accented) and weak (nonaccented, or less-accented) beats, whereas **tempo** is the speed at which music is performed. The following considerations will help us define these "temporal" aspects of musical style in specific pieces.

1. Are *rhythmic patterns* varied and contrasting? Or is the music under consideration mostly based on a single rhythmic figure?

2. Are there any *rhythmic motives* (rhythmic patterns that recur)? Are these motives part of the accompanying figures, or are they part of the essential melodic/thematic material?

3. Are there rhythmic figures that *conflict* with the meter of the passage, such as cross rhythms, hemiola, or syncopation?

4. Is *meter* consistent throughout the piece or passage? Or are there any metric changes?

5. Is the meter symmetrical or asymmetrical?

6. Does the music consistently follow and reflect the notated meter, or is there conflict between musical flow and notated meter?

7. What is the *tempo* of the piece? Are there any tempo changes?

8. Are there any tempo alterations notated on the score (such as *rubato, accelerando* or *ritardando*)?

Melody

We will consider in this section single melodic lines. This "horizontal" component of music is not only extremely important perceptually (the average listener will perceive melody immediately, along with rhythm, as the primary element of music), but also formally (the thematic material that generates a composition is, more often than not, melodic).

1. Does the **melody** break up into clear *motives* (brief, characteristic figures made up of clearly recognizable rhythmic or pitch patterns)? Or does it flow and unfold without clear motivic definition?

2. Is the *contour* (the shape) of this melody smooth and curvelike, or jagged and abrupt?

3. Does this melody include any *sequences* (that is, sections based on the repeated statement of a melodic segment at different tonal levels, usually in a pattern ascending or descending by steps)?

4. What *intervals* are used in this melody? Is it mostly by steps, with some small leaps, or does it include numerous leaps, some of them large? Is the melody mostly diatonic, or does it include chromaticism?

5. Are melodic motives in this piece important in the *generation of form?* Does this melodic material play an important role in later thematic development?

6. What is the *character* of this melody? Is it rhythmic and vigorous? Is it lyrical and songlike (cantabile)? Is it particularly expressive?

7. What is the *formal function* of this specific melodic passage? Does it present new material, repeat known material, or present contrasting material? Does it function as a *refrain* (a passage that recurs more or less periodically)? Does it have a *developmental* character?

Harmony and Harmonic Rhythm

We could say that this constitutes the "vertical" component of music. **Harmony** is closely associated with melody, in that it both "accompanies" and generates melody. Harmony also moves forward melodically. That is, the connection of chords with one another introduces a linear, melodic component (which we call *voice leading*) into the realm of harmonic sonority.

1. What is the *harmonic style* of this piece? Is it *functional* (chord roots related mostly by 5ths and steps, following the principles of functional harmony which we will study throughout the first part of this book)? Is it *modal* (triadic, but based on modal and contrapuntal principles rather than on functional tonality)? Is the harmony *nontriadic* (chords are not triads)?

2. What is the *formal function* of harmony? Does it create *tension and motion* toward goals (cadences and points of arrival)? Is it of a more *coloristic and static* nature (roots often related by third)?

3. Is the harmony mostly *diatonic?* Or is it mostly *chromatic?*

4. What is the *role of dissonance* in this harmonic style? Is it used sparingly, controlled, and resolved? Or is prominent dissonance an essential component of this harmonic language?

5. Does harmony in this specific passage have a stable role, or is it a passage of unstable, developmental harmonic relationships?

6. Does this piece include some *harmonic sequences* (harmonic patterns repeated at different tonal levels, in some ascending or descending pattern)?

7. Examine the *harmonic rhythm* in the passage (that is, the rate of harmonic or chordal change). Is it fast (chords changing, say, every beat) or slow (chords changing, say, every measure or even less often)?

Tonality

This section addresses long-range tonal relationships in the piece, and, in a more general sense, the tonal system on which the piece is built.

1. What *set of tonal relationships* is this piece based on? That is, what *tonal system* underlies its structure?

2. Is the piece based on the *functional,* major-minor tonal system? Or is this a *modal* piece? Or is it perhaps a *post-tonal* piece loosely based on nonfunctional triadic relationships?

3. What is the main *key* of the piece (the "tonic key")? Does the piece *modulate* to other keys?

4. Are there large sections in keys other than the tonic key? What are these important *secondary tonal areas?*

5. What is the long-range *tonal design* of the composition? To what extent does this tonal shape, or *tonal motion,* determine the form of the composition?

Texture

We will examine here the relationship between the horizontal and vertical components of music and between different and simultaneous musical elements.

1. Is the **texture** mostly *homophonic* (a melodic line with chordal accompaniment), *polyphonic* or *contrapuntal* (different independent lines moving simultaneously), or a combination of both?

2. Is the texture *homorhythmic* (all voices have the same, or very similar, rhythm)?

3. If the texture is mostly homophonic, how is the harmonic accompaniment presented? Is it written in keyboard style? Or is it written as sustained chords?

4. If it is polyphonic, does the contrapuntal texture follow a functional harmonic design? This is the type of counterpoint we call "tonal counterpoint." In "modal counterpoint," on the other hand, voices are related by the principles of consonance and dissonance, but the resulting triads do not necessarily follow functional progressions.

5. Is the counterpoint imitative (motives appear in different voices in imitation of each other)?

Form and Formal Growth

In this section we will examine how the composition unfolds in time, and how different sections are related tonally and thematically.

1. What *techniques of thematic growth* are used in this composition? Some of the most frequent techniques you may find are repetition, sequence, fragmentation, and variation.

2. Is the thematic material organized in clearly articulated *phrases and periods,* or does it seem to *spin out* without clear breaks?

3. Is the composition based on a *single motive* or theme, or are there statements of *contrasting thematic material?* Is the contrasting material presented in the form of an independent section?

4. How are the different sections of this composition related thematically? What is the *formal design* or formal type that results from sectional relationships? Some possible formal types are binary, ternary, sonata form, and rondo.

5. How do the *thematic formal design* and the *long-range tonal design* correlate?

Dynamics

This term refers to the levels of loudness in music.

1. Does the score include *dynamic markings?*

2. If it does not, how would you make *performance decisions* regarding **dynamics**? You may want to listen to a recorded performance of the piece, and determine whether or not you agree with that rendition.

3. If dynamic markings are included, how *detailed* are they? Are they so detailed that they become an indispensable part of musical expression as imagined by the composer (as you will find, for instance, in late-Romantic orchestral compositions)?

4. Do dynamic marks *correlate* with other musical events (such as motivic or thematic units, rhythmic figures, harmonic motion)?

Timbre and Instrumentation

We will finally examine sound quality (**timbre**) as a stylistic feature, as represented by instrumentation and orchestration.

1. Is this composition *vocal, instrumental,* or both?

2. What voice or voices, instrument or instruments is the piece written for?

3. Were the specific *technical and idiomatic characteristics* of the instrument taken into account by the composer?

4. What kind of *ensemble* is the piece written for? Is it a small chamber ensemble? Are all instruments of the same family (say, strings), or is it a mixed ensemble?

5. Are any instruments used as *soloists,* or in a soloistic style? Are other instruments used in a subordinate, accompanying role?

6. What kind of *orchestra* did the composer write for? Is it a small or a large orchestra? What size woodwind, brass, and percussion sections are required?

7. What orchestral instruments are used with prominent *melodic functions?* Does the composer exploit the characteristic *timbre of instruments* and the characteristic *color of instrumental families?* Examine instrumental doublings.

8. Is there any correlation between *formal sections and orchestration?*

9. In how much *detail* does the composer indicate *articulations, bowings, and special effects* such as mutes, harmonics, and different colors within the same instrument?

Again, you should remember that you may not be able to address fully each of the questions asked in the above discussion until you have studied all of the textbook, or at least most of it. But you should keep referring to the above guidelines as you advance in your study of music and as you listen to music with an increasingly discerning musical mind.

THE MUSICAL STYLE PERIODS

Writing about the historical style periods can easily lead into *a number of pitfalls.* We will thus begin this section with several disclaimers.

1. The development of musical style through the centuries has been *gradual,* with *overlapping trends* rather than abrupt change. It would be misleading, then, to think of style periods as closed compartments. Quite to the contrary, they are open on both ends. Take, for instance, the Classical period, which is preceded by the baroque period and followed by the Romantic period. The end of the baroque era, however, overlaps with the styles we call preclassical and galant, which prefigure the classical style. Classical style traits, on the other hand, can be traced in composers well into the Romantic period (such as Schubert, Mendelssohn, and Brahms, especially in their symphonic compositions and chamber music).

2. Because *periods overlap,* it is misleading to think of them as beginning and ending on some specific years or coinciding with some specific events (in the case of the baroque period, for instance, one often reads that it begins in 1600 and ends the year Bach dies, 1750).

3. The division of music history into major style periods (such as Renaissance, baroque, Classical, and Romantic) does not take sufficiently into account the wealth of *intermediate, transitional developments.*

4. Discussions of style within one period often disregard the fact that several *different, sometimes contrasting, styles coexist within each period.* Periods such as the Renaissance and the twentieth century, in particular, are especially rich in their abundance of contrasting styles. Discussing only mainstream developments usually does not serve the stylistic wealth of a period.

5. Within the same period, musical style may vary drastically, depending on the genre in which a work was composed, the musicians and listeners likely to play and hear it, and the social function or occasion for which it was intended (e.g., dance music, as opposed to sacred music for liturgical use).

Having thus warned you about these potential pitfalls, we will proceed to fall into each one of them in the following pages. We will knowingly need to do so in order to present a summarized account of style through the ages. As inadequate and simplified as this outline may be, it will provide you with some ideas and principles to (1) listen to music from each period with some basic knowledge of what to expect in terms of mainstream style (against which you may compare the composition at hand), and (2) research and study on your own the style of composers or schools that may not quite fit the mainstream stylistic traits put forth in our discussion.

Because musical styles in the Middle Ages are quite different, in almost every aspect, from the styles we will study in this book, we will begin our discussion with the Renaissance. And, here again, the Renaissance is too rich a period for us to be able to account for all coexisting styles, especially because this book is not meant to cover Renaissance music. We will thus focus on one specific style of the late Renaissance, which had a substantial impact on later compositional styles: sixteenth-century sacred vocal polyphony.

Before we begin with each period, we should also note that instead of listing style characteristics in an abstract way, we will focus on the style of one or two representative pieces for each period, from which we should be able to extrapolate some general stylistic traits. Our discussion of each of these pieces will not necessarily follow in an orderly way each of the stylistic categories we have outlined in the section "The Elements of Style," but will rather focus on stylistic categories pertinent to the specific pieces and periods.

A CHARACTERISTIC RENAISSANCE STYLE: SACRED VOCAL POLYPHONY

The term *Renaissance* ("rebirth") refers to the renewed interest in the art and culture of ancient Greece and Rome, a period usually known as "classical antiquity." The Renaissance in general comprises the fifteenth and sixteenth centuries. The musical Renaissance spans approximately from the year 1430 to the year 1600. Among the many styles we can find in Renaissance music, the style of sacred vocal polyphony has become a model of compositional restraint, perfection of craft, purity of sound, and expressive serenity and objectivity. Several generations of composers practiced and developed this international style throughout the fifteenth and the sixteenth centuries. The last of these generations, best represented by Palestrina, Victoria, and Lassus (second half of the sixteenth century), achieved the highest level of stylistic consistency in sacred vocal polyphony. The contrapuntal techniques we studied in chapter D (species counterpoint) are a pedagogical adaptation by Fux of the contrapuntal style practiced by these composers.

We will now examine the characteristics of this style as illustrated by Spanish composer Tomás Luis de Victoria's *Kyrie,* from the Mass *O magnum mysterium* (anthology, no. 1). This Mass movement is clearly structured in three sections (which we will label I, II, and III), corresponding with the three sentences of the text: "Kyrie eleison. Christe eleison. Kyrie eleison" ("Lord, have mercy. Christ, have mercy. Lord, have mercy").

Texture

1. The prevalent texture in this style is **imitative counterpoint**. Each of the three sections begins with a point of imitation (mm. 1, 13, and 20) in which an opening *motive* is presented by each of the four voices. Are there any inner points of imitation? (Explain, for instance, mm. 25–27.) The intervals of imitation are unison, 8ve, 5th, and 4th.

2. Other than the points of imitation, *lines are thoroughly independent* from the point of view of contour and shape, and each of them is melodically self-sufficient.

Melodic lines

1. *Melodic curves are smooth and wavelike.* A characteristic shape for phrases is to build up to a *single, high focal point* (zenith), and then to descend back gradually.

2. A lot of the *melodic motion* is stepwise, although there are also numerous 3rds, and some 5ths, 4ths, and 8ves. Every time there is a leap it is balanced by motion in the opposite direction immediately before or after the leap.

3. Melodic lines flow freely: repetition of motivic cells and sequences is *not* idiomatic in this style. The *overall rhythm* of the combined voices also produces a flowing effect: Victoria avoids simultaneous attacks in all four voices, in such a way that when some of the voices move at least one of the other voices is sustained (this type of rhythmic relationship among voices is called *complementary rhythm*).

Tonality

1. The piece is "in G," but the signature features a single ♭, so it is not Gm. G with a single ♭ means that it is a "minor" type of key, but with a raised $\hat{6}$ (E♮). Of course, we know that *Dorian* fits this definition. The example is indeed in the Dorian mode on G, that is, Dorian transposed up a 4th.

2. Most of this music is based on the Church modes rather than on major-minor tonality.

Harmony

1. This music functions, above all, *linearly.* That is, the essential musical concept in this style is the independence of horizontal lines.

2. Vertical sonorities are *triadic,* although not ruled by the principles of functional tonality we will study in this book. What propels the music forward is not the play of chordal tensions we find in later functional progressions, but the abundance of *contrapuntal dissonance* and its tendency to resolve to consonance.

3. *Dissonance is strictly controlled* (prepared and resolved), following the same type of principles we studied in chapter D. That is, dissonances are mostly passing tones, occasional lower neighbor notes, and suspensions.

Chromaticism

1. This music is *essentially diatonic.*

2. The main chromatic alterations in this piece are (a) scale degree $\hat{7}$ raised to become the *leading tone* (a half step below the final or tonic) at cadences (in our example, F♯ resolving to G), (b) scale degree $\hat{6}$ lowered to become ♭$\hat{6}$ (E♭), normally functioning as an upper neighbor to $\hat{5}$ (D–E♭–D). The occasional alterations (two, to be exact) of scale degree $\hat{3}$ which we find in sections II and III are unusual in Dorian.

Form

The two main genres composers of sacred vocal polyphony practiced were *the Mass and the motet.* Masses use the text from the Mass (the central liturgical service of the Roman Catholic Church), whereas motets use other sacred Latin texts.

1. From a formal point of view, both Mass movements and motets often consist of a succession of sections, each of which begins with a point of imitation and closes on a cadence on one of the main degrees of the mode.

2. Each of the three sections in our example begins with a point of imitation, and ends on a cadence. The cadential scheme, considering final cadences in each section, is G–D–G (the main degrees in transposed Dorian mode).

3. If you compare initial subjects in each of the sections, you will see that there is an interesting thematic symmetry in the movement: subject I (mm. 1–2) and subject III (mm. 20–21) are related by *inversion* (the same intervals, but in opposite directions). This A–B–A formal scheme mirrors the symmetrical shape of the three-sentence text.

THE BAROQUE STYLE

The baroque period may be said to begin around 1600 and to end in mid-eighteenth century. Some major baroque composers are Claudio Monteverdi, Jean-Baptiste Lully, Archangelo Corelli, Antonio Vivaldi, Johann Sebastian Bach, Jean-Philippe Rameau, and George Frideric Handel. The following are some of the general characteristics of this musical period:

1. Music in the baroque period focuses around two major areas: the development of *opera* as a musical-dramatic genre, and the development of *instrumental virtuosity.*

2. *Opera* and the musical techniques associated with it (especially the recitative) allow composers to depict human passions and the emotional states of the soul in a musical setting. Operas and other dramatic genres (such as *oratorios* and *cantatas*) make use of a great variety of styles and vocal settings (from solo voice to multiple choirs).

3. *Instrumental virtuosity* allows for the development of numerous instrumental genres, both for solo instruments and for various instrumental ensembles.

4. Common to both vocal and instrumental genres is the *concertato* **style,** in which different vocal or instrumental groups are combined and contrasted. The instrumental concerto is one possible manifestation of the *concertato* style. Baroque concertos are either of the solo type, for a single solo instrument and ensemble accompaniment, or the *concerto grosso* type, for a group of solo instruments (the *concertino*) and ensemble accompaniment (the *ripieno*).

We will now examine some of the specific aspects of baroque style, using four pieces from the anthology as references: Henry Purcell's "Ah, Belinda" (anthology, no. 3), Vivaldi's Concerto, op. 3, no. 3, II (anthology, no. 5), and Bach's Invention no. 3 in DM (anthology, no. 13) and Fugue no. 2 in Cm, from *The Well-Tempered Clavier* I (anthology, no. 14).

Texture

1. Perhaps the most significant innovation in seventeenth-century music was the ***basso continuo*** or **thoroughbass**. We have already discussed this technique in chapter F, and demonstrated it in examples F.4 and F.5. Composers using

thoroughbass techniques wrote a two-voice frame consisting of a melody and a figured bass. The figures, indicating intervals above the bass, are realized as chordal, harmonic accompaniment, usually at the keyboard.

2. The *basso continuo* is not only a technique, but also a texture. The Purcell and Vivaldi examples in the anthology illustrate what we can call *continuo texture:* an outer-voice duet constitutes the main structure of the piece, and the inner voices provide the harmonic accompaniment. In the Purcell example the melody is vocal, whereas Vivaldi's upper voice is a solo violin.

Harmony and Tonality

1. Although the principles of *functional tonality* were not formulated until 1722 (in Rameau's *Traité de l'harmonie*), throughout the seventeenth century functional tonality and the *major-minor tonal system* became progressively established and refined. What we hear in the Purcell and Vivaldi examples are functional harmonic progressions of the type we will study in this book.

Counterpoint

1. In the mature or late baroque, composers often favored *highly contrapuntal textures,* as illustrated by the two Bach examples mentioned above. The two voices in the invention, and the three voices in the fugue, function as independent lines, all sharing an equal melodic status.

2. Baroque counterpoint is **tonal counterpoint**. That is, it proceeds according to the principles of functional tonality. Baroque counterpoint can be reduced to functional harmonic progressions.

3. Baroque counterpoint is highly *imitative and motivic.* If you examine the invention or the fugue, you will see that each of them in based almost exclusively on a single theme or motive, and that there are numerous cases of imitation among the voices, both at the beginning and within the pieces.

Melody and Rhythm

1. A look at the melodies in the Vivaldi and Bach examples will tell us that complete compositions or movements could be generated by a *single theme,* or by one or two very characteristic motivic figures.

2. We will also see that instrumental melodies become much more *angular and jagged* than the type of Renaissance vocal line we discussed above. Notice, particularly, the contour of Vivaldi's violin part. In mm. 5–6 (top voice) of the Bach fugue you will see a melody which, as a matter of fact, is actually like two independent lines in different registers. This type of "double melody" presented as a single melody is called a **compound melody** and is often found in baroque music. Can you identify any passages of compound melody in the Vivaldi example?

3. Unlike melody in the Renaissance, baroque melody has its basis to a great extent in *motivic repetition and sequences.* Notice especially the numerous sequences in Bach's fugue.

4. Unlike Renaissance flowing rhythms, baroque composers do not hesitate to write complete movements on a *repeated rhythmic figure*. See the rhythmic repetitions in the Vivaldi example and the almost constant (and almost obsessive) string of sixteenth notes in both of Bach's examples.

Thematic and Formal Growth

1. Although baroque composers used preestablished formal types, especially in their dance suites and concertos, they also favored freer types of form, which were generated either by text interpretation or by purely musical unfolding of ideas.

2. We will soon see that composers in the Classical period often organized their music in symmetrical phrases and periods. Baroque composers frequently favored instead a melodic technique known as **Fortspinnung**, or "spinning out." In Vivaldi's example you can see that the complete movement seems to freely "spin out" of the motives in mm. 1–2. The music grows naturally and freely, without clear phrase articulations or sectional divisions. Bach's fugue conveys the same effect of a continuous, almost uninterrupted flow of music generated by the initial motivic gesture.

3. In Purcell's example, two contrasting techniques of formal growth are presented simultaneously. The bass features a repeated four-measure phrase (a bass *ostinato,* or ground bass). The voice, on the other hand, "spins out" its melody in a much freer style, aside from some motivic repetitions associated with the words "Peace and I."

THE CLASSICAL STYLE

The musical period we know as Classical overlaps the previous period (the baroque) in the mid-eighteenth-century decades, and with the following period, the Romantic, in the early decades of the nineteenth century. Major Classical composers are Joseph Haydn, Wolfgang Amadeus Mozart, and Ludwig van Beethoven, although the life and stylistic development of the latter overlap the transition from the Classical to the Romantic periods. Classical composers are generally concerned with form, formal and tonal symmetry and balance, and the simplification of melodic, harmonic, and textural means (although simplified means can, of course, lead to richly complex results, as in the best works of Mozart). This is the period in which such formal types as binary, ternary, sonata form, and rondo became the standard models for movements of instrumental sonatas, concertos, and symphonies.

NOTE

The term classical *is often used to refer to several different concepts. Here, it means a specific historical and stylistic period, and this is what the term will usually mean in this book. Thus, when we refer to* classical *composers, we mean "composers of the Classical period." We can also use the term to refer to a more general approach to art and music (as in "classical antiquity"). Finally, the term* classical music *is commonly used to refer to Western art music of the past (as in "this radio station plays classical music"), as opposed to popular music, jazz, and so on. We will not use the term in the latter way in this book.*

Our musical references for the following discussion of classical style will be Haydn's Menuet and Trio from the Divertimento in CM, Hob. XVI:1 (anthology, no. 19), Mozart's Piano Sonata K. 333 in B♭M, III (anthology, no. 28), and Maria Theresia von Paradis's *Sicilienne* (anthology, no. 31).

Melody and Phrase Structure

1. As you listen to the three examples listed above you will hear that a common trait among them is the organization of the thematic and melodic material. Melodies are modular, built on distinctive *motivic gestures.*

2. All three examples begin with modular phrase structures in which thematic units or phrases are preferably grouped by multiples of two measures (2 + 2, 4 + 4, 8 + 8).

3. This music is often organized in eight-measure symmetrical periods (combinations of two phrases) which end on a cadence. See, for instance, Mozart's mm. 1–8 and 9–16, and Haydn's mm. 1–8.

Form and Formal Growth

1. The Mozart example is an excellent illustration of the classical approach to form. Two of the main elements of formal growth in this music are **variation and contrast**.

2. For an example of *variation,* compare mm. 1–8 with 9–16.

3. *Thematic and motivic contrast* is built into this music at every step. First, compare mm. 1–2 with 3–4 (the first phrase) for two contrasting motivic ideas. Then, compare mm. 1–16 (the first section) with mm. 16–24 (a transitional section, with new thematic material), and with mm. 24–36 (the second section, itself based on new, contrasting material). Notice also the variety of rhythmic figures in these two initial sections.

4. When you listen to the complete movement (in *rondo* form), you will notice that its form is based on the periodic return of the opening material (the *refrain*). Sections in between refrains are based on contrasting thematic material.

Harmony and Tonality

1. Classical music is firmly rooted in the *major-minor tonal system.*

2. Opening thematic gestures normally establish the key of the piece or movement unequivocally. Phrases are based on clear *functional progressions,* which normally produce strong harmonic *motion directed toward the cadence.*

3. *Harmonic rhythm* tends to be slow in classical music. Often the chords change every measure or half-measure (see the Mozart and Paradis examples).

4. Formal contrast is not only thematic, but also *tonal.* In the Mozart example, for instance, the refrain is always in the tonic key, B♭M. The first contrasting section (mm. 24–36) is in the key of the dominant, FM. The second contrasting section begins in the relative minor key, Gm (m. 65) and moves through several keys before returning to B♭M and the refrain in m. 112.

5. In other words, **classical form** *is closely associated with* **tonal design**. The standard classical tonal design is based on the following principle: *the tonic key is established, tension is created by moving away from the tonic key, tension is released by a return to the tonic key.*

Texture

1. Classical composers strove for *simple, transparent textures,* as illustrated by our three examples.

2. The preferred texture was usually **homophonic**, in which a melodic-thematic line is supported by a harmonic accompaniment.

3. The *harmonic accompaniment* is often in *block chords* (as in the Paradis example) or in *arpeggiated chords* (as in much of Mozart's example).

Dynamics and Articulation

1. Although *dynamics and articulation* are rarely indicated on Renaissance and baroque scores (which is not the same as saying that these scores should be performed without recourse to dynamics and articulation!), they become an essential element in the notation of classical music.

2. Dynamics provide a further element of contrast. In the Mozart example, the first statement of the initial phrase (mm. 1–8) is marked *p,* whereas its varied restatement (mm. 9–16) is marked *f.*

3. Articulation can be used to stress the contrast between different themes, or also as an element of variation used for expressive variety. Compare, for instance, the initial theme in the Mozart movement (mm. 1–4) with the transitional contrasting theme in mm. 16–20. What is the role of articulation as an element of contrast between these two themes? Now look at mm. 24–25, and to the variation of the same motive, which appears in mm. 26–27. Is articulation a factor in this variation?

4. Effects such as *crescendo, diminuendo,* and *sforzando* are often used by classical composers.

THE ROMANTIC STYLE

The leading composers of the Romantic age (early nineteenth century to early twentieth century) turn away from formal and objective models. They focus on their inner world, where they usually find contradiction, complexity, irrationality, and unresolved tension. Some of the notable Romantic composers are Franz Schubert, Felix Mendelssohn, Hector Berlioz, Frédéric Chopin, Robert Schumann, Clara Schumann, Johannes Brahms, Piotr Ilyich Tchaikovsky, Anton Bruckner, Richard Wagner, Franz Liszt, Giuseppe Verdi, and Gustav Mahler. Romantic music is an art of intense personal and subjective expression. Its essence is well represented by the *Lied* (song) and by the short character pieces for piano. Both of these genres are used to depict and capture intimate moods and emotions. (There was also a complementary tendency toward creating very long works for massive ensembles, well represented, for instance, by Bruckner's and Mahler's symphonies).

Our examples for the following discussion will be the songs "Bitte," by Fanny Mendelssohn Hensel (anthology, no. 43), and "Am leuchtenden Sommermorgen" by Robert Schumann (anthology, no. 49).

Melody and Rhythm

1. A salient feature of Romantic music is its **lyricism**: melody is often the most important element, and harmony helps enhance the beauty of melody.

2. *Romantic melody* is often nonmotivic. It unfolds and spins out in a similar way as Baroque melody did, but not necessarily from an initial motive. Romantic melodies are often *through-composed* (that is, without any motivic recurrences). This is indeed the case of the melody by Fanny Mendelssohn, and, to a great extent also, of the Schumann song.

3. The classical wealth of contrasting rhythms is often lost in Romantic music. *Rhythms often become repetitive and obsessive.* Rather than pursuing rhythmic contrast, Romantic composers often pursue rhythmic homogeneity.

Harmony and Tonality

1. Whereas the classical composer was concerned with establishing tonality at the outset of the piece (with both a clear key-defining thematic gesture and an early strong cadence in the tonic key), *clear tonal definition is not the concern of the Romantic composer.*

2. **Tonal ambiguity** (often in the service of some poetic purpose), on the other hand, is favored by Romantic composers. The Fanny Mendelssohn song is in A♭M, and it begins with a tonic chord. We do not find, however, a cadence in A♭M in the whole song, until the very final cadence. The cadence in mm. 6–7 resolves to A♭m, not A♭M. In the Schumann song, in B♭M, we hear an opening measure which is unusually ambiguous from the tonal point of view.

3. As illustrated by both songs, Romantic harmony is *highly chromatic.* Not only are chordal progressions chromatic, but modulations are often to unexpected and distant keys.

4. *Coloristic, nonfunctional harmonic progressions* (for instance, using third-related root motion) are often used to depict mood.

Form and Formal Growth

1. Romantic composers often focus more on *spontaneous poetic expression* than on the abstract constructive and thematic aspects of music. Form may grow from a text, or a poetic or programmatic idea.

2. *Phrases and phrase structure* are not symmetrical or clearly delimited by cadences. Standard formal types are often avoided or used in nonconventional ways.

3. *Long-range tonal relationships* often obscure rather than clarify the formal structure. Tonal designs are not conventional or standard. In the Schumann song, for instance, the main key is B♭M and secondary key areas are EM (only suggested, mm. 9–10) and GM (m. 17), both distant and unexpected keys.

THE TWENTIETH CENTURY

The study of twentieth-century post-tonal art music falls beyond the scope of this book. Stylistically, the twentieth century is one of the most complex, and one of the richest, and also fragmented, periods in music history. Any attempt to summarize it in a few paragraphs would fall short of doing justice to this stylistic wealth and complexity. Rather than attempt such a general summary, then, we will simply point out some stylistic aspects that are relevant to (and connect with) our discussion of style and tonality in previous periods.

1. The progressive *weakening (and eventual breakdown) of the tonal system* which we find in much late-nineteenth-century music led some early twentieth-century composers to look for *alternative methods of pitch organization.* Composers such as Arnold Schoenberg, Alban Berg, and Anton Webern based their music on radically new approaches to pitch organization, including *nontonal (or **atonal**)* intervallic and motivic cells and nontriadic sonorities. In the early 1920s, Schoenberg (followed by Berg and Webern) began to use a new system of pitch organization, which we know as the *twelve-tone system* or **serialism**. From a general point of view, a lot of Schoenberg's atonal music, as well as Berg's, is a continuation of Romantic stylistic features. Webern's music, on the other hand, and some of Schoenberg's twelve-tone music, displays strongly classical stylistic traits.

2. After World War II, some composers first continued to investigate serial compositional techniques in the tradition of Schoenberg, Berg, and Webern. Soon, however, a variety of other compositonal styles replaced serialism as the technique of choice for many European composers. *Postserial styles* in the 1960s and 1970s place great emphasis on elements such as texture, timbre, and dynamics, whereas pitch or rhythm structures are often not exactly determined by the composer. Major European composers in this period are Pierre Boulez, Karlheinz Stockhausen, Luciano Berio, Witold Lutosławski, György Ligeti, and Krzysztof Penderecki. In the United States, composers such as Milton Babbitt have continued to develop serial techniques in their music, whereas other composers, such as Elliott Carter, George Crumb, Morton Feldman, or Pauline Oliveros, have explored a variety of postserial techniques and styles in their compositions.

3. Some prominent twentieth-century composers defy classification, because of their very personal, individualistic approaches to composition and style. Among these, we will mention Charles Ives, Edgard Varèse, Olivier Messiaen, and John Cage.

4. Rather than break away with the tonal system, other composers in the first half of the century sought to **extend the concept of tonality** in a variety of ways, and at the same time break away from the Romantic tenets of style. Among the

composers who somehow preserved the concept of **pitch centricity** in their music (that is, who used various methods of organizing the pitch content of their compositions around some central pitch or collection of pitches) are Claude Debussy, Igor Stravinsky, Béla Bartók, Benjamin Britten, Sergei Prokofiev, Dmitri Shostakovich, Darius Milhaud, and Paul Hindemith, to name just a few. Modal, pentatonic, whole-tone, and other nonfunctional scales, as well as nonfunctional tertian (or or at times nontertian) harmony, are some of the alternative methods of pitch organization used by some of these composers.

5. *Rhythm, timbre, and dynamics* often became essential elements in the music of composers such as Stravinsky, Bartók, and Prokofiev. The general approach to texture, form, and types of genres in much of the music by these and other composers of the first half of the century also leads to their frequent characterization as **neoclassical**.

6. Other composers, on the other hand, stayed even *closer to the traditional tonal system,* while also extending it in their own way. Maurice Ravel, Manuel de Falla, Jean Sibelius, Sergei Rachmaninoff, George Gershwin, Aaron Copland, Samuel Barber, and Ralph Vaughan Williams represent in many ways the continuation of the tonal and stylistic traditions we will study in this book.

7. Similarly, we find in the late twentienth century numerous composers who base their music on extensions of the concept of tonality and pitch centricity (in styles that have often been called **neotonal** or "neo-Romantic"), in some cases featuring a clear *revitalization of traditional tonality.* This rediscovery of tonality and its expressive power in the late years of the century is patent in (otherwise stylistically diverse) works by composers such as David Del Tredici, George Rochberg, Joan Tower, and "minimalist" composers Philip Glass, Steve Reich, and John Adams, or in recent works by Penderecki and Hans Werner Henze.

8. The tonal tradition, moreover, underlies the music of several other mainstream twentieth-century styles. **Musical comedies**, **film music**, **jazz**, **pop**, **and rock** are all based to a great extent on the principles of functional tonality that we will study in this book, and as such these repertoires will be broadly represented in the book's musical examples.

CONCLUSIONS

We should stress again that the history of musical style, in spite of the contrasting approaches we have identified in the different periods, constitutes an unbroken continuum. Periods overlap, and transitions from one style to the next are often extended over decades. Although we have pointed out important differences between musical style in the Classical and Romantic periods, for instance, some Romantic composers preserved various classical principles in certain of their compositions. This has led some authors to stress not so much the differences, but rather the continuities between the two periods. Both differences and continuities do exist between periods, and the above discussions on stylistic elements will perhaps help you to determine to what extent a particular composition does or does not fulfill the standard characterizations of style for the period it belongs to.

Terms for Review

Musical style:
    Rhythm
    Meter
    Tempo
    Melody
    Harmony
    Tonality
    Texture
    Form and formal growth
    Dymanics
    Timbre
Musical style periods
Renaissance style:
    Sacred vocal polyphony
    Imitative counterpoint
Baroque style:
    Concertato style
    Basso continuo, thoroughbass
    Tonal counterpoint

Compound melody
Fortspinnung
Classical style:
    Variation and contrast
    Classical form and tonal design
    Homophonic textures
Romantic style:
    Lyricism
    Tonal ambiguity
Twentieth-century styles:
    Atonality
    Serialism
    Extended tonality
    Pitch centricity
    Neoclassicism
    Neotonal styles in late twentieth
        century
    Musical comedies, film music, jazz,
        pop, and rock

Worksheet G

LISTENING ASSIGNMENT Your assignment for this chapter will be to listen to as much of the music listed below as possible (the recordings should be available at your school's music library). As you listen to each composition, follow the score, if it is available at the music library.[1] The composers are listed in alphabetical order. Find the dates for each composer, and place him or her in the appropriate historical period. Then determine whether or not each of the compositions is representative of the period it belongs to, based on the general stylistic guidelines for each period that you have learned in this chapter. Take notes on the style characteristics for each piece, and be ready to discuss in class why each piece is or is not a good example of its period's style.

Notice that the following list does not intend to represent all the major styles and genres for each period. To be minimally representative, such a list would be of a much larger size than what is intended here. This also applies, of course, to twentieth-century compositions. Rather than being representative in any way, the few twentieth-century compositions in the list simply sample some of the main stylistic trends in the first half of the century.

1. Johann Sebastian Bach, Brandenburg Concerto no. 5

2. J. S. Bach, Cantata no. 4, "Christ lag in Todesbanden"

3. Béla Bartók, *Concerto for Orchestra*

4. Archangelo Corelli, *Concerti Grossi,* op. 6 (selected concertos)

5. Claude Debussy, *La mer*

6. George Frideric Handel, *Water Music*

7. Joseph Haydn, Symphony no. 99, in E♭M

8. Elizabeth Jacquet de la Guerre, Suite in Dm

9. Fanny Mendelssohn Hensel, *Lieder,* op. 9

10. Gustav Mahler, Symphony no. 5, I

11. Marianne Martinez, Piano Sonata in EM

12. Wolfgang A. Mozart, Symphonies no. 39, in E♭M, K. 543, and 40, in Gm, K. 550

13. Giovanni Pierluigi da Palestrina, *Missa Brevis*

14. Arnold Schoenberg, *Pierrot Lunaire,* selected songs

15. Franz Schubert, *Winterreise,* selected songs

16. Robert Schumann, *Davidsbündlertänze*

17. Igor Stravinsky, *Symphony of Psalms*

18. Richard Wagner, *Tristan und Isolde,* "Prelude and Transfiguration"

19. Anton Webern, Concerto, op. 24

---

[1] If individual scores or recordings of the works by women composers such as Jacquet de la Guerre, Mendelssohn Hensel, or Martinez are not available at your school's library, you can find examples of their compositions in James Briscoe, ed., *Historical Anthology of Music by Women* (Bloomington: Indiana University Press, 1987).

PART 1

Diatonic Harmony

Chapter 1

The Connection of Chords

If you listen to a recording of the opening fanfare of Claudio Monteverdi's *Orfeo* (1607), you will hear that it is based on a single chord. Tonality is here defined by the assertion of this single chord, the tonic triad. This is, however, a very unusual musical occurrence. Music is normally based on more than one chord, and tonality established by means other than assertion. In this chapter we will first examine the most frequent root relationships among successive chords, and then we will study the principles of part writing which regulate the connection of chords in tonal harmony.

HARMONIC PROGRESSION

A **harmonic progression** is a succession of two or more chords. In the tonal system, a given chord is not allowed to follow randomly any other chord. Some progressions are better than others, some are more idiomatic or typical than others, and conversely some chord successions are so atypical that, in principle, they sound "wrong" in the tonal language, and hence should be avoided. If chords constitute our harmonic vocabulary (like words in a spoken language), harmonic progressions are sentences, which we put together according the correct syntax of the tonal language. Throughout this book we will study both the harmonic vocabulary and the tonal syntax.

Basic Types of Progression

Taking into account the relationship between chord roots, there are *three basic types of chord progression: by 5th, by 2nd, and by 3rd.* Listen to the ***ritornello*** (the refrain, or recurring musical idea) from movement I of Antonio Vivaldi's "Winter" (*The Four Seasons*). The main melodic line, the bass line, and the Roman numerals for this musical phrase are reproduced in example 1.1. This is a progression in which all roots (also bass notes, in this case) are *related by 5th:* C–F–B♭–E♭–A♭–D–G–C–F.

The **5th progression**, in which chord roots are a 5th (or its inversion, a 4th) apart, is the most essential root relationship in tonal music. The root motion *down a*

Example 1.1   Antonio Vivaldi, *The Four Seasons,* "Winter," I, *Ritornello*

5th or up a 4th has the property of propelling the music forward, of creating a harmonic motion that calls for continuation. The fundamental progression in tonal music, I–V–I, is based on this relationship: the root of V is a 5th above (or a 4th below) the root of I. Moreover, V is frequently preceded by ii, whose root ($\hat{2}$) is itself a 5th above $\hat{5}$. Any chord may be preceded by the chord a 5th above it; ii may thus be preceded by vi, and if we continue this same process, after seven chords we will use up all the available diatonic triads in a key (example 1.2). The bass line of the resulting progression, the **circle of 5ths** progression, contains, in its complete form, all

Example 1.2

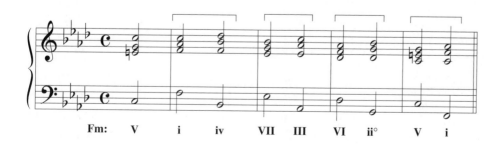

the pitches of the diatonic scale organized in descending 5ths, or ascending 4ths, or, as it is found most often in music, in descending 5ths alternating with ascending 4ths. Such is the case of the Vivaldi phrase, and of the circle of 5ths triadic progression reproduced in example 1.2.

Both example 1.1 and example 1.2 illustrate the specific type of harmonic progression we call **sequence**. As we studied in chapter G, a sequence is a melodic-harmonic pattern that is restated, literally or with slight modifications, at different tonal levels, often up or down a step. In example 1.1, both the upper voice and the bass feature **melodic sequences**. In example 1.2, however, we see that the realization of the Roman numerals (the harmonies) from the Vivaldi example also displays a **harmonic sequential pattern** in which a pair of chords (the second and third chords) is restated in each of the following measures, and each statement is a step lower than the previous one. The circle of 5ths usually supports this type of sequence descending by steps, as we will often see in this book.

NOTE
_____

In a diatonic circle of 5ths not all the 5ths or 4ths are perfect. Which 5th or 4th is not perfect in example 1.2, and what kind of 5th or 4th is it?
_____

Example 1.3, on the other hand, features several cases of **root motion by 2nd**, or stepwise progressions. Beginning with the second chord (iii), the progression iii–IV–V–vi–V is all by 2nds. Stepwise progressions are also very common in tonal music, although not all progressions by 2nd are equally idiomatic. The step progressions shown in example 1.3 (marked with brackets) are all standard: iii–IV, IV–V, V–vi, and vi–V. I–ii is also found in the literature, although less often. Progressions such as ii–iii, IV–iii, and stepwise progressions to or from vii° in root position (vi–vii°, vii°–vi, I–vii°, or vii°–I) are seldom found and may be considered unidiomatic. Finally, the progression V–IV is very unusual in common practice harmony, although it is quite common in blues and rock music.

Example 1.4a illustrates the third type of standard progression, a **progression by 3rds**, in this case descending. An ascending progression by 3rds also appears in m. 1

♪♪♪ Example 1.3

CM: I   iii   IV   V   vi   V   I

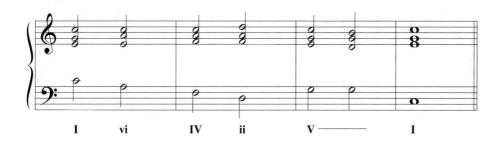

Example 1.4a

I   vi   IV   ii   V ——————— I

Example 1.4b   John Lennon–Paul McCartney, "All My Loving," from the album *With the Beatles*

EM: I   vi   IV   ii

♮VII   V₇

of example 1.3. Here again, not all progressions by 3rds are equally idiomatic. The two most frequent cases are the ascending progression I–iii–V, or the descending progression I–vi–IV, which can be extended to I–vi–IV–ii, as in example 1.4a. Example 1.4b illustrates a progression by descending 3rds moving all the way from I to V: I–vi–IV–ii–♮VII–V$_7$.[1]

---

[1] For a detailed and compelling study of the music of The Beatles, see Walter Everett, *The Beatles as Musicians: Revolver to the Anthology* (New York: Oxford University Press, 1999).

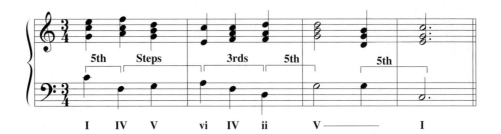

Although examples 1.2, 1.3, and 1.4 illustrate progressions largely based on a single type of root motion, the three types are usually combined in music. Example 1.5 shows a progression combining root motion by 5th, 2nd, and 3rd.

The detailed study of specific diatonic triads and the idiomatic progressions they are associated with in a musical context will be taken up in various chapters throughout part 1 of this book. In the remainder of this chapter we will review the general principles of chord connection, and we will also discuss specific guidelines to connect chords whose roots are related by 5th, 2nd, or 3rd.

NOTATING, VOICING, AND SPACING CHORDS

Notation of Triads in Four Voices

We will begin by notating triads in *four voices* (or *parts,* as voices are often called) on two staves, according to the notational and musical conventions of vocal ensemble style (*vocal scoring*). To begin with, we must keep each of the voices within possible (and comfortable) ranges. The four voices are called, from top to bottom, **soprano, alto, tenor,** and **bass** (**SATB**). Their ranges are represented in example 1.6. In vocal scoring, soprano and alto are notated in the upper staff in treble clef, tenor and bass in the lower staff in bass clef. The direction of the stems, as illustrated in example 1.7a, is essential to the immediate visual identification of each of the four voices.

Voicing a Triad in Four Voices: Doublings

The term *voicing* refers to the distribution of pitches among the four voices, SATB. Because triads have three pitches and we write in four voices, a pitch must always be doubled. Once we connect several chords in harmonic progressions, *doubling will be determined mostly by voice leading*. If you have a choice, however, preferably double the root of the chord if possible (example 1.7b). Doubling the fifth is your second choice (example 1.7c), followed by doubling the third (example 1.7d). These doubling preferences refer to *major and minor triads only*. The strongest and most stable interval in M and m triads is the P5 which frames them. For this reason, it is preferable to

♪♪♪Example 1.6

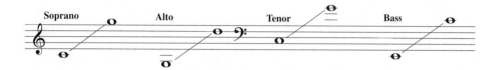

stress the root (the main pitch in a triad) or the fifth, rather than the third (unnecessarily stressing the third usually weakens the sound of a triad, an effect which, however, may be used to good advantage for expressive purposes).

NOTE

Because of the dissonant 5th which frames them, diminished and augmented triads present specific voicing problems that often depend on their harmonic context. Different criteria apply to doublings in these two types of triads, as will be discussed later in the book.

♪♪♪Example 1.7

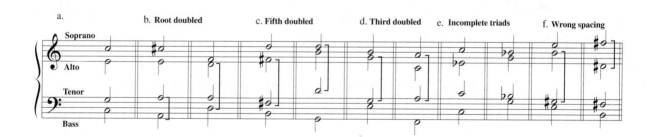

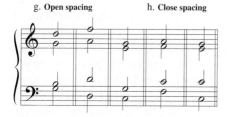

You should avoid doubling the leading tone (LT). Because it has a strong melodic tendency toward the tonic, the LT (the third of V, or the root of vii°) usually resolves to Î. Doubling it not only would stress a pitch which, because of its tendency, needs no additional emphasis, but also is likely to result in parallel 8ves if both LTs are resolved to Î (see discussion of parallel 8ves in rule 5 in the next section).

M or m triads may occasionally, if rarely, be incomplete (one pitch left out). The only pitch that may be omitted is the fifth. The root and the third should never be omitted. (Omitting the root would create an identity crisis for the triad, and omitting the third would turn the triad into an open 5th, a perfect interval which may sound quite hollow in a triadic context.) If a chord has no fifth, you may either double the third or triple the root (example 1.7e)

Spacing

There should be no more than one 8ve between soprano and alto or alto and tenor. Tenor and bass, however, may be more than one 8ve apart (see example 1.7f).

Triads may be in open or close spacing. In **open spacing** there is one 8ve or more between soprano and tenor (example 1.7g). In **close spacing** there is less than an 8ve between soprano and tenor (example 1.7h). In other words, in open spacing you should be able to insert one or more chord notes between some of the adjacent three upper voices. For instance, in the first chord in example 1.7g you could insert a D between tenor and alto, and a B between alto and soprano. What pitches could you insert between adjacent upper voices in the second and third chords? In close spacing, on the other hand, you cannot insert any chord notes between any of the adjacent three upper voices. Verify whether this is true in example 1.7h.

EXERCISE

To practice notating triads in four voices, refer to exercise 1.2 in worksheet 1 at the end of this chapter.

CHORD CONNECTION: THE PRINCIPLES OF PART WRITING

We will now focus on the techniques of chord connection. A smooth, stylistically correct connection between two chords follows a number of principles, which we will summarize in the following paragraphs. These principles reflect *general harmonic conventions in common practice tonal music.* But even within this stylistic frame, some of the usual conventions of chord connection and melodic style are closely linked to *vocal music,* and specifically to **chorale-style harmonizations**. These are four-part vocal harmonizations of hymn tunes, in which the actual tune is usually placed in the soprano. This type of composition started being widely used in Lutheran services in the baroque period (to be sung by the congregation) and is still used in the same context. You should keep in mind that some of the conventions you will study below do not

necessarily apply to, say, instrumental music. Because of idiomatic writing, for instance, instrumental lines often include numerous large leaps of types which you will
not find in chorale textures (or in choral music in general), and which you will need to
avoid in your vocal four-part harmonizations.

In the anthology, nos. 8–10, you can examine some of the 371 chorale harmonizations by J. S. Bach that have reached us. In these chorales you can clearly hear
the two simultaneous dimensions of sound: the horizontal dimension provided by the
independent lines, and the vertical dimension that results from pitch simultaneities
among the four lines, and which produces chordal sonorities. In our chord connections we need to keep both dimensions in mind. The motion of voices between
chords is regulated by the principles of **part writing**. But at the same time we need
to think of all four voices as interacting, independent lines, an element of harmony
we refer to as **voice leading**.

Basic Voice-Leading Conventions

Example 1.8 shows several connections between tonic and dominant chords. Although
the principles of part writing and voice leading apply to all types of chord connections
regardless of their root motion, we will begin by illustrating these principles with

♪♪♪ Example 1.8

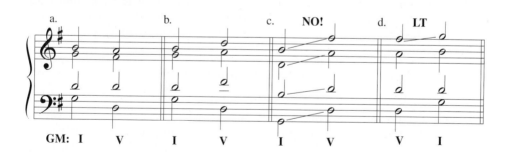

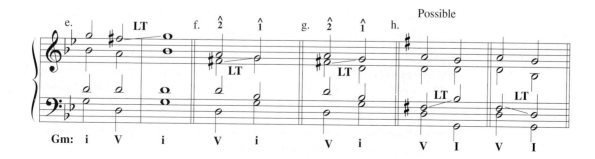

progressions based only on the tonic and the dominant triads. **Nine basic rules of voice leading** follow.

1. *General principle.* When connecting two chords, leave any *common tone(s)* between the chords in the same voice(s); take all other voices to the nearest possible pitch from the second chord, as long as doing so does not create some other kind of voice-leading problem, such as faulty parallel 5ths or 8ves (examples 1.8a, d, and e).

2. *Leaps.* Melodic motion by step (conjunct motion) is preferred. Avoid large leaps whenever possible, unless they are musically justified. Although leaps of 3rd, P4, and P5 are frequent in the bass (and so is the 8ve), leaps larger than a P4 or P5 should rarely be used in the upper voices. Leaps of a 7th should especially be avoided. The part writing in example 1.8b, although less smooth than example 1.8a because of leaps in three voices, is quite acceptable. Example 1.8c, on the other hand, presents some seemingly unnecessary large leaps in all four voices which result in quite faulty part writing. Because a part-writing flaw often engenders other troubles, example 1.8c illustrates two more problems we will point out below.

3. *Augmented and diminished intervals.* Melodic augmented intervals should in principle be strictly avoided. Beware especially of the augmented second, $\flat\hat{6}$–$\natural\hat{7}$, in the minor mode. Diminished intervals, usually descending and most often in the bass (such as the diminished fifth $\hat{4}$–$\hat{7}$, the diminished fourth $\hat{3}$–$\sharp\hat{7}$ in minor, and even the diminished seventh $\hat{6}$–$\sharp\hat{7}$ also in minor), are possible in some progressions. They usually resolve by step in the opposite direction of the leap ($\hat{4}$–$\hat{7}$–$\hat{1}$ or, in minor, $\hat{3}$–$\sharp\hat{7}$–$\hat{1}$ or $\hat{6}$–$\sharp\hat{7}$–$\hat{1}$).

4. ***Contrapuntal motion*** *between voices.* As we studied in chapter D, the simultaneous presentation of independent lines (melodies) is known as *counterpoint.* The term also refers to the technical principles that regulate the simultaneous combination of voices.

    In chapter D we also saw that there are four possible types of motion between voices.

    Parallel motion: Voices move in the same direction preserving the harmonic interval between them. In example 1.8a, soprano-alto move in parallel motion (they preserve the 3rd, even though the first one is a M3 and the second a m3), as they do in example 1.8d, now preserving the 6th.

    Similar motion: Voices move in the same direction, but the harmonic interval between them is not preserved. Both the soprano-tenor and alto-bass pairs in example 1.8f move in similar motion.

    Oblique motion: A voice moves (up or down) and the other voice stays on the same pitch. The tenor-bass motion in both examples 1.8a and d illustrates oblique motion.

    Contrary motion: Voices move in opposite directions. In example 1.8b, the tenor and bass move by contrary motion.

♪♪♪ Example 1.9

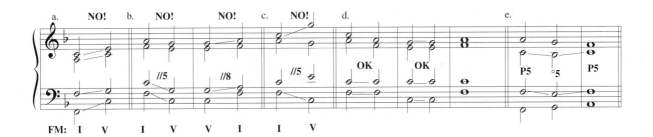

Contrapuntal motion among the four voices. Try to avoid moving all four voices in the same direction, as in example 1.9a. If possible, at least one of the voices should move in contrary or oblique motion with respect to the other three (although at times a perfectly acceptable voice leading will include motion of all voices in the same direction). All the progressions in example 1.8 follow this voice-leading principle, except for example 1.8c. Not only do all voices leap, but they all do so in the same direction, contributing to the poor realization of the part writing.

5. *Forbidden parallels.* **Parallel 5ths** or **parallel 8ves** result when two voices move by parallel motion from a P5 to another P5, or from an 8ve to another 8ve. Parallel perfect 5ths (//5) and 8ves (//8) are strictly forbidden (example 1.9b). Consecutive **P5s or P8s by contrary motion** are equally forbidden (example 1.9c). This is a strong stylistic feature in tonal music and is based on the principle of voice independence: If two voices move in parallel 8ves (and, to a certain extent, also in parallel 5ths), their individuality and independence are lost. Moreover, because the 5th is a very stable and strong interval, the sound of parallel 5ths is particularly characteristic, and in a triadic texture of independent voices it tends to stand out as unstylistic. We mentioned above that voice-leading woes rarely come alone. All voices leaping in the same direction in the faulty I–V progression in example 1.8c results in some problematic parallels. Can you find them?

NOTE

5ths or 8ves repeated *in the same voices, without motion, are not incorrect parallels (see example 1.9d).*

Consecutive 5ths are allowed only if one of them is diminished (*unequal 5ths*), although they should be avoided between the outer voices (bass and soprano). Example 1.9e illustrates a progression that features two sets of acceptable unequal 5ths in succession (P5–°5 and °5–P5).

NOTE

Instrumental or choral 8ve doubling is totally correct and is not of the same nature as voice-leading parallel 8ves. It is commonly used to strengthen a voice (as in 8ve doubling of a melody or bass at the piano) or for coloristic purposes (an oboe melody doubled at the upper 8ves by a flute and a piccolo).

6. *Direct or hidden 5ths or 8ves.* A **direct or hidden 5th or 8ve** results when a P5 or an 8ve between *outer voices* is approached by similar motion and with a leap in the soprano (example 1.10a). If the soprano is approached by step, the 5th or 8ve is perfectly acceptable (example 1.10b). This latter case happens frequently in what is called "horn 5ths." In example 1.10c, from Mozart's Sonata in FM, K. 332, I, brackets indicate two standard cases of horn 5ths. In the first type, a 5th is preceded by a 3rd, in a descending motion in which the soprano moves by step. The second type features an ascending motion from a 6th to a 5th, also with a soprano moving by step. (The 8ves between the top and middle voices in this example are not a case of faulty "parallel 8ves," but rather of correct 8ve doubling of a melody.)

7. *Leading tone.* As a general principle, **resolve the leading tone** up a half step, to the tonic, especially when the LT is in one of the outer voices. See examples 1.8d, e, and f; see also the section "Voicing a Triad in Four Voices: Doublings" on pages 138–140.

   If the LT is in an inner voice, however, exceptions to this principle are possible. If the voice above the LT moves to $\hat{1}$ in the same octave as the LT, then we hear the resolution to $\hat{1}$ in the upper voice as a satisfactory resolution. This allows the LT to move down a 3rd, as illustrated by example 1.8g. Occasionally a LT in an inner voice leaps up a 4th or down a 3rd, as demonstrated in example 1.8h. Although both of these LT motions are possible and found in Bach chorales, you should use them with moderation because they contravene the strong melodic tendency of $\hat{7}$ towards $\hat{1}$.

♪♪♪**Example 1.10**

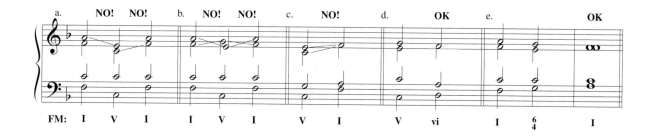

♪♪♪Example 1.11

8. *Voice overlap and voice crossing.* In example 1.11a, the soprano moves to a pitch (E) lower than the adjacent voice (alto, F) in the previous chord. The alto then moves from C to F, a pitch higher than the adjacent voice (soprano, E) in the previous chord. These are all examples of **voice overlap**, which in principle should be avoided in part writing. As a reminder that often troubles do not come alone, what else is dubious in the connection of these three chords?

In Example 1.11b, the soprano and alto cross twice. **Voice crossing** should also be avoided in part-writing exercises, especially when it involves one of the outer voices. In other words, you should try to keep the proper order of voices: soprano above alto above tenor above bass. Occasional and brief voice crossing between the tenor and alto is possible as long as it does not create other voice-leading problems.

The reason for these guidelines concerning voice crossing and overlap has to do again with the independence of the parts: Voices that cross or overlap tend to get confused with each other, thus losing their individuality. These are not, however, absolute rules. You will find occasional overlaps and voice crossings in Bach chorales, and you can also use them occasionally if you have some musical reason for it.

9. *Unison.* **Unison** between two voices is correct as long as it is approached and left by contrary or oblique motion. Do not approach or leave it by similar motion. The result will be an awkward voice overlap, as in example 1.11c. Two unisons in a row in the same voices involving successive different pitches (*parallel unisons*) are strictly forbidden, as much as parallel 8ves are. (Unisons repeated in the same voices, without change of pitch, are perfectly acceptable.) Examples 1.11d and e show two cases of correct unisons that occur frequently in progressions we will study.

EXERCISE

To practice error detection in chord connections, refer to exercise 1.3 in worksheet 1 at the end of this chapter.

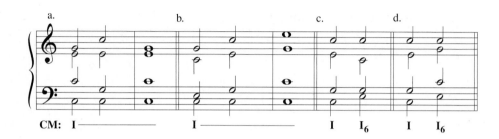

Changes of Voicing or Position

In a change of voicing, a chord remains the same, but its voicing changes. The change of voicing may affect one or more of the three upper voices, or it may also affect the bass. If the bass position changes, the position of the chord changes (from root position to an inversion or vice versa, or from one inversion to another).

Examples 1.12a and b illustrate **changes of voicing** in the upper voices on a static bass. In example 1.12a only two voices change, whereas in example 1.12b all three voices change.

In four-voice connections involving a **change of position** (from root position to first inversion, for instance), at least one voice should remain static. Example 1.12c is an example of change of position in which only two voices change (including, of course, the bass). Example 1.12d illustrates a change of position in which three voices change.

EXERCISE

To practice changes of voicing and position, refer to exercise 1.4 in worksheet 1 at the end of this chapter.

Voice-Leading Guidelines for the Three Basic Types of Progression

We studied at the beginning of this chapter that the three basic types of progression involve root motion by descending 5th, by step, or by 3rd, respectively. We will now review some general guidelines for voice leading in each of these progression types. All of the following guidelines assume that all chords are in root position, and that the root is doubled in all chords. Many other voice-leading possibilities are afforded by different doublings and by chord inversions, as will become apparent to you as you begin writing progressions in the following chapters.

♪♪♪ Example 1.13

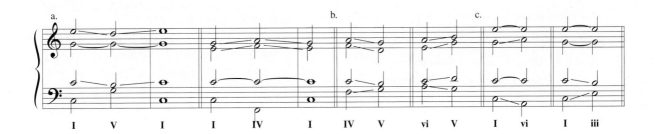

Roots by Fifth

The voice leading for the 5th progression allows for several equally good possibilities. The most standard, and most smooth voice leading, however, is illustrated in example 1.13a: the common tone between the two chords remains in the same voice, while the other two upper voices move by step to the closest pitch in the next chord. This same principle applies to both the ascending 5th and the descending 5th progression, as both examples in example 1.13a illustrate (I–V–I, ascending-descending, and I–IV–I, descending-ascending).

Roots by 2nd

Progressions by 2nd do not allow for various possibilities without risk of parallel 5ths and 8ves. The best and safest voice leading is shown in example 1.13b: all three upper voices move in contrary motion with the bass (two of them by steps, one by 3rd). The same principle applies to roots ascending by step (such as IV–V) or descending by step (such as vi–V).

Roots by 3rd

Diatonic triads whose roots are related by a 3rd have two common tones. The smoothest voice leading in this progression keeps both common tones in the same voices, while the remaining voice moves by step. A descending 3rd progression (I–vi) and an ascending 3rd progression (I–iii) appear in example 1.13c.

EXERCISE

To practice part writing in four voices, refer to exercise 1.5 in worksheet 1 at the end of this chapter.

VOICE-LEADING GUIDELINES

1. Common tones between two chords preferably remain in the same voice(s). In 5th and 3rd progressions, the other pitches move to the nearest possible pitch in the second chord. In step progressions upper voices move in contrary motion with the bass.

2. Avoid unnecessary leaps. Conjunct motion is preferred.

3. Avoid augmented melodic intervals. Diminished intervals are acceptable, especially in the bass, and usually resolve by step in the opposite direction.

4. Try not to move all four voices simultaneously in the same direction.

5. Parallel perfect 5ths, 8ves, and unisons are forbidden. P5s and 8ves by contrary motion are also forbidden.

6. Avoid direct 5ths or 8ves between outer voices, unless the soprano moves by step.

7. It is best to resolve the LT up a half step to $\hat{1}$, especially in the outer voices.

8. Avoid crossing voices, especially above the soprano or below the bass. Avoid voice overlap.

9. Approach and leave unisons by contrary or oblique motion (not by similar motion).

MELODIC STYLE

As much as possible, your individual lines should be melodically satisfying. This applies especially to the *soprano line.* You should also craft the shape of your voices, especially the outer voices (soprano and bass). Some of the criteria for doing so are similar to those you studied in chapter D with reference to melody in species counterpoint. Because Renaissance style, however, was more strict than common practice style, the following melodic principles in four-part, chorale-style harmony are not quite as rigorous as those in species counterpoint.

Basic Melodic Conventions

1. *Stepwise motion* is always preferred. If possible, it is desirable to balance a leap in the melody with motion in the opposite direction before or after the leap, although this is considered a stricter guideline in counterpoint than in harmonic part writing. We have already seen that large leaps and augmented intervals should be avoided. Diminished melodic intervals, on the other hand, are acceptable. The bass line is likely to have more leaps than the upper voices, including frequent skips of 3rd, P4, P5, and 8ve.

2. Two *consecutive leaps* in the same direction are awkward unless they outline a triad (or, in the bass, an 8ve split by a 5th, as in $\hat{1}$–$\hat{5}$–$\hat{8}$), and in all cases it is best to balance them with motion in the opposite direction *before and after* the leaps.

3. Melodies should have a smooth (not jagged) contour. The best melodies have a single focal point (highest or lowest pitch). Repeating a pitch more than twice results in a static, uninteresting line. This may often happen, however, in the alto and tenor; inner voices will tend to be more static because of the preference to leave common tones in the same voice if possible. Avoid excessive or unmusical pitch repetition in the soprano.

All the above principles of good melodic style are illustrated in the four chorale melodies in example 1.14. Read the melodies carefully, sing them, and verify the application of the above guidelines. Observe especially how leaps are balanced, and how consecutive leaps in the same direction outline a triad or an 8ve split by a 5th. Basic contours are indicated under three of the melodies, and focal points are marked with arrows.

Example 1.14

EXERCISE

To practice critical analysis of melodic style, refer to exercise 1.6 in worksheet 1 at the end of this chapter.

VOICE INDEPENDENCE

Voices, especially outer voices (soprano-bass) must be as independent as possible. This principle is not different from what you learned in chapter D regarding voice independence in species counterpoint. Contrary or oblique motion is preferred, whereas parallel motion should be limited to three or four consecutive pitches. Contours should be independent, and focal points should, if possible, not happen at the same time. The outer voices of a phrase from a chorale by J. S. Bach are reproduced in example 1.15a.

♪♪♪ Example 1.15a   J. S. Bach, Chorale 80, "O Haupt voll Blut und Wunden," mm. 1–4

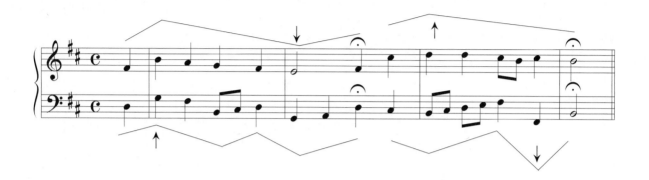

♪♪♪ Example 1.15b   J. S. Bach, Chorale 160, "Gelobet seist du," mm. 1–4

♪♪♪ Example 1.15c   J. S. Bach, Chorale 181, "Gott hat das Evangelium," mm. 1–4

Examine them for independence of contour and focal points. Notice that the leap of a 5th in the soprano after the first fermata is not balanced by motion in the opposite direction before or after the leap. This is quite acceptable in this case because the F♯ and the C♯ belong to different phrases, as indicated by the fermata, and hence are not heard as a melodic unit.

Voice Leading and Species Counterpoint

Most of the voice-leading principles we have just studied have their origin in Renaissance counterpoint and its pedagogical adaptation, species counterpoint. In chapter D you were introduced to species counterpoint, and you must certainly have recognized, in the present chapter, such principles as moving the voices mostly by steps, balancing leaps with motion in the opposite direction, avoiding parallel perfect intervals, avoiding direct 5ths and 8ves, and so forth.

As soon as we start realizing harmonic progressions, you will observe that *outer-voice motion is usually ruled by the principles of first- or second-species counterpoint.* This is often true also of inner voices, but in four-part harmonic realizations the shape of inner voices may have to be sacrificed in order to achieve smooth overall voice leading, especially if we are to keep common tones in the same voice as much as possible. Your focus should be mostly on outer-voice independence and shape.

In example 1.15b you can see the outer-voice frame for a fragment of a Bach chorale. Verify that it is written according to the principles of first-species counterpoint. Here again, some of the conventions of common practice counterpoint are slightly different than those of the Renaissance. In chapter D, for instance, you learned that, in first species, all harmonic intervals should be consonant. In the Bach example, a harmonic °5 has been marked. Both harmonic and melodic diminished intervals, such as °5 or °7, are quite idiomatic, and hence quite acceptable, in common practice harmonic style. Refer to example E.1a, another Bach chorale fragment in which outer voices are ruled by first-species counterpoint, and identify two correct harmonic diminished intervals in the outer-voice frame.

EXERCISE

To practice critical analysis of part writing, voice leading, and melodic style, refer to exercise 1.1 in worksheet 1 at the end of this chapter.

WHY ALL THESE RULES

In order to be effective, the principles and conventions of voice leading and chordal connection must be understood in their proper context.

1. Voice-leading rules reflect conventions that for centuries have been considered the foundation of compositional craft.

2. The rules are stylistic in nature, and limited to a relatively short historical period. Although most voice-leading principles were already in effect in the sixteenth century, the style of chordal functional harmony which this book represents was practiced from mid- to late seventeenth to mid- to late nineteenth centuries. It is still practiced to the present day in most commercial music: Music composed for movies, television, musicals, and entertainment or background music in general is usually solidly grounded on the principles of tonal voice leading.

   Tonal music is written according to a number of conventions of good craft which make it "sound as it does," that is, which make it sound "stylistically correct." A fifteenth-century 8ve-leap cadence sounds very different than a Mozart cadence because of the different conventions involved. And, to use another example, frequent series of parallel 5ths are stylistically correct in the music of Debussy, whereas they would be totally out of place (stylistically wrong) in the music of Haydn or Mozart.

3. Even in the stylistic time span mentioned above, one finds numerous exceptions to the rules in actual music by composers of the period. The reasons are multiple: (1) Four-part, chorale-style harmony reflects mostly a vocal style. Instrumental styles may at times be less strict in their observance of some rules. (2) Harmony and its principles, as studied in a book like this, are pedagogical in nature. Rules have an important function for beginning musicians, in helping them acquire technique, discipline, and control over the music they write. (3) All composers of the past acquired their solid craft through elaborate studies that included many more rules than the ones presented in this book. Once they possessed technique and control, at times they consciously ignored some convention for good musical reasons. But although good musical reasons always have priority over rules and conventions, careless craft only reflects (and produces) poor musicianship.

ASSIGNMENT AND KEYBOARD PRACTICE
For a written assignment and keyboard practice of the materials learned in this chapter, refer to chapter 1 in the workbook.

Composers and Their Music 1

In this section you will be asked to write short biographies of several of the new composers mentioned in each chapter. Biographies should be no longer than one page, written in good style, and they should include basic information about composers: dates and places of birth and death; major professional appointments and places of residence; a brief comment on the role of the composers within the context of their historical periods; and a list of major compositions. You should use the *New Grove Dictionary of Music and Musicians* as your primary source, along with one additional source for each composer (such as a music history textbook or a monograph on the composer), which you should cite in full at the end of your biography. For correct citation style, consult Kate Turabian, *A Manual for Writers of Term Papers, Theses, and Dissertations* (University of Chicago Press, 1996). Your biographies should not be copied literally from your sources. Write *summaries* of information taken from the sources, and make sure that the data you select for your paper are always significant and important, not just secondary or anecdotal, in the life of a composer.

In this section you will also find suggested listening assignments, including representative works by some of the composers cited in the course of each chapter. Most of the compositions listed should be easily available at your school's music library. Some of the compositions by women composers appear in James Briscoe, *Historical Anthology of Music by Women* (Indiana University Press, 1987), which comes with an accompanying set of recordings.

This section is an important component of your training as a musician. Familiarizing yourself with some of the most significant compositions by composers of all periods will help you know and understand your rich historical background as a Western musician. Moreover, listening to this music should prove to be an enjoyable and enriching activity.

Biographies

Write short biographies of the following composers mentioned in this chapter: Johann Sebastian Bach, Claudio Monteverdi, Antonio Vivaldi, John Lennon, and Paul McCartney.

Listening

Listen to the following compositions by composers mentioned in this chapter:

Monteverdi: *Orfeo* (selections)
Bach: Brandenburg Concerto No. 5
Vivaldi: *The Four Seasons*
The Beatles: *Sgt. Pepper's Lonely Hearts Club Band*
Follow the score while you listen (if one is available). Be able to place these compositions in one of the style periods and to comment on why and how they represent the musical characteristics of that period.

Terms for Review

Harmonic progression
Ritornello
Progression by 5th
Circle of 5ths
Sequence (melodic and harmonic)
Progression by 2nd
Progression by 3rd
Soprano, alto, tenor, bass (SATB)
Voicing a triad in four voices; doublings
Spacing:
    open, close

Chorale-style harmonizations
Part writing and voice leading

Voice leading conventions (nine basic
    rules)
Contrapuntal motion:
    parallel, similar, oblique, contrary

Parallel 5ths and 8ves
5ths and 8ves by contrary motion
Direct (hidden) 5ths and 8ves
Leading-tone resolution
Voice overlap, voice crossing
Unison
Changes of voicing or position
Melodic style
Voice independence

Worksheet 1

EXERCISE 1.1   Analysis.

1. a) Analyze example 1.16 with Roman numerals. What is the key of the passage? Notice that chords are presented in a characteristic keyboard figuration (the *bass afterbeat* pattern typical of waltzes and marches) in which a chord is broken into a bass note on the downbeat and the remaining pitches as a block chord in the following beats. The *complete measure* is analyzed as one chord, with the position determined by the bass on the downbeat.

> **Procedure to analyze progressions with Roman numerals**: First determine the key for the passage. Then, identify the root and type of each chord by organizing its pitches in thirds. Once you know the root of the chord, determine on what scale degree the chord is built in the specific key for the passage, and assign the correct Roman numeral (capital or lowercase) depending on the chord type.

   b) How does the voice leading in the left hand reflect the guidelines studied in this chapter?

   c) How does the melody reflect the changes of harmony? Does it also display good voice leading in its motion from chord 1 to chord 2?

   d) Comment on the melody. Although it is an instrumental melody, is it "well written" by our vocal melodic standards?

♪♪♪ Example 1.16   Franz Schubert, *Walzer, Ländler und Ecossaisen*, op. 18, Ländler, no. 3, mm. 1–8

e) Admitting that Schubert certainly knew what he was doing, could you comment critically on the melody in mm. 1–5?

2. Study the part writing and voice leading in the following example from a Bach chorale. Identify one case of each of the following events, and label each one with the corresponding "event number" (1, 2, 3, etc.) with an arrow pointing at the exact location of the event. For each example of chord connection, write "yes" or "no" to indicate whether Bach follows the guidelines for voice leading according to the corresponding root motion.

　1. A root-position chord connection with root motion by descending 5th.

　2. A root-position chord connection with root motion by step.

　3. A root-position chord connection with root motion by 3rd.

　4. A root-position chord connection with root motion by ascending 5th (or descending 4th).

　5. A chord in open position.

　6. A chord in close position.

　7. A V–I progression in AM in which the LT resolves in the same voice.

　8. A V–I progression in AM in which the LT resolves in the voice above it.

　9. A melodic double leap which outlines a triad.

　10. A single leap balanced by contrary motion before or after the leap.

　11. A descending diminished leap in the bass. Label the exact interval. Notice that this chord is immediately followed by a change of position. Does the diminished leap resolve up by step *after* the change of position?

　12. A triad in $^6_3$ position.

　13. A seventh chord in root position.

　14. A seventh chord in $^6_5$ position.

　15. A seventh chord in $^4_2$ position.

　16. A unison approached and left by contrary or oblique motion.

♪♪♪Example 1.17   J. S. Bach, Chorale 7, "Nun lob', mein' Seel', den Herren," mm. 1–8

EXERCISE 1.2   Write root-position triads in four voices with the requested spacing (o for open, c for close), without key signatures (write only the necessary accidentals before each triad).

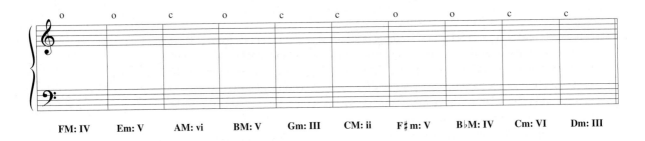

FM: IV   Em: V   AM: vi   BM: V   Gm: III   CM: ii   F♯m: V   B♭M: IV   Cm: VI   Dm: III

EXERCISE 1.3   Identify and mark all the voice-leading mistakes in the following progressions.

EXERCISE 1.4   Complete the following changes of voicing or position in four voices.

EXERCISE 1.5   Complete the following progressions in four voices on the given bass notes. All your chords should be in root position, and you should apply the principles of voice leading according to root motion, which you studied above.

EXERCISE 1.6   The following melody is very weak according to the criteria for melodic style discussed in this chapter. Criticize the melody, circle all the faulty spots, and annotate the specific problem for each of the weak spots.

Chapter 2

The Tonic and Dominant Triads in Root Position

The tonic and the dominant triads (I and V in major keys, or i and V in minor keys) constitute the basic two-chord unit of the tonal system. **Structural chords** are those that can have the role of beginning or ending musical units. The tonic and dominant harmonies are structural chords: only the tonic triad is a true point of departure; both the dominant and the tonic may function as points of arrival.

Many musical units are built on only these two chords. Listen to the opening of Giuseppe Verdi's drinking song from *La traviata* ("Libiamo ne' lieti calici," see anthology, no. 52). The section is based only on I and V_7 in the key of B♭M. The accompaniment features a chordal texture which was discussed in worksheet 1, the **bass afterbeat figuration** typical of waltzes and marches. In this figuration, the chord is broken into a bass note on the downbeat and a block chord in the following beats. The *complete measure* is analyzed as one chord, with the position determined by the bass on the downbeat.

NOTE

You will notice that, in actual music, the dominant chord often appears as a seventh chord, V_7, rather than a triad, V. Although we must first learn how to connect triads before we can deal with seventh chords, you will have to recognize the dominant seventh in actual musical examples from the outset. Following the study of diatonic triads, chapter 12 will be entirely devoted to V_7 and its inversions.

Examine now example 2.1, and identify the key and the chords on which the piece is based. To help you recognize the chords and to understand their relationship within the key, label each of them with the correct Roman numeral.

All of example 2.1 is based on two chords, I and V_7. The chords are here presented in a type of **arpeggiated keyboard figuration**, rather than as block chords. (This type of arpeggiated keyboard figuration follows the pattern low note—high note—middle note—high note and is called **Alberti bass**.) Measures 1–2, left hand,

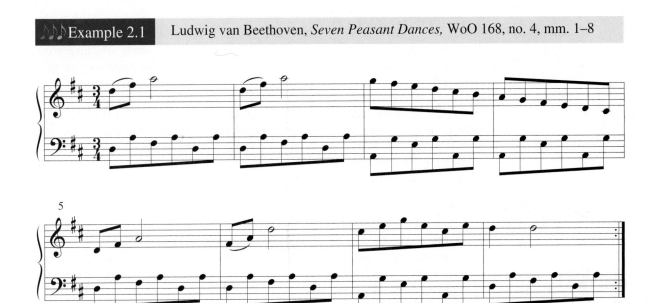

♪♪♪Example 2.1   Ludwig van Beethoven, *Seven Peasant Dances,* WoO 168, no. 4, mm. 1–8

contain only three pitches, D–F♯–A, the tonic triad (I) in DM. The right-hand melody in these measures is based on these pitches exclusively. Measures 3–4, left hand, feature also three pitches, A–E–G. These pitches do not form a triad, but they outline a seventh chord, and if we imply the missing pitch, A–C♯–E–G, we have the complete V_7 harmony in DM. We need not imply the missing pitch, though. The descending scale in the right hand actually contains all the pitches in V_7, including our "missing" C♯, plus, admittedly, a few more. If you circle the V_7 pitches in this scale (in descending order, G–E–C♯–A–G–E–C♯), you will see that the remaining pitches connect the chord tones by filling in the intervals between them by steps. They are, as you know from chapter D, **passing tones**. Passing tones belong to a general melodic category of pitches we call **nonchord tones**, which we will study at length in chapter 8. Nonchord tones are not part of the chord in which they appear, and they have a melodic, embellishing function. Measures 5–8 should be easy to figure out after mm. 1–4, especially because there are no new chords here, and these measures contain no nonchord tones at all. Notice that in m. 7, V_7 is now very clearly stated, if we consider all pitches in both hands.

In the two examples above you will have observed that V (V_7) has a tendency to resolve to I and, in these particular examples, does indeed invariably resolve to I. This tension-resolution pattern between V and I is the defining harmonic force underlying the tonal system. In this chapter we will examine what creates this tension-resolution pattern, and we will review specific voice-leading issues regarding these two chords.

THE TONIC TRIAD

The tonic is the central pitch in a key, and the triad built on the tonic (the tonic triad, made up of scale degrees $\hat{1}$, $\hat{3}$, and $\hat{5}$) is the central triad in the tonal system. Self-contained musical units (such as phrases, periods, or complete pieces) frequently begin and end on the tonic. Beginning on the tonic provides the listener with a sense of tonal center. Ending on the tonic provides a sense of conclusion (formal units that end on the tonic are said to be **closed**). The tonic is the tonal goal to which musical tensions and processes are ultimately directed, as well as the element of stability and release in which these tensions resolve. The dominant harmony, on the other hand, provides the most immediate factor of harmonic tension that requires resolution to the tonic.

NOTE

Compositions often modulate, *that is, they move temporarily to another key (for instance, the key of the dominant—GM if the original key is CM). In passages in which the music has modulated, the tonic is temporarily the I or i chord in the new key. In such passages, closed formal units will thus not begin and end in the original tonic, but rather in the new tonic.*

THE DOMINANT TRIAD

The dominant triad (scale degrees $\hat{5}$–$\hat{7}$–$\hat{2}$) follows the tonic in importance within the hierarchy of the tonal system. The leading tone, contained in the dominant triad, is a **tendency tone**: It creates a tension because it has a tendency to resolve to $\hat{1}$ by half-step motion. This tendency and its resolution are two of the fundamental tenets of tonality. Another member of V, scale degree $\hat{2}$, is also an unstable tone because of its dissonance with $\hat{1}$. $\hat{2}$, although not properly a tendency tone, is melodically directed toward $\hat{1}$ or $\hat{3}$, both members of the tonic triad. Thus, whereas V, as a M triad, is not in itself unstable or dissonant, it is so in the context of a key in which a tonic has been heard and established. As an unstable chord with respect to I, V requires resolution to a more stable harmony. For the time being, V will move exclusively to I (or i), thus resolving the tonal tension created by the leading tone and by $\hat{2}$.

EXERCISE

To practice harmonic analysis of tonic-dominant progressions, refer to exercises 2.1.1 and 2.1.2 in worksheet 2 at the end of this chapter.

THE I–V–I PROGRESSION: THE PRINCIPLES OF PROLONGATION

Because the I–V–I progression is essential in defining common practice tonality, we call it the **fundamental progression** of tonal music. The tonic and dominant chords can be combined at several different levels of musical activity and structure. In the first

♪♪♪Example 2.2

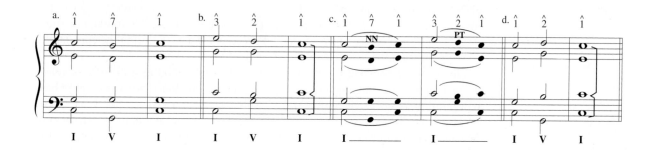

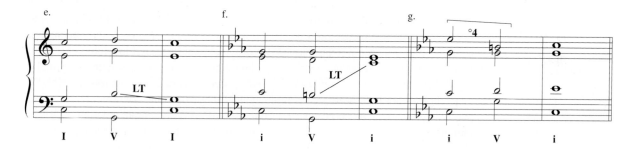

place, the I–V–I progression is often found as a harmonic unit of adjacent chords at the local level. Tonic and dominant, on the other hand, constitute the basic harmonies in several cadential types. In this category, they have a role in the articulation of form. Finally, the I–V–I progression underlies larger formal and compositional spans, and from this point of view these harmonies represent the structural pillars on which larger formal units and complete compositions are built. In the following sections we will examine these three levels of harmonic activity involving the tonic and dominant chords.

Several realizations of the fundamental progression appear in example 2.2. In example 2.2a, we see a I–V–I progression in which the bass effects the $\hat{1}$–$\hat{5}$–$\hat{1}$ motion characteristic of this progression, and the upper voice moves from $\hat{1}$ down by half step to $\hat{7}$ and back to $\hat{1}$. The type of melodic motion featured in the soprano, which was already introduced in chapter D, is called **neighbor motion**: A note moves stepwise to the closest note above or below it, and then back to the original note. The $\hat{1}$–$\hat{7}$–$\hat{1}$ motion is a **lower neighbor figure**, and $\hat{7}$ functions here as a **neighbor note** to $\hat{1}$ (NN). The I–V–I progression in example 2.2d, on the other hand, features an **upper neighbor figure** in the soprano, $\hat{1}$–$\hat{2}$–$\hat{1}$.

In example 2.2b, the same bass now supports a descending $\hat{3}$–$\hat{2}$–$\hat{1}$ line in the soprano. The motion here takes us from one member of the tonic triad, $\hat{3}$, to another member, $\hat{1}$, by means of a descending stepwise motion through $\hat{2}$. This type of stepwise motion in which a note fills in the space of a 3rd between two other notes is called **passing motion**. The $\hat{3}$–$\hat{2}$–$\hat{1}$ motion is a *passing figure*, and $\hat{2}$ functions here as a *passing tone* (PT).

In a neighbor-note motion, the embellished note is both approached and left by step. Melodic motion in which the embellished note is either approached *or* left by step, but not both, results in what is known as an **incomplete neighbor** (IN). Whereas a NN figure embellishing the pitch C, for instance, is C–B–C, incomplete neighbor figures are either C–B or B–C (with B being the IN in both cases). The soprano in example 2.2g illustrates a case of the incomplete neighbor figure (B♮–C) in the context of a i–V–i progression.

In all of the above cases, the soprano can be understood as a melodic or *linear* elaboration of tonic triad members. Similarly, the bass motion $\hat{1}$–$\hat{5}$–$\hat{1}$ represents a **bass arpeggiation**, or horizontal unfolding, of two members of the tonic triad, $\hat{1}$ and $\hat{5}$. The I–V–I progression can thus be understood as a harmonic elaboration or extension of the tonic triad, by means of arpeggiation in the bass, and by either neighboring or passing motion in the soprano. These are examples of **prolongation**. By prolongation we mean the extension of a musical element (a pitch or a chord) in such a way that its influence remains in effect although it might not actually be present at all moments. Some frequent means of prolongation are arpeggiation, neighbor and incomplete neighbor motions, and passing motion, all of which are illustrated in examples 2.2a, b, and g. If in these examples you think of the outer-voice frame as a unit, we can also say that *the tonic triad is prolonged by contrapuntal means:* Arpeggiation and NN, IN, or PT figures are here presented simultaneously in a two-voice contrapuntal structure. We will often refer to chords with a contrapuntal, prolongational function as **linear chords**, because they result from melodic motion (lines) rather than vertical processes.

Harmonic Reduction

The I–V–I progression thus constitutes the primary *harmonic prolongation of the tonic triad.* We can express this graphically as in example 2.2c. We call this type of graph a **harmonic reduction** (or also a **voice-leading reduction**). A harmonic reduction is a nonmetrical representation of harmonic motion and harmonic hierarchy in a musical passage. Harmonic reductions usually represent prolongational structures (we could also call them "prolongational reductions"). That is, this type of reduction shows that some pitches or chords are structurally more important than others, and some other pitches or chords have a subordinate role. The function of the latter is to extend a harmony that is structurally more important by some prolongational means.

A prolongational reductive graph should clearly show (1) the pitches that have a structural function and those that have a prolongational role, (2) the extent of the prolongation, and (3) the specific prolongational technique used in a particular passage. A number of musical **graphic symbols** (notes, stems, slurs, etc.) are used for these purposes in reductions, and their meaning here is different than in actual music scores. The following comments will help you understand and produce this type of reductive graph.

1. In these particular examples, we use *open notes* or *white notes* to notate the tonic triad, the harmonic unit we are prolonging. Open notes look like half notes, but here they do not denote rhythmic duration. In this type of graph they will denote structural importance: open notes represent the most structurally important pitches in a passage, those that are prolonged by other, subordinate pitches.

2. We will represent these subordinate pitches as *stemmed black notes* (next in importance) or as *unstemmed black notes* (third in the pitch hierarchy).

3. *Slurs* are used to connect pitches related by prolongational means, and to unify prolongational structures. A slur, for instance, may begin at the pitch being prolonged and show the extent of the prolongational figure.

4. The graphic notation in example 2.2c thus simply means that we are prolonging a tonic triad by means of a progression that features a soprano NN figure in the first case, and a soprano PT figure in the second case. The prolonging, subordinate nature of chords 2 and 3 is expressed by the unstemmed black note heads and the slurs.

Connecting the Tonic and Dominant Chords

Example 2.2 shows several possible connections between I and V. More are possible, especially with different doublings (all the illustrations in example 2.2 begin with a tonic triad in which the root is doubled). These are, however, the most standard voice-leading possibilities. We will now comment briefly on each of them.

Voice Leading in the I–V–I Progression

1. Because the I–V–I progression is made up of two *root motions by 5th,* the simplest and smoothest voice leading follows the principles for this type of progression discussed in chapter 1. This is the "lower-neighbor progression" represented in example 2.2a. ("Lower neighbor" denotes that the soprano effects a NN motion, $\hat{1}$–$\hat{7}$–$\hat{1}$, to the note *below,* the "lower-neighbor note"). As you can see in example 2.2a, in the three upper voices of both the I–V and V–I connections, the common tone remains in the same voice, while the other two voices move by steps.

2. Remember to avoid doubling the leading tone (LT) in V. In the V–I or V–i connection, in principle the leading tone *resolves* up a half step to the tonic. Remember also that in minor you need to raise $\hat{7}$ so it becomes the LT.

3. Example 2.2b features a "passing progression," with a $\hat{3}$–$\hat{2}$–$\hat{1}$ passing figure in the soprano, as we discussed above. This upper-voice motion requires some voice-leading adjustment in the lower voice. If we want to resolve the LT, we end up with three voices on $\hat{1}$ in the last I chord. This tripled root is acceptable as long as we include the third of the chord as part of the incomplete triad. The alto moves from $\hat{5}$ to $\hat{3}$ for this purpose.

4. The progression in example 2.2d is an "upper-neighbor progression" because the soprano effects a NN motion to the note above it, $\hat{1}$–$\hat{2}$–$\hat{1}$. This soprano figure results in 3rd arpeggiations in the inner voices. Here again, we end up with an incomplete final triad if we want to resolve the LT to $\hat{1}$.

5. A possible alternative to the incomplete triads from examples 2.2b and d is shown in example 2.2e. Here the LT leaps down to $\hat{5}$ and is thus left unresolved, in exchange for a complete final triad. Unresolved LTs should be used only when they are in an inner voice. This is a type of voice leading often found in Bach chorales.

6. The solution in example 2.2f is perfectly acceptable, as we saw in chapter 1. In this voice leading we can hear the LT resolve to $\hat{1}$ in the adjacent upper voice.

7. Our final example, example 2.2g, shows an "incomplete neighbor" V–I progression in which one voice (here the soprano) leaps down a 4th from $\hat{3}$ to $\hat{7}$. In minor modes, this voice leading features an acceptable diminished-fourth leap, which, as we saw in chapter 1 and as illustrated by our example, should be balanced with motion by step in the opposite direction of the leap.

NOTE

We mentioned above that the outer-voice frames of the progressions in example 2.2 can be considered contrapuntal structures. You should keep in mind that, as we discussed in chapter 1 and you can verify in example 2.2, the voice-leading principles you learned in species counterpoint are present in harmonic progressions, even in such short instances as the ones in this example. In chapter 1 we also noted that one of the adjustments made to species counterpoint in common practice voice leading is a more liberal treatment of diminished intervals, both melodically and harmonically. The melodic °4 in the soprano in example 2.2g, although perfectly acceptable in this harmonic context, would be objectionable in a strict species-counterpoint context.

> ### *Typical Errors to Avoid*
>
> ---
>
> 1. Doubling the LT (and resolving both of them to $\hat{1}$, with resulting parallel 8ves).
> 2. Not raising $\hat{7}$ in minor modes.
> 3. Not resolving the LT, especially when it is placed in the soprano.
> 4. Omitting the third in an incomplete triad (instead of omitting the fifth).

EXERCISES

To practice realizing I–V–I progressions in four voices, refer to exercise 2.2 in worksheet 2 at the end of this chapter.

To practice specific voice-leading models in I–V–I progressions, refer to exercise 2.3 in worksheet 2 at the end of this chapter.

THE I–V–I PROGRESSION AS A FORM-GENERATING STRUCTURE

The I–V–I progression is the fundamental harmonic unit of the tonal system. It represents the statement of a tonal center (I), the momentary departure from that center and the creation of a tension (V), and the return to the center by means of the resolution of the tension. The I–V–I progression unequivocally *defines and establishes a key*.

The I and V chords (the latter usually in the more frequent form of V₇) provide sufficient harmonic support for short, simple compositions, such as Franz Schubert's "Originaltänze," op. 9, no. 26 (anthology, no. 40). Listen to this piece, examine the score, and analyze the chords with Roman numerals. (Beware of the first chord: What is the key of the piece? On what chord does it begin?)

The significance of I and V in tonal music goes much beyond the immediate chord-to-chord type of progression we first think of when we think of chord connections. The I–V–I progression also has an essential long-range, formal significance in music. Complete compositions and formal structures are built on the harmonic structure provided by the tonic and dominant relationship. In this section we will examine some of the formal aspects of I and V, beginning with their cadential functions.

Cadences Involving I and V

Musical formal units (such as phrases, periods, sections, or complete pieces) are usually articulated by means of **cadences**, musical points of arrival defined both melodically and harmonically. We will study cadences in more detail in chapter 5 and basic formal units in chapter 6. As a preview of chapter 5, however, we can observe that several cadence types involve tonic and dominant harmonies.

The familiar V–I cadence, the most common closing gesture in the tonal system, is known as an *authentic cadence* (AC). An authentic cadence in which both chords are in root position and $\hat{1}$ is in the top voice in the final chord (approached by step from $\hat{2}$ or $\hat{7}$) is called a **perfect authentic cadence** (PAC) and has a conclusive effect (examples 2.3a and b). A V–I cadence in which at least one of the two chords is not in root position, or in which $\hat{1}$ is not in the top voice in the final chord, is called an **imperfect authentic cadence** (IAC) and has a less conclusive effect (examples 2.3c to e). A musical statement, however, may also end on V (usually with $\hat{2}$ or $\hat{7}$ in the top voice). Because V is not a stable harmony, such a statement is inconclusive, and continuation is necessary (such formal units are said to be **open**). A cadence on V is called a **half-cadence** (HC) (example 2.3f).

♪♪♪ Example 2.3a to f

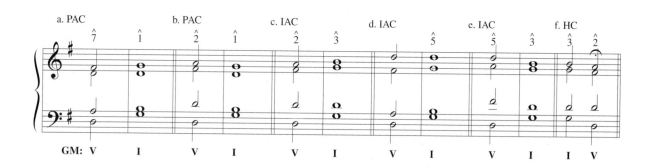

GM: V   I   V   I   V   I   V   I   V   I   I   V

♪♪♪ Example 2.3g   Fred Neil, "Everybody's Talkin'"

FM: V₇

♪♪♪ Example 2.3h   Otto Harbach–Jerome Kern, "Smoke Gets in Your Eyes," from *Roberta*

E♭M: V₇

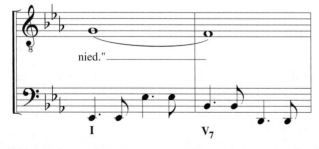

We can appreciate the different effects of the cadential progressions V–I or I–V by comparing the cadences in examples 2.3g and h. In the verse of Nilsson's 1969 hit "Everybody's Talkin'," we hear a V_7–I authentic cadence (which is actually an IAC; why?). In the song from the show *Roberta* reproduced in example 2.3h, on the other hand, the verse ends with a I–V_7 cadence. What kind of a cadence is this, and what is its effect?

Cadence, Phrase, and Period

The two fragments by Bach reproduced in example 2.4 illustrate all of the above types of cadences, as well as two primary types of formal units. A **phrase** has been defined as "a directed motion in time from one tonal entity to another."[1] A phrase is a

♪♪♪ **Example 2.4a**   J.S. Bach, Chorale 14, "O Herre Gott, dein göttlich Wort," mm. 1–5

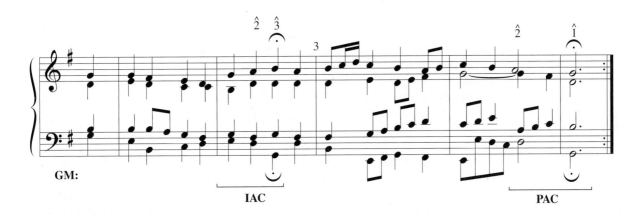

♪♪♪ **Example 2.4b**   J. S. Bach, Chorale 67, "Freu'dich sehr, o meine Seele," mm. 1–4

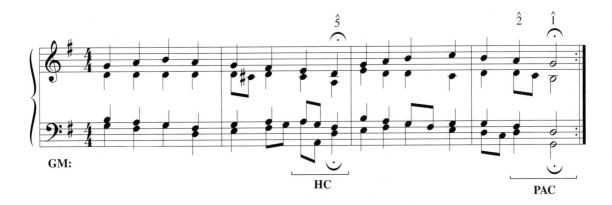

---

[1] William Rothstein, *Phrase Rhythm in Tonal Music* (New York: Schirmer, 1989), p. 5.

self-sufficient musical statement, and it delineates a clear motion between two tonal points. In example 2.4a you can hear two phrases, indicated by the fermatas. The first phrase begins on I in GM and ends on an IAC on G. The tonic in this V–I cadence functions as a tonal goal for the phrase, but it does not sound like a conclusive tonal goal because $\hat{3}$, not $\hat{1}$, is in the upper voice. Compare the ending of the first phrase with the ending of the second phrase, which closes with a PAC on G. This time the tonal goal has a clearly conclusive character because of the $\hat{2}$–$\hat{1}$ motion in the soprano. Both phrases together constitute a formal unit we call a **period**. A period consists of at least two phrases, the last of which closes with a PAC.

Example 2.4b features another two-phrase period. The open character of the first phrase is even more evident in this case, because of the HC on D (V in GM). The long-range tonal motion of the first phrase is I–V. The closing cadence in this period is, again, a conclusive PAC with a $\hat{2}$–$\hat{1}$ motion in the soprano. Considering the beginning harmony, the temporary tonal goal at the HC, and the final tonal goal at the end of the period, the long-range tonal motion in this example is I–V–I, a tonic-dominant-tonic progression at the formal level.

Listen now to mm. 1–8 of Mozart's Piano Sonata in AM (anthology, no. 27), a period which begins on I and ends with a V–I PAC. You will hear that the period consists of two subunits or phrases, that the melodic material is the same in both phrases, and that the first phrase (mm. 1–4) seems inconclusive, whereas the second phrase (mm. 5–8) does reach the sense of completion not achieved at m. 4. What kind of cadence closes the first phrase in m. 4? Notice also that the last pitch of the melody in m. 4 is B ($\hat{2}$), accompanied by a G♯ ($\hat{7}$) in the alto, both of which create a tension toward $\hat{1}$. Instead of reaching a conclusion in m. 5, the phrase is **interrupted, both harmonically and melodically**, then starts all over again, and it finally reaches its goal in m. 8, where both B ($\hat{2}$) and G♯ ($\hat{7}$) resolve to $\hat{1}$, and V resolves to I. The graph in example 2.5 shows this long-range harmonic process, and illustrates how the **I–V–I progression provides the structural frame** for this musical unit. This type of reduction, which we call a **bass reduction**, is especially useful to illustrate the underlying harmonic motion in a passage or a piece. In our example, the first slur shows phrase 1 and its tonal motion from I to V. A possible conclusion at m. 5 is thwarted by a new phrase beginning on the tonic, which this time leads to the conclusive cadence in m. 8. The long-range tonal motion in this period can thus be summarized as I———V//I———V–I. The double vertical lines above the staff represent the harmonic *interruption* at the HC, which, as is most often the case, supports a melodic interruption at $\hat{2}$. (The technique of interruption will be discussed further in chapter 6.)

Bass Reductions

In the bass reduction in example 2.5 we can see the meaning of the reductive symbols in this type of graph:

1. Tonic and dominant harmonies that begin or end phrases are usually shown as open or white notes. In V–I cadences, we will also show the cadential V as an open note. Although they look like half notes, here these symbols do not denote any durational meaning.

♪♪♪Example 2.5

2. The motion from one harmony to another, that is, between harmonies which delimit phrases, is shown by a slur.

3. Sometimes an inner phrase begins with the same harmony that ended the previous phrase, or with some subordinate harmony that prolongs the previous cadential chord. In these cases we will consider this beginning to be an extension of the previous cadential harmony. We will not notate this type of beginning harmony as an open note, but rather as a black note, normally without a stem, to signify its subordinate, prolongational role. An example of this type of situation and notation appears in example 2.6.

4. A double vertical line after a V harmony indicates a melodic interruption on $\hat{2}$.

5. Measure numbers are placed above the staff, and Roman numerals indicating the function of the notated harmonies are placed under the corresponding pitches.

Identifying Cadences and Phrases

Because cadences and phrases are largely defined by harmonic criteria, identifying them should ideally involve examining both melody and harmony. There is also a lot we can tell, however, from melody alone. The following steps will help you identify cadences and phrases, in either a melodic/harmonic context, or also if all you have is an unaccompanied melody.

1. Look for places in the score where the music seems to reach some kind of momentary repose: a fermata; a melodic long note perhaps followed by a rest; the end of a sentence or verse in the text if the music is vocal; or a clear melodic point of arrival after a musical statement, perhaps indicated but such elements as melodic shape or direction, or phrasing slurs and articulation.

2. Verify whether the point of repose you have identified is supported by a harmonic cadential gesture: an arrival on V, or a clear cadential V–I. Keep in mind that not all V–I or I–V progressions are cadences. Inside a phrase, these harmonies simply constitute noncadential harmonic progressions. At the end of a phrase, they are cadences.

3. Melodic cadences can also be confirmed by the scale degree motion involved. In a conclusive PAC, the melody will effect a $\hat{2}$–$\hat{1}$ or $\hat{7}$–$\hat{1}$ motion (examples 2.3a and b). In a less conclusive IAC, frequent melodic gestures will be $\hat{2}$–$\hat{3}$, $\hat{5}$–$\hat{5}$, or $\hat{5}$–$\hat{3}$ (examples 2.3c to e). Finally, a HC will probably feature a $\hat{3}$–$\hat{2}$ melodic motion (example 2.3f), or possibly also $\hat{1}$–$\hat{7}$.

4. In the sections "Further Analysis" and "Practical Application and Discussion" you will analyze the cadential and phrase structures of several short pieces from the anthology (Mozart's AM Sonata, Haydn's CM Divertimento, and a Minuet from the *Notebook of Anna Magdalena Bach*). Verify how the criteria discussed above apply to cadences and phrases in each of these pieces.

5. Sing "Oh! Susanna," without any harmonic accompaniment. As you sing, hear the phrases and the melodic cadences that close each of them. What kind of cadences are you hearing? What scale degrees does the melody feature in each of the cadences?

EXERCISES

To practice cadence identification in musical contexts, refer to exercise 2.1 in worksheet 2 at the end of this chapter.

To practice analyzing the role of I and V as structural harmonies in a formal context, as well as realizing bass reductions showing long-range harmonic motion, refer to exercises 2.1.2 and 2.1.3 in worksheet 2 at the end of this chapter.

FURTHER ANALYSIS

The structural function of tonic and dominant, as well as the fundamental architectural paradigm "tonic established/departure from tonic/return to tonic" can be heard at an even larger level (in this case underlying a complete piece) in the Minuet from Joseph Haydn's Divertimento in CM, Hob. XVI/1 (anthology, no. 19). As you listen to the piece, you will notice that it has two main sections, indicated by the repeat signs in m. 8. The main points of formal articulation are m. 4 (end of the first phrase, on I), m. 8 (end of the third phrase and of the first main section, on V), m. 12 (end of the third phrase on V), m. 13 (return of the opening two phrases and of I), and mm. 19–20 (PAC, which closes the piece).

The key is firmly established in mm.1–4 by a succession of V₇–I progressions. The first main section (mm. 1–8) closes on a HC, and thus represents a departure from the tonic. Notice the inconclusive melodic gesture in m. 8, featuring an interruption at $\hat{2}$, as in the Mozart example we discussed above. The HC does not fully resolve to a tonic in root position in m. 9. Rather than a return to the tonic, mm. 9–12 are a prolongation (or extension) of the area "away from the tonic." With the new HC reached in m. 12, the tension for the return of the tonic is intensified and resolved in m. 13 with the return, not only of I, but also of the complete opening section. The latter now concludes with a PAC, thus closing the musical idea which had been left open in m. 8, and also resolving the $\hat{2}$ from the interruption in m. 8 to its final goal, $\hat{1}$. The structural tonic-dominant frame of this piece is summarized graphically in example 2.6. Notice the graphic notation for the extension of V in mm. 9–12.

♪♪♪ Example 2.6

PRACTICAL APPLICATION AND DISCUSSION

1. Discuss the structural role of the I–V–I progression in the following two complete pieces: anthology, no. 27 (Mozart, Piano Sonata in AM, I, theme) and anthology, no. 6 (*Minuet from Notebook for Anna Magdalena Bach*). Play or listen to the pieces, and determine their phrase and cadential structure. For the Mozart example, make a bass reduction in the style of those in examples 2.5 and 2.6, showing the tonal motion within the phrases, and the role of I and V in shaping the form of this short composition.

2. Examine the compositions you are presently practicing or performing on your instrument, looking for examples of concepts discussed in this chapter. Look prefer-

ably at some short pieces such as minuets or other dance types. Answer the following questions:
   a) Do the main formal units begin and end on the tonic? If the piece modulates to another key, do formal units begin and end on the tonic of the new key?
   b) Do main formal units conclude with a PAC?
   c) Are there any important cadences on V (HCs)?
   d) Do PACs and HCs affect your sense of phrasing?
   e) Identify some I–V and V–I progressions, and examine their voice leading, comparing it with the normative voice leading studied in this chapter.
   f) How does the material studied in this chapter affect your musical experience both as a listener and as a performer?

ASSIGNMENT AND KEYBOARD PROGRESSIONS

For analytical and written assignments and keyboard progressions based on the materials learned in this chapter, refer to chapter 2 in the workbook.

PITCH PATTERNS

Sing (and listen to while you sing) the pitch patterns in example 2.7, in both the major and minor modes, as an aural practice of the tonic and dominant triads and their connections. Notice the leading tone and hear its resolution. Singing these patterns with scale degree numbers will help you understand their relationship to harmonic degrees and chordal functions. You may also use *solfège* syllables (do-re-mi-fa-sol-la-ti-do) if you wish, depending on what sightsinging system is used at your school.

♪♪♪ Example 2.7

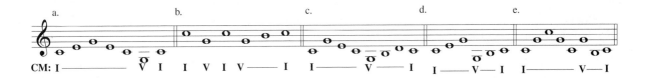

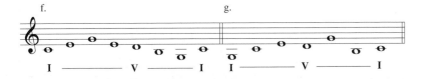

Composers and Their Music 2

Biographies

Write short biographies of the following composers mentioned in this chapter: Wolfgang Amadeus Mozart, Ludwig van Beethoven, Franz Schubert, Jerome Kern.

Listening

Listen to the following compositions by composers mentioned in this chapter:

    Mozart: Symphony no. 40 in Gm, K. 550
    Beethoven: Symphony no. 3 in E♭M, op. 55,
      Eroica
    Schubert: Symphony no. 8 in Bm, *Unfinished*
    Harbach-Kern: *Roberta*

Follow the score while you listen. Be able to place these compositions in one of the style periods and to comment on why and how they represent the musical characteristics of that period.

As you listen to these pieces, try to pay attention to endings of formal units, to hear the type of cadence that closes a particular unit, and to hear possible long-range tonal motion involving the tonic and the dominant. Movement III in the Mozart symphony (Minuet) is particularly appropriate for this aural exercise, and so is the beginning of movement IV in the Beethoven symphony. In the latter, notice particularly the numerous half cadences and their effect in propelling the music forward.

Terms for Review

I and V as structural chords
Bass afterbeat figuration
Arpeggiated keyboard figuration
Alberti bass
Passing tone
Nonchord tone
Tonic triad and its function
Closed formal units
Dominant triad and its function
Tendency tone
Fundamental progression
Neighbor motion
Upper and lower neighbor figures
Neighbor note
Passing motion
Incomplete neighbor motion

Bass arpeggiation
Prolongation
Linear chords
Harmonic (voice-leading) reductions
Graphic symbols in reductions
Voice leading in the I–V–I progression
Cadence
Perfect authentic cadence
Imperfect authentic cadence
Open formal units
Half cadence
Phrase
Period
Melodic and harmonic interruption
Structural role of the I–V–I progression
Bass reduction

Worksheet 2

EXERCISE 2.1   Analysis

1. a) Analyze example 2.8 with Roman numerals.
    b) What types of cadences can you identify in mm. 4 and 8? How are they differ-
        ent, and what are their different effects?

    c) Granting that melody and harmony are always interdependent, how is this de-
        pendence or relationship even more evident than usual in this fragment?

♩♩♩♩ Example 2.8   L. v. Beethoven, *Für Elise,* mm. 1–8

2. a) Analyze example 2.9 with Roman numerals. What kind of chordal figuration is used for the piano's left hand?

   b) Think of this passage as a period made up of two contrasting phrases (mm. 1–5 and 6–9). On what type of cadence does each phrase end?

   c) Write a brief statement (one paragraph) explaining the harmonic motion within each of these two phrases and in the complete period as a whole. Using your own music paper, provide a bass reduction of the harmonic motion in these phrases, showing the beginning and ending harmony for each of the phrases, and paste the reduction to your statement. Notice that the opening of the second phrase is a harmonic extension of the end of the first phrase, and notate that appropriately on your graph.

3. In a brief essay, discuss the structural role of the I–V–I progression in the following two fragments: anthology, no. 7 (Bach, Polonaise from *Notebook for Anna Magdalena Bach*), mm. 1–8, and anthology, no. 21 (Haydn, Piano Sonata in DM, Hob. XVI:37, III), mm. 1–20. Play or listen to these examples. Determine their phrase and cadential structures, as well as the role of I and V in shaping the form of these fragments. As an additional exercise, make a bass reduction for each of these examples, similar to those in examples 2.5 and 2.6, showing the tonal motion within the phrases. In the Haydn fragment, consider mm. 9–12 as a harmonic extension of the cadence on A in m. 8.

♪♪♪Example 2.9   L. v. Beethoven, Sonata for Violin and Piano, *Spring,* op. 24, II, mm. 1–9

EXERCISE 2.2   Write the following progressions in four voices, with correct voice leading. Always PLAY and LISTEN to your part-writing exercises before you turn them in to your teacher.

General procedure for realizing a progression from given Roman numerals:

1. If the bass is not given, write out the complete bass line for the progression.
2. Write the first chord with correct doubling and spacing.
3. You will want to ascertain that your outer-voice frame is made up of independent, satisfactory lines. For this purpose, you might want to sketch out the soprano right after you write the bass, making sure that you have a good upper line, and that the outer-voice duet follows the principles of first-species counterpoint.
4. Fill in inner voices chord by chord with the smoothest possible connection between chords: think of all the pitches for each chord, leave common tones in the same voices, take the remaining pitches from one chord to the closest possible pitches from the next chord, and check the resolution of the LT.
5. Double-check the connection for possible mistakes (parallel or hidden 5ths or 8ves, augmented melodic intervals, failure to raise $\hat{7}$ in minor keys, doubled LT, etc.).

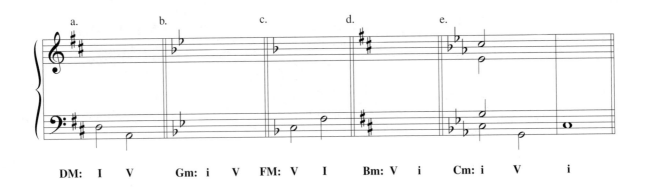

DM: I   V   Gm: i   V   FM: V   I   Bm: V   i   Cm: i   V   i

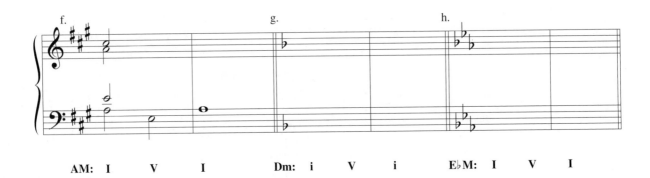

AM: I   V   I   Dm: i   V   i   E♭M: I   V   I

EXERCISE 2.3   Realize the following I–V–I (or i–V–i) progressions in four voices. In each of the progressions, use the required voice-leading model.

2.3a: Lower-neighbor progression.

2.3b: Upper-neighbor progression.

2.3c: Passing progression.

2.3d: Resolve the LT in the voice above it.

2.3e: Upper-neighbor progression with an unresoved LT (and a complete final triad).

2.3f: A descending °4 leap in the soprano.

2.3g: A prolongational reduction graph for your progression in exercise 2.3a (see example 2.2c).

2.3h: A prolongational reduction graph for your progression in exercise 2.3c.

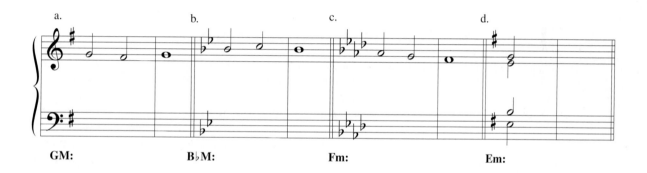

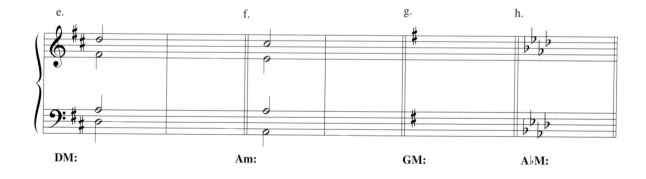

Chapter 3

Harmonic Function; The Subdominant Triad in Root Position

THE BASIC HARMONIC FUNCTIONS

In chapter F we defined **harmonic function** as the relationship of a chord with the other chords in the key, and very especially its relationship with the tonic. Functions may also be grouped according to their type. Whereas the tonic is the only chord in the system that provides conclusive repose (the **tonic function**), several chords that contain the leading tone provide a tension which needs to resolve. Some of these chords are V, V_7, vii°, vii°$_7$, and vii°$_7$. We will refer to all these chords as having a **dominant function**. A number of other chords are used to precede the dominant (or a chord with a dominant function). Chords in this group include mainly IV, ii, and ii$_7$. These chords have the function of preparing the dominant. We will refer to this function as **predominant**.

Some chords function at times as **substitutes** for other chords. Although V must in principle resolve to I, in the "deceptive progression," V–vi, it resolves to a tonic substitute, vi. We will also see occasional examples of iii functioning as a dominant substitute. Finally, chords at times have the function of extending or embellishing other chords contrapuntally. This is a frequent function, as we will see throughout part 1, of first- and second-inversion chords, as well as of such chords as IV, vi, and iii. We will refer to this extending or embellishing function as **prolongational function**. A prolongational chord extends linearly the area of influence of another chord that is more important structurally.

NOTE

Chordal function is entirely dependent on context, and one same chord can have different functions in different contexts. In this chapter we will see that IV can function as a predominant but, in a different context, it can also function as a tonic prolongation. Chords in the dominant family (such as vii°$_6$, V_5^6, or V_3^4), on the other hand, usually appear as linear chords, as we will study in chapters 4, 12, and 13. Thus, a chord can also have two simultaneous functions (such as a member of the dominant family actually functioning as a contrapuntal chord prolonging the tonic).

Summary of the Most Common Harmonic Functions of the Diatonic Triads

I (i)	Tonic
ii (ii°)	Predominant (precedes V)
iii (III)	Tonic prolongation (or dominant substitute)
IV (iv)	Tonic prolongation (subdominant) or predominant (precedes V)
V	Dominant
vi (VI)	Tonic prolongation or tonic substitute or predominant (precedes V)
vii°	Dominant

From a broader perspective, we can also think of three major harmonic functions: *structural chords, predominant chords,* and *prolongational chords.*

1. *Structural chords* are those that can have a beginning or ending function within musical units. Only I (i) and V are truly structural in functional tonality.

2. *Predominant chords* have the function of preparing the dominant, or more specifically of preparing structural arrivals. ii, IV, and vi can function as predominant chords.

3. *Prolongational chords* have the function of extending the structural frame in time or of extending other nonstructural chords. We will study a variety of prolongational structures throughout this book.

THE SUBDOMINANT TRIAD

The subdominant triad (IV in major keys, iv in minor) is built on $\hat{4}$. It comprises scale degrees $\hat{4}$–$\hat{6}$–$\hat{1}$. The tonic, dominant, and subdominant triads can be considered the basic chords in the tonal system, and they illustrate all the main functions defined above (tonic, dominant, predominant, and prolongation). For this reason they are known as the **primary triads**.

IV as Prolongation of I

In the opening measures of example 3.1a, the harmonic progression is V_7–I–IV–I–V_7–I–V_7–I. The phrase is thus based mostly on dominant-tonic progressions, with the only exception of the third chord, a subdominant triad which follows and precedes tonic triads. Examine the voice leading of this I–IV–I progression: The roots are related by descending 5th; one pitch (scale degree $\hat{1}$, B♭) is common to both chords and remains in the same voice; the other two pitches in I, F–D, move up by steps to their upper neighbors, G–E♭, and down by steps again. IV functions here as a true **subdominant**, as opposed to a predominant. In its subdominant function, IV embellishes the tonic triad and extends the tonic harmony by means of an upper-neighbor progression. This is an example of **IV as a prolongational chord**.

Examine the harmonic reduction of the left hand in example 3.1b. In chapter 2 you learned to read this type of reductive notation: The open notes indicate that I is the most important harmony in this passage, and the slurred, unstemmed black notes after I show that the progression I–V–I prolongs the tonic by means of a neighbor figure (NN). The initial V_7 harmony is also an elaboration of the tonic harmony that follows it. In this case you can also recognize upper-neighbor figures in the two upper voices, but instead of complete NN motions (D–E♭–D and B♭–C–B♭) we see only incomplete ones (E♭–D and C–B♭), without the initial note of the NN figure. As we saw in chapter 2, this type of melodic motion in which a NN (say, $\hat{1}$–$\hat{2}$–$\hat{1}$) is missing either the initial pitch ($\hat{2}$–$\hat{1}$) or the final pitch ($\hat{1}$–$\hat{2}$) is called an *incomplete neighbor* (abbreviated IN). The initial V_7–I progression elaborates the tonic harmony linearly by means of an IN figure.

♪♪♪ Example 3.1a   F. Chopin, Mazurka, op. 7 no. 1, mm. 1–8

♪♪♪ Example 3.1b   Harmonic Reduction of 3.1a

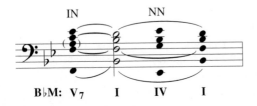

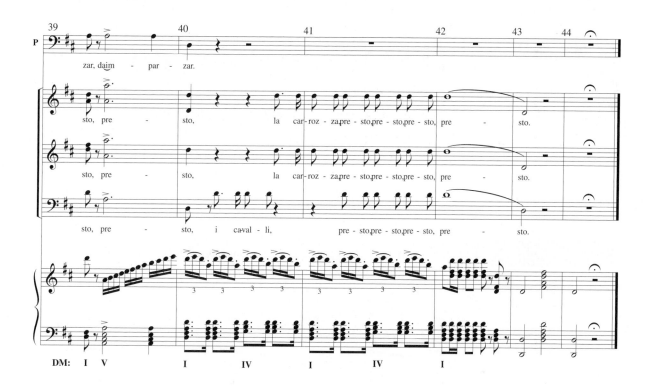

♪♪♪Example 3.2   Gaetano Donizetti, *Don Pasquale,* Act III, "Introductory Chorus," mm. 39–44

The Plagal Cadence

Sometimes composers write an authentic cadence at the end of a piece and prolong the final I by means of a IV–I cadence (the complete progression may thus be V–I–IV–I). The IV–I cadence (often sung to the word *Amen* at the end of Protestant hymns) is called a **plagal cadence**. In example 3.2, Gaetano Donizetti ends the "Introductory Chorus" of *Don Pasquale,* Act III, with a PAC followed by a reiterated plagal cadence. Observe that, in mm. 40–42, the repeated cadential I–IV–I progression in the orchestra (the piano reduction in our example) harmonizes an extended scale degree $\hat{1}$ in the chorus.

EXERCISE

To practice realizing progressions using IV as a prolongation of I, refer to exercises 3.2a to d and 3.3a in worksheet 3 at the end of this chapter.

♪♪♪ Example 3.3a   R. Schumann, "War Song," from *Album for the Young,* op. 68, mm. 21–26

DM: IV   V   I   IV   V   I

♪♪♪ Example 3.3b   F. Schubert, *Walzer, Ländler und Ecossaisen,* op. 18, Ecossaise no. 2

IV as Predominant

We have just seen that, in the I–IV–I progression, IV prolongs I. The I–V–I progression, on the other hand, is often elaborated by the introduction of a IV between I and V: I–IV–V–I. Although this IV may still be seen as extending the tonic harmony, the step progression $\hat{4}$–$\hat{5}$ in the bass creates a melodic drive toward V. When IV precedes (and proceeds to) V, its function is to prepare the dominant. This is the *predominant function* which we defined earlier. In example 3.3a, both subdominants in mm. 23 and 25 function as predominant chords because they precede (and prepare) the authentic cadences that follow.

The second part of Schubert's "Ecossaise" no. 2 is based only on the I–IV–V$_7$–I progression. Analyze this complete little piece (example 3.3b), writing the correct Roman numerals under each measure.

Typical Errors to Avoid

1. Writing parallel 5ths or 8ves in the IV–V connection.
2. Writing an augmented 2nd in the iv–V connection (minor modes) if ♭$\hat{6}$ and ♯$\hat{7}$ are left in the same voice.
3. Writing the bass of the IV–V progression ($\hat{4}$–$\hat{5}$) as a 7th rather than a 2nd.

EXERCISES

To practice analyzing musical fragments based on I, IV, and V harmonies, refer to exercise 3.1 in worksheet 3 at the end of this chapter.

To practice realizing progressions using IV as a predominant chord, refer to exercises 3.2e to g and 3.3b to d in worksheet 3 at the end of this chapter.

To practice harmonizing melodic fragments with I, IV, and V chords, refer to exercise 3.4 in worksheet 3 at the end of this chapter.

NOTE

*The last chord in example 3.5g is a major tonic triad (notice that the third has been raised) in a minor mode. This is a device frequently used by composers (especially during the Renaissance and baroque periods) to close a piece in the minor mode, called **Picardy third**. Ending a minor mode piece with a major tonic triad gives the final cadence a stronger sense of conclusion.*

VOICE-LEADING GUIDELINES

1. The IV chord includes two tonally strong degrees ($\hat{4}$ and $\hat{1}$, the root and fifth, respectively), either of which is perfectly suitable for doubling. Doubling the third ($\hat{6}$) produces a weaker sonority.

2. In the I–IV–I progression, the roots are a 5th (or a 4th) apart. The chords have one common tone which remains in the same voice. The other two pitches move by steps in the same direction (example 3.4a).

   The harmonic reduction in example 3.4b reflects the fact that this progression is a prolongation of the tonic: $\hat{1}$ is retained as the common tone, while the voices with $\hat{3}$ and $\hat{5}$ are embellished with *upper neighbor-note figures* (up a step, and return to the original note). From a voice-leading point of view, IV functions here as a **neighbor chord** (a chord that results from linear neighbor-note motion).

   The I–IV–I progression can be used to harmonize a soprano that repeats or holds $\hat{1}$ (as in example 3.4a), or one that features either of two neighbor figures: $\hat{5}$–$\hat{6}$ –$\hat{5}$ or $\hat{3}$–$\hat{4}$–$\hat{3}$ (example 3.4c).

3. Example 3.4c illustrates a plagal cadence in block-chord style. A V–I authentic cadence is followed by a IV–I cadence in which the voice leading follows the same guidelines as in no. 1.

4. The IV–V connection, however, presents new difficulties. This progression features root motion by 2nd. As you learned in chapter 1, to connect chords whose roots are a second apart, *the three upper voices should move in contrary motion with the bass* (two of the voices by step, one by leap of a 3rd). This connection is illustrated in example 3.5a.

5. Several soprano melodic patterns can be harmonized with a IV–V–I cadential progression. Among them, $\hat{1}$–$\hat{7}$–$\hat{1}$ and $\hat{4}$–$\hat{2}$–$\hat{1}$ provide a conclusive effect appropriate for PACs, whereas $\hat{4}$–$\hat{2}$–$\hat{3}$ and $\hat{6}$–$\hat{5}$–$\hat{5}$ are used in IACs or in progressions inside phrases (examples 3.5a to c). Here again, notice that the outer-voice frames in these examples follow the principles of first-species counterpoint.

6. If you wish to harmonize a $\hat{6}$–$\hat{7}$–$\hat{1}$ motion in the soprano with a IV–V–I progression, you must beware of multiple voice-leading problems. Parallel 8ves and 5ths are a frequent error in such harmonization (example 3.5d). Example 3.5e shows a possible voice-leading solution to this problem. In the minor mode, however, the same progression would be flawed by a melodic augmented 2nd ($\flat\hat{6}$–$\sharp\hat{7}$) in the soprano (example 3.5f). Examples 3.5g and h illustrate two ways of avoiding the augmented 2nd in minor. Example 3.5g features identical voice leading as does example 3.5c (the normative voice leading in progressions with roots a 2nd apart): $\flat\hat{6}$ and $\sharp\hat{7}$ are simply placed in different voices. At other times the melodic minor scale is used in its ascending form ($\hat{5}$–$\sharp\hat{6}$–$\sharp\hat{7}$–$\hat{1}$), thus avoiding the awkward melodic augmented 2nd. As you will see in example 3.5h, such use of the melodic minor scale results in a major IV (rather than iv) in a minor key, with the same voice leading as in example 3.5e. In practice, the melodic turn $\hat{5}$–$\sharp\hat{6}$–$\sharp\hat{7}$–$\hat{1}$ is more frequently harmonized with the progression i–IV–vii°$_6$–i (or I–IV–vii°$_6$–I in major), which we will study in chapter 13, because it allows for a smoother voice leading than i–IV–V–i.

♪♪♪ Example 3.4

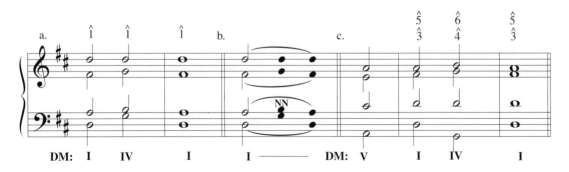

♪♪♪ Example 3.5

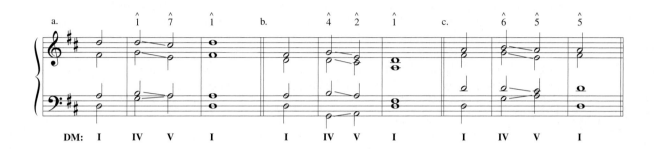

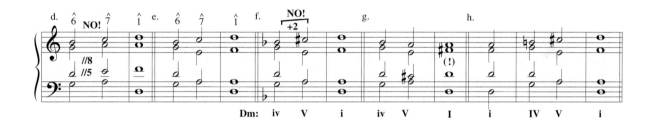

ELABORATING THE I–V–I PROGRESSION

The fundamental progression I–V–I can be elaborated in many ways. With the harmonic elements we have learned in this chapter, we can expand the I–V–I progression by means of two subordinate progressions. First, we can prolong the initial I with a contrapuntal I–IV–I progression. Then, we can prepare the V–I cadence with a predominant IV. Example 3.6a illustrates this elaboration of the fundamental progression. The

♪♪♪ Example 3.6

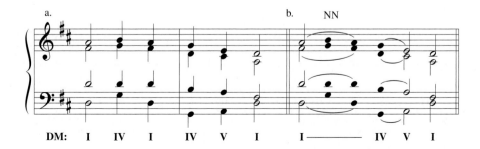

harmonic reduction in example 3.6b tells us how these chords function within the harmonic phrase as a whole. The I–V–I progression is notated as open notes because these chords constitute the fundamental structure of the phrase. The I–IV–I progression prolongs the initial tonic, as shown by the slurs that tie these chords together. The second IV chord is connected to the cadential V, thus showing its predominant function. The Roman numeral notation under each of these examples demonstrates that *we can hear two levels of harmony in this progression*. At one level, we hear each chord in isolation, as in example 3.6a. At the next, deeper level (example 3.6b), the initial tonic triad and its elaboration are heard as a single harmony extended by a neighboring motion.

EXERCISE

To practice harmonic reduction, refer to exercises 3.3e and 3.4e in worksheet 3 at the end of this chapter.

ASSIGNMENT AND KEYBOARD PROGRESSIONS

For analytical and written assignments and keyboard progressions based on the materials learned in this chapter, refer to chapter 3 in the workbook.

PITCH PATTERNS

Sing the pitch patterns in example 3.7, both in major and minor modes. Listen to the chords and progressions which are either implied (as in patterns a and b) or actually spelled out linearly (as in pattern c, where the tonic and subdominant chords have been "horizontalized").

Example 3.7

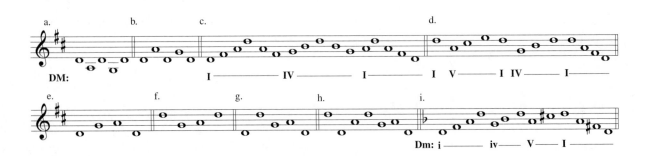

Composers and Their Music 3

Biographies

Write short biographies of the following composers mentioned in this chapter: Robert Schumann, Frédéric Chopin.

Listening

Listen to the following compositions by composers mentioned in this chapter:

R. Schumann: Symphony no. 3 in E♭M, op. 97, *Rhenish*

Chopin: 24 Preludes, op. 28

Follow the score while you listen. Be able to place these compositions in one of the style periods and to comment on why and how they represent the musical characteristics of that period.

Terms for Review

Harmonic function
Tonic function
Dominant function
Predominant function
Substitution
Prolongational function
Primary triads

Subdominant triad
IV as a prolongation chord
Plagal cadence
IV as predominant
Picardy third
Neighbor chord

Worksheet 3

EXERCISE 3.1   Analysis.

1. a) Analyze example 3.8 with Roman numerals (RNs). The second sixteenth note in each of the sixteenth-note figures should be analyzed as a nonchord tone, an ornamental pitch foreign to the chord against which it sounds as a dissonance. In this case, the second sixteenth note is always a melodic lower-neighbor note (a note a step below a chord tone).

   b) On the other hand, the chord in m. 2, beat 1, is also an ornamental chord with a similar function. Study the voice leading to and from this chord, and explain its function with precise musical terms. Show the voice-leading structure of mm. 1–2 (using only chord tones) in the staves in example 3.8b, using a reductive notation modeled after example 3.4b. With what kind of cadence does the passage close? Explain.

♪♪♪Example 3.8a   F. Schubert, Ecossaise D.158

♪♪♪Example 3.8b

2. Identify and explain the cadence type at the end of example 3.9.

♪♪♪ Example 3.9   J. S. Bach, "Vor deinen Tron tret'ich hiermit," from *18 Chorale Preludes,* mm. 40–45

3. a) Analyze the complete example 3.10 with RNs (one chord per measure, except for m. 15 which has two chords). Beware of—and for the time being ignore—the numerous nonchord tones.

   b) Section 1 (mm. 1–8). On what progression is this section based?

♪♪♪Example 3.10   F. Schubert, *Zwanzig Walzer,* op. 127, no. 13

c) Chords in section 1 change every measure. How does Schubert achieve a sense of motion within mm. 1–2 and 5–6?

d) How does the bass reflect the melody in mm. 1–2 and 5–6?

e) The most dissonant beat in section 1 (m. 3, beat 1) is a dominant ninth chord (a V$_7$ chord with one more third on top of the seventh) resulting from the melodic line. How does Schubert stress this dissonant spot?

f) The resolution of the progression, in mm. 4 and 8, also receives a special articulation treatment. How?

g) Section 2 (mm. 9–16). On what progression is this second section based?

h) Chords change here every two measures. By what means does Schubert extend each chord for two measures?

i) Changes of harmony, as well as dissonance, and also harmonic function (tension/release) are all reflected in this section by specific articulation marks. Explain.

j) Compare the cadences in mm. 8 and 16. What are their types, and how are they different?

EXERCISE 3.2   Realize the following progressions in four voices. First add RNs if missing, then write the bass line if it is not provided. Next, write a good soprano line, making sure that it forms a good contrapuntal frame with the bass. Finally, add inner voices using correct voice leading. Use only, in all cases, tonic, dominant, or subdominant chords in root position. *Remember:* Before turning in a part-writing exercise, play it and listen to it.

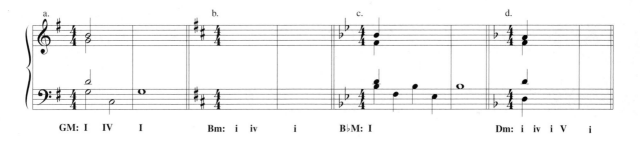

EXERCISE 3.3

1. Write four-voice harmonizations for the following melodic fragments. Write the bass first, and then fill in with the inner voices. Sing each melody before writing the harmonization, and after writing it play the complete harmonization at the piano.

2. The complete progression in exercise 3.3a is a prolongation of the tonic triad by means of two progressions which we have studied in this and the previous chapters. In exercise 3.3e, provide a harmonic reduction of your realization of exercise 3.3a, following the reductive models studied in examples 2.2e and 3.4b.

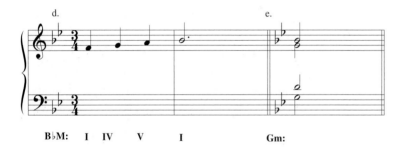

EXERCISE 3.4

1. The following soprano fragments are made up of melodic tonal patterns which in this chapter have been associated with specific harmonic patterns. Harmonize each fragment with the corresponding harmonic pattern or patterns. First, write scale degrees over the melodic fragments. Then, provide the *bass line and RNs* for your harmonization. You need not fill in the inner voices, although you may do so for additional practice. The melody in exercise 3.4d is made up of two segments which you can harmonize with two different patterns. To connect both segments, harmonize m. 1, beats 3–4 with a single chord.

2. Measure 1 in the progression in exercise 3.4d functions as a linear prolongation of the tonic triad. Measure 2, on the other hand, consists of a predominant-dominant-tonic cadential gesture. In exercise 3.4a, provide a harmonic reduction of your realization of exercise 3.4d, showing the linear function of each of these chords within the harmonic phrase as a whole. Model your reduction after example 3.6b.

EM:

Gm:

Am:

FM:

FM:

Chapter 4

Texture; Triads in First Inversion

TEXTURE

The term **texture** refers to the relationship between different musical lines and between the horizontal and vertical components of music. Music in which there is a single, unaccompanied line is said to be **monophonic**. In example 4.1a, on the other hand, two voices are presented simultaneously. Music that has more than one voice is **polyphonic**. In the type of polyphony illustrated by our example, voices are independent, and they are equally important. Because polyphonic textures are ruled by the principles of **counterpoint**, they are also called **contrapuntal textures**. In example 4.1a, not only are the voices independent (in contour, rhythm, type of motion, etc.), but so is the thematic material. This is an example of **free counterpoint**, as opposed to the fragment in example 4.1b, written in **imitative counterpoint**. In the latter type of polyphony, voices share the same motives or themes, and hence "imitate" each other. Although voices here are still independent, their thematic material is the same. **Imitation** in example 4.1b is present not just at the beginning. The first three entries of the initial motive are marked with brackets on the score. Find and mark all the subsequent statements of this motive. Beginning with the bass in mm. 9–10, moreover, a second motive is repeatedly stated in all voices. Mark all the entries of this second motive from m. 10 to the end of the piece. The words mean: "Blessed is He who comes in the name of the Lord." Do the words have anything to do with the motivic content of the piece? That is, are the two motives we have identified related to specific words?

In example 4.2a, on the other hand, there is only one melody (the top line), while the function of the left-hand lines is to provide a chordal accompaniment (the parallel sixths added for two beats in m. 3 do not constitute an independent line, but simply a **supporting parallel melody**). The accompanying lines are thus subordinate to the melody. Such a texture is called **homophonic**. In a homophonic texture the accompaniment may be in the form of block chords, as in example 4.2a (in which some of the pitches that complete the chord are presented by the right-hand melody), or the chords may be broken into a variety of figurations. In example 4.2b, the chordal accompaniment is arpeggiated, but the texture is still purely homophonic.

♪♪♪ Example 4.1a   J. S. Bach, Sarabande, from Partita no. 2 in Cm, for Harpsichord, mm. 9–12

♪♪♪ Example 4.1b   Orlande de Lassus, "Benedictus," from *Missa pro defunctis*

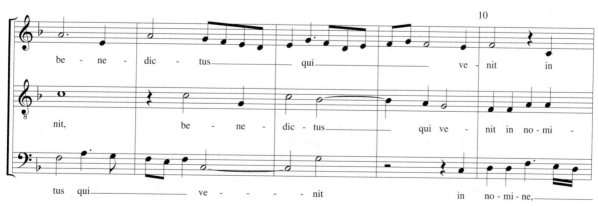

♪♪♪ Example 4.1b   **Continued**

NOTE

Even in homophonic textures such as these, outer voices are normally ruled by contrapuntal principles. If you play the outer-voice notes on each beat in example 4.2b (circled on the example), for instance, you will hear a satisfactory two-voice frame in first-species counterpoint.

Chorale Texture

In chapter 1 you were introduced to **chorale texture**. In chorale harmonizations, the original hymn tune is usually placed in the upper voice, which thus becomes the main voice. Chorale harmonizations, however, feature four independent lines, and as such they are contrapuntal. At times, chorale harmonizations are **homorhythmic**, that is, all

♪♪♪ Example 4.2a   Joseph Haydn, Piano Concerto in DM, II, mm. 1–4

♪♪♪ Example 4.2b   F. Schubert, *Phidile,* mm. 1–4

voices have the same or nearly the same rhythm. In such cases, the effect is of a chordal texture, and it is clearly apparent that harmonies result from the simultaneous presentation of independent lines, as in the chorale fragment we discussed in example E.1a. In other cases, the four voices include numerous nonchord tones, as in anthology, no. 9 (Bach, "Was Gott tut"). In chapter 2 we explained that nonchord tones have a melodic, embellishing function, and that they are not part of the chord with which they are simultaneously sounded. (We will study nonchord tones in detail in chapter 8.) Nonchord tones in chorales break the homorhythmic character of the texture and contribute to voice independence.

EXERCISE

To practice analysis of a variety of textures, refer to exercise 4.1.1 in worksheet 4 at the end of this chapter.

TRIADS IN FIRST INVERSION

Analyze anthology, no. 9 (Bach, "Was Gott tut") with Roman numerals. When the beat is subdivided into eighth notes in this particular example, the first eighth note is always the actual chord, and the second one is either a nonchord tone or a change of voicing. Analyze, then, the first eighth note for each chord. You will notice that, other than the third chord from the end (a ii$^6_5$), all the other chords are either I, IV, or V. They are not all, however, in root position. If this were the case, there would be only three possible different bass notes for these three chords. Counting root position and first inversion, on the other hand, we have six possible bass notes, which allow for a much more interesting bass line.

NOTE

The progression V–IV is very unusual in common practice tonal harmony, and in principle it must be systematically avoided. The progression V–vi, on the other hand, is common, and it constitutes what we know as deceptive resolution of V (*or* **deceptive cadence**)*, which we will study in chapter 5 and also in more detail in chapter 14. In the deceptive resolution of V, the bass motion is $\hat{5}$–$\hat{6}$. An occasional (not frequent, but possible) substitute for the V–vi deceptive resolution is V–IV$_6$, which features the same $\hat{5}$–$\hat{6}$ bass motion. A case of V–IV$_6$ progression can be found in "Was Gott tut." This is the only case of V resolving to the subdominant which will be practiced in this book, and it should only be used very occasionally.*

EXERCISE

To practice writing isolated triads in first inversion from given Roman numerals, refer to exercise 4.2 in worksheet 4 at the end of this chapter.

The Triad in First Inversion: Uses and Function

First-inversion triads are used to provide for better voice-leading, to increase the number of available pitches for the bass (and thus to provide for a richer bass line), or to provide variety to the types of sonorities in a texture. In "Was Gott tut," the chords in first inversion introduce an element of variety in a passage that contains basically only three triads. By using I$_6$, IV$_6$, and V$_6$, the number of both sonorities and pitches for the bass are doubled. In example 4.3, on the other hand, one can see the logic of voice leading as a reason to use inverted triads. The I$_6$ in m. 14 is the tonic chord keyboard position closest to the IV in m. 13 (following our voice-leading guideline 1 in chapter 1), whereas the tonic at m. 16 is approached through a V$_6$ (also the closest dominant position), thus stressing the $\hat{7}$–$\hat{1}$ voice leading by exposing it in the bass.

Because triads in first inversion are less stable than root-position triads, composers have used them for expressive or formal purposes, when the stability of a root position triad is not desired. In a PAC, for instance, both V and I are in root position. If the composer wishes to have a V–I cadence without a fully conclusive effect, one of the two chords may be used in first inversion. The V$_6$–I or V–I$_6$ cadences, known as

♪♪♪Example 4.3   W.A. Mozart, Piano Sonata in B♭M, K. 570, I, mm. 1–20

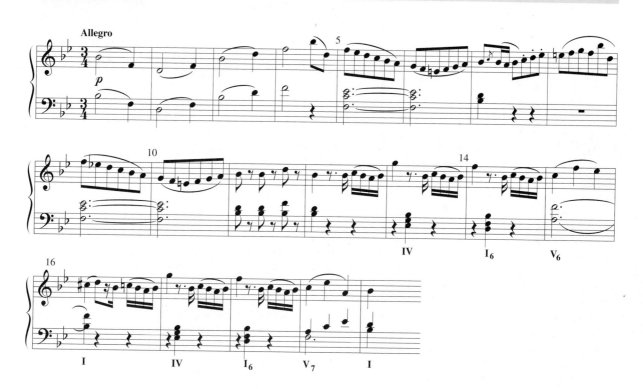

imperfect authentic cadences (IACs), are often used for this purpose, because they are less conclusive and stable than a PAC. We will study IACs in more detail in chapter 5.

Prolongation as a Function

As you will remember from chapter 3, a prolongational or contrapuntal chord extends the "area of influence" of another chord that is more important structurally. One of the most direct ways of extending a harmony in time is to change the position of the chord from root position to first inversion. *Prolongation is indeed the most frequent function of triads in first inversion.* In example 4.4 you can see how first-inversion chords (marked with a 6) extend two of the harmonies: the initial i and the iv that precedes the final HC. (The circled bass pitches are nonchord tones.) In other words, first-inversion triads are usually *prolongational chords*.

Arpeggiation and Voice Exchange

In examples 4.5a and b, which summarize the voice leading of the first-inversion chord used as a **prolongation**, a i₆ extends the previous i: The chord (the harmony) does not change between chords 1 and 2; only the position changes. The tonic function is thus

♪♪♪Example 4.4   J. S. Bach, Chorale 111, "Herzliebster Jesu, was hast du verbrochen," mm. 1–3

Positions: 5   6   6   6   6
Chords: Am: i ——————— V ——— i vii° i ——————— iv ——— V

prolonged by means of **arpeggiation** or chordal skip, as indicated by means of reductive notation in example 4.5c. The main (or only) voice-leading motion within the chord is what we call a **voice exchange**, produced by arpeggiation in two voices: the soprano and bass lines (C–A and A–C, respectively) exchange pitches, while $\hat{1}$ and $\hat{5}$ are sustained in the other two voices. Voice exchange is indicated graphically by a cross symbol showing the exchange of pitches between two voices in this type of voice leading. The same voice leading and function apply if the first inversion precedes the root position, as in example 4.5d.

In example 4.6a, the subdominant triad (and function) is similarly extended by a iv$_6$, and both of them function as predominants. In example 4.6b, V$_6$ extends the dominant chord and function. In both examples 4.6a and b, the Roman numeral notation in parentheses remind us that, as we saw in chapter 3, we can hear two levels of harmony

♪♪♪Example 4.5

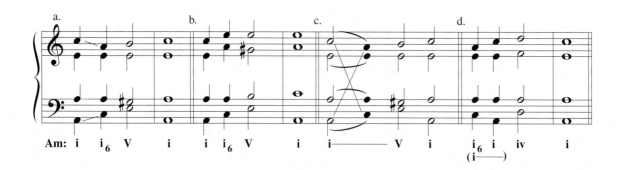

a.   b.   c.   d.

Am: i   i$_6$ V   i   i   i$_6$ V   i   i —————— V   i   i$_6$ i   iv   i
                                                       (i ———)

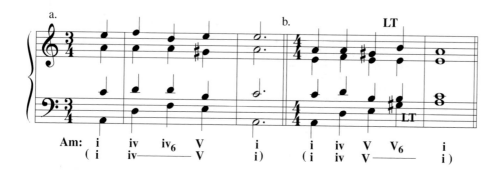

♪♪♪Example 4.6

in these progressions. At one level, we hear each chord in isolation. At the next, deeper level, the root-position triad and its inversion are heard as a single harmony in which a voice-leading change (a change of position or arpeggiation) is operated.

EXERCISE

To practice realizing short progressions using changes of position and voice exchange, refer to exercises 4.3a to c in worksheet 4 at the end of this chapter.

THE NEIGHBOR V₆

In chapters 2 and 3 we studied cases of dominant and subdominant harmonies that function as neighbor chords to I by means of neighbor figures. In example 4.7a you will see a similar type of voice leading, this time featuring V_6 as a neighbor chord: In the progression $I–V_6–I$, one voice remains static while the other three perform neighbor-note figures (two lower neighbors—down a step, back up a step—and one upper neighbor—up a step, down a step). The function of V_6 here is to prolong the tonic, and so is the function of the following neighbor IV, which completes the progression in our example. The reduction in example 4.7b shows graphically how this complete progression prolongs the tonic triad by means of a series of neighbor notes. An example by J. S. Bach illustrates the use of the $I–V_6–I$ progression in a chorale texture, with slightly embellished voice leading (example 4.7c). Compare Bach's realization with the model in example 4.7a, and comment on the differences. Possible melodic patterns to be harmonized with the neighbor $I–V_6–I$ progression are $\hat{1}–\hat{2}–\hat{1}$ (example 4.7a), and also $\hat{3}–\hat{2}–\hat{3}$ or $\hat{5}–\hat{5}–\hat{5}$ (example 4.7c).

In an alternative, and very frequent, voice leading, the neighbor-note figure in the two upper voices is replaced by a *passing-tone figure*. The B in the soprano in example 4.7d functions as a passing tone between A and C♯, and so does the B in the tenor. In this voice leading, summarized in example 4.7e (where PT means passing tone), the two voices that have the PT figures also feature voice exchange: The soprano and tenor

♪♪♪ Example 4.7a and b

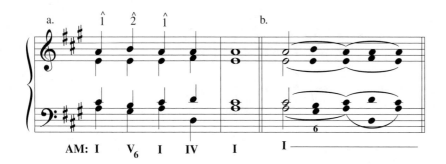

♪♪♪ Example 4.7c   J. S. Bach, Chorale 196, "Da der Herr Christ zu Tische sass," mm. 1–2

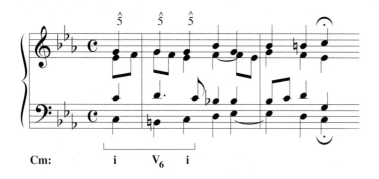

♪♪♪ Example 4.7d and e

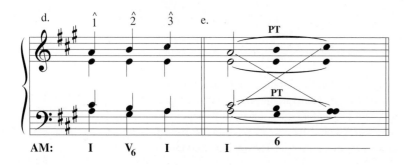

♪♪♪ Example 4.7f   Stephen Sondheim–Leonard Bernstein, "Somewhere," from *West Side Story*

E♭M: ii₇   V₆   I♭₇   IV

exchange the pitches A–C♯, with an intervening passing tone B in each voice. A common melodic pattern often harmonized with the passing I–V₆–I progression is $\hat{1}$–$\hat{2}$–$\hat{3}$ (or $\hat{3}$–$\hat{2}$–$\hat{1}$). Bach's chorale "Was Gott tut" (anthology, no. 9) opens with this type of realization of the I–V₆–I progression. Both examples 4.2a and b begin with slight variations of this progression. Study these examples, and discuss their characteristics in class.

As we already saw in chapter 2, in the type of nonchord tone which we call *incomplete neighbor* (IN), the embellished note is either approached *or* left by step, but not both (see also chapter 8 for more details on INs). In example 4.7f you can see a well-known case of **V₆ as an incomplete neighbor** to the tonic (which in this case appears as a tonic-seventh chord). Notice the incomplete neighbor figure, D–E♭, in the bass.

NOTE

Although we will not study diatonic seventh chords formally until chapters 12 (dominant seventh) and 15 (all other diatonic seventh chords), seventh chords are very much part of the harmonic vocabulary of popular music, and as such they will appear in many of our examples of popular music, as is the case of example 4.7f. The incomplete neighbor function illustrated by this example, however, would be exactly the same if the ii and the I chords were triads instead of seventh chords. Besides seventh chords, other chords, which we will not study until later in the book, will also appear occasionally in our popular music examples. Extended tertian chords (in which one or more thirds are added on top of a seventh chord, as in V_7^9 or V_9^{11}) and added-sixth chords (triads with an added sixth, such as $I^{add\,6}$) are common occurrences in the pop and jazz repertoires. Their appearance in a particular example should not detract you from whatever point is being made about that particular example.

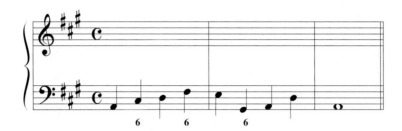

Example 4.8

First-inversion triads allow us to write longer progressions than the ones possible so far. In example 4.8, the primary progression I–IV–V–I has been elaborated by means of first-inversion triads and by a closing plagal cadence. Analyze this figured-bass progression: Find the basic root-position chords, and understand how our three fundamental functions are prolonged to generate this nine-chord harmonic phrase. Write Roman numerals under each of the bass notes, and then a second set of Roman numerals under the first one to indicate the deeper level of prolonged harmonies. Finally, add a soprano line to this bass and include voice exchanges for two of the three changes of position.

EXERCISES

To practice realizing short progressions using V_6 as a neighbor chord, refer to exercises 4.3d to f in worksheet 4 at the end of this chapter.

To practice analysis of musical fragments including triads in first inversion, refer to exercise 4.1.2 in worksheet 4 at the end of this chapter.

To practice realizing figured basses using first-inversion triads, refer to exercises 4.4a and b in worksheet 4 at the end of this chapter.

To practice harmonizing melodic fragments with progressions that include first-inversion triads, refer to exercises 4.5a and b in worksheet 4 at the end of this chapter.

ELABORATING THE I–V–I PROGRESSION

In chapter 3 we saw that we can elaborate the fundamental progression by extending the initial tonic triad and by preparing the cadential dominant. In this chapter we have learned more means to extend not only the initial tonic triad, but also actually any triad. Example 4.9a shows one of the many elaborations of the I–V–I progression that

♩♪♪ Example 4.9

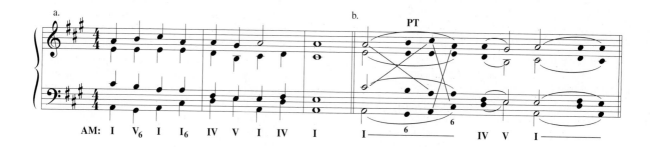

we could write at this point. First, we extend the initial tonic by means of two first-inversion triads (a passing V_6 and a I_6). Then, we continue with a complete cadential gesture, IV–V–I. Finally, we extend the final tonic triad by means of a neighbor I–IV–I progression (a plagal cadence). A harmonic reduction of this progression (example 4.9b) shows the linear function of all these chords within the complete harmonic phrase. Notice that the initial extension of I includes two voice exchanges. What do the Roman numerals in example 4.9b tell us as compared with the Roman numerals in example 4.9a?

EXERCISE

To practice harmonic reduction, refer to exercises 4.5c and d in worksheet 4 at the end of this chapter.

Typical Errors to Avoid

1. Doubling the LT in V_6.
2. Not resolving the first LT in the V–V_6 progression (or doubling one of the leading tones).
3. Not approaching and leaving the doubled note in the $^6_3$ chord by contrary or oblique motion, with resulting parallel 8ves.
4. Writing parallel 5ths or 8ves as a result of a chordal skip in the bass or any other voice.

VOICE-LEADING GUIDELINES

1. *Doubling.* In primary triads in first inversion it is preferable to double the root or the fifth. Double the third only if doing so produces the best possible voice leading. Otherwise, double the root or the fifth. Doubling the bass in a $^6_3$ chord (especially if it is doubled by the soprano) strongly emphasizes the third of the chord, an effect which, unless specifically desired by the composer, unnecessarily weakens the sound of the triad.

2. Do not double the bass (the LT) in a V_6 chord. Because the LT is in the bass, the V_6 chord will always resolve to a root-position tonic chord.

3. In example 4.6b the change of position involves the dominant triad. Because we cannot double the leading tone, when the bass moves to it in V_6, the previous LT in another voice must move to a different pitch (in this case, G♯–B in the soprano). This previous LT *should not be left unresolved.* Notice that the G♯–B line in the soprano moves on to A, thus resolving the G♯ two beats later. Refer to example 4.4, m. 1, beats 3–4, for a similar situation regarding the LT, except that in this case it does not arise from a change of position, but simply from a change of voicing (and also of spacing, from open to close). In any case, you will see that Bach does not leave either of the two LTs unresolved when the V chord resolves to i_6 on the downbeat of m. 2.

4. The best voice leading in a change of position (from root position to first inversion or vice versa) is illustrated in example 4.5a: A voice exchange is effected between the bass (A–C) and another voice (in this case the soprano, C–A). In such a voice exchange, two voices exchange pitches, while the other two do not move.

5. An alternative voice leading can be seen in example 4.5b: One voice remains static, while the other three move in the same direction. Other combinations are also possible. In all cases, the voice leading involves chordal skips in one or more voices.

6. To avoid parallel 8ves between two different chords, one of which is in root position and the other in first inversion (as in I–V_6, V_6–I, IV–V_6, IV_6–I, etc.), approach and leave the doubled note in the $^6_3$ chord by contrary or oblique motion. The lines in example 4.10 show how the doubled notes in both V_6 in example 4.10a (B) and iv_6 in example 4.10b (D) are approached and left by contrary motion. Without changing the voice leading in the remaining voices, try approaching or leaving any of the doubled notes in these two examples by parallel motion, and verify the resulting parallel 8ves.

7. Chordal figuration, such as changes of position or voicing, can be used to *prevent parallel 5ths or 8ves,* as illustrated by examples 4.10c and d. In example 4.10c, a chordal skip in the tenor prevents what otherwise would have been parallel 8ves between bass and tenor. Similarly, a change of position (a chordal skip in the bass) prevents parallel 5ths in example 4.10d. On the other hand, the same type of chordal skips can *produce parallel 5ths or 8ves,* as illustrated in examples 4.10e and f. In example 4.10e, a change of position produces parallel 8ves and a direct 5th; in 4.10f the chordal skip in the alto results in parallel 5ths.

♪♪♪ Example 4.10

PARALLEL $^6_3$ CHORDS

Because a chord in first inversion (made up of a 6th and a 3rd above the bass) does not contain a 5th if it is presented in close position, $^6_3$ chords may be used in succession without the difficulty of having to avoid parallel fifths. Composers have used parallel $^6_3$ sequences in passages in which the effect of a smooth, linear flow of parallel voices is desired (often in transitional passages). Parallel $^6_3$ sequences, which have a contrapuntal origin, momentarily suspend the functional character of harmony. Because they are perceived as parallel lines, their character is more melodic (linear) than harmonic (vertical). The passage in parallel $^6_3$ sonorities in anthology, no. 32 (Beethoven, Sonata op. 2, no. 1, III, Trio, mm. 59–62), shows indeed how a single melody (mm. 55–57) is first reinforced with a supporting melody in parallel 3rds (mm. 57–59), and finally with full parallel $^6_3$ chords.

The fragment by Mozart reproduced in example 4.11a (Piano Sonata K. 283, III, mm. 9–14) is a sequence based on parallel $^6_3$ sonorities, as you may see clearly in the chordal reduction of the passage that appears in example 4.11b. In three voices, the connection of parallel $^6_3$ chords does not present any difficulty as long as the 6th above the bass (the chordal root) is in the soprano (example 4.11c). If the 3rd above the bass (the chordal fifth) is in the soprano (open $^6_3$ position), parallel 5ths will result (example 4.11d). In four voices, because one of the voices must be doubled, parallel 8ves will result if the same voice is always doubled. This is exactly what happens in the Mozart example. While the parallel 8ves in example 4.11a, however, either result from instrumental octave doubling (in the left hand) or are minimized by an instrumental broken-chord figuration (in the right hand), the octaves in the four-voice reduction (example 4.11b) have no justification. In order to avoid them, one of the voices will not move in parallel motion with the other three, and the doubled voice will not always be the same. Examples 4.11e and f illustrate this technique known as **alternate doublings**. Notice that in all cases the doubled notes (marked in the examples) are approached and left by oblique or contrary motion, and that the LT should still not be doubled if it appears in a chord that is followed by the tonic triad (as in the next to last chord in examples 4.11e and f).

EXERCISE

To practice realizing a sequence of parallel $^6_3$ chords, refer to exercise 4.4c in worksheet 4 at the end of this chapter.

HARMONIZING A MELODY

So far, you have written chordal realizations in four voices of given bass or soprano lines with Roman numerals (the harmonization) also provided, or harmonizations of brief melodic patterns, which we have associated with standard harmonic patterns. In this chapter you will start to compose your own harmonizations of longer soprano lines. For the time being, you will write *only the bass line and Roman numerals,* omitting the two inner voices.

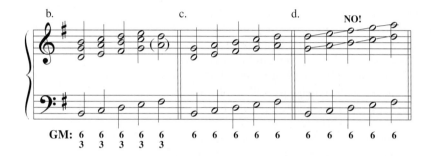

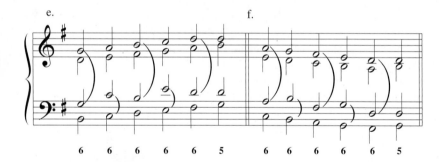

Harmonic Rhythm

The rhythmic pattern created by the change of chords is known as **harmonic rhythm**. (We will study harmonic rhythm in detail in chapter 11.) The rhythmic phrase under the Roman numerals in example 4.13f, for instance, indicates the harmonic rhythm (HR) for the progression. Notice that a change of position is not counted as a change of chord (I–I₆ is the same chord). The harmonic rhythm for the melodies you will harmonize will be given. Sometimes you will be asked to write a chord for each soprano note (example 4.12a). Sometimes, however, two soprano notes belong to the same chord and can be harmonized with a single chord, as in example 4.12b. In most of these cases, using a change of position within the same chord contributes to the melodic

♪♪♪Example 4.12

motion and variety of the bass (example 4.12c). Conversely, if a soprano note is long (two or more beats, or, in compound meter, a dotted quarter or longer), you may be able to harmonize it with two different chords (example 4.12d), or you may need to use only one chord and its first inversion (example 4.12e).

Procedure

The basic procedure for harmonizing a melody is as follows:

1. For the time being progressions will begin and end on the tonic chord.

2. First, try to identify any possible melodic patterns we may have associated with standard harmonic patterns. A scale degree analysis of the melody will help you in this process. In example 4.12a, for instance, we recognize two familiar scale degree patterns, $\hat{1}$–$\hat{2}$–$\hat{3}$ and $\hat{4}$–$\hat{2}$–$\hat{1}$, and both are harmonized with corresponding harmonic patterns which we have already studied. The same $\hat{4}$–$\hat{2}$–$\hat{1}$ pattern also appears in examples 4.11b, c, and e. In example 4.12d we see the $\hat{1}$–$\hat{2}$–$\hat{3}$ pattern which we can harmonize with the I–V$_6$–I progression, except in this case the initial I can itself be extended by means of a i–iv–i neighbor progression.

3. In example 4.13 you can see a detailed illustration of an alternative (and complementary) method to the identification of patterns. This method is more laborious, but it will be useful when you do not recognize any particular standard

♪♪♪ Example 4.13

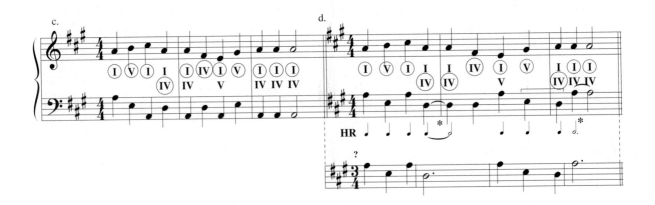

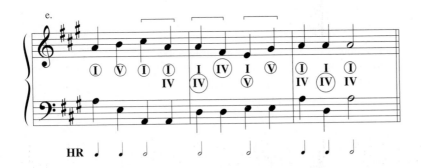

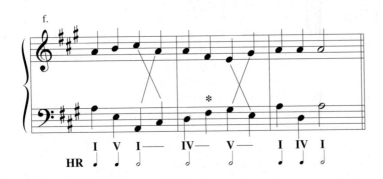

pattern in a passage. First, think what possible chords each given note belongs to in the given key, using only chords and inversions you have already studied in this book.

4. From the possible chords, choose the ones that result in a *good progression,* that is, in a progression that follows the criteria we have studied so far: V should resolve to I and not to IV, IV may follow I and precede V, and so forth. If the HR is given, look for melodic fragments that may be harmonized by a single chord with change of position (two notes that belong to the same chord, or a long note).

5. Avoid sustaining a chord (or a chord and its first inversion) over the bar line, or, in quadruple meter, over beats 2 and 3. In both cases, the chord would begin on a weak beat and end on a strong beat, creating a **harmonic syncopation** that produces a blurring of meter and a conflict between meter and harmony. We will study harmonic syncopation and the relationship between harmony and meter in more detail in chapter 11.

6. Once you have the correct progression, write a bass line for it. If your line is monotonous or repetitive because you are using only root-position triads, try to enrich your bass by using some first inversions in the spots you previously identified as possible for changes of position. Think of the outer-voice frame you are writing in terms of first-species counterpoint, and remember to check for voice-leading errors.

Practicing the Process

Let us try to harmonize the melody for example 4.13a. After singing the melody, list the possible chords for each note, as in example 4.13b. Assume for a moment that you were not given the HR and that you could choose freely from the possible chords. The circled chords in example 4.13c seem to be a possible good progression, for which we write a bass line. The progression is correct but produces a poor and repetitive bass, because the progression itself has several repeated connections (as in the two I–IV pairs). The last measure, of course, is too simple. Look now at the harmonization in example 4.13d. The bass is not only weak melodically, but also there are several obvious errors: two harmonic syncopations (marked with asterisks) and a V–IV progression. We mentioned before that harmonic syncopations blur the sense of meter. The lower staff in example 4.13d illustrates this point: Because the HR in this progression creates a grouping of chords in 3, we may hear this bass line as if it were in $\frac{3}{4}$, as notated in the lower staff, thus producing a conflict with the $\frac{4}{4}$ meter of the given melody.

Considering the lack of success of our attempted harmonizations, we might as well go back to the given HR. According to it, there are three pairs of notes that should be harmonized with the same chord, as shown by the brackets in example 4.13e. These same fragments indicated by brackets are all subject to harmonizations using a change of position. The progression circled in this example follows the given HR and makes sense harmonically, although the bass that results from it is quite poor because of the various repeated notes. For the final version in example 4.13f, we have improved the bass by changes of position, and we have also taken advantage of two possible voice exchanges. The last measure, with its plagal cadence, is now also much improved.

One should always double-check carefully to make sure that all voice leading and doubling between the two voices is correct. The only thing that might be criticized in example 4.13f is that in the IV₆ at m. 2 we have doubled the third between bass and soprano (see asterisk). This doubling, however, allows for very smooth and effective voice leading between the two voices, whereas trying to avoid it would lead to a variety of other problems or to a weaker bass line (try it if you wish). The doubling is then fully justified musically.

The outer-voice frame we have written works just fine as a first-species counterpoint duet. In example 4.13f we could be picky about the unbalanced leap in the bass, m. 2, but considering the various problems we have had to deal with, this seems a very minor flaw in this context, and we can let it pass. Sing all four versions in class or with some friend (examples 4.13c, d, e, and f), and notice the different points we have discussed. Now try your own harmonization of the following melody (example 4.14), using only I, IV, V, and their first inversions.

🎵🎵🎵 Example 4.14

PRACTICAL APPLICATION AND DISCUSSION

1. Identify all first-inversion triads in anthology, no. 8 (Bach, "Was mein Gott will"), mm. 1–5, and discuss their function within the passage.

2. J. S. Bach's Chorales 29 and 64 (anthology, nos. 10a and b) provide two different harmonizations of the same chorale melody. Compare how the initial $\hat{1}$–$\hat{2}$–$\hat{3}$ melodic gesture is harmonized in each chorale, and discuss the details of voice leading in each case. In Chorale 29, identify the cadence types in mm. 6, 8, and 13.

3. Find several first-inversion triads in a composition you are currently performing (or in its piano accompaniment). What is the function of each of them? Why do you think that the composer chose to use each of them instead of a root-position triad? How do these inverted triads make the music more interesting?

EXERCISE

To practice harmonizing melodies, refer to exercise 4.6 in worksheet 4 at the end of this chapter.

ASSIGNMENT AND KEYBOARD PROGRESSIONS

For analytical and written assignments and keyboard progressions based on the materials learned in this chapter, refer to chapter 4 in the workbook.

PITCH PATTERNS

1. Practice singing triads in first inversion up from various pitches. The ascending scale degree (assuming a tonic triad) and intervallic patterns for M and m triads in first inversion are as follows:

   M triad in first inversion: $\hat{3}$–$\hat{5}$–$\hat{1}$ (m3 + P4)

   m triad in first inversion: ♭$\hat{3}$–$\hat{5}$–$\hat{1}$ (M3 + P4)

2. Sing the pitch patterns in example 4.15 (and hear the horizontalized harmonies) in the major and minor modes.

♪♪♪ Example 4.15

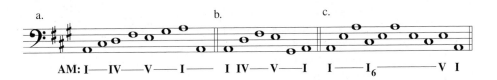

AM: I—IV—V—I— I IV—V—I I——I₆——V I

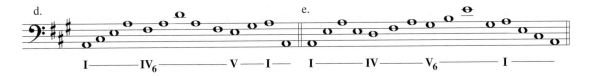

I———IV₆————V—I— I——IV——V₆——I—

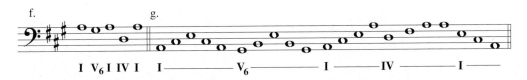

I V₆ I IV I   I————V₆———— I ——IV ——I——

Composers and Their Music 4

Biographies

Write short biographies of the following composers mentioned in this chapter: Orlande de Lassus, Joseph Haydn, Leonard Bernstein.

Listening

Listen to the following compositions by composers mentioned in this chapter:

Lassus: *Missa pro defunctis* in four voices, or another Mass, or selected motets

Haydn: Symphonies no. 94, *Surprise,* and no. 101, *The Clock*

Bach: *The Well-Tempered Clavier,* Book I, preludes and fugues 1–5

Beethoven: Symphonies no. 6 in FM, op. 68, and no. 7 in AM, op. 92

Sondheim-Bernstein: *West Side Story*

Follow the score while you listen. Be able to place these compositions in one of the style periods and to comment on why and how they represent the musical characteristics of that period.

Listen especially for texture. Some of the compositions or movements in this list are strictly contrapuntal; others are not. Identify contrasting textures within the same movement or composition. Does the composer use contrapuntal and homophonic sections as a means of contrast? Do some of the sections combine both contrapuntal and homophonic textures? Are contrapuntal sections imitative, or are they based on free counterpoint?

Terms for Review

Texture

Monophonic

Polyphonic

Counterpoint

Contrapuntal texture

Free counterpoint

Imitative counterpoint

Imitation

Supporting parallel melody

Homophonic

Chorale texture

Homorhythmic

Deceptive cadence

Triads in first inversion:

    functions and voice leading

Imperfect authentic cadence

$^6_3$ chords as prolongation (arpeggiation)

Voice exchange

Neighbor V_6

V_6 as an incomplete neighbor

Parallel $^6_3$ chords

Alternate doublings

Harmonic rhythm

Harmonic syncopation

Worksheet 4

EXERCISE 4.1   Analysis.

1. Texture. Briefly discuss the texture of the following examples:
   a) Anthology, no. 31, Maria Theresia von Paradis, *Sicilienne.*

   b) Anthology, no. 34, Beethoven, op. 13, III, mm. 1–17.

   c) Anthology, no. 37, Friedrich Kuhlau, Sonatina, mm. 1–8.

   d) Example 4.16.

♪♪♪ Example 4.16   J. S. Bach, Fugue no. 1, from *The Well Tempered Clavier, II*

♪♪♪ Example 4.16   Continued

♪♪♪ Example 4.17   Antonio de Cabezón, Hymn on *Pange lingua*

e) Example 4.17.

In each of these examples, answer the following questions:
1) Is it homophonic or polyphonic (contrapuntal)?
2) If it is homophonic, what kind of accompaniment does it feature?
   a. Melody with block chords.
   b. Melody with broken (arpeggiated) chords.
   c. Melody, chords, and a parallel supporting melody.
   d. Accompaniment is (mostly) homorhythmic with melody.
   e. Other (explain).
3) Is an outer-voice contrapuntal frame evident in each of these homophonic examples?
4) If it is polyphonic, explain the exact relationship among voices.
   a) Chorale texture.
   b) Free counterpoint: voices unrelated, nonimitative counterpoint.
   c) Imitative counterpoint: voices share same thematic material.
   d) All voices are similar in importance.
   e) One voice is in long notes (probably a borrowed tune, or *cantus firmus*) whereas the others are in faster figurations. In which voice is the *cantus firmus*? (You will remember that in chapter D we defined *cantus firmus* as a preexistent melody used as the basis for polyphonic composition.)
   f) If there is a *cantus firmus,* are the other voices imitative or free?

2. Harmony.
   a) Provide a RN analysis of example 4.18 and explain the function of the chords in this passage. Comment briefly on the voice leading. How can the passage be explained as a prolongation of the tonic triad?

♪♪♪Example 4.18   Maria Szymanowska, Nocturne in B♭M, mm. 17–19

b) Explain the basic harmonic motion in example 4.19 (the RN for the chord in mm. 107–109, a first inversion of a V_7 chord, is V_5^6), which can be summarized as a six-chord progression with changes of position. Mark all the changes of position in the fragment with a bracket, and explain their role. Explain also by what harmonic means is the tonic triad prolonged in mm. 104–112.

♪♪♪♪ **Example 4.19**   Gioachino Rossini, *Il barbiere di Siviglia,* Overture, mm. 104–115

♪♪♪Example 4.20   J.S. Bach, Chorale 54, "Lobt Gott, ihr Christen allzugleich," mm. 1–2

c) Analyze example 4.20 with RNs. Remember our definition of *passing tone*
   (PT): a pitch that fills in a gap of a 3rd by steps. A PT is an ornamental melodic
   pitch, and it does not change the harmonic nature of a chord.
   1) Circle all the PTs in the fragment.
   2) Mark all the changes of position with a bracket. Explain their role, espe-
      cially in view of the soprano line Bach harmonized.

   3) Mark any voice exchange with the usual cross sign.
   4) Study the voice leading in the last three chords. Does the IV–V connection
      feature our standard voice leading? What about the V–I connection? Does
      Bach allow himself any voice-leading license? After you find it, make sure
      you first scream the customary, "If Bach does it, why can't I do it too???"☺
      Then, explain why you think Bach chose this particular voice leading. His
      alternative could have been to write a B in the tenor for the last chord. What
      advantage did he find in writing a D instead?

EXERCISE 4.2   Write the following triads in four voices with correct doubling.

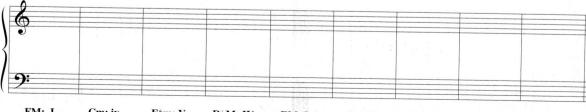

FM: I_6 Cm: iv_6 F♯m: V_6 D♭M: IV_6 EM: I_6 Gm: V_6 A♭M: I_6 Dm: V_6 BM: IV_6

EXERCISE 4.3   Realize the following progressions in four voices. Use voice exchange where possible. *Always verify (and enjoy) the sound of what you write* by playing and listening to it.

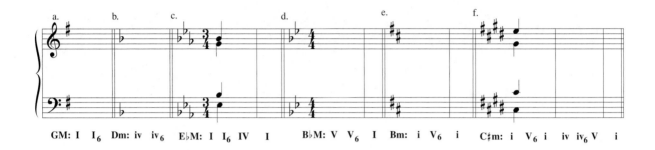

GM: I I₆   Dm: iv iv₆   E♭M: I I₆ IV   I   B♭M: V V₆   I   Bm: i V₆   i   C♯m: i V₆ i   iv iv₆ V   i

EXERCISE 4.4   *Figured-bass realization.* Provide a RN analysis and a four-voice realization of the following figured basses. You need not provide a RN analysis of exercise 4.4c, which you should realize as a series of parallel $^6_3$ chords.

> **Procedure to realize a figured bass:** Review the section "Figured Bass" in chapter F.
> 1. First provide a RN analysis of the figured bass.
>   a) Bass notes with no figures (or with a $^5_3$, a 5, or a 3) indicate root-position chords.
>   b) Accidentals alone refer to the third above the bass.
>   c) A note with only an accidental indicates a root-position triad with an altered third. For instance, a ♯ under a $\hat{5}$ in a minor key reminds you to raise $\hat{7}$ in a root position V chord; a ♯ under a $\hat{1}$ in a minor key indicates a Picardy third.
>   d) A 6 (or a $^6_3$) indicates a first-inversion triad.
>
> 2. Then realize the figured bass with your RNs as you have already been doing. Remember to write a good soprano line first, and to check your outer-voice first-species contrapuntal frame.

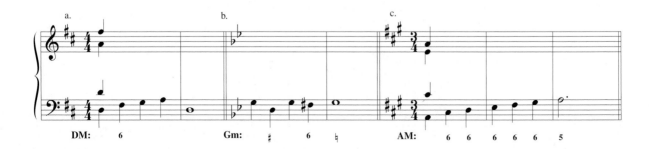

DM: 6   Gm: ♯   6   ♮   AM: 6   6   6   6   6   5

EXERCISE 4.5

1. Harmonize the following melodic patterns in four voices, using standard harmonic patterns that correspond with each of the melodic patterns. Exercise 4.5a is made up of three 3-note overlapping patterns, whereas exercise 4.5b consists of two 3-note patterns.

2. After you write each of the four-voice harmonizations, provide harmonic reductions of your realizations in exercises 4.5c and d. The phrase in exercise 4.5a can be understood in its entirety as a prolongation of I. You can model your reduction after examples 4.7b and e above. Mark any voice exchanges with the customary cross symbol. The progression in exercise 4.5b consists of an extension of the initial tonic followed by a predominant-dominant-tonic cadential gesture. Models for this reduction can be examples 3.6b and 4.10b above.

EXERCISE 4.6   *Melody harmonization.* Write a bass and RNs (no inner voices) harmonizing the following melodies. The harmonic rhythm (HR) is given.

1. Sing each melody several times before writing the harmonization.

2. Use only I, IV, or V in root position or first inversion.

3. First try to identify any melodic patterns that may be harmonized with some of the harmonic patterns you have learned.

4. Harmonize the notes marked with a 6 with first-inversion triads. (If necessary, a 5 is used to indicate a root-position triad.)

5. Check your two-voice contrapuntal frame to verify good voice leading.

6. Always *play your harmonizations* (as well as all your other exercises) before you turn them in. Make sure you are satisfied with them, and enjoy them!

Chapter 5

Cadences

A **cadence** is a musical point of arrival, normally produced by harmonic and melodic means, which articulates the end of a musical group (such as a phrase, a period, a section, or, of course, a complete movement or piece). Cadences provide musical punctuation, and their function is similar to the function of periods and commas in written language. Some are conclusive and final (like periods), some are conclusive in a weaker way (like semicolons), and others are used to confirm or reiterate a conclusion. Or, in some other cases, cadences are not meant to produce any kind of closing effect, but rather to suspend momentarily musical motion (like commas). Because they mark the end of phrases, periods, and other musical units, cadences have an essential role in defining musical sections. The tonal, rhythmic, and thematic relationships among units or sections (the "shape" of a composition) constitutes musical **form**. As we will see in chapter 6, cadences are an element of *formal articulation:* They are sectional markers and also define the tonal goal or direction of sections. In this chapter we will study in some detail all the most frequent cadence types found in tonal music. Although we have already seen, in previous chapters, the authentic, half, plagal, and deceptive cadences, we will now discuss each of them more specifically.

AUTHENTIC CADENCES

An **authentic cadence** includes a chord of the dominant family resolving to a tonic chord (for instance, V–I, V_7–I, V_6–I, V–I_6, or $vii°_6$–I). As we saw in chapter 2, authentic cadences can be of two types, perfect and imperfect, depending on the scale degrees in the upper voice and the position of the chords involved.

The Perfect Authentic Cadence

Mozart closes the last movement of his Piano Sonata in B♭M, K. 333 (anthology, no. 28) with a V_7–I cadence, in which both V_7 and I are in root position, $\hat{1}$ is in the top voice in the final tonic, and it is approached by step from $\hat{7}$. This type of V_7–I or V–I

Example 5.1   J. Haydn, Piano Sonata no. 32 in C♯m, Hob. XVI:36, I, mm. 94–97

cadence is the most conclusive of all authentic cadences, and it is known as a **perfect authentic cadence** (PAC). *In a PAC, $\hat{1}$ is in the top voice in the last chord, it is approached by step from $\hat{2}$ or $\hat{7}$, and both the dominant and the tonic chords are in root position.*

Many pieces and movements end with a PAC, and at times the cadence is reiterated several times to stress the sense of closure. To conclude the first movement of his Piano Sonata no. 36 in C♯m (example 5.1), Haydn wrote a string of five cadential gestures, all of the PAC type. Verify that these are all indeed PACs, and notice the strongly conclusive effect of the example.

EXERCISES

To study voice leadings for PACs, refer to examples 5.7a and b.

To practice realizing PACs in four voices, refer to exercises 5.2a and b in worksheet 5 at the end of this chapter.

The Cadential $^6_4$: A Preview

In both the Mozart and Haydn examples we just discussed, we can see a very common cadential figure, which we will study in more detail in chapter 9. Because you are likely to encounter this figure in numerous cadences, however, we will introduce it now as a preview of our discussion in chapter 9. Examine and play the PAC cadence we just studied in Mozart's B♭M sonata, mm. 7–8. In m. 7, beat 2, notice that, above a half-note F in the bass, the soprano effects a 4–3 motion (B♭–A), whereas the tenor effects a 6–5 motion (D–C). If we consider both motions above the bass together, we come up with the intervals $^{6-5}_{4-3}$ above the $\hat{5}$ in the bass. This very common harmonic gesture is called a **cadential $^6_4$**, and its function is to embellish melodically a dominant chord (the V$^5_3$ to which the linear $^6_4$ resolves). The symbol V$^{6-5}_{4-3}$, which we will use to refer to this cadential figure, expresses its function in an appropriate way: The harmony is really a V, and the voice motions 6–5 and 4–3 are melodic embellishments of the real harmony, the dominant chord represented by the $\frac{5}{3}$. In the Mozart half cadence (HC) in m. 4, the V is also preceded by a cadential $\frac{6}{4}$. In this case, the 6–5 motion is in the soprano, ornamented with an upper-neighbor figure, and the 4–3 is in the tenor. In the Haydn example above (example 5.1), the V_7 in m. 95 is equally preceded by a cadential $\frac{6}{4}$. You can verify the standard $\frac{6-5}{4-3}$ voice leading in the piano's right hand.

NOTE

In four-voice realizations of the cadential $\frac{6}{4}$, it is customary to double the bass ($\hat{5}$).

Example 5.2 shows three examples of cadential $\frac{6}{4}$. In the first case, V is preceded by IV. This allows for the 4th in the $\frac{6}{4}$ (which, as we know from our studies of species counterpoint, is a dissonant interval because it involves the bass) to be treated (prepared and resolved) as a 4–3 suspension. In example 5.2b, V is preceded by ii_6, a chord that very often replaces IV as a predominant. This is indeed the chord that precedes the cadential V_{4-3}^{6-5} in both the Mozart and Haydn examples we discussed above. In this case, both the 6th and the 4th function as passing tones above $\hat{5}$. Because, unlike the type of passing tones we have seen so far, these appear on a strong fraction of the beat, we call them *accented passing tones* (APT).

Study the cadence in example 5.2c. First, find the $\frac{6}{4}$ pitches in the melody (m. 5 of the example, to the words "Ev'rythin's"). Does this melodic $\frac{6}{4}$ resolve to $\frac{5}{3}$ in the next measure ("goin' my")? Notice that the B♭ which doubles the bass in the melody in m. 5 moves to an A♭ in m. 6, the seventh of the V_7 chord. The complete melodic figure in mm. 5–6 can then be represented as V_{6-5}^{8-7}. If you look at the accompaniment you will see another frequent possibility for approaching the seventh in the V_7. First, find the $\frac{6}{4}$ in the piano part (m. 5). Then, verify that, instead of moving down in a 6–5 figure, the 6th of the $\frac{6}{4}$ moves up to the seventh in a 6–7 figure, hence the Roman numeral V_{4-3}^{6-7}.

♪♪♪ Example 5.2a and b

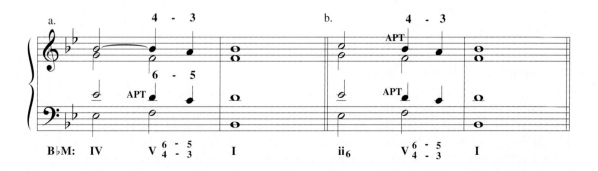

♪♪♪Example 5.2c   Oscar Hammerstein II–Richard Rodgers, "Oh, What a Beautiful Mornin,'" from *Oklahoma!*

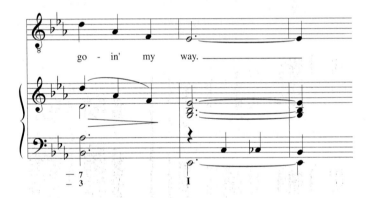

EXERCISES

To practice writing the cadential $^6_4$ in four voices, refer to exercises 5.2c and d in worksheet 5 at the end of this chapter.

Imperfect Authentic Cadences

Composers at times wish to end a musical statement with a less-conclusive gesture than the PAC. In the section immediately before the PAC cadence by Mozart mentioned above (anthology, no. 28), he avoids a conclusive cadence in order to build up tension toward the end and also to achieve a stronger closing effect once he finally reaches the final PAC. The series of V–I$_6$ cadences that he writes (mm. 206–222; see especially mm. 207, 210, 213, 218, and 222) do not create a sense of conclusion because the tonic in first inversion is a weak sonority to end a piece on. These are **imperfect authentic cadences** (IAC). In an IAC, *one of the chords is not in root position (or both chords are not), or $\hat{1}$ is not in the top voice.* The cadences in mm. 206–222 of anthology, no. 28 illustrate the first type (a chord is in inversion). An example of the second type is found earlier in the same movement: Although in m. 20 Mozart closes a phrase with a V–I cadence and both chords are in root position, it is a nonconclusive IAC because $\hat{3}$ is in the top voice (the upper-voice cadential motion is here $\hat{5}$–$\hat{3}$). The vii°$_6$–I cadence (which we will study in chapter 13) is a special type of IAC called **leading-tone cadence**, and it is more common in Renaissance music than in the common practice repertoire.

EXERCISES

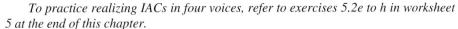

To study voice leadings for IACs, refer to examples 5.7d to h.

*   To practice realizing IACs in four voices, refer to exercises 5.2e to h in worksheet 5 at the end of this chapter.*

THE HALF CADENCE

Examine now the opening period of the same sonata movement by Mozart (anthology, no. 28, mm. 1–8). The statement ends on a PAC. At m. 4, however, the first phrase ends on a V chord, creating a definite need to resolve the harmonic tension, and thus to continue to the second phrase, as in a question-answer structure. A *cadence on V* (often preceded by the tonic or by a predominant chord) is called a **half cadence** (HC). The most frequent melodic motion at a HC is $\hat{3}$–$\hat{2}$, and the $\hat{2}$ usually represents the type of melodic interruption we studied in chapter 2. Instead of immediately effecting a melodic resolution down to $\hat{1}$, a phrase interrupted at a HC usually begins all over again, and eventually reaches closure with the resolution of the melodic $\hat{2}$ to $\hat{1}$ in the PAC at the end of the period.

Half cadences are very effective musical "marks of punctuation": They allow for clear articulation of the musical flow (we can clearly finish a phrase on a HC), and yet they create a harmonic need to "move forward." Listen to the Fm phrase by Pauline Viardot–Garcia in example 5.3, and you will hear that, although we realize that this is indeed a phrase, we also know that the music will go on. Further, we expect the next phrase to begin on an Fm tonic chord because the phrase ends on a dominant harmony in Fm, a half cadence.

The Phrygian Cadence

Refer to anthology, no. 50 (Schumann, *Album for the Young,* "Folk Song"). The first phrase ends at m. 4 with a half cadence (on V of Dm). Because V is preceded by iv$_6$, $\hat{5}$ in the bass is approached by half-step motion, B♭–A. This special type of half cadence

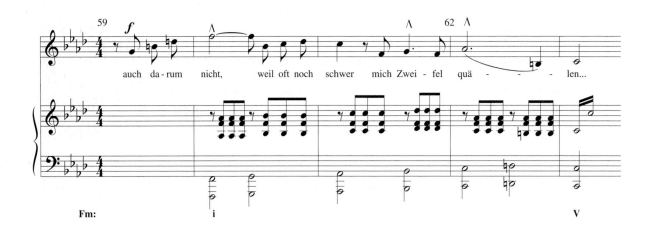

Example 5.3   Pauline Viardot-Garcia: "Die Beschwörung," mm. 60–63

in minor in which V is preceded by iv$_6$ is called **Phrygian cadence** (Ph.C.), because of the prominent half-step motion in the bass (which, in the Phrygian mode, takes place both between degrees $\hat{1}$–$\hat{2}$ and $\hat{5}$–$\hat{6}$).

EXERCISES

To study voice leadings for HCs, refer to examples 5.7i to l.

    To practice realizing HCs in four voices, refer to exercises 5.2i to l in worksheet 5 at the end of this chapter.

THE PLAGAL CADENCE

The IV–I cadence is known as a **plagal cadence** (PC). In chapter 3 we explained that the plagal cadence is sometimes used by composers to prolong the final tonic, following a more conclusive PAC. After a PAC, a plagal cadence has the effect of strongly confirming the conclusion of a piece. Such an extended prolongation of the final tonic can be seen in example 5.4. Brahms closes his Romance in FM, op. 118, no. 5 with a PAC in mm. 53–54, followed by four measures of tonic prolongation, which include a prominent plagal cadence in mm. 55–56. Notice the unusual final sonority in this piece. In what position is the final tonic chord in m. 57?

Example 5.4   J. Brahms, Romance, op. 118, no. 5, mm. 53–57

THE DECEPTIVE CADENCE

A **deceptive cadence** (DC) is a cadential progression of the dominant to a chord other than the expected (and, in principle, prescribed) tonic. In example 5.5, Mozart first delays the PAC which eventually will close the Fantasia in Cm, K. 475, by means of a deceptive cadence, V_7–VI, in m. 179 (the V_7 chord is preceded by a slight elaboration of the standard cadential $^6_4$ figure). A repeat an octave lower of the same cadential gesture leads to a PAC in m. 180, confirmed by a second PAC in mm. 180–181 (this time with a standard voice leading for the cadential $^6_4$, that is, $^{8-7}_{6-5}$). $^{4-3}$

The V–vi (or V–VI in a minor key) progression is the most frequent type of deceptive cadence. (A slight variation of this progression is occasionally found in the literature: V may resolve deceptively to IV_6 instead of to vi, as we mentioned in the note on page 198 in the previous chapter.) In a deceptive cadence the leading tone still resolves

♪♪♪ Example 5.5   W. A. Mozart, Fantasia in Cm, K. 475, mm. 179–181

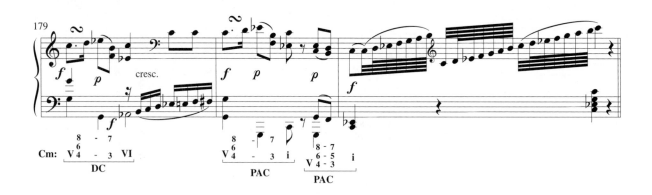

to the tonic ($\hat{7}$–$\hat{1}$), thus providing melodic closure, as in the top voice of the Mozart example. But because the $\hat{5}$ in the bass resolves to $\hat{6}$ instead of $\hat{1}$, we hear this cadence as an inconclusive (and usually unexpected and surprising) harmonic motion. Because it requires continuation to some kind of closure, it is often used to delay the end of a harmonic phrase as in example 5.5.

The passage by Palestrina in example 5.6 combines two of the cadences we just studied. In m. 40 we hear what might be the approach to a PAC. Instead, the dominant at the end of m. 40 resolves deceptively, to the VI in m. 41, which immediately turns into an extended iv chord. What kind of cadence is, then, the final cadence in mm. 42–44?

♪♪♪ Example 5.6   Giovanni Pierluigi da Palestrina, "Hosanna in excelsis," from *Missa Gabriel Archangelus,* mm. 40–44

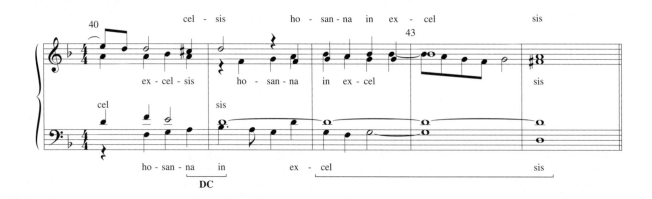

What kind of tonic chord do we end on? This beautiful cadence, which definitely has a conclusive effect, does not include a PAC at all. Moreover, although the movement could end on a PAC in m. 41 (we actually reach melodic closure in this cadence, with the $\hat{7}$–$\hat{1}$ in the soprano), the deceptive and plagal cadences that follow allow for a few measures of *cadential extension,* a concept we will study in more detail in the next two chapters.

EXERCISES

To study voice leadings for plagal and deceptive cadences, refer to examples 5.7m to o.

*   To practice realizing plagal and deceptive cadences in four voices, refer to exercises 5.2m and n in worksheet 5 at the end of this chapter.*

Typical Errors to Avoid

1. Doubling the LT (and resolving both of them to $\hat{1}$, with resulting parallel 8ves).
2. Not raising $\hat{7}$ in minor modes.
3. Not resolving the LT, especially when it is placed in the soprano.
4. Writing parallel 5ths or 8ves in progressions by step, such as IV–V and V–vi.
5. Writing parallel 5ths or 8ves in the progression IV$_6$–V$_6$ (double-check the part writing for this progression in example 5.7e).

CADENCES: SUMMARY AND VOICE LEADING

Example 5.7 provides a variety of voice-leading models for each of the cadences discussed above. Authentic and half cadences are represented by three-chord progressions using only the chords we have studied so far: I, IV, and V. The following comments will help you understand these examples.

1. Examples 5.7a–c illustrate three frequent upper-voice figures in PACs: $\hat{4}$–$\hat{2}$–$\hat{1}$, $\hat{1}$–$\hat{7}$–$\hat{1}$, and, with a dominant embellished by a cadential $^6_4$, $\hat{4}$–$\hat{3}$–$\hat{2}$–$\hat{1}$. Notice that, in the cadential $^6_4$, $\hat{5}$ (the bass) is doubled.

2. Examples 5.7d–e show IACs in which one of the two cadential chords is in first inversion. In 5.7e, moreover, the upper voice cadential pattern, $\hat{1}$–$\hat{2}$–$\hat{3}$, does not end on $\hat{1}$.

3. Examples 5.7f–h feature root-position chords, but the upper voice does not end on $\hat{1}$ in the last tonic chord. All three melodic patterns, $\hat{4}$–$\hat{2}$–$\hat{3}$, $\hat{6}$–$\hat{5}$–$\hat{3}$, and $\hat{6}$–$\hat{5}$–$\hat{5}$, are typical of IACs.

4. Examples 5.7i–l show four HCs. The first two represent frequent melodic patterns in HCs, $\hat{1}$–$\hat{7}$ and $\hat{3}$–$\hat{2}$. The $\hat{3}$–$\hat{3}$–$\hat{2}$ pattern in example 5.7k results from a $^{6-5}_{4-3}$ embellishment of the cadential V. Finally, a Phrygian cadence appears in example 5.7l.

5. The plagal cadence in example 5.7m does not require any comment, other than noticing that, in this case, the sustained $\hat{1}$ appears in the upper voice.

6. Two deceptive cadences (V–vi and V–IV$_6$) appear in examples 5.7n–o. The progression V–vi is a progression by step, of the type in which, in principle, we recommended that all three upper voices move in contrary motion with the bass. The LT in this cadence, however, should still resolve. The root and third of V will thus move a step up, while the other two voices move down. This voice leading results in a *doubled third* in the vi chord (or a doubled fifth in the V–IV$_6$ variant).

♪♪♪ Example 5.7

We mentioned above that cadences have a function similar to punctuation marks in language. Musical flow or "musical discourse" is indeed articulated by cadences, which in turn delimit phrases and other musical units. Understanding cadences and their function is essential to the proper rendition of a "musical text." Let's listen, for instance, to example 5.8. Not every V–I in music marks a cadence, of course (we should not confuse simple V–I progressions with cadences). For there to be a cadence, something must stop, even if only momentarily. Where are the cadences in this example? Where does the flute part, for instance, come to a rest?

You will have identified clear points of arrival, or breaks in the melodic flow, in mm. 54, 60, and 69–70. These cadential points tell us, indeed, that this passage contains three phrases. Awareness of phrase endings and of their relative role is obviously a central element to perform this (or any other) passage properly. Why is it that only the last of these three cadences is really conclusive? What is the function of the first two cadences within the general context of this example?

Both of them allow for phrase articulation (and for the flutist to breathe!) while not interrupting the musical flow. The cadence in mm. 53–54 is a dominant-tonic cadence, but not a PAC. Why not? Are both V and I in root position? What scale degree does the melody come to rest on in m. 54? Now look at the cadence in m. 60. Why is this an inconclusive cadence? What scale degree does the flute come to rest on? Is it a comfortable degree for a "rest"?

Of course, the final cadence in mm. 68–70 is a PAC (What makes it so?). What about the V–I cadence in mm. 66–67? Could the movement have ended there? Yes, if the flute had resolved the G down to F ($\hat{2}$–$\hat{1}$) instead of up to A ($\hat{2}$–$\hat{3}$). As it is, this cadence is not conclusive: It is an IAC that allows for a four-measure cadential extension leading to the true PAC in mm. 68–70.

♪♪♪ Example 5.8   Anna Amalie, Sonata for Flute in FM, I, mm. 51–70

♪♪♪Example 5.8   Continued

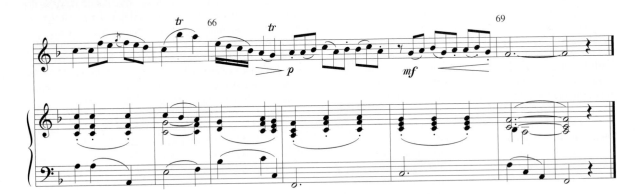

EXERCISES

To practice analyzing a variety of cadences, refer to exercise 5.1 in worksheet 5 below.
    To practice writing progressions ending on one of the cadences we have studied in this chapter, refer to exercise 5.3.
    To practice realizing a figured bass and harmonizing a melody, refer to exercises 5.4 and 5.5.

ASSIGNMENT AND KEYBOARD PROGRESSIONS

For analytical and written assignments and keyboard progressions based on the materials learned in this chapter, refer to chapter 5 in the workbook.

PITCH PATTERNS

Sing the pitch patterns in example 5.9. Hear the different cadences as you sing them, and understand the characteristics that define each of the cadences, as well as their functions.

♪♪♪ Example 5.9

Composers and Their Music 5

Biographies

Write short biographies of the following composers mentioned in this chapter: Pauline Viardot–Garcia, Johannes Brahms, Richard Rodgers.

Listening

Listen to the following compositions by composers mentioned in this chapter:

Viardot–Garcia: "Die Beschwörung," from *Zwölf Gedichte von Pushkin* (recording in Briscoe anthology)

Mozart: piano sonatas in DM, K. 284; AM, K. 331; B♭M, K. 333

Brahms: symphonies no. 3 in FM, op. 90, and no. 4 in Em, op. 98

Hammerstein-Rodgers: *Oklahoma!*

Follow the score while you listen. Be able to place these compositions in one of the style periods, and to comment on why and how they represent the musical characteristics of that period.

Listen particularly for cadences, and hear how they articulate form by closing phrases and other formal units. Try to identify PACs as you hear them, and hear their conclusive function, as opposed to the role of HCs, which you can also identify easily by hearing their role as "open" cadences, requiring continuation of the harmonic motion. Try to identify also some less-conclusive cadences, such as IACs and deceptive cadences.

Terms for Review

Cadence
Form
Authentic cadence
Perfect authentic cadence
Cadential $^6_4$
Imperfect authentic cadence

Leading-tone cadence
Half cadence
Phrygian cadence
Plagal cadence
Deceptive cadence

Worksheet 5

EXERCISE 5.1 Analysis. Study and label each of the following cadences. Name the cadence type, and provide specific (Roman numerals) RNs and other characteristics (such as upper-voice melodic motion) to justify your choice.

1. Example 5.10.

Example 5.10   J. S. Bach, Chorale 143, "In dulci jubilo," mm. 29–32

2. Example 5.11.

Example 5.11   R. Schumann, "Wenn ich in deinen Augen seh," from *Dichterliebe,* op. 48, no. 4, mm. 8–12

3. Example 5.12.

   a) Identify the two cadences as marked.

   b) Comment on the resolution of the first cadence to the chord at the beginning of the next measure.

Example 5.12   J. S. Bach, Chorale 197, "Christ ist erstanden," mm. 27–29

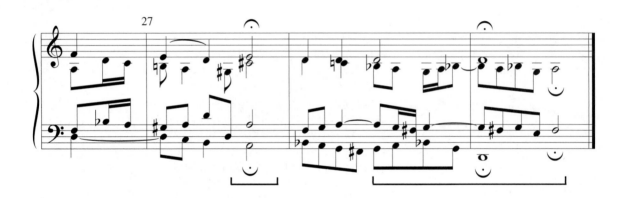

4. Example 5.13.

Example 5.13   J. Lennon–P. McCartney, "Got to Get You into My Life," from the album *Revolver* (verse)

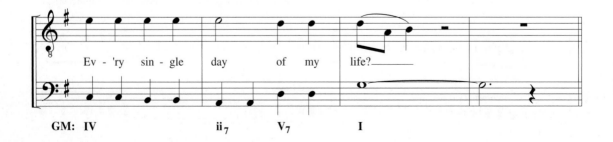

5. Anthology, no. 26, Mozart, Sonata in CM, III, m. 8.

6. Anthology, no. 18, Amalie, Sonata in FM, m. 21.

7. Anthology, no. 11, Bach, Minuet from *French Suite* no. 3, m. 8.

8. Anthology, no. 47, Schumann, "Ich grolle nich," mm. 11–12.

9. Anthology, no. 32, Beethoven, Sonata in Fm, op. 2, no. 1, m. 8.

EXERCISE 5.2   Realize the following cadences in four voices as required. Some so-prano melodic patterns are provided, and so are some Roman numerals. Provide RNs where missing.

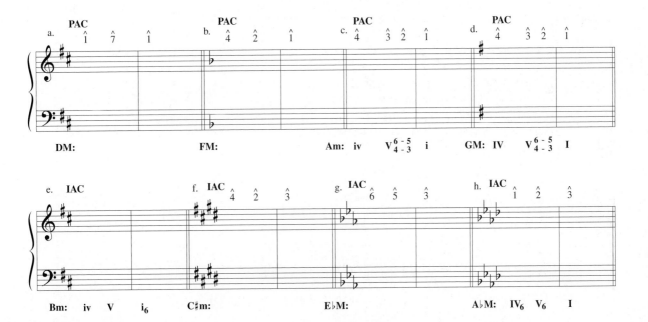

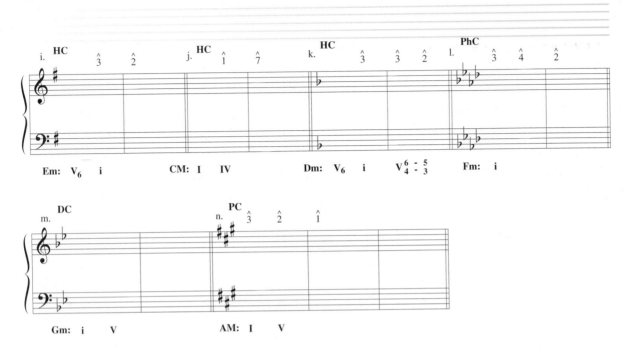

Em: V₆   i   CM: I   IV   Dm: V₆   i   V⁶⁻⁵₄⁻₃   Fm: i

Gm: i   V   AM: I   V

EXERCISE 5.3   Finish each of the following short progressions with the required cadence type (and realize the complete progression in four voices).

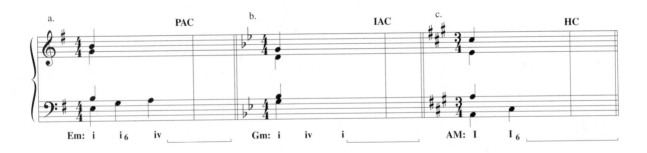

Em: i   i₆   iv _____   Gm: i   iv   i _____   AM: I   I₆ _____

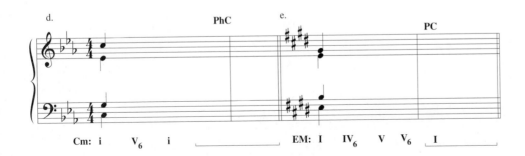

Cm: i   V₆   i _____   EM: I   IV₆   V   V₆   I _____

EXERCISE 5.4   Analyze the progression with RNs and realize the figured bass in four voices. Always play the exercises you write to know what they sound like. Remember to double-check your outer-voice frame for good first-species counterpoint.

Em:

EXERCISE 5.5   Harmonize the following melody with a bass and RNs (no inner voices) following the given harmonic rhythm. Harmonize the notes marked with a 6 with a first-inversion triad (5 indicates a root-position triad). Use only I, IV, and V in root position and first inversion.

AM:

HR

Chapter 6

Melodic Organization I: Phrase Structure

Similar to language syntax, musical thoughts and statements are grouped into units of varied length and function, in which melodic, rhythmic, and harmonic factors play a determining role, and in which cadences are an element of punctuation. As we noted in the previous chapter, the tonal, thematic, and rhythmic relationships among musical units constitute what we know as musical **form**. In this chapter we will study the basic types of musical statements and their groupings, with emphasis on melodic and tonal organization. You should keep in mind that music allows for an enormous variety of formal possibilities at any level. In this and other chapters we will discuss specific formal models that may be considered standard, at least in some repertoires. Not all the music you perform or listen to, however, conforms to these models. There are other possible models, and in many cases music does not conform to any preestablished formal type. The principles you will study in this and other chapters will provide you with criteria to approach the formal aspects of music, as well as a basis for comparison of specific formal arrangements with standard methods of musical organization.[1]

MOTIVE

A **motive** is a short, recurring musical figure, consisting of a characteristic rhythmic or pitch pattern, identifiable throughout a composition or a musical section. A **rhythmic motive** is a rhythmic figure which has, by its repetition, a structural role in a piece or passage. The accompaniment in anthology, no. 57 (Wolf, "Das verlassene Mägdlein") is based exclusively on the rhythmic motive quarter note/two eighth notes. The motive in example 6.1, on the other hand, presents both a clearly identifiable pitch pattern (a lower-neighbor-note figure) and a characteristic rhythmic pattern (two sixteenth notes/one eighth note).

---

[1] For further study of this chapter's topics, you can find a thorough coverage of phrase structure in Douglass Green, *Form in Tonal Music* (New York: Holt, Rinehart and Winston, 1979) and W. Rothstein, *Phrase Rhythm in Tonal Music.* For a study of phrase structure in the Classical period, see William Caplin, *Classical Form* (New York: Oxford University Press, 1998).

♪♪♪Example 6.1   J. S. Bach, Brandenburg Concerto no. 3, I, mm. 1–2

PHRASE

In our preview of phrase structure in chapter 2, we used the following definition of **phrase**: "a directed motion in time from one tonal entity to another" (W. Rothstein). In other words, a phrase takes us from a certain tonal point to another tonal point. A phrase presupposes *motion*, although the motion may well take us back where we started (motion from, say, I to I is perfectly acceptable within a phrase). Moreover, a phrase usually ends with a cadence of some type, and gives us a sense of being a self-sufficient musical unit (although not necessarily a closed or conclusive one).

Refer, for instance, to example 6.2. Although mm. 1–2 display some degree of musical independence, at least melodically, we would not call this fragment a phrase because it does not feature any kind of harmonic motion (the linear neighbor figure in the piano's right hand, m. 1, beat 2, is certainly not what we consider "harmonic motion"). The same can be said of mm. 3–4. Whereas mm. 1–2 are a linear elaboration of I, mm. 3–4 constitute in turn a linear elaboration of V. We do hear, on the other hand, the complete mm. 1–4 as a self-sufficient unit that effects a motion from tonic to a half cadence (HC) on V. This is the first phrase in this example. But, of course, a HC is not conclusive, and the music continues until it reaches another tonal goal, in this case a more stable one, the tonic in m. 8. Measures 5–8 are also a phrase by our definition.

A NOTE ABOUT IMPLIED HARMONY

*As we discussed in chapter 2, one should in principle examine both melody and harmony in order to identify cadences and phrases. At times, however, only a melody may be available. The harmony at the beginning or end of a phrase, if the melody alone is provided, may be implied from the melodic pitches (scale degrees). For structural purposes within a phrase, you will only need to identify implied tonic or dominant harmonies. The following suggestions will help you identify **implied harmonies**:*

1. Are I or V outlined melodically at the beginning or end of the phrase?
2. Are the beginning or end of the phrase built around (or based on) characteristic pitches of I or V?

3. *Can you harmonize the beginning or the end with a I or a V?*
4. *A phrase ending on $\hat{1}$ indicates a perfect authentic cadence (PAC). Possible* **melodic cadential patterns** *will be $\hat{2}$–$\hat{1}$ or $\hat{7}$–$\hat{1}$.*
5. *A phrase ending on $\hat{3}$ indicates an imperfect authentic cadence (IAC). Likely cadential patterns will be $\hat{2}$–$\hat{3}$ or $\hat{5}$–$\hat{3}$. An ending on $\hat{5}$, with the pattern $\hat{5}$–$\hat{5}$, is more ambiguous, and could mean both an IAC (V–I) or a HC (I–V).*
6. *A phrase ending on $\hat{2}$ ($\hat{3}$–$\hat{2}$) or $\hat{7}$ ($\hat{1}$–$\hat{7}$) is a clear sign of a HC.*

♪♪♪ Example 6.2   Louise Reichardt, "Frühlingsblumen," mm. 1–8

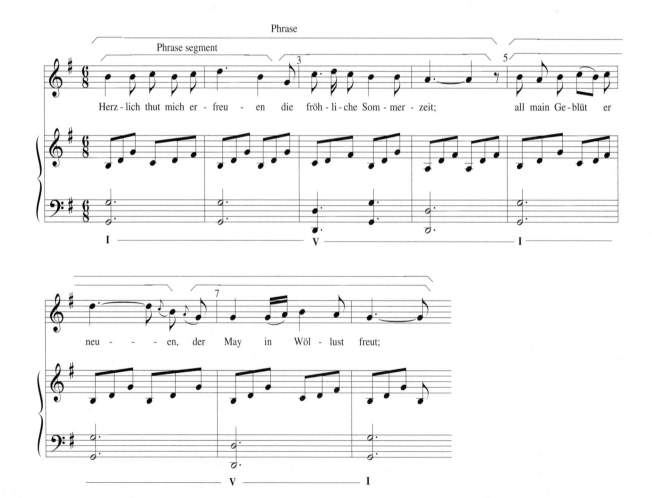

Phrase Segment

The two phrases in the Reichardt example (mm. 1–4 and 5–8) can each be broken up into smaller segments. We mentioned that mm. 1–2 display some degree of musical independence, at least melodically. The same is true for mm. 3–4, 5–6, and 7–8, as indicated by the lower level of brackets. The divisions of a phrase are called **phrase segments** or **subphrases**. The second phrase (mm. 4–8) is equally made up of two phrase segments.

Sentence Structure

The first phrase of anthology, no. 50 (R. Schumann, *Album for the Young,* "Folk Song," mm. 1–4) also features two distinctive segments, mm. 1–2 and 3–4. Phrase segments may contain contrasting thematic material, as in Schumann's example, or similar material, as in anthology, no. 27 (Mozart, Sonata in AM, K. 331, I). The latter example also illustrates a particular type of phrase structure known as **sentence**. A sentence opens with a melodic segment (m. 1 in Mozart's K.331) which is immediately restated, transposed or untransposed (m. 2 in K.331, a transposition down a step of m. 1). This is usually followed by a passage twice the length of the original segment (mm. 3–4 in our case), which leads to a cadence. Refer now to anthology, no. 32 (Beethoven, Sonata in Fm, op. 2, no.1, mm. 1–8) and explain why this phrase is a sentence.

Phrase Connections: Elision

Phrases may be distinctly separated, or they may overlap. Musical factors such as rests, fermatas, or long notes can help in the determination of phrase length. In Reichardt's example above, the HC in m. 4 supports a long A in the melody followed by a rest, all of which stresses the cadence's role as a point of momentary repose. Each phrase in Bach's Chorale 29 (anthology, no.10a) closes with a fermata, leaving little doubt as to the length and number of phrases in this example.

The end of a phrase, however, may also overlap with the beginning of the next phrase (that is, end and beginning may share the same pitch) in what we know as an **elision.** In example 6.3, the first phrase ends on the downbeat of m. 5, while the second phrase begins on the same downbeat. The brackets above and below this excerpt show that the two phrases are connected by means of elision. Do the two-measure phrase segments also feature elision? You may also study the elisions in anthology, no. 25 (Mozart, Sonata in CM, K. 309, I, mm. 7–8) and example 2.1 (Beethoven, *Seven Peasant Dances,* no. 4).

EXERCISE

To practice the analysis of phrase and cadence structures, refer to exercise 6.1 (questions 1 to 3) in worksheet 6 at the end of this chapter.

PERIOD STRUCTURE

Phrases are often grouped into larger units. A **period** is a group of two or more phrases that ends on a conclusive cadence (normally PAC, occasionally IAC), and that contains one or more inner cadences (normally HC or IAC) *weaker* than the final one. Three of the examples we have discussed above meet these conditions. In the Reichardt example (example 6.2), the first phrase ends on a HC, while the second phrase closes with a PAC, thus confirming its periodic structure. Discuss how both R. Schumann's "Folk Song" fragment (anthology, no. 50) and Mozart's Sonata in AM (anthology, no. 27), mm. 1–8, are examples of periods.

Antecedent-Consequent Structure

Now refer back to Reichardt's example. We know that the first phrase reaches a HC in m. 4, which, of course, is inconclusive harmonically. You could think of this type of phrase as a "question." The second phrase, conclusive because of the PAC at the end of it, can be thought of as the "answer." Two phrases that form a period and which have this type of musical "question-answer" relationship because the first phrase ends on a HC, while the second one ends on a PAC, are called **antecedent** (the first phrase) and **consequent** (the second phrase). Antecedent-consequent structures are very common in music, especially in the Classical period. Are the Schumann and Mozart periods which we just mentioned above also antecedent-consequent structures?

♪♪♪Example 6.4   S. Foster, "Gentle Annie" (Verse)

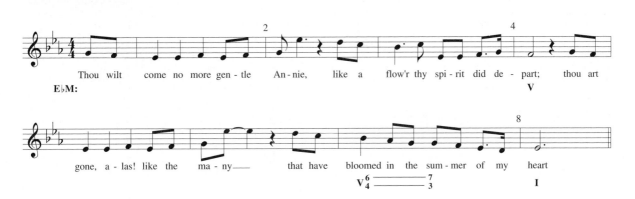

Thou wilt   come no more gen - tle   An - nie,   like a   flow'r thy spi - rit did de - part;   thou art

E♭M: V

gone, a - las! like the   ma - ny——   that have   bloomed in   the sum - mer   of my   heart

$$V^6_4 \text{———} ^7_3 \qquad I$$

Parallel Period

The two phrases in an antecedent-consequent structure do not necessarily need to be related thematically. In Mozart's AM sonata, however, they obviously are, at least for two measures (mm. 1–2 are the same as mm. 5–6). This is an example of a **parallel period**. A parallel period has two phrases that are in antecedent-consequent relationship, and both *begin* with the same (or similar) material. Phrase endings are different, however, because the first phrase ends on a HC and the second phrase ends on a PAC. A parallel period appears in anthology, no. 28 (Mozart's Piano Sonata in B♭M, K. 333, III), mm. 1–8. Discuss the motivic, phrase (Are there phrase segments? Are they contrasting or similar?), and cadential structures in this example. Now sing the melody in example 6.4, and comment on its phrase structure. Is it an antecedent-consequent structure? And a parallel period? Why?

EXERCISE

To practice writing a parallel period, refer to exercise 6.2 in worksheet 6 at the end of this chapter.

FORM DIAGRAMS

We will use graphic **form diagrams** of the type known as **line** or **bubble diagrams** to summarize visually the form and formal relationships of a composition or a section. Sections of a composition and their length are represented on a line, and slurs ("bubbles") are used for the same purpose as additional visual references. The bubbles, moreover, are hierarchical: A bubble may include other bubbles, which in turn may include other bubbles, and so on, to indicate different formal levels. We indicate thematic relationship between phrases by means of lowercase letters. Phrases with the same thematic material are designated with the same letter, whereas different letters indicate contrasting material.

♪♪♪Example 6.5   Form Diagram for Anthology, no. 27 (Mozart, AM Sonata), mm. 1–8

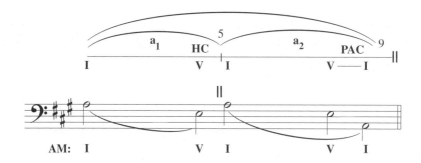

The diagram in example 6.5 refers to the period in anthology, no. 27 (Mozart, AM sonata, mm. 1–8): The letters a_1–a_2 indicate that the two phrases are related thematically. Capital letters will be used to indicate thematic relationships between formal units at a higher level than the phrase (phrase pairs, periods, etc.).

The long-range tonal motion of phrases and periods, essential to the articulation of form, is mostly determined by their beginning and cadential harmonies. In our diagrams, tonal motion is represented by Roman numerals under the line, and cadences will be labeled with the usual abbreviations (PAC, HC, etc.). You will find this type of graph very useful to express the main formal characteristics of a piece, and to compare different pieces among themselves at a glance. The graph in example 6.5, for instance, tells us that Mozart's period is made up of two phrases related thematically, that the first phrase begins on I and ends on a HC (antecedent), and that the second phrase also begins on I but ends on a PAC (consequent). Hence, the two phrases constitute a parallel period.

BASS REDUCTIONS

In chapter 2 you were introduced to a type of graph we call *bass reductions*. We can use bass reductions to show in a graphic way harmonic motion, harmonic function, and harmonic hierarchy in a formal context. For the time being, our bass reductions will include only tonic and dominant chords that have a formal or structural significance, in other words, those that determine the beginning and ending of phrases and periods, in the way we already discussed in chapter 2. Example 2.5 in that chapter consisted of the bass reduction for the initial period of Mozart's AM sonata, the same period we have diagrammed above. Under the bubble diagram in example 6.5 you can see the same bass reduction reproduced again and how the information in the reduction matches the information in the bubble diagram. As a matter of fact, both types of graphs can be used together very effectively. To review the exact meaning of symbols in bass reductions, refer back to chapter 2.

NOTE

Form diagrams indicate formal design, *that is, length of formal units and thematic relationships among them. Bass reductions, on the other hand, indicate* tonal structure, *or tonal motion. Both types of graphs should not contradict each other (for instance, an important cadence closing a formal unit should also appear as structurally important in the bass reduction). However, because they actually show different things, formal diagrams and bass reductions may or may not correspond exactly with each other. For instance, in a four-phrase design, phrase 1 may begin and end on the tonic, phrase 2 may lead to and cadence on the dominant, phrase 3 may begin and end on the dominant (and thus it will function as a prolongation of the dominant established at the end of phrase 2), and phrase 4 may again begin and end on the tonic. Whereas in this case the formal diagram will show a four-phrase design, the bass reduction will show a three-part tonal structure (I—I V—V I—I). You will find a structure with these characteristics if you look ahead at examples 20.4 and 20.5.*

EXERCISE

To practice realizing form diagrams and bass reductions, refer to the section, "Further Analysis," on page 253, and to exercise 6.1 in worksheet 6 at the end of this chapter.

MORE ON PERIOD STRUCTURE

Contrasting Period

Unlike a parallel period, the two phrases in a **contrasting period** are not based on the same thematic material, as illustrated by anthology, no. 37 (Kuhlau, Sonatina, op. 55/4, II, mm. 1–8). The letters a and b in example 6.6 indicate that the two phrases in this fragment are not related thematically. Harmonically, this is still an antecedent-consequent structure, because the first phrase ends on a HC and the second on a PAC. You may remark that the second phrase does not begin on the tonic, but rather on the dominant. The chord at m. 5, a V_7 in third inversion (V_2^4), prolongs the dominant harmony on which the first phrase ends. The complete second phrase may actually be seen as a dominant prolongation, which does not fully resolve until the final tonic.

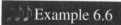Example 6.6   Form Diagram for Anthology, no. 37 (Kulhau, Sonatina), mm. 1–8

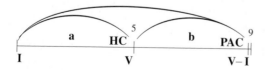

Example 6.7   W. A. Mozart, Sonata in FM, K. 332, I, mm. 1–12

Symmetrical and Asymmetrical Periods

In a **symmetrical period**, both phrases have the same length. Both examples 6.5 (Mozart, AM sonata) and 6.6 (Kulhau, sonatina) represent symmetrical periods. Considering the number of measures in each of the phrases, we can describe both of these periods as having a 4 + 4 phrase structure. In an **asymmetrical period**, phrases are not of equal length. Example 6.7 illustrates a twelve-measure period, in which the two contrasting phrases (mm. 1–4 and 5–12) are, respectively, four and eight measures long (4 + 8). Although the rest in the melody in m. 4 clearly separates the first phrase from the second, could one argue for elision considering the harmonic phrase in the left hand?

Three-Phrase Period

Listen to anthology, no. 30 (Mozart, "Die Zufriedenheit"). The first phrase ends in m. 5, with an inconclusive cadence on D, V in GM. The second phrase ends again on a HC in m. 9. A third phrase finally brings the song to a conclusion, in m. 14, with a PAC on G. Because this final cadence is conclusive and the previous two are not, the three phrases constitute a period, in this case **three-phrase period**. The diagram and bass reduction in example 6.8 show the formal characteristics of this song. Because phrases 2 and 3 are related motivically (compare mm. 6–7 with mm. 10–11), we assign to them the letter symbols b_1 and b_2. The second phrase begins and ends on V, and thus we consider it a harmonic prolongation of the cadential V in m. 5. The bass reduction shows this extension of V by means of a black, unstemmed D connected to the open D in m. 5 with a slur.

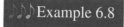Example 6.8   Form Diagram and Bass Reduction for Anthology, no. 30 (Mozart, "Die Zufriedenheit")

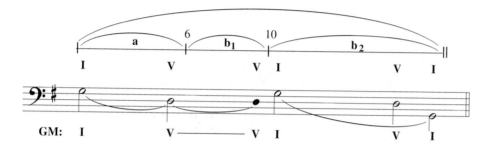

EXERCISE

To practice writing a three-phrase period, refer to exercise 6.3 in worksheet 6 at the end of this chapter.

Double Period

Listen now to anthology, no. 33 (Beethoven, Sonata in Cm, op. 10/1, II, mm. 1–16), marking phrases and cadences on the score as you listen. You will hear and see that the complete passage forms a single period (the only PAC is at the end), and that it has four phrases, each four measures long. Moreover, you will hear that the four phrases are grouped in pairs. This type of four-phrase period with phrases grouped in pairs is called **double period**. The first part of such a period (which ends on a weak cadence) thus comprises two phrases. The second part consists of two more phrases and ends on a PAC. In anthology, no. 33, phrases 1 and 2 are contrasting (a_1 and b_1, mm. 1–4 and 5–8), and both end on HCs. Phrase 3 (a_2, mm. 9–12) is a varied repetition of the first phrase (the accompaniment changes), and phrase 4, b_2, is itself a variation of phrase 2, leading in this case to the conclusive PAC. Considering the two parts of the period (A_1 and A_2, mm. 1–8 and 9–16), this is an antecedent-consequent structure, as well as a parallel and symmetrical period.

Study and understand the form diagram and bass reduction in example 6.9, and listen again to the fragment while following and "hearing" the diagram/reduction. Notice that the different formal levels are notated with different symbols in the bass reduction. The HC cadence in m. 8 and the PAC in m. 16 are more important than the cadences in mm. 4 and 12 because they represent a higher grouping of phrases (2 + 2) than the level of the individual phrase. The cadence in m. 8, moreover, not only closes the first pair of phrases, but also features a melodic interruption at $\hat{2}$, before the music starts all over again at the beginning of the consequent. The final cadence in m. 16 provides the closing resolution which the melody did not reach in m. 8. In the graph, both

♪♪♪ **Example 6.9**   Form Diagram and Bass Reduction for Anthology, no. 33 (Beethoven, Sonata op. 10/1)

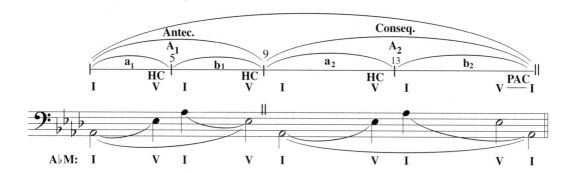

cadences in mm. 8 and 16 are notated as open notes, whereas the single-phrase cadences in mm. 4 and 12 are notated with stemmed black notes to signify their secondary role within the double period.

Modulating Period

Music does not always stay in the same key. The process of moving from one key to another is known as **modulation**. Examine the parallel period in example 6.10. The key signature and the beginning of the period establish the key of FM. The antecedent ends on a HC in FM (m. 4). The end of the consequent, however, features a

♪♪♪ **Example 6.10**   S. Foster, "Jeanie with the Light Brown Hair" (Chorus)

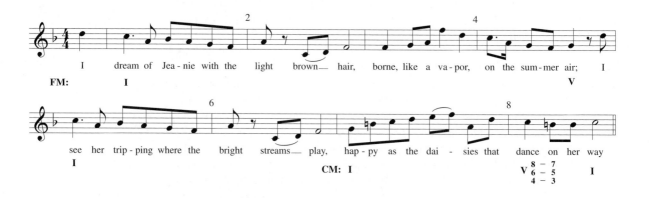

The Technique of Interruption

In the above section on antecedent-consequent structure, we discussed that the HC in m. 4 of the Reichardt period is inconclusive. The phrase that ends on this HC is also inconclusive melodically, because the melodic motion in m. 4 stops on the pitch A, $\hat{2}$ in GM, a degree that obviously has a tendency, in this context, to continue or resolve to $\hat{1}$ (notice the line descending from D to A in mm. 3–4). In chapter 2 we discussed a very similar situation (in Mozart's AM sonata), and we explained that the harmonic and melodic motions toward I and $\hat{1}$ are interrupted at this point in this type of phrase. Instead of resolving the tension by a melodic motion to $\hat{1}$, the phrase begins all over again, and finally reaches its goal in m. 8, where the resolution of $\hat{2}$ to $\hat{1}$ is completed.

1. The following fragments feature examples of melodic interruption. Identify the exact location for the interruption, as well as the eventual resolution of the interrupted line to $\hat{1}$: anthology, no. 28 (Mozart, Piano Sonata in B♭M, K. 333, III, mm. 1–8) and anthology, no. 26 (Mozart, Piano Sonata in CM, K. 309, III, mm. 1–19). Because in a period you can expect to find the interruption on $\hat{2}$ at a HC, you should first determine the cadential and phrase structure of these fragments.

2. Realize bubble diagrams and bass reductions for the following periods: Reichardt, "Frühlingsblumen," mm. 1–8 (example 6.2), and R. Schumann, "Folk Song," mm. 1–8 (anthology, no. 50).

PAC in CM (m. 8). Although the key signature is still FM because that is the main key of the complete song, by mm. 7–8 we have modulated to CM, as confirmed by the clear PAC in the new key. A period may indeed begin in a key, modulate to a different key, and end on a PAC *in the new key*. Such a period is a **modulating period**. Explain how this same process works in anthology, no. 24 (Mozart, Sonata in DM, K. 284, I, mm. 1–8) and in anthology, no. 12 (Bach, *French Suite* no. 5, "Gavotte," mm. 1–8).

EXERCISE

To practice analysis of a variety of period structures, refer to exercise 6.1 (questions 4 to 7) in worksheet 6 at the end of this chapter.

PHRASE GROUP

A group of two or more phrases that does not end on a PAC or a IAC is not a period. We refer to such a musical unit as a **phrase group**. Examine the two initial phrases in anthology, no. 57 (Hugo Wolf, "Das verlassene Mägdlein," mm. 5–12). The first phrase, in Am, closes on a HC, and so does the second phrase. Because both phrases end on half cadences and the unit does not end on a conclusive cadence, this is a phrase group and not a period.

EXERCISE

To practice realizing a figured bass and harmonizing a given melody, in application of concepts learned in previous chapters, refer to exercises 6.4 and 6.5 in worksheet 6 at the end of this chapter.

PRACTICAL APPLICATION AND DISCUSSION

1. The types of structures we have discussed in this chapter are best found in compositions of the Classical period (by composers such as Haydn, Mozart, Beethoven, and their contemporaries, and also by nineteenth-century composers such as Schubert, Mendelssohn, and Chopin) and in dance pieces by late-baroque composers (such as minuets, bourrées, gavottes, etc., by Bach, Handel, and many others). Try to find, in the pieces you perform (by these or any other composers), examples of some of the following items: a phrase (or larger unit) based on a motive, two phrases connected by an elision, a parallel period, an antecedent-consequent structure, a three-phrase period, a double period, a modulating period, and a phrase group. You will probably not find examples of all these in the pieces you play, but try to find as many as you can, and bring your findings to class for possible class discussion.

2. How does your understanding of cadences, phrase and period structure, and types of periods affect your appreciation of the music you listen to and perform? Why is the understanding of form and long-range tonal relationships among formal units important for a musician? Apply this discussion to one of the examples from the anthology you have analyzed in this chapter (such as the fragments from Mozart's AM sonata, I; Mozart's CM sonata, III; or Beethoven's Cm sonata, op. 10/1, II). How does the knowledge of form and tonal relationships affect the way you hear and would perform any of these examples?

ASSIGNMENT

For an analytical assignment based on the materials learned in this chapter, and for a variety of writing assignments, refer to chapter 6 in the workbook.

 Composers and Their Music 6

Biographies

Write short biographies of the following composers mentioned in this chapter or in worksheet 6: Louise Reichardt; Manuel de Falla; Joseph Boulogne, Chevalier de Saint–Georges; Amy Beach.

Listening

Listen to the following compositions by composers mentioned in this chapter:

Reichardt: Selected songs, as available in your music library.

Chevalier de Saint–Georges: A *symphonie concertante* or a violin concerto, as available in your music library.

Beach: Symphony no. 1 in Em.

Falla: *The Three-Cornered Hat.*

Follow the score while you listen. Be able to place these compositions in one of the style periods, and to comment on why and how they represent the musical characteristics of that period.

As you listen, apply as many of the concepts you have learned in this chapter as possible. For instance, try to identify important cadences visually (if the score is available) and aurally (directly from the recording). Hear phrases and their possible relationships. Are some of them grouped into periods and antecedent-consequent structures? If you hear a period, is it parallel or contrasting? Is the music motivic (that is, is it built on a clearly recognizable motive)?

Terms for Review

Form
Motive
Rhythmic motive
Phrase
Implied harmony
Melodic cadential patterns
Phrase segment, subphrase
Sentence structure
Elision
Period
Antecedent
Consequent

Parallel period
Form diagram
Line (bubble) diagram
Contrasting period
Symmetrical period
Asymmetrical period
Three-phrase period
Double period
Modulation
Technique of interruption
Modulating period
Phrase group

Worksheet 6

EXERCISE 6.1   Analysis. Study the phrase/period structure of the following examples. For each of the examples, provide a brief discussion of structure, including at least the following information:

1. Is the fragment based on a motive?

2. How many phrases are there? Provide measure numbers and phrase numbers for each. Are any phrases connected by elision?

3. Identify the cadences at the end of each phrase. In cases where only a melody is given, you can identify cadences on the basis of the given Roman numerals and the cadential melodic gestures.

4. Is there any antecedent-consequent phrase structure?

5. What kind of a period is this? One or several of the following may apply to each example: parallel, contrasting, symmetrical, asymmetrical, three-phrase (or four-phrase), double, modulating, phrase group (not a period).

6. Provide a line (bubble) diagram for each of the examples, indicating the following items: phrases/measure numbers; phrase relationship with letters; cadences at the end of each phrase (with a cadence-type abbreviation); and long-range harmonic motion from beginning to end of each phrase.

7. In the blank staff provided for exercise 6.1.6, realize a bass reduction of anthology, no. 23 (Chevalier de Saint–Georges, Symphonie Concertante, II, mm. 1–24), following the models provided in this chapter.

Examples for Analysis

1. Example 6.11. (Do not count phrase repetitions as independent phrases in this example.)

Example 6.11   J. Haydn, String Quartet, op. 76/3, II

Discussion:

Form diagram:

2. Example 6.12.

Example 6.12   Amy Beach, "Oh Were My Love Yon Lilac Fair!" from *Twenty-Three Songs,* op. 43, no. 3, mm. 3–10

Discussion:

Form diagram:

3. Example 6.13.

Example 6.13   Manuel de Falla, *The Three-Cornered Hat,* "The Neighbor's Dance," mm. 1–16

Discussion:

Form diagram:

_____

4. Anthology, no. 31 (Paradis, *Sicilienne,* mm. 1–10)

Discussion:

Form diagram:

_____

5. Example 6.14.

Example 6.14   Chevalier de Saint–Georges, Symphonie Concertante in AM, op. 10, no. 2, I, mm. 1–16

Discussion:

Form diagram:

_____

6. Anthology, no. 23 (Chevalier de Saint–Georges, Symphonie Concertante, II)

Discussion:

Form diagram:

_____

EXERCISE 6.2   Write a melody in antecedent-consequent form (a parallel period). The beginning is given. Be ready to sing or play your melody if asked by your instructor.

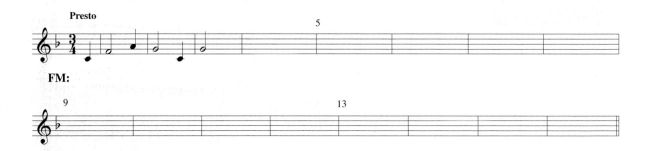

FM:

EXERCISE 6.3   Write a melody with the following characteristics: a three-phrase period, form a–b–a or a_1–b–a_2, twelve measures long. Make it musical, and be able to sing or play it. Indicate (with cadence-type abbreviations) what cadences are implied at the end of each phrase.

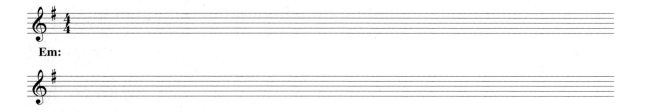

Em:

Although the present chapter did not cover any new chords or part-writing material, you should keep practicing the skills you have learned in previous chapters. The following part-writing exercises are included here for this purpose.

EXERCISE 6.4   Analyze the following progression with RNs, and realize in four voices. Remember to verify the outer-voice frame for good first-species counterpoint.

EXERCISE 6.5   Harmonize the following melody with a bass and RNs, following the given HR. Harmonize the notes indicated by a 6 with triads in first inversion. Use only i, iv, and V in root position and first inversion.

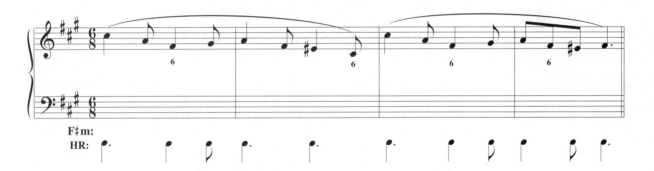

Chapter 7

Melodic Organization II: Thematic Development; Phrase Extension; Formal Functions

Along with harmonic development, melodic or thematic development is one of the basic forces of musical growth. The term **thematic development** refers to the musical process by which melodic material is derived from a previously presented theme or melody, or to the process of musical growth by which themes or melodies generate extended sections. Such musical growth is effected by means of a variety of developmental techniques. Thematic development is both a melodic and a harmonic process, and both processes interact and influence each other. In this chapter we will first focus specifically on some of the standard techniques of melodic development. The techniques we will examine may be found even within the scope of a period (for instance, when the two phrases in a parallel period are related but not identical) or within a phrase (when, for instance, the phrase is derived from a single motive). After studying melodic developmental techniques, we will focus on *phrase extension*. Phrases can be expanded in a variety of ways, often using the same means of melodic development we will discuss in the first part of the chapter.

MELODIC DEVELOPMENTAL TECHNIQUES

Compositions or movements usually begin with one or more sections in which the musical materials on which the piece is based are presented. Later sections in the piece, however, often have the function of developing the material that was presented earlier. At times, the new material presented at the beginning is very brief, perhaps just a short motive (what Beethoven symphony is based on a very brief and well-known motive presented at the very outset?), and even the initial section is based on the immediate development of that motive. We will now examine some of the most common techniques of melodic and motivic development.

Repetition and Transposition

The **repetition** of a motive or a phrase is a basic means of formal growth. Repetition implies restatement of a segment at exactly the same tonal level. Examine example 7.1a and identify several instances of repetition of a motive or a melodic segment, in

Example 7.1a   J. S. Bach, Brandenburg Concerto no. 2, I, mm. 1–5

Example 7.1b   J. S. Bach, Invention no. 1 in CM, mm. 1–2

Example 7.1c   F. Chopin, Mazurka no. 45 in Am, op. posth. 67, no. 4, mm. 1–8

Example 7.1d   Nikolay Rimsky-Korsakov, *Scheherazade,* III, mm. 1–4

this case all within a single phrase. A repetition stated at a different tonal level than the original segment is a transposed repetition, or a **transposition**. In example 7.1b, the motive which begins Bach's Invention in CM is first stated at the level of the tonic (m. 1), and then repeated a 5th higher, at the level of the dominant. In chapter 6 we studied the sentence, a type of phrase structure that includes repetition or transposition (of the intial segment) as a means of formal growth. Example 7.1c shows a sentence by Chopin, in which the first phrase segment (mm. 1–2) is repeated a 3rd lower in mm. 3–4.

Variation

Repetition may be literal, as in example 7.1a, or varied. In a *varied repetition* (or **variation**) the basic frame of the melody is preserved, but the original motive or phrase is now altered in some way (embellished with added notes or figuration, simplified, rhythmically altered, etc.). An example of varied repetition by Nikolay Rimsky-Korsakov appears in example 7.1d. Circle, in m. 3 (the varied repetition of m. 1), the notes from the original statement in m. 1.

Melodic Sequence

In a **melodic sequence**, several immediate restatements of a melodic *segment* occur at a lower or higher tonal level. A melodic sequence thus involves transposition of a melodic segment, but usually the original segment is immediately transposed several times in a row, in a pattern of transpositions that rises or falls by intervals of the same size (often, but not necessarily, by steps) or by patterns of paired intervals (a motive may be sequentially transposed, for instance, following the pattern "down a 3rd, up a step"). Notice that in a sequence the restatement takes place *in the same voice,* as opposed to imitation, where a theme is restated in a different voice. The melody by George Gerswhin reproduced in example 7.2a includes a three-measure sequence descending by steps (each sequence segment, marked with brackets on the example, is a step lower than the previous segment).

In example 7.2a, the sequence goes down by steps following the diatonic scale of CM, which means that the exact relationships of steps and half steps between segments are not preserved, as you will see immediately by playing or singing the Gershwin melody. This type of sequence is called a **tonal sequence**. Look now at anthology, no. 24 (Mozart, Sonata in DM), m. 9, a two-segment sequence. You will notice that, because some of the pitches have been altered, the first and second segments feature exactly the same intervallic relationships. This is a **real sequence**, in which the exact intervallic relationships are preserved. What kind of sequence can you identify in m. 10 of the same Mozart example?

A sequence in which the restatement of the segment is not literal, not because of the normal step and half-step diatonic relationships, but because some variation has been introduced, is called a **modified sequence**. Some intervals, for instance, may have been expanded or contracted (see "Intervallic Expansion and Contraction," on page 267). In anthology, no. 20 (Haydn, Sonata in DM), mm. 1–2 present an example of modified sequence. What interval has been altered?

♪♪♪Example 7.2a   Ira Gershwin–George Gershwin, "Someone to Watch Over Me," from *Oh, Kay!*

There's a some-bo-dy I'm   long-ing to see   I hope that he   turns out to be   some-one to

watch o - ver   me.

♪♪♪Example 7.2b   J. S. Bach, Invention no. 1 in CM, mm. 3–5

CM   GM

Sequences are often used as a means to modulate, and they are then called **modulating sequences**. In some cases the sequence begins in one key and leads to a different key by the introduction of accidentals proper to the new key. Such is the case of example 7.2b, a sequence that begins in CM and ends in GM after the introduction of the F♯ which leads into the new key. In anthology, no. 32 (Beethoven, Sonata op. 2/1), mm. 68–73, the left hand features a modulating sequence in which each segment is in a different key. What is the key for each segment? Is this a real or a tonal sequence?

Change of Mode

The theme of Vivaldi's "Spring" (from *The Four Seasons*), III, as shown in example 7.3, mm. 58–61, is in EM. In m. 61, however, Vivaldi begins a sequence on this theme by stating the first sequence segment (derived from the theme) in Em rather than EM. Besides featuring repetition and descending sequence by steps, this example is thus also an illustration of **change of mode** as a technique of melodic development. In change of mode the key remains the same, but the mode changes from major to minor, or vice versa.

Example 7.3   A. Vivaldi, *The Four Seasons,* "Spring," III, mm. 58–64

Fragmentation

Melodic development is often based on a fragment of the original theme rather than the complete unit. Such technique is known as **fragmentation**. The fragment may be repeated, presented as a sequence, or subjected to any other kind of developmental transformation. Example 7.4 illustrates Beethoven's use of fragmentation in his Symphony no. 6 in FM, I. Example 7.4a presents the first theme of the movement. The theme begins with two characteristic motives, labeled "a" and "b" in example 7.4a. The initial motive of the theme (motive "a") is treated sequentially in example 7.4b, whereas motive "b" generates the repeated figure represented in example 7.4c. A similar instance of combined fragmentation and sequence appears in example 7.5 (Beethoven, Symphony no. 7 in AM, I). The phrase in example 7.5a (part of the first theme) includes the fragment or motive labeled "a" in the example. This motive later generates the sequence reproduced in example 7.5b. Taking into consideration the accidentals in example 7.5b, what other type of developmental technique is used in this passage?

Example 7.4   From L. v. Beethoven, Symphony no. 6, I

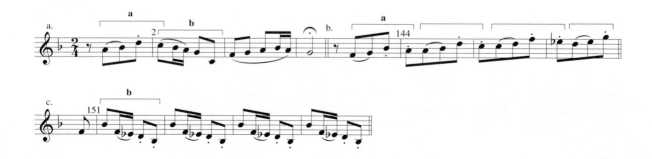

♪♪♪ Example 7.5   From L. v. Beethoven, Symphony no. 7, I

Intervallic Expansion and Contraction

You may have observed that, although example 7.4c is clearly derived from m. 2 in example 7.4a, the intervals are not at all the same. In thematic development, motives are at times immediately recognizable by their characteristic contour and rhythm, although some intervals may have been replaced by other larger or smaller intervals, in what we call **intervallic expansion** or **contraction**. Example 7.6a shows how the first interval in Beethoven's motive has been expanded from a M2 to a P4 and the last interval has been contracted from a P5 to a M3. Are there any examples of intervallic expansion or contraction in example 7.5b? The passage in example 7.6b is highly motivic, and it includes several cases of intervallic expansion or contraction. Explain what the exact transformation is in each case.

♪♪♪ Example 7.6a

♪♪♪ Example 7.6b   Marianne Martínez, Sonata in AM, mm. 4–5

♪♪♪ Example 7.7   J. S. Bach, *The Well-Tempered Clavier*, I, Fugue no. 8 in D♯m, Subject

Inversion

An **inversion** is a mirror image of a melody. In an inversion the contour of the melody and the direction of intervals are reversed: ascending motion becomes descending, and vice versa. In Bach's Fugue in D♯m (*Well-Tempered Clavier,* I, no. 8), some statements of the subject (the main theme of a fugue) are presented in inversion. Compare the original form and its inversion, reproduced in example 7.7. Compare also the two phrases in the opening period of Mozart's Sonata in DM, K. 284, I (anthology, no. 24,

♪♪♪ Example 7.8   J. S. Bach, *A Musical Offering* (Retrograde Canon)

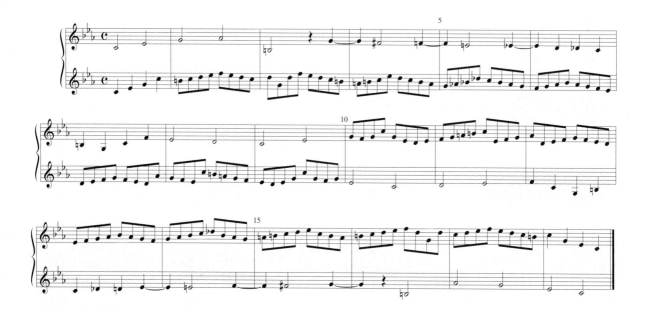

mm. 1–8). The eighth-note figure in the second half of m. 5 and first half of m. 6 is an inversion of the equivalent figure in mm. 1–2. Inversion can thus also be used as a variation device between two parallel phrases.

Melodic Retrograde

Whereas inversion involves reading a melody upside down, to **retrograde** a melody is to read it backward. Although melodic retrograde is seldom used in homophonic music, it is a device found in contrapuntal music. Example 7.8 is a two-voice **retrograde canon** by Bach. A **canon** is a "rule" by which a voice is derived from another voice (a **round** is a type of perpetual canon, in which several voices sing the same melody but each voice comes in when the previous voice reaches a certain point). Bach's original score provides only the top voice. The bottom voice is derived from the top by a canon (rule) which can be very simply expressed. Find the canon in this composition, and discuss in class why this is called a retrograde canon (or, also, a crab canon).

Augmentation

Augmentation and its equivalent, *diminution,* are examples of rhythmic transformations of motives or themes. Augmentation is the statement of a theme in proportionally longer rhythmic values. Most often, rhythmic values are doubled, tripled, or quadrupled. In the same fugue by Bach which we mentioned in example 7.7 (Fugue in D♯m), the subject is also presented in augmentation, with doubled values. Example 7.9 compares the original statement of the theme with its augmented version.

Diminution

The opposite process to augmentation, **diminution**, is the statement of a theme in proportionally shorter rhythmic values. Example 7.10 reproduces two instances of diminution from Beethoven's Symphony no. 3 in E♭M (*Eroica*), IV. In example 7.10a,

♪♪♪ Example 7.9

a.

b.   Augmentation

one of the two main themes in the movement is first stated in its original form, and toward the end of the movement it appears in diminution. Example 7.10b reproduces a fragment by the second violins in which a three-note figure is stated four times in descending sequence, twice in original values, twice more in diminution.

EXERCISES

To practice the analysis and recognition of various techniques of melodic development, refer to exercise 7.1 (items 1 to 9) in worksheet 7 at the end of this chapter.

To practice writing various techniques of melodic transformation, refer to exercise 7.2 in worksheet 7 at the end of this chapter.

PHRASE EXTENSION

In chapter 6 we studied a variety of phrase and period structures. A phrase can be lengthened by adding a melodic fragment to it, and developmental techniques such as the ones we studied above are often used in the process. A transformation that adds length to a phrase is called a **phrase extension**. Repetition, variation, and sequence are some techniques frequently found in phrase extensions. An extension may take place at the beginning of a phrase (*initial extension*), within a phrase (*internal extension* or *interpolation*), or at the end of a phrase (*cadential extension*). We will now study some specific examples of each of these three types of extension.

Initial Extension

A melodic unit may be lengthened by adding notes to its beginning, in what we call **initial extension**. The theme from Bach's Invention no. 3 in DM appears in example 7.11a. In later statements, this theme includes an initial extension, which lengthens its anacrusic (or pickup) segment (example 7.11b).

Initial extensions are not always melodic. Opening phrases, especially in songs, are often preceded by an introductory accompanimental figure that functions as a har-

♪♪♪Example 7.11   J. S. Bach, Invention no. 3 in DM, Theme

monic prefix. Examples of this type of initial extension can be found in anthology, no. 42 (Schubert, "Auf dem Flusse") and no. 48 (Schumann, "Widmung").

Cadential Extension

Refer back to example 5.1, the closing passage for the first movement of a Haydn sonata. You will see that mm. 95–97 are made up of a series of cadential gestures. The cadence in m. 95 is a perfect authentic cadence (PAC), and it could have been the concluding cadence of the movement, had Haydn wished to stop there. Instead, he wrote four additional PACs, further strengthening the sense of final closure. We can say that the four additional cadences in mm. 95–97 are a **cadential extension**, because their function is to expand the PAC cadence in m. 95. A cadential extension is a fragment added at the end of a musical unit, usually after the cadence. It may take the form, as in the Haydn example, of a few re-iterations of the V–I cadence, as if to confirm that this is indeed the final cadence; it may also be a slightly longer addition (often called a **codetta**), including some thematic material; or it may be an extended section, sometimes of substantial length, at the end of a movement. We call the latter case a **coda**. We will now examine some of the shorter types of cadential extension (for a discussion and example of coda, refer to page 277).

Refer to anthology, no. 25 (Mozart, Sonata in CM, K. 309, I), mm. 54–58. This passage closes the first large section of this movement and leads to a PAC in GM in mm. 57–58. Now look at the end of the movement, mm. 148–155. We first recognize the same passage from mm. 54–58, now in mm. 148–151, and in the key of CM. We would expect this passage to end on a PAC in CM in mm. 151–152. It does indeed, but instead of concluding with this cadence in m. 152, the music goes on for four more measures. A final statement of the theme that opened the movement appears in mm. 152–153, followed by a cadential gesture repeated three times in mm. 153–155. Measures 152–155 thus constitute a four-measure cadential extension.

A common type of cadential extension by means of a deceptive resolution of V is illustrated by example 7.12. Instead of resolving the V_7 directly to I in a PAC which could have ended the phrase in m. 2 of our example, Lennon and McCartney extended the phrase for three more measures by means of a deceptive resolution of V_7. (Notice that the specific type of deceptive cadence in this example involves an inverted seventh chord on ♭VI, the chromatic submediant, as indicated by the Roman numeral ♭VI$_5^6$, rather than the simpler type of resolution to the diatonic submediant, vi. ♭VI is a chromatic chord, which we will study in chapter 22.)

A slightly longer type of cadential extension, one we call a *codetta*, can be found in anthology, no. 27 (Mozart, AM sonata), variation VI. This variation closes the first movement of this sonata. By comparison with the original theme, presented at the

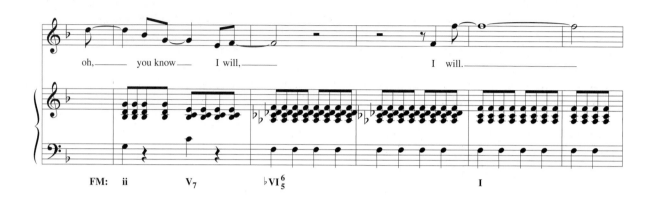

♪♪♪ Example 7.12   J. Lennon–P. McCartney, "I Will," from the Album *The Beatles* ("The White Album")

beginning of the movement, we know that the final cadence could come in m. 19, beat 3. We see a PAC in that spot, but we also see that the music then picks up new strength, to continue for eight more measures. Where is the material for this cadential extension derived from within this same variation? What role do repetition and variation play in this eight-measure codetta?

Internal Extension: Interpolation

An **interpolation** is an internal addition to a phrase. The clearest type of interpolation occurs when a phrase which has been previously stated is stated again, and this second statement includes material that has clearly been added to the original version. This is the case of example 7.13a. The opening phrase of Beethoven's Symphony no. 5, III, closes with a fermata in m. 8. The phrase is immediately repeated, but this time it closes with a fermata in m. 18. The second phrase, then, is ten measures long instead of the intial eight. The two added measures, bracketed in the example, constitute a clear interpolation.

Internal extensions provide a rich resource for a composer to vary and extend musical materials in unexpected ways, and to break the predictable balance of parallel periods and equal phrase lengths. And although an interpolation becomes obvious if there was a previous unextended original statement of the same material, very often interpolations can easily be identified even if there was no previous unextended model. We can also (ar least usually) base our recognition of extensions on criteria provided by our stylistic expectations, especially when we are dealing with periodic structures. In example 7.13b, for instance, a period by Mozart begins with a four-measure antecedent made up of two phrase segments (2 + 2 measures), and closing on the HC in m. 4. By analogy, we could expect the characteristic four-measure consequent of a parallel period, closing in m. 8 with a PAC. The PAC comes indeed, but in m. 10, not m. 8 as expected, because of the interpolation of two measures, mm. 7–8, bracketed in our example. If you play the consequent skipping from m. 6 to m. 9, you will hear the phrase as it would have been without the interpolation. Much more predictable and also less interesting, to be sure. Looking at the interpolation itself, what developmental technique does Mozart use in these two measures?

♪♪♪ Example 7.13a   L. v. Beethoven, Symphony no. 5 in Cm, op. 67, III, mm. 1–18 (violin 1 and cello parts)

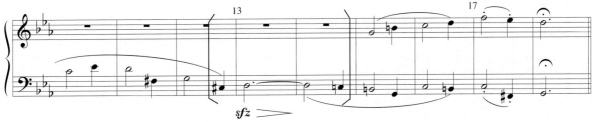

♪♪♪ Example 7.13b   W. A. Mozart, Piano Sonata in CM, K. 279, III, mm. 1–10

EXERCISE

To practice the analysis of various techniques of phrase extension, refer to exercise 7.1 (items 10 and 11) in worksheet 7 at the end of this chapter.

FURTHER ANALYSIS

Extending Period Structures

In this section we will study two somewhat more complex cases of period extension: a further case of interpolation by Mozart and a cadential extension by Beethoven.

Recomposing an extended phrase

Mozart's Piano Concerto in Dm, K. 466, III, begins with the period reproduced in example 7.14. Although we do not have any previous unextended model for this period, we can immediately see that the first phrase is four measures long (mm. 1–4), and that the consequent, instead, goes on for nine measures. This is, clearly, an extended consequent phrase, as we can easily tell by listening to it. How was this phrase extended, based on the model provided by the antecedent?

A useful way to analyze phrase extension is to "recompose" the phrase as if it were not extended, and to rework the process of extension to see how many steps are needed to achieve the final result. Example 7.15 illustrates a process of "recomposition" for the Mozart passage from example 7.14 (to simplify this example, we show the piano's right hand only). First, we can imagine the consequent to be symmetrical with the antecedent, in a 4 + 4 parallel period. Example 7.15a shows this possibility, in which the music skips from m. 7 directly to the cadence in m. 12. Although this would be a perfectly satisfactory solution (resulting in a very common type of period), it is also quite predictable in its simplicity and offers no surprise to the listener.

Now play example 7.15b. A two-measure interpolation breaks the symmetry of the period, and also the expectations of the listener, based on the model established in the antecedent. This solution would also be satisfactory, and it would introduce an element of surprise and asymmetry (this would now be a 4 + 6 asymmetrical period). Mozart, however, did not settle for this solution either. In another surprising turn which further foils our expectation, a new, four-measure interpolation extends the period to a highly asymmetrical 4 + 9 phrase structure. The new interpolation

includes a complete repetition of the previous interpolation (both are marked with brackets over the music in example 7.15c), and both statements are linked by two beats of connective material (marked with a slur). Listen to this passage again, anticipating the possible (and frustrated) resolutions to the cadence indicated in example 7.15. What is the effect of this extension process on the listener and the performer?

An extended period by Beethoven

As a final example of cadential extension, we will look at the opening period of Beethoven's Piano Sonata in Cm, op. 13, III (anthology, no. 34, mm. 1–17). The first phrase (mm. 1–4) ends on a half cadence (HC). The second and contrasting phrase (mm. 5–8) ends on a PAC, which could conclude the period if it were going to have only two phrases. The period is prolonged, however, by a third phrase, actually a repetition of the second phrase (mm. 9–12). The PAC in mm. 11–12 could again end the period. Instead, we now have a six-measure cadential extension that is more than a simple reiteration of the cadential gesture. The thematic material in mm. 12–17 is actually new, although we do not hear these final measures quite as a new phrase. They really function as a cadential extension, because their harmonic function is to prolong the tonic reached at m. 12. The final set of PAC cadences at mm. 16–17 assert and confirm both the tonal goal and the end of this rather complex period.

As a final observation on this example, notice that the cadential extension itself has two segments (mm. 12–13 and 14–17), and that the second one is a varied repetition of the first one. The extension could have ended in m. 14 if the V_7 in m. 13 had resolved to i in 14. How did Beethoven resolve this V_7 in order not to stop the harmonic motion at this point?

Listen to the Beethoven period several times, and hear each of the formal and harmonic relationships that have been discussed. How is your listening (and your performance if you were to play this piece) enriched by the understanding of the harmonic and formal function of the different parts of this fragment?

♪♪♪ Example 7.14   W. A. Mozart, Piano Concerto in Dm, K. 466, III, mm. 1–13

♪♪♪ Example 7.15

EXERCISE

To practice writing phrase extensions, refer to exercise 7.3 in worksheet 7 at the end of this chapter.

INTRODUCTION TO FORMAL FUNCTIONS; THEMATIC DEVELOPMENT IN DEVELOPMENTAL SECTIONS

Although the techniques of melodic or thematic development we have studied in this chapter can be found in any section of a composition (and, as we have seen, are even present at the phrase and period level), some sections are actually built on them. These are developmental sections, and also often transitional sections, both of which are part of a variety of formal types. We will study large formal types in chapter 26. But before we get that far, it will be useful for you to be able to hear that, depending on their context within a large-scale design, musical units have different formal functions. Specifically, you should be able to locate and understand the function of developmental sections. The following comments, although no more than an introduction to these topics, will help you listen to larger movements with some general criteria to identify formal functions.

Compositions usually have an initial, tonally stable section in which thematic material is presented and tonality is established. The formal function of such a section is *expository* (and sometimes it is even called *exposition*). Very often the expository material and key return either at the end of the composition in the form of a *recapitulation* or several times during the movement in the form of a **refrain**. The formal type based on a refrain which always returns in the same key is called a **rondo**. Listen to anthology, no. 34 (Beethoven, Sonata op. 13 in Cm, III), a rondo, and identify all the returns of the expository material (mm. 1–17, the extended period we just analyzed). The contrasting sections between refrains are called **episodes**.

Now listen to anthology, no. 32 (Beethoven, Sonata op. 2, no. 1, I). This is a *sonata allegro,* in a formal type which is usually called **sonata form**. The initial section, up to the repeat signs, is called the **exposition**. First you will hear a theme stated in Fm, the home key (mm. 1–8), then a section that takes us from Fm to AbM (mm. 9–20), followed by the new section in the latter key, in which several new themes are presented. Notice, for instance, the theme in mm. 20–24, another one in mm. 33–36, and a third one in mm. 41–43. A sonata form exposition usually has two key areas.

Now refer, as you listen, to m. 101. You will hear that the initial theme is stated again, in the original key. Not only this, but the complete exposition is repeated with a few changes, and the main one is that here the themes, which in the exposition were in AbM, now remain in the original key of Fm. This section (m. 101–end) is called the **recapitulation**, and it ultimately leads to the closing cadence. In a sonata form recapitulation, the material from the exposition returns, but now it is usually all in the main key, rather than in the two keys that were featured in the exposition. Refrains and recapitulations, which musically represent a *return,* not only of thematic material, but also of the main key, have a *resolutive function,* that is, they resolve a tension created by contrast, harmonic instability, and so forth.

Let us now focus on two sections of this movement. In the first place, the passage in mm. 9–20, as we just saw, has the function of taking us from Fm to A♭M, in other words, to modulate. This is a **transition**, hence the term *transitional function.* Transitional sections are often (although not always) developmental, that is, they build on a theme previously presented, and develop it by means of some of the techniques we have discussed in this chapter. Is this transition developmental? Is it based on the first theme? How?

The section between the exposition and the recapitulation (mm. 49–100) in a sonata form is called the **development**. This is the freest section in the movement, one in which composers may use any developmental technique to expound on some thematic material previously presented or, if they so wish, on new material. This type of section, in which thematic material is freely developed by means of any type of developmental technique, has what we call a *developmental function.* Developmental sections are harmonically unstable, that is, they modulate to a variety of keys as part of the developmental process. Discuss the development in Beethoven's sonata in terms of thematic (melodic) developmental techniques. What themes is it based on, and what techniques of melodic development can you identify?

Finally, movements, especially long ones, sometimes end with a *coda,* which, as we defined, is a large cadential extension. Codas have a *conclusive function* and bring movements to a close by means of reiterated cadential gestures. Mozart closes the third movement of his B♭M Sonata, K. 333 (anthology, no. 28) with a coda. The last section of the movement, beginning in m. 200, is a return to the refrain, and it includes a cadential extension (mm. 207–214) in which the refrain is expanded by means of inconclusive imperfect authentic cadences (IACs). After the big cadential gesture of mm. 212–214, Mozart could have written a final confirmation of the cadence, such as the one he wrote in the last two measures of the movement. Instead, he appended yet one more brief section, a conclusive coda, meant to provide still some more space for reiterated cadential gestures. Cadential extensions and codas such as these provide ample musical space for the grounding of the tensions accumulated throughout long movements.

In summary, the **formal function** of musical material may be **expository** (to present the material), **transitional** (to take us from one key area and formal section to another key area and formal section), **developmental** (to expand and develop material that, most often, has been previously presented), **resolutive** (to resolve a tension created by previous material), or **conclusive** (to bring movements or large formal sections to a close). These functions may, of course, be combined in a variety of ways (a section, for instance, may be both transitional and developmental, or resolutive and conclusive).

As an additional exercise, you may listen to two other sonata form movements in the anthology and comment on the developmental techniques used in their development sections: anthology, no. 25 (Mozart, Sonata in CM, K. 309, I; development: mm. 59–93), and anthology, no. 35 (Beethoven, Sonata in CM, op. 53, "Waldstein," I; development: mm. 90–156).

PRACTICAL APPLICATION AND DISCUSSION

1. Find examples of thematic development in at least one of the compositions you play. Identify any of the developmental techniques you have just learned.

2. If you play a sonata, or if there is one that you like to listen to, is the first movement in sonata form? If so, what developmental techniques are used in the development section? Where do the themes and motives for the development come from?

Is the last movement of your sonata in rondo form? If so, identify all the returns of the refrain. Are there any transitional sections leading into the refrain that use developmental techniques?

3. Comment on your findings in class, and discuss whether this chapter has helped you discover something interesting you did not know about the music you perform.

ASSIGNMENT

For an analytical and compositional assignment based on the materials learned in this chapter, refer to chapter 7 in the workbook.

 Composers and Their Music 7

Biographies

Write short biographies of the following composers mentioned in this chapter: Nikolay Rimsky-Korsakov, Maria Theresia von Paradis, Marianne Martínez, George Gershwin.

Listening

Listen to the following compositions by composers mentioned in this chapter:

Rimsky-Korsakov: *Sheherazade.*
Paradis: *Sicilienne.*
Beethoven: Symphony no. 5 in Cm, op. 67.
Gershwin: *Oh, Kay!*

Follow the score while you listen. Be able to place these compositions in one of the style periods, and to comment on why and how they represent the musical characteristics of that period.

As you listen to each of these pieces, pay attention to their formal aspects. Hear possible period structures, important cadences, and pay attention to formal growth and developmental processes. How would you say each of these pieces and movements grows formally? You will hear that repetition is an important factor in some of these pieces. Others are based on periodic structures. Still others are highly motivic and include extensive developments. As you listen, try to hear formal functions of different sections (expository, transitional, developmental, resolutive, or conclusive). In sections that are clearly developmental, can you recognize some of the specific developmental techniques being used?

Terms for Review

Thematic development
Repetition
Transposition
Variation
Melodic sequence
Tonal sequence

Real sequence
Modified sequence
Modulating sequence
Change of mode
Fragmentation
Intervallic expansion

Intervallic contraction
Inversion
Retrograde
Retrograde (crab) canon
Round
Augmentation
Diminution
Phrase extension
Initial extension
Cadential extension
Codetta
Coda
Internal extension (interpolation)

Refrain
Rondo
Episodes
Sonata form
Exposition
Recapitulation
Transition
Development
Formal functions:
    expository, transitional,
    developmental, resolutive,
    conclusive

Worksheet 7

EXERCISE 7.1   Analysis. Identify and name the technique(s) of thematic development or phrase extension in the following examples. In the case of sequences, identify the exact type.

1. Anthology, no. 26 (Mozart, Sonata in CM, III), mm. 5–7.

2. Anthology, no. 32 (Beethoven, op. 2, no. 1, I):

    mm. 56–59:

    mm. 61–62:

    mm. 95–100 (compare to mm. 1–2):

3. Refer back to example 4.16. The subject (theme) of this fugue is stated by the alto, mm. 1–4. What technique does Bach use for the right-hand development in mm. 13–18?

4. Example 7.16. How is fragment b related to fragment a?

 **Example 7.16**   J. S. Bach, *The Well-Tempered Clavier*, II, Fugue no. 2 in Cm

a.

b.

5. Example 7.17. How is fragment b related to fragment a?

 **Example 7.17**   J. S. Bach, *The Well-Tempered Clavier*, II, Fugue no. 3 in C♯M

a.

b.

6. Example 7.18. How is fragment b related to fragment a?

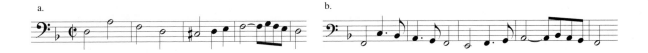

Example 7.18   J. S. Bach, *The Art of Fugue*

7. Example 7.19. Fragment b is a variation on fragment a. What technique(s) of thematic development can you identify?

Example 7.19   Sergei Rachmaninoff, *Rhapsody on a Theme of Paganini*, op. 43

8. Example 7.20.

9. Example 7.21.

10. In anthology, no. 26 (Mozart, Sonata in CM, III), the antecedent has eight mea-
    sures (mm. 1–8), and the consequent has eleven (mm. 9–19). Why? What is the
    formal role of mm. 16–18?

11. Refer to anthology, no. 31 (Paradis, *Sicilienne*).

a) Phrase 1 (mm. 1–4) is four measures long; phrase 2 (mm. 5–10) is six measures long. A possible phrase proportion for this period would be 4 + 5 instead of 4 + 6. What measure has been clearly interpolated?

b) How is the interpolated measure related with the previous one?

c) What technique of formal growth is used in mm. 11–14?

d) And in mm. 15–16?

e) How is m. 17 related to the previous two?

f) Could the cadence at m. 23 have taken place in m. 21?

What is the formal function of mm. 21–22?

By what means is this function effected (that is, how are mm. 21–22 related to mm. 19–20?)

g) Could the cadence at m. 28 have taken place in m. 27?

What is the formal function of m. 27?

How is m. 27 related to m. 28?

EXERCISE 7.2   Write new versions of the following melodies using the devices specified in each case.

a.   Bach, *The Art of Fugue.* Inversion.

b.   Bach, *The Well-Tempered Clavier* II, Fugue no. 22 in B♭m. Inversion.

c.   Bach, *The Art of Fugue.* Diminution.

d. Inversion, augmentation.

e. Luther, "Ein feste Burg." Retrograde.

f. Mozart, Symphony no. 39 in E♭M, IV. Descending sequence on the given segment: Write three missing segments, and end on 1̂ in Cm.

EXERCISE 7.3

1. Complete the following parallel period from Mozart's Symphony no. 39 in E♭M with a consequent. How was the sequence segment in exercise 7.2f above derived from this theme?

2. After you write your consequent, and using your own music paper, write four more versions of the same consequent, using the following extensions in each of them. Think musically, and write extensions that you think make good musical sense in the context of this period.

   a) An interpolation using fragmentation and sequence.

   b) An interpolation using repetition and variation.

   c) An interpolation using new melodic material.

   d) A cadential extension.

EXERCISE 7.4   Harmonize the following melody *in four voices.* Add a bass, Roman numerals (RNs), and the two inner voices. Use only I, IV, and V in root position and first inversion (for the notes indicated with a 6). Remember to double-check your outer-voice frame for good first-species counterpoint.

GM: 6   6   6

Chapter 8

Nonchord Tones

Refer again to anthology, no. 9 (Bach, "Was Gott tut"). You will remember that when you analyzed this fragment with Roman numerals in chapter 4, you were told to consider the first eighth note in each beat as the actual chord, while the second eighth note was, in this example, either a nonchord tone or a change of voicing. Examine, for instance, the first chord. It is a tonic GM triad, G–B–D, with the root doubled. The pitches A–C do not belong to the chord and create dissonances with some of the chord tones. A and C are here nonchord tones. **Nonchord tones** (NCT), also called *nonharmonic tones,* are pitches foreign to the chord with which they sound simultaneously. Nonchord tones may be consonant or dissonant but, most often, they create dissonances within the chord that contains them, and for this reason they cannot be used freely in tonal music. Rather, their use is regulated by a number of conventions to control dissonance. In general, the tenets of dissonance control require *resolution to a consonance* and, in many cases, also *preparation* (that is, a predetermined way of approaching the dissonant pitch).

In previous chapters we have already introduced both the concept of nonchord tones and some specific types of nonchord tones. In chapter D, for instance, we discussed the passing tone and the neighbor note in the context of second-species counterpoint (see examples D.6b to d), and suspensions were studied as part of fourth species. In chapter 2 we discussed again the passing tone and the concept of nonchord tones (example 2.1), and we introduced the principles of passing and neighbor motions in I–V–I progressions (example 2.2). In this chapter we will study the most common types of NCTs and their normative behavior within the consonant frame of the tonal system. The most common NCTs fall into one of the following categories: passing tones, neighbor notes, anticipations, incomplete neighbors, or suspensions. *NCTs are melodic in nature.* That is, they are not harmonic (vertical) events, but rather linear (horizontal) events. NCTs provide both tonal variety (by introducing pitches foreign to the harmonic framework) and musical tension (by introducing dissonances that need to resolve to consonances).

NOTE

An important factor to consider in the study of nonchord tones is their placement on metrically strong or weak beats or beat divisions. As you will remember from chapter B, in duple meter beat 1 is strong and beat 2 is weak. In quadruple meter, beats 1 and 3 are strong, and 2 and 4 weak. And in triple meter, only beat 1 is strong. The same principles apply to beat divisions or fractions. In a beat divided into two eighth notes, the first one is strong, the second one weak. If the division is into four sixteenth notes, notes 1 and 3 are strong, and notes 2 and 4 are weak. In beats divided into three notes (in triplets or compound meters), note 1 is strong and notes 2 and 3 are weak.

THE PASSING TONE

A **passing tone** (PT) is a NCT that fills in the gap between two chord tones (normally a 3rd). Example 8.1 features a PT in every measure but the last (the circled notes). In all six cases you will see that PTs are approached and left by step (both in the same direction), and that regular PTs fall on a weak beat or beat fraction.

PTs may occur simultaneously in two voices (**double passing tones**). Find several instances of double PTs in anthology, no. 9 ("Was Gott tut").

NOTE

The passing tones we are studying in this section are purely melodic nonchord tones. You should not confuse this type of passing tone with the type of linear passing motion that results in some harmonic progressions. In examples 2.2c and 4.7e we discussed this type of linear passing motion in the context of chordal voice leading. The same comment applies to the difference between melodic neighbor notes, which we will study later in the chapter, and linear neighbor motion in a chordal context, which we also discussed in examples 2.2c and 4.7b. The nonchord tone and the chordal voice-leading types of passing or neighboring motion result from interpretations of melodic motion at different musical levels.

A PT which fills in a 3rd is usually diatonic. A **chromatic PT**, on the other hand, fills in a whole-step gap by means of two half steps. In Beethoven's Sonata in Cm, op. 10/1, II (anthology, no. 33), chromatic PTs can be found in the top voice, mm. 2 and 4. The D♯ circled in m. 3 of example 8.3 is a chromatic PT closing the step between D and E.

An **accented passing tone** (APT) is a passing tone that falls on a strong beat or beat fraction. All the circled pitches in example 8.2a are APTs. If the gap to be filled is a 4th rather than a 3rd (as in a melodic fragment $\hat{5}$–$\hat{6}$–$\hat{7}$–$\hat{1}$ filling a $\hat{5}$–$\hat{1}$), two PTs are needed. Two such successive PTs are shown in example 8.2b, m. 8, beat 2. In this case, the first PT is unaccented and the second one accented. (The same figure in compound meter or a triplet results in two successive unaccented PTs.)

A final example by the Beatles will help you review all the different types of PTs we have discussed above. The initial harmonic progression in example 8.2c is simply I–IV–V–I in GM. And yet this simple harmony is greatly enriched by a variety of

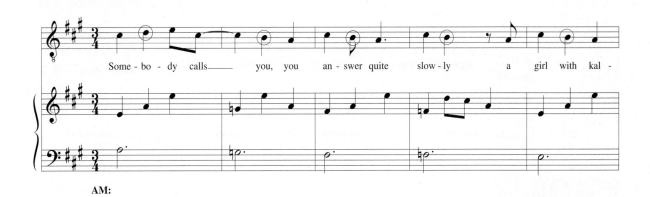

Example 8.1   J. Lennon–P. McCartney, "Lucy in the Sky with Diamonds," from the Album
Sgt. Pepper's Lonely Hearts Club Band (Verse)

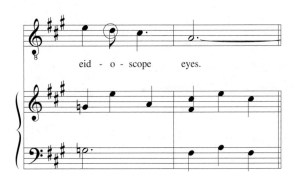

Example 8.2a   W. A. Mozart, Piano Sonata in B♭M, K. 333, I, mm. 1–4

♪♪♪ Example 8.2b   W. A. Mozart, Piano Sonata in AM, K. 331, I, Var. VI, mm. 9–10

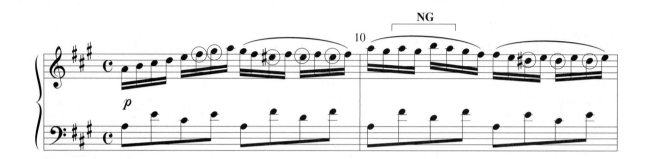

♪♪♪ Example 8.2c   J. Lennon–P. McCartney, "A Hard Day's Night," from the Film and Album *A Hard Day's Night* (Final Cadence of Verse)

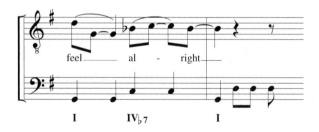

double PTs in the two vocal parts in parallel 3rds. Examine the vocal parts, circle the chord tones, and then determine whether each PT is diatonic or chromatic, accented or unaccented. What kind of cadence closes this phrase?

NOTE

Whereas parallel 5ths and 8ves have been considered unstylistic in Western "art music," and we know that common practice composers have, as a general principle, avoided them, popular music often revels in the bald expressive power of parallel perfect intervals. Thus, parallel 5ths and 8ves are not unstylistic or avoided in popular music. Examine the voice leading from IV to V in example 8.2c. If you disregard the PTs, you will discover that avoiding parallel 5ths was indeed not the concern of the Beatles! This type of voice leading is certainly fully acceptable in the stylistic context of a rock song.

THE NEIGHBOR NOTE

A **neighbor note** (NN) is a NCT that departs by step from a pitch and returns, also by step, to the same pitch. The NN is thus a step above (upper NN) or below (lower NN) the embellished pitch. NNs usually fall on weak beats or beat fractions, although they may also fall on accented metric divisions (**accented NN**). The initial motive of Mozart's Sonata in AM, K. 331 (anthology, no. 27) is based on an upper NN figure.

NNs may also be *chromatic* (a half step above or below the embellished pitch). In example 8.3, m. 3, the pitch D is first embellished by a diatonic upper NN, and then by a chromatic lower NN, followed by a chromatic PT between D and E. Notice that at m. 5, the pitch A is also embellished by two NN figures. What is the rhythmic relationship between the motive around D in m. 3 and the equivalent motive around A in m. 5?

Examine now the successions of NNs circled in example 8.2b, second half of each measure. You will see that each of them falls on either the beat or the third sixteenth note of the beat. In other words, these are all *accented NNs* (ANN).

♪♪♪Example 8.3   F. Chopin, Mazurka in Am, op. 7, no. 2

♪♪♪Example 8.4   W. A. Mozart, Piano Sonata in AM, K. 331, I, Var. III, mm. 1–2

Neighbor Group

You may have seen that in example 8.2b, m. 2, beats 1 to 2, the melodic turn A–G♯–B–A contains a lower NN of A immediately followed by the upper NN, before the figure returns to the chord tone, A. Such a figure is called a **neighbor group** (NG) or *double neighbor,* and it consists of two NNs (one upper and one lower, or vice versa) immediately following each other. The passage in example 8.4, from Mozart's AM sonata, features two NGs. Identify and circle them on the score.

THE ANTICIPATION

An **anticipation** (ANT) is a nonchord tone that anticipates a pitch from the next chord. An ANT is approached by step and left by repeating the same note, and is placed on a weak beat or beat fraction.

The period by Beethoven reproduced in example 8.5 opens with two anticipation figures. In the anacrusis (pickup) to m. 1, the F♯ sounded against the GM chord anticipates the F♯ in m. 1, where it is a member of the V$_7$ chord. Similarly, the nonchord tone G at the end of m. 1 anticipates the chord tone G in m. 2.

INCOMPLETE NEIGHBORS

We know that a neighbor note is approached by step from the note it embellishes and then returns to the same note also by step. Now examine the three examples in example 8.6. In example 8.6a, a nonchord tone (E in the alto) is approached by leap and left by step, whereas in example 8.6b the nonchord tone C in the soprano is approached by step and left by leap. Both of these NCTs are placed in metrically weak beat divisions. The G in the alto in example 8.6c, on the other hand, is also approached by leap and left by step, but its position is metrically strong. All three NCTs have in common that they function as neighbor notes to a chord tone which they approach *or* leave by step. In other words, they are all neighbor notes which do not effect the complete two-step neighbor motion we are familiar with, and for this reason we call them **incomplete neighbors** (IN). The first example (example 8.6a) is the least frequently found in

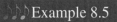Example 8.5   L. v. Beethoven, Sonata in GM, op. 49, no. 2, II, mm. 1–8

music. Examples 8.6b and c, on the other hand, represent two types of incomplete neighbors that are found more often and which are usually called escape tone and appoggiatura, respectively.

The Escape Tone

An **escape tone** (ET) is approached by step and left by leap, normally in the opposite direction (example 8.6b). It occurs on a weak beat or beat fraction. Refer to anthology, no. 9 ("Was Gott tut"), m. 3. The chord on beat 4 is IV_6 in DM (a CM chord in first inversion). The NCT in the bass is, of course, a familiar PT. The D in the soprano, on the other hand, is an ET, approached by step up and left by leap down.

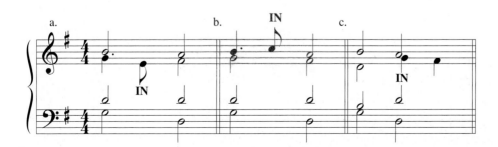

Example 8.6

The Appoggiatura

An **appoggiatura** (AP) is approached by leap and left by step (normally in the opposite direction from the approaching leap), and usually falls on a strong beat or beat division (although metrically weak appoggiaturas are also possible, as illustrated by example 8.6a).

The opening phrase in anthology, no. 33 (Beethoven's Sonata op. 10/1, II) contains two APs. In m. 1, the C in the top voice does not belong to the underlying chord (a V_5^6 in A♭M, which includes the pitches E♭–G–B♭–D♭, with G in the bass), and it is approached by leap and left by step in the opposite direction. Examine and discuss the equivalent AP in m. 3. Instances of APs may also be found in example 8.2a, m. 2, and 8.3, m. 4. Identify and circle them.

Examples 8.7a and b will allow you to compare (and to make sure you do not confuse) the opposite characteristics of the escape tone (weak placement, approached by step, left by leap, as in example 8.7a) and the appoggiatura (strong placement, approached by leap, left by step, as in example 8.7b).

♪♪♪ Example 8.7a   J. Haydn, Piano Sonata in CM, Hob. XVI:3, II, mm. 1–2

♪♪♪ Example 8.7b   W. A. Mozart, Piano Sonata in CM, K. 309, I, mm. 54–56

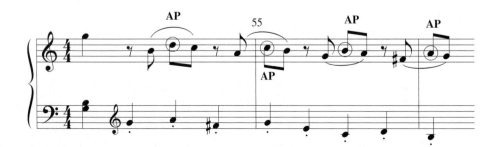

VOICE-LEADING GUIDELINES

1. NCTs do not prevent or hide faulty parallel perfect intervals, although they may easily create them. The poor voice leading in example 8.8a is not hidden or improved by a few passing tones: The parallel 5ths between bass and tenor (beats 1 and 2), between bass and soprano (beats 2 and 3), and the 8ves in contrary motion between bass and tenor (8ve C–C in m. 1, beat 3, followed by unison G in m. 2, beat 1) are incorrect in spite of the intervening passing tones. On the other hand, the passing tone in example 8.8b creates parallel 5ths in a chord connection, which otherwise would be correct.

2. Simultaneous NCTs in different voices are possible and occur frequently in chorale textures. Simultaneous NCTs, however, sound better if they are *consonant among themselves* (although, of course, they may be dissonant with the chord tones that sound at the same time). Anthology, no. 8 (Bach, "Was mein Gott will") features a variety of simultaneous NCTs. Examine this example, and notice how NCTs are indeed consonant among themselves.

3. As a summary of the NCTs studied above, each of them is briefly demonstrated in example 8.9.

♪♪♪♪ Example 8.8

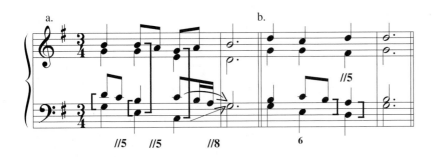

♪♪♪♪ Example 8.9

♪♪♪ Example 8.9   Continued

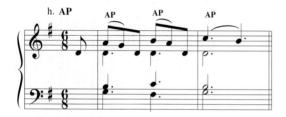

EXERCISE

To practice adding NCTs to four-voice textures, refer to exercises 8.2.1 and 8.3 in worksheet 8 at the end of this chapter.

SUSPENSIONS

In chapter D you were introduced to the study of **suspensions**. You learned that, for instance, if in two consecutive thirds in first species you delay the upper-voice motion by one beat, the 3–3 counterpoint becomes 3–4–3, a figure that includes a 4–3 suspension, as was illustrated in examples D.8a and b. If you examine example 8.10a, you will see a similar process, only now it takes place in a four-voice chordal frame. First, we see a plain I–V–I progression. Then, the motion from 1̂ to 7̂ in the upper voice is delayed by one beat. Counting intervals from the bass, we see that the delayed pitch and its resolution form a 4–3 suspension with the bass note A.

A suspension thus involves two chords (in our example, the D and A chords in m. 1). A note from the first chord is sustained and then resolved into the second chord. The actual suspension (marked S in our example), which occurs over the second chord, is the *sustained note*. The **preparation** (P) and the **resolution** (R), however, are required components that precede and follow a suspension. Example 8.10a illustrates the

♪♪♪ Example 8.10

parts in a suspension figure: the pitch D, which belongs to the DM triad, is suspended over the AM triad as a NCT, and then resolved down to C. The components are as follows:

1. *Preparation (P).* The suspended note must be a chord tone in the previous chord and must appear in the same voice as (and usually, but not necessarily, tied to) the suspension.

2. *Suspension (S).* The preparation note is suspended, or delayed, into the second chord, where it usually creates a dissonance. The suspension must fall on a *strong beat* and must be *at least as long as (or longer than) the preparation.* The suspension is often tied to the preparation, but it may also be rearticulated and still be a suspension, as long as it is prepared by the same pitch in the same voice.

3. *Resolution (R).* The suspension resolves *downward* to a member of the second chord.

Types of Suspension

Suspensions are labeled by means of two Arabic numerals which indicate *intervals with the bass.* The first numeral refers to the interval between *the bass and the suspension;* the second numeral indicates the interval between *the bass and the resolution.*

1. In a **4–3 suspension** (example 8.10a), the suspension is a 4th above the bass, and resolves down to the pitch a 3rd above the bass.

2. In a **7–6 suspension** (example 8.10b), the suspension is a 7th above the bass, and resolves down to the pitch a 6th above the bass. Because the chord of resolution contains a 6, a 7–6 suspension does not resolve to a root-position triad, but rather to one of the chord inversions that contain a 6 (for the time being, only a triad in first inversion).

3. A **9–8 suspension** (example 8.10c), features a suspension a 9th (*not* a 2nd) above the bass, resolving to the 8ve.

4. The **2–3 suspension** is the only one in which a suspension is actually *in the bass*. Look at example 8.10d carefully to understand how the 2–3 suspension works. The suspended C, in the bass, creates a dissonance of a 2nd (or a 9th) with another voice (in this case, the tenor). The bass dissonance resolves down to a pitch which forms a 3rd with the tenor, hence the 2–3 label (in which, of course, intervals are still counted from the bass upward). The 2–3 suspension often resolves to a first-inversion triad, as in our example. The $\frac{5-6}{2-3}$ figures simply indicate that the A in the alto is a 5th over the delayed D, which then becomes a 6th over the pitch of resolution, C.

5. A different category of suspension (one that is often not considered a true suspension) is represented in example 8.10e. The **6–5 suspension** is different from the previous four types in that it is a *consonant* suspension, and therefore its musical effect is much less dramatic than in the case of dissonant suspensions.

NOTE

The note of resolution should not sound at the same time as the suspension, except in a 9–8 suspension. Example 8.10f illustrates an incorrect version of the 7–6 suspension from example 8.10b: The note of resolution (G) is present in the soprano at the same time as the suspension (A). In example 8.10b, it is not. The problem in example 8.10f is that while we are delaying the motion to G in one voice (creating an expectation), we hear the delayed pitch in another voice (thus frustrating the expectation). The suspension and its resolution sounding at the same time, moreover, make for an unclear sonority. The effect is similar to giving away the punch line beforetime. In a 9–8 suspension, on the other hand, the note of resolution (D in example 8.10c) is present in the bass, by definition, at the same time as the suspension, because the resolution is to the 8ve above the bass (that is, to the same note as the one in the bass, in a higher 8ve).

EXERCISE

To practice writing suspensions, refer to exercises 8.2.2, 8.3b, and 8.4 in worksheet 8 at the end of this chapter.

Embellished Suspensions

Suspensions are often **embellished** with some of the NCTs we have studied. In example 8.11a, the suspension presented in its plain version in example 8.10a has been embellished with an anticipation of the resolution. Example 8.11b features an

♪♪♪Example 8.11a to e

♪♪♪Example 8.11f   J. S. Bach, Chorale 32, "Nun danket alle Gott," mm. 2–4

appoggiatura to the resolution; example 8.11c, an escape tone (which, however, in this case is a chord tone); example 8.11d, a neighbor note to the anticipation-resolution; and example 8.11e, a neighbor note (also a chord tone in this particular example) to the suspension. An embellished suspension appears in the last measure of example 8.11f. Discuss the suspension and its embellishment, as well as all the other NCTs in this phrase.

Suspensions with Change of Bass (or Change of Part)

Occasionally the bass note changes between the suspension and the resolution. This produces a rearrangement of the interval between the bass and the resolution, but the basic frame of the suspension remains unchanged. The suspension, which in example 8.10c was a 9–8, becomes a 9–6 in example 8.12a because of a change of chord position and hence of bass note. The 7–6 suspension from example 8.10b, on the other hand, becomes a 7–3 in example 8.12b because of a complete change of chord between the suspension and the resolution. Similarly, the 4–3 suspension from example 8.10a turns into a 4–6, involving a complete change of chord, in example 8.12c. Notice, though, that the structure of the suspension (P–S–R) has not changed in any of these

♪♪♪ Example 8.12

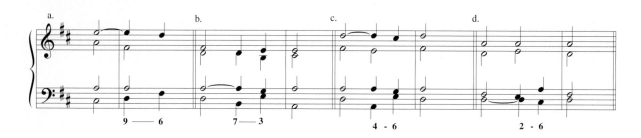

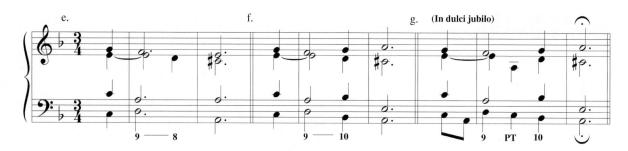

cases. Finally, a similar process turns the 2–3 suspension from example 8.10d into a 2–6 suspension in example 8.12d. Notice, however, that the voice that changes here is not the bass (which carries the 2–3 suspension in both examples), but one of the upper voices, in this case the tenor. Rather than "change of bass," in 2–3 suspensions we speak of "change of part."

A complex example of embellished suspension with change of bass is illustrated by examples 8.12e to g. A simple frame for a 9–8 suspension appears in example 8.12e. In example 8.12f the same suspension is resolved with a change of bass (and a change of chord). Finally, example 8.12g reproduces a passage from Bach's chorale "In dulci jubilo," in which the suspension is ornamented with a chord tone (A), and a passing tone is added in the bass.

Chain of Suspensions

A **chain of suspensions** is an uninterrupted succession of several suspensions. In a chain of suspensions the resolution of a suspension becomes the preparation for the next one. In the excerpt by J. S. Bach reproduced in example 8.13, the resolution of a 9–8 suspension on F becomes the preparation for a 4–3 suspension on C, and the resolution of the latter becomes the preparation for a 9–8 suspension on D.

Sequences are often based on chains of suspensions of the same type. The most frequent sequential series of suspensions is the *chain of 7–6 suspensions*. The Handel fragment in example 8.14 is based on such a chain. In three voices, the third voice in

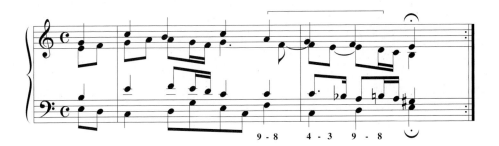

♪♪♪Example 8.13   J. S. Bach, Chorale 34, "Erbarm dich mein, O Herre Gott"

this sequence doubles the bass in parallel 10ths, as shown in the Handel fragment by the circled pitches. In four voices, the voice leading (illustrated in example 8.15a) also includes a voice which alternates doubling each of the voices in parallel 10ths (avoiding always to double the suspension resolution). Notice that *parallel 5ths on weak beats resulting from a chain of suspensions are perfectly acceptable* (as in the 5ths between tenor and alto in our example). The octaves on strong beat (alto-soprano) are not a problem because they are separated by chordal skips, which, as we saw in chapter 4, prevent parallel 5ths and 8ves.

   Chains of 2–3 suspensions are also common. The chain in example 8.15b results from a series of parallel $\frac{5}{3}$ chords. Here again, the 5ths on weak beat (bass-tenor) separated by a suspension are not objectionable. In example 8.15c, the chain of 2–3 suspensions results from a series of parallel $\frac{6}{3}$ chords. The parallel 5ths on strong beats (bass-tenor) are not a problem because they are separated by consonant intervals, and neither are the 8ves on strong beat (tenor-soprano) because of the chordal skips in the tenor.

♪♪♪Example 8.14   G. F. Handel, "Chaconne," from *Trois Leçons,* Var. 9, mm. 1–5

♪♪♪Example 8.15

Finally, although parallel 5ths on weak beats resulting from suspensions are not considered faulty, parallel 8ves resulting from a chain of 9–8 suspensions are more objectionable (example 8.15d). Because a series of 9–8 suspensions is too close to a series of parallel octaves, chains of 9–8 suspensions are usually avoided.

EXERCISE

To practice writing chains of suspensions, refer to exercise 8.5 in worksheet 8 at the end of this chapter.

Retardation

A suspension figure that resolves upward is called a **retardation.** In example 8.2a the C on the downbeat in m. 4 would be a 9–8 suspension over B♭ if it resolved down by step. Its upward resolution to D, however, makes it a retardation. Examine the cadence in anthology, no. 33, m. 16 (Beethoven, Sonata in Cm, op. 10/1, II). Three NTCs sound on the final A♭. How does each of them resolve? What is each of them?

PEDAL POINT

A **pedal point** is a tone that is sustained, usually in the bass (although it may occur in any other voice), while a variety of changing harmonies (some consonant, some dissonant) sound over it. Most often, pedal points have the function of prolonging the tonic

♪♪♪ Example 8.16   J. S. Bach, Fugue no. 2 in Cm, from *The Well-Tempered Clavier*, I, mm. 28–end

or dominant harmonies (pedals on $\hat{1}$ and $\hat{5}$, respectively). A pedal on $\hat{1}$ usually comes as a cadential extension after a PAC, whereas a pedal on $\hat{5}$ often leads to an important return of the tonic, toward the end of a composition, usually after a developmental excursion away from the tonic.

Example 8.16 shows a characteristic tonic pedal point in the bass, closing a fugue by J. S. Bach. The pedal in this example begins after a PAC on C in m. 29. As is usually the case, the material over the pedal begins and ends with statements of the chord that is being prolonged, hence with consonances. To analyze harmonies over a pedal, you should in principle ignore the pedal note and think of the lowest voice in the chordal texture above the pedal as the bass voice. After you have identified the type of harmonies over the pedal, however, it is useful to verify their level of consonance or dissonance against the pedal tone. For examples of *upper-voice pedal points,* refer to examples 3.2 and 3.8.

FURTHER ANALYSIS

For further study and class discussion, refer to anthology, no. 18 (Amalie, Sonata for flute), mm. 1–8 and 13–21.

1. Analyze all the chords in these measures with Roman numerals, identifying at the same time the numerous and interesting NCTs in both the flute and the piano parts. Label all suspensions with the correct figures. You will need to apply yourself diligently to the study of this piece, because this is the most challenging analytical assignment you have been given so far. You

will find in it many interesting and beautiful instances of NCTs embellishing harmonies you are already capable of analyzing.

NOTE: M.5 begins with a ii₆ which, in beat 3, becomes a ii₆⁶. The third chord in m. 7, on the other hand, is a vii°₇/V. You need not worry for now about these chords because we have not studied them yet.

2. Explain how NCTs are used to embellish and prolong the tonic harmony in mm.1–2.

Summary of Nonchord Tones

NCT	Approached by	Left by	Metric Position
Passing tone	Step	Step (same direction)	Weak
Accented PT	Step	Step (same direction)	Strong
Neighbor note	Step	Step (opposite dir.)	Weak
Accented NN	Step	Step (opposite dir.)	Strong
Anticipation	Step	Repeated note	Weak
Escape tone	Step	Leap (normally opposite direction)	Weak
Appoggiatura	Leap	Step (normally opposite direction)	Strong (sometimes weak)
Suspension	Repeated note (from preparation)	Step down (to resolution)	Strong
Retardation	Repeated note (from preparation)	Step up (to resolution)	Strong

EXERCISES

To practice harmonizing melodies that include a variety of NCTs, refer to exercises 8.6 and 8.7 in worksheet 8 at the end of this chapter.
   To practice identifying and labeling NCTs, refer to exercise 8.1.

PRACTICAL APPLICATION AND DISCUSSION

1. Find examples of as many as possible of the types of NCTs studied in this chapter in compositions you are practicing or performing on your instrument.

2. How do NCTs affect performance? How do you perform different NCTs? For instance, how does the way you approach the performance of a passing tone or a neighbor note differ from the way you perform an appoggiatura or an accented passing tone? Composers often stress this by means of articulation marks. How?

Use the initial period from anthology, no. 28 (Mozart, Sonata in B♭M, III, mm. 1–8) as a reference for your discussion. Notice that in the cadential $^6_4$ at the HC (m. 4), the D and the B♭ can actually be interpreted as APTs.

3. Composers through the centuries have been very fond of suspensions. Why? What is the effect of a suspension as perceived by the performer and the listener? What effect do suspensions have on musical motion? Do you perform suspensions in any specific way?

ASSIGNMENT

For analytical and written assignments based on the materials learned in this chapter, refer to chapter 8 in the workbook.

 Composers and Their Music 8

Biographies

Write short biographies of the following composers mentioned in this chapter or in workbook chapter 8: Anna Amalie, Archangelo Corelli.

Listening

Listen to the following compositions by composers mentioned in this chapter:

Amalie: Sonata in FM for Flute and Continuo (recording in Briscoe anthology).
Corelli: Sonata "La Folia," op. 5, no. 12.

Mozart: Symphony no. 41 in CM, K. 551, *Jupiter.*
Beethoven: Sonata no. 21 in CM, op. 53, *Waldstein.*

Follow the score while you listen. Be able to place these compositions in one of the style periods and to comment on why and how they represent the musical characteristics of that period. As you listen, can you identify cases of melodic dissonance produced by nonchord tones? When you hear it, what effect does it have on the music and on you as a listener? Do any of these pieces in particular use extensive melodic dissonance?

Terms for Review

Nonchord tone
Passing tone
Double PT
Chromatic PT
Accented PT
Neighbor note
Accented NN
Neighbor group
Anticipation
Incomplete neighbors
Escape tone
Appoggiatura
Suspension

Preparation and resolution
4–3 suspension
7–6 suspension
9–8 suspension
2–3 suspension
6–5 suspension
Embellished suspension
Suspension with change of bass or change of part
Chain of suspensions
Retardation
Pedal point

Worksheet 8

EXERCISE 8.1 Analysis. Identify and label all NCTs in the two excerpts by Bach reproduced in example 8.17. Label suspensions with the correct figures.

♪♪♪ Example 8.17a   J. S. Bach, Chorale 29, "Freu dich sehr, o meine Seele," mm. 1–4

♪♪♪ Example 8.17b   J. S. Bach, Chorale 76, "Freu dich sehr, o meine Seele," mm. 1–5

Note: At this stage, you will not be able to analyze and understand all the chords and harmonic processes in these excerpts. This should not hinder you, however, from identifying and understanding most of the NCTs and their function.

EXERCISE 8.2

1. Add NCTs (no suspensions yet) to the chorale in example 8.18a.

Procedure for embellishing a given texture with NCTs:

1. Identify spots where you may use PTs (filling a 3rd).

2. Identify spots where you may use NNs (such as repeated notes in the given texture).

3. Locate other possible places for other NCTs. For an ANT, for example, you need a voice ascending or descending by step. Write one in the next-to-last chord (**).

4. Be sparing in your use of NCTs. An overloaded texture may turn unmusical. You may use simultaneous NCTs in different voices, but only as long as they are consonant among themselves. Some suggested spots for simultaneous NCTs are marked with a +.

♪♪♪ Example 8.18a   (Based on Bach, Chorale 72)

2. Add three suspensions to the phrase in example 8.18b, as required.

Procedure for embellishing a given texture with suspensions: You first need to identify spots where you may use a suspension. For this purpose you will need a voice that descends by step, in such a way that the second note of the step is an 8ve (for a 9–8), a 6th (a 7–6), or a 3rd (4–3 or 2–3) above the bass. In example 8.18a, m. 5, the chord marked with an asterisk (*) allows for a 7–6 suspension. Why? Write it. Can you add a suspension to the second chord in m. 1 in example 8.18a? And to the second chord in m. 2?

♪♪♪Example 8.18b   (Based on Bach, Chorale 64)

9-8   7-6   4-3

EXERCISE 8.3   Realize the following two progressions in four voices. Then, add NCTs to both of them (no suspensions in exercise 8.3a; include a suspension in exercise 8.3b, m. 3).

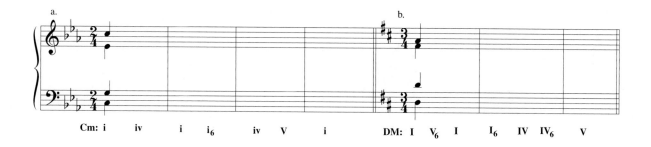

a.   b.

Cm: i   iv   i   i₆   iv   V   i   DM: I   V₆   I   I₆   IV   IV₆   V

EXERCISE 8.4   Realize the following suspensions in four voices. Write the actual suspension in the specified voice. Remember not to double the note of resolution (except in 9–8 suspensions). Notice that the Roman numeral V^{5-6}_{2-3} simply refers to a V_6 with a 2–3 suspension in the bass.

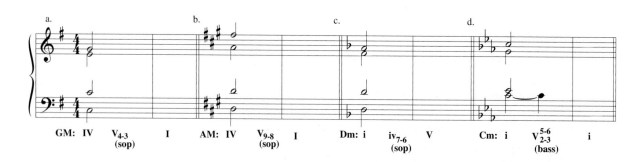

a.   b.   c.   d.

GM: IV   V₄₋₃   I   AM: IV   V₉₋₈   I   Dm: i   iv₇₋₆   V   Cm: i   V⁵⁻⁶₂₋₃   i
           (sop)   (sop)   (sop)   (bass)

EXERCISE 8.5

1. Complete the chain of 4–3/9–8 suspensions that has been started for you in exercise 8.5a. The first four suspensions are part of the chain and will all be in the same voice. The last 4–3 suspension will be in a different voice.

2. Complete the chain of 7–6 suspensions that has been started for you in exercise 8.5b.

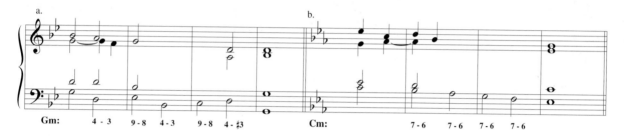

EXERCISE 8.6   Harmonize the melody in exercise 8.6 in four voices, using only i, iv, V, and their first inversions, following the given harmonic rhythm (HR) (harmonize the notes marked with a 6 with a first inversion of the previous chord). Sing the melody and the harmonization in class or with friends.

Procedure to harmonize a melody with NCTs:

1. Sing the melody, and identify (or verify the given) HR.

2. Identify, mark, and label the NCTs in the melody. In m. 2, for instance, all three pitches on beat 1 may not belong to the same chord; but pitches 1 and 3 may, which leaves pitch 2 as a likely PT. Beat 2 in the same measure, however, features a melodic figure that is part of the same triad.

3. Harmonize the melody as if it did not have NCTs (that is, base your harmonization on the chord tones). In m. 2, for example, the beat 1 chord will include the pitches C–E♭ (a likely iv). Write Roman numerals for your chords, then write a bass line and fill in the inner voices according to the rules of correct voice leading and doubling.

EXERCISE 8.7

1. Harmonize the following folk melody with a bass and RNs (no inner voices), using only I, IV, V, and their first inversions. Notice its slow harmonic rhythm.

2. Using the line below, provide a form diagram (with bubbles, measure numbers, cadences, and letters to indicate phrase relationships) for the complete melody, identifying its three phrases.

Chapter 9

$^6_4$ Chords

In chapter E we studied that a triad is in second inversion if its fifth is in the bass. The two intervals above the bass in this position are a 6th and a 4th, hence the figured bass $^6_4$ to indicate second inversion. The category of chords which we know as "$^6_4$ chords," however, presents some conceptual difficulties. In the first place, although they all *look* like triads in second inversion, most of them *do not function or sound* like triads in second inversion. In most cases, $^6_4$ chords *behave linearly and not functionally.* Hence, we hear them melodically rather than as a harmonic inversion. In chapter D, moreover, we learned that the P4 is a dissonant interval if it involves the bass, as is the case in $^6_4$ chords. As a result, $^6_4$ chords *may be dissonant chords,* because they contain a dissonance—the P4 between the bass and another voice.

Indeed, both of the above criteria are true for most types of $^6_4$ chords: they are linear and hence do not funtion like second inversion triads, and they are dissonant. These criteria, however, do not apply to some categories of $^6_4$ chords (such as *arpeggiated* or *oscillating* $^6_4$s), which we will study first under the general heading of *consonant* $^6_4$s. We will then study three types of *dissonant* $^6_4$s: the *neighbor,* the *passing,* and the *cadential* $^6_4$s. All $^6_4$ chords that you write should belong to one of the above categories, and their voice leading should follow the conventions for each of the types that will be studied in this chapter. In any case, whether they are consonant or dissonant, $^6_4$ chords always function as *prolongational chords.*

EXERCISE

To practice spelling single $^6_4$ chords in four voices, refer to exercise 9.2 in worksheet 9 at the end of this chapter.

CONSONANT $^6_4$ CHORDS

Sometimes a $^6_4$ chord is heard as an inversion of a root-position triad, which it actually extends. Because this type of $^6_4$ chord sounds like triadic inversions in the context of an extended consonant harmony, we do not think of them as dissonant chords. Let's examine two types of chords within this category.

The Arpeggiated $^6_4$

Listen to the beginning of Beethoven's Symphony no. 3 (*Eroica*), III, mm. 167–173 (example 9.1). The phrase is based on an arpeggiation of the tonic triad in all voices. The bass arpeggiation produces an obvious unfolding of the tonic harmony, which may be read as I–I$_6$–I$^6_4$–I–I$^6_4$–I$_6$–I, or simply as an extended I. Because the role of I$^6_4$ in this context (the **arpeggiated $^6_4$**) is clearly to extend a consonant harmony by means of triadic inversion, without actually departing from the consonant frame established in m. 1, we hear it as a **consonant $^6_4$**.

The Oscillating $^6_4$

A type of consonant $^6_4$ also results from a common accompaniment figure in which the bass of a tonic chord alternates (or "oscillates") between $\hat{1}$ and $\hat{5}$, a pattern frequently found in waltzes and marches. The song "Die Beschwörung," by Viardot-García, begins with such a left-hand pattern (example 9.2). Here again, we hear all of m. 1 in this example as a consonant tonic chord.

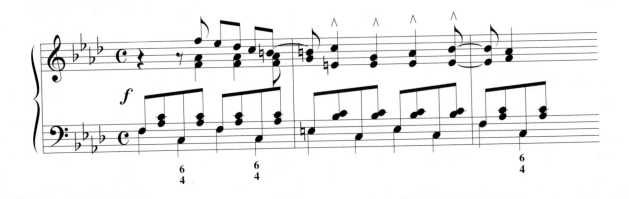

DISSONANT $^6_4$ CHORDS

In this section we will discuss the three most common types of **dissonant** $^6_4$ chords. All of these $^6_4$ chords are *linear* in nature (that is, they result from contrapuntal and melodic processes) and they do not constitute independent harmonic entities. Their function is to embellish or intensify other, more important harmonies. In other words, they are all *prolongational chords.* Because of their linear nature, we do not hear them as triads in second inversion in a consonant context. The 4th with the bass results here from melodic, contrapuntal processes, and for this reason we treat it as a dissonance. Thus, *these $^6_4$ chords are dissonant* themselves. As we learned in the chapter on nonchord tones, dissonances may not be used freely in tonal music. They must resolve, and normally also be prepared, according to standard voice-leading principles. Such is also the case with dissonant $^6_4$ chords. Because they are treated as dissonances, they may not be used freely. We will now study the voice-leading conventions that regulate the normative behavior of linear $^6_4$ chords.

♪♪♪Example 9.3a   Elton John, "Candle in the Wind," from the Album *Goodbye Yellow Brick Road*

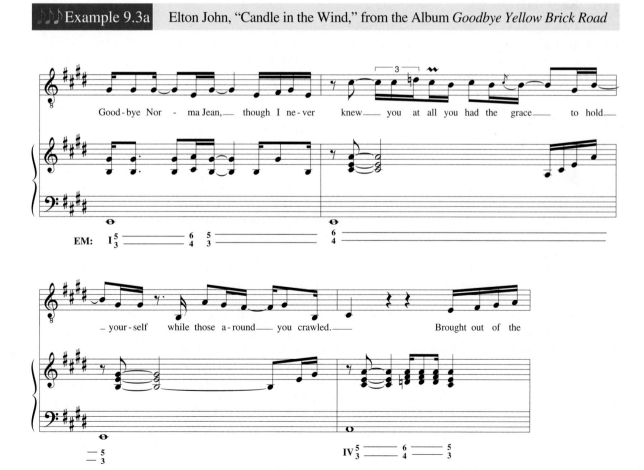

♪♪♪Example 9.3b   F. Schubert, *Valses Sentimentales,* op. 50, no. 3, mm. 1–8

THE NEIGHBOR $^6_4$

Examine the phrase by Elton John in example 9.3a. The first three measures feature a bass pedal on $\hat{1}$. The only harmonic change occurs briefly in m. 1, and then again in the complete next measure. In both cases, two of the tones from the tonic triad ($\hat{3}$ and $\hat{5}$) move to their upper neighbors ($\hat{4}$ and $\hat{6}$), and then back, in a motion over the bass which we can represent as $^{5-6-5}_{3-4-3}$. In chapter 3 we studied that when IV functions as a prolongation of I (in the progression I–IV–I), one of the upper voices sustains the common tone $\hat{1}$, while the other two voices feature neighbor-note (NN) figures. If the common tone is also left in the bass instead of only one of the upper voices, a I–IV$^6_4$–I progression results, as in example 9.3a. This is a very common progression, which clearly functions as a linear prolongation of I. $\hat{1}$ is present in the bass as a pedal (and also usually doubled in one of the upper voices), while the other two voices realize a double NN figure. For this reason, this type of $^6_4$ chord is known as a **neighbor** $^6_4$ (N$^6_4$) or also *embellishing* $^6_4$ or *pedal* $^6_4$. Identify the N$^6_4$ chord in example 9.3b, and verify its voice leading. The standard voice leading for the N$^6_4$ is summarized in example 9.4a.

The most frequent occurrence of the N$^6_4$ is as an elaboration of the tonic. Other similar progressions are possible, as illustrated by the N$^6_4$ elaboration of IV which appears in example 9.3a, m. 4, and the elaboration of V illustrated in example 9.4b. The graph in example 9.4c summarizes the linear character of N$^6_4$ progressions: rather than "chords," these are linear harmonies that result from two nonchord tones (two NNs). Although using Roman numerals for these progressions can be practical because they help determine the exact pitches in the $^6_4$ chord, Roman numerals distort the linear nature of these chords. We do not really hear a N$^6_4$ to I as a subdominant in second inversion (IV$^6_4$), but as a melodic double NN figure elaborating I. For this reason, we will not use Roman numerals to refer to dissonant $^6_4$ chords. The label "N$^6_4$" (as in I– N$^6_4$ –I) describes much better the musical process taking place in the neighbor $^6_4$ progression, as shown in example 9.4.

♪♪♪ Example 9.4   The Neighbor $^6_4$

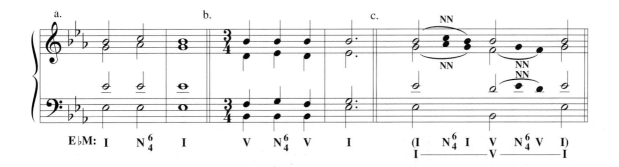

E♭M: I   N$^6_4$ I   V   N$^6_4$ V   I   (I   N$^6_4$ I   V   N$^6_4$ V   I)

I ———————————— V ———————————— I

FURTHER ANALYSIS

Compound Melody

1. Identify and label the nonchord tones (NCTs) in example 9.3b. You will see that the explanation for some of them is not immediately obvious, especially for the A in m. 1 and the F♯–A in m. 3. The concept of **compound melody** will help you understand the melodic structure of this phrase. A compound melody comprises two (or three) strands in different registers in such a way that it may be understood as several different, independent lines (voices) brought together into a single melody, as in "one-line counterpoint." Play the Bach theme in example 9.5a. Then, think of it as two independent melodies, and play it as in example 9.5b. This is a compound melody which contains the two hypothetical lines shown in example 9.5b.

    Thinking of the Schubert melody as a compound melody will help you account for some of the NCTs. Example 9.6a breaks the compound melody into its constituent voices, making the role of the A in m. 1 and the F♯–A in m. 3 more clear. Example 9.6b shows the contrapuntal relationship between the two voices, and example 9.6c presents a reduced version of the melodic structure for this phrase. Play all of these examples, hearing and understanding how the two melodic strands are related contrapuntally, and how this reading of the phrase as a compound melody helps account for all the NCTs in the passage. Notice especially the following points:

    a) In examples 9.6a and b we see that the upper voice, after the anacrusic D, basically consists of an ascending motion from G to B and descending back to G. In this context, the A in m. 1 is a passing tone, whereas the A in m. 3 is an accented passing tone.

    b) The first half of the middle voice in examples 9.6a and b is simply an extension of $\hat{5}$, elaborated by means of upper neighbors. The second half of the middle voice is a linear descent from G to D. We can now see that that both the F♯ and A in m. 3 function as accented passing tones in two different voices.

    c) The lower voice is a sustained G (the bass of the texture), over which we see, in the piano's left hand, a $^{5-6-5}_{3-4-3}$ neighbor motion.

    d) The reduction in example 9.6c shows the complete passage as a harmonic prolongation of I. The upper voice effects a passing motion from $\hat{1}$ to $\hat{3}$ and back, whereas the middle voice features an extension of $\hat{5}$ followed by a descent from $\hat{1}$ to $\hat{5}$ by means of two passing tones.

2. The phrase by Mozart reproduced in example 9.7 includes several of the neighbor chords which we have studied so far. The complete phrase is a harmonic prolongation of I, achieved exclusively by means of a variety of NN relationships. Identify all the NN relationships and label the resulting sonorities in each case with the corresponding Roman numerals (or linear $^6_4$ labels), understanding their harmonic and linear functions. You will find only one chord you have not studied yet: the first chord in m. 2 is a second inversion of V_7, labeled as V^4_3, which here also functions as a neighbor chord.

Example 9.5 J. S. Bach, Fugue no. 3 in C♯M, from *The Well-Tempered Clavier,* I, Subject

Example 9.6 F. Schubert, *Valses Sentimentales,* op. 50, no. 3, mm. 1–4 (Melody)

EXERCISE

To practice analyzing and composing compound melodies, refer to exercises 9.1.3 and 9.6 in worksheet 9 at the end of this chapter.

Example 9.7   W. A. Mozart, Piano Sonata in CM, K. 545, mm. 1–4

THE PASSING $^6_4$

In example 9.8, m. 2, you will see another case of a dissonant $^6_4$ chord resulting from linear motion. I and I_6 in this example are connected by means of an intervening PT in the bass and another one in the top voice ($\hat{2}$ in both cases). The resulting V^6_4 is an example of a **passing** $^6_4$ chord (which we will label as P^6_4), a chord normally used to connect melodically two chords with the same function, most often a root-position triad and its first inversion (or vice versa). Notice that the two voices with PT figures (the outer voices in this case) perform a voice exchange. Another voice sustains $\hat{5}$, while the fourth voice features a leading-tone NN figure, $\hat{1}–\hat{7}–\hat{1}$. Study carefully the voice leading in both examples 9.8 and 9.9, noticing the linear character of each voice, the

Example 9.8   Meredith Willson, "Goodnight My Someone," from the Show *The Music Man*

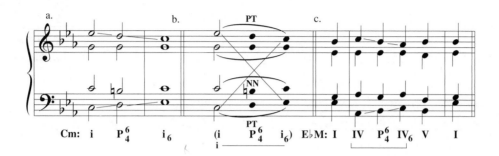

voice exchange, the doubled bass (fifth) in the P^6_4, and the prolongational function of the complete i–P^6_4–i$_6$ progression (example 9.9b). Because the P^6_4 (a *passing chord*) has the same linear function as a PT, it normally appears on a *weak beat*.

This progression is not found in the literature as frequently as the neighbor $^6_4$, although it is still a standard progression. Composers often prefer to use V^4_3 or vii°$_6$, rather than V^6_4, in their passing progressions between I and I$_6$ (we will study passing progressions with V^4_3 and vii°$_6$ in chapters 12 and 13, respectively). Besides the P^6_4 linking I and I$_6$, other passing $^6_4$ progressions may possibly be found, such as IV–P^6_4–IV$_6$ (example 9.9c).

EXERCISE

To practice writing short progressions including neighbor and passing $^6_4$ chords, refer to exercises 9.3a to d in worksheet 9 at the end of this chapter.

THE CADENTIAL $^6_4$

In chapter 5 you were introduced to the cadential $^6_4$, the last type of $^6_4$ chord we will study in this chapter, and also the type most commonly found in the literature. An example from Donizetti's *Lucia di Lammermoor* will serve as a reminder of this chord's characteristics. In example 9.10a you will recognize the basic frame for a PAC: a V_7–I in GM (mm. 4–5) preceded, in m. 3, by IV. In the first half of m. 4, however, you will hear a $^6_4$ sonority over $\hat5$. Although the chord produced by this $^6_4$ sonority looks like a I$^6_4$, this chord does not function at all as a tonic. It is a dissonant linear sonority over $\hat5$ resulting from NCTs, and its function is to intensify and embellish melodically the dominant chord that follows it and to which it resolves. The voice leading for this chord, known as the **cadential $^6_4$** (cad. $^6_4$), is summarized in examples 9.10b to d and in the following points:

1. When the cadential $^6_4$ is preceded by IV, as in our examples, *the 6th above the bass,* which *resolves down to the 5th above the bass* (6–5), functions as an accented PT in the figure $\hat4$–$\hat3$–$\hat2$; *the 4th above the bass,* which *always resolves down to the 3rd above the bass* (4–3), functions as a 4–3 suspension ($\hat1$–$\hat7$), *including its correct preparation.* The fourth voice holds the doubled bass, $\hat5$.

♪♪♪Example 9.10a   G. Donizetti, *Lucia di Lammermoor,* Act III, Final Aria, "Tu che a Dio spiegasti l'ali"

♪♪♪Example 9.10b to d   The Cadential $^6_4$

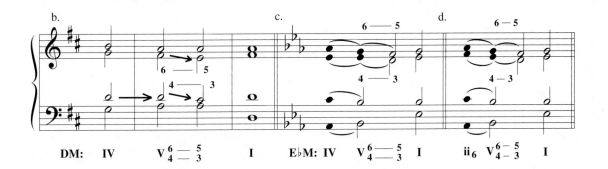

2. When the cadential $^6_4$ is preceded by ii or ii$_6$, both the 6th and the 4th above the bass function as accented passing tones, as illustrated by example 9.10d.

3. Because, according to the linear explanation of the cadential $^6_4$, the **voice leading,** *which intensifies V, can be summarized by the figures* $^{6-5}_{4-3}$, the notation V$^{6-5}_{4-3}$–I expresses more accurately the true nature of this progression than the alternative notation I$^6_4$–V–I found in some books. The complete $^{6-5}_{4-3}$ figure, over $\hat5$ in the bass, has a *dominant function* (as expressed by the V$^{6-5}_{4-3}$ notation) and not a tonic function, as could be misinterpreted from the I$^6_4$–V notation. Identify all the linear elements of voice leading (especially the $^{6-5}_{4-3}$ and the preparation of the 4–3 suspension) in the Donizetti cadential $^6_4$ (for the time being, focus on the left-hand chords, and ignore the 7th of the V$_7$, which appears in the right hand).

PRACTICAL APPLICATION AND DISCUSSION

1. Composers often write cadential $^6_4$ progressions embellished with additional NCTs or other melodic devices. This is the case in the examples by Marianne Martínez and Felix Mendelssohn (examples 9.11 and 9.12). Study the voice leading in these two cadences and discuss it in class. Where are the $^{6-5}_{4-3}$ figures? (Circle the pitches that constitute the 6–5 and 4–3 lines.) How is the $^6_4$ prepared by Martínez? What other elements of dissonance, (delayed or embellished resolution, for example) are introduced by each of the composers? In the Martínez example, observe also that there are two similar cadences, one in m. 33, the other in mm. 34–35. What is the difference between them? What is the function of the cadence in m. 33? And what is the melodic/harmonic/formal function of mm. 35–36?

2. Try to find some $^6_4$ chords in the music you perform, bring them to class, and discuss how they function. You are most likely to find examples of cadential $^6_4$ chords. How do they resolve? Are they embellished with additional NCTs? Are they preceded by IV, by ii or ii$_6$, or by ii$^6_5$?

3. Can you remember, or find, any compound melodies in your musical repertoire? If you can, bring them to class and explain how your melodies actually contain two or more independent lines. Think about how being aware of these lines affects your performance. Do you bring out some notes more than others? Are the distinct lines easily heard by the listener?

Example 9.11   M. Martínez, Sonata in AM, mm. 32–36

♪♪♪Example 9.12   Felix Mendelssohn, Caprice op. 33, no. 1, mm. 302–306

NOTE

Because of its linear function as a suspension/accented PT figure, the cadential $^6_4$ usually falls on a strong beat. In triple meters, however, the cadential $^6_4$ is often found on beat 2, with the resolution to $^5_3$ on beat 3. As we studied in chapter B, beat 2 in triple meter may be perceived as either weak or strong depending on the context, and, as a matter of fact, beat 2 is sometimes stressed in a variety of ways (such as dynamic or agogic accents, or phrasing). Placing a cadential $^6_4$ (which we perceive as an accented harmonic event) on beat 2 is in itself a way of emphasizing this beat.

VOICE-LEADING GUIDELINES

1. *Doubling* As a rule, **double the bass (the fifth) in a $^6_4$ chord**. You will rarely find any other triad member doubled in $^6_4$ chords. On occasions you may find the third of the chord (the 6th above the bass) doubled because of strong voice-leading reasons. The root (the 4th above the bass) is never doubled because it is the dissonant pitch, and dissonances are not doubled.

2. *Neighbor $^6_4$*. In the most common N^6_4 progression (I–N^6_4–I), the bass and the voice that doubles it sustain $\hat1$, while the other voices perform NN figures ($\hat3$–$\hat4$–$\hat3$ and $\hat5$–$\hat6$–$\hat5$). In the V–N^6_4–V progression, $\hat5$ is sustained and doubled, and the other two voices also perform NN figures over the $\hat5$ pedal.

3. *Passing $^6_4$*. Most often used to connect a triad and its first inversion (or vice versa). Because of its function as a passing chord, it is usually placed on a weak beat. In the most common passing $^6_4$ progression (I–P^6_4–I_6), the bass and one of the upper voices feature a voice

exchange ($\hat1$–$\hat2$–$\hat3$ and $\hat3$–$\hat2$–$\hat1$), a third voice sustains $\hat5$, and the fourth voice performs a leading-tone neighbor figure, $\hat1$–$\hat7$–$\hat1$.

4. *Cadential $^6_4$*. It is normally placed on a strong beat (or in beat 2 in triple meter). In the V^{6-5}_{4-3} figure, $\hat5$ is in the bass and doubled. The $^6_4$ above $\hat5$ resolves to $^5_3$ in the V chord, following the voice-leading 6–5, 4–3. If the $^6_4$ is preceded by IV, the 4th must be prepared as a suspension by keeping $\hat1$ in the same voice in the IV and $^6_4$ chords. If it is preceded by ii or ii_6, both the 6th and the 4th function as accented PTs.

5. *Errors to avoid*. Because neighbor, passing, and cadential $^6_4$ chords are dissonant, their doubling, preparation, and resolution should follow the voice-leading conventions summarized above. In principle, any departure from these conventions should be considered a voice-leading error to be avoided.

EXERCISES

To practice writing short progressions including cadential $^6_4$ chords, refer to exercises 9.3e to g in worksheet 9 at the end of this chapter.

  To practice analyzing musical examples including a variety of $^6_4$ chords, refer to exercises 9.1.1 to 9.1.2 in worksheet 9 at the end of this chapter.

  To practice realizing a figured bass including all types of dissonant $^6_4$ chords, refer to exercise 9.4 in worksheet 9 at the end of this chapter.

HARMONIZING MELODIES WITH $^6_4$ CHORDS

A variety of melodic patterns may be harmonized with $^6_4$ chords, as you can verify in examples 9.4, 9.9, and 9.10b and c (notice that any of the inner voices can also become the upper voice in each of these examples). Some of the most common patterns and their harmonizations are illustrated in example 9.13.

1. In example 9.13a you can see a string of melodic neighbor patterns, all of which allow harmonizations using N^6_4 chords. In the most frequent N^6_4 progression (I– N^6_4 –I), the melodic patterns may be $\hat{5}$–$\hat{6}$–$\hat{5}$ or $\hat{3}$–$\hat{4}$–$\hat{3}$, but other patterns and progressions are possible, as shown by mm. 3–4 in the same example.

2. Example 9.13b shows possible patterns to be harmonized with P^6_4 progressions. In general, the melodic patterns will be either a lower-neighbor figure or a passing figure. In the I–P^6_4–I_6 progression, such patterns will be $\hat{1}$–$\hat{7}$–$\hat{1}$ and $\hat{3}$–$\hat{2}$–$\hat{1}$ (or

Example 9.13

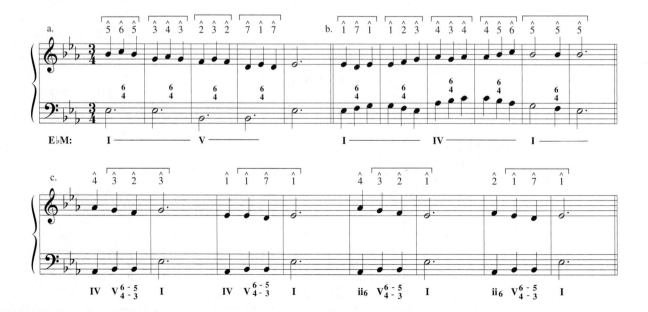

$\hat{1}$–$\hat{2}$–$\hat{3}$, depending on the direction of the bass). A sustained $\hat{5}$ can also be harmonized with this same progression.

3. Finally, example 9.13c shows patterns that may be harmonized with a cadential $^6_4$. The possibilites for the actual cadential $^6_4$ figure are $\hat{3}$–$\hat{2}$–$\hat{3}$ (or $\hat{3}$–$\hat{2}$–$\hat{1}$), $\hat{1}$–$\hat{7}$–$\hat{1}$, or $\hat{5}$–$\hat{5}$–$\hat{5}$. Notice how the approach to the $\hat{1}$–$\hat{7}$–$\hat{1}$ pattern changes depending on whether we use a IV to precede the $^6_4$ (and then the pattern is $\hat{1}$–$\hat{1}$–$\hat{7}$–$\hat{1}$) or a ii$_6$ (and then the pattern is $\hat{2}$–$\hat{1}$–$\hat{7}$–$\hat{1}$).

EXERCISE

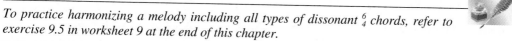

To practice harmonizing a melody including all types of dissonant $^6_4$ chords, refer to exercise 9.5 in worksheet 9 at the end of this chapter.

ASSIGNMENT AND KEYBOARD PROGRESSIONS

For analytical and written assignments and keyboard progressions based on the materials learned in this chapter, refer to chapter 9 in the workbook.

PITCH PATTERNS

Sing the following pitch patterns. As you sing, understand the harmonies that are linearized in them. Hear the various $^6_4$ chords, as well as their characteristic voice leading and linear function.

♪♪♪ Example 9.14

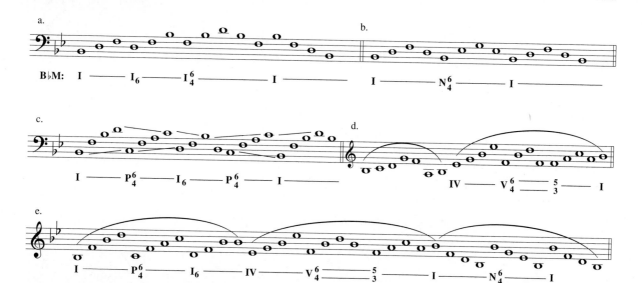

Composers and Their Music 9

Write short biographies of the following composers mentioned in this chapter: Gaetano Donizetti, Florence Price.

Listening

Listen to the following compositions by composers mentioned in this chapter:

> Donizetti: *Don Pasquale* (selections) or *Lucia di Lamermoor* (selections).
> Martínez: Sonata in AM (recording in Briscoe anthology).

Haydn: String Quartet in Gm, op. 74, no. 3.
Price: Symphony in Em (or any other orchestral composition available at your library).

Follow the score while you listen. Be able to place these compositions in one of the style periods and to comment on why and how they represent the musical characteristics of that period. Try to hear and identify as many cadences as possible and to verify whether or not a cadential $^6_4$ is used in the case of authentic or half cadences.

Terms for Review

Arpeggiated $^6_4$
Consonant $^6_4$ chords
Oscillating $^6_4$
Dissonant $^6_4$ chords
Neighbor $^6_4$

Compound melody
Passing $^6_4$
Cadential $^6_4$
$^{6-5}_{4-3}$ voice leading
Doubling in $^6_4$ chords

Worksheet 9

EXERCISE 9.1   Analysis.

1. Identify and list in the spaces below the type of $^6_4$ chords used in each of the following short excerpts by Florence Price, F. Schubert, and Gioachino Rossini.

   a) Example 9.15a (list type and measure numbers):

♪♪♪Example 9.15a   Florence Price, *Fantasie Negre,* mm. 141–148

   b) Example 9.15b: For this example, mark on the score—with lines—the characteristic voice leading for this type of $^6_4$ chord. Does the melody also reflect the voice leading?

♩♩♪Example 9.15b   F. Schubert, *Valses Nobles*, op. 77, no. 6, mm. 1–8

c) Example 9.15c: Identify and mark on the score the characteristic voice leading for the type of $^6_4$ represented by this example.

♩♩♪Example 9.15c   G. Rossini, *Il barbiere di Siviglia*, Act V, no. 3, mm. 139–144

2. Analyze anthology, no. 26 (Mozart, Piano Sonata in CM, K. 309, III).

   a) On the line below, provide a complete form diagram, including bubbles, measure numbers, cadences, and letters for form. What kind of period is this?

   _____

   b) On the score, provide a complete RN analysis of mm. 1–8. What types of $^6_4$ chords can you identify?
   c) What is the harmonic/linear function of each chord in mm. 1–8?

   What is the overall harmonic motion from m. 1 to m. 8?

   What is the long-range harmonic function of all the harmonies in mm. 1–7?

   d) Analyze and explain the final cadence (mm. 18–19). Provide RNs and explain the voice leading .(Is it of a type we have studied in this chapter?)

   e) Circle and label all NCTs in mm. 1–8.
   f) Describe the texture of this passage. What is the term that best applies to this type of texture?

3. Example 9.16 reproduces a compound melody. In the staff below it, renotate the passage clearly showing the various melodies that make up the compound melody. Refer to Examples 9.5 and 9.6b for models of notation.

Example 9.16   Henryk Wieniawski, Scherzo-Tarantella, op. 16, mm. 4–13

EXERCISE 9.2   Write the following triads in four voices with correct doubling.

Em: iv$^6_4$ A♭M: V$^6_4$ C♯m: i$^6_4$ GM: IV$^6_4$ Fm: V$^6_4$ DM: I$^6_4$ E♭M: V$^6_4$ Bm: iv$^6_4$ B♭M: I$^6_4$ AM: V$^6_4$

EXERCISE 9.3   Realize the following short progressions in four voices. Provide RNs where needed.

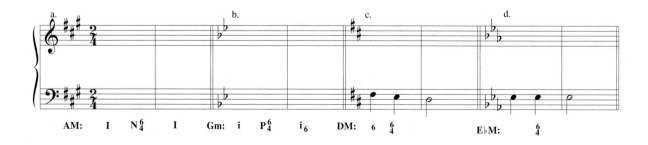

AM: I   N$^6_4$ I   Gm: i   P$^6_4$ i$_6$ DM: 6 $^6_4$ E♭M: $^6_4$

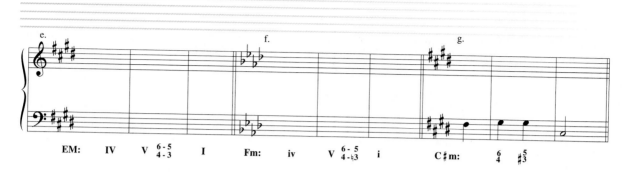

EM: IV   V $^{6-5}_{4-3}$ I   Fm: iv   V $^{6-5}_{4-\natural3}$ i   C♯m: $^6_4$ $♯^5_3$

EXERCISE 9.4   Analyze the following progression with RNs and realize it in four voices, using only i, iv, V and their inversions. Remember to double-check your outer-voice frame for good first-species counterpoint.

EXERCISE 9.5   Provide a four-voice harmonization of the following melody. As a practice of $^6_4$ chords, this melody allows you to use one in each measure (including m. 4), except for mm. 7 and 8 (an unlikely situation in the music literature, to be sure). First, write a good bass line, taking into account the possible $^6_4$ chord in every measure. Then, add the inner voices, following the voice-leading guidelines for $^6_4$ chords studied in this chapter. Indicate all the $^6_4$ chords you use, and provide a RN analysis of your harmonization. Notice that, other than m. 7, which will require three different RNs, all other measures require only one RN each.

FM:

EXERCISE 9.6 On your own music paper, write a compound melody using the examples studied in this chapter as models. A possible beginning is provided for you to use, although you may use your own beginning if you prefer.

Note:

1. Always listen to everything you write: Play through your exercises, or have a friend play through them while you listen.

2. When you listen to progressions, do not listen chord by chord. Rather, hear (a) harmonic patterns (bass patterns), and (b) linear patterns in the upper voices. In the I–P$_4^6$–I$_6$ pattern, for instance, first hear the $\hat{1}$–$\hat{2}$–$\hat{3}$ in the bass and then the voice exchange between the bass and an upper voice. In the I–N$_4^6$–I pattern, focus on the double-neighbor motion over the static bass.

Chapter 10

The Supertonic; Metric Reduction

You are already familiar with the concept of predominant function and with IV as a predominant chord. The **supertonic triad** is another chord whose function is almost exclusively to precede and prepare the dominant. The supertonic (ii in major, ii° in minor) is the triad on $\hat{2}$, and it contains scale degrees $\hat{2}$, $\hat{4}$, and $\hat{6}$.

THE SUPERTONIC IN ROOT POSITION

In example 10.1, observe the most characteristic harmonic context for **ii in root position**, which may be summarized as follows:

1. Because ii has two common tones with IV ($\hat{4}$ and $\hat{6}$), the two chords are very closely related tonally and functionally; ii often follows IV (examples 10.1 and 10.2a).

2. Because of the 5th relationship with V, **ii functions as a very strong predominant chord**. Whereas the relationship between IV and V is melodically strong (the roots are related by 2nd, and that provides a melodic tendency of IV toward V), ii and V have the strongest harmonic relationship (roots related by 5th; examples 10.1 and 10.2a).

3. The cadential progression ii–V–I is often used to harmonize the melodic patterns $\hat{2}$–$\hat{2}$–$\hat{1}$ or $\hat{2}$–$\hat{7}$–$\hat{1}$ as shown in examples 10.2a and b.

4. The progression I–ii (both in root position), although quite possible and correct, is not very frequent in the tonal repertoire because of its weak harmonic nature (roots by second). ii is more often preceded by I_6 (as in I–I_6–ii–V–I, example 10.2c) or by IV (I–IV–ii–V–I, example 10.2a). I–ii–I_6, or the even weaker I–ii–iii, are not suitable progressions to harmonize a $\hat{1}$–$\hat{2}$–$\hat{3}$ bass (the passing $^6_4$ progression, I–P^6_4–I_6 is a much stronger harmonization, and so is I–vii°$_6$–I_6, which we have not studied yet). If you do write a I–ii progression, beware of parallel 5ths or 8ves: as in any progression by steps, the best voice leading results from moving the three upper voices in contrary motion with the bass; see example 10.2d.

5. ii° (root position supertonic in a minor key) is a dissonant chord—it contains a °5th—and it is rarely found in root position. The supertonic in minor is more likely to appear as ii°₆.

Before we leave example 10.1, we can use it to review some familiar concepts. How are the two phrase segments in the first phrase related melodically? Look now at the second phrase (mm. 5–8). What is the harmonic function of the complete phrase? Does the V at the half cadence in m. 4 resolve before the end of the period? Analyze the chord in m. 6. What kind of chord is it? What is its function in the context of the complete second phrase? Notice that this chord actually has the characteristics of *two* of the chord types that we studied in the previous chapter. How and why is that so?

♪♪♪Example 10.1   F. Schubert, Originaltänze, op. 9, no. 3, mm. 1–8

♪♪♪Example 10.2

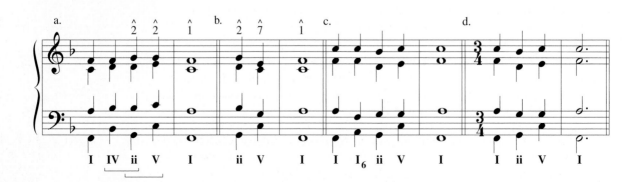

Doubling and Voice Leading

The usual progressions with ii do not present any special doubling or voice-leading difficulty, as illustrated by example 10.2. Any of the members of ii in root position may be doubled, and doubling should be determined by voice leading. In ii° (root position in minor), an infrequent but possible chord, it is better to double the third (the root and the fifth form a dissonant °5th, and one should not double dissonant pitches).

IV and ii have two common tones, which in principle should be left in the same voices, while the other voice moves up by step. ii and V have one common tone. In example 10.2a (soprano pattern $\hat{2}$–$\hat{2}$–$\hat{1}$), the common tone is sustained, while the other two upper voices move up by step. An alternative and correct voice leading is shown in example 10.2b (soprano pattern $\hat{2}$–$\hat{7}$–$\hat{1}$), where all voices move down in contrary motion with the bass. I and ii have no common tones, and all three voices should move down in contrary motion with the bass (example 10.2d).

EXERCISE

To practice realizing short progressions using supertonic chords in root position, refer to exercises 10.2a and b in worksheet 10 at the end of this chapter.

THE SUPERTONIC IN FIRST INVERSION

The supertonic chord appears most often in **first inversion**. ii$_6$ (ii°$_6$ in minor) may be found even more frequently than IV as the chord preparing the dominant. ii$_6$ is indeed a very effective predominant harmony because it has both the harmonic strength of the ii–V relationship (roots by 5th) and the melodic strength of the IV–V progression (a bass by steps, $\hat{4}$–$\hat{5}$). The close relationship between ii and IV, as well as their identical function, is best understood by comparing the ii$_6$–V and IV–V progressions, which differ in only one note (see examples 10.3a to c). As a matter of fact, IV and ii$_6$ may appear in succession over a sustained bass note $\hat{4}$, in such a way that IV is transformed into ii$_6$ by means of a simple **5–6 melodic motion** (the 5th above the bass turns into a 6th above the bass) in one of the upper voices, as illustrated by example 10.3b.

Doubling and Voice Leading

ii$_6$ (in major) appears very often with a doubled third ($\hat{4}$, a tonally strong scale degree), as in example 10.3c. Doubling the root (example 10.3d) is perfectly acceptable, whereas doubling the fifth (example 10.3e) is possible but less frequent. In the minor mode, ii°$_6$ normally appears with a doubled third (example 10.3f), possibly with a doubled root. Doubling the fifth in ii°$_6$ is likely to result in an augmented 2nd, $\flat\hat{6}$–$\natural\hat{7}$ (compare examples 10.3e and h), so in general it should be avoided.

The progression ii$_6$–V–I (or ii°$_6$–V–i) is a common cadential formula. An ornamented version of this formula appears in example 10.3i (Bach, Chorale 194, "Liebster Immanuel, Herzog der Frommen," mm. 14–16). Compare the voice leading in this example with example 10.3c, and identify all the NCTs in the Bach fragment.

♪♪♪ Example 10.3

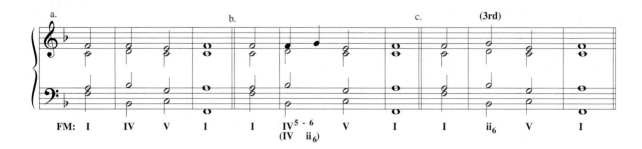

FM: I　　IV　　V　　I　　　I　　IV⁵⁻⁶　V　　I　　　I　　ii₆　V　　I
　　　　　　　　　　　　　　　　　　　(IV　ii₆)

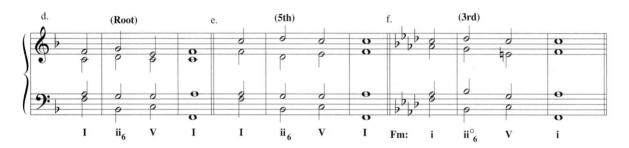

　　　I　　ii₆　V　　I　　　I　　ii₆　V　　I　　　Fm: i　ii°₆　V　　i

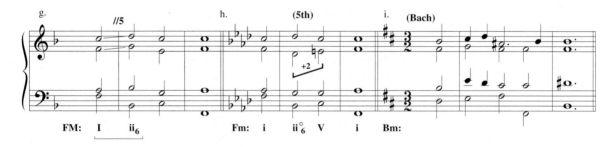

FM: I　　ii₆　　　　　Fm: i　ii°₆　V　i　　Bm:

NOTES

Compare examples 10.3f and g. In the progression I–ii₆, parallel 5ths may easily result if the root of I is doubled, as in example 10.3g. The problem can be avoided by doubling the third in I, as in example 10.3f (although the problem arises only in major keys; in minor, the consecutive 5ths in the same progression would be perfectly acceptable unequal 5ths, P5–°5). This is an example of doubling of the third in a root-position triad totally justified by voice-leading considerations.

　　Compare also examples 10.3d and g. In 10.3d, the parallel 5ths are avoided by switching the position of the voices involved (that is, the soprano line from example 10.3g is taken an octave lower in example 10.3d, and becomes the alto line, and the alto in example 10.3g becomes the soprano in example 10.3d). Parallel 5ths thus become correct parallel 4ths. In general, parallel 5ths among upper voices can often be avoided (and turned into parallel 4ths) by switching the voices that produce the faulty voice leading.

THE SUPERTONIC AND THE CADENTIAL $^6_4$

The supertonic, both in root position or first inversion, may (and most often does) precede a cadential $^6_4$. Because, unlike IV and I, ii and I do not have a common tone, the 4–3 figure in a cadential $^6_4$ preceded by ii or ii$_6$ will not be prepared as a suspension. Examine example 10.4a. If the cadential $^6_4$ were preceded by IV, we would prepare the 4–3 figure ($\hat{1}$–$\hat{7}$–$\hat{1}$) by placing $\hat{1}$, a member of IV, in the same voice as the following $\hat{1}$–$\hat{7}$–$\hat{1}$ (the top voice in this case). $\hat{1}$, however, is not a member of ii. The correct preparation of a cadential $^6_4$ preceded by ii (or by ii$_6$) is to approach both the 6th and the 4th in the $^6_4$ *by steps,* as shown in examples 10.4a and b, and as we already pointed out in chapter 9. With this voice leading, both the 6th and the 4th function as accented PTs over $\hat{5}$ (rather than the 4th being a suspension). Comparing examples 10.2b and 10.4a will help you hear the $^6_4$ as a double APT.

NOTE

Parallel 5ths may easily result when ii or ii$_6$ precedes a cadential $^6_4$. Here again, the solution is to switch the voices that produce the parallel 5ths and turn them into parallel 4ths (compare examples 10.4b and c).

EXERCISE

To practice realizing short progressions using supertonic chords in first inversion, refer to exercises 10.2c and d in worksheet 10 at the end of this chapter.

♪♪♪Example 10.4

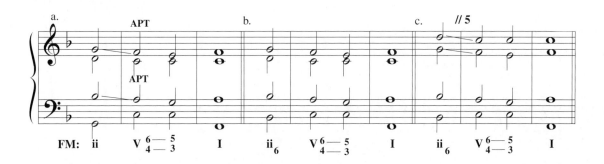

Typical Errors to Avoid

▶ Doubling the fifth in ii°₆, with a resulting augmented 2nd in the ii°₆–V progression
▶ Writing parallel 5ths in the I–ii or I–ii₆ progression
▶ Writing parallel 5ths in the ii₆–cadential $^6_4$ progression

---

Numerous examples of the ii₆–V$^{6-5}_{4-3}$–I progression may be found in the literature. As a matter of fact, this is perhaps the most common cadential formula (even more standard than the IV–V$^{6-5}_{4-3}$–I or the ii₆–V–I). Example 10.5 presents several such cadences by various composers. Analyze all of them, labeling them with Roman numerals and discussing their voice leading as compared with the examples studied in example 10.4. Make sure you identify both the 6–5 and the 4–3 in Haydn's cadential $^6_4$ progression. (Example 10.5b; the 4–3 is quite obvious, but where is the 6–5?). Discuss the harmonic/linear techniques used to prolong the final tonic chord in Haydn's example (mm. 145–149), as well as in example 10.5c, mm. 8 and 9, and in example 10.5d, m. 16.

EXERCISES

To practice realizing a progression using supertonic and $^6_4$ chords, refer to exercise 10.3 in worksheet 10 at the end of this chapter.

To practice harmonizing a melody using supertonic and $^6_4$ chords, refer to exercise 10.4 in worksheet 10 at the end of this chapter.

To practice analyzing a variety of musical examples that include supertonic and $^6_4$ chords, refer to exercise 10.1 in worksheet 10 at the end of this chapter.

♪♪♪ Example 10.5a   G. Donizetti, *Lucia di Lammermoor,* Act I, no. 3 ("Regnava nel silenzio"), Final Cadence

♪♪♪ Example 10.5b   J. Haydn, Trio in FM, Hob. XV:6, I, mm. 142–149

♪♪♪ Example 10.5c   G. Donizetti, *Don Pasquale,* Act II, Scene IV, mm. 7–11

♪♪♪ Example 10.5d   Felix Mendelssohn, "Duett," from *Zwölf Gesänge*, op. 8, no. 12, mm. 14–17

METRIC REDUCTION

In chapter 2 you were introduced to the concept of reduction. We saw two specific types of reduction, which were used in several examples in the preceding chapters: prolongational reduction, and bass reduction. *Prolongational reductions* show, by means of graphic symbols, the hierarchical structure of a passage from the tonal point of view. That is, they tell us what pitches are structurally more important, what other pitches have a subordinate role of extending or prolonging the structural pitches, and the means by which prolongation takes place. We have used prolongational reductions to show that a variety of harmonic progressions, which have a linear function, prolong a harmony that is structurally more significant (say, a neighbor $^6_4$ figure which prolongs a tonic harmony). Prolongational graphs also show that voice leading in this type of progression results from melodic and contrapuntal relationships. We have also used a particular type of reduction, which we have called *bass reduction,* to show long-range harmonic motion in extended passages (such as phrases, periods, or complete pieces). Bass reductions are especially useful to represent tonal motion as it relates to form.

In this section we will learn about **metric reduction**, a type of reduction that can have direct practical applications, such as, for instance, helping a performer understand the underlying melodic and harmonic framework of a texturally complex passage and hence make decisions regarding grouping and phrasing. In a metric reduction a musical texture is simplified to its *basic harmonic and melodic structure*. The essential process of reduction consists of removing NCTs and condensing arpeggiated chordal patterns into block chords. We refer to such harmonic reduction as metric reduction because the placement and duration of harmonies within the metric structure are preserved.

The process of reduction, moreover, may involve several stages. Examine, for instance, example 10.6. Example 10.6a shows the score for the first period of Mozart's DM Sonata, K. 284. In the first level of metric reduction in the system below the score

Example 10.6   W. A. Mozart, Piano Sonata in DM, K. 284, I

(example 10.6b), NCTs have been removed and arpeggiated patterns have become block chords. This is the underlying harmonic and melodic frame of this passage, with register, metric placement, and durations preserved. In a second level of reduction (example 10.6c) the pitches in the melody have been grouped (mostly in 3rds) following the harmonic structure provided by the left hand.

In the first level of reduction, we left pitches in the same register where they appear on the score. Occasionally, changing the octave of a pitch or a pattern may help construct a linear pattern, which was otherwise concealed by a change of register. In example 10.6c, for instance, hearing the A in m. 2 in the upper register helps us understand the nature of this melody: The structural frame of the first phrase is an ascending arpeggiated tonic triad, A–D–F♯–A, with a passing tone G. The linear nature of the segment F♯–G–A–B (mm. 1–3) is best understood if we hear the A at m. 2 in the upper register. In a similar way, changing the register of the C♯ in m. 8 helps us hear the completion of the linear descending pattern F♯–E–D–C♯. Notice, finally, that although the G in m. 3 (right hand) moves down to E by steps (through the accented PT, F♯), the B does not resolve to A as you could expect, but is rather left "dangling" in its register (as indicated by the A in parentheses and the question mark in example 10.6c). When the high register is revisited in m. 6, however, the B does resolve to A, thus achieving closure in the high register (as shown by the arrow and the exclamation mark).

PRACTICAL APPLICATION AND DISCUSSION

Metric Reduction and Performance

Simplifying a piece of music by means of metric harmonic reduction has immediate practical applications for the performer. In the first place, it helps understand the melodic and harmonic structure of the music, its voice leading, and its underlying linear patterns. In the second place, practicing a chordal reduction of a piece or fragment helps memorize it, phrase it, and, in the case of string instruments, work at intonation. Example 10.6 illustrates these points as applied to a composition for piano. Example 10.7 shows how a passage from the solo violin repertoire (Bach's "Chaconne") may be practiced in a reduced version to help improve musical understanding, intonation, and memorization. (In order to make it more idiomatic for the violin, the violinist would be likely to omit some of the notes in this reduction while practicing it.)

In example 10.7b we can see how a reduction helps us appreciate (and hear) the numerous sequential and linear patterns in all voices. The top voice features the sequence F–G/E–F/D–E, followed by another sequence F–D–B♭/E–C–A/D–B♭–G and a closing descending line (G–F–E–D). Each of the sequences, moreover, contains several linear designs. In mm. 57–60, notice the F–E–D–C♯ pattern (one pitch per measure, in parallel 3rds with the bass), and the G–F–E–D pattern mostly on the third beats. Identify the melodic linear patterns in mm. 61–65. Similarly, two basic linear patterns can be heard in the bass in mm. 57–60. The repeated **chaconne bass** on which Bach writes this composition (the descending melodic 4th D–C–B♭–A) comes out clearly in the reduction. If you consider all the bass notes in mm. 57–60 (D–G–C–F–B♭–E–[D]–A), what harmonic/melodic pattern do you recognize? Look now at the bass in mm. 61–65, and find the chaconne bass and other sequential and linear patterns. Finally, study the interesting voice leading in mm. 64–65. (Do you see any voice exchange?)

Example 10.7   J. S. Bach, "Chaconne," from Partita no. 2 in Dm for Violin Solo, BWV 1004, mm. 57–65

EXERCISE

To practice realizing a metric reduction, refer to exercise 10.5 in worksheet 10 at the end of this chapter.

ASSIGNMENT AND KEYBOARD PROGRESSIONS

For analytical and written assignments and keyboard progressions based on the materials learned in this chapter, refer to chapter 10 in the workbook.

PITCH PATTERNS

Sing the pitch patterns in example 10.8, listening to and understanding the various uses of the linearized supertonic chords.

♪♪♪ Example 10.8

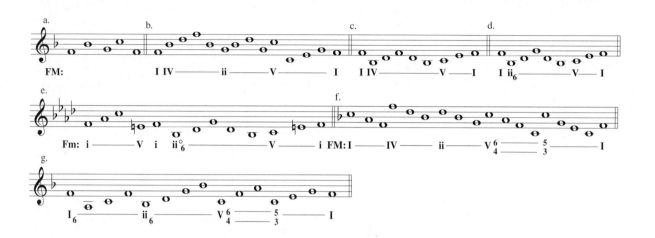

FM: I IV ——————— ii —— V ————— I   I IV ————— V —— I   I ii₆ —————— V — I

Fm: i ——— V i ii°₆ ————— V ——— i   FM: I ——— IV ——— ii — V ⁶₄ ——— ⁵₃ ——— I

I₆ ————— ii₆ ————— V ⁶₄ ——— ⁵₃ ——— I

Composers and Their Music 10

Biographies

Write short biographies of the following composers mentioned in this chapter: Felix Mendelssohn, Carl Maria von Weber.

Listening

Listen to the following compositions by composers mentioned in this chapter:

Schubert: *Die schöne Müllerin* (selected songs).

Mendelssohn: Symphony no. 4 in AM, op. 90, *Italian.*

J. S. Bach: Partita no. 2 in Dm for Violin Solo, BWV 1004.

Follow the score while you listen. Be able to place these compositions in one of the style periods and to comment on why and how they represent the musical characteristics of that period.

Terms for Review

Supertonic triad
Function of the supertonic triad
ii in root position
Relationship of ii with IV and V
ii and ii° in first inversion

5–6 melodic motion
Supertonic and cadential ⁶₄
Metric reduction
Metric reduction and performance
Chaconne bass

Worksheet 10

EXERCISE 10.1   Analysis.

1. Refer to Example 10.9 and answer the following questions:

   a) Analyze the phrase structure of mm. 1–8. How many phrases are there? On what cadences do they end? How are the phrases related, and what kind of formal structure do they constitute?

♪♪♪ Example 10.9	Carl Maria von Weber, Theme from "Variations on an Original Theme," op. 2

b) How are the phrases in mm. 9–16 related? (Are they parallel, contrasting, etc.?)
What is the formal/thematic function of mm. 9–16 as a whole with respect to
mm. 1–8 (answer/contrasting/variation)? How do the textures of these two sections compare? Assign lowercase letters to each of the phrases in this piece, expressing their parallel or contrasting relationships:

c) What cadential pattern do you recognize in the following measures:

m. 2:   m. 4:   m. 6:

m. 7, beat 3 (Where is the $^{6-5}_{4-3}$?):

m. 15 (Where is the $^{6-5}_{4-3}$?):

What harmonic/linear pattern do you recognize in mm. 9–11?

d) Circle and label all the NCTs in mm. 9–16.

e) Provide a complete RN analysis of mm. 1–8.

f) On your own music paper, provide a bass reduction for the complete example,
showing tonal motion and hierarchy within each of the phrases and over the
complete piece.

2. Compare the cadences in examples 10.10a, b, and c. What do they have in common? How do they differ? (Take into account the complete predominant-
dominant-tonic pattern.)

Example 10.10a   Giuseppe Verdi: *Il trovatore,* Act II, no. 15, "E deggio e posso crederlo?"

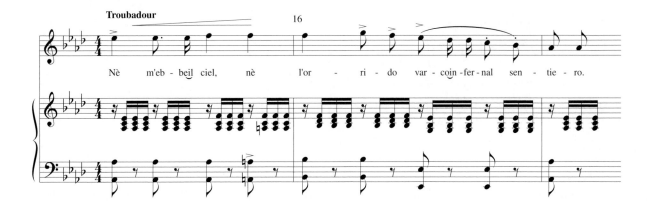

Example 10.10b   G. Donizetti, *Lucia di Lammermoor,* Act. II, no. 6, "Il pallor funesto?"

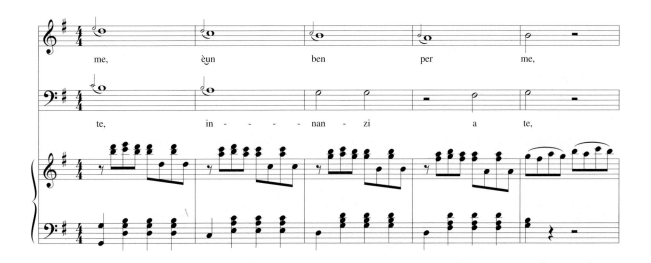

🎵🎵 Example 10.10c   Notebook of Anna Magdalena Bach, "Aria di Govannini"

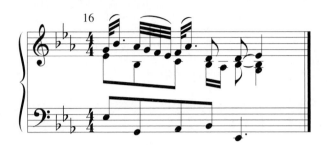

EXERCISE 10.2   Realize the following short progressions in four voices. Add Roman numerals (RNs) where missing.

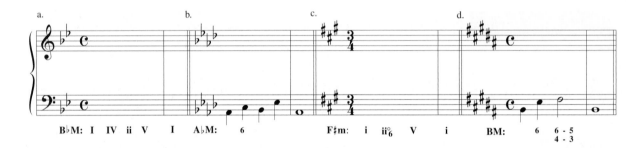

B♭M: I IV ii V I   A♭M: 6   F♯m: i ii°₆ V i   BM: 6 6 - 5
                                                                    4 - 3

EXERCISE 10.3   Realize the following progression in four voices. Remember to double-check your outer-voice frame for good first-species counterpoint.

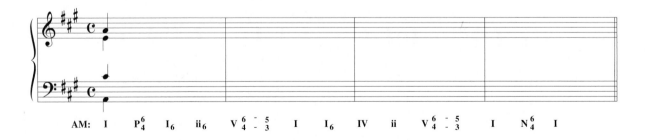

AM: I P⁶₄ I₆ ii₆ V⁶₄ - ⁵₃ I I₆ IV ii V⁶₄ - ⁵₃ I N⁶₄ I

EXERCISE 10.4   Harmonize the following melody with bass and RNs. Use i, iv, V, ii, and their inversions. Include one or more of each of these: passing $^6_4$, neighbor $^6_4$, cadential $^6_4$. Remember to double-check your outer-voice frame for good first-species counterpoint.

EXERCISE 10.5   Metric reduction. Provide a metric reduction of anthology, no. 27, mm. 1–8. (Mozart, Sonata in AM, K. 331, Theme).

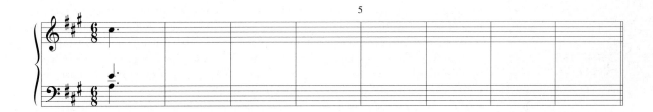

Chapter 11

Harmonic Rhythm; Hypermeter

In this chapter we will study relationships between harmony and other primary parameters of music: rhythm, meter, and melody. Harmonic progressions do not occur in isolation. Rather, they form harmonic phrases that are usually part of a melodic/harmonic complex appearing in a rhythmic and metric context. Although the possible interrelations among all these elements are endless, and good composers often surprise us with unexpected possibilities, here again we can examine some standard relationships commonly found in Western tonal art music. Doing so will allow us to understand better how specific examples sometimes depart from this standard behavior, and what the resulting effect is. We will also learn that meter can be heard at various hierarchical levels; that accents created by meter, rhythm, or harmony may or may not correlate; and that all of it affects the way we hear music.

HARMONIC RHYTHM

While listening to a recording of anthology, no. 52 (Verdi, "Libiamo ne'lieti calici," from *La traviata*), consider these questions. How many different chords are there in the complete excerpt? How often do chords change? We will refer to the rate of chord change with the term **harmonic rhythm** (HR). The harmonic rhythm in anthology, no. 52 is certainly very slow: There are only four chord changes in twenty-one measures (using only two different chords), and the first chord does not change for eight measures. A diagram for the harmonic rhythm of this excerpt appears in example 11.1.

Now examine example 11.2a, the first period of Verdi's famous aria, "Sempre libera" (also from *La traviata*). Although the harmonic rhythm may still be considered slow, it is not quite as slow as in the previous example. The rate of change is here one chord per measure, except in mm. 12–13. Because m. 12 ends a phrase and m. 13

Example 11.1

Example 11.2a   G. Verdi, *La traviata,* "Sempre libera," mm. 8–16

Sem pre li - be - ra deg-g'i - o fol - leg - gia - re di gio-ja in gio - ja, vo' che

scor - ra il vi - ver mi - o pei sen - tie - ri del pia - cer.

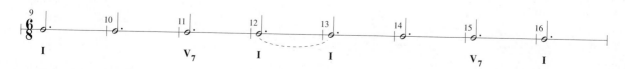

Example 11.2b

begins the next phrase, however, we do not really hear these two measures as being one single harmonic unit. Example 11.2b represents graphically the harmonic rhythm of this passage.

NOTE

Although the chord in m. 10 is a type of diminished seventh chord, which we will not study until chapter 18, you should be able to discuss its function if you examine its voice leading with respect to the previous and following chords. Is it really a chord with a harmonic function, or does it have a well-defined linear function?

The harmonic rhythm in example 11.3a, on the other hand, is quite different from what we have seen in the two examples above. Throughout most of this excerpt, chords change every beat, producing a fast harmonic rhythm as indicated by the diagram in example 11.3b. Chorale harmonizations usually feature this same type of fast harmonic rhythm (a chord per beat).

Notice that the terms *slow* and *fast* as applied to harmonic rhythm have nothing to do with how slow or fast the tempo of the music is. They simply refer to the rate of chordal change, and in this context *slow* means "not very often," whereas *fast* means "often or very often." We can also say that in a slow harmonic rhythm chords usually (and approximately) change every measure or even less often, whereas in fast harmonic rhythms they change every beat or even more often, with numerous possible gradations in between. We will discuss possible interactions between harmonic rhythm and tempo in the next section.

♪♪♪Example 11.3a   Josephine Lang, "Gott sei mir Sünder gnädig," mm. 5–10

nom - men, auch Du   wirst auf - ge - nom - men!

♪♪♪ Example 11.3b

Harmonic Rhythm and Tempo

One may find fast or slow harmonic rhythms in a variety of contexts. In general, a fast harmonic rhythm creates a sense of harmonic activity which may enliven and add motion to the music, whereas a slow harmonic rhythm may produce a more static effect. Although there is no preestablished relationship between harmonic rhythm and tempo, faster tempos often feature slower harmonic rhythms (see example 11.2, and anthology, no. 52, Verdi, "Libiamo"), and slow tempos may display faster harmonic rhythms (see, for instance, anthology, no. 33, Beethoven, Sonata op. 10, no. 1, and anthology, no. 50, Schumann, "Folk Song"). A fast harmonic rhythm in a fast tempo may produce a blurred or crowded effect, whereas a slow harmonic rhythm in a slow tempo may result in a static musical passage. Composers, on the other hand, use these effects to their advantage for expressive and formal purposes. If you refer back to example 2.9, for instance, you will see that by using a slow harmonic rhythm with a slow tempo, Beethoven emphasizes the melody, which is the active factor in that passage and which must be played "molto espressivo." Conversely, whereas a slow harmonic rhythm is often found at the beginning of fast movements to allow for a clear establishment of the key, fast harmonic rhythms in such movements may appear in harmonically unstable developmental sections and in other passages in which the composer wishes to create a sense of harmonic unrest.

Irregular Harmonic Rhythm

In examples 11.2 and 3 the rate of chord changes is quite regular (every measure, every beat). These are cases of **regular harmonic rhythm**. Harmonic rhythm is not always regular, though. Changes in harmonic rhythm are an element of musical variety, and they may be used to prevent predictability. Different sections in a composition often feature contrasting and characteristic harmonic rhythms. Moreover, the harmonic rhythm may change within one single section.

Listen to the opening twenty-three measures of Mozart's *Jupiter* Symphony. As you listen, mark the chord changes on the keyboard reduction provided in example 11.4a. Then compare your notes with the diagram in example 11.4b. This is an example of **irregular harmonic rhythm**. Comment on the different sections of the passage, and how the harmonic rhythm functions in each of them. The upper line of Roman numerals under the diagram indicates the rhythm of the basic tonic and dominant functions on which the excerpt is built at the surface level (other chords are not indicated by these Roman numerals). What kind of cadence does the passage end on? What happens to the harmonic rhythm, as we approach the cadence, in mm. 19–21? The *acceleration of harmonic rhythm* is a device often used by composers to create a *drive toward a cadence*, thus stressing the function of the cadence as a harmonic goal.

Now listen to the fragment again, listening to the harmonic rhythm indicated by the lower line of Roman numerals. You are now hearing a deeper level of harmonic rhythm, one determined by the structural chords that are being prolonged rather than by each particular chordal change at the surface level. At this deeper level of harmonic activity, we first hear a motion from I to V and back to I (mm. 1–8), then we hear an area in which I is prolonged (mm. 9–18), and finally a prolongation of V leading to the half cadence (mm. 19–23). At this level, the tonic harmony in mm. 9–18 is prolonged by several linear chords (What is their exact linear function?), and the "tonic" chords in mm. 19–23 also have the function of embellishing the underlying dominant harmony by linear means (What are these means exactly?). In other words, the diagram shows that we can hear **harmonic rhythm at various levels**. *At the surface level, the harmonic rhythm is often bound to melodic and rhythmic activity, whereas at the next deeper level it is associated with such formal factors as phrase and period structure.*

As an aural exercise, listen to the opening twenty-two measures of Mozart's Symphony no. 40 in Gm, K. 550. On the diagram provided in example 11.5, notate the harmonic rhythm of the passage (by ear) and also the long-range harmonic motion. Then discuss what you have heard in class. The slurs over the diagram should help you listen to this fragment and also determine its long-range harmonic motion.

EXERCISE

To practice analysis of harmonic rhythm, refer to exercises 11.1.1 and 11.1.2 in worksheet 11 at the end of this chapter.

Example 11.4b

Example 11.5

HYPERMETER

In chapter B we studied the concept of **metric accent**. Metric accents result from the organization of pulses into regularly recurring patterns. Within a measure, beats are differently accented depending on specific meters. In essence, we studied that in duple meters the pattern of metric accents is strong-weak, in quadruple meters it is strong-weak-strong-weak, and in triple meters it is strong-weak-weak (although beat 3 is the weakest). These metric patterns are summarized in the following figures, where the symbol – means strong and ‿ means weak.

$$\overset{-\,\smile}{}\,\overset{-\,\smile}{} \qquad \overset{-\,\smile\,-\,\smile}{}\,\overset{-\,\smile\,-\,\smile}{} \qquad \overset{-\,\smile\,\smile}{}\,\overset{-\,\smile\,\smile}{}$$

$$\tfrac{2}{4}\; 1\;2\;|\;1\;2\;\| \qquad \tfrac{4}{4}\; 1\;2\;3\;4\;|\;1\;2\;3\;4\;\| \qquad \tfrac{3}{4}\; 1\;2\;3\;|\;1\;2\;3\;\|$$

NOTE

In $\frac{4}{4}$, beat 3 is weaker than beat 1. Thus, if the harmonic rhythm is a half note, the second half note is weaker than the first one (the relationship that we are hearing then is the same as in $\frac{2}{2}$ – ‿ for the whole measure).

Whereas the strong-weak relationships we have just noted above are applied to beats, similar patterns can be found at higher metric levels. In other words, we can think of whole measures as "beats," and then think of their relative accentual value with respect to each other. This will provide us with an interesting type of phrase rhythm with immediate implications for performance. Take, for instance, the familiar Mozart melody in example 11.6. If you play it hearing the metric accents indicated above each measure, you will discover that we perceive meter at several different levels. In the lower level (the measure level), we hear the standard alternation of strong and weak beats in duple meter. By grouping measures in pairs, we can hear two-bar units featuring a strong-weak-strong-weak quadruple pattern of metric accents (lower brackets). If we think of each measure as a "beat," we can then hear the whole period as two "big measures" in $\frac{4}{4}$ (second level of brackets). A metric unit larger than a measure is called a **hypermeasure**. In the second level of our example, we hear two four-bar hypermeasures, featuring the typical alternation of strong-weak metric accents. Moreover, we can also hear the phrase rhythm at a higher level, and think of the period as a single $\frac{4}{4}$ hypermeasure. This provides us with two accented metric impulses (mm. 1 and 5) and two phrase upbeats (mm. 3 and 7).

Just as *meter* refers to the combination of beats in a metrical context, the term **hypermeter** refers to the combination of measures in a metrical context. Not all music is hypermetric. Two conditions for hypermeter to exist are the recurrence of equal-sized measure groups (such as 2 + 2 + 2 + 2, 4 + 4, etc.), and a pattern of alternation between strong and weak measures. Both of these conditions are met and illustrated in example 11.6. Notice, moreover, that hypermeter is based on the concept of *metric hierarchy:* Beats are contained in measures, which in turn are contained in larger hypermeasures, which are themselves contained in larger hypermeasures, and so on. *A beat perceived as strong in one level becomes a beat in the next level,* as you can also verify in our example.[1]

---

[1] For further study of hypermeter and related issues, refer to W. Rothstein, *Phrase Rhythm in Tonal Music*, pp. 8–13.

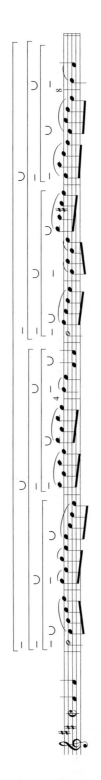

Example 11.6 W. A. Mozart, Piano Sonata in DM, K. 284, III

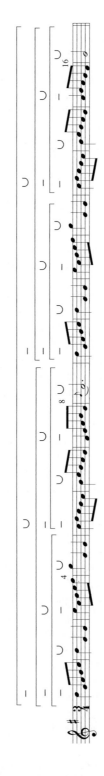

Example 11.7a Minuet from *Notebook for Anna Magdalena Bach*

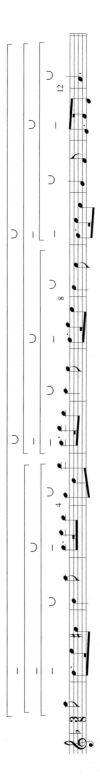

Example 11.7b G. F. Handel, "But Who May Abide the Day of His Coming?" from *Messiah*

Irregular Harmonic Rhythm

In examples 11.2 and 3 the rate of chord changes is quite regular (every measure, every beat). These are cases of **regular harmonic rhythm**. Harmonic rhythm is not always regular, though. Changes in harmonic rhythm are an element of musical variety, and they may be used to prevent predictability. Different sections in a composition often feature contrasting and characteristic harmonic rhythms. Moreover, the harmonic rhythm may change within one single section.

Listen to the opening twenty-three measures of Mozart's *Jupiter* Symphony. As you listen, mark the chord changes on the keyboard reduction provided in example 11.4a. Then compare your notes with the diagram in example 11.4b. This is an example of **irregular harmonic rhythm**. Comment on the different sections of the passage, and how the harmonic rhythm functions in each of them. The upper line of Roman numerals under the diagram indicates the rhythm of the basic tonic and dominant functions on which the excerpt is built at the surface level (other chords are not indicated by these Roman numerals). What kind of cadence does the passage end on? What happens to the harmonic rhythm, as we approach the cadence, in mm. 19–21? The *acceleration of harmonic rhythm* is a device often used by composers to create a *drive toward a cadence,* thus stressing the function of the cadence as a harmonic goal.

Now listen to the fragment again, listening to the harmonic rhythm indicated by the lower line of Roman numerals. You are now hearing a deeper level of harmonic rhythm, one determined by the structural chords that are being prolonged rather than by each particular chordal change at the surface level. At this deeper level of harmonic activity, we first hear a motion from I to V and back to I (mm. 1–8), then we hear an area in which I is prolonged (mm. 9–18), and finally a prolongation of V leading to the half cadence (mm. 19–23). At this level, the tonic harmony in mm. 9–18 is prolonged by several linear chords (What is their exact linear function?), and the "tonic" chords in mm. 19–23 also have the function of embellishing the underlying dominant harmony by linear means (What are these means exactly?). In other words, the diagram shows that we can hear **harmonic rhythm at various levels**. *At the surface level, the harmonic rhythm is often bound to melodic and rhythmic activity, whereas at the next deeper level it is associated with such formal factors as phrase and period structure.*

As an aural exercise, listen to the opening twenty-two measures of Mozart's Symphony no. 40 in Gm, K. 550. On the diagram provided in example 11.5, notate the harmonic rhythm of the passage (by ear) and also the long-range harmonic motion. Then discuss what you have heard in class. The slurs over the diagram should help you listen to this fragment and also determine its long-range harmonic motion.

EXERCISE

To practice analysis of harmonic rhythm, refer to exercises 11.1.1 and 11.1.2 in worksheet 11 at the end of this chapter.

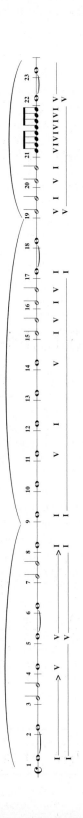

Example 11.4b

Example 11.5

Example 11.7a demonstrates how a hypermetric analysis of a sixteen-measure period allows us to hear it, at the highest level, as a single $\frac{4}{4}$ hypermeasure providing strong accents at the beginning of each eight-measure phrase. Lower hypermetric levels tell us about the relative metric accentuation for eight-bar and four-bar hypermeasures. Play this melody several times (you can find the complete score in anthology, no. 6), hearing the hypermetric patterns at each level, and notice how the highest level produces a musically convincing long-range phrase rhythm.

Example 11.7b features a slightly more complex phrase rhythm. The passage includes three four-bar hypermeasures. At the middle hypermetric level we hear a grouping of 4 + 8 measures, in which mm. 1 and 5 are beginning strong hyperbeats, and m. 9, although still strong, is not really an initial downbeat. At the highest level, it all becomes a $\frac{3}{4}$ hypermeasure, with a single initial strong beat. Play this phrase, and determine whether you hear its rhythm as notated on the example, or whether, perhaps, you could argue for a different interpretation.

Then realize (and discuss in class) your own hypermetric analyses of the complete Haydn Menuet in anthology, no. 19 (Divertimento in CM), Mozart's "Theme" from Sonata in AM, K. 331 (anthology, no. 27), and Mozart's Sonata in CM, K. 309, III, mm. 1–19 (anthology, no. 26). In the last two cases, the phrase extensions at the end of each fragment will require some metric adjustment (explore the possibility of a shorter hypermeasure at the end of the AM sonata example and an interrupted or incomplete measure in the CM fragment).

What is the effect of hypermetric analysis on performance? Far from hearing or performing the Mozart period "note by note" or "measure by measure," the concept of hypermeasure allows us to hear and perform it as a whole, single metric unit, with its inner phrase downbeats and upbeats. Hypermeter is thus allowing us to hear large-scale metric organization at the phrase level.

HARMONY, RHYTHM, AND METER: TONAL AND METRIC ACCENTS

The relationship between harmony and meter is free and flexible. In order to understand it better, we will define a new type of accent, which we will call **tonal accent**. Whereas metric accents are regular and result from a metric structure that in some ways is superimposed to music, *tonal accents result from harmonic events* and hence come from the music itself. Tonal accents may result from elements such as harmonic progression or tonal motion within phrases. In the first case, for instance, one could interpret the tonic in a V_7–I progression as *rhythmically accented,* because after the unstable and dissonant V_7, the stable and consonant tonic is heard as a point of arrival or repose.[2] We will refer to the type of tonal accent created by harmonic progression as **harmonic accent**. In the case of tonal motion within a phrase, we typically hear tonal accents at the beginning and at the end of a phrase. In other words, points of initiation or arrival (cadences) are rhythmically accented. We will call this type of tonal accent (which begins and ends musical units) **structural accent**.

Tonal accents are thus rhythmic rather than metric. (You will remember that in chapter B we defined rhythmic accents as those that result from "grouping, note length, a sense of harmonic or tonal arrival, and other nonmetrical factors.") Moreover, *tonal*

---

[2] From a different perspective, however, some performers may argue that dissonance should receive a stronger emphasis than consonance, and that V_7, rather than I, should be heard as rhythmically accented.

accents are totally independent from metric accents. Tonal and metric accents may or may not coincide, as the discussion of the following examples will illustrate.

Example 11.8 shows the initial four measures of Mozart's familiar DM sonata, III, which we have already discussed. The arrows over mm. 1 and 4 represent structural accents (the initial and cadential accents, respectively). From example 11.6, on the other hand, we know that the **hypermetric pattern of accents for this four-bar phrase** is strong-weak-strong-weak. This pattern is indeed the most standard metric design for four-bar (or eight-bar) phrases. In other words, we usually think of this type of formal unit as $\frac{4}{4}$ hypermeasures with a strong-weak-strong-weak accentual pattern. Such a pattern presupposes that, at the hypermetric level, regular phrase beginnings are metrically strong, whereas cadences are *metrically* weak, a concept you can very well apply (and verify) in performance. *Rhythmically,* on the other hand, we saw that cadences receive a structural accent (the arrow in our example). In this type of hypermetric pattern (strong-weak-strong-weak), the initial structural accent coincides with the initial metric accent, while the cadential structural accent falls on a metrically weak measure.

The phrase in example 11.9, on the other hand, represents a less frequent, but equally possible, type of relationship between structural and metric accents. In this ex-

ample, structural accents fall on mm. 1 and 8. Thinking of the passage, however, as two four-bar hypermeasures, we notice immediately that metric accents fall on measures 2, 4, 6, and 8, while the odd-numbered measures, in this case, are clearly unaccented. Unlike the Mozart example above, the four-bar metric pattern weak-strong-weak-strong produces a coincidence of final structural accent (the cadence) with final metric accent, whereas the initial structural accent falls on a metrically weak measure.

A final example in this discussion will further stress the independence between tonal and metric accents. The Chopin passage in example 11.10 actually illustrates how structural, harmonic, and metric accents can all be independent of each other (and in conflict with each other). Because the harmonic rhythm in this passage establishes a pattern of two-bar hypermeasures, and we clearly hear m. 1 as metrically accented, we can think of the whole passage as consisting of four two-bar hypermeasures with a strong-weak-strong-weak metric pattern. The structural accents fall on m. 1 (the beginning of a metrically accented hypermeasure) and m. 7 (the arrival on the tonic, in a metrically weak hypermeasure), establishing the first conflicting relationship between tonal and metric accents. Looking now at the harmony for the passage, a possible interpretation would be to hear a harmonic accent in m. 3, because of the arrival on a tonic harmony after the dominant harmony in mm. 1–2. Following the same interpretation, we can hear m. 7 as harmonically accented. The arrows over the Roman numerals

Example 11.10   F. Chopin, Prelude in AM, op. 28, no.7, mm. 1–8

FURTHER ANALYSIS

Metric-Harmonic "Rhyme" and Conflict

Analyze, and discuss in class, the harmonic rhythm and the metric placement of chords in anthology, no. 9 ("Was Gott tut"), mm. 1–4. In the possible interpretation of the dominant-tonic progression we discussed earlier in the chapter (and on which we will base the following comments), we hear a harmonic accent on the tonic resolution. In the Bach passage, you can verify that all tonic chords fall on a metrically strong beat (1 or 3), whereas all dominant chords fall on a metrically weak beat (2 or 4) except for the V in m. 4, beat 1. This V, however, also resolves to a tonic on strong beat (beat 3) after a passing deceptive resolution on beat 2. When, in a passage like this, tonic chords are placed on strong beats, and dominant chords are placed on weak beats, we can speak of a correspondence between metric and harmonic accents that creates a **metric-harmonic "rhyme"** (a poetic term we use metaphorically).

A further example of metric-harmonic rhyme is provided by the phrase from Mozart's Sonata in DM reproduced in example 11.8 above. Analyze its harmonic rhythm, and identify the metric location of all tonic and dominant chords. After you do so, examine the diagram in example 11.11.

The diagram indicates that all tonic chords are placed on strong beats, and that the V in m. 2 is on a weak beat. The V in m. 4, on the other hand, falls on a strong beat because it is the half cadence (HC) that closes the phrase. At the hypermetric level, however, we have already seen that m. 4 in this phrase is weak. In the hypermetric design of the complete phrase, then, the V in m. 4 is actually on a weak beat, confirming the metric-harmonic rhyme for the whole phrase.

Metric-harmonic rhyme is a factor of formal balance which can easily be found in music, especially in the baroque and Classical periods. We can also find, however, many passages in which metric and harmonic accents do not correspond, creating a **metric-harmonic conflict**, which may be used to good advantage to propel the music forward or for dramatic purposes. We already discussed an example of metric-harmonic tension (Chopin's Prelude no. 7). Examples 11.2a and b (Verdi's "Sempre libera") provide a further instance of noncorrespondence between metric and *har*monic accents. The four-bar hypermetric design in this example follows the standard strong-weak-strong-weak pattern. The I on which the phrase ends (m. 12 or m. 16) is placed in a relatively weaker measure than the preceding V_7 (m. 11 or m. 15), producing a metrically accented dominant chord which resolves to a less accented tonic. As you listen to this period, hear the difference between the metric-harmonic rhyme in mm. 9 and 13 (the tonic chords that initiate each of the two phrases) and the lack of such rhyme in mm. 12 and 16 (the tonic chords that close the phrases, both on metrically weak measures).

Examples 11.12 and 11.13 illustrate two simple but effective cases of conflicting metrical and harmonic accents. In example 11.12, each of the two pairs of four-measure phrases features a different relationship between metric and harmonic accents. Discuss the metric accents for each of the measures in the four-measures phrases and whether the harmonic accents do or do not correlate with the metric accents.

Listen to example 11.13, and make a diagram of its harmonic rhythm, structural accents, metric accents at the measure level, and correlation among structural, metric, and harmonic accents. After you do this, discuss your findings in class. Notice especially the opening gesture (mm. 60–61): Is it a typical beginning gesture? Or would you be more likely to find such a gesture elsewhere in a piece? What kind of metric-harmonic ambiguity is established by this gesture? Does Mozart follow through with this ambiguity for the rest of the passage?

Finally, example 11.14 shows a case of conflict between metric accent and harmonic rhythm. While the violin features a melody in unequivocal $\frac{3}{4}$, the rhythm of the piano chords establishes a conflicting and simultaneous $\frac{2}{4}$ grouping. In chapter B we studied the type of rhythmic event featured here in the piano part (hemiola), in which beats in triple meter are grouped in pairs, as in duple meter (or, conversely, triple grouping in duple meter). Hemiola is a device commonly found in baroque instrumental music and often used by Schumann and Brahms to create a conflict between metric and rhythmic accents produced by grouping.

♪♪♪ Example 11.11

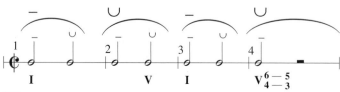

♪♪♪Example 11.12   F. Schubert, *Twelve Waltzes, Seventeen Ländler, and Nine Ecossaises,* op. 18, Waltz no. 6, mm. 17–33

♪♪♪Example 11.13   W. A. Mozart, Symphony no. 41 in CM, K. 551, *Jupiter,* III, mm. 60–67, (Piano Reduction)

under example 11.10 show these harmonic accents. It is interesting, then, to observe the following characteristics of this piece: (1) the initial structural accent falls on a measure that is not harmonically accented; (2) the first harmonic accent according to the above interpretation (m. 3) comes on a metrically weak hypermeasure; and (3) the final structural accent and the final harmonic accent in this passage coincide (m. 7), but the same measure is metrically weak at the hypermetric level. Are there other possible interpretations of harmonic accent in this phrase? What are they, and how would they change your reading of rhythmic emphasis as related to metric structure? Does an interpretation different from the one we have just discussed perhaps seem more convincing to you? If so, can you articulate your interpretation and present your arguments in class? In any case, the complex interaction of structural, harmonic, and metric accents in this prelude accounts for the highly dynamic character of this seemingly

♪♪♪ Example 11.14   J. Brahms, Sonata no. 2 for Violin and Piano, op. 100, I, mm. 116–120

PRACTICAL APPLICATION AND DISCUSSION

1. Find examples of fast and slow harmonic rhythm in your performance repertoire. How does the harmonic rhythm relate, in each case, to the tempo? What is the combined effect of harmonic rhythm and tempo in each of your examples? If, for instance, you find a case of slow harmonic rhythm with slow tempo, is it meant to focus the attention on an expressive melody? How do these tempo/harmonic rhythm relationships affect the way you would hear or perform your examples?

2. In a section with fast harmonic rhythm, examine the metric placement of dominant and tonic sonorities. Do they correspond with metric accents, or do they create metric-harmonic conflict?

3. If you find a section with four- or eight-measure phrases and slow harmonic rhythm, study the relationship between hypermetric and tonal accents. Does the design in your example correspond with either of the designs we have discussed in examples 11.8 or 11.9?

4. Can you find any examples of conflicting metrical and harmonic accents? Can you discuss different possible interpretations of the passages you find, and perhaps argue in favor of the interpretation you find the most musically satisfying?

(and deceptively) simple short composition. Understanding these accentual conflicts can only help the performer and the listener to transmit and appreciate the elements that propel this music forward in such a convincing way.[3]

---

[3] The above discussion on the relationship between tonal and metric accents is largely based on the following two sources, which you may wish to consult for further study of the topic: Jonathan Kramer, *The Time of Music* (New York: Schirmer, 1988), pp. 83–98, and Fred Lerdahl and Ray Jackendoff, *A Generative Theory of Tonal Music* (Cambridge, MA: MIT Press, 1996), pp. 17–18 and 30–35. See also David Epstein, *Beyond Orpheus* (Oxford: Oxford University Press, 1987), pp. 60–71.

WRITING YOUR OWN PROGRESSIONS

Beginning with this chapter, you will be asked to write your own progressions using the chords we have already studied. Being able to compose correct, musical harmonic progressions is an essential part of understanding and knowing tonal harmony. Your progressions should be metrical, and in order to avoid the needless four-voice realization of possibly faulty progressions, you will normally be asked to write only a bass line and Roman numerals. Before we discuss specific guidelines to write your own progressions, however, we will see how the relationship between metric and harmonic accents can affect the progressions you write.

Metric-Harmonic Relationships in Harmonic Progressions

We know by now that the relationship between harmony and meter is free and flexible, and that depending on the metric placement of certain chords, we can create what we have called metric-harmonic "rhyme," or we can instead create metric-harmonic conflict. Examine, for instance, the progression in example 11.15a. In this progression all dominant chords fall on a metrically weak beat (including the passing V_4^6 in m. 3) and resolve to I or vi on strong beats. Harmonic accents in this case correspond with metric accents, and thus we can speak of metric-harmonic rhyme.

Now examine example 11.15b. Dominant chords (including the passing V_4^6 in m. 3) are now on strong beats and resolve to I or vi on weak beats. This progression illustrates the concept of conflict between harmonic and metric accents. In example 11.15c, the same progression is renotated in $\frac{3}{4}$, and you can verify that the metric-harmonic conflict disappears. Compare and play the notations in examples 11.15b and c. The

♪♪♪ Example 11.15

former creates ambiguity between harmonic accents and notated meter; the latter establishes an unequivocal correlation between the two types of accent. Notice especially that the last two measures in example 11.15b contain a dissonant $^6_4$ on a strong beat and a final tonic on beat 4. Compare the metric placement of these two chords in the triple-meter version in example 11.15c.

We saw above that conflicts between harmonic and metric accents are abundant in music. When used skillfully, they are a powerful tool to create musical tension for expressive or formal purposes. Because writing such conflicts effectively, however, presupposes substantial skill, we will first concentrate on writing progressions in which *metric and harmonic accents correspond,* that is, progression in which there is metric-harmonic rhyme.

EXERCISE

To practice analyzing the relationship between metric and harmonic accents, refer to exercise 11.1.3 in worksheet 11 at the end of this chapter.

Harmonic Syncopation

In writing your own progressions, you should also be careful to avoid what we know as **harmonic syncopation**. The harmonic accents created by all chords in example 11.16a confirm the accentual metric pattern of triple meter. While the V in m. 4 is on a strong beat, it does not resolve to a weak beat, but rather is prolonged in beat 3 to resolve in the next measure. A dominant such as this, beginning on a strong beat and resolving on the next strong beat, is perfectly correct. You can find a similar case in example 11.15c, m. 3, this time including a passing vi between V and V_6.

Now examine example 11.16b. The four brackets indicate chords that begin on a weak beat and continue to the next strong beat. Such metric events are called *harmonic syncopations* and should be systematically avoided for now, because they have a

♪♪♪ Example 11.16

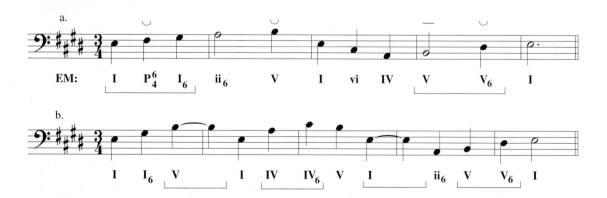

weakening effect on the metric character of a progression. In other words, *do not write chords that begin on a weak beat and continue to a strong beat.* This applies also to changes of position, as in brackets 2 and 4 in example 11.16b.

Guidelines for Writing Your Own Progressions

The following guidelines should be observed in writing your progressions:

1. Begin and end with tonic in root position (unless you choose to finish on a HC).

2. Establish a harmonic rhythm, and keep it as regular as possible.

3. Avoid harmonic syncopation.

4. For the time being, strive for correspondence between harmonic and metric accents. Pay special attention to these points:

   a) Place chords with a dominant function preferably on a weak beat (or, if they are on a strong beat, prolong them through the next weak beat).

   b) Resolve chords with a dominant function to a strong beat.

   c) Passing and neighbor $^6_4$s should be placed on weak beats.

   d) The cadential $^6_4$ falls on a strong beat, whereas its resolution to $^5_3$ falls on a weak beat. The $^6_4$ may be on beat 2 of a $^3_4$ measure if it resolves to $^5_3$ on beat 3, because beat 3 is weaker than beat 2 in $^3_4$ (see example 11.17a, m. 4).

5. Follow the fundamental principles of correct harmonic progression as we have learned them so far:

   a) Any chord may be used in root position or first inversion to provide variety to the bass line. You may effectively use first-inversion chords to prolong (or precede) the same chord in root position.

   b) V resolves only to I, I_6, or (deceptively) to vi. Do not resolve V to IV or ii.

   c) V is usually preceded by a predominant chord (IV or ii).

   d) All $^6_4$ chords should belong to one of the categories we have studied, and should resolve accordingly.

   e) Finish your progression with one of the cadence types we have studied.

   f) Strive for harmonic and bass-line melodic variety.

The progression in example 11.17a illustrates many of the points outlined above. Discuss this progression, and remark on everything that is correct in it. On the other hand, many things in example 11.17b are wrong or dubious. Find the weaknesses in this progression, and learn to avoid these mistakes. Finally, analyze in class the Bach chorale reproduced in example 11.17c. Think about the succession of chords (after you have analyzed them with Roman numerals), their metric placement, and the relationships between metric and harmonic accents in this chorale. (The last chord in m. 6 is a secondary dominant of vi, a type of chord we will study in chapter 17.)

NOTES

1. *Harmonic syncopation involving the initial tonic is possible and frequently found in Bach chorales. Its function is to reinforce the tonality at the outset of a phrase.*

2. *Half cadences are often placed on strong beats. In order to prepare the arrival of V on a strong beat, the chords that lead to the HC may emphasize the dominant on strong beats (and then the tonic falls on weak beats). Example 11.18a illustrates a syncopated initial tonic and a HC on a strong beat, which, nonetheless, does not require any metric adjustments. The HC in example 11.18b, on the other hand, is preceded by a dominant on a strong beat and a tonic on a weak beat, thus preparing the strong arrival on V at the HC.*

♪♪♪ Example 11.17a and b

♪♪♪ Example 11.17c   Bach, Chorale 159, "Als der gütige Gott"

♪♪♪Example 11.18a   J. S. Bach, Chorale 193, "Was bist du doch, O Seele, so betrübet"

♪♪♪Example 11.18b   J. S. Bach Chorale 45, "Kommt her zu mir"

EXERCISE

To practice writing your own progressions, refer to exercise 11.2 in worksheet 11 at the end of this chapter.

HARMONIZING A MELODY WITH KEYBOARD FIGURATION

Your melody harmonizations so far have been in vocal block-chord or chorale texture or in two voices (soprano and bass) with Roman numerals. Melodies are very often harmonized at the piano. Because simple sustained block chords are not a very idiomatic piano technique (the piano does not really sustain the sound, which is instead produced by a percussive attack), a variety of more active figurations are used to extend the sound of a chord, especially in slow harmonic rhythms. In all the fragments reproduced in example 11.19, for solo piano, a melody in the right hand is accompanied by some characteristic left-hand chordal figurations: **repeated block chords** in example 11.19a, the **bass afterbeat** pattern in example 11.19b (typical of waltzes and marches), a pattern of **repeated broken chords** in example 11.19c, **arpeggiated chords** in examples 11.19d

♪♪♪ Example 11.19a   L. v. Beethoven, Piano Sonata op. 14, no. 1, I, mm. 1–4

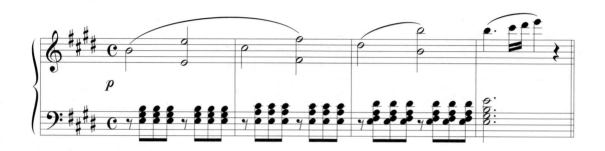

♪♪♪ Example 11.19b   F. Schubert, Waltz, op. 9, no. 13, mm. 1–4

♪♪♪ Example 11.19c   L. v. Beethoven, Rondo, op. 51, no. 1, mm. 1–2

and e, and a particular type of arpeggiation called **Alberti bass** in example 11.19f (in which the arpeggiation follows the pattern low note-high note-middle note-high note). In all these cases the principles of voice leading are preserved: Although chords may be broken, arpeggiated, and so on, their connections follow the familiar voice-leading guidelines as if we were dealing with block chords. (One may add, however, that you will find many more exceptions to the voice-leading norms in piano music and piano accompaniments in general than in four-voice vocal realizations.)

♪♪♪Example 11.19d and e | W. A. Mozart, Piano Sonata K. 457, II, mm. 1–2 and W. A. Mozart, Piano Sonata, K. 330, I, mm. 26–28

♪♪♪Example 11.19f | W. A. Mozart, Piano Sonata, K. 457, I, mm. 63–65

In all the fragments in example 11.19 the piano displays both the melody and the accompaniment. Very often, however, the melody is performed by a voice or a melodic instrument, while the piano provides only the accompaniment. In these cases, the chordal figuration is distributed between both hands, normally with the more active figuration in the right hand and a slower-moving bass in the left hand. The four fragments in example 11.20 are taken from Schubert songs, and show the same techniques we saw in example 11.19, here performed with both hands: repeated chords in example 11.20a, bass afterbeat in 11.20b, repeated broken chords in example 11.20c, and arpeggiation in example 11.20d. Examine now the following examples in the anthology, and notice the chordal figuration and the voice leading: anthology, no. 37, mm. 9–16 (Kuhlau, Sonatina); no. 24, mm. 7–8 (Mozart, DM sonata); no. 26 (Mozart, CM sonata, III); no. 32, mm. 1–8 and 125–131 (Beethoven, op. 2, no. 1); no. 34, mm. 1–8 (Beethoven, op. 13); 40 (Schubert, op. 9, no. 26); no. 52 (Verdi, "Libiamo"); no. 20, mm. 1–8 and 9–22 (Haydn, Hob. XVI: 24); no. 38 (Schubert, *Erlkönig*); and no. 47 (Schumann, "Ich grolle nicht").

Example 11.20a   F. Schubert, "Aufenthalt," from *Schwanengesang*, no. 5

Rau - schen-der Strom,   brau - sen - der   Wald,

Example 11.20b   F. Schubert, "Ungeduld," from *Die schöne Müllerin*, no. 7

Ich schnitt' én ger'n in al - le Rin-den ein,   ich griib'

Writing a Keyboard Harmonization

We will now write a left-hand keyboard accompaniment for the melody given in example 11.21a. The procedure is as follows:

1. Write a Roman numeral harmonization of the melody on the basis of the given harmonic rhythm, and taking into consideration the possible nonchord tones (NCTs) (marked with asterisks in example 11.21a). Anacrusic beginnings ("pickups") are not usually harmonized.

2. Examine the harmonic rhythm, and think about what kind of rhythmic figuration may be used that would correspond with the duration of the harmonies.

♪♪♪ Example 11.20c   F. Schubert, "Ständchen," from *Schwanengesang,* no. 4

Lei - se fle - hen mei - ne Lie - der   durch   die Na cht zu   dir;

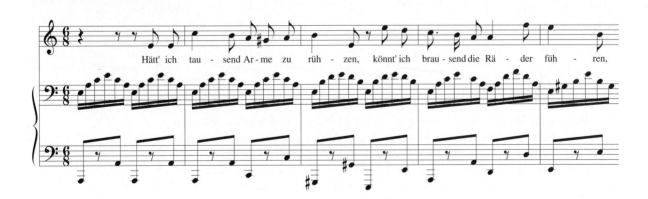

♪♪♪ Example 11.20d   F. Schubert, "Am Feierabend," from *Die schöne Müllerin,* no. 5

Hätt' ich tau - send Ar - me zu   rüh - zen,   könnt' ich brau - send die Rä - der füh - ren,

3. Choose a figuration, and realize the Roman numerals following the figuration and observing the usual voice-leading rules.

NOTE

Notice that the process here is the opposite from the process we learned to realize metric reductions in chapter 10. In a metric reduction, idiomatic instrumental figurations are reduced to block-chord style in order to simplify a texture for the sake of analysis or practice. When you write a keyboard harmonization, you first think of harmonies in a reduced form, such as Roman numerals or block chords, and then convert them into a more complex texture in the form of idiomatic keyboard figuration.

♪♪♪Example 11.21

After singing or playing the melody in example 11.21a several times, and after thinking of possible chords for each measure, we realize that it may be harmonized with one of our standard progressions: I–IV–ii–V/V–I–V–I. Because the melody is in $\frac{3}{4}$, a bass afterbeat pattern would be appropriate (a waltz accompaniment), as illustrated by our realization in example 11.21b. If we wish to provide an accompaniment with more rhythmic vitality than the bass afterbeat, an Alberti bass pattern like the one in example 11.21c would also be a good possibility.

You can now try to harmonize the melody in example 11.22, as a class exercise or on your own. A suggested pattern is provided, although you might prefer to use a different one. In m. 3, beat 1 (*), you may use an inversion of the chord from m. 2. In m. 5, beat 2, and m. 7, beat 1 (**), you may use $\frac{6}{4}$ chords.

ASSIGNMENT

For analytical and written assignments based on the materials learned in this chapter, refer to chapter 11 in the workbook.

♪♪♪Example 11.22

Paisiello, "Nel cor più non mi sento"
(La Molinara)

Composers and Their Music 11

Biographies

Write short biographies of the following composers mentioned in this chapter: Giuseppe Verdi, Josephine Lang.

Listening

Listen to the following compositions by composers mentioned in this chapter:

    Bach: Cantata 140, "Wachet auf, ruft uns die Stimme."

    Verdi: *La traviata* (complete opera if possible, following the translation of the libretto).

    Lang: "Frühzeitiger Früling" (recording in Briscoe anthology).

Follow the score while you listen. Be able to place these compositions in one of the style periods and to comment on why and how they represent the musical characteristics of that period. Pay attention to the harmonic rhythm in some of the cantata and opera sections you listen to. Is it fast or slow? How is it related to the tempo of the section? How does it contribute to the musical character of the section? Try also to hear harmonic accents in some of the sections you listen to, and how they are related to metric accents.

Terms for Review

Harmonic rhythm (HR)
HR and tempo
Regular and irregular HR
Levels of HR
Metric accents
Hypermeasure
Hypermeter
Tonal accent
Harmonic accent
Structural accent

Hypermetric accents in a four-bar hypermeasure
Metric-harmonic rhyme and conflict
Harmonic syncopation
Keyboard figurations
Repeated block chords
Bass afterbeat
Repeated broken chords
Arpeggiated chords
Alberti bass

Worksheet 11

EXERCISE 11.1   Analysis.

1. Determine and notate the harmonic rhythm (HR) for Bach's Chorale 153 (example 11.23). Write note values for the length of each chord under the chorale's score. Beware that changes of position, suspensions, and other NCTs do not affect the harmonic rhythm.

♪♪♪ Example 11.23   J. S. Bach Chorale 153, "Alle Menschen müssen sterben"

2. Notate with note values the HR for Haydn's Sonata in DM, Hob. XVI: 24, II (anthology, no. 20), mm. 1–8. Is this a fast or slow HR?

3. Analyze the opening phrase from Bach's Chorale 1 (example 11.24) with Roman numerals (RNs). Then, write strong and weak metric symbols on top of the score (− ⌣ ⌣), and comment briefly on the relationship between metric and harmonic accents in this passage. Why is the V in m. 4 on a strong beat? The dominant in m. 5, beat 1, is also on a strong beat. Considering that both the chords that follow in the same measure function as passing chords, where does the dominant on beat 1 resolve?

♪♪♪ Example 11.24   J. S. Bach, Chorale 1, "Aus meines Herzens Grunde," mm. 1–7

EXERCISE 11.2   *Writing harmonic progressions.* Be careful with the correlation of metric and harmonic accents, and write harmonic phrases that are logical and musical. Play your progressions and make sure you like them!

1. In exercise 11.2a write a progression (bass and RNs only) in AM, in $\frac{2}{4}$, using only I, IV, and V, and their first inversions.

a.

AM:

2. In exercise 11.2b write a progression (bass and RNs) in E♭M, in $\frac{3}{4}$, using only I, IV, and V, ii, and their first inversions.

b.

E♭M:

3. In exercise 11.2c write a progression in Dm, in $\frac{4}{4}$, including a passing $\frac{6}{4}$, a neighbor $\frac{6}{4}$, and a cadential $\frac{6}{4}$. Use only i, iv, and V in any of their inversions.

c.

Dm:

EXERCISE 11.3

1. On your own music paper, provide a bass reduction for example 11.17c above (Bach, Chorale 159), showing tonal motion and hierarchy within each of the phrases and over the complete piece.

2. On your own music paper, provide a metric reduction for anthology, no. 6 (Minuet from *Notebook for Anna Magdalena Bach*). Your reduction should furnish an accurate account of the harmonic content for the complete piece.

Chapter 12

The Dominant Seventh and Its Inversions

In previous chapters we have often seen musical examples utilizing dominant seventh chords. Nevertheless, we have delayed its study until the basic consonant triads were introduced because this is a chord that normally presents some voice-leading difficulties for the beginning harmony student.

V_7 IN ROOT POSITION

This chord comprises the dominant triad (a M triad) and an added minor seventh (a diatonic seventh above the root). V_7 is always a Mm_7 sonority including scale degrees $\hat{5}$–$\hat{7}$–$\hat{2}$–$\hat{4}$, and it contains two dissonant intervals: the m7 between $\hat{5}$ and $\hat{4}$, and the °5 (or +4, depending on the voicing) between $\hat{7}$ and $\hat{4}$. Because of its dissonant quality, V_7 is a very effective chord in which the tendency of V to resolve to the tonic is further enhanced by the tendency of dissonance to resolve to consonance. V_7 thus contains *two tendency tones* (example 12.1a): the *leading tone,* (LT) which, as we know, has a tendency to resolve *upward to* $\hat{1}$, and the dissonant *seventh* ($\hat{4}$), which in V_7 will as a principle resolve *down to* $\hat{3}$. Example 12.1b summarizes the linear tendencies in this chord. Identify the V_7 chord in the cadence reproduced in example 12.1c, and verify the resolution of the two tendency tones. Notice also the unusual voice leading in the resolution of the cadential $^6_4$ in this example. Is the dramatic change of register in both the vocal part and the cadential $^6_4$ voice leading justified in any way by the text?

Doubling

A four-pitch chord in principle requires no doubling in four voices. As we will see immediately, though, V_7 appears sometimes in an incomplete form, with the fifth ($\hat{2}$) omitted (the fifth is the only member of a seventh chord which may be omitted: We already know that the root and third of any chord may not be left out, and the omission

♪♪♪Example 12.1a and b

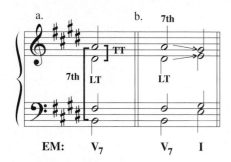

♪♪♪Example 12.1c   M. Willson, "I Ain't Down Yet," from *The Unsinkable Molly Brown* (Final Cadence)

of the seventh in a seventh chord is obviously a contradiction in terms). Because tendency tones and dissonant pitches should not be doubled, the only member of V_7 which may be doubled if the fifth is omitted is the root.

EXERCISE

To practice spelling Mm₇ chords in root position, refer to exercise 12.2 in worksheet 12 at the end of this chapter.

♪♪♪ Example 12.2   R. Schumann, "Ein Choral," from *Album for the Young,* op. 68

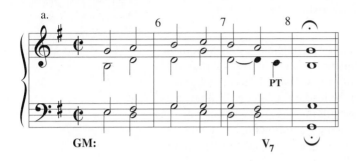

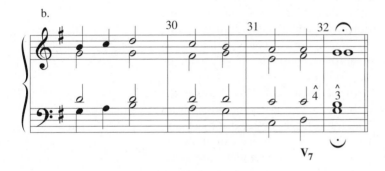

The V₇–I Progression: Voice-Leading Guidelines

The two phrases from R. Schumann's "Ein Choral" reproduced in example 12.2 illustrate the most important aspects regarding the voice leading of V_7. In example 12.2a (m. 7) we see *the melodic nature (and origin) of the seventh in V_7*: the voice that doubles the root of the V triad, $\hat{5}$, moves to $\hat{3}$ by means of a dissonant passing tone, $\hat{4}$. In example 12.2b (m. 31), the seventh is not a passing tone (PT), but rather a member of the harmonic sonority, V_7. Because it is a dissonance, Schumann prepared it by presenting the same pitch ($\hat{4}$) in the same voice as a consonance in the previous chord. By preparing it in this way, the seventh is here treated as if it were a suspension. Although it may not always be possible, *it is preferable to prepare the seventh* when you write in vocal chorale style by approaching it either by step or by repetition, as in the Schumann examples. (Can you identify an example of voice overlap in one of these phrases?)

Both examples 12.2a and b depict the same type of resolution of V_7, which may be summarized as follows:

1. The third ($\hat{7}$ or LT) moves up to $\hat{1}$, especially when it is in an outer voice.

2. The seventh ($\hat{4}$) moves down to $\hat{3}$.

3. The fifth ($\hat{2}$) may move up to $\hat{3}$ or down to $\hat{1}$.

4. The same melodic fragments which you learned could be harmonized with a V–I progression can also be harmonized with a V$_7$–I progression ($\hat{2}$–$\hat{1}$, $\hat{2}$–$\hat{3}$, $\hat{7}$–$\hat{1}$, and $\hat{5}$–$\hat{5}$). To these, you can now add $\hat{4}$–$\hat{3}$ as a characteristic melodic pattern for a V$_7$–I harmonization.

If you apply these guidelines to the resolution of a complete V$_7$, as Schumann does, you will necessarily end up with an incomplete I as a chord of resolution (see both cadences in example 12.2). *In the V$_7$–I progression, one of the two chords is usually incomplete* in order to exercise correct voice leading. Example 12.3 presents all the standard resolutions of V$_7$ to I, beginning with the one that you must *avoid*: If you insist on resolving a complete V$_7$ to a complete I following the guidelines listed above, you will end up with parallel 5ths (example 12.3a). If the V$_7$ is complete, the resolving I will usually be incomplete. This **complete-incomplete (C–IN)** voice leading includes two possibilities: If you resolve the fifth up, the incomplete I will include a doubled root and a doubled third (example 12.3b); if you resolve the fifth down, the incomplete I will include a tripled root and a single third (as in the Schumann example, and in example 12.3c). In another correct voice leading, V$_7$ is incomplete and resolves to a complete I (**incomplete-complete, IN–C**, example 12.3d).

The "complete-incomplete" issue is most crucial when the $\hat{7}$–$\hat{1}$ motion is in the soprano. *If the LT is in an inner voice,* some alternative voice-leading possibilities allow for two complete chords. In example 12.3e, for instance, we see that by resolving the LT in an inner voice to the voice immediately above it, we can allow the voice with $\hat{7}$ to leap down to $\hat{5}$, thus completing the tonic triad (**complete-complete, C–C**). In yet another possible voice leading illustrated by example 12.3f (acceptable, if less desirable), we see that we can also come up with two complete chords by not resolving the inner-voice LT at all. (To review the options regarding the resolution of the LT, refer to chapter 2 section, "Connecting the Tonic and Dominant Chords," points 5 and 6.)

♪♪♪ Example 12.3

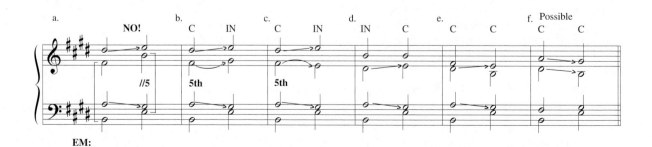

EXERCISE

To practice realizing V₇–I progressions, refer to exercise 12.3 in worksheet 12 at the end of this chapter.

Preparing the Seventh in V_7

Although numerous approaches to V_7 are possible, we will examine here some of the most frequent cases involving the chords we have already studied. In both the IV–V_7 (or iv–V_7) and ii$_6$–V_7 (ii°$_6$–V_7) progressions, the seventh may be properly prepared by repetition (examples 12.4a and b). In the IV–V_7 connection you should still pay attention to the same parallel fifths which we learned to avoid in the IV–V connection (chapter 3). In the ii$_6$–V_7 progression, it is possible to have scale degrees $\hat{6}$–$\hat{7}$–$\hat{1}$ in the same voice in the major mode. The same progression in the minor mode, on the other hand, will result in an objectionable melodic +2 (examples 12.4c and d).

   V_7 often follows a V triad, in such a way that the only harmonic or voice-leading change is the addition of the seventh. The best voice leading in this case is demonstrated in example 12.4e: the only voice that moves is the one that is *doubling the root of V*. This voice approaches the seventh by step, in an 8–7 motion over the bass. A

♪♪♪ Example 12.4

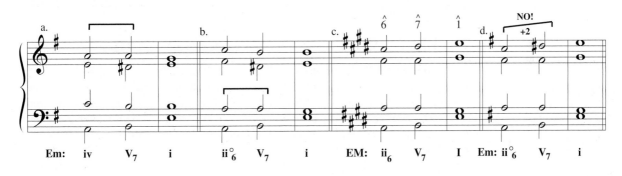

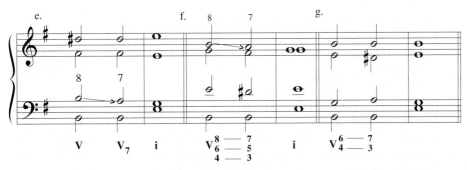

PRACTICAL APPLICATION AND DISCUSSION

Many examples of V_7 can easily be found throughout the musical literature, especially in authentic cadences. As a sample of various uses of V_7, look at these excerpts from the anthology: no. 24 (Mozart, Sonata in DM, mm. 7–8 and 15–17); no. 27 (Mozart, Sonata in AM, Theme, mm. 7–8 and 17–18); no. 19 (Haydn, Divertimento, mm.1–3); no. 31 (Paradis, *Sicilienne,* mm. 3–4 and 8–10); and no. 52 (Verdi, "Libiamo").

In studying these examples, first identify the key of each passage (note that the keys are different in the two passages from the Mozart DM sonata, as well as in the two passages from Paradis's *Sicilienne*). After you know the correct key, label the chords with exact Roman numerals. Then, observe the doubling and voice leading of the progressions. Are the chords complete or incomplete? Do tendency tones resolve as expected? Are all the voice-leading guidelines studied on pages 379–380 followed?

Pay special attention to the two passages in Mozart's DM sonata. Because chord tones are presented melodically in the right hand, the voice leading may not be immediately obvious. Make sure, though, that you identify the complete voice-leading figure $\begin{smallmatrix}8-7\\6-5\\4-3\end{smallmatrix}$ in both cadences. Does the seventh resolve? Where? Notice that the line $\hat{5}$–$\hat{4}$–$\hat{3}$ (the preparation of the seventh, the seventh, and its resolution) is interrupted by a change of register, or a *register transfer:* By displacing the pitch D down an octave, the line has been brought to (and continued in) a lower register. What kind of double nonchord tone takes place on the final tonic in each of the two cadences?

---

similar voice leading is also the best for the cadential $^6_4$ progression with V_7 (example 12.4f): The doubled $\hat{5}$ in the $^6_4$ chord moves down by step to the seventh of V_7 (in an 8–7 motion over the bass). Notice the complete voice leading indicated by the figures $\begin{smallmatrix}8-7\\6-5\\4-3\end{smallmatrix}$. In a possible alternative to this voice leading, the 6th in the cadential $^6_4$ moves *up* to the 7th, in the $\begin{smallmatrix}6-7\\4-3\end{smallmatrix}$ motion shown in example 12.4g.

EXERCISE

To practice realizing short progressions using V_7 in root position, refer to exercise 12.4 in worksheet 12 at the end of this chapter.

INVERSIONS OF THE DOMINANT SEVENTH

Listen to example 12.5, and analyze all its chords. (Remember to transpose the horn in E♭ as you read the passage: As we studied in chapter C, in this transposing instrument a notated C sounds as an E♭—a M6 below.) You will see that the opening phrase (mm. 1–4) has a familiar bass line ($\hat{1}$–$\hat{7}$–$\hat{1}$–$\hat{2}$–$\hat{3}$–$\hat{4}$–$\hat{5}$) which could be harmonized using only triads. The chord in m. 2 ($\hat{7}$ in the bass) could be a V_6, prolonging the initial I with a neighbor motion. The first three bass notes in m. 3 could be harmonized with a passing $^6_4$ progression, I–P$^6_4$–I$_6$. Mozart, however, used inversions of V_7 in both m. 2 and m. 3: V^6_5 instead of V_6, and V^4_3 instead of P$^6_4$. (In the second phrase, mm. 7–8, you will also find two V_7 chords. Review doubling and voice leading in both of them.)

All three inversions of V_7 are frequently used in tonal music. They normally appear in complete form, and resolve to a complete tonic triad following the same guidelines we studied for V_7. As the following comments will show, *all three inversions usually function as linear chords.*

First Inversion

In the first inversion of V_7, V^6_5 (complete figures: $^6_5$), the leading tone is in the bass. Its standard resolution is thus to a tonic triad in root position, with the bass moving up to $\hat{1}$. The most common functions of V^6_5 (as those of V_6) are to prolong the tonic as a

♪♪♪♪Example 12.5   W. A. Mozart, Concerto in E♭M for Horn and Orchestra, K. 447, II, mm. 1–8

neighbor chord (example 12.5, mm. 1–2, and example 12.6a), or to approach I from below as a passing chord between vi or IV$_6$ and I, in a progression which also prolongs I: I–IV$_6$–V$_5^6$–I (example 12.6b).

Second Inversion

In the second inversion of V$_7$, V$_3^4$ (complete figures: $^6_{4\ 3}$), the fifth is in the bass, which allows for two possible resolutions: down to tonic in root position or up to tonic in first inversion. Its most frequent function is to prolong the tonic, either as a neighbor chord (example 12.6c) or as a passing chord between I and I$_6$, or vice versa (example 12.6d).

♪♪♪Example 12.6

An example of the latter (I_6–V_3^4–I) may be seen in the Schumann chorale reproduced in example 12.2, m. 30. This passing function of V_3^4 is equivalent to the passing function of P_4^6, and thus V_3^4 is an alternative to P_4^6 in the harmonization of a $\hat{1}$–$\hat{2}$–$\hat{3}$ or $\hat{3}$–$\hat{2}$–$\hat{1}$ bass segment. The prolongational reductions in example 12.6e represent graphically the linear functions of both V_5^6 and V_3^4.

NOTE

*Study the resolution of V_3^4 in m. 3 of Mozart's horn concerto (example 12.5). The outer voices in the I–V_3^4–I_6 progression (bass and horn/violins) move in parallel 10ths, with the result that the seventh ($D\flat$) resolves upward. When V_3^4 moves to I_6, **the seventh may resolve upward** as in the Mozart example. This exception to the downward resolution of the seventh is justified by the linear voice-leading pattern in parallel 10ths or 3rds. The 5ths that may result in this progression are perfectly acceptable unequal 5ths, as illustrated by example 12.6f.*

Third Inversion

In the third inversion of V_7, V_2^4 (complete figures: $_2^{\overset{6}{4}}$), the seventh is in the bass. Because the seventh must resolve downward, V_2^4 will always resolve to I_6, as shown in the Haydn excerpt reproduced in example 12.7 (mm. 26–27). A frequent function of V_2^4 is to prolong V by means of a passing tone in the bass, in the progression $V–V_2^4–I_6$ (example 12.6g). The Haydn example depicts another standard application of V_2^4: A predominant chord with $\hat{4}$ in the bass (IV or ii$_6$) moves to V_2^4 on a repeated $\hat{4}$ in the bass, as in example 12.6h. (Find two other inversions of V_7 in example 12.7, and observe their resolutions.)

EXERCISES

To practice spelling Mm$_7$ chords in inversion, refer to exercise 12.5 in worksheet 12 at the end of this chapter.

To practice realizing short progressions using inversions of V_7, refer to exercise 12.6 in worksheet 12 at the end of this chapter.

To practice harmonizing a bass line, realizing a figured bass, and harmonizing a melody using V_7 chords in various positions, refer to exercises 12.7 to 12.9 in worksheet 12 at the end of this chapter.

Typical Errors to Avoid

▶ Not resolving the seventh of V_7 downward by step (or the LT in an outer voice up to $\hat{1}$).
▶ Writing parallel 5ths in a V_7–I progression if both chords are complete.
▶ Not resolving V_2^4 to I_6.

♪♪♪ Example 12.7   J. Haydn, Trio in GM, Hob. XV:5, III, mm. 25–28

PRACTICAL APPLICATION AND DISCUSSION

As an application of concepts which you have learned so far, you may analyze the following two excerpts from the anthology: no. 33 (Beethoven, op. 10, no. 1) and no. 37 (Kuhlau, Sonatina).

1. Anthology, no. 33 (Beethoven):
   a) Review the formal characteristics of this passage.
   b) What is the linear function of the inverted V$_7$ chords in mm. 1–3?
   c) The first of these inverted V$_7$ chords is on a weak beat; the second one on a strong beat. What causes the discrepancy?
   d) What is the harmonic rhythm in mm. 5–8? How is harmonic motion achieved in mm. 5–6? Does Beethoven do something in mm. 6–7 (a harmonic-metric event) which you have been told to avoid? What is the effect of this event, and how does Beethoven emphasize it by other means (consider the dynamic and performance indications for the second chord in m. 6)?
   e) What is the linear function of the inverted V$_7$ in m. 7?
   f) In spite of its complex appearance because of contrapuntal activity in the upper voices, the cadence at mm. 15–16 is of a simple and familiar type. Identify the type, and mark on the score the specific $\begin{smallmatrix}8-7\\6-5\\4-3\end{smallmatrix}$ voice leading.
   g) Realize a metric reduction of mm. 9–16.

2. Anthology, no. 37 (Kuhlau):
   a) Find two inverted V$_7$ chords in mm. 1–8, and discuss their linear functions.
   b) The complete phrase in mm. 9–16 may be considered a harmonic prolongation of the tonic which was reached at m. 8. What is the chord used for this prolongation, and how is it used linearly? Pay special attention to mm. 14–15 and to the means used to prolong I in these measures.

How would the points raised in this discussion affect your perception and your performance of these pieces? For instance, could your phrasing be affected by hearing groups of chords as linear prolongations of a tonic harmony, rather than as individual entities? Does the concept of harmonic prolongation help you understand better the harmonic coherence and function (as well as the long-range direction) of these phrases?

Think, for example, of the Kuhlau phrase in mm. 9–16. Where does it come from? Where does it lead? How does it do so? And, in the opening phrase of the Beethoven example (mm. 1–4), how does the change in the relationship between harmonic and metric accent affect you as listener or performer? Where does it direct your attention, and hence toward what goal does it direct the phrase?

🎵♪♪ Example 12.8a   J. Haydn, Piano Sonata in Cm, Hob. XVI:20, I, mm. 32–35

Combining Prolongational Chords

In the preceding chapters we have studied a variety of chords that have a linear function. We have usually seen such chords in isolation, illustrating how each of them is used to prolong a previous chord, normally, a tonic or a dominant. Examples of isolated harmonic linear patterns are I–IV–I, I–N$_4^6$–I, I–P$_4^6$–I$_6$, V–N$_4^6$–V, IV–P$_4^6$–IV$_6$, I–V$_5^6$–I, I–V$_3^4$–I$_6$, V–V$_2^4$–I$_6$. By combining several of these chords or patterns, composers may extend (and provide variety to) passages of **harmonic prolongation**. The passage by Haydn that appears in example 12.8a can be interpreted as a single prolongation of I by means of two chords we have learned in this chapter: V$_3^4$ and V$_5^6$. Each can be used as a linear neighbor chord. The combination of both results in a neighbor-group figure, a linear gesture used very frequently by composers to prolong the tonic. The prolongational reduction of the left-hand part in example 12.8b shows the linear nature of this harmonic phrase. Compare the Haydn passage with the phrase by Enrique Granados reproduced in

example 12.9a, and write a prolongational reduction of the latter's left-hand part in the space provided under it.

Two examples by Saint-Georges will further illustrate the combination of linear chords as a tool for prolongation. The phrase in example 12.10a (in EM) contains two familiar neighbor chords in succession: N$_4^6$ and V$_5^6$. The left-hand reduction in example 12.10b shows that each of the pitches in these two chords, as presented in the left-hand figuration, is a neighbor note to one of the members of the tonic triad.

Finally, you may provide a harmonic analysis of example 12.11a. First, analyze the passage with Roman numerals. Then, identify the chords that have a linear function, provide a prolongational reduction in the space provided below, and explain the prolongation of I in mm. 87–90. The V$_7$ in m. 90 does not resolve to I until m. 93. Measures 91–92 delay this resolution also by linear means. How do these two measures extend the V$_7$ in m. 90?

♪♪♪Example 12.8b   Prolongational Reduction

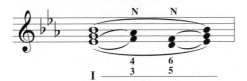

♪♪♪Example 12.9a   Enrique Granados, *Escenas Románticas,* no. 5, mm. 40–42

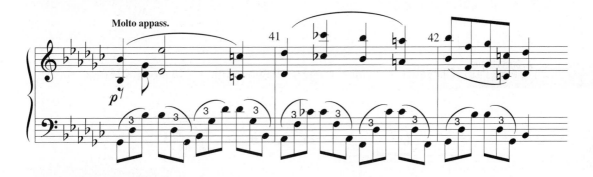

♪♪♪Example 12.9b   Prolongational Reduction

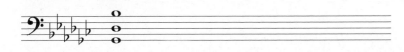

Example 12.10a   Chevalier de Saint–Georges, Sonata no. 2, for Violin and Piano, mm. 13–16

Example 12.10b   Prolongational Reduction

Example 12.11a   Chevalier de Saint–Georges, Adagio in Fm, for Piano, mm. 86–93

♪♪♪ Example 12.11b   Prolongational Reduction

EXERCISE

To practice analysis of musical fragments including V_7 *chords in various positions, refer to exercise 12.1 in worksheet 12 at the end of this chapter.*

ASSIGNMENT AND KEYBOARD PROGRESSIONS

For analytical and written assignments and keyboard progressions based on the materials learned in this chapter, refer to chapter 12 in the workbook.

PITCH PATTERNS

Sing the pitch patterns in example 12.12, and as you sing listen to the linearized V_7 chords in root position or inversion and to their resolution.

♪♪♪ Example 12.12

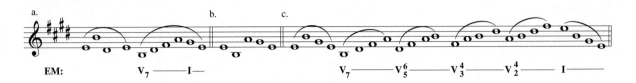

EM:　　　　　　V₇ ——— I —

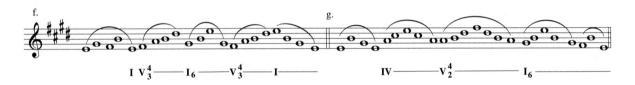

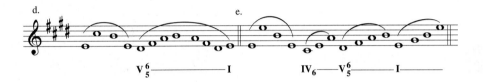

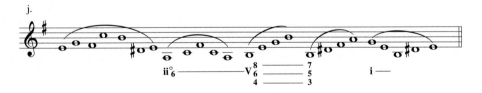

Composers and Their Music 12

Biographies

Write short biographies of the following composers mentioned in this chapter: Friedrich Kuhlau, Enrique Granados, Edvard Grieg.

Listening

Listen to the following compositions by composers mentioned in this chapter:

  Granados: *Spanish Dances.*

Beethoven: Piano Sonata in Cm, op. 10, no. 1.
Haydn: *Lord Nelson Mass.*
Grieg, *Peer Gynt* (Suite II).

Follow the score while you listen. Be able to place these compositions in one of the style periods and to comment on why and how they represent the musical characteristics of that period.

Terms for Review

Resolution and function of V_7

Resolution of the seventh

Doubling in V_7

Preparation of the seventh

Voice-leading possibilities: C–IN, IN–C,   C–C

V–V_7

V_{6-5}^{8-7} (4–3)

Register transfer

Resolution and function of V_5^6

Resolution and function of V_3^4

Upward resolution of the seventh in V_3^4

Resolution and function of V_2^4

Harmonic prolongation by combination
  of several linear chords

Worksheet 12

EXERCISE 12.1   Analysis.

1. a) Provide a Roman numeral (RN) analysis for example 12.13.

    b) Explain the linear function of each inversion of the dominant seventh used in this passage.

    c) Comment on the textural and instrumental variations between mm. 1–8 and 9–16.

    d) In the staff system below, provide a *prolongational reduction* of mm. 1–8, including only bass notes and a "verticalization" of the compound melodic motive (the reduction of the first measure is provided for you). Indicate, with the type of reductive notation we have used in this and other chapters (see examples 12.6e, 12.8b, and 12.10b for models), the linear/prolongational function of pitches in both the melody and the bass.

    e) On your own music paper, provide a *metric reduction* of mm. 9–16 (piano part only). After you do so, add to your metric reduction an analysis of metric and tonal accents. Indicate the hypermetric accentual pattern for the complete period, and provide a brief discussion of whether metric, structural, and harmonic accents do or do not coincide.

♪♪♪ Example 12.13   W. A. Mozart, Sonata for Violin and Piano, K. 377, II, mm. 1–16

2. a) Analyze with RNs the passage from Edvard Grieg's *Peer Gynt* reproduced in example 12.14 (beware of transposing instruments!).

  b) The complete passage functions like a harmonic prolongation of i. In the space below, explain the linear function of each chord and how it contributes to this extended prolongation. Then, express these linear functions graphically in the staff provided after example 12.14, using the same notation you have used in exercise 12.1.1d above, now applied *only to the bass line* (that is, realize a *bass reduction* showing linear harmonic functions).

Example 12.14   Edvard Grieg, "The Rape of the Bride (Ingrid's Lament)," from *Peer Gynt,* Suite II, op. 55, I, mm. 35–42

V₇ in Root Position

EXERCISE 12.2   Write Mm₇ chords in root position (in four voices, with correct spacing) above the following pitches. Indicate under each chord the key in which it functions as V₇.

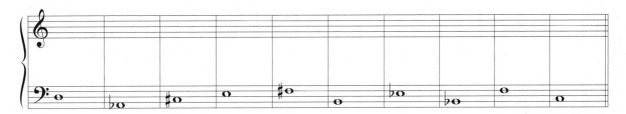

Key:

EXERCISE 12.3   Resolve each of the following V₇ chords three times, illustrating each of the three possible ways of resolving V₇ to the tonic (C–IN, IN–C, C–C).

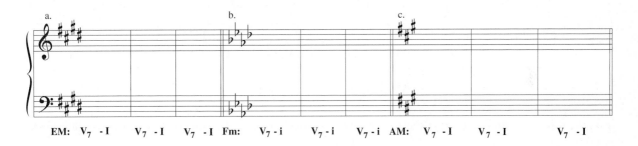

EXERCISE 12.4   Realize the following short progressions in four voices.

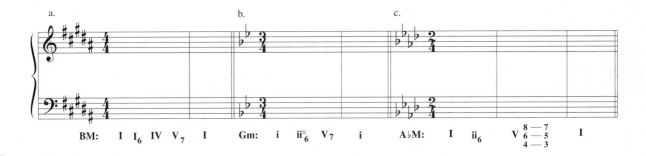

Inversions of V₇

EXERCISE 12.5   Write the following inverted V₇ chords, and indicate the key for each of them.

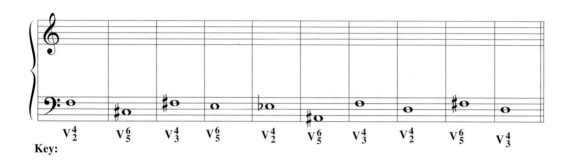

V^4_2 V^6_5 V^4_3 V^6_5 V^4_2 V^6_5 V^4_3 V^4_2 V^6_5 V^4_3

Key:

EXERCISE 12.6   Realize the following short progression in four voices.

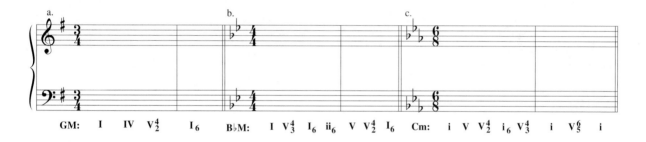

GM: I   IV V^4_2 I_6 B♭M: I V^4_3 I_6 ii_6 V V^4_2 I_6 Cm: i   V V^4_2 i_6 V^4_3 i V^6_5 i

EXERCISE 12.7   Provide correct RNs for the following bass. Include three types of $^6_4$ chords and all three inversions of V₇.

EXERCISE 12.8   Analyze the bass with RNs and realize in four voices. Remember to double-check your outer-voice frame for good first-species counterpoint.

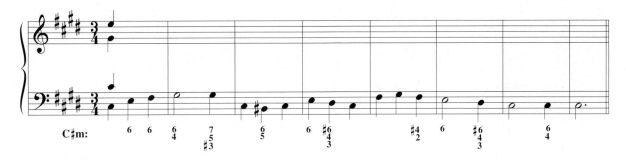

EXERCISE 12.9   Harmonize the following melody with a bass and RNs (no inner voices). Include a passing and a cadential $^6_4$, and harmonize the notes marked with an X with inversions of V_7 (all three inversions should be present). The harmonic rhythm is one chord per note, except for the two notes marked with a bracket, which will be harmonized with a change of position (a voice exchange). Remember to double-check this outer-voice frame for good first-species counterpoint.

Chapter 13

The Leading-Tone Triad

The triad built on the leading tone (LT), vii° (in both major and minor keys), comprises scale degrees $\hat{7}$–$\hat{2}$–$\hat{4}$. It thus has two common tones with V, and three common tones with V_7. The **leading-tone triad** has a dominant function, and as such may substitute for V, V_7, or for some of their inversions. Unlike V or V_7, however, vii° is not a structural chord, but rather functions as a *prolongational chord*. vii° contains the same two tendency tones as V_7, $\hat{7}$ and $\hat{4}$, which produce a harmonic dissonance (°5, or +4 when inverted). Because it is a dissonant chord, doubling and resolution in vii° follow the usual conventions: Dissonant tones should not be doubled, and dissonant intervals should be resolved.

DOUBLING AND VOICE LEADING

1. The leading-tone triad usually appears in first inversion. While in the root-position vii° the dissonance (the °5) is above the bass, in **vii°₆** the dissonance does not involve the bass, but rather two upper voices.

2. Because the root (the LT) and the fifth (the dissonant tone) form a °5, neither is usually doubled. As a norm, **double the third (the bass) in vii°₆**.

3. The °5 (or +4) may be resolved as a dissonance. $\hat{7}$ must resolve to $\hat{1}$ as usual, whereas $\hat{4}$ may resolve by step down to $\hat{3}$. This **resolution of the tritone** (°5 or +4) is desirable and is the same as the resolution of the same tritone, $\hat{7}$–$\hat{4}$, in V_7. Example 13.1 shows three cases in which the tritone is resolved. (Notice that when the tritone is spelled as a °5, the resolution is inward to a 3rd; when the tritone is presented as an +4, it resolves outward to a 6th.) In all these cases the chord of resolution is incomplete (doubled root and third).

4. The **resolution of the tritone**, although desirable, is not indispensable. In example 13.2, both $\hat{7}$ and $\hat{4}$ move upward by step. This voice leading is found very frequently in the literature, and it allows for a complete chord of resolution. The 5ths in example 13.2b are acceptable unequal 5ths (°5–P5).

5. In all cases, $\hat{2}$ may move down to $\hat{1}$ or up to $\hat{3}$.

♪♪♪ Examples 13.1 and 13.2

THE PASSING vii°₆

The function of vii°₆ is most frequently linear, connecting I and I₆ (or I₆ and I) as a passing chord. In example 13.3a Bach uses vii°₆ in this contrapuntal context between i and i₆ in Am. (The phrase is indeed in Am, although the ♯ in the key signature suggests a modal scale on A; what mode on A has an F♯ in the key signature?) Study the voice leading in this example. In the first place, you will see that this progression is built on a $\hat{1}$–$\hat{2}$–$\hat{3}$ (or $\hat{3}$–$\hat{2}$–$\hat{1}$) bass segment connecting i and i₆. This is, then, the third possible alternative that we learn to harmonize this bass line, along with i–P$_4^6$–i₆ and i–V$_3^4$–i₆. *All three progressions prolong the tonic harmony by means of a passing chord of the dominant family.* Moreover, you will notice in example 13.3a that the outer voices feature a *voice exchange,* and that another voice carries a $\hat{1}$–$\hat{7}$–$\hat{1}$ leading-tone figure. Both voice-leading properties are common to the passing vii°₆ and P$_4^6$ progressions. The same as the P$_4^6$ progression, the passing vii°₆ can be used to harmonize $\hat{1}$–$\hat{2}$–$\hat{3}$ or $\hat{3}$–$\hat{2}$–$\hat{1}$ melodic segments. Analyze now the rest of example 13.3a. The complete progression up to the very last chord may be read as a prolongation of the tonic. By what harmonic/linear means is this prolongation effected?

♪♪♪ Example 13.3a   J. S. Bach, Chorale 3, "Ach Gott vom Himmel, sieh darein," mm. 1–2

Example 13.3b   M. Martínez, Sonata in AM, I, mm. 1–2

Example 13.3c   W. A. Mozart, Sonata in FM, K. 280, mm. 136–142

Two instances of passing vii°₆ in keyboard texture appear in examples 13.3b and c. Analyze both passages with Roman numerals (RNs) and study their voice leading. Notice that both examples contain numerous octave doublings that result from melodic and harmonic arpeggiations and changes of register. Writing metric reductions for each example might help you understand their voice leading.

EXERCISE

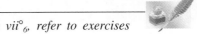

To practice realizing short progressions using the passing vii°₆, refer to exercises 13.2a to c in worksheet 13 at the end of this chapter.

vii°₆ AS A DOMINANT SUBSTITUTE

vii°₆ functions as a dominant substitute (an alternative to P$_4^6$ and V$_3^4$) in the passing vii°₆ progression. The function, however, is all the more evident when vii°₆ substitutes for V in such a standard progression as IV–V–I, which with the substitution becomes **IV–vii°₆–I**. Bach's Chorale 42 opens with this progression, which clearly establishes the AM key with a tonic-predominant-dominant-tonic harmonic phrase (example 13.4a). This progression is used especially to harmonize ascending $\hat{1}$–$\hat{2}$–$\hat{3}$ or $\hat{6}$–$\hat{7}$–$\hat{1}$ segments in the soprano. Examples 13.4b and c illustrate correct voice-leading possibilities for this progression. In minor, the melodic segment $\hat{6}$–$\hat{7}$–$\hat{1}$ may produce an +2 between ♭6 and ♯7, as in example 13.4d. The solution to avoid the +2 is to place ♭6 and ♯7 in different voices, or to use an ascending melodic minor scale (♯$\hat{6}$–♯$\hat{7}$–$\hat{1}$), with the resulting major subdominant chord in a minor key (IV–vii°₆–i), as in example 13.4e.

NOTE

You may have realized that in example 13.4a, Bach wrote the progression I–V₆–IV₆–V$_5^6$ –I. An obvious problem with this progression, according to what we have studied in this book, could be the resolution of V₆ to IV₆, and the downward motion of the LT which it implies. Harmonically, this progression could then be considered dubious. If we explain it linearly, however, we see that the progression is perfectly acceptable. V₆ is actually not a functional chord in this context, but rather a passing chord between I and IV₆. The function of this V₆ is thus not harmonic, but contrapuntal, and as such its resolution to a subdominant chord does not present any problem. Notice also the ii$_5^6$ at the end of this passage, a chord which we will study in chapter 15.

♪♪♪ Example 13.4a   J. S. Bach, Chorale 42, "Du Friede fürst, Herr Jesu Christ," mm. 1–4

AM: I   IV vii°₆ I   V₆   IV₆ V$_5^6$ I——   IV₆   I   ii$_5^6$ V   I

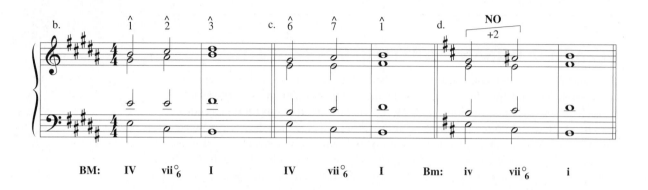

EXERCISE

To practice realizing short progressions using vii °₆ as a dominant substitute, refer to exercises 13.2d and e in worksheet 13 at the end of this chapter.

THE LEADING-TONE CADENCE

The progression vii°₆–I, when used as a cadential gesture, is called the **leading-tone cadence**. This type of cadence is not very common in music after the seventeenth century. In the fifteenth and sixteenth centuries (the Renaissance), however, it was one of the standard cadential formulas. The structural frame in this cadence is the $\hat{2}$–$\hat{1}$ motion in the bass and the $\hat{7}$–$\hat{1}$ motion in one of the upper voices. In example 13.5, the structural frame is found in the alto-bass voice pair. Notice the 7–6 suspension at the cadence between these two voices. This "cadential suspension" (effected by the voice which carries the $\hat{1}$–$\hat{7}$–$\hat{1}$ figure) is a characteristic stylistic feature of this cadence in the Renaissance. Study the reductions of this passage in example 13.4f, including a version without the cadential suspension and one with it.

VOICE-LEADING GUIDELINES

1. In vii°₆ it is best to double the bass (the third of the chord, $\hat{2}$). It is permissible to double the fifth ($\hat{4}$), but you should never double the root ($\hat{7}$).

2. It is desirable to resolve the tritone $\hat{7}$–$\hat{4}$ to the 3rd $\hat{1}$–$\hat{3}$ (or $\hat{4}$–$\hat{7}$ to the 6th $\hat{3}$–$\hat{1}$). It is also possible to move $\hat{4}$ upward by step to $\hat{5}$. In the first case, the tonic of resolution is incomplete. In the second case, it is complete.

3. The most frequent use of vii°₆ is as a passing chord between I and I₆, or vice versa. Standard voice-leading patterns for this progression appear in example 13.6.

The bass and another voice (in this example the soprano) feature a voice exchange; all the other voices carry neighbor-note or passing figures. The linear nature of the passing vii°₆ is graphically expressed in example 13.6c. The passing vii°₆ progression may be used to harmonize $\hat{1}$–$\hat{2}$–$\hat{3}$ or $\hat{3}$–$\hat{2}$–$\hat{1}$ in either the bass or the soprano.

4. $\hat{1}$–$\hat{2}$–$\hat{3}$ or $\hat{6}$–$\hat{7}$–$\hat{1}$ (in major) in the soprano may also be harmonized with the progression IV–vii°₆–I, in which vii°₆ functions as a dominant substitute.

♪♪♪ Example 13.6

Typical Errors to Avoid

▶ Doubling the LT.
▶ Not resolving the LT in vii°₆.
▶ Writing an +2 between ♭6 and ♯7 in the progression iv–vii°₆–i (in minor).

EXERCISES

To practice realizing a progression using various vii °₆ chords, refer to exercise 13.3 in worksheet 13 at the end of this chapter.

To practice writing your own progressions using vii °₆ chords, refer to exercise 13.4 in worksheet 13 at the end of this chapter.

To practice analysis of musical fragments including vii °₆ chords, refer to exercise 13.1 in worksheet 13 at the end of this chapter.

ASSIGNMENT AND KEYBOARD PROGRESSIONS

For analytical and written assignments and keyboard progressions based on the materials learned in this chapter, refer to chapter 13 in the workbook.

PITCH PATTERNS

Sing the pitch patterns in example 13.7, listening to the vii°₆ chords, their function within the phrase, and their resolution.

♪♪♪ Example 13.7

Composers and Their Music 13

Biographies

Write short biographies of the following composers mentioned in this chapter: Elizabeth Jacquet de la Guerre, Antonio Caldara (compare with the biographies of Alessandro Scarlatti, G. F. Handel, and Jean-Baptiste Lully), and Giovanni Pierluigi da Palestrina.

Listening

Listen to the following compositions by composers mentioned in this chapter:

Jacquet de la Guerre: Suite in Dm for Harpsichord; excerpts from Cantata *Semelé* (Briscoe anthology).

Listen (at least partially) to a baroque opera by Caldara, A. Scarlatti, or Handel. Then, listen to parts of an opera by Lully.

Palestrina: *Missa Papae Marcelli,* or *Missa Brevis,* or another Mass.

Follow the score while you listen. Be able to place these compositions in one of the style periods and to comment on why and how they represent the musical characteristics of that period.

Terms for Review

Leading-tone triad

vii°$_6$

Doubling and resolution of vii°$_6$

The passing vii°$_6$

vii°$_6$ as a dominant substitute

IV–vii°$_6$-I progression

Leading-tone cadence

Worksheet 13

EXERCISE 13.1   Analysis

1. Study mm. 21–29 of Chevalier de Saint-Georges's *Adagio* (example 13.8).

   a) Analyze the complete passage with RNs.

   b) Measures 21–24 are a prolongation of the tonic triad, and mm. 25–29 prolong the dominant. Explain the linear function of each chord, and provide a reductive graph of the left-hand harmonies showing their prolongational role with respect to I and V.

   c) Notice that, in m. 27, the dominant "resolves" unusually to a chord of the predominant family. If you think of this chord linearly (as a motion toward the next chord), however, its explanation becomes clear. Explain. Where does the V thus *really* resolve?

♪♪♪Example 13.8   Chevalier de Saint–Georges, *Adagio,* mm. 21–29

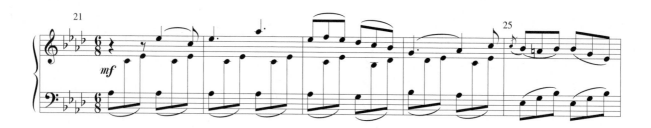

2. Analyze the passage by Antonio Caldara reproduced in example 13.9. Provide RNs for the complete passage, and answer the following questions.

   a) Identify two harmonic patterns studied in this chapter, in mm. 23–24.

   b) What harmonic/linear means are used to prolong the tonic in mm. 23–24?

   c) And in mm. 27–28?

   d) What dissonance type do you identify in the keyboard's right-hand part, m. 29, beat 1 (provide exact label)?

   e) Circle and label all the nonchord tones (NCTs) in the voice part.

   f) What kind of periodic structure is this? Label the cadences, discuss the relationship between phrases, and label the type of period.

♪♪♪ Example 13.9   Antonio Caldara, "Alma del core," from *La constanza in amor vince l'inganno,* mm. 23–30

3. Identify and circle a passing vii°₆ in example 13.10. Explain (and provide the exact label for) the dissonance that is also present in the same measure.

Example 13.10   Elizabeth Jacquet de la Guerre: Suite in Am, Sarabande, mm. 1–8

4. Identify a leading-tone triad in anthology, no. 19 (Haydn, Minuet in CM), Trio. What is its function? What NCT is used to embellish both the leading-tone triad and the chord it resolves to?

EXERCISE 13.2   Realize the following short progressions in four voices.

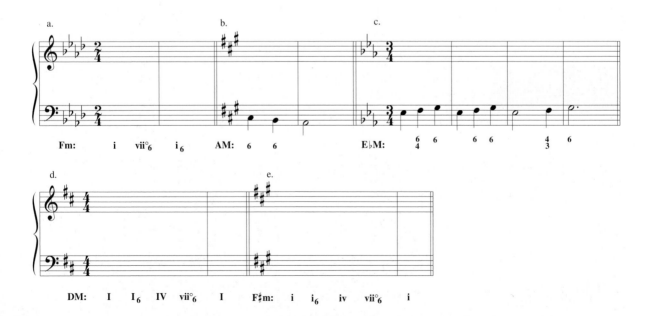

EXERCISE 13.3   Realize the following progression in four voices. Remember to double-check the outer-voice frame for good first-species counterpoint.

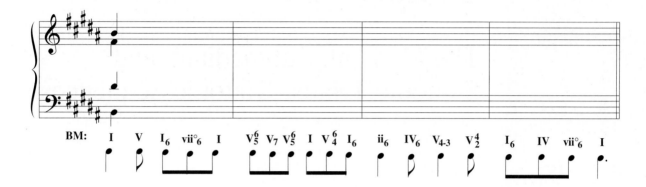

EXERCISE 13.4

1. Write your own progressions in the keys and meters indicated, using the required chords (along with any of the other chords and inversions we have studied so far).

    a) F♯m. Include a passing vii°$_6$, a V$_2^4$, and a neighbor $_4^6$.

    b) A♭M. Include a V$_3^4$, a ii in root position, a V$_5^6$, and a vii°$_6$ as a dominant substitute in the cadence.

2. Choose one of your own progressions from above, and use it as a harmonic basis to compose a phrase for keyboard. Your phrase should consist of a simple melody (right hand) with keyboard-style accompaniment (left hand).

Chapter 14

The Mediant, Submediant, and Subtonic Triads; Diatonic Sequences

The last diatonic triads we will study are the *mediant, submediant,* and *subtonic* chords. The mediant is built on $\hat{3}$, the submediant on $\hat{6}$: a 3rd above the tonic in the first case, a 3rd below in the latter case. Both chords have a weaker functional character than the triads we have studied so far, and both (especially iii) appear less frequently in tonal progressions. We will also see that the subtonic triad (built on $\flat\hat{7}$, and hence a diatonic triad in the minor mode) may be found at times associated with III in minor keys.

THE MEDIANT AND SUBMEDIANT TRIADS

The triad built on $\hat{3}$ (the **mediant**) includes scale degrees $\hat{3}$–$\hat{5}$–$\hat{7}$; it is a minor triad (iii) in major keys, and a major triad (III) in its most frequent minor key form (notice that, in minor, the fifth of III is *not* the leading tone [LT], but rather $\flat\hat{7}$). The triad built on $\hat{6}$ (the **submediant**), on the other hand, includes scale degrees $\hat{6}$–$\hat{1}$–$\hat{3}$; it is a minor triad (vi) in major keys, and a major triad (VI) in minor keys.

The Mediant and Submediant as Prolongations of the Tonic

Because both iii and vi have two common tones with I, and because the root of each is a 3rd from $\hat{1}$, they are often used as chords prolonging the tonic by arpeggiation.

Two instances of *mediant chords prolonging the tonic* appear in examples 14.1a and b. In example 14.1a Bach prolongs i through all of m. 1 by means of arpeggiation of the bass: $\hat{1}$ moves a 3rd up to $\hat{3}$, then down a 5th to $\hat{6}$, and up a 3rd again to $\hat{1}$ (the 3rds are, of course, filled in by passing tones). Voice leading in the upper voices emphasizes the prolongational character of the complete measure: A passing tone (PT) connects two members of i in the soprano ($\hat{5}$–$\hat{4}$–$\hat{3}$), the alto moves also between two members of i ($\hat{3}$–$\hat{1}$), while the tenor moves from $\hat{1}$ to $\hat{5}$ by means of two PTs, $\hat{7}$–$\hat{6}$. Harmonically, the progression prolongs i by means of an arpeggiation *to* III, and another arpeggiation *from* iv$_6$ (i–III–iv$_6$–i).

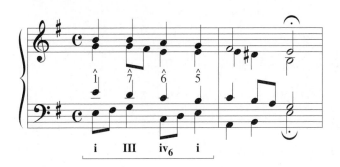

♪♪♪Example 14.1a   J. S. Bach, Chorale 138, "Jesu, meine Freude," mm. 1–2

♪♪♪Example 14.1b   J. Brahms, Symphony no. 4, op. 48, III, mm. 1–6

In example 14.1b we have a similar example by Brahms. In m. 1 the tonic is extended by a bass arpeggiation supporting a mediant chord, in the progression I–iii–IV–V. Observe that in both examples 14.1a and b one of the voices displays a descending line, $\hat{1}$–$\hat{7}$–$\hat{6}$–$\hat{5}$, and that in both cases $\hat{7}$ (actually ♭7 in minor) does not function (or resolve) like a leading tone. *The progression I–iii–IV, in which iii prolongs I and in which $\hat{7}$ does not resolve like a LT (it is not part of a dominant harmony), is often used to harmonize the melodic segment $\hat{1}$–$\hat{7}$–$\hat{6}$.*

Example 14.2 presents a summary of some usual progressions involving the mediant as a prolongation of I. In example 14.2a, the space between I and V is divided by iii. Compare this to example 14.2b, in which I is similarly prolonged by a I_6 which also divides the fifth by arpeggiation. In both examples 14.2c and d a predominant chord has been added between iii and V; notice the characteristic descending $\hat{1}$–$\hat{7}$–$\hat{6}$–$\hat{5}$ in the

♪♪♪Example 14.2

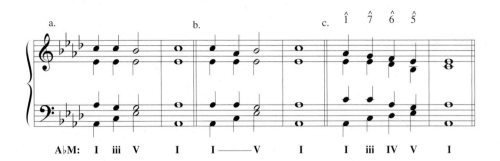

soprano. Example 14.2e summarizes graphically the functions in this progression: iii prolongs I, IV prepares V, and both iii and IV are steps in the motion from I to V (or, melodically, from $\hat{1}$ to $\hat{5}$).

Turning now to example 14.3, we see two instances of the *submediant as a prolongation of the tonic* by downward bass arpeggiation. This very common progression usually takes the form of a *succession of descending 3rds*. In its simplest form (two descending 3rds), the progression may be I–vi–IV–V, I–vi–ii₆–V, or I–vi–ii⁶₅–V. In all three cases, *vi functions as a divider of the space between I and a predominant chord.* Which of these progressions can you identify in examples 14.3a and b? Observe also the use of chomaticism in the bass in each of these examples. In example 14.3a, we can interpret the second chord in m. 4 as a passing chord including a chromatic passing motion in the bass (notice the passing motion in each of the voices), whereas the D♯ in example 14.3b, m. 43, also functions as a chromatic PT between the previous D and the E in m. 44.

Three **progressions in descending 3rds** using only triads appear in examples 14.4a, b, and c. In example 14.4c the progression is extended by the addition of one more third. Example 14.4d expresses graphically the linear function of chords in these two progressions.

♪♪♪ Example 14.3a   L. v. Beethoven, Seven Variations on "God Save the King," mm. 1–6

♪♪♪ Example 14.3b   Chevalier de Saint–Georges, Symphonie Concertante in AM, op. 10, no. 2, I, mm. 41–45

NOTE

An important voice-leading principle in third-related chords (such as I–iii and I–vi), which, of course, have two common tones, is that you should retain both common tones in the same voices, *as you may verify in all such connections in examples 14.2 and 14.4.*

EXERCISE

To practice realizing short progressions using mediant and submediant chords, refer to exercises 14.2a to c in worksheet 14 at the end of this chapter.

♪♪♪Example 14.4

THE SUBTONIC

In the minor mode, III is often preceded by VII (the **subtonic triad**, made up of ♭$\hat{7}$–$\hat{2}$–$\hat{4}$), as illustrated by example 14.5a. In this progression, III divides the space between i and V, but it is now preceded by VII, which, in this context, sounds like a *momentary dominant of III*. If you play this progression and hear the VII–III motion as if III were a momentary tonic and VII its dominant, you will indeed get a taste of what's to come in chapters 16 and 17 (the concepts of tonicization and secondary dominant).

In m. 6 of example 14.5b you can hear the VII–III progression in the context of a chorale by Johann Hermann Schein. In mm. 3–5 and 7–8, on the other hand, you can hear two progressions in which VII is preceded by III and followed by i (see brackets). The progression III–VII–i–V is a very common progression in the music of the sixteenth and seventeenth centuries, and its voice leading is related to a sequential paradigm we will study below (see example 14.5c; notice that the VII between III and i prevents the parallel 8ves and 5ths that could result if the triads moved directly down a 3rd, from III to i, a technique that we will also see in example 14.18c). Two very popular **ground basses** (repeated harmonic phrases on which performers would improvise) from the sixteenth and seventeenth centuries, the **romanesca and folia** basses (example 14.5c), include this progression. The *romanesca* phrase is based exclusively on the III–VII–i–V progression, and the *folia* phrase includes the i–VII–III progression we just studied.

Gm: i   VII   III   ii₆   V 6−5 / 4−3   i

Johann Hermann Schein, "Wir Christenleut," from *Cantional*

Gm:

i   VII   III   VII   i   V 4-3   i

The *Romanesca* and *Folia* Basses

Romanesca   Folia

Gm: III   VII   i   V   III   VII   i   V   I   i   V   i   VII   III   VII   i   V   I

EXERCISE

To practice realizing short progressions using the subtonic triad, refer to exercises 14.2e and f in worksheet 14 at the end of this chapter.

OTHER USES OF THE MEDIANT AND SUBMEDIANT

vi as a Predominant

Example 14.6a reproduces the first two phrases of Bach's Chorale 135. The vi in m. 3, beat 1, is not a tonic prolongation (it follows a ii chord). Its function is, rather, to precede a dominant harmony (V_6), and therefore it may be interpreted as a predominant. The submediant may indeed function as a predominant if it precedes the dominant. Its function, however, is often ambiguous, as shown in example 14.4e. Although vi pre-

♪♪♪ **Example 14.6a**   J. S. Bach, Chorale 135, "Gott der Vater, wohn uns bei," mm. 1–4

♪♪♪ **Example 14.6b**   J. S. Bach, Chorale 14, "O Herre Gott, dein göttlich Wort," mm. 1–2

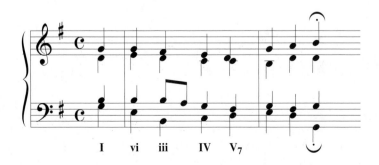

♪♪♪Example 14.6c   Camille Saint-Saëns, *Christmas Oratorio,* no. 8, mm. 5–7

cedes V and may be heard associated with the dominant, it still acts as a prolongation of the opening tonic, hence its ambiguous function. The vi in m. 2 of the same example is part of a $\hat{6}$–$\hat{7}$–$\hat{1}$ bass motion, and it moves to a dominant chord (V_5^6) which is itself a passing chord between vi and I. Here again the function of vi is ambiguous: It prolongs I (and proceeds to I through a passing chord), but it also precedes a dominant harmony.

In example 14.6a, mm. 1 and 3, you may also find two vii°$_6$ chords of the types we have studied. Identify the chords and their harmonic/linear function within the phrase.

iii and vi as 5th-Related Chords

Because of their root relationship by 5th (or 4th), iii and vi can effectively be paired in harmonic progressions. In example 14.6b (and example 14.4f), the standard I–vi–IV–V$_7$ progression is slightly altered by the insertion of iii between vi and IV: I–vi–iii–IV–V$_7$. By doing so, Bach prolongs the tonic harmony one more beat (both vi and iii in this phrase prolong I by arpeggiation) while taking advantage of the strong root relationship (ascending 5th) between vi and iii. Moreover, notice that the melodic fragment that Bach harmonizes with this progression is the familiar $\hat{1}$–$\hat{7}$–$\hat{6}$–$\hat{5}$, and that iii allows for the standard harmonization of the descending $\hat{7}$ which we have studied above.

The progression iii–vi–ii–V–I, on the other hand, is based on a pattern of roots related by descending 5ths (a fragment of the circle of 5ths). As we will see when we study the circle-of-5ths sequence on page 423, this progression can frequently be found as part of a larger descending-5ths pattern. Moreover, it often also appears in isolation (that is, without being part of a broader circle of 5ths), as you can see in example 14.6c. This example features a slight variation of the above progression (notice the incomplete iii, the ii$_6$, and the cadential $^6_4$ figure), which is otherwise based on a pattern of roots related by descending 5ths, F♯–B–E–A, or $\hat{3}$–$\hat{6}$–$\hat{2}$–$\hat{5}$ in DM.

The Dominant as an "Apparent Mediant"

Occasionally, a chord that looks like a mediant in first inversion moves directly to a tonic chord. This is the progression represented in example 14.7a. In these cases, $\hat{5}$ is in the bass and it is doubled, and $\hat{7}$ does act as a LT. *We will not think of this chord as being a "mediant" at all, but rather a dominant harmony.* In major, this dominant chord looks like iii$_6$. In minor, however, it looks like an augmented triad, III$^+_6$ (III with a raised $\hat{7}$: $\flat\hat{3}$–$\hat{5}$–$\hat{7}$, as in example 14.7b. You can find a clear example of an authentic cadence with an apparent "III$^+_6$–i" instead of the usual V–i in anthology, no. 50 (Schumann, "Folk Song"), m. 8. The apparent mediant in first inversion at a cadence can best be explained as a dominant harmony embellished by a nonchord tone. In example 14.7a, the soprano's $\hat{3}$ in iii$_6$ may be heard as an anticipation of the $\hat{3}$ in the following I chord. The voice leading in example 14.7b is very characteristic of this progression (see also the Schumann "Folk Song" cadence): $\hat{3}$ in the soprano can be heard as an escape tone (notice the $\hat{3}$–$\hat{1}$ motion in the soprano which replaces the familiar $\hat{2}$–$\hat{1}$ from the V–i progression). In example 14.7c, the escape-tone function of the same $\hat{3}$–$\hat{1}$

♪♪♪ Example 14.7

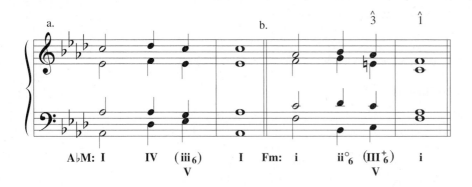

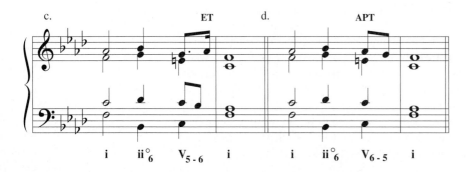

figure (as part of a $\hat{2}$–$\hat{3}$–$\hat{1}$ motion) is perfectly apparent. Finally, in example 14.7d, $\hat{3}$ may be interpreted as an accented PT between $\hat{4}$ and $\hat{2}$, over a V chord (compare with example 14.7b). Notice that in both examples 14.7c and d, the "embellished dominant" figures result from a 5–6 or 6–5 motion over the bass $\hat{5}$.

The Deceptive Resolution of V: vi as a Tonic Substitute

In previous chapters we have already introduced the **deceptive cadence** (a V–vi cadence which usually delays momentarily an authentic cadence) or deceptive progression (a V–vi progression within a phrase, with no cadential function). In both cases, V resolves "deceptively" (that is, in an unexpected way) to vi, which functions here as a tonic substitute. Find a deceptive resolution of V or V_7 in each of the following examples: examples 14.1b and 14.6b, and Schumann's "Folk Song" (anthology, no. 50). Notice, however, that in example 14.1b—Brahms—the deceptive progression is not V–vi, but rather an alternative form that we discussed in chapters 4 and 5. Refer now to anthology, no. 20 (Haydn, Sonata in DM), and study the closing section (mm. 20–24). Is there a deceptive resolution of V in the passage, and if so, what is its formal function?

The voice leading of the deceptive progression requires some considerations. As a principle, the LT should still resolve up to $\hat{1}$. In order to avoid possible parallel 8ves or 5ths, the other two voices should move in contrary motion with the bass. This correct voice leading, illustrated in example 14.8a, results in a vi with a *doubled third*. In the V_7–vi progression in example 14.8b, both the LT and the seventh should resolve as usual (the LT up, the seventh down), and the result is also a doubled third in vi.

EXERCISE

To practice realizing progressions using deceptive resolutions of V, refer to exercises 14.2d and 14.4 in worksheet 14 at the end of this chapter.

♪♪♪ Example 14.8

a.   b.
                          7th
                     LT   LT

A♭M: V   vi V_7 vi

VOICE-LEADING GUIDELINES

1. In progressions by 3rds (I–iii, I–vi, vi–IV, etc.), retain common tones in the same voices.

2. Use the progression I–iii–IV to harmonize a descending melody, $\hat{1}$–$\hat{7}$–$\hat{6}$.

3. The "apparent" iii$_6$–I or III$^+_6$–i progressions are really dominant-tonic progressions with a nonchord tone em-

bellishment. For this reason, you should double the bass ($\hat{5}$) and not the LT ($\hat{7}$).

4. In the deceptive resolution of V (V–vi), beware of parallel 8ves and 5ths: resolve the LT to $\hat{1}$, and move the other two voices in contrary motion to the bass. This will result in a doubled third in vi.

EXERCISES

To practice harmonizing a bass and a melody using mediant and submediant chords, refer to exercises 14.3 and 14.5 in worksheet 14 at the end of this chapter.

To practice writing your own progressions using mediant and submediant chords, refer to exercise 14.6 in worksheet 14 at the end of this chapter.

To practice analysis of musical fragments including mediant and submediant chords, refer to exercises 14.1.1 to 14.1.3 in worksheet 14 at the end of this chapter.

HARMONIC SEQUENCES

In chapter 7 we studied melodic sequences, and we defined them as the restatement of a melodic segment at a higher or lower tonal level. A melodic sequence is often accompanied by a **harmonic sequence**. In example 14.9a you will see that the violin performs a melodic sequence in which each segment is one measure long and is transposed a 3rd below the previous segment. You will also see that the sequence is diatonic: it stays within the key of FM, and has no accidentals outside this key. Now examine the accompaniment. Assign a Roman numeral (RN) to each chord, and pay attention to the harmonic pattern for the complete phrase. Mozart wrote a harmonic diatonic sequence to accompany the melodic sequence. In each measure the root relationships (of descending 4ths) are preserved, and so are the exact spacing and voice leading, although each measure is *transposed a 3rd below the previous measure* (we will return to this sequence and this example on pages 427–428, when we study sequences by descending 3rds). In the staff provided under the example, write a four-voice metric reduction of the piano accompaniment, and notice how each complete harmonic unit (one measure) is transposed as a whole, without any voice-leading alterations.

We will now study the three most common types of harmonic sequences: by descending 5ths (the circle of 5ths), by steps (including the 7–6 and 5–6 techniques), and by descending 3rds. At this point, it may be useful for you to review the sections "Basic Types of Progression" and "Voice-Leading Guidelines for the Three Basic Types of Progression" in chapter 1.

The Diatonic Circle-of-5ths Sequence

The circle of descending 5ths is the harmonic sequence most widely used by composers of tonal music. It is a progression that provides a very strong harmonic support (root relationships by 5th) for melodic sequences descending by step. In example 14.10, a melodic sequence first begins with two two-measure segments, followed by

Example 14.9a   W. A. Mozart, Sonata for Violin and Piano, K. 372, I, mm. 34–38

Example 14.9b

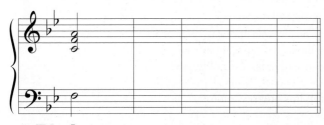

FM: I

♪♪♪Example 14.10   S. Rachmaninoff, *Rhapsody on a Theme of Paganini,* op. 43, Theme, mm. 17–24

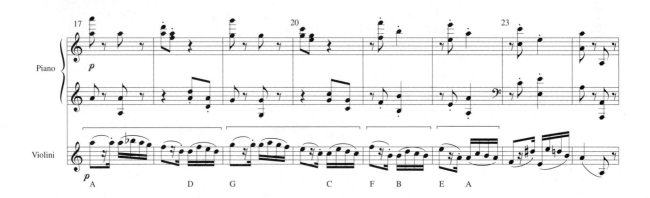

two one-measure segments. The accompaniment (in the piano part) features a circle-of-5ths bass, first with a harmonic rhythm of a chord per measure, then a chord per beat. The complete circle-of-5ths bass line is A–D–G–C–F–B–E–A, with an added C–E–A cadential figure.

Rachmaninoff's lean harmonic realization of this bass as presented by the piano includes full chords only in mm. 18 and 21. Possible complete realizations of this progression in minor and major appear in examples 14.11a and b.

We should remark on several harmonic and voice-leading characteristics for the circle-of-5ths progression:

1. The descending-5ths bass most often appears as alternating descending 5ths and ascending 4ths.

2. In a complete diatonic circle of 5ths, one of the 5ths will be diminished (it may also appear as an ascending +4). In major, the °5 or +4 occur between $\hat{4}$ and $\hat{7}$. In minor, between $\hat{6}$ and $\hat{2}$.

3. One of the triads in the diatonic circle of 5ths is diminished: vii° in major, and ii° in minor.

4. Because the circle of 5ths is a descending harmonic sequence on a two-chord segment, the voice leading of chord pairs should be preserved.

5. In a harmonic sequence, preserving voice-leading patterns has priority over dealing with scale degrees functionally. In the major mode, vii° appears in root position, $\hat{7}$ is usually doubled, and it does not resolve to $\hat{1}$ (that is, it is not treated as a LT). vii°, moreover, proceeds to iii—not to I (see chords 3 and 4 in example 14.11b). In the minor mode, VII is usually major in this progression (on ♭$\hat{7}$, not on the LT), and ii° appears in root position.

♪♪♪Example 14.11

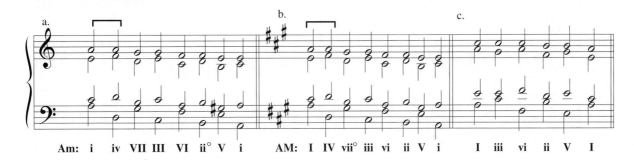

Am: i   iv VII III VI ii° V   i   AM: I   IV vii° iii vi   ii V   i   I   iii   vi   ii   V   I

Although the circle-of-5ths progression is often used in its complete form, it may also appear partially. A shorter circle-of-5ths segment sometimes found in music literature is I–iii–vi–ii–V–I. In this segment, all chords preserve the normative diatonic functions, and the chord on $\hat{7}$ is avoided (example 14.11c). Study example 14.12, and identify a complete circle-of-5ths progression underlying the contrapuntal texture. Because this passage is polyphonic, you might be tempted to confuse sequence and imitation. Make sure you mark all the melodic sequences in each voice and also all the cases of polyphonic imitation in the passage.

Voice-Leading Variants for Circle-of-5ths Sequences

Example 14.13 shows several standard voice-leading paradigms for sequences based on the circle of 5ths. Paradigms in examples 14.13a, b, and c are exclusively based on root-position triads. Their differences affect mostly the intervallic patterns between outer voices. In example 14.13a, you can see a linear pattern of parallel 10ths every other chord, with octaves in between (resulting in a 10–8–10–8 design). Example 14.13b features parallel 10ths by contrary motion throughout, and the outer-voice pattern in example 14.13c is 8–5–8–5.

♪♪♪Example 14.12   J. S. Bach, Fugue 2 in Cm, from *The Well-Tempered Clavier,* I, mm. 22–25

♩♪♪Example 14.13

AM: 10 8 10 8   10 8 10 8   10 10 10 10   10 10 10 10   8 5 8 5   8 5 8 5   10 6 10 6   10 6 10 6

6 5 6 5   6 5 6 5   10 5 10 5   10 5 10 5   10 10 10 10
                                                6   6   6   6
                                               10 10 10 10
                                                6   6   6   6

A realization of the circle of 5ths frequently found in the literature alternates chords in $\frac{5}{3}$ and $\frac{6}{3}$ positions. Two voice-leading paradigms resulting from this alternation of root position and first-inversion triads appear in examples 14.13d and e. In the first of these, which begins with a $\frac{5}{3}$ triad, the outer-voice pattern is 10–6–10–6, whereas the second paradigm, which begins with a $\frac{6}{3}$ triad, displays the outer-voice pattern 6–5–6–5.

You can find an example of a circle-of-fifths sequence in which root-position and first-inversion triads alternate in anthology, no. 32 (Beethoven, Sonata in Fm, op. 2, no. 1, I), mm. 73–78. Which of the above voice-leading patterns can you recognize in this passage? Now go back to examples 14.10 and 14.12, and identify the basic underlying voice-leading patterns for each. Consider especially the outer voices, and compare the basic voice leading (disregard melodic elaboration) with the outer-voice patterns in the paradigms we have studied. Finally, discuss and identify in class the voice-leading sequential paradigm in mm. 18–21 of example 14.14. Notice that in the upper voice there is a change of octave (a register transfer) every two beats. For your outer-voice paradigm, assume that all pitches are in the same octave.

NOTE

Sequences based on the ascending circle of fifths _are also possible, although they are found much more rarely in the literature. Examples 14.13f and g show two sequential paradigms based on ascending fifths. In the first one, all triads are in root position. The second type alternates root-position and first-inversion triads. The ascending-fifths_

♪♪♪ Example 14.14   W. A. Mozart, Piano Sonata in CM, K. 545, mm. 16–22

sequence is not usually found in minor, and when it appears in major it is often limited to the I to iii segment (that is, I–V–ii–vi–iii), thus avoiding the final vii°–IV–I segment (a very awkward cadential gesture, unlike the usual ii–V–I that closes the descending circle of 5ths).

Sequences by Descending and Ascending Steps: The 7–6 and 5–6 Techniques

We will now study two sequential techniques which are based on the principles of fourth-species counterpoint (syncopated counterpoint). In chapter D we learned how to write a series of 7–6 suspensions (see example D.10b). We also learned that a string of 6–5 suspensions is perfectly acceptable because 5ths separated by a consonant interval (a 6th in this case) are not parallel 5ths, and that, by the same token, parallel 5ths between strong beats are correct in fourth species as long as they are separated by consonances (see example D.12c).

Refer first to example 14.15a. Without the syncopated upper voice, this sequential paradigm would simply be based on a descending series of parallel $^6_3$ chords of the type we studied in chapter 4. By syncopating the upper voice (the 6th above the bass) we elaborate this sequence with a series of 7–6 suspensions (the **7–6 technique**). The Mozart fragment reproduced in example 14.16 is based on this paradigm, as you can verify in the reduction below it.

♪♪♪Example 14.15

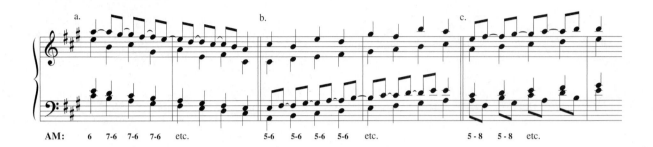

♪♪♪Example 14.16   W. A. Mozart, Piano Sonata in GM, K. 283, I, mm. 48–51

Example 14.15b, on the other hand, is based on an ascending succession of $\frac{5}{3}$ chords. By moving one of the voices in syncopation by step, a 5–6 pattern is produced above the bass. This contrapuntal procedure, which we know as the **5–6 technique**, breaks the faulty parallel 5ths that would result if the successive $\frac{5}{3}$ chords were not elaborated. Example 14.15c shows a variant of this sequence in which the bass moves down a third to the same pitch that forms the 6th in the 5–6 motion, thus turning the sequence into a succession of root-position triads. The 5–6 sequence works best in major. It is also possible in minor, although the best segment in which to use it in this mode is usually from III to vi. An example of the ascending 5–6 sequence appears in example 14.17.

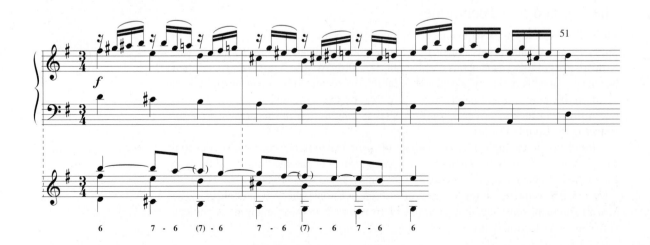

Example 14.17   E. Y. Harburg-Harold Arlen, "If I Only Had a Brain," from the Film *The Wizard of Oz*

NOTE

In chapter 4 we discussed that a succession of parallel $^6_3$ chords is essentially a three-voice procedure, and we learned that, in four voices, doubling requires special care. If the same voice is always doubled, parallel 8ves will result. We also learned the technique of "alternate doublings," in which the fourth voice does not move in parallel motion with the remaining voices, and the doubled voice is not always the same. Review the section of chapter 4 in which parallel $^6_3$ chords are discussed, and verify the technique of alternate doublings in examples 14.15a and b.

Sequences by Descending 3rds

In a sequence by descending 3rds based only on successive root-position triads, parallel 8ves and 5ths are likely to result, as illustrated by example 14.18a. Two common ways of avoiding the problem in this sequence are shown in examples 14.18b and c. In example 14.18b, a passing $^6_3$ chord connects the roots by 3rds (circled in

Example 14.18

♪♪♪ Example 14.19a Carl Philipp Emanuel Bach, Piano Sonata no. 4, from *6 Sonaten für Kenner und Liebhaber*, I, mm. 5–8

the bass line). The resulting sequential pattern features an alternation of $^5_3$ and $^6_3$ chords over a bass descending by steps. Compare this sequential design with the passage by Carl Philipp Emanuel Bach reproduced in example 14.19a. In this example, circle the roots by descending 3rds, and label each of the intervening passing chords with a $^6_3$ below the corresponding bass note. Then, study example 14.19b. Whereas in the C. P. E. Bach example the sequence by 3rds was quite literal both harmonically and melodically, the James Taylor song features the same sequence in a slightly altered form, both melodically and harmonically. What are these slight alterations and how are they produced? This example appropriately introduces at the end of this chapter a taste of what is to come in the next chapter: diatonic seventh chords.

Example 14.18c, on the other hand, shows a paradigm in which the intervening chord is in root position and the resulting bass pattern is a descending 4th followed by an ascending 2nd. This a very common harmonic paradigm, especially in the baroque and Classical periods. The Mozart passage which we discussed in example 14.9 is indeed based on this paradigm, and so is the famous Canon in D by Pachelbel (listen to a recording of this piece, and hear the repeated sequential pattern and the variations that Pachelbel writes on it).

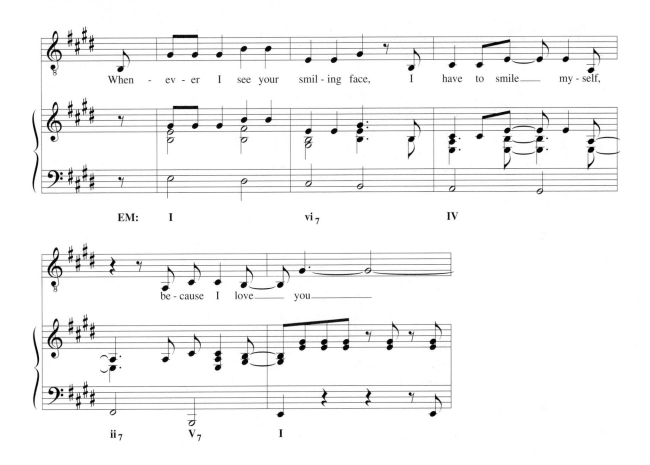

Example 14.19b   James Taylor, "Your Smiling Face" (Beginning of Verse)

EXERCISES

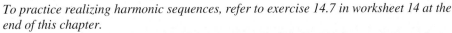

To practice realizing harmonic sequences, refer to exercise 14.7 in worksheet 14 at the end of this chapter.

   To practice analysis of musical fragments including harmonic sequences, refer to exercises 14.1.5 to 14.1.7 in worksheet 14 at the end of this chapter.

MORE ON THE 5–6 TECHNIQUE

As we saw, the 5–6 technique is a linear procedure in which a voice moves by step, producing the intervals 5–6 (or 6–5) over a stationary bass. This motion creates what may appear to be two different chords, but is better interpreted as a contrapuntal

Example 14.20   F. Schubert, "Des Fischers Liebesglück," mm. 4–6

motion. This procedure may be used sequentially, or it may also be used in isolation, over a variety of scale degrees. We saw in chapter 10 that the relationship between the subdominant in root position and the supertonic in first inversion (IV–ii₆) is a 5–6 motion over $\hat{4}$. Can you identify a 5–6 motion of this type in example 14.20? Now refer back to example 13.9 (worksheet 13, exercise 13.1.2, Caldara, "Alma del core"). Identify an example of the 5–6 technique somewhere in mm. 28–30. What kind of suspension takes place at the same time?

EXERCISE

To practice analysis of musical fragments including 5–6 techniques, refer to exercise 14.1.4 in worksheet 14 at the end of this chapter.

ASSIGNMENT AND KEYBOARD PROGRESSIONS

For analytical and written assignments and keyboard progressions based on the materials learned in this chapter, refer to chapter 14 in the workbook.

PITCH PATTERNS

Sing the pitch patterns in example 14.21. As you sing, listen to the chords we have studied in this chapter, and understand their function within the phrase.

♪♪♪ Example 14.21

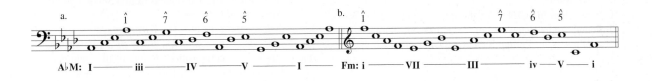

a.
$\hat{1}$ $\hat{7}$ $\hat{6}$ $\hat{5}$
b. $\hat{1}$ $\hat{7}$ $\hat{6}$ $\hat{5}$

A♭M: I ——— iii ———— IV ——— V ——— I   Fm: i ——— VII ———— III ——— iv — V — i

c.   d.   e.

A♭M: I ———— vi ———— ii$_6$——— V ———— I

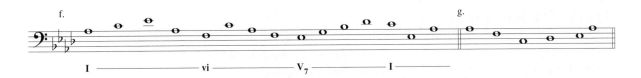

f.   g.

I ——————————— vi ———————— V$_7$ ———— I ————

h.
(ET)   (AP)

Fm: i——— ii°$_6$ ———— V ———— i ———— V ———— i ——— (III$_6^+$)——— i
                                                        V

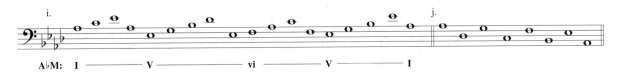

i.   j.

A♭M: I ——————— V ——————— vi ——————— V ——— I

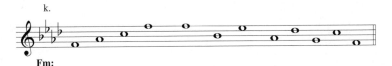

k.

Fm:

Composers and Their Music 14

Biographies

Write short biographies of the following composers mentioned in this chapter: Camille Saint-Saëns, Sergey Rachmaninoff, Carl Philipp Emanuel Bach, Harold Arlen.

Listening

Listen to the following compositions by composers mentioned in this chapter:

Saint-Saëns, *The Carnival of the Animals.*
Rachmaninoff, *Rhapsody on a Theme of Paganini,* op. 43.

C. P. E. Bach, selected sonatas from *6 Sonaten für Kenner und Liebhaber.*
Arlen, score for the film *The Wizard of Oz.*

Follow the score while you listen (if available). Be able to place these compositions in one of the style periods and to comment on why and how they represent the musical characteristics of that period. Try to identify harmonic sequences aurally and to determine what type of sequences they are (circle of 5ths, descending or ascending by steps, decending 3rds, etc.).

Terms for Review

Mediant triad
Submediant triad
iii and vi as tonic prolongations
Progression by 3rds
Subtonic triad
Ground bass
Romanesca and folia basses
vi as a predominant
iii and vi as 5th-related chords

Dominant as an "apparent mediant"
vi as a tonic substitute
Deceptive cadence
Harmonic sequence
Diatonic circle-of-5ths sequence
Sequences ascending or descending by steps
7–6 and 5–6 techniques
Sequences by descending 3rds

Worksheet 14

EXERCISE 14.1   Analysis.

1. Identify the progression in example 14.22. What is the function of the second chord?

Example 14.22   F. Schubert, "Ständchen," from *Schwanengesang,* no. 4, mm. 1–4

2. a) Analyze example 14.23 with RNs.

   b) The complete passage is a harmonic prolongation of I. Explain very specifically how each chord functions in this extended prolongation.

   c) What kind of cadence closes the passage?

Example 14.23   J. S. Bach, Chorale 143, "In dulci jubilo," mm. 1–4

3. a) Analyze example 14.24 with RNs.

   b) How does vi function in this example?

   c) What kind of cadence closes the passage?

Example 14.24   J. S. Bach, Chorale 69, "Komm, Heiliger Geist, Herre Gott," mm. 1–2

4. Refer back to example 13.10 (worksheet 13, exercise 13.1.3, Jacquet de la Guerre, Suite in Am, Sarabande), and identify several examples of 5–6 techniques.

5. a) Identify the sequential progression in example 14.25, mm. 1–4. Analyze it with RNs.

   b) Compare mm. 1–4 to the voice-leading paradigms studied. What paradigm or paradigms do you recognize?

   c) The three phrases in example 14.25 present three different realizations of the same progression. How are they different?

♪♪♪ Example 14.25   G. F. Handel, Passacaglia, from *Suite de Pièces,* 1st coll., no. 7, IV, mm. 1–12

6. Study the contrapuntal sequence in example 14.26. In the staff under it, write a chordal metric reduction using the pitches circled in the example (the chordal tones). What voice-leading paradigm can you identify?

Example 14.26   J. S. Bach, Invention no. 4 in Dm, mm. 7–11

7. a) What are the underlying progressions in examples 14.27a and b? Identify the roots for each chord in the progressions, and circle these roots in the bass. In example 14.27b, be sure to take into account the change of registers in the bass. What exact sequential type does this example represent?

   b) Consider melodic/contrapuntal relationships in each of these passages. What are the basic principles of melodic growth in each individual line?

   c) In example 14.27a, how are the lines related on a measure-by-measure basis? And how are they related as a whole, considering the complete example? What specific interval regulates this contrapuntal relationship?

♪♪♪ Example 14.27a   W. A. Mozart, Symphony no. 39, K. 543, in E♭M, IV, mm. 125–133

♪♪♪ Example 14.27b   J. S. Bach, Fugue no. 16 in Gm, from *The Well-Tempered Clavier,* I, mm. 24–28

EXERCISE 14.2   Realize the following short progressions in four voices. Provide RNs where missing.

DM: I   vi   IV   V₇   I   Fm: 6   7   EM: I   iii   vi   ii   V   V₂⁴   I₆

BᵇM: I   IV   V   vi   V₅⁶   I   Dm: i   VII   III   iv   V₄⁶⁻₃⁵   i   F♯m: ♯

EXERCISE 14.3   Provide a RN analysis for the following bass line. Include the following chords: III, two VIs (one of them as part of a deceptive cadence), V₅⁶, V₂⁴, all three types of dissonant ₄⁶s (passing, neighbor, cadential), and a 4–3 suspension (you should not realize it, just write the figures under a bass note on which a 4–3 suspension would work).

EXERCISE 14.4   Realize the following figured bass in four voices. Provide a RN analysis. Remember to double-check the outer-voice frame for good first-species counterpoint.

Gm: ♯₄⁶   6   9-8   7♯   ♯   ♯₂⁴   6   ♯6   4-3   6   8-7 / 6-5 / 4-♯   ♮

EXERCISE 14.5   Harmonize this melody in four voices, using the given HR. Include the following chords in your harmonization: iii, vii°$_6$, V$_3^4$, V$_5^6$, a cadential $_4^6$, a deceptive resolution of V, and a neighbor $_4^6$. Use voice exchange between bass and melody wherever it is possible. Write your bass and RNs first, and make sure they make harmonic and metric sense. Then add the inner voices. Remember: Always play (and make sure you like) your exercises.

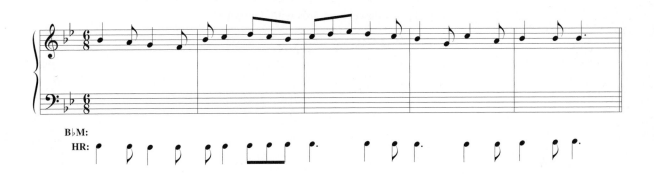

EXERCISE 14.6

1. Write progressions (bass and RNs) using the chords indicated in each case in the required meters. Be careful with the metric placement of your chords.

   a)   iii, deceptive resolution of V, neighbor $_4^6$.

   b)   Passing $_4^6$, V$_2^4$, VI.

   c)   V$_5^6$, V$_3^4$, ii°$_6$, a fragment of a circle of 5ths.

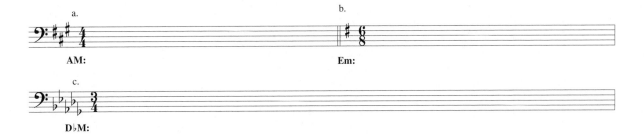

2. Choose one of your own progressions from above, and use it as a harmonic basis to compose a phrase for a melodic instrument of your choice (such as flute, clarinet in B♭, violin, etc.) and keyboard accompaniment. Your phrase should consist of a simple melody (for the melodic instrument) with a keyboard-style accompaniment (both hands).

EXERCISE 14.7   On your own music paper, realize the following harmonic sequences in four voices (two $\frac{4}{4}$ measures each).

1. A root-position circle of 5ths with a 10–8–10–8 outer-voice paradigm, in FM.

2. A circle of 5ths alternating first-inversion and root-position chords, with a 6–5–6–5 outer-voice paradigm, in Cm.

3. A sequence ascending by steps using the 5–6 technique, in B♭M.

4. A sequence by descending 3rds with interpolated $\frac{6}{3}$ chords, in Gm.

Chapter 15

Other Diatonic Seventh Chords

We have now studied all of the diatonic triads and the dominant seventh chord. Seventh chords may also be built on any diatonic scale degree. You may wish to review the quality of seventh chords on each of the diatonic degrees of major and minor keys in the chapter E section, "Diatonic Seventh Chords in the Major and Minor Keys." The function of seventh chords is usually the same as the corresponding diatonic triad. Although all seventh chords may be found in music, we will focus on those that appear most frequently: the leading-tone sevenths (vii°_7 and $\text{vii}^{\varnothing}_7$), the supertonic seventh (ii_7 or $\text{ii}^{\varnothing}_7$), and the subdominant seventh (IV_7 or iv_7).

GENERAL DOUBLING AND VOICE-LEADING GUIDELINES

Because seventh chords in four voices will usually be complete, you need not double any pitch. If a seventh chord cannot be complete because of voice-leading considerations, you may omit the fifth of the chord. You should not double the seventh or the leading tone (LT). It is best to double the root unless it is the LT (as in vii°_7). Two voice-leading conventions apply to all seventh chords:

1. The seventh must resolve downward by step.
2. It is better to prepare the seventh if possible, by approaching it as a repeated note or by step. It is less desirable to approach it by leap, but if you must do so it is better to approach it by ascending leap.

Doubling and voice-leading principles apply equally to seventh chord inversions. For inversions we will use the same symbols we already learned as applied to the dominant seventh: $^6_5$ indicates first inversion (third in the bass), $^4_3$ indicates second inversion (fifth in the bass), and $^4_2$ indicates third inversion (seventh in the bass).

♪♪♪ Example 15.1

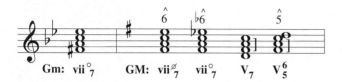

♪♪♪ Example 15.2   A. Beach, "Barcarolle," from *Three Pieces*, op. 28, no. 1, mm. 1–6

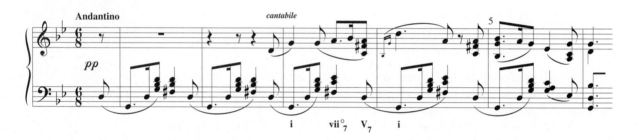

THE LEADING-TONE SEVENTHS

The diatonic seventh chord on the LT is half-diminished in major keys (**vii**^ø₇) and fully diminished in minor keys (**vii**°₇). The fully diminished chord, however, is also used in major keys, with exactly the same spelling as vii°₇ in minor. This is not properly a diatonic chord, because it requires a lowered $\hat{6}$ ($\flat\hat{6}$), a degree "borrowed" from minor. vii°₇ actually appears in major keys more often than the purely diatonic vii^ø₇, a fairly infrequent chord.

Both vii^ø₇ and vii°₇ resolve to the tonic, and both have a dominant function. Both chords are very **closely related to V₇**: The LT sevenths have three common tones with V₇ ($\hat{7}$–$\hat{2}$–$\hat{4}$, bracketed in example 15.1), and one pitch a step away from the root of V₇ ($\hat{6}$ in vii^ø₇, $\flat\hat{6}$ in vii°₇, $\hat{5}$ in V₇), as illustrated by example 15.1. The close relationship may best be observed by comparing the two LT sevenths with V$^6_5$: All three chords are built on the LT, and all three chords share the LT triad ($\hat{7}$–$\hat{2}$–$\hat{4}$). Because of this close relationship, LT seventh chords often move to V₇ before resolving to the tonic, as in the phrase by Beach reproduced in example 15.2 (see mm. 3–4).

THE HALF-DIMINISHED SEVENTH

The *half-diminished seventh* sonority comprises a diminished triad and a m7. vii^ø₇ appears only in major keys, although it is found less often than vii°₇. Example 15.3 (m. 15) shows a standard context for vii^ø₇: It functions as a dominant, it is preceded by a predominant chord (IV), and it resolves to I.

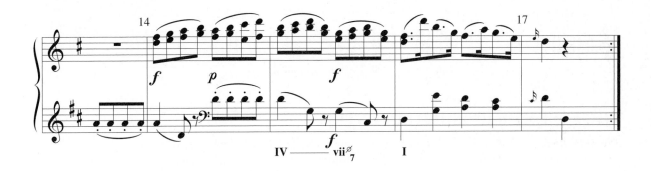

♪♪♪Example 15.3   W. A. Mozart, Piano Sonata in DM, K. 284, III, Var. V, mm. 13–17

Example 15.4 illustrates the main voice-leading characteristics for this chord. The °5, $\hat{7}$–$\hat{4}$ (common to both vii°$_7$ and V$_7$) must be resolved inward to $\hat{1}$–$\hat{3}$ (or outward to $\hat{3}$–$\hat{1}$ if it appears as a +4, $\hat{4}$–$\hat{7}$ as in example 15.4d); the seventh resolves down by step; and the third ($\hat{2}$) may in principle move up to $\hat{3}$ or down to $\hat{1}$. If it moves down to $\hat{1}$, however, parallel 5ths may result (as in example 15.4b); $\hat{2}$ should then move up to $\hat{3}$, as in example 15.4a (of course, you could also switch the soprano and alto parts in example 15.4b to avoid the parallel 5ths).

Examples 15.4c and d represent the two most usual inversions of vii°$_7$: vii°$^6_5$ and vii°$^4_3$ (the 3rd inversion is much less frequent). vii°$^6_5$ should not resolve to I in root position for the same reason we already discussed (the bass $\hat{2}$–$\hat{1}$ would produce parallel 5ths with another voice). And because the fifth of this chord ($\hat{4}$) resolves down by step to $\hat{3}$ as part of the tritone $\hat{4}$–$\hat{7}$, vii°$^4_3$ will also usually resolve to I$_6$, as in example 15.4d. In all these examples you may note that in the normative resolution of this chord (which does not allow for much voice-leading freedom), the *third* of the tonic chord is doubled.

♪♪♪Example 15.4

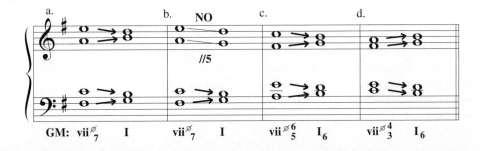

♪♪♪ Example 15.5

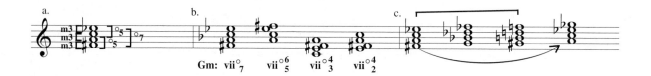

Gm: vii°₇   vii°⁶₅   vii°⁴₃   vii°⁴₂

THE FULLY DIMINISHED SEVENTH

The *fully-diminished seventh chord* is made up of a diminished triad and a diminished 7th. The **intervallic content** of this chord is highly uniform, as you can see in example 15.5a: You can indeed build a °7 chord by stacking *three minor 3rds,* or also by overlapping *two diminished 5ths.* The result is that you come up with the same intervals if you read from the bottom up or from the top down. We call this type of sonority a *symmetrical* sonority. Imagine the pitch F♯ placed on top of the °7 chord in example 15.5a. The resulting division of the octave into four minor thirds (F♯–A–C–E♭–F♯) is indeed symmetrical around the axis C, that is, the upper and lower halves of the sonority are, intervallically, mirror inversions of each other.

Because of its symmetrical nature and its highly uniform intervallic content, the °7th chord is a characteristic sonority with strong expressive power and a variety of harmonic possibilities, some of which we will study in the second part of this book. A result of this symmetrical intervallic content is that, although we can determine the position of a vii°₇ chord by its spelling, the *sound* of each inversion is intervallically identical to any other inversion. In example 15.5b you can see the different spelling for each inversion. Play each of the chords, and notice that you are still playing stacked 3rds (+2 = m3 in sound), overlapping tritones, and a °7th outer-voice interval.

Another property of °7th chords is that, if we consider their actual pitch content, regardless of possible enharmonic spellings, there are only **three possible different chords**, as illustrated by example 15.5c. Play a °7th chord on any pitch and on the two following pitches in the chromatic scale (such as F♯, G, and G♯). These are three different chords. The fourth chord, however (on A) contains exactly the same pitches as the first one, on F♯. All of these properties of the °7th chord have been widely used by composers as a means to modulate, to create harmonic ambiguity, and to create dramatic tension. For the time being we will limit our study of this chord to its most elementary function as a member of the dominant family in both major and minor keys.

Voice Leading

Example 15.6 shows a frequent function of vii°₇: It embellishes I as a linear neighbor chord (m. 1). Here you will see the normative voice-leading principles in the resolution of vii°₇: The LT (A♯) moves up to 1̂, the seventh (G♮) moves down (♭6̂–5̂), and the pitch that forms a °5 with the bass (E) also moves down (4̂–3̂). These standard voice-leading guidelines are clearly shown in example 15.7.

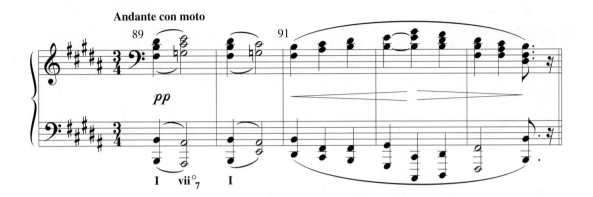

♪♪♪ Example 15.6   J. Brahms, Ballade, op. 10, no. 4, mm. 89–93

The third of vii°$_7$ may either move up or down. If it moves up (as in example 15.7a), a satisfactory resolution of both °5ths occurs. In example 15.7b the third moves downward, producing unequal 5ths. This voice leading is often found in music and is quite acceptable. If the third moves down to $\hat{1}$, however, a more satisfactory voice leading results when the unequal 5ths appear inverted, as 4ths (example 15.7c).

vii°$^6_5$

The first inversion of vii°$_7$, vii°$^6_5$, may then resolve *either to I or to I$_6$* (the third in the bass may move up or down). In the vii°$^6_5$–I progression (as well as I–vii°$^6_5$) unequal 5ths will also occur, and here again they are quite acceptable, although not ideal (because they involve the bass). The progression vii°$^6_5$–I$_6$ produces a more satisfactory resolution of both tritones. Example 15.7d illustrates the use of vii°$^6_5$ as a passing chord between I and I$_6$.

vii°$^4_3$ and vii°$^4_2$

Because the fifth of vii°$_7$ ($\hat{4}$) must resolve down as part of the tritone $\hat{7}$–$\hat{4}$, the second inversion, vii°$^4_3$, usually resolves to I$_6$ (or i$_6$, as in example 15.7e). In the third inversion (which is found less often than the other two inversions), on the other hand, the seventh ($\flat\hat{6}$) should resolve down to $\hat{5}$, resulting in a $^6_4$ chord which must be treated as one of the standard types of $^6_4$ chords. Most frequently, vii°$^4_2$ resolves to a cadential $^6_4$, although it may also resolve to a passing $^6_4$. In both cases it is possible to find the voice-leading license used in examples 15.7f and g: in example 15.7f, in order to preserve the customary doubling in the $^6_4$ chord ($\hat{5}$ is doubled), the °5 in vii°$^4_2$ (F♯–C, or $\hat{7}$–$\hat{4}$) does not

♪♪♪ Example 15.7

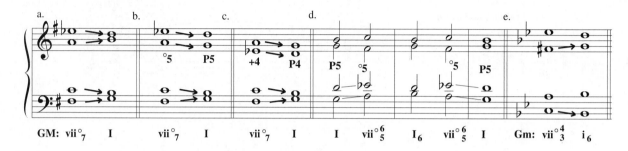

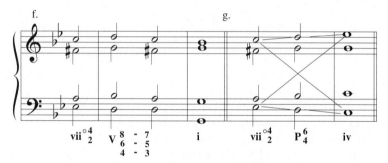

resolve inwards but rather moves up producing unequal 5ths; in example 15.7g the same unequal 5ths occur because of the voice exchange effected by the passing $^6_4$ figure.

Now go back to the Brahms passage in example 15.6 and study the resolution and voice leading of the fourth chord: What chord is it? To what chord does it resolve? How does Brahms avoid unequal 5ths? You may also notice some other harmonic aspects of the passage: How does Brahms prolong the tonic in m. 91? The second chord in m. 92 is also a seventh chord which we will study in this chapter. Which one? Does Brahms prepare the seventh in this chord?

vii°$_7$ and V$_7$

vii°$_7$ and V$_7$ have the same function, share three common tones, and by moving the fourth pitch by step, one of the chords may be converted into the other. Because of this close relationship, both chords often appear together. Example 15.8 shows several possibilities of vii°$_7$ chords moving to V or V$_7$ chords (in either root position or inversion). In all these cases, the vii°$_7$ chord is heard as a contrapuntal elaboration of V$_7$, in which ♭6 functions as a neighbor note (NN) or passing tone (PT) (depending on the context) moving to $\hat{5}$.

PRACTICAL APPLICATION AND DISCUSSION

Example 15.9 begins with a statement of the tonic, a "dominant area," and a return to the tonic. How is the dominant area extended? Explain the linear relationships between the opening and closing tonic and the central dominant area (look at both the two upper voices and the left-hand chords).

Interesting linear designs involving vii°₇ chords may be found in two examples from the anthology. In anthology, no. 34 (Beethoven, Sonata op. 13, III), the first phrase ends at m. 4 on a V chord, and the beginning of the second phrase extends this dominant harmony to resolve it in m. 6. What is the chord at m. 5 which prolongs the V from m. 4?

Now turn to anthology, no. 56 (Clara Schumann, Trio). In mm. 269–270, two inversions of vii°₇ are connected linearly by a passing chord. What are the two inversions, what is the passing chord, and where is the voice exchange which connects the progression linearly? Look also at the resolution to I in m. 271. How is I prolonged in this measure? What seventh chord can you identify?

As a final example for this discussion, study example 15.10. First, think of mm. 1–8 as a single harmonic unit (underlying a phrase with two parallel phrase segments). The long-range motion is from i to i₆, hence a prolongation of i; how are i and i₆ connected? i₆ is itself extended through m. 14, and at m. 15 it descends back to i. How is i₆ extended linearly in mm. 9–14? What chord is used for this extension and how does it function? How does i₆ go back to i in m. 15? How is i prolonged in mm. 16–18? In other words, all of mm. 1–18 are a prolongation of the tonic. Discuss the cadential gesture in mm. 19–22, and prepare a complete bass reduction for the example, showing graphically the linear prolongation of i by means of the appropriate reductive notation.

Example 15.8

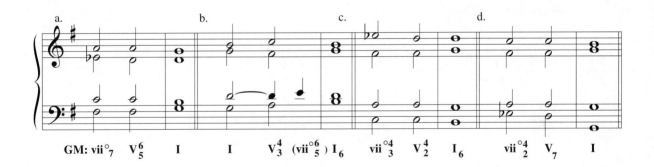

Example 15.9 W. A. Mozart, Piano Sonata in Cm, K. 457, I, mm. 1–8

♪♪♪ Example 15.9   Continued

♪♪♪ Example 15.10   L. v. Beethoven, Piano Sonata in Cm, op. 10, no. 1, I, mm. 1–22

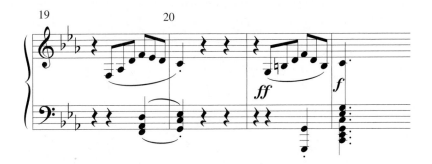

EXERCISES

To practice spelling and resolving leading-tone seventh chords, refer to exercise 15.2 in worksheet 15 at the end of this chapter.

To practice realizing short progressions using LT seventh chords, refer to exercises 15.3a and b in worksheet 15 at the end of this chapter.

THE SUPERTONIC SEVENTH

The seventh chord on $\hat{2}$, along with V_7, is one of the most commonly used seventh chords in the tonal literature. It is a mm chord in major keys (ii_7) and a half-diminished chord in minor keys ($ii^{\o}_7$). Its function is the same as the ii triad: to precede the dominant, most often in cadential gestures. Mendelssohn concludes the opening phrase of his violin concerto with an authentic cadence preceded by a $ii^{\o}_7$ dominant preparation (example 15.11). You will remark that the $ii^{\o}_7$ "grows" from the previous chord, iv (which has three common tones with it). The voice leading of the passage is as smooth as it can possibly be. The three common tones are retained in the same voices, including the seventh, which is thus prepared. The seventh resolves down to $\hat{7}$, and moreover the seventh in V_7 ($\hat{4}$) is also prepared (and, of course, resolved). Measures 1–8 in this phrase are a prolongation of the tonic. What harmonic/linear means does Mendelssohn use for this prolongation?

♩♩♪Example 15.11   Felix Mendelssohn, Concerto for Violin, op. 64, mm. 1–11

Even more common than ii₇ is its first inversion. **ii$_5^6$** is one of the strongest and most frequently used predominant chords. By combining the strong melodic bass motion ($\hat{4}$–$\hat{5}$) and the dissonant clash of a 2nd ($_5^6$ above the bass), this chord creates a powerful drive toward V. The cadential formula ii$_5^6$–V₇–I is one of Bach's favorites (as well as of most other composers). In Bach's realizations of this formula we can see the melodic origin of this chord (as of dissonance in general): The dissonance (the seventh of the chord) is normally prepared as a suspension that resolves in the next chord, with a change of bass. Two cadences by Bach reproduced in examples 15.12a and b confirm this voice leading.

The excerpt in example 15.12b is in Fm, despite the key signature. How do you explain the final FM chord? Observe that both examples illustrate the melodic origin of V₇: What is the function of the seventh in both final cadential dominants?

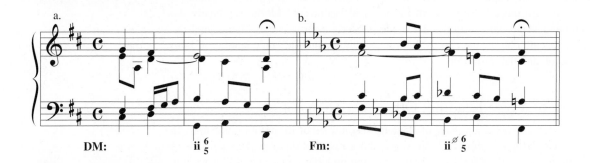

Example 15.12a and b   J. S. Bach, Chorale 20, "Ein feste Burg ist unser Gott" (Final Cadence) and J. S. Bach, Chorale 25, "Wo soll ich fliehen hin" (Final Cadence)

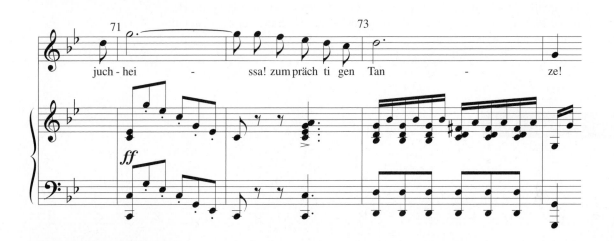

Example 15.12c   Felix Mendelssohn, "Hexenlied," *Zwölf Gesänge,* op. 8, no. 8, mm. 71–74

Example 15.12d   M. Szymanowska, Nocturne in B♭M, mm. 53–55

Two examples by nineteenth-century composers show the use of ii$_5^6$ (or ii$_5^{\circ 6}$) in a keyboard texture (examples 15.12c and d). Even in this context in which dissonance is often treated with more freedom, both Felix Mendelssohn and Maria Szymanowska approach the seventh with careful voice leading. Study both passages, identifying the supertonic seventh chords, the chords that precede them, and the voice leading of both the preparation and the resolution.

Summary of Voice Leading; Other Inversions of ii$_7$

Example 15.13 presents a summary of standard resolutions of ii$_7$ and its inversions. In all of these cases the seventh ($\hat{1}$) is prepared, and it resolves down to $\hat{7}$. The ii$_7$–V$_7$–I progression is especially effective to harmonize the melodic patterns $\hat{4}$–$\hat{4}$–$\hat{3}$ (example 15.13b) and $\hat{1}$–$\hat{7}$–$\hat{1}$, whereas the ii$_5^6$–V–I or ii$_5^6$–V$_7$–I progressions are often used for the patterns $\hat{2}$–$\hat{2}$–$\hat{3}$ (example 15.13c), $\hat{6}$–$\hat{5}$–$\hat{5}$, or $\hat{1}$–$\hat{7}$–$\hat{1}$. Notice the close relationship of ii$_5^6$ as a predominant (example 15.13c) with both IV and ii$_6$ (two chords that are contained in ii$_5^6$). In example 15.13d you will see another standard progression involving ii$_5^6$: Because ii$_5^6$ and V$_2^4$ have the same bass, $\hat{4}$, the progression ii$_5^6$–V$_2^4$ allows for very smooth voice leading over a stationary bass.

♪♪♪ Example 15.13

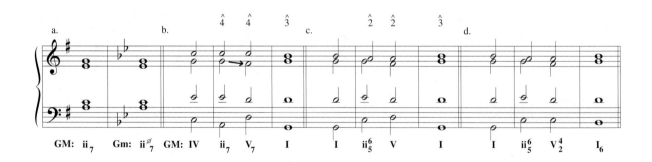

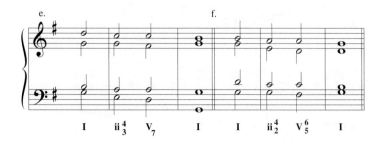

The second inversion of ii$_7$, ii$_3^4$, is not found as frequently as ii$_5^6$. Example 15.13e shows the standard resolution of ii$_3^4$, down to V or V$_7$. The third inversion, on the other hand, is often used as part of the progression illustrated in example 15.13f. Because ii$_2^4$ is built on $\hat{1}$, it allows for a smooth connection with I. The seventh is thus prepared in the bass and, as usual, is resolved down to $\hat{7}$, and hence to V$_6$ or V$_5^6$. Study the harmonization of the opening period of Mozart's Gm Symphony (example 15.14). What are the only four chords used by Mozart? What is the complete progression? How does the second chord resolve?

♪♪♪ Example 15.14   W. A. Mozart, Symphony no. 40 in Gm, K. 550, I, mm. 1–9

THE SUBDOMINANT SEVENTH

IV$_7$ is the most common among the remaining diatonic seventh chords. The subdominant seventh is a MM$_7$ sonority in major keys (IV$_7$) and a mm$_7$ sonority in minor keys (iv$_7$). IV$_7$ is also a chord that often illustrates the melodic origin of seventh chords. In example 15.15a you can find a IV$_7$ chord which results melodically from a PT in the soprano. (How do you explain each of the notes over the bass $\hat{5}$ in m. 4?) In example 15.15b, on the other hand, IV$_7$ appears as an independent chord. In both cases, however, the seventh over $\hat{4}$ ($\hat{3}$) is approached by step from above (prepared) and resolved by step downward. If IV$_7$ is preceded by I, as in example 15.15c, the seventh may be prepared as a repeated note. In any case, the progression IV$_7$–V$_7$–I works well to harmonize the melodic pattern $\hat{3}$–$\hat{2}$–$\hat{1}$.

♪♪♪ Example 15.15a and b   J. S. Bach, Chorale 5, "An Wasserflüssen Babylon," mm. 3–4 and J. S. Bach, Chorale 117, "O Welt, ich muss dich lassen" (Final Cadence)

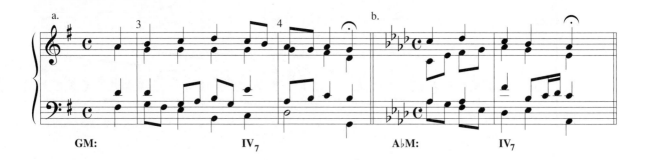

♪♪♪ Example 15.15c to e

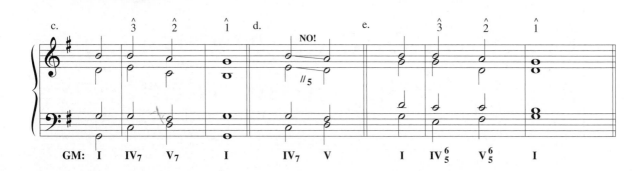

Example 15.15f   G. F. Handel, "Surely He Hath Borne Our Griefs," from *Messiah*, mm. 19–24 (Simplified)

A♭M:

NOTE

Beware of parallel 5ths between IV₇ and V, as shown in example 15.15d.

IV$_7$ can often be found in first inversion, also harmonizing the $\hat{3}$–$\hat{2}$–$\hat{1}$ melodic pattern. The progression IV$_5^6$–V$_5^6$–I creates an effective contrapuntal motion toward I. Notice, in example 15.15e, the outer voices moving in contrary motion toward a common goal, $\hat{1}$: $\hat{3}$–$\hat{2}$–$\hat{1}$ in the soprano, and $\hat{6}$–$\hat{7}$–$\hat{1}$ in the bass. Identify, in example 15.15f, the same progression in the context of a well-known passage by Handel. In m. 23 of this same fragment, moreover, you will also find a IV$_5^6$ used as part of a two-beat predominant complex. What chord does IV$_5^6$ move to in this measure? Finally, mm. 19–21 are based on an interesting harmonic sequence, which you can identify in the bass. What sequence is it (provide Roman numerals, and comment on root motion)? What nonchord tones are used to embellish the whole passage?

IV$_7$, as well as all other diatonic seventh chords, can be found much more frequently in twentieth-century popular music (such as jazz, musical theater, or rock) than in common practice art music. Chordal dissonances in popular music are often more "harmonically" than "linearly" conceived. That is, they are often conceived more as an integral part of the chordal sonority, rather than as a result of linear voice leading. For this reason, the principles of preparation and resolution of sevenths in popular music are not always followed as strictly as in common practice art music. An example of a characteristic popular music progression involving IV$_7$ appears in example 15.16a.

Example 15.16b shows the final section of a well-known refrain based on the **blues progression**. The complete blues progression may include several seventh chords, as it does in the form it appears in this song: I♭$_7$–IV♭$_7$–I♭$_7$–V$_7$–IV♭$_7$–I–V. You may observe some interesting aspects in the blues harmonic phrase. First, the progression V–IV (with or without sevenths), so unusual in common-practice music, is an essential component of the blues progression. Second, the tonic and subdominant seventh chords in this example are not really diatonic. While the diatonic seventh

Example 15.16a   Alan Jay Lerner–Frederick Loewe, "Almost Like Being in Love," from *Brigadoon* (Refrain)

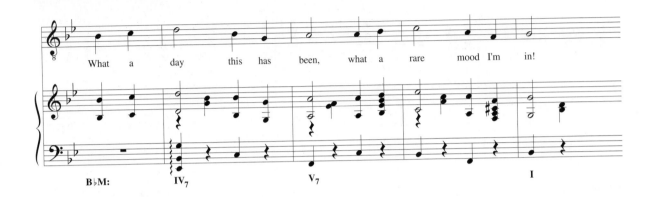

Example 15.16b   J. Lennon–P. McCartney, "Can't Buy Me Love," from the Film and Album *A Hard Day's Night* (Refrain)

chords on both of these degrees are MM$_7$ sonorities, the ♭7th turns these chords into Mm$_7$ sonorities in which two chromatic degrees are used: ♭$\hat{7}$ in I$_{♭7}$, and ♭$\hat{3}$ in IV$_{♭7}$. You may remember, however, that in chapter C we studied the "blues scale" (see example C.8d), a "major" scale that includes both ♭$\hat{3}$ and $\hat{3}$, as well as ♭$\hat{7}$ and $\hat{7}$. Thus, we see that the chromatic sevenths in both I$_{♭7}$ and IV$_{♭7}$ are actually part of the regular blues scale.

EXERCISES

To practice realizing short progressions using supertonic and subdominant seventh chords, refer to exercises 15.3c to e in worksheet 15 at the end of this chapter.

To practice realizing a progression using a variety of seventh chords, refer to exercise 15.4 in worksheet 15 at the end of this chapter.

To practice harmonizing a melody using a variety of seventh chords, refer to exercise 15.5 in worksheet 15 at the end of this chapter.

To practice writing your own progressions using a variety of seventh chords, refer to exercise 15.6 in worksheet 15 at the end of this chapter.

THE DIATONIC SEVENTH CIRCLE OF 5THS

In chapter 14 we studied the diatonic circle of 5ths as a harmonic sequence. A similar sequential progression results from a chain of diatonic seventh chords built on a circle-of-5ths bass, as in example 15.17. The best voice leading for this progression consists of alternating complete (C) and incomplete (IN) chords, beginning with a complete one. This allows for preparation and resolution of all the sevenths. As you may see in example 15.17, all seven diatonic seventh chords appear in this progression, and voice leading is treated as is customary in harmonic sequences. (In this case, the sequence segment is made up of two chords.)

As in the case of the circle of 5ths with triads, the progression with seventh chords might appear complete or, very often, only as a segment of the complete circle. The excerpt in example 15.18a is based exclusively on a circle of 5ths. Think of m. 22 as a tonic chord prolonged contrapuntally (embellished by a NN and two PTs—one in the violin, and one in the keyboard's right hand); similarly, m. 23 functions as a iv chord with linear embellishments (two NNs, and a PT in the violin—notice that the second chord in m. 23 is actually a "dominant of iv," that is, again a "secondary dominant" of the type we will study in the next chapter). If this accounts for the initial i–iv of the circle, analyze now the chords in mm. 24–25 for the rest of the progression, comparing it with example 15.17 for Roman numerals (RNs) and voice leading. The circle of 5ths with seventh chords is as common in popular music as it is in common-practice art music. An example from the popular repertoire appears in example 15.18b. Play through this example, and realize the Roman numerals either at the piano or on paper.

♪♪♪ Example 15.17

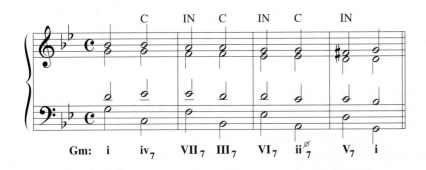

Gm: i   iv₇   VII₇   III₇   VI₇   ii°₇   V₇   i

♪♪♪ **Example 15.18a**   J. S. Bach, Concerto for Two Violins, BWV 1043, I, mm. 22–26

Dm: i ——————   iv ——————

♪♪♪ **Example 15.18b**   Bart Howard, "Fly Me to the Moon (In Other Words)" (Opening)

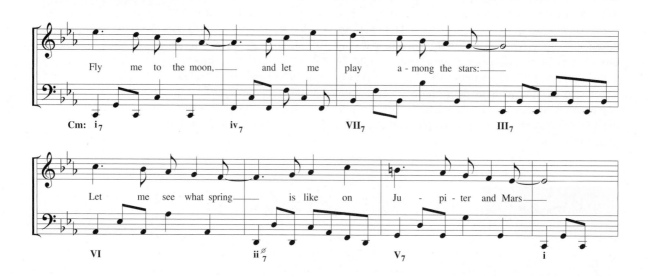

Cm: i₇   iv₇   VII₇   III₇

VI   ii°₇   V₇   i

EXERCISES

To practice writing seventh-chord circles of 5ths, refer to exercise 15.7 in worksheet 15 at the end of this chapter.

To practice analysis of musical fragments including diatonic seventh chords, refer to exercise 15.1 in worksheet 15 at the end of this chapter.

ASSIGNMENT AND KEYBOARD PROGRESSIONS

For analytical and written assignments and keyboard progressions based on the materials learned in this chapter, refer to chapter 15 in the workbook.

PITCH PATTERNS

1. Be able to sing $^{\varnothing}7$, $^{\circ}7$, mm$_7$, and MM$_7$ sonorities in root position on any pitch.

2. Sing the pitch patterns in example 15.19, listening to the linearized harmonic progressions as you sing.

♪♪♪ Example 15.19

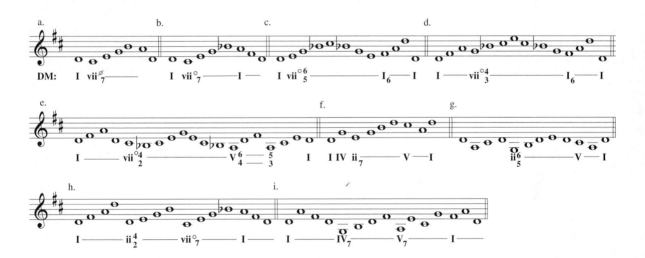

 Composers and Their Music 15

Biographies

Write short biographies of the following composers mentioned in this chapter: Frederick Loewe, Maria Szymanowska, Clara Schumann.

Listening

Listen to the following compositions by composers mentioned in this chapter:

   Frederick Loewe, *My Fair Lady* or *Brigadoon*.

Maria Szymanowska: Nocturne in B♭M (Briscoe anthology).
Clara Schumann: Trio in G minor.
Felix Mendelssohn: Concerto for Violin, op. 64.

Follow the score while you listen. Be able to place these compositions in one of the style periods and to comment on why and how they represent the musical characteristics of that period.

Terms for Review

Leading-tone sevenths

$\text{vii}^{\varnothing}_{7}$

vii°_{7}

$\text{vii}^{\varnothing}_{7}$ and vii°_{7} as related to V_7

The $^{\circ}_{7}$ sonority:
    intervals, inversions, possible
    different $^{\circ}_{7}$ chords

Resolution of inversions of $\text{vii}^{\varnothing}_{7}$ and vii°_{7}

Supertonic seventh

ii^{6}_{5}; other inversions of ii_{7}

Subdominant seventh

Blues progression

Diatonic seventh circle of 5ths

Worksheet 15

EXERCISE 15.1   Analysis.

1. Study example 15.20, focusing on the following aspects.

   a) *Texture.* Compare and discuss texture in mm. 1–4 and 5–9. What is the role of
       the harpsichord in mm. 1–4? And in mm. 5–9? What is the role of the flute in
       mm. 5–9 with regard to the harpsichord's right hand?

♪♪♪Example 15.20   J. S. Bach, Sonata no. 1 for Flute and Keyboard, BWV 1030, IV, mm. 1–9

b) *Melody.* What kind of melody did Bach write in this example, if you consider the type of line (or lines)? Focus especially on mm. 1–2 and 3–4. How does the melody grow in mm. 1–2? Is it generated by a motive (comment on its rhythmic characteristics)? What technique of melodic growth does Bach use? Is this technique accompanied by a similar harmonic procedure?

c) *Harmony.* Analyze mm. 1–4 with RNs (focus on the keyboard part only).

  1) What is the linear function of the seventh chord in m. 1, beat 2?

  2) What are the two seventh chords in m. 2, beats 1–2? What is their linear function? What two chords do they connect, and by means of what voice leading (examine both the bass and the keyboard's top voice)?

  3) The chord in m. 2, beat 3, has two nonchord tones which resolve in beat 4. Explain.

  4) Measure 3, beat 3: What chord is this, and how does it resolve? The chord of resolution, in beat 4, is itself a dissonant chord. What is its linear function?

  5) What is the basic progression in mm. 5–6, as outlined by the keyboard's left hand? What is the linear function of the chord at m. 6, beats 1–2?

  6) If you look closer and consider both hands of the keyboard, you will find an example of the sequential 5–6 technique in mm. 5–6 (beginning on beat 3 of m. 5). Mark it clearly on the score.

2. Analyze example 15.21 with RNs. What familiar linear gesture opens the excerpt? What is the seventh chord in m. 13, and how does it function?

♪♪♪Example 15.21   L. Reichardt, *From Ariel's Revelation,* mm. 9–17

ich   bin   fröh - lich,   Ro - - fe kenn   mich   duf - te

fe - lig   bei   dir   fühl'   ich   Freu - - - den.

3. Play and analyze the progressions in the keyboard part of example 15.22. Notice the basic two-measure harmonic rhythm, although you should pay attention for possible chordal alterations in the second measure of each harmony. What is the underlying root progression? Are any seventh chords used and how? What is the structure of the melody this progression harmonizes?

♪♪♪ Example 15.22   F. Kreisler, *Liebesleid*, mm. 1–16

EXERCISE 15.2   Write the following leading-tone seventh chords in each of the indicated keys (provide key signatures) and resolve them appropriately. If the resolution is to a $^6_4$ chord, resolve the $^6_4$ chord, too.

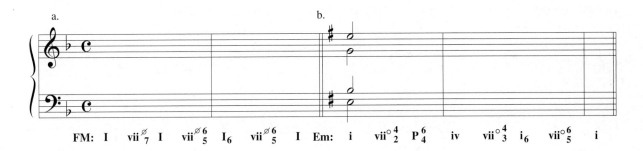

EXERCISE 15.3   Realize the following short progressions in four voices.

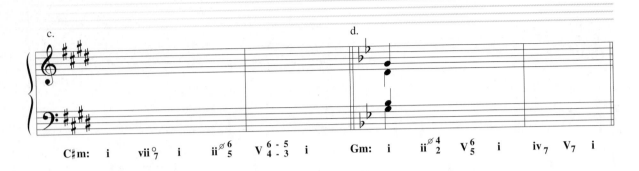

c.

C#m: i   vii°₇ i   ii°⁶₅   V⁶⁻⁵₄⁻₃ i

d.

Gm: i   ii°⁴₂   V⁶₅   i   iv₇   V₇   i

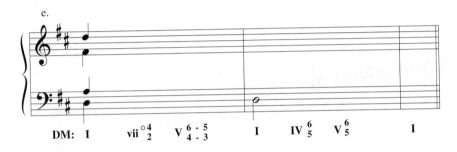

e.

DM: I   vii°⁴₂   V⁶⁻⁵₄⁻₃   I   IV⁶₅   V⁶₅   I

EXERCISE 15.4   Realize the following progression in four voices. Verify that your outer-voice frame follows the conventions of first-species counterpoint.

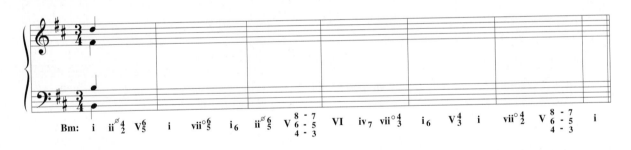

Bm: i   ii°⁴₂ V⁶₅   i   vii°⁶₅   i₆   ii°⁶₅ V⁸⁻⁷₆⁻₅₄⁻₃ VI   iv₇ vii°⁴₃   i₆   V⁴₃ i   vii°⁴₂ V⁸⁻⁷₆⁻₅₄⁻₃ i

EXERCISE 15.5   Harmonize the following melody with a keyboard texture. Include two leading-tone seventh chords, a deceptive cadence, and a cadential ⁶₄ preceded by a predominant seventh chord.

Dm:
HR:

EXERCISE 15.6

1. Write progressions (bass and RNs) in the keys and meters indicated below. Use the following chords (in any order, but correctly resolved):

   a) $ii^{\varnothing6}_{5}$, $vii^{\circ4}_{3}$, $vii^{\circ4}_{2}$

   b) ii^{4}_{2}, V^{4}_{2}, $vii^{\varnothing4}_{3}$

   c) $ii^{\varnothing4}_{3}$, $vii^{\circ6}_{5}$, iv_{7}

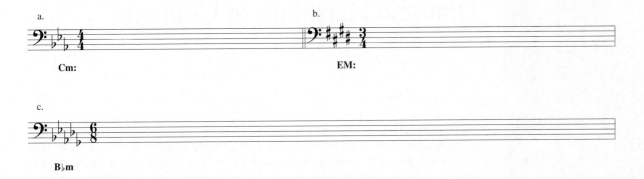

2. Choose one of your own progressions from above, and use it as a harmonic basis to compose a phrase for the keyboard. Your phrase should consist of a simple melody (right hand) with keyboard-style accompaniment (left hand).

EXERCISE 15.7   Using your own music paper, write two complete seventh chord circle-of-5ths sequences, in AM and Fm, respectively.

Appendix to Part I

Summary and Application: Diatonic Harmony in Context

We have now completed our study of diatonic harmony. And we can now ask the familiar question again: How is our knowledge of diatonic harmony relevant to the way we hear and perform music? It would be pretentious to argue that everything you have learned is relevant to performance. We have discussed many harmonic and voice-leading details, for instance, which are about how we *write* music, or how music *was written* by the masters of the past, and not necessarily about how we *perform* music. Acquiring a solid craft and a good understanding of how music is composed and how it works is a valuable goal in itself, even if not everything we know has a direct bearing on performance.

Having said this, however, we may add that a great deal of what we have studied *does* have a direct application in contributing to our improved perception and understanding of musical structure, and hence in making us better performers. We will now discuss an example from this perspective, but first it will help to understand the general musical context for diatonic harmony.

1. Music is seldom totally diatonic.

2. Music does not usually stay in one key for very long. Modulation is an essential element in musical growth and development, and it provides tonal variety.

3. The basic long-range musical (and formal) design consists of *exposition* (statement of musical materials), *development,* and *return* (conclusion or resolution). When music is diatonic, it is usually so in expository and resolutive processes. In expository sections (the beginning of a piece) the key is established and the thematic material is first heard. In resolutive sections (the return or conclusion, after a central developmental section), the main key is reestablished after sections in which tonal instability and modulation are likely, and the original material is restated in its original key. Both the exposition and the return are possibly diatonic, especially in the Classical period.

4. In the following chapters we will begin our study of harmonic chromaticism and modulation. Chromatic chords are very often linear, or they are harmonically subordinate to diatonic chords. Diatonic chords usually provide the frame for chromaticism, which often has an ornamental function.

5. We have learned in the previous chapters that diatonic triads (and seventh chords) have a variety of functions, and also that triads can have very different roles within a musical phrase or section. In summary, these roles can be stated as follows:

a) *Structural.* Structural triads are placed at *points of departure* (beginnings) and *points of arrival* (cadences). Only one triad is a true point of departure: the tonic; both the tonic and the dominant may end sections. The tonic and the dominant are the only truly structural chords (example 15A.1a).

b) *Chords that prepare a structural arrival.* These are the predominant chords (ii or IV, occasionally vi), which prepare either an authentic cadence (AC) or a half cadence (HC) (examples 15A.1b and c).

Example 15A.1   A Summary of Diatonic Functions

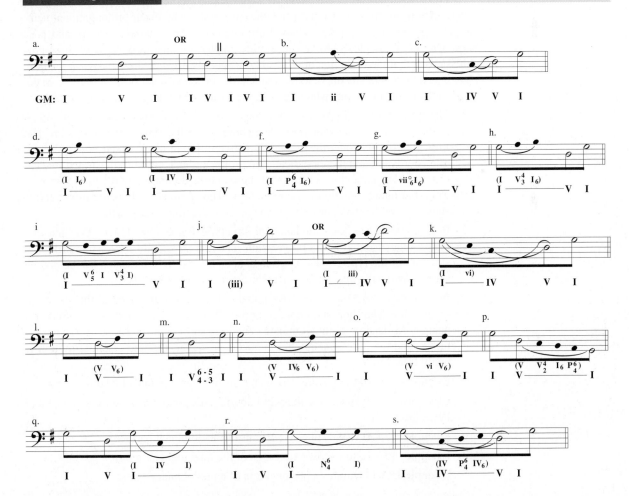

c) *Prolongational chords.* These are chords whose function is to extend a structural frame in time, either by prolonging the initial tonic, by prolonging a dominant, by prolonging the final tonic, or by prolonging some chord other than the tonic or the dominant. Triads (or seventh chords) in inversion may prolong other chords, as in many of the progressions we have seen involving $^6_3$ or $^6_4$ chords. Progressions such as I–(I$_6$)–V–I, I– (P$^6_4$–I$_6$)–V–I, I–(vii°$_6$–I$_6$)–V–I, or I–(V$^6_5$–I–V$^4_3$–I$_6$)–V–I use inverted chords to prolong the initial tonic (the prolongational chords are here shown in parentheses). Progressions such as I–V–(V$_6$)–I, I–V–(IV$_6$–V$_6$)–I, or I–V–(V$^4_2$)–I$_6$ include a dominant prolongation. Nonstructural chords such as IV, vi, or iii also function often as prolongations of the initial final tonic, in progressions such as I–V–I–(IV–I), I–V–I–(N$^6_4$ –I), I–V–I–(vi–IV–I), and I–(iii)–IV–V–I. Finally, these same nonstructural chords can themselves be prolonged in progressions such as I–IV–(P$^6_4$ –IV$_6$)–V–I.

Prolongational chords are *linear* (or contrapuntal) rather than purely harmonic, because they result from horizontal (melodic) processes. The linear prolongational techniques (or functions) we have studied are *neighbor chord, passing chord,* and *bass arpeggiation.* Examples 15A.1d to s provide graphic summaries of some of these progressions and of the basic functions of diatonic chords. Realize these basses at the keyboard as a review of the diatonic harmonic structures and functions you have learned. Notice the following points which refer to the harmonic paradigms in example 15A.1:

1. The structural I–V–I progression in these examples is connected by a beam. Each of these examples shows a possible elaboration of the structural progression. The Roman numerals under the graphs show two different levels of harmonic activity. The chords in parentheses indicate the prolongational structure illustrated in each example. The parentheses mean that these chords do not really function harmonically, but rather linearly or contrapuntally. The chord actually being prolonged is shown under the parentheses as a Roman numeral followed by a line.

2. In example 15A.1a two fundamental structural frames are shown. The first one features the essential I–V–I progression. The second one illustrates an interruption structure of the type we discussed in chapters 2 and 6, as indicated by the double slash showing the interruption after the HC on V (I–V//I–V–I).

3. In examples 15A.1b and c a predominant chord has been added to the structural progression. The short slur connecting ii or IV to V means that these are predominant chords leading to the dominant. The long slur connecting I and V (and curving around the predominant chord) means, however, that the essential motion is really from I to V.

4. Examples 15A.1d to i feature various means of extending the initial tonic harmony.

5. Examples 15A.1j to k show iii and vi dividing the space between I and V or I and IV, respectively.

6. Examples 15A.1l to p display extensions of the dominant harmony.

7. Examples 15A.1q to r show extensions of the final tonic harmony.

8. Example 15A.1s features a prolongation of a predominant chord.

Diatonic Functions and Performance

How does our knowledge of diatonic functions help us understand (and transmit through performance) the structure of a fragment like Haydn's Sonata in DM, II (anthology, no. 20)? The movement is (and begins) in Dm. A *first cadence* (a HC in Dm) is reached at m. 8. A "new beginning" in m. 9 unexpectedly establishes the relative major key, FM. We will soon study modulation, and we will see that modulation is a process in which a key moves into another key, usually smoothly and by means of elements common to both keys. This is not the case here: FM is directly established, without transition (this may be called a "direct modulation" or, even better, simply a "change of key"). The *second cadence* in the fragment, in m. 16, is also a HC, now in FM. An AC in FM is prepared in mm. 20–21, deceptively resolved in m. 22, and finally reached, after a cadential extension, in m. 24. This is the *first perfect authentic cadence* (*PAC*) in the fragment. In m. 25 we see a return to the original key of Dm and to the opening thematic material.

The harmonic goals for the fragment are, then, m. 8 (HC), m. 16 (HC in F), m. 22 [deceptive cadence (DC)], m. 24 (PAC in F), and finally m. 25 (the return to Dm). We have now established the harmonic frame for the passage: two "points of departure" in D and F (mm. 1 and 9), two open (inconclusive) points of arrival (the HCs in mm. 8 and 16), a final point of arrival on F (delayed by a DC), and a return to D. The next questions are: How do we get from one point to another, and how do we tie it all together?

We have already analyzed most of this example by fragments in previous chapters. We will provide here a brief summary. The graph in example 15A.2c, a bass reduction for the complete excerpt, may serve as a visual reference to the following analytical outline.

1. Measures 1–4. A prolongation of i by means of a passing vii°_{6} (or, to be more exact, a $vii^{\circ 6}_{5}$ if we consider the high B♭), leading to a predominant-dominant progression.

2. Measures 5–8. A prolongation of i by arpeggiation, a predominant-dominant-tonic progression, a vi chord which functions both as a prolongation of i and as a predominant, and the final HC, which functions as the goal of the complete passage. The HC is ornamented linearly by a cadential $^{6}_{4}$ and a chromatic neighbor note (NN). Instead of resolving to i in Dm, the half cadence moves abruptly into a new key, FM.

3. Measures 9–16. A prolongation of I in FM first by means of a neighbor-group figure (V^{4}_{3}–V^{6}_{5}, mm. 9–12), then a neighbor $^{6}_{4}$ (mm. 13–14), and a neighbor $^{6}_{5}$ (m. 15). The HC in F (m. 16) is ornamented by a cadential $^{6}_{4}$, and preceded by a chromatic predominant chord (a chord with a secondary dominant function of the type we will study in the next chapters).

4. Measures 17–24. The V in F reached in m. 16 moves to I_{6} through a passing V^{4}_{2}, and a series of V^{4}_{2}–I_{6} progressions prolong this first-inversion tonic. A new predominant-dominant progression announces a PAC in mm. 20–21, resolved deceptively in m. 22. A cadential extension repeats the cadential progression (including another chromatic chord, also a secondary dominant to be studied in the next chapter), prolonging the dominant harmony for two more measures, and finally resolving it to I at m. 24, the ultimate goal for the complete passage in FM (mm. 9–24).

How does it all tie together? The excerpt is a long prolongation of Dm. Just as a Dm tonic may be prolonged by arpeggiation to a mediant chord (i–III–i), the Dm key (i) moves here, by a long-range bass arpeggiation, to FM (III), and back to Dm (i) in m. 25. The two graphs in examples 15A.2a and b show this long-range tonal motion, and show moreover that the main tonal frame of the example outlines the Dm tonic triad which it thus prolongs ($\hat{1}$, $\hat{5}$ in m. 8, $\hat{3}$ in the FM section, and $\hat{1}$ again).

The slurs above example 15A.2c indicate the phrase structure of the fragment. We can break the passage into three eight-measure phrases. The first two phrases can themselves be divided into 4 + 4 segments. The division of the third phrase (6 + 2), on the other hand, is not symmetrical, and is determined by the deceptive cadence in m. 22 and the two-measure extension that follows. Notice that this division of the passage into phrases and phrase segments corresponds exactly with the long-range harmonic analysis represented in the graph.

What conclusions can we draw from the above analysis that would apply to the performance and perception of the piece? It is easy to argue that our understanding of *long-range tonal goals,* of the excerpt as an *organic tonal whole,* and of how the different sections are *connected* by tonal design should help in our rendition or perception of the piece: We know where the music is coming from, where it is going (what is its tonal purpose or goal), and why. Furthermore, we also know *how.* Because we understand the difference between *structural chords* and *linear prolongational chords,* we have established a hierarchy, we have plotted a "tonal path" from one structural point to another, and we can follow and understand the role of each chord as a linear step toward the goal (or, say, as words within sentences, themselves part of a paragraph).

All of this should help us propel the music toward the tonal goals through phrasing. By hearing phrases as musical units that prolong a harmony linearly and move toward a goal, we can create the appropriate tension for the music to move forward. Arrivals on HCs enhance the tension. And although the "new beginning" in m. 9 could be seen as a point of momentary release of tension, the fact that we are abruptly taken away from the main key is in itself a source of tension (also enhanced by the increase of rhythmic activity in the right hand throughout this FM section). The only true point of arrival in the complete passage, and hence the only place where we can really feel the release of tension, is the return to Dm in m. 25. We should now be able to avoid listening to or playing this piece mechanically, or "chord by chord." Try listening to the passage several times (or, if possible, play it), hearing (and enjoying!) your knowledge of its long-range tonal design and following the "musical story" that the harmony unfolds.

♪♪♪ Example 15A.2

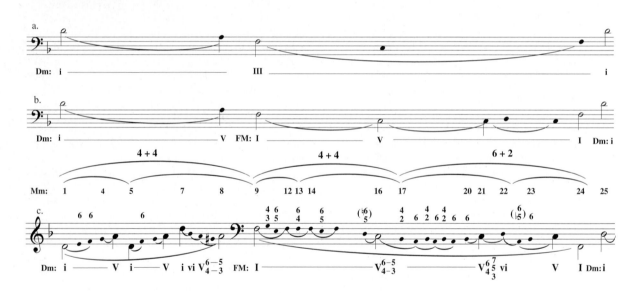

PART 2

Chromatic Harmony and Form

Chapter 16

Secondary Dominants I

CHROMATIC HARMONY

So far we have studied only chords constructed with pitches from the diatonic major or minor scales. The different types of minor scale (natural, melodic, and harmonic) are all considered diatonic in spite of the various alterations of $\hat{6}$ and $\hat{7}$. The only true **chromatic tones** (foreign to the diatonic scale being used) we have encountered are chromatic nonchord tones (NCTs) such as neighbor notes (NNs) and passing tones (PTs), and these are purely melodic in nature.

Beginning with this chapter, and for the remainder of the book, we will study **chromatic harmony**, that is, harmony in which chromatic alterations other than NCTs are introduced. At times these alterations result from *modulation*, the establishment of a new, different key. When music modulates, a new scale (with different accidentals than the original scale) is used, and this produces chromaticism with respect to the original key. The fragment in example 16.1a begins in DM and ends in Bm. The accidental in the second phrase, A♯, is the leading tone (LT) in the new key and results from the switch to the Bm scale.

Chromaticism, however, is very often present within a single key, resulting from **chromatic**, or **altered**, **chords**, chords that use a tone or tones foreign to the diatonic scale of the key they are used in. The passage in example 16.1b is all in Em, and yet in m. 7, beat 4, we see a chord that includes an A♯ and a C♯. Although these two pitches are part of a chord (A♯–C♯–E–G), this type of chromaticism is often a consequence of melodic, linear processes. *Chordal chromaticism often results from a linear elaboration of a diatonic framework.* Example 16.1c shows the diatonic framework the chorale phrase in example 16.1b elaborates. In this context, we see that the chromatic chord results from a chromatic passing-tone motion in the bass ($\hat{4}$–$\hat{5}$–$\hat{1}$ becomes $\hat{4}$–♯$\hat{4}$–$\hat{5}$–$\hat{1}$).

As illustrated in example 16.1, chordal or linear chromaticism may be used at the local level to provide pitch variety and to increase tonal "color" (the term *chromaticism* is derived from the Greek *chroma*, "color"). Moreover, chromaticism enhances voice-leading tension and direction. In example 16.1a, the A–A♯ line produces a strong pull toward B, the new tonic. In example 16.1b, the bass motion $\hat{4}$–♯$\hat{4}$–$\hat{5}$ is much stronger linearly than only $\hat{4}$–$\hat{5}$. Long-range chromaticism as represented by modulation, on the other hand, is an essential type of tonal process whose function is to define formal organization, as we will study in future chapters.

Example 16.1a   J. S. Bach, Chorale 80, "O Haupt voll Blut und Wunden," mm. 1–4

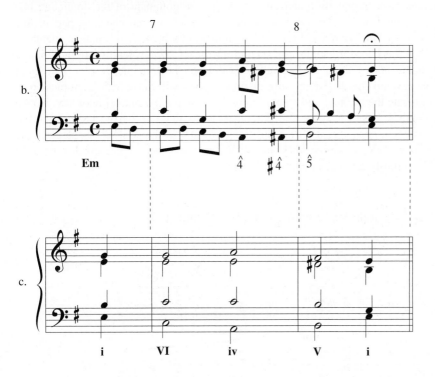

Example 16.1b and c   J. S. Bach, Chorale 167, "Du grosser Schmerzensmann," mm. 7–8, and Harmonic Reduction of Example 16.1b

TONICIZATION: SECONDARY DOMINANTS

The first type of chromatic chord we will study results from the concept of **toniciza-tion**: Any major or minor triad may become a momentary tonic if it is preceded by its dominant (that is, by the major triad or Mm_7 chord whose root is a 5th above—or a 4th below—the root of the tonicized chord). The fragment in example 16.2 is in CM throughout. The GM chord (V) in m. 1, beat 3, however, is preceded by its dominant (a Mm_7 chord on D, V_7 of G). Although we still hear the G chord as V in C (a half cadence), V is here momentarily tonicized because of the preceding chord.

Such dominant chords, whose function is to tonicize the triad that follows, are known as **secondary dominants** (some authors also call them **applied dominants**). Their Roman numeral (RN) abbreviation includes two symbols separated by a slash, as in V_7/V or V_7/IV. The first symbol indicates the secondary dominant function; the second symbol after the slash indicates the triad being tonicized. We read the slash as "of," thus V_7/V is "V_7 of V," and V_7/IV is "V_7 of IV." Although secondary dominants may appear as simple M triads (V/V of V/IV), most often they appear as Mm_7 chords (V_7/V).

V_7 OF V

The degree most frequently tonicized is $\hat{5}$. V_7/V, the dominant of the dominant, is a Mm_7 chord built on $\hat{2}$. The first "harmonic" accidental we introduce, as part of this chord, is $\sharp\hat{4}$ (by "$\sharp\hat{4}$" we mean "raised $\hat{4}$," regardless of whether the actual accidental is $\sharp$ or $\natural$). $\sharp\hat{4}$ in this chord functions as a **secondary**, or *temporary*, **leading tone** of $\hat{5}$, and hence should not be doubled. Secondary dominants, in principle, resolve as regular dominant seventh chords (LT up, seventh down), so $\sharp\hat{4}$ will move to $\hat{5}$. Examples 16.3a and b illustrate the spelling and resolution of V_7/V in a major and a minor key. Notice that in minor, besides $\sharp\hat{4}$, we also need to raise $\hat{6}$ to $\sharp\hat{6}$, in order to have a Mm_7 sonority. Examples 16.3c to f present all the positions of V_7/V in the context of characteristic progressions. V_7/V, as well as V_5^6/V and V_3^4/V, can resolve to a V embellished by a cadential $_4^6$, as illustrated by examples 16.3g and h.

🎵🎵🎵 Example 16.2   J. S. Bach, Chorale 40, "Ach Gott und Herr," mm. 1–2

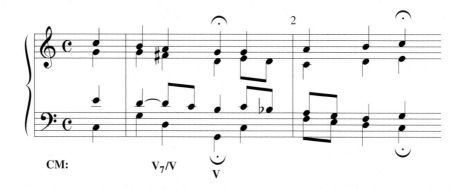

CM: V_7/V V

In example 16.3 you can see that a frequent melodic gesture which can be harmonized with a progression using V_7/V is $\hat{4}$–$\#\hat{4}$–$\hat{5}$. Other possible melodic fragments which can be harmonized with a secondary dominant of V and its resolution to V are $\hat{6}$–$\hat{5}$, $\hat{1}$–$\hat{7}$, and $\hat{2}$–$\hat{2}$ (which can be harmonized with an inverted secondary dominant of V). Among these, $\#\hat{4}$–$\hat{5}$, $\hat{6}$–$\hat{5}$, and $\hat{1}$–$\hat{7}$ can also be found as bass fragments in one of the progressions using an **inversion of V_7/V**, as you can verify in example 16.3.

EXERCISES

To practice spelling secondary dominants of V in root position and inversions, refer to exercise 16.2 in worksheet 16 at the end of this chapter.

To practice spelling and resolving secondary dominants of V, refer to exercise 16.3 in worksheet 16 at the end of this chapter.

♪♪♪ Example 16.3

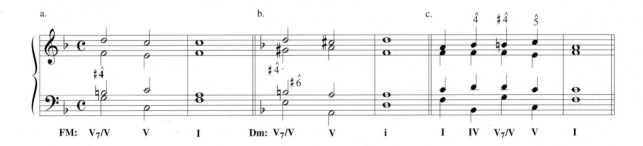

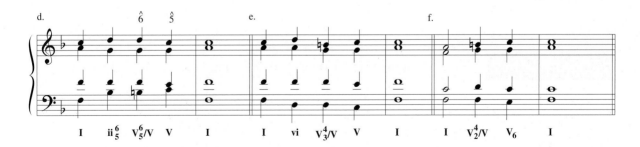

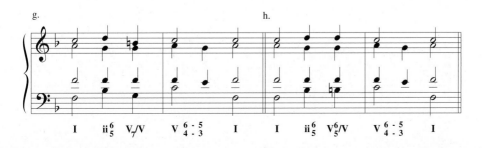

V_7/V in root position is often found in cadential gestures. In example 16.3c, V_7/V precedes an authentic cadence. The bass $\hat{2}$–$\hat{5}$–$\hat{1}$, a very strong cadential gesture which we have previously harmonized diatonically as ii (or ii$_7$)–V–I, is strengthened by the chromatic tension provided by $\sharp\hat{4}$. As you will see, ii$_7$ and V_7/V differ only in one pitch: $\hat{4}$ in ii$_7$, or $\sharp\hat{4}$ in V_7/V. In this context, V_7/V functions as a chromatic predominant chord.

In example 16.4 Haydn closes the phrase on a half cadence (HC), preceded by V_7/V which functions, in the way we have just discussed, as a chromatic predominant chord. In m. 3 we see another very frequent form of the secondary dominant of V: V^6_5/V, which allows for the strong linear motion $\hat{4}$–$\sharp\hat{4}$–$\hat{5}$ in the bass. If V^6_5/V is preceded by ii$^6_5$, no motion is needed in any voice other than the bass chromaticism (see example 16.3d). The function of this type of secondary dominant is not harmonic, but rather linear. V^6_5/V is here a chromatic, embellishing chord with a passing function.

V^4_3/V, on the other hand, is the least frequent form of the dominant of V. In example 16.5a we can see a linear use of this chord by C. Schumann. Explain how V^4_3/V functions here as a neighbor chord. Mark, on the score, all the NN figures that involve this secondary dominant. Then verify how the change of bass in m. 2 of the Duke Ellington example (example 16.5b) turns an incomplete neighbor figure into a double-neighbor (or neighbor-group) figure involving both V^6_5/V and V^4_3/V.

Because in V^4_2/V $\hat{1}$ is in the bass, the chord can be effectively used after I, with $\hat{1}$ carried over in the bass as a common tone between the two chords. Mozart does just that at the beginning of his Finale for Symphony no. 40, reproduced in example 16.6a. Compare Mozart's opening progression (mm. 1–4) with example 16.3f (and remember that, of course, V^4_2/V resolves to V_6). Analyze Mozart's second phrase (mm. 5–8) harmonically. What kind of phrase structure can you identify in the complete passage? In the phrase by Andrew Lloyd Webber (example 16.6b), on the other hand, V^4_2/V results from a passing motion in the bass (D–C–B, or $\hat{2}$–$\hat{1}$–$\hat{7}$) between V/V and V_6.

♪♪♪Example 16.4   J. Haydn, String Quartet, op. 76, no. 5, I, mm. 1–4

♩♩♩ Example 16.5a   Clara Schumann, Trio in Gm, op. 17, I, mm. 273–275

♩♩♩ Example 16.5b   Duke Ellington, "Don't Get Around Much Anymore" (Perfect Authentic Cadence in Verse)

VOICE-LEADING GUIDELINES

1. The principles for doublings and resolution that we applied to the dominant seventh chord also apply to secondary dominants.

2. Do not double the secondary LT ($\sharp\hat{4}$ in V_7/V).

3. Resolve the secondary LT up and the seventh down.

4. *Cross relations*. You may have observed that in examples 16.1a and b, and example 16.4 at least one of the voices moves by chromatic half step (as in A–A♯ or C–C♯). When two adjacent chords include pitches related by chromatic half step, *it is better to keep the chromatic motion in the same voice*. Chromatically related pitches in different voices create what are known as cross relations. Although cross relations are found in music, they have not been used indiscriminately by composers. Because cross relations produce a dissonant clash between two voices, and because the smoothest voice leading results from keeping the chromatic motion in the same voice, as a principle we will avoid cross relations.

Sing or play the progressions in example 16.7, and hear the chromatic relationships among voices. Examples 16.7a and c illustrate cross relations between the outer voices. Listen to these realizations, and compare them with the smoother realizations presented in examples 16.7b and d. Although in example 16.7b the cross relation between outer voices remains, its effect is softened by the chromatic motion in the bass.

5. *The chromaticized voice exchange*. The progression in example 16.7e shows a specific type of cross relation which, besides being quite acceptable, actually results in an especially effective voice leading. Notice the voice exchange between the figures D–B♮ in the soprano and B♭–D in the bass, indicated by the usual voice exchange cross. This is a *chromaticized voice exchange* which includes a cross relation (B♭–B♮). As shown in our example, this progression is often embellished with a passing $^6_4$ which makes the cross relation even less problematic.

♪♪♪Example 16.6a   W. A. Mozart, Symphony no. 40 in Gm, K. 550, IV, mm. 1–8

♪♪♪Example 16.6b   Tim Rice–Andrew Lloyd Webber, "Don't Cry for Me Argentina," from *Evita* (Verse)

♪♪♪Example 16.7   J. Haydn, String Quartet, op. 76, no. 5, I, mm. 1–4

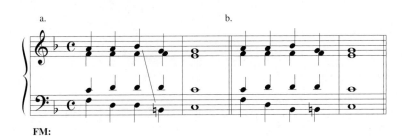

V₇ OF IV (iv)

Along with V₇/V, the dominant of IV (iv in minor) is very frequently found in music. V₇/IV is the Mm₇ chord built on $\hat{1}$. In major keys, V₇/IV consists of the I triad with an added m7. The new accidental introduced by this chord is thus ♭$\hat{7}$. In minor keys, ♭$\hat{7}$ is a diatonic pitch, and we need instead to raise the minor $\hat{3}$ to ♯$\hat{3}$, the LT of $\hat{4}$. Examples 16.8a and b show the spelling and resolution of this chord in both M and m. You will observe that in example 16.8b, ♭$\hat{3}$ and ♮$\hat{3}$ have been kept in the same voice, and that the voice leading from example 16.8a has been changed in example 16.8b to avoid the +2 between ♭$\hat{6}$ and ♮$\hat{7}$ in the soprano.

The most frequent melodic pattern harmonized with a secondary dominant of IV and its resolution to IV is ♭$\hat{7}$–$\hat{6}$ (as part of the motion $\hat{1}$→♭$\hat{7}$–$\hat{6}$), as shown in example 16.8a. Other possible patterns are $\hat{3}$–$\hat{4}$, $\hat{5}$–$\hat{4}$, or $\hat{5}$–$\hat{6}$.

EXERCISES

To practice spelling secondary dominants of IV in root position and inversions, refer to exercise 16.2 in worksheet 16 at the end of this chapter.

To practice spelling and resolving secondary dominants of IV, refer to exercise 16.3 in worksheet 16 at the end of this chapter.

♪♪♪ Example 16.8

Example 16.8 illustrates the use of the dominant of IV in the context of cadential progressions. V_7/IV in root position is also often used in opening progressions, with the function of both prolonging the opening I and of creating a pull toward the subdominant. In example 16.9 you will see how Beethoven begins his Trio, op. 1, no. 1, with a very effective use of such a progression. Analyze the complete passage.

♪♪♪ Example 16.9   L. v. Beethoven, Trio, op. 1 no. 1, I, mm. 1–9

Example 16.10   C. Schumann, Trio in Gm, op. 17, I, mm. 1–9

The prolongation of the tonic may be stressed even more by resolving V_7/IV to IV_4^6 (N_4^6) on a tonic pedal, as in example 16.8c. Example 16.8d shows the linear prolongational character of this progression, where all pitches are either PTs or NNs in a change of voicing within the tonic harmony. This is also a frequent opening progression because it establishes the tonic in a strong and colorful way. Discuss in class

C. Schumann's use of this progression in the opening measures of her Gm Trio (example 16.10, mm. 1–3).

The most frequent **inversions of V_7/IV** are V_5^6/IV and V_2^4/IV, normally used in the standard progressions shown in examples 16.8e and f. V_2^4/IV usually follows I to create a very effective linear progression in which the upper voices do not move, as shown in example 16.8f. The bass moves down by step from $\hat{1}$ to $\flat\hat{7}$, and then to $\hat{6}$, and the other voices complete the IV$_6$ to which V_2^4/IV must resolve. Example 16.11 shows a version of this progression taken from the closing measures of C. Schumann's Trio in Gm. How do you explain the pitches with sharps in the piano's right hand, m. 283? See also example 16.10 (mm. 6–7) for further examples of the dominant of iv in inversion.

EXERCISES

To practice realizing progressions including tonicizations of V and IV, refer to exercises 16.4 and 16.5 in worksheet 16 at the end of this chapter.

To practice harmonizing a melody including tonicizations of V and IV, refer to exercise 16.6 in worksheet 16 at the end of this chapter.

To practice writing your own progressions using tonicizations of V and IV, refer to exercise 16.7 in worksheet 16 at the end of this chapter.

To practice analysis of musical fragments including tonicizations, refer to exercise 16.1 in worksheet 16 at the end of this chapter.

♪♪♪ Example 16.11   C. Schumann, Trio in Gm, op. 17, I, mm. 282–287

FURTHER ANALYSIS

Elaborating a Diatonic Framework with Chromatic Harmony

We have mentioned that chromatic chords often result from linear **elaborations of a diatonic framework**. Example 16.12 illustrates exactly that. We begin, in example 16.12a, with the fundamental frame I–V–I. In example 16.12b we add a predominant chord, IV (note values do not denote duration in this example, but rather structural prominence). The predominant could also be ii$_5^6$, or both IV and ii$_5^6$. In 16.12c we see that a PT, E♭, between I and IV generates a V$_7$/IV. Moreover, another chromatic PT in the bass, B♮ (which we can also interpret as a simple chromatic alteration of the ii$_5^6$ chord) creates a V$_5^6$/V. As a final elaboration (in this case diatonic), we embellish V with a cadential $_4^6$ figure. The phrase in example 16.12d illustrates a chromatic elaboration of the basic I–IV–V progression by means of secondary dominants. Play the phrase at the piano, and as you play provide an inner-voice realization of the Roman numerals.

Let us refer back to example 16.10, the opening phrase of C. Schumann's Trio. Not only is the complete passage a prolongation of the opening tonic, but all of its chromaticism can be easily understood as an elaboration of a simple diatonic framework. As an exercise, or as a class exercise, try to determine, on a separate piece of staff paper, and by means of a bass reduction, what the underlying diatonic progression is. You can explain all bass prolongations as PTs, NNs, or arpeggiations. After you have come up with your own bass reduction you may compare it with the one offered in example 16.13.

In example 16.13a (which represents the "surface" level) we see, with the help of a very cumbersome line of Roman numerals, that, after the initial pedal prolongation of i, the bass effects a descending arpeggiation by 3rds connected by PTs, leading to the predominant ii$^{ø6}_5$ and to the V at m. 4. The resolution to i (through a V$_2^4$–i$_6$) is prolonged by a neighbor-group figure (m. 5). It then continues to another descending arpeggiation, connected by PTs (m. 6), and also leads to a predominant-dominant figure with a chromatic PT, which generates a connecting secondary vii°$_7$ chord (C♯, m. 7), of the type that we will study in chapter 18. The V in m. 8 is prolonged by means of three PTs leading to i.

In example 16.13b we get rid of all PTs and NNs, and we see two sets of 3rd arpeggiations of the tonic-predominant-dominant-tonic figures. Because the 3rd arpeggiations prolong the tonic, we delete them in example 16.13c, showing only the two underlying tonic-predominant-dominant-

Example 16.12a to c

a.

I   V   I

b.

I   IV   (ii$_5^6$)   V   I

c.

I   V$_7$/IV   IV   V$_5^6$/V $\begin{array}{c}6-5\\4-3\end{array}$ I

tonic frames. The first progression, however, also prolongs the initial tonic, so a further deletion in example 16.13d leaves only the underlying harmonic frame, a tonic-predominant-dominant-tonic progression.

Example 16.12d Roy Orbison–Joe Melson, "Only the Lonely (Know How I Feel)" (from Verse)

Example 16.13

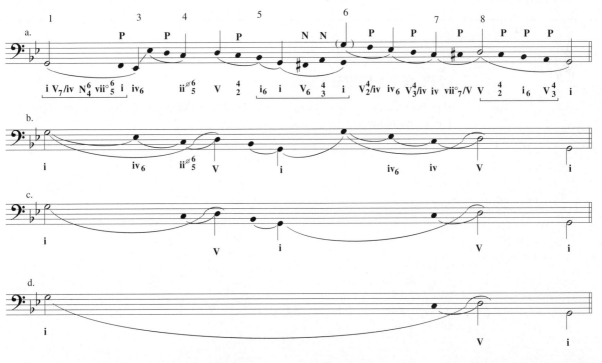

PRACTICAL APPLICATION AND DISCUSSION

1. Listen to example 16.10 several times, following the graphs in example 16.13. Focus on the following aspects:
   a) Not all pitches in the bass, or all chords, have the same importance. Arpeggiations, PTs, and NNs prolong a previous pitch and harmony.
   b) Arpeggiations, PTs, and NNs create a forward motion (they lead somewhere). Harmonic and linear chromaticism creates an even stronger forward motion (a tension that requires resolution). Hear the sense of forward direction provided by the secondary chords in the passage.
   c) Try to hear the different levels of the harmony: on the one hand, some pitches (and chords) create a motion; on the other hand, some pitches (and chords) act as goals. All of it is visually expressed in example 16.13.

   After you do all of this, discuss in class how this analytical exercise has affected your listening. Has it helped you understand and hear the elements of tension and directed motion in the passage? Do you hear the unity of the phrase better? Don't you find it more musical to hear this fragment as one or two sweeping arches (as represented in examples 16.13b, c, and d) than chord by chord? If you were to perform this passage, how would the understanding of example 16.13 affect your performance?

2. Find some instances of harmonic chromaticism in the pieces you perform or know well. Do your examples have a linear/melodic origin? Do they elaborate a diatonic frame? How is your sense of musical direction in these passages affected by your awareness of these concepts? Bring some of these examples to class, perform them, and explain how you hear them in the light of this discussion.

ASSIGNMENT AND KEYBOARD PROGRESSIONS

For analytical and written assignments and keyboard progressions based on the materials learned in this chapter, refer to chapter 16 in the workbook.

PITCH PATTERNS

Sing the melodic pitch patterns in example 16.14. As you sing, listen to the secondary dominants and their resolutions.

♪♪♪ Example 16.14

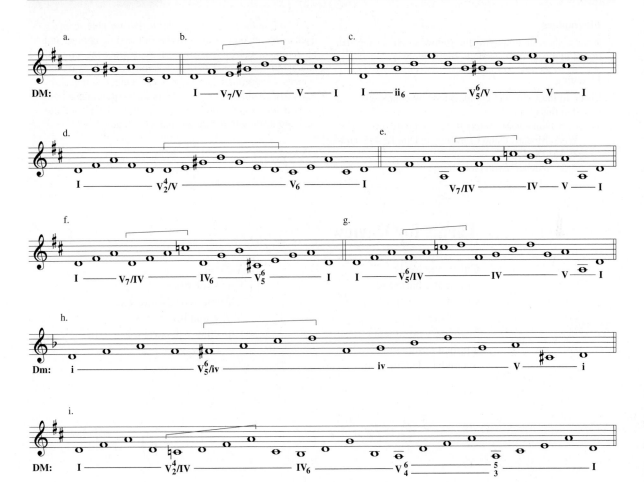

Composers and Their Music 16

Biographies

Write a short biography of the following composer mentioned in this chapter: Andrew Lloyd Webber.

Listening

Listen to the following compositions by composers mentioned in this chapter:

C. Schumann, *Six Songs from "Jucunde,"* op. 23.
W. A. Mozart, Piano Concertos in Dm, K. 466, and AM, K. 488.
A. L. Webber, *Evita* (selections).

Follow the score while you listen. Be able to place each of these compositions in one of the style periods and to comment on why and how it represents the musical characteristics of that period. As you listen, identify instances of chromaticism. Is it local, embellishing chromaticism resulting from linear processes and tonicization, or is it long-range chromaticism resulting from modulation and leading to the establishment of a new key?

Terms for Review

Chromatic tones
Chromatic harmony
Chromatic (altered) chords
Tonicization
Secondary dominants
Applied dominants
Secondary leading tone

V_7/V and inversions
Cross relations
Chromaticized voice exchange
V_7/IV and inversions
Chromatic elaboration of a diatonic
    framework

Worksheet 16

EXERCISE 16.1 Analysis.

1. Refer to anthology, no. 19, Haydn, Menuet and Trio in CM. Identify two cases of tonicization in mm. 9–12. What are the degrees tonicized? How does each of the tonicizations work? What are the chromatic degrees introduced and the Roman numerals in each of the tonicizations?

2. Play through the period in example 16.15.

   a) What degree is tonicized in the first phrase?

   b) How many times, and by means of which secondary chords?

   c) One of these tonicizations is linear and embellishing, whereas the other one is functional. Explain.

   d) Where do these tonicizations lead to within the period?

   e) Does the second phrase also include a similar tonicization?

   f) Using your own music paper, realize a bass reduction for the passage. Use example 16.13 as a reference for your reduction, in which you will show several levels of harmonic activity. In the first level (the "surface" level), show the role of tonic, dominant, and predominant chords using appropriate symbols. If any of these chords is prolonged or embellished by any other chord (such as secondary dominants), show it accordingly. In the following levels, first delete the prolongational chords, leaving only the underlying harmonic structure at the phrase level, and finally the basic structure at the period level.

Example 16.15   W. A. Mozart, "Là ci darem la mano," from *Don Giovanni*, m. 1–8

3. a) Two tonicizations take place in example 16.16. Identify both, provide exact RNs for each, and mark on the score any linear voice leading resulting from the tonicizations.

   b) This period features four clear harmonic units, of two measures each. Comment on the formal/harmonic function of each of these units within the period. For instance, the first unit establishes the key (by what means?).

   c) On your own music paper, provide a metric reduction for the passage (both hands). Provide Roman numerals under the reduction, and show the form of the fragment by means of a bubble diagram over the reduction.

♪♪♪Example 16.16   L. v. Beethoven, Sonatina in GM, II, mm. 1–8

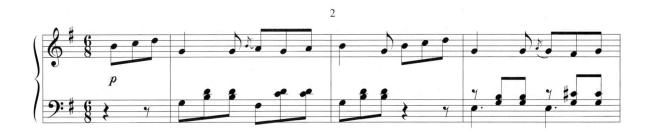

4. The opening of the chorale in example 16.17 features a tonicization. Explain what degree is tonicized, provide a RN analysis for the complete passage, comment on the voice leading for the tonicization, and explain the linear character of the complete example.

♪♪♪Example 16.17   J. S. Bach, Chorale 8, "Freuet euch, ihr Christen," mm. 1–2

EXERCISE 16.2

1. Write the following secondary dominants in root position, in four voices, with correct spacing. Provide key signatures.

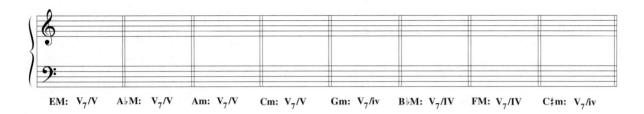

EM: V₇/V   A♭M: V₇/V   Am: V₇/V   Cm: V₇/V   Gm: V₇/iv   B♭M: V₇/IV   FM: V₇/IV   C♯m: V₇/iv

2. Write the following secondary dominants in inversion, in four voices, with correct spacing. Provide key signatures.

Procedure for spelling secondary dominants:

a) The root of a secondary dominant is the pitch a 5th above (or a 4th below) the tonicized degree. The root of V₇/V, for instance, is $\hat{2}$, the pitch a 5th above $\hat{5}$.

b) On the root, you need to build a Mm₇ chord. Check carefully for possible accidentals you may need: the third should be major, the fifth perfect, and the seventh minor.

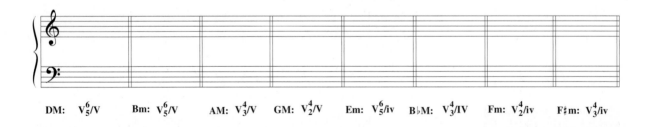

DM: V⁶₅/V   Bm: V⁶₅/V   AM: V⁴₃/V   GM: V⁴₂/V   Em: V⁶₅/iv   B♭M: V⁴₃/IV   Fm: V⁴₂/iv   F♯m: V⁴₃/iv

EXERCISE 16.3   Spell and resolve the following secondary dominants of V and IV.

Bm: V₇/V V   FM: V₇/V V   B♭M: V⁶₅/V V   GM: V⁴₃/V V   F♯m: V⁴₂/V V₆   Em: V⁴₂/V V₆

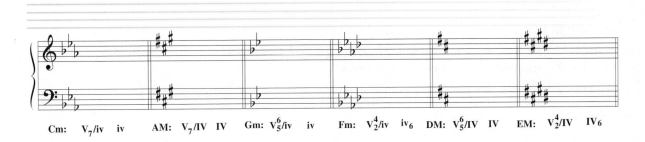

Cm: V₇/iv iv   AM: V₇/IV IV   Gm: V⁶₅/iv iv   Fm: V⁴₂/iv iv₆   DM: V⁶₅/IV IV   EM: V⁴₂/IV IV₆

EXERCISE 16.4   Realize the following short progressions in four voices. Provide RNs for exercise 16.4b. Be careful to check the outer-voice frame for good counterpoint.

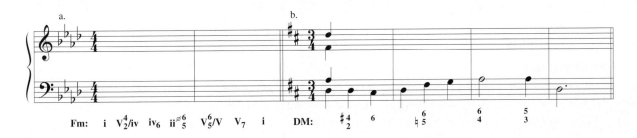

Fm: i   V⁴₂/iv iv₆ ii°⁶₅ V⁶₅/V   V₇   i   DM:

EXERCISE 16.5   Realize the following progression in four voices. Be careful to check the outer-voice frame for good counterpoint.

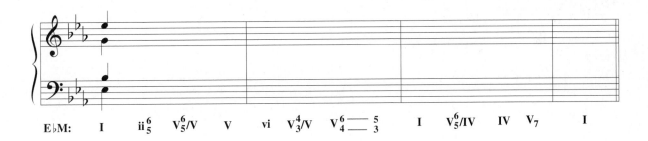

E♭M: I   ii⁶₅   V⁶₅/V   V   vi   V⁴₃/V   V⁶₄ — ⁵₃   I   V⁶₅/IV   IV   V₇   I

EXERCISE 16.6

1. Harmonize the following melody with a bass and RNs or a figured bass. Include a tonicization of iv and one of V. The harmonic rhythm is one chord per beat.

2. Once you are sure that your harmonization is correct, copy the melody again on your own music paper and, below it, provide a left-hand keyboard realization of your harmonization.

Em:

EXERCISE 16.7

1. Write your own progressions (bass and RNs) in the keys and meters indicated below. Use the required chords, besides any of the other chords we have already studied. Make sure you resolve secondary dominants (and any other chords that require resolution) correctly.

   a) Gm; include V_5^6/iv and V_7/V.

   b) E♭M; include V_2^4/IV, V_5^6/V, and V_2^4/V.

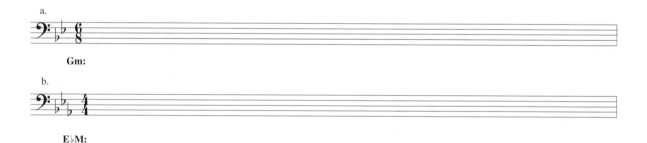

2. Choose one of your own progressions from above, and use it as a harmonic basis to compose a phrase for keyboard. Your phrase should consist of a simple melody (right hand) with keyboard-style accompaniment (left hand).

Chapter 17

Secondary Dominants II

In this chapter we will continue the study of secondary dominants. We will first examine the dominants of ii (VI in minor), iii (III in minor), and the less frequent V_7/VII. We will also study the deceptive resolution of secondary dominants, the connection of consecutive secondary dominants and the irregular resolution resulting from this connection, and we will introduce secondary key areas.

The dominants of the supertonic, submediant, and mediant can frequently be found in music, and in principle they may appear in any inversion. To simplify our presentation, however, we will focus only on those inversions which appear most often in the form of standard harmonic patterns.

V_7 OF ii

Because the supertonic in minor keys is a diminished triad and composers have avoided secondary dominants of diminished triads, V of ii is usually found only in the major mode. It is a Mm_7 chord built on $\hat{6}$, and it includes the accidental $\sharp\hat{1}$, the secondary leading tone (LT) of $\hat{2}$. In example 17.1, by nineteenth-century American composer Clara Scott, V_7/ii is used to approach the cadential gesture $ii_7-V_{4-3}^{6-5}-I$. The progression V_7/ii–ii–V–i (see also example 17.3) is especially strong because of the succession of 5th-related roots ($\hat{6}-\hat{2}-\hat{5}-\hat{1}$). Examine also Scott's voice leading: $\sharp\hat{1}$ (D$\natural$) functions as a chromatic passing tone (PT) between $\hat{1}$ and $\hat{2}$.

The most frequent inversion of V_7/ii is V_5^6/ii, in which $\sharp\hat{1}$, the secondary LT, is emphasized in the bass (see example 17.3). The opening of Chevalier de Saint–Georges's Sonata no. 2 for violin and piano shows an effective use of this inversion. Notice that while the chord in both m. 3 and m. 7 is V_5^6/ii, the root of the chord, F$\sharp$, appears only in the melody, thus further stressing $\sharp\hat{1}$ in the bass. Is the chromaticism in m. 5 melodic or harmonic? What about the D$\sharp$ in m. 6? Does it imply a secondary dominant harmony?

Example 17.1   Clara Scott, *Twilight Fancies*, mm. 1–8

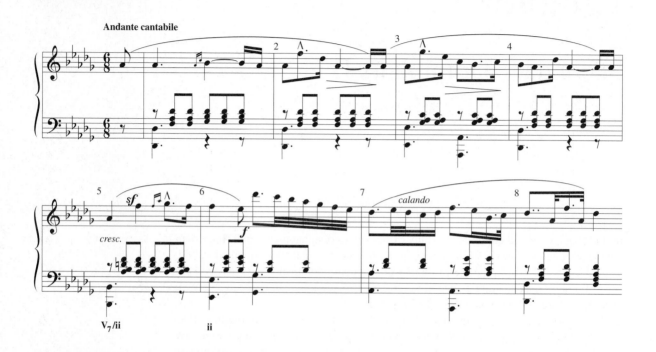

Example 17.2   Chevalier de Saint–Georges, Sonata no. 2 for Violin and Piano, mm. 1–10

EXERCISE

To practice spelling and resolving secondary dominants of ii, refer to exercise 17.2 in worksheet 17 at the end of this chapter.

V₇ OF vi (VI)

The dominant of the submediant is found equally in major or minor modes. In major, V_7/vi is built on $\hat{3}$ and includes $\sharp\hat{5}$, the LT of $\hat{6}$. In minor, V_7/VI includes the M triad III (diatonic), with an added m7, $\flat\hat{2}$. The opening phrase from the Étude-Mazurka "La Favorite," by nineteenth-century American composer Jane Sloman, illustrates the use of V_7/vi within a period in FM (example 17.4). After the first phrase establishes the key with a very standard diatonic progression, the V_7/vi at the beginning of the second phrase introduces an element of harmonic variety. Notice the tonally strong bass in this second phrase (two consecutive sets of P4-related pitches), the chromatic voice leading in the left hand, and the numerous chromatic nonchord tones (NCTs) in the right hand.

♪♪♪ Example 17.3

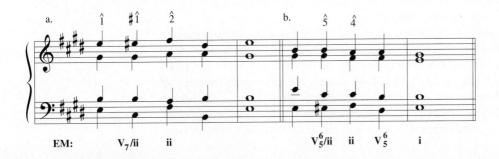

♪♪♪ Example 17°.4   Jane Sloman, "La Favorite," Étude-Mazurka, mm. 1–8

As with all secondary dominants, this chord is often found in first inversion (V$^6_5$/vi), because of the linear strength of the LT in the bass. Examine example 17.5, identify V$^6_5$/VI (the passage is in Dm), and verify its voice leading. What other secondary chords can you identify in the fragment? Are there any other chords taking advantage of the LT in the bass? The chord on G♯ in m. 77 is a chord on a secondary LT (♯$\hat{4}$), but it is not exactly a secondary V$_7$. What is it? We will study this type of chord in the next chapter. Notice the top line which Mozart was able to write in mm. 76–77 using only chord tones! Finally, compare this passage with Saint–Georges's passage in example 17.2. What do they have in common?

The second inversion of V$_7$/vi, V$^4_3$/vi, allows for a good linear bass line descending by steps from $\hat{1}$. Another example by Mozart (example 17.6) demonstrates this progression on the bass $\hat{1}$–$\hat{7}$–$\hat{6}$, I–V$^4_3$/vi–vi. Analyze the first five chords in this passage (mm. 20–21; notice that the key here is E♭M, despite the key signature), paying attention not only to function and RNs, but also to voice leading. What is the linear function of the second chord? And of the fourth chord? The remainder of the passage presents some interesting challenges which we will discuss later in this chapter (see p. 509).

♪♪♪ Example 17.5   W. A. Mozart, String Quartet K. 173, IV, mm. 73–77

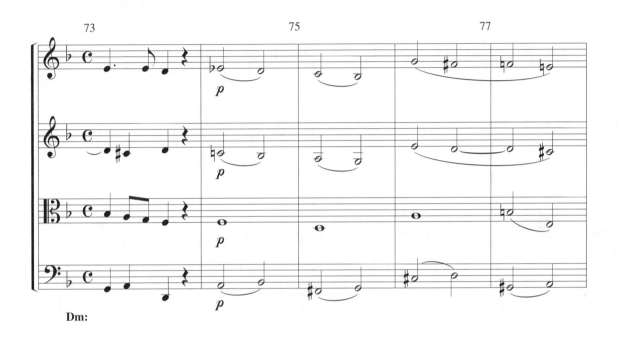

Dm:

♪♪♪ Example 17.6   W. A. Mozart, Sonata for Violin and Piano, K. 481, II, mm. 20–24

E♭M: I

♪♪♪ Example 17.7

Consult example 17.7 for a summary of progressions involving the dominant of vi. Make sure you notice the difference between the V_3^4/vi progression (example 17.7d) and the progression with V_2^4/IV (example 16.8f). The last progression in this example (example 17.7e) shows a very effective use of V_5^6/vi as a chromatic passing chord embellishing a deceptive cadence. Play this progression first omitting the V_5^6/vi (you will thus hear a simple deceptive cadence, I–V_7–vi), and then with the passing V_5^6/vi inserted between V_7 and vi.

EXERCISE

To practice spelling and resolving secondary dominants of vi, refer to exercise 17.2 in worksheet 17 at the end of this chapter.

V_7 OF iii (III)

The secondary dominant of the mediant in the major mode is a Mm$_7$ chord on $\hat{7}$, with two accidentals: ♯$\hat{2}$ (LT of $\hat{3}$) and ♯$\hat{4}$. In the minor mode, on the other hand, V_7/III is built on ♭$\hat{7}$, and it does not involve any chromatic alteration (the scale degrees are

Example 17.8

b̂7̂–2̂–4̂–♭6̂, all members of the natural minor scale). Consult example 17.8 for spelling and resolution of this chord.

Because in minor modes the mediant key is the relative major (III), a key very closely related to the minor tonic key, the secondary dominant of the mediant appears more often in minor than in major. This chord also appears frequently in first inversion, although you will find examples of it in both root position and other inversions. The connection I–V$_7$/iii requires special voice-leading care because of the danger of parallel 5ths and a melodic +2 between 1̂ and ♯2̂ (try it and you will see; a solution is to double the third in I, as in example 17.8a). In example 17.9a, Schubert partially avoids the problem by writing leaps in two voices (right hand). Does he avoid, however, the +2? Example 17.9b, on the other hand, illustrates a standard use of V$_7$/III in minor. By writing the chord in first inversion (V$_5^6$/III), Chopin can take advantage of the linear bass progression, 1̂–2̂–3̂. Notice also how natural and diatonic this chord sounds in the minor mode as compared to the equivalent progression in major.

Example 17.9a   F. Schubert, Symphony in Bm, "Unfinished," II, mm. 268–274

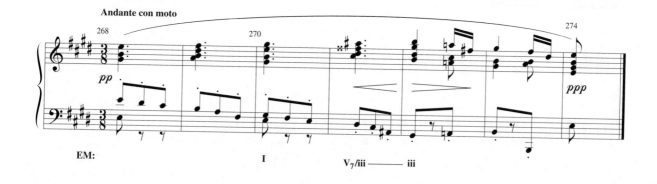

Example 17.9b   F. Chopin, Mazurka 43 in Gm, op. posth. 67, no. 2, mm. 1–6

EXERCISE

To practice spelling and resolving secondary dominants of iii, refer to exercise 17.2 in worksheet 17 at the end of this chapter.

V₇ OF VII

The dominant of vii (a diminished triad) is normally not found in music. As we studied in chapter 14, however, ♭$\hat{7}$ in minor is a diatonic degree, the root of a M triad, VII. This degree is sometimes tonicized. The secondary dominant of VII is built on $\hat{4}$, and includes the raised $\hat{6}$. Although V₇/VII may be used as an independent tonicization, it is often found as part of a circle of 5ths of secondary dominants. Refer to anthology, no. 5 (Vivaldi, Concerto, op. 3, no. 3), mm. 15–22. This passage, in Em, begins with a sequence based on a circle-of-5ths bass: B–E–A–D. What harmonies does Vivaldi assign to the bass B–E–A in mm. 16–18? In mm. 19–20, we have an example of V₇/VII–VII, to the bass A–D, $\hat{4}$–♭$\hat{7}$. A four-voice realization of the same progression appears in example 17.10.

Example 17.10

Because ♭$\hat{7}$ is not a diatonic degree in major, one would not expect to find many tonicized ♭VIIs in major keys. In a crossover between modes, however, ♭VII does appear in major occasionally. The phrase in example 17.11 is unquestionably in CM throughout, and it includes three tonicized chords. The most striking of all, taking the place of the inner cadence with fermata included, is a tonicized ♭VII. What other two degrees are tonicized?

EXERCISES

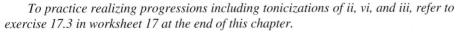

To practice spelling and resolving secondary dominants of VII, refer to exercise 17.2 in worksheet 17 at the end of this chapter.

To practice realizing progressions including tonicizations of ii, vi, and iii, refer to exercise 17.3 in worksheet 17 at the end of this chapter.

To practice harmonizing a melody including various tonicizations, refer to exercise 17.4 in worksheet 17 at the end of this chapter.

DECEPTIVE RESOLUTIONS OF SECONDARY DOMINANTS

Just as a dominant chord may resolve deceptively to vi or VI, a secondary dominant may resolve deceptively by upward stepwise root motion, to the triad which would function as vi or VI in the tonicized area. The Haydn fragment reproduced in example 17.12, for instance, illustrates a deceptive resolution of V$_7$/vi. The passage is in DM, and we first hear a deceptive resolution of V$_7$ to vi, followed by a tonicization of the submediant (V$_7$/vi) which also resolves deceptively to VI/vi (that is, to a GM chord which, in the tonicized key area of the submediant, Bm or vi, would itself be VI). Notice that the chord on G♯ is, again, a secondary vii°$_7$/V, a chord we will study in the next chapter.

♪♪♪Example 17.12   J. Haydn, String Quartet, op. 77, no. 1, I, mm. 43–46

CONSECUTIVE SECONDARY DOMINANTS: CHROMATIC SEQUENCES

The following comments refer to example 17.13. Play through all the progressions if possible, listen to them, and sing them in class.

1. In example 17.13a you will recognize a succession of secondary dominants with their respective resolutions. The resulting bass pattern is a circle of 5ths.

♪♪♪Example 17.13a

2. In example 17.13b, we have deleted the intervening triad of resolution between secondary dominants. Each secondary V_7 now resolves to another secondary V_7 whose root is a 4th above (or 5th below). In chapter 15 we studied the circle of 5ths of diatonic seventh chords. Now we can write a circle of 5ths of secondary dominants.

♪♪♪Example 17.13b

3. The connection of two secondary V_7s requires an **irregular resolution** of the LT and the seventh. In the first place, notice that the chords in succession alternate between complete (C) and incomplete (IN). Then, observe the voice leading (and see example 17.13c).

   a) The seventh of the first chord moves down chromatically to become the LT of the next chord.

   b) The LT of the first chord moves *down* chromatically to become the seventh of the next chord.

   You will also observe that in this progression (see example 17.13b) *two of the voices move chromatically* as long as you have successive V_7s.

♪♪♪Example 17.13c, d, and e

4. *Chromatic sequences using inverted secondary dominants.* If you place either of the chromatic voices in the bass, you will end up with a sequence of alternate secondary V^6_5s and V^4_2s, all of them complete. Compare example 17.13c (root position) with example 17.13d and e. In the latter two, each of the chromatic voices has been placed in the bass, with the same results (in different order) in the inversions: $^6_5$–$^4_2$ or $^4_2$–$^6_5$. This is a common **sequential pattern,** as well as one of the most effective chromatic progressions.

In example 17.13f you can see this pattern applied to a closed progression in CM. Notice that we can now harmonize a descending chromatic bass. Moreover, we still think of this progression as being in CM—a very chromatic CM, to be sure, but CM nonetheless. So, what happened then to our good old white-key CM scale? Once you introduce wholesale chromaticism, you will see that the chromatic scale ends up substituting for the diatonic scale (for any diatonic scale, in any key). These examples also show the harmonic power of secondary dominants. In only two chapters and with a single harmonic concept, we have gone from all-diatonic harmony to the type of thoroughly chromatic progression we are discussing now.

♪♪♪ Example 17.13f

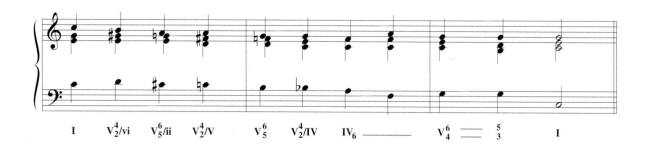

| I | V^4_2/vi | V^6_5/ii | V^4_2/V | | V^6_5 | V^4_2/IV | IV_6 ——————— | V^6_4 —— $^5_3$ | I |

5. *Harmonizing complete chromatic scales in the bass.* The progressions in examples 17.13g and h are two extreme examples of the "power of secondary dominants." Example 17.13g is a **harmonization of a complete descending chromatic bass**, using only the secondary dominant $^4_2$–$^6_5$ patterns we have just studied. Whereas in example 17.13f we have stayed well within the limits of CM, in example 17.13g we really push the limits towards an all-chromatic linear tonality, although the progression is still in CM. Play, write, or listen to someone play this progression. Although accidentals have been omitted in the figures to avoid clutter, all these sonorities should be secondary dominant sevenths in inversion. While the first two measures stay within the tonicization of diatonic degrees in CM, where do you think we start getting away from CM proper? An interesting property of this type of chromatic sequence is that it *suspends tonality* momentarily. We hear it as a process moving somewhere, but we don't really know where it will take us until we get there.

♪♪♪Example 17.13g

I   4   6   4   6   4   6   4   6   4   6   4   6   4   6   4   6   I!
     2   5   2   5   2   5   2   5   2   5   2   5   2   5   2   5

Finally, example 17.13h shows the **harmonization of a complete ascending chromatic bass**, and this time we are not even "pushing the limits": the progression *is* in CM. Study it, make sure you understand it, and play, sing, or listen to it.

♪♪♪Example 17.13h

I   V$_5^6$/ii   ii   V$_5^6$/iii   iii   ii$_6$ V$_5^6$/V   V   V$_5^6$/vi   vi   V$_5^6$/VII   V/iii ——— iii$_6$ ii$_6$ V$_4^6$ — $_3^5$ I

6. *Some examples from the literature.* First, refer back to example 17.11, Bach's Chorale 11, and look at m. 1, beats 3–4. In CM, beat 3 is a V$_6$ chord. What chord does it move to? What happens to the LT in the V$_6$ as it moves to the next chord?

Refer now to example 17.6, Mozart's violin sonata K. 481, and analyze mm. 2–3. The V$_5^6$/vi in m. 2, beat 1, resolves to a major VI, or V/ii, which immediately becomes V$_2^4$/ii. What does the V$_2^4$/ii move on to? What happens to the bass B♭, the seventh of V$_2^4$/ii, as it moves to the next chord? And to the E♮, the LT in V$_2^4$/ii? Complete the analysis of m. 3, tracing the voice leading of the LTs and sevenths.

Finally, refer to anthology, no. 44 (Chopin, Mazurka 43). First, analyze mm. 25–32, in B♭M. You will find consecutive V$_7$s in mm. 25–26 (repeated in mm. 27–28), and especially in mm. 29–30, a circle-of-5ths fragment. In mm. 29–30, look at the right hand, and trace the voice leading of the LTs and sevenths for each chord. Do they follow the criteria we have established above? What about the left hand in these measures: Does it follow our voice-leading principles? Well, composers *do* take liberties. In a case like this, with the left-hand parallel 5ths, Chopin is reinforcing the already strong bass by 5ths, in contrast to the smooth, chromatic right hand. Of course, Chopin did this in a deliberate way to emphasize musically an instrumental bass, and in no way are these 5ths "voice-leading errors."

The passage in mm. 29–30 tonicizes only diatonic degrees in B♭M. What about the similar but longer linear sequential passage in mm. 21–25? Some nondiatonic degrees are tonicized here, beginning with the $V_7/\flat VII$ in m. 23. Of course, the circle of 5ths leads from V_7/IV to $V_7/\flat VII$, and after that on to the tonicization of $\flat\hat{3}$, $\flat\hat{6}$, $\flat\hat{2}$, and so forth. One could continue like this for the complete twelve-pitch cycle of the chromatic scale (as in example 17.13g). In order to avoid this, Chopin breaks the circle of P5ths in m. 25, with a °5th from G♭ to C (instead of C♭), thus getting the sequence back into B♭M through V_7/V.

EXERCISES

To practice realizing chromatic sequences including secondary dominants, refer to exercise 17.5 in worksheet 17 at the end of this chapter.

To practice analysis of musical fragments including various tonicizations, refer to exercise 17.1 in worksheet 17 at the end of this chapter.

SECONDARY KEY AREAS

Listen to example 17.14. The song is in CM, but in our fragment you will first hear a tonicization of iii, then one of ii (or, as we find out in m. 4, actually II), and finally a half cadence (HC) in C. Each of these tonicizations, however, involves more than the secondary dominant and its resolution to the chord on the tonicized degree. In mm. 1–2 of our example, we hear a ii–V–i (actually ii_7–V_7–i_7) progression tonicizing iii, or, in other words, "ii_7–V_7–i_7 of iii." Similarly, in mm. 3–4 we hear essentially the same progression, but now "of ii (or II)." We will use the concept of **secondary key area** to refer to short passages in which there is a progression that involves more secondary chords than just the dominant, or in which a degree is tonicized more than once. Measures 1–2 in our example are, then, a secondary key area of iii, and mm. 3–4 are a secondary key area of II, both within the overall key of CM. The Roman numeral (RN) analysis under this score shows our notation for secondary key areas: The RN under the line indicates the degree tonicized (iii and II in our case), and the RNs above the line indicate the chords within the key area analyzed and labeled in the secondary key, in this case Em and DM.

NOTE

In chapter 27 we will study extended tertian chords (ninth, eleventh, and thirteenth chords) in detail. Although extended tertian chords are usually generated linearly, we can also think of them as being built by adding thirds on top of a seventh chord. In a ninth chord, for instance, a third has been added on top of a seventh chord. As a preview of chapter 27, in example 17.14 you can see three examples of the most common type of ninth chord, V_7^9, and you can also verify that in all cases the ninth functions linearly and resolves downward as a 9–8 suspension.

FURTHER ANALYSIS

Two examples from the anthology will further help you understand the concept of secondary key area.

1. *Anthology, no. 54 (Verdi, Il trovatore, Act II, no. 14, mm. 15–24).*

   a) The passage begins in Cm. Does it end in Cm?

   b) Analyze the complete fragment harmonically, identifying all the secondary dominants.

   c) Is there any harmonic section you may label as a secondary key area? Could mm. 19–21 be one? Of what tonicized degree?

   d) Write your RN analysis of the passage under the bass line in example 17.15, making sure you notate the secondary key area correctly. Be careful to indicate the correct mode (with capital or lowercase RNs) of the tonicized triad (under the "secondary area" line). The repetition of mm. 15–16 has been omitted in example 17.15.

2. *Anthology, no. 34 (Beethoven, Sonata op. 13, III), mm. 18–25.* The first period of the piece ends in m. 17 with a perfect authentic cadence (PAC) in Cm. Two brief secondary key areas (four measures each) follow, the first one in the Fm area (iv in Cm), the second one in the EbM area (III in Cm). As it turns out, the second key area, of III, is here to stay: It proves to be a full modulation to EbM, on which the second section of the piece is built, beginning in m. 25. But in mm. 22–24 we don't know this yet. We only find out after EbM is established in m. 25, and we hear the new phrase continuing in EbM. So, by analogy with mm. 18–21 (key area of iv), we will consider mm. 22–25 a secondary key area of III. Listen to the piece, and notice the transitional character of these two passages in iv and III. Example 17.16 provides the bass line and the secondary key area indications. Fill in the specific RNs for each chord within the two key areas (above the key area line).

Example 17.15

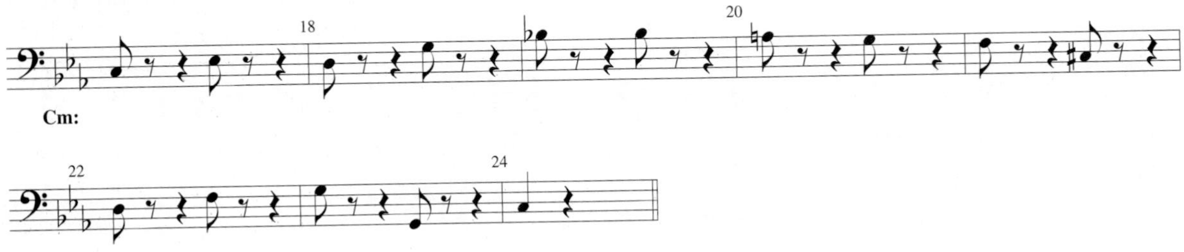
18
20
Cm:
22
24

Example 17.16

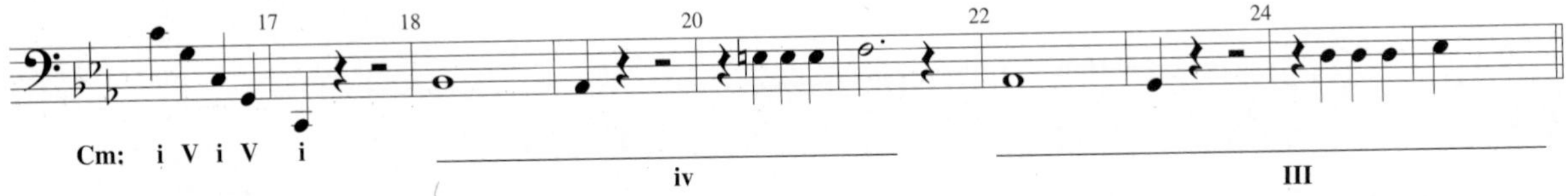
17
18
20
22
24
Cm: i V i V i
iv
III

ASSIGNMENT AND KEYBOARD PROGRESSIONS

For analytical and written assignments and keyboard progressions based on the materials learned in this chapter, refer to chapter 17 in the workbook.

PITCH PATTERNS

Sing the melodic pitch patterns in example 17.17, paying attention to the sound of the various secondary dominants marked by brackets.

Example 17.17

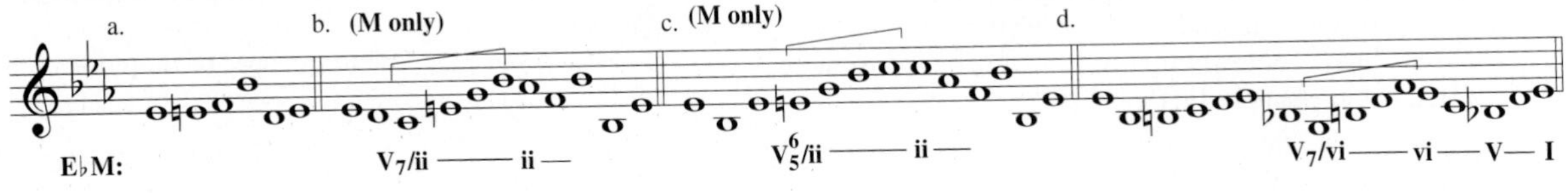
a.
b. (M only)
c. (M only)
d.
E♭M:
V7/ii — ii —
V6/5/ii — ii —
V7/vi — vi — V — I

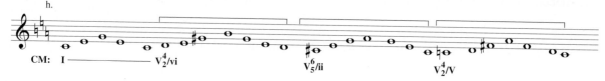

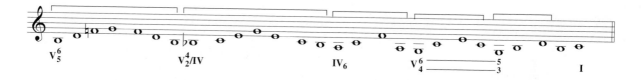

Composers and Their Music 17

Biographies

Write short biographies of the following composers mentioned in this chapter: Clara Scott, Jane Sloman, Cole Porter.

Listening

Listen to the following compositions by composers mentioned in this chapter:

Verdi, *Il trovatore* (complete opera if possible, or selections).

Vivaldi, *L'estro armonico*, op. 3.
Porter, *Jubilee* (selections).
Follow the score while you listen. Be able to place each of these compositions in one of the style periods and to comment on why and how it represents the musical characteristics of that period.

Terms for Review

V_7/ii and inversions
V_7/vi and inversions
V_7/iii and inversions
V_7/VII and inversions
Deceptive resolution of secondary dominants

Consecutive secondary V_7s
Irregular resolution of V_7s
$^6_5$–$^4_2$ sequential pattern
Harmonizing the descending and ascending chromatic bass lines
Secondary key areas

Worksheet 17

EXERCISE 17.1 *Analysis.* The following examples include tonicizations of various degrees. Identify the degree or degrees tonicized in each case, and provide exact RNs if required.

1. Anthology, no. 31, Paradis, *Sicilienne*, mm. 7–8. Provide RNs for these two measures (the piece is in GM).

2. Example 17.18. Provide RNs for the secondary dominants in m. 3 and m. 6.

♪♪♪ Example 17.18   L. v. Beethoven, Piano Sonata, op. 13, II, mm. 1–8

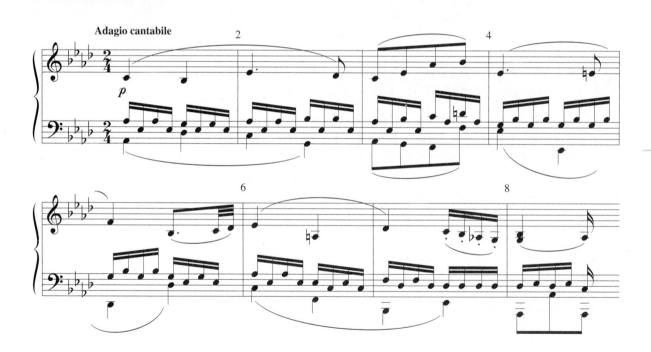

3. Example 17.19. Tonicization plays an essential role in this brief piece. What two degrees are tonicized in mm. 1–8? And what two degrees are tonicized in mm. 9–16? Provide RNs for all four secondary dominants. Comment on the melodic and harmonic sequential patterns that result in each of these two cases.

♪♪♪Example 17.19   F. Schubert, *Originaltänze*, op. 9, no. 16

4. Example 17.20. Which two degrees are tonicized in this example? Can you identify one or more linear patterns in the voice leading for one of these tonicizations?

5. Example 17.21. What progression is this passage based on? What kind of chords is the progression built on? Does it illustrate some special voice-leading properties we have studied in this chapter?

6. Example 17.22. The song from which this passage is taken is in CM. Provide a harmonic analysis for the passage. Analyze mm. 5–7 as a secondary key area, providing the correct analytical notation under the score.

Example 17.20   L. v. Beethoven, Piano Concerto no. 4, op. 58, II, mm. 1–13

Example 17.21   W. A. Mozart, String Quartet, K. 421, III, mm. 21–29

♪♪♪Example 17.22   Cole Porter, "Begin the Beguine," from *Jubilee* (End of Refrain and Beginning of Bridge)

EXERCISE 17.2   Write and resolve the following secondary dominant chords. The resolution should be to the appropriate tonicized chord, in root position or inversion as required by the voice leading in the bass.

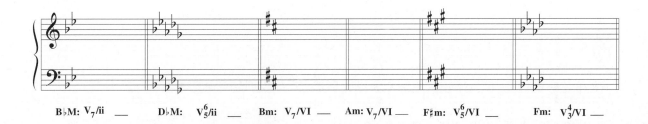

B♭M: V₇/ii ___   D♭M: V⁶₅/ii ___   Bm: V₇/VI ___   Am: V₇/VI ___   F♯m: V⁶₅/VI ___   Fm: V⁴₃/VI ___

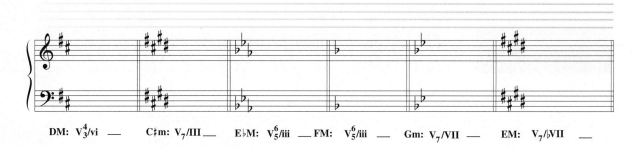

DM: V_3^4/vi ___   C♯m: V_7/III ___   E♭M: V_5^6/iii ___ FM: V_5^6/iii ___   Gm: V_7/VII ___   EM: V_7/♭VII ___

EXERCISE 17.3   Realize the following progressions in four voices, and provide RNs for progression b.

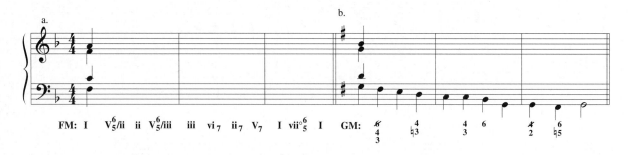

FM: I V_5^6/ii   ii V_5^6/iii   iii   vi$_7$ ii$_7$ V$_7$ I vii°$_5^6$ I   GM: $\frac{6}{4}$ $\frac{4}{3}$ $\frac{4}{3}$ 6 $\frac{4}{2}$ $\frac{6}{5}$

EXERCISE 17.4   Harmonize the following melody (based on Bach's Chorale 105) in four voices, in chorale style, and include a RN analysis of your harmonization. The notes marked with an asterisk should be harmonized with secondary dominants. Include tonicizations of III, iv, and V (although not necessarily in this order). Double-check your outer-voice frame for good counterpoint.

Bm:

HR:

4 - 3

EXERCISE 17.5   Realize the following sequential patterns involving consecutive secondary dominants. Be careful with the voice leading and the irregular resolution of the LT and the seventh. Provide RNs for progression b.

E♭M: I V_7/iii V_7/vi V_7/ii V_7/V   V$_7$ I   AM: $\frac{\#4}{2}$ $\frac{6}{\natural5}$ $\frac{\#4}{2}$ $\frac{6}{\natural5}$ $\frac{4}{2}$ 6

Chapter 18

Secondary Leading-Tone Chords

In example 18.1 you will recognize a familiar harmonic structure: two phrases in Gm, the first one ending on a half cadence (HC), the second one on a perfect authentic cadence (PAC). In the approach to V at the HC, you will also recognize a familiar bass line, the secondary leading-tone figure $\hat{4}$–$\#\hat{4}$–$\hat{5}$. On the basis of our studies so far, we might expect $\#\hat{4}$ to be harmonized with V_5^6/V. A closer look will show that Bach chose to harmonize it with another familiar chord, a $vii°_7$ chord, that close cousin and frequent substitute of V_5^6. In this case, $vii°_7$ is not "of i" (Gm), but rather, because it is built on C$\#$, "of V" or "of D" in this example. (Incidentally, what unusual voice-leading event do you see in m.1, in the right hand? To help explain it, remember that Bach was harmonizing a given, existing melody, which he was not going to change just because of a leading tone [LT] resolving in an unusual manner. Does the "voice overlap" help with the harmonic voice leading?)

| ♪♪♪Example 18.1 | J. S. Bach, Chorale 19, "Ich hab' mein' Sach' Gott heimgestellt," mm. 1–4 |

SECONDARY LEADING-TONE SEVENTH CHORDS

The chord on $\sharp\hat{4}$ in example 18.1 is vii°$_7$/V, a secondary vii°$_7$ chord. Just as secondary dominants can tonicize any degree, the other members of the dominant family can also be used to tonicize chords. A **secondary leading-tone chord** is a triad or seventh chord built on a secondary LT. vii°$_7$/V, for instance, is a fully diminished seventh chord built on $\sharp\hat{4}$, and it will resolve to V as if V were a momentary tonic and as if $\sharp\hat{4}$ were a momentary LT resolving to its momentary tonic, $\hat{5}$. You will find secondary vii°$_6$, vii$^\varnothing_7$, and vii°$_7$ chords tonicizing the same degrees you can tonicize with V$_7$ chords. Secondary LT sevenths are more frequent than vii°$_6$, and among them vii°$_7$ is by far the most commonly found chord, in root position or inversion. You may refer to anthology, no. 18 (Amalie, sonata for flute) for an example of a secondary vii°$_7$. In m. 8 you will see a HC on V, preceded by a $\sharp\hat{4}$ (B$\natural$) in the bass. The complete chord is B$\natural$–D–F–A, or vii°$_7$/V. How does this LT chord compare with the other chord on $\sharp\hat{4}$ (B$\natural$) in m. 11? What other secondary chord do you recognize in m. 10?

Chord Types, Resolution, and Voice Leading

Example 18.2 illustrates the three possible seventh chord harmonizations of a secondary LT. Choosing V$^6_5$, vii$^\varnothing_7$, or vii°$_7$ is totally up to the composer. vii$^\varnothing_7$ may be used to tonicize major triads (such as V or IV), but not usually for minor triads (such as ii or

♪♪♪ Example 18.2

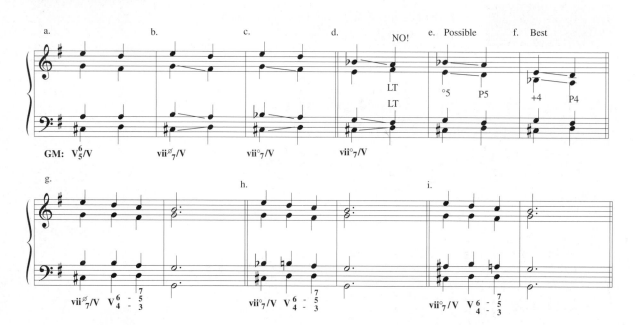

vi). vii°₇, on the other hand, appears in tonicizations of both major and minor triads. All three chords stress the LT in the bass, with its strong linear pull. vii°₇ has the advantage of, in some cases, introducing a new accidental. In example 18.2c, vii°₇/V in M introduces ♭$\hat{3}$ besides ♯$\hat{4}$; in example 18.4a, vii°₇/IV includes ♭$\hat{2}$ besides ♭$\hat{7}$; and in example 18.4b, vii°₇/ii adds ♭$\hat{7}$ to ♯$\hat{1}$. These chords intensify the chromaticism of a passage and also create two strong linear tensions, the LT and the seventh.

Voice Leading

As usual, the secondary LT resolves up, and the seventh down. Otherwise, all the same voice-leading principles (and problems) we studied regarding leading-tone seventh chords apply to secondary LT sevenths. You may want to review chapter 15 to refresh your knowledge of these principles, especially the resolution of the tritone (root and fifth) and the possible parallel 5ths resulting from the downward resolution of the third in vii°₇ (see examples 15.4 and 15.7). Resolving the third upward in vii°₇/V (or vii⌀₇/V), as in example 18.2d, results in a doubled LT in the V of the resolution, which you want to avoid. Example 18.2e shows a possible resolution with unequal 5ths (which, in vii°₇ would be faulty parallel 5ths), and example 18.2f shows the best possibility, with 4ths instead of 5ths. (Examples 18.2b and c avoid the problem altogether by voicing the chord differently.)

The resolution of vii°₇/V or vii⌀₇/V to V$^{6-5}_{4-3}$, a very frequent occurrence, is illustrated in examples 18.2g to i. You may notice that the notation in example 18.2h is a bit awkward: The seventh, B♭, first has to go up a half step to B♮, before resolving down to A. Although awkward, the notation B♭–B♮–A is perfectly acceptable and found in many scores. At times, however, composers choose an alternative, and also perfectly correct, notation, which reflects the voice-leading motion better by using the enharmonic A♯ instead of B♭, as in example 18.2i.

Study Bach's use of vii°₇/V in example 18.3. In m. 9, beats 2–3, the LT, seventh, and tritone (TT) are perfectly resolved as we would expect. How does Bach deal with the voice leading of the problematic third? Then, in m. 10, notice an interesting possibility: instead of preceding a V$^{6-5}_{4-3}$ figure, as in example 18.2h, Bach's vii°₇/V acts as an

♩♩♩Example 18.3   J. S. Bach, Chorale 94, "Warum betrübst du dich, mein Herz," mm. 9–10

♪♪♪Example 18.4

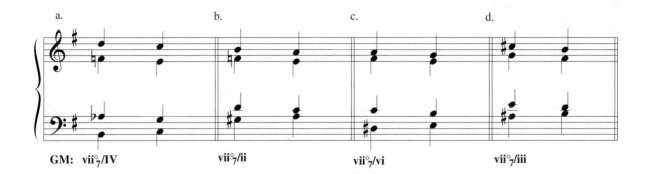

GM: vii°₇/IV   vii°₇/ii   vii°₇/vi   vii°₇/iii

ornamental neighbor chord between the $\frac{6}{4}$ and the $\frac{5}{3}$, creating a beautiful linear elaboration of V. One more observation before we leave this example: What secondary chord is used at the beginning of the phrase?

Example 18.4 shows some frequently found secondary vii°₇ chords besides vii°₇/V. As we mention above, they all increase the chromatic intensity of the harmony, as well as the dissonant and linear tension of the voice leading. These are all dramatically effective chords.

EXERCISE

To practice spelling secondary diminished seventh chords in root position, refer to exercise 18.2 in worksheet 18 at the end of this chapter.

Examples from the Literature

The following examples demonstrate the use of the secondary vii°₇ chord in a variety of contexts. In the Granados fragment (example 18.5), vii°₇/ii in m. 43 stands out as the only chromatic harmony in the passage. The voice leading in and out of this vii°₇/ii is perfectly smooth in spite of the broad, open left-hand piano figuration. Notice also the linear function of vii°₇/ii as a passing chord between the previous and following chords. Explain how each of the pitches of vii°₇/ii functions as a passing tone (PT) in this example. Explain also how this complete passage prolongs the opening tonic harmony.

Example 18.6, on the other hand, features vii°₇ chords in a more chromatic context. The first one, in m. 5, is also a vii°₇/ii with a passing function. Now look at the resolution of the V₇ at the end of m. 6. Just by altering one pitch in the chord, $\hat{5}$ to $\sharp\hat{5}$, the chord becomes a passing vii°₇/vi which connects V₇ with its deceptive resolution to vi (m. 7, beat 2). As we continue listening, however, we realize that all of m. 7 and m. 8 are actually *a secondary key area of vi*. Analyze these two measures as such, as if vi were the tonic. Is there any deceptive resolution within the secondary key area (in

♩♪♪Example 18.5   E. Granados, *Escenas Románticas*, no. 5, mm. 40–48

other words, a deceptive resolution of a secondary dominant, of the type we studied in the previous chapter)? Is there any secondary function *within* the secondary key area (for instance, a dominant of the dominant of vi)?

The phrase by Schumann in example 18.7a has two parallel phrase segments. What harmony is tonicized at the end of the first phrase segment? Both dotted figures include secondary vii°₇ chords, of iii in m. 1, and of vi in m. 4. Verify the spelling and resolution of each of them, and explain how they connect the previous and following chords linearly. Verify also the spelling and resolution of the secondary leading-tone seventh chord in example 18.7b, m. 2. What type of leading-tone chord is it, and what degree does it tonicize? Does it resolve to the tonicized degree, or does it resolve in an unexpected (or at least unconventional) way?

♪♪♪ Example 18.6   J. Lang, *Frühzeitiger Frühling*, mm. 5–11

Days of delight, are you here so soon?
Are you giving me the sun, hills, and forest?
The little brooks flow more fully.

♪♪♪Example 18.7a   R. Schumann, "An Important Event," no. 6 from *Scenes from Childhood*, op. 15, mm. 1–4

♪♪♪Example 18.7b   Paul McCartney, "My Love" (Refrain)

SECONDARY vii°₇ CHORDS IN INVERSION

All inversions of the LT seventh chords may in principle be used, and they should all resolve according to the usual conventions of resolution of LT seventh chords. In summary, these are as follows:

1. The bass in vii°⁶₅ (the third of the chord) may resolve down to a root-position tonicized chord, or up to a chord in first inversion. In vii°⁶₅/V, however, the fifth of the chord resolves down, as part of the TT, to the LT, $\hat{7}$ (see example 18.8a). The bass

♪♪♪ Example 18.8

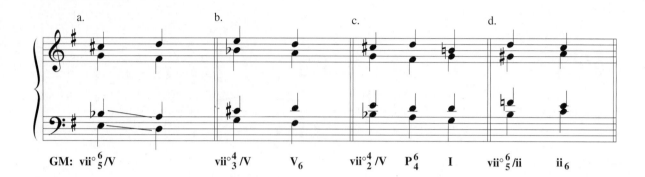

GM: vii°$^6_5$/V   vii°$^4_3$/V   V$_6$ vii°$^4_2$/V   P$^6_4$ I   vii°$^6_5$/ii   ii$_6$

must not, in this case, double $\hat{7}$, so it should not resolve up, but only down. The unequal 5ths that result are awkward, but possible. The same inversion as vii°$^6_5$, however, is not possible because it would produce parallel 5ths.

vii°$^6_5$ tonicizing chords other than V does not present the problem of doubling the LT, so it may resolve up or down without difficulties. In example 18.8d, vii°$^6_5$/ii appears to be resolving upward to ii$_6$. Compare this resolution with Haydn's resolution of the same chord in example 18.9. Are they the same?

2. According to the conventional resolution of the TT between the root and the fifth, vii°$^4_3$, which has the fifth in the bass, should resolve downward to a tonicized chord in first inversion, as in example 18.8b. In example 18.10, Kreisler resolves a vii°$^4_3$/ii to ii$_6$, following exactly the conventions we have studied. Find the chord, study the voice leading of the resolution, and notice also how Kreisler leads *into* the chord: He takes advantage of all common tones by keeping them sustained, and by introducing a passing chord between I and vii°$^4_3$/ii (which chord?) he can

♪♪♪ Example 18.9   J. Haydn, Piano Sonata in DM, Hob. XVI:37, III, mm. 110–114

DM: vii°$^6_5$/ii

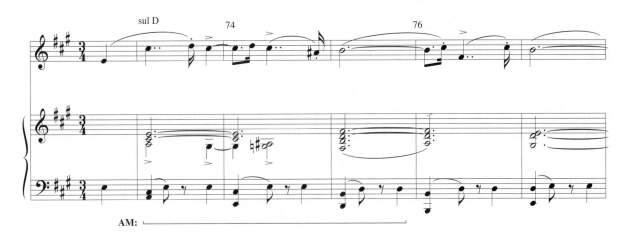

♪♪♪ Example 18.10   F. Kreisler, *Liebesleid*, mm. 73–80

write a nice descending chromatic line in an inner voice. Study the harmonies and voice leading in the passage and, as you play it or listen to it, hear the descending chromatic line in the inner voice.

3. vii$^{\circ 4}_{2}$ has the seventh in the bass, which resolves down to the fifth of the tonicized chord. The resulting $^{6}_{4}$ position will need to be treated as a dissonant $^{6}_{4}$ chord in one of the familiar ways. In example 18.8c, the V$^{6}_{4}$ moves on to I as a passing $^{6}_{4}$ chord. In example 18.11, on the other hand, vii$^{\circ 4}_{2}$/V resolves to V$^{4}_{3}$. Verify the spelling of vii$^{\circ 4}_{2}$/V in this phrase. Then, notice that, following the same voice leading we learned in irregular resolutions of secondary dominants, the leading tone in vii$^{\circ 4}_{2}$/V becomes the seventh in the following V$^{4}_{3}$. After you verify this, why do you think Maurice Jarre chose to spell the secondary LT as D♭ instead of C♯? Does this en-harmonic spelling make more sense from a melodic point of view?

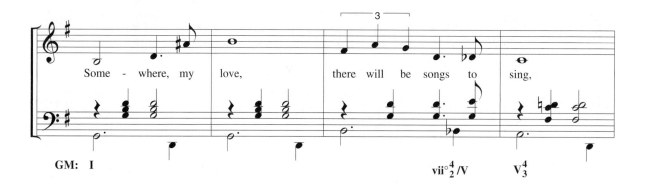

Example 18.11   Paul Francis Webster–Maurice Jarre, "Somewhere, My Love," from the Film *Doctor Zhivago* (Opening Phrase)

EXERCISES

To practice spelling secondary diminished-seventh chords in inversion, refer to exercise 18.2 in worksheet 18 at the end of this chapter.

To practice analyzing figured basses including secondary diminished-seventh chords, refer to exercise 18.4 in worksheet 18 at the end of this chapter.

To practice realizing progressions including secondary diminished seventh chords, refer to exercises 18.3 and 18.5 in worksheet 18 at the end of this chapter.

THE vii°₇ OVER A PEDAL POINT

vii°₇ chords are often used over pedal tones, creating a very expressive multiple dissonance. The fragment in example 18.12, from a Bach Prelude in B♭m, features a pedal point on $\hat{5}$. As he does in many other pedal points, Bach writes a vii°₇/V over the pedal at the end of m. 20. Notice the delayed resolution of the right-hand pitches. If you disregard the pedal, what is the inversion of vii°₇ which Bach writes? Does he resolve this inversion as we have learned we should? To what position of V (again, disregard the pedal) does he resolve it? Finally, notice that the fermata in m. 22 indicates a dramatic stop on a dominant harmony (a HC). On what dominant harmony does Bach pause?

In anthology, no. 56 (C. Schumann, Trio) you may see examples of vii°₇ over a $\hat{1}$ pedal. What degree does the vii°₇ over $\hat{1}$ in m. 265 tonicize? What is the inversion of this vii°₇? Find the two appearances of the same secondary chord, also over $\hat{1}$, in mm. 275–278. What other vii°₇ chord does Clara Schumann use repeatedly, over the same tonic pedal, in mm. 276–281?

♪♪♪Example 18.12   J. S. Bach, Prelude 22 in B♭m, from *The Well-Tempered Clavier*, I, mm. 20–24

B♭m:

A CHROMATIC HARMONIZATION OF A DIATONIC TUNE: BACH, CHORALE 21

As a summary of secondary LT chords, we may now go back to an example we looked at a long time ago: example E.1a, reproduced again as example 18.13. Now we have all the tools we need to understand this beautiful chorale phrase. First sing the tune (the soprano line), and notice how simple and diatonic it is. Then play or listen to the harmonization, and notice how chromatic it is, and how much intensity and drama is added to the melody through this chromaticism. First analyze the chorale harmonically, and *then* continue reading.

1. The beginning and end of the phrase tell us that it is in Am. In m. 1, beat 2, a vii°₇ chord tonicizes iv. Does the tonicization of iv continue? How do you hear the cadence in m. 2? It sounds like a HC in the key of iv (Dm). What specific kind of HC (consider the previous chord and bass note!)? The whole fragment from m. 1, beat 2, to the first fermata is, then, a *secondary key area of iv*. What kind of tonicizing chord appears in m. 1, beat 4, and how does it function linearly?

Example 18.13   J. S. Bach, Chorale 21, "Herzlich thut mich verlangen," mm. 1–4

Am:

2. The chords in m. 3, beats 1–3, tonicize V. What is the first of these chords? And the third one? What chord is used to connect them, in what position is it, and how does it function linearly? Notice the voice exchange figure characteristic of this type of linear function.

3. Example 18.14 shows the long-range tonal plan for the phrase, by means of a bass reduction. Seen from this perspective, the tonal motion is an extended i_6–iv–V–i, in which iv and V appear as tonicized secondary areas. Notice the role of the numerous passing chords in this phrase.

EXERCISES

To practice harmonizing a melody including secondary diminished seventh chords, refer to exercise 18.6 in worksheet 18 at the end of this chapter.

To practice analysis of musical fragments including secondary diminished seventh chords, refer to exercise 18.1 in worksheet 18 at the end of this chapter.

Example 18.14

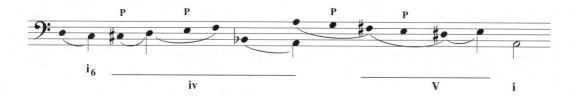

i_6 _____   iv   _____   V   i

Secondary Functions in Context: Two Songs by Mozart

1. Telling a story through harmony: "Wie Unglücklich bin ich nit" (anthology, no. 29).

We will use this Mozart song to illustrate the role of secondary functions in a long-range tonal structure and their relationship to the text. First, read the text. Then, analyze the complete song harmonically (use Roman numerals). Break the song into harmonic phrases (units). What is their tonal direction? How do they correspond with textual units and phrases? Can we tell a story through harmony? How does Mozart use chromaticism as a dramatic means?

a) *Harmonic unit 1, mm. 1–4.* This phrase establishes the key, by means of mostly diatonic progressions leading to the PAC in m. 4. The words in mm. 3–4 are "how languishing are my steps." How does the voice leading depict these words musically? See, for instance, the static lines, the dragging half-step motion in the bass (the only chromaticism in the whole phrase), and also the repeated G in the voice part, the lowest point in the section.

b) *Harmonic unit 2, mm. 5–6.* As you work through these comments, follow also the bass reduction in example 18.15. What happens harmonically in this section? It is all a secondary key area of V, leading to a PAC on a tonicized V in m. 6. The music has *turned away* from the tonic and moved *toward* the dominant. The text in these measures is: "When I turn them (my steps) towards you"!

c) *Harmonic unit 3, mm. 7–10.* "Only my sighs console me." The music is chromatic, with half steps in the bass and the voice part (the sighs, of course), and with the expressive vii°$_7$ tonicizing ii. Notice, in m. 7, the change of position within vii°$_7$/ii by means of a voice exchange and a passing $^6_4$. Tonally, this unit takes us back toward the tonic. The "moving towards you" was short-lived; there does not seem to be much of a response from "you"! When we get back to the tonic, however, the words are "all my pains multiply." So the tonic that we reach in m. 9 is in minor mode, a sad and chromatic tonic, with numerous half-step sighs. The section closes on a tonicized HC on V (perhaps a sign of hope?).

d) *Harmonic unit 4, mm. 11–15.* So, is there hope? If I cannot be with "you," at least I can think of "you," and that is apparently as positive as things will get. So, to the words "when I think of you," the mode becomes major again, and the harmony diatonic, to the end of the song.

e) *In summary,* this song (1) *establishes* I, (2) *moves away* from I to V, (3) *returns* to the tonic, now minor, through a tonicization of ii, and (4) *reaffirms* I diatonically in a closing phrase. And all of this is telling a story through harmony, through chromaticism, and by means of secondary functions, tonicization, and changes of mode. Listen again to the song, or even better perform it, and hear the long-range tonal motions, the tonal direction of phrases, follow (and understand) the bass reduction in example 18.15, and, most important, *hear the story* as it is told by the music!

2. Long-range tonal plan in "Die Zufriedenheit" (anthology, no. 30).

We can now study in more detail a piece which we already discussed in chapter 6. Analyze "Die Zufriedenheit" harmonically and formally, and review example 6.7 and the brief discussion of the song's phrase structure which accompanies that example in chapter 6. You will remember that the song has three phrases, clearly delineated by rests. Sing the melody several times, and discuss the form of the song motivically and thematically (assign letters to the phrases, indicating their formal relationship). If you consider the beginning and ending harmonies (cadences) for each phrase, what is the long-range tonal plan for the song? Within this harmonic plan, what harmonies are tonicized? After you think about these matters, you may discuss them in class and read the following notes.

a) *The song has three phrases (mm. 1–5, 6–9, and 10–14).* Phrases 1 and 2 are unrelated thematically. Phrases 2 and 3 are related motivically (see mm. 6–7 and 10–11). We can express the form by the letter scheme a–b$_1$–b$_2$.

b) *Phrase 1 begins with a prolongation of I: on a $\hat{1}$ pedal, I is prolonged by IV$^6_4$ and V$^4_3$. V is tonicized at the cadence (m. 5) by means of a brief secondary key area of V, a cadential figure ii$_6$–V$^{6-5}_{4-3}$–I "of V" (or "in DM"). The long-range motion of phrase 1 is then I–V.

c) *Phrase 2 begins and ends on V,* and it all can be interpreted as a prolongation of V leading to the HC in m. 9. ii is tonicized in mm. 6–7.

d) *Phrase 3 begins and ends on I.* The phrase is a prolongation of I, including two tonicizations of IV in mm. 10–11.

e) *The long-range tonal plan* is, then, as follows:

$$\text{I} \text{———} \text{V} \quad \text{V} \text{———} \text{V} \quad \text{I} \text{———} \text{I}$$

In other words, in phrase 1 I is *established*, and we *move away* to V by the end of the phrase. In phrase 2, V is prolonged throughout, creating a central area of *tonal contrast* (and also of tonal tension) ending on a HC. In phrase 3, we *return* to I and we stay there. This short song is thus based on the same general tonal plan that may be found underlying most of the formal schemes in the music of the eighteenth and nineteenth centuries: **establishment** of the tonic, **departure** from the tonic, **return** to the tonic.

531

f) *Listen to the song*, and/or perform it in class if possible. Hear the three phrases as harmonic/tonal units, hear their long-range motion, and the general tonal plan of the song. How is this discussion helping you understand the unity of this composition? If you perform it, how is it helping you with the interpretation and rendition of the phrases? Does it help you be aware, for instance, that phrase 2 is all an extension of the V cadence in m. 5 (hence a "departure from"),

creating a tension toward the return in phrase 3? Does it help to hear in this way the *direction* of the music?

g) If you are currently performing some short piece or movement on your instrument in which you can identify the same basic tonal scheme (establishment, departure, return), bring it to class, perform it, explain how you hear its overall tonal plan, and discuss how being aware of the plan might affect your performance.

♪♪♪ Example 18.15

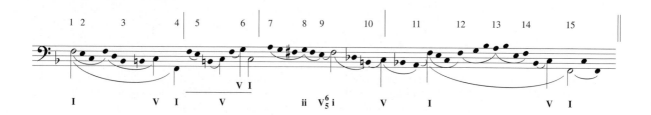

ASSIGNMENT AND KEYBOARD PROGRESSIONS

For analytical and written assignments and keyboard progressions based on the materials learned in this chapter, refer to chapter 18 in the workbook.

PITCH PATTERNS

Sing the pitch patterns in example 18.16, hearing the secondary LT seventh chords and their tonicizing effect. In examples 18.16f and g, hear the bracketed fragments as secondary key areas of IV and V, respectively.

♪♪♪ Example 18.16

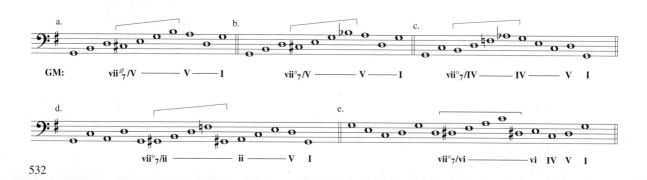

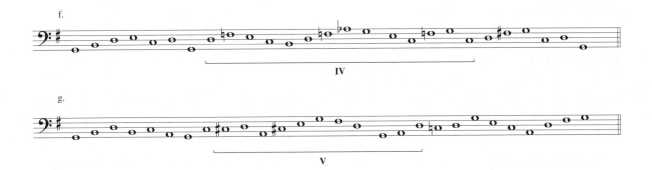

f.

IV

g.

V

Composers and Their Music 18

Biographies

Write short biographies of the following composers mentioned in this chapter: Fritz Kreisler, Maurice Jarre.

Listening

Listen to the following compositions by composers mentioned in this chapter:

    R. Schumann, *Carnaval*, op. 9, and *Kinderscenen*
      (*Scenes from Childhood*).

    J. S. Bach, Mass in Bm (complete is possible, or
      selected movements).

    M. Jarre, film score for *Doctor Zhivago* (selections).

Follow the score while you listen. Be able to place each of these compositions in one of the style periods and to comment on why and how it represents the musical characteristics of that period.

Terms for Review

Secondary leading-tone chords
Secondary leading-tone seventh chords:
    spelling, resolution, voice leading,
    inversions

vii°$_7$ over a pedal point
The "establishment-departure-return"
    tonal paradigm

Worksheet 18

EXERCISE 18.1   Analysis.

1. Refer to anthology, no. 25 (Mozart, Sonata in CM, I).

   a) What two degrees are tonicized in mm. 13–14? Provide Roman numerals (RNs) for each secondary chord and its resolution in each measure.

   b) The key beginning in m. 35 is GM. In this key, what is the secondary chord in m. 50, and how does it resolve?

   c) Think of mm. 73–74 as a secondary key area of vi, or Am. *In this key*, provide RNs for the tonicization in m. 74.

   d) The key in mm. 103–108 is Cm. Provide RNs for the complete passage. Be careful to identify all nonchord tones: The harmonic rhythm is a chord per measure.

> ♪♪♪ Example 18.17   M. Szymanowska, Nocturne in B♭M, mm. 27–31

2. Identify with RNs all the tonicizations and secondary functions in the following examples.

   a) Anthology, no. 31 (Paradis, *Sicilienne*), mm. 19–23.

   b) Example 18.17.

   c) Example 18.18.

     1) What happens to the mode after m. 32?

     2) Label the tonicizations in the following measures:

      Mm. 30–31:

      Mm. 34–35:

      Mm. 35–36 (Can this be a secondary key area? Why?):

      Mm. 38–39:

     3) What familiar progression can you identify in mm. 36–37? Comment on the voice leading required in this particular type of progression, and verify it in these measures.

   d) Example 18.19.

   What is the harmonic function of this complete passage (notice especially the bass)?

Example 18.18   Carl Friedrich Zelter, "Abschied," mm. 28–39

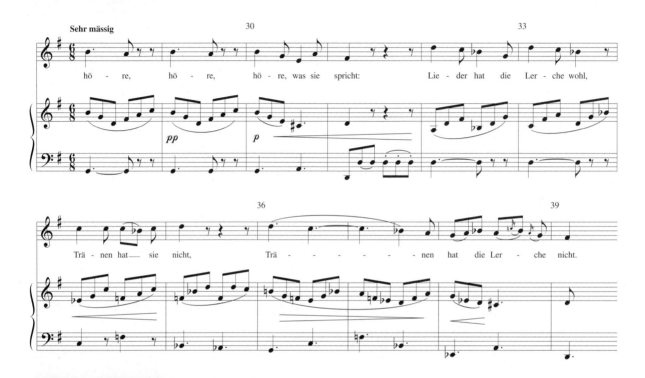

Example 18.19   J. S. Bach, Prelude no. 3 in C♯M, from *The Well-Tempered Clavier* I, mm. 87–104

EXERCISE 18.2   Write the following secondary diminished seventh chords in four voices.

FM: vii°₇/V   Cm: vii°₇/III   GM: vii°₇/IV   Gm: vii°₇/ii   Bm: vii°⁴₃/iv   A♭M: vii°⁴₂/IV   B♭M: vii°⁶₅/V   C♯m: vii°⁴₂/V

E♭M: vii°⁴₃/vi   DM: vii°⁶₅/ii   F♯m: vii°⁴₃/III   D♭M: vii°⁴₂/vi   Am: vii°⁶₅/iv   Em: vii°⁴₃/III   Dm: vii°⁴₂/V

EXERCISE 18.3 Realize the following short progressions in four voices, and provide RNs where needed.

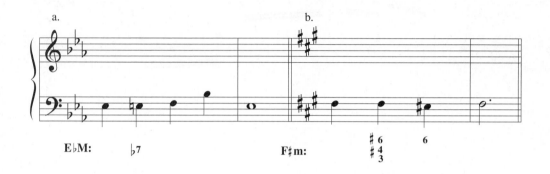

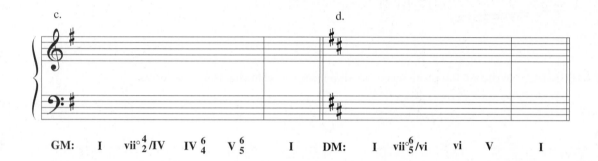

GM: I   vii°$^4_2$/IV   IV$^6_4$ V$^6_5$ I   DM: I   vii°$^6_5$/vi   vi   V   I

EXERCISE 18.4 Write the correct RNs for the following figured basses.

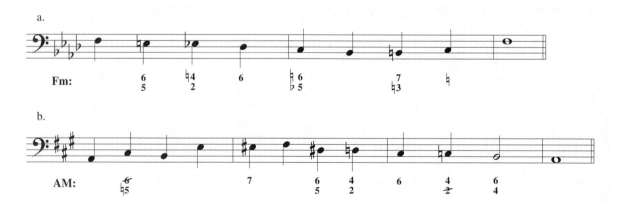

EXERCISE 18.5   Realize the following progression in four voices. Double-check your outer-voice frame for good counterpoint.

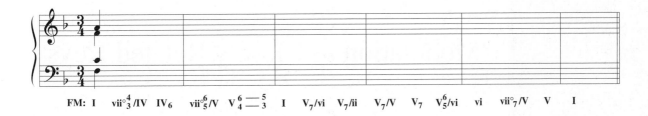

EXERCISE 18.6   Harmonize the following melody (based on Bach's Chorale "O grosser Gott von Macht") in four voices, in chorale style. The melody allows for various tonicizations, some of which are indicated under the staff. Use some kind of a secondary chord (a secondary dominant or, where possible, a secondary diminished seventh) to harmonize the indicated pitches.

Chapter 19

Modulation to Closely Related Keys

So far we have studied only music that stays in the same key. Because the change of key center in a secondary key area is only momentary, it does not really displace the main key center of the passage. Complete pieces, however, rarely remain in the same key. Changing the key center within a composition provides tonal variety to the music, and often is a major element in long-range formal designs. The process of moving from one key center to another is known as **modulation**. In chapters 20 and 26 we will see that in formal types such as binary, sonata form, and rondo, large-scale tonal plans (achieved by means of modulation) are essential to the definition of form. And in chapter 21 we will study that in contrapuntal genres such as the invention and the fugue, modulation is a fundamental component in the processes of formal growth and development.

It should be stressed that modulation implies a change of key center. A **change of mode** between parallel keys, as between CM and Cm, is not considered a modulation, because the key center does not change (C in both cases). We should also note that the exact difference between a secondary key area and a modulation is not always clear. In general, a modulation will take place if the new key is clearly established by a complete predominant-dominant-tonic progression, and preferably if it is confirmed unequivocally by means of an authentic cadence. These factors of tonal confirmation create a clear sense of a new key, as opposed to secondary key areas, where the presence of the main key is still felt. In this chapter we will study some of the most frequent techniques used by composers in modulations among *closely related keys*.

KEY RELATIONSHIPS: CLOSELY RELATED KEYS

Motion from one key to another is often accomplished in a smooth way, by means of a variety of techniques that make the key change as musically and perceptually logical as possible. A smooth modulation will be easier to accomplish if the scales of the keys involved are very similar in pitch content. The most similar scales occur between keys that either have the same key signature (such as CM and Am, the relative major/minor relationship), or the key signatures do not differ by more than one accidental (such as CM and GM/Em, a one-sharp difference, or CM and FM/Dm, a one-flat difference). Groups of keys whose signatures do not differ by more that one accidental are **closely related**. **Distantly related keys**, on the other hand, feature key signatures that differ by more than one accidental, such as CM and EM, A♭M, or C♯m.

The five keys that are closely related to any given key are its relative M/m key, those adjacent above and below this key in the circle of fifths, and their respective relative M/m keys, as illustrated in example 19.1. Thus, the keys closely related to DM are its relative minor Bm, AM (a fifth above D) and its relative minor F♯m, and GM (a fifth below D) and its relative minor Em. The same system applies to minor keys: The keys closely related to Dm are its relative major FM, Am (a fifth above D) and its relative major CM, and Gm (a fifth below D) and its relative major B♭M. Verify all these rela-

♪♪♪ Example 19.1

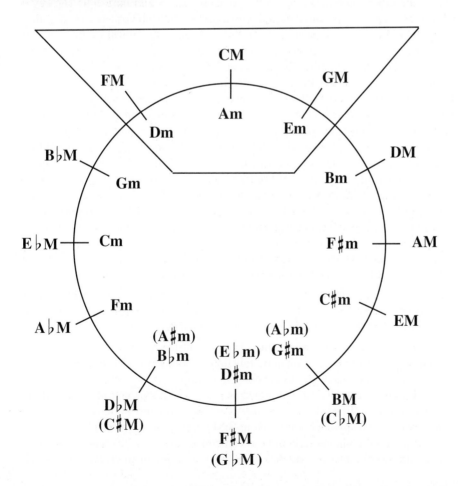

tionships in the circle of keys reproduced in example 19.1. From a different perspective, notice also that the closely related keys are those whose tonic triad is one of the diatonic major or minor triads within the original key. In CM, for instance, the closely related keys are Dm, Em, FM, GM, and Am, corresponding with all the major or minor triads that result from the CM scale.

EXERCISE

To practice determining the set of closely related keys for a given key, refer to exercise 19.2 in worksheet 19 at the end of this chapter.

DIATONIC PIVOT CHORD MODULATION

Examine now example 19.2. Analyze the first four measures with Roman numerals (RNs), and you will see that the key of B♭M is clearly established by means of a standard diatonic progression that leads to the authentic cadence in mm. 3–4. The key is confirmed at the end of the initial period with a perfect authentic cadence (PAC) (mm. 9–10). The beginning of the new phrase in m. 11 is almost identical to m. 1. In mm. 12–13, however, we find an extended V_7 in FM, which indeed resolves to I in m. 14. The following measures confirm the new key, FM, by means of a series of V_2^4–I_6 progressions. The key center has thus changed from B♭ to F. The modulation from B♭M to FM, however, has been effected very smoothly and in a musically natural way. If you examine mm. 11–12, you will notice that we hear the first chord in m. 11 clearly as I in B♭M. In m. 12, however, we hear that a resolution to FM is coming, not only because of the clear V_7, but also because of the melodically striking E♮ (compare it with the equivalent E♭ in m. 2). How does the chord in between (m. 11, beats 1–2) function? In m. 1 we heard exactly the same chord functioning as vi_6 in B♭, and this is how it functions also in m. 11. In retrospect, however, we also hear this same chord as ii_6, moving on to V_7, in FM. The chord then has a double function, serving as a **diatonic pivot chord** between the two keys, that is, *a chord that has a diatonic function in both of the keys for which it acts as a connection.*

The modulation which we have just studied is a *diatonic pivot chord modulation*, and it contains all the elements of a correct, smooth modulation:

1. *The first key* is established harmonically with a progression that includes a V–I, and is preferably confirmed by an authentic cadence (notice that a key is not really established unless there is a V–I progression which defines it unequivocally).

2. *A diatonic pivot chord* connects the old key with the new key. A diatonic pivot chord is a chord that has a diatonic function in both keys. Modulations often involve more than one single pivot chord. In example 19.2, for instance, the initial B♭M I in m. 11 can also be interpreted as a IV in FM, thus providing us with the perfectly standard progression IV–ii_6–V_7 in FM. Measure 11 thus actually contains two diatonic pivot chords (I–vi_6 in B♭M become IV–ii_6 in FM).

Any chord common to both keys can conceivably be a diatonic pivot chord. The best chords, however, are those that function as *predominants in the new key,*

Example 19.2   W. A. Mozart, Piano Sonata in B♭M, K. 333, I, mm. 1–16

because they can be naturally followed by the new dominant. The dominant of the old key, on the other hand, is a possible pivot chord, *but it is not normally a good one*, because it requires resolution to the tonic of the old key, and resolving it otherwise usually breaks the functional logic of the harmonic phrase.

The double function of pivot chords will be indicated visually by means of a "bracket" (as indicated in both examples 19.2 and 19.3) which allows for the notation of both its old and its new functions.

3. *The new key* is itself established harmonically with a progression including V–I and is confirmed by further progressions or preferably by an authentic cadence.

All the above elements are clearly summarized in the modulating progression in example 19.3. (In our schematic examples of modulations in this and other chapters, keys will be minimally established by means of a simple progression.) Observe that in this example we could also label two diatonic pivot chords: I–vi$_6$ in AM become IV–ii$_6$ in EM.

EXERCISE

To practice determining the pivot function of a chord between two keys, refer to exercise 19.3 in worksheet 19 at the end of this chapter.

Determining the Diatonic Pivot Chord

The process we have followed to analyze the Mozart modulation shows you the way to determine a diatonic pivot chord:

1. Find the first chord which clearly indicates that we are moving to a new key (in the Mozart example, the V$_7$ in m.12). Typically (although not always), this "first chord" in the new key will contain an accidental.

2. Look at the chord immediately before this clear sign of a new key, and read it in both the old key and the new key. If you find more than one chord that can be read in both keys, you may interpret them as a pivot group.

♪♪♪ Example 19.3

AM: I   vi$_6$ ii$_5^6$ V$_7$ I   vi$_6$

EM: ii$_6$ V   I   vi   ii$_6$ V$_7$ I

3. In other words, the best way to determine the pivot chord is to analyze the passage from the beginning (in this case in B♭M) and from the end (in FM) at the same time, and see where the two keys "meet" by means of a common element that acts as a diatonic pivot. In our discussion, the "meeting point" turned out to be clearly the second chord of m. 11, or also possibly all of m. 11. We will practice this process many times in the course of this chapter.

MODULATION TO V

We will refer to keys by the Roman numeral that represents their relationship to the original key. Thus the modulation to the key of the dominant (from CM or Cm to GM) will be "to V," or also I→V. A modulation from a major key to its relative minor (CM to Am) will be I→vi, and from a minor key to its relative major i→III. The supertonic key is ii, and a modulation to this key from a major key (CM to Dm) will be I to ii, or I→ii. And so on.

I to V

The most common modulation from a major key is to the key of the dominant, V. This is the modulation which we already discussed in example 19.2. Refer now to example 19.4. E♭M is established in mm. 6–9, and the fragment ends on a PAC in B♭M. In m. 9 we hear the E♭ chord as I in E♭M, but in m. 10–11 two dominant-tonic progressions in B♭M leave little doubt we are modulating to V, as the cadence in mm. 12–13 confirms. What are the exact Roman numerals for the chords that establish B♭M in mm. 10–11? Notice that the resolution to I in m. 11 is preceded by a triple nonchord tone sonority in the right hand, beats 1 and 2, creating an "appoggiatura chord," a "chord of nonchord tones (NCTs)" that resolves in beat 3. Explain each of the three pitches as individual NCTs.

Because m. 9 is I in E♭M, and m. 10 already establishes B♭M, the only possible chord that may be interpreted as a diatonic pivot chord is precisely the E♭ chord in m. 9, which will be I in E♭M and IV in B♭M. This is a common pivot chord in the modulation from I to V, allowing for a very direct and quick switch of tonal center. Study this type of modulation as shown, in chorale style, in example 19.5.

In order to understand the possible diatonic pivot chords between two keys that hold a I–V relationship, you can imagine the triads in both CM and GM. By comparing their pitch content you can determine which triads are common to both keys.

Triad on	C	D	E	F (F♯)	G	A	B
CM	**I**	ii	**iii**	IV	**V**	**vi**	vii°
GM	**IV**	*V*	**vi**	*vii°*	**I**	**ii**	*iii*

The triads that include an F♯ in GM (V, vii°, and iii) are not found in CM, and they are indicated in italics in the above chart. These three triads are not possible pivot chords because they are not common to both keys. The remaining four triads (in bold

Example 19.4   C. Schumann, "Ich stand in dunklen Träumen," mm. 6–13

I stood in dark dreams and gazed at her portrait,
And the beloved features mysteriously came to life.

face), on the other hand, are common to both keys. Because V in the original key is not usually the best pivot (it calls for a resolution to the original tonic), the preferable pivot chords are then I/IV, iii/vi, and vi/ii, all of which can function as predominants in the new key.

EXERCISE

To practice analyzing a modulation to V from a given modulating bass line, refer to exercise 19.4a in worksheet 19 at the end of this chapter.

♪♪♪Example 19.5

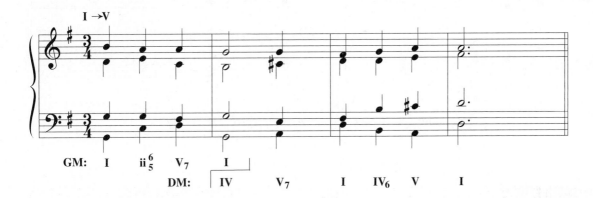

Modulating from V Back to I

After having modulated from I to V, say CM to GM, sooner or later the music is likely to return to the original "home key" by means of a V to I modulation, GM to CM, that is, up a P4. Refer to anthology, no. 28 (Mozart, Piano Sonata in B♭M, III). The movement is in B♭M. The section beginning in m. 24 and ending with a PAC in mm. 35–36, however, is in FM, the key of V. First, discuss in class the modulation from B♭M to FM, in mm. 20–21. Although you can explain it as a pivot chord modulation, you will notice that, in m. 20, the element that leads our ear toward FM is not so much a pivot chord process as a single, unaccompanied pitch. The *melodic introduction of the leading tone in the new key* is sometimes a sufficiently strong factor to support a modulation.

Beginning in m. 41 of this same example you will see that there is a return of the original material, again in B♭M, although just a few measures earlier the previous section closed on a strong PAC in FM. How did we go back to the "home key"? If you disregard the series of ornamental chromatic passing tones in mm. 37–38, all that happens from m. 36 (I in FM) to m. 39 is that the pitch E♭ is added to the FM triad, turning it into V_7 of B♭M. Because in the modulation V→I the tonic in the original key is the same chord as the dominant in the new key, this is the most commonly (and effectively) used diatonic pivot chord for this modulation, as summarized in example 19.6.

The modulation from I to V and back is one of the fundamental long-range tonal plans in Classical period formal designs, which we discuss in chapters 20 and 26. But it can also be found, in a condensed form, in the beginning of tonal fugues. A **fugue** is a contrapuntal (that is, polyphonic) genre in which a **subject** is stated in the tonic key, then imitated (literally or slightly varied) a fifth above and leading to the key of the dominant (**answer**), then stated again, back in the original tonal level and in the tonic key, in a third voice (the process may go on similarly if there are more voices).

The subject in Bach's Fugue in B♭M (example 19.7) is stated by the soprano voice in mm. 1–5. In m. 5, the alto begins the answer. Measure 5 is still in B♭M, but in m. 6 the answer leads toward FM by introduction of the E♮ (♯$\hat{4}$ in the original key). How does this pivot chord modulation work? The answer continues in FM until the subject

♪♪♪ Example 19.6

V → I

DM: I   ii₆   V⁶₅/V   V | I |
                    GM: | V ——— 7   I   V⁴₃/vi   vi   V₇   I

♪♪♪ Example 19.7   J. S. Bach, Fugue 21 in B♭M, from *The Well-Tempered Clavier*, I, mm. 1–13

Subject

B♭M:

Answer

to FM:

Subject

to B♭M:

comes in again in the bass, in m. 9, at the original tonal level. What we first hear, in m. 9, as I in FM, immediately becomes V_7 in B♭M by the introduction of the E♭ ($♭\hat{7}$ in FM). The return to the original key is confirmed in the following measures.

These initial measures of Bach's fugue thus summarize the process of modulation from I to V and return to I. As you can observe in this passage, the essential pitch, from a melodic point of view, in the modulation from I to V is $♯\hat{4}$, the leading tone in the new key. In the modulation from V back to I, the essential pitch is $♭\hat{7}$ in the key of V, which becomes the seventh of V_7 in the tonic key.

NOTE

It is interesting to observe that the modulation from the tonic directly to the subdominant key (I to IV) is quite unusual. If you think of it, however, as a modulation a P4 up, the relationship between keys is the same as in V back to I (a P4 up). In both cases (I to IV and V to I) the tonic in the first key is the same as the dominant in the second key. Practice writing or playing a modulation from GM (I) to CM (IV) using I in GM as the pivot chord.

Modulation to v in Minor Keys

In minor keys, modulations to the dominant are usually to *minor* v, instead of V. The initial measures of Bach's Fugue 16 in Gm appear in example 19.8. Analyze the modulations in the passage and discuss them in class in a way similar to what we have just done with the B♭M fugue.

♩♪♪ Example 19.8   J. S. Bach, Fugue 16 in Gm, from *The Well-Tempered Clavier*, I, mm. 1–6

MODULATION TO THE RELATIVE MAJOR AND MINOR KEYS

The most common modulation from a minor key is not to the key of the dominant, but rather to the relative major key, i to III. Because these two keys share the same scale, with the only exception of the raised $\hat{7}$ (the leading tone) in harmonic minor, the possible diatonic pivot chords are many, and the modulation is easily effected. The chart below illustrates the triad relationships in CM and Am, indicating the possible diatonic pivot chords in bold face.

Triad on	C	D	E	F	G(G♯)	A	B
CM	**I**	**ii**	iii	**IV**	V	**vi**	**vii°**
Am	**III**	**iv**	*V*	**VI**	*vii°*	**i**	**ii°**

The only triads in this chart that do not qualify as diatonic pivots are those in Am which include a G♯, that is, V and vii°. Otherwise, all the remaining triads can be used in the modulation between these keys. Example 19.9 illustrates several of these modulations schematically. Play or sing these modulations in class, and hear the different double functions of the various pivot chords.

i to III

Example 19.10 shows how simple and direct the modulation from i to III can be. The first phrase establishes Bm and cadences in this key in m. 5. This same tonic chord is immediately reinterpreted as vi in the relative major, DM, and used as a predominant moving to V₇ of DM in mm. 6–7. Notice that to make the modulation even smoother, Haydn reharmonizes the same melodic passage: The motive in the first violin in mm. 2–3 is harmonized with a predominant chord in Bm, and its repetition in mm. 6–7 appears over V₇ in the new key, DM. Refer to anthology, no. 11 (Bach, French Suite no. 3, Minuet), and study the modulation between these same two keys, Bm and DM, in mm. 1–16. Reading the music from the beginning, in Bm, you will find that the last clear sign of this key is the progression in mm. 12–13. Reading from the end, in DM, we see that the key is established in the last three measures of the passage, beginning with the V in m. 14. What is, then, the diatonic pivot chord, and how does it function in both keys?

EXERCISE

To practice writing a modulation from i to III from given Roman numerals, refer to exercises 19.4b and 19.6 in worksheet 19 at the end of this chapter.

I to vi

The modulation from a major key to its relative minor, or I to vi, can use any of the same pivot chords we indicated in the chart above. The passage by Schubert reproduced in example 19.11 begins in FM and ends in Dm (the song as a whole is in Am). Measure 51 features the last FM tonic, while the cadence in Dm first appears in mm. 55–56. The two chords in between can be analyzed as diatonic pivot chords.

Example 19.10   J. Haydn, String Quartet, op. 64, no. 2, Menuetto, mm. 1–14

Example 19.11   F. Schubert, "Am Feierabend," from *Die schöne Müllerin*, mm. 45–59

What are the functions of these chords in each of the keys? Now look at the relationship between this modulation and the text. The boy speaking is a worker at a mill, sitting with his fellow workers in the quiet evening hour of leisure in the presence of the miller and the lovely millermaid. The translation of the text is as follows: "And the master speaks to all: your work has pleased me. And the maiden, my delight, wishes all a good night." How is the master represented tonally? What are the characteristics and register of the master's melody? Compare all of these with the music depicting the millermaid: How is the text reflected in the key, the harmonic progression, the melody, and the register? (The second chord in m. 56, ♭II₆, is a type of chromatic predominant chord known as the "Neapolitan sixth," which we will study in chapter 23.)

WRITING PIVOT CHORD MODULATIONS

We will now practice writing modulating progressions using diatonic pivot chords. We will write these progressions in the usual form of a bass line with Roman numerals, following this procedure:

1. Write a progression in the original key, using any of the chords you have learned so far, including secondary dominant functions. The progression should establish the key by means of at least one predominant-dominant-tonic chordal unit.

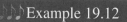Example 19.12

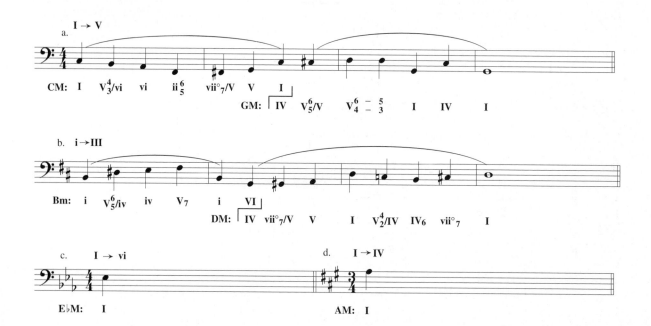

2. Think of a possible chord common to both keys which you may use as a diatonic pivot in the modulation. Write the chord, and provide its double interpretation by means of the usual pivot symbol.

3. Write a progression in the new key. Establish the key immediately. Ideally, your pivot will act as predominant in the new key and will lead to a dominant-tonic progression. Once the key is thus established, continue the progression as you wish, and close with an authentic cadence (or perhaps a plagal cadence) which confirms the new key.

Study (and play if possible) the modulating progressions proposed in example 19.12. Then write a couple of modulating progressions in the spaces provided, using the keys indicated in each case.

EXERCISE

To practice writing your own diatonic pivot-chord modulations, refer to exercises 19.7a and 19.7b in worksheet 19 at the end of this chapter.

MODULATIONS TO ii AND iii FROM A MAJOR KEY

Modulations from a major key to the submediant and mediant keys are not quite as frequent as those we have studied so far, because they do not have the structural, form-defining role of modulations to V or to the relative major. They both can be effected by means of pivot chords, although in the case of I→ii only two common chords are available. Between CM and Dm, for instance, ii in CM is the same as i in Dm, and IV in CM the same as III in Dm. More possible diatonic pivot chords are available between the keys of I and iii. As an exercise, figure out all the possible diatonic pivot chords in a modulation from CM to Em. Then refer to anthology, no. 59 (Amy Beach, *Ecstasy*), mm. 5–12. In spite of the numerous embellishing nonchord tones in the passage, the chordal harmony is quite simple: E♭M is established in mm. 5–8, and the last three measures of the passage (10–12) are an authentic cadence in Gm, the mediant key. What is the function of the intervening Cm chord in m. 9?

CHROMATIC MODULATION

Chromatic Pivot Chords

More often, however, modulations to ii or iii are of the type known as chromatic. Consider, for instance, the modulation from FM to Gm in example 19.13. Measure 17 begins on an FM tonic chord, which is not a possible diatonic pivot with Gm. The introduction of the pitch F♯, ♯$\hat{2}$, in the outer voices, and its subsequent resolution to the Gm tonic chord in the next measure announce the modulation to ii, confirmed by the repetition of the cadence. From a voice-leading point of view, the modulation proceeds by melodic chromatic motion: the F in m. 17 becomes F♯, the leading tone in the new key, leading to G. From a harmonic point of view, there is no diatonic pivot chord in this modulation. We can speak, however, of a **chromatic pivot chord**. This is a

♪♪♪Example 19.13   J. S. Bach, Fugue 21 in B♭M, from *The Well-Tempered Clavier*, I, mm. 13–19

FM: V₇   I   V⁶₅/ii

Gm: V⁶₅ ——— i

chord that is chromatic (such as a secondary dominant) in one, or both, of the keys. In our example, the chord in beats 3–4 of m. 17, which includes the chromatic F♯, is chromatic in FM (V⁶₅/ii) and diatonic in Gm (V⁶₅). In other words, we first hear the dominant of the new key, Gm, as a secondary dominant, and only after that do we realize that it is actually a modulation. This modulation, then, is achieved by means of both, chromatic voice leading (F to F♯), and a chromatic pivot chord.

A **chromatic modulation** to a closely related key is one in which one or both of the following conditions apply:

1. The main modulating procedure is ascending linear chromatic motion in at least one voice, which normally introduces the leading tone of the new key.

2. The pivot chord is not diatonic in both keys. It is frequently a secondary dominant or diminished seventh chord in the first key, while being the diatonic (primary) dominant or diminished seventh chord in the new key (the dominant of the new key is first introduced as if it were a secondary dominant in the original key, but then the new key is confirmed).

Some possibilities of chromatic modulations are schematically illustrated in example 19.14.

a. I → ii

CM: I   ii⁶₅   V⁸⁻⁷₆⁻⁵₄⁻³   I   V⁶₅/ii
                                    Dm: V⁶₅   i   VI   iv   V₇   i

b. I → ii

I   ii⁶₅   V⁶₄⁻⁵³   I   V₇/ii
                           Dm: V₇   i   ii°⁶₅   V⁶₄⁻⁵³   i

c. I → iii

CM: I – 6   ii⁶₅   V₇   I   IV   ii   V⁶₅/iii
                                    Em: V⁶₅   i   ii°⁶   V⁶₄⁻⁵³   i

d. I → iii

I – 6   ii₇   V₇   I – 6   ii⁶₅ vii°⁶₅/iii
                              Em: vii°⁶₅   i₆   iv   V⁶₄⁻⁵³   i

Chromatic modulations are not exclusive to tonal motions to the keys of iii or ii. The modulation to V is often effected chromatically (can you figure out and explain a possible chromatic modulation from I to V?). In example 19.15a, moreover, you may analyze a modulation from GM to its relative minor, Em, which includes not only chromatic voice leading, but also a chromatic pivot chord. GM is established in m. 4. What linear chromatic motion leads to Em in the next measure? The chord in m. 5, beat 1, is diatonic in GM (What is its function?), but not in Em. The second chord, on the other hand, is diatonic in Em, but not in GM. No diatonic pivot is present in this modulation. What is the chromatic function of this second chord (on the bass pitch B) in GM? Notice that this function, however, does not account for the nonfunctional succession between these two chords. Only voice leading and chromatic linear motion can really explain this modulating progression.

A curious case of chromatic-pivot modulation appears in example 19.15b. In principle, in a simple diatonic modulation from Gm to its relative major, BbM, i in Gm could become vi in BbM. Our example's opening phrase ends on a Gm tonic chord in m. 4, which could conceivably function as such a pivot. Because of the strong Gm bass motion in this measure (G–D–E♮–F♯), however, we do not hear this chord as a pivot leading toward BbM. The first chord we hear moving toward the new key (in m. 5), hence as a likely pivot chord, is actually a chromatic chord (a secondary dominant) in both keys. No diatonic pivot chord between Gm and BbM is present in this modulation, which is thus a chromatic pivot chord modulation.

♪♪♪ Example 19.15a   J. S. Bach, Chorale 167, "Du grosser Schmerzensmann," mm. 3–8

Example 19.15b   Irving Mills–D. Ellington, "It Don't Mean a Thing (If It Ain't Got That Swing)" (Refrain)

EXERCISE

To practice analyzing a chromatic modulation from a given modulating bass line, refer to exercise 19.5 in worksheet 19 at the end of this chapter.

WRITING CHROMATIC MODULATIONS

The following steps to write chromatic modulations to ii and iii are illustrated by the progressions in example 19.14. After you study these examples, practice writing your own chromatic modulations from a major key to the keys of ii and iii.

1. First establish the original key in the usual way.

2. Write a chromatic motion in the bass introducing the new leading tone. If you want to modulate to ii, the bass may move directly from $\hat{1}$ to $\sharp\hat{1}$, and on to $\hat{2}$

(example 19.14a). If the modulation is to iii, the bass should not move, of course, from $\hat{1}$ to #$\hat{2}$ (an augmented second). A bass motion $\hat{1}$–$\hat{4}$–$\hat{2}$–#$\hat{2}$–$\hat{3}$, for instance, allows for a good harmonization which will also produce another chromatic motion ($\hat{4}$–#$\hat{4}$) in an upper voice, besides the bass's $\hat{2}$–#$\hat{2}$: I–IV–ii–V$^6_5$/iii–iii, and on to confirm the key of iii. You may also use the $\hat{4}$–#$\hat{4}$ chromatic motion in the bass for this modulation, and then $\hat{2}$–#$\hat{2}$ will be in an upper voice (examples 19.14c–d). In any case, you will need to provide the appropriate Roman numerals for your chromatic bass.

3. If you do not want to write the chromatic motion in the bass, just introduce the dominant of the new key in root position first as a secondary dominant in the original key, and do not return to the original key, but move on to confirm the modulation (example 19.14b).

4. Finally, confirm the new key with a good progression and a cadence.

EXERCISE

To practice writing your own chromatic modulation, refer to exercise 19.7c in worksheet 19 at the end of this chapter.

MODULATION TO VII IN MINOR

VII in a minor key is a closely related key (as in Am to GM, the reverse relationship from between I and ii). This modulation is found occasionally, and it can be easily achieved simply by using the tonic in the original key as a diatonic pivot, reinterpreted as ii in the new key. Identify this exact process in the modulation from Gm to FM featured in example 19.16. Notice how Bach leads the bass from $\hat{1}$ down to a raised $\hat{6}$, which becomes the leading tone for the new key, harmonized as V$_6$/VII. Can you think of a good chromatic modulation from i to VII? (Hint: Start the chromatic modulation from iv or iv$_6$ in the original key.)

♪♪♪Example 19.16   J. S. Bach, Chorale 297, "Jesu, der du meine Seele," mm. 7–10

MODULATION AND PHRASE STRUCTURE: SEQUENTIAL AND PHRASE MODULATION; MODULATING PERIODS

Modulations have a primary role in formal processes. Long-range tonal designs are realized by means of modulatory processes that provide tonal direction to complete movements. In the next chapter we will study some formal paradigms and we will see that they are closely associated with long-range tonal schemes. At a more local level, however, tonicization and modulation often have a structural role in generating phrase and period structures, as we will discuss in the following examples.

Sequential Modulation

In a **sequential modulation** or tonicization, the sequence is used as a means to change tonal center. This is often done by stating each sequence segment in a different key, as in the case of Bach's Minuet from French Suite no. 3 (anthology, no. 11). The key in mm. 23–24 is F♯m. In m. 25 an ascending sequence consisting of two segments first tonicizes Em (the key of iv with respect to the home key of the piece, Bm) in mm. 25–26, and then F♯M (the key of V) in mm. 27–28. This tonicized V leads to the return of the tonic key in m. 31. The long-range tonal plan outlined by this sequential passage is thus iv–V–i as key areas, or, in other words, a large authentic cadence at the phrase level, as opposed to the chord level.

Descending melodic sequences, normally accompanied by a circle-of-fifths harmonic sequence, are also a strong modulating procedure at the formal level. A circle of fifths can be used to modulate virtually to any key, depending only on where the composer stops the circle. The circle can thus be used to go from one key to another, and moreover it may also tonicize each of the steps in the process. In example 19.17, a six-measure sequence is used to modulate from Fm to Cm (a modulation which, of course, Bach could have realized with only a couple of chords had he wished to do so). Are any other degrees (that is, pitches) tonicized in the process? Play the melody, and identify its two registral layers as a compound melody (if you need to do so, you may review this concept in chapter 9). Notice the strongly linear character of the passage, and identify some of the long-range lines in both the upper voices and the bass (think in groups of two measures for these long-range linear relationships). Are there any instances of voice exchange?

The well-crafted modulation by Chevalier de Saint–Georges reproduced in example 19.18 is interesting for several reasons. It is a sequential modulation from a minor key to the ♭VII key which, moreover, also benefits from chromatic linear motion in the top voice and from a chromatic pivot chord. Provide a chromatic pivot chord interpretation of the modulation, while understanding its sequential and linear/chromatic characteristics. How are the two upper voices related?

Phrase (or Direct) Modulation; Abrupt Modulation

Not all modulations proceed smoothly by means of a pivot chord. In the type of modulation known as **phrase modulation**, a phrase is in a key, and the next phrase is in a different key, which is presented more or less suddenly. In the passage by Grieg which

♪♪♪Example 19.17   J. S. Bach, French Suite no. 2, Minuet, mm. 15–24

appears in example 19.19, the first period (two phrases, mm. 1–8) is in Bm. The second period, mm. 9–16, is in F♯m, the key of the minor dominant. There is no transition between the keys, but rather the new key is presented suddenly as the new phrase begins in m. 9. This is a phrase modulation. Because in this type of modulation there is no transitional process between the two keys, it is also called **direct modulation**. Refer, for another example, to anthology, no. 32 (Beethoven, Sonata in Fm, op. 2 no. 1, III). The first phrase of the minuet, mm. 1–4, is in Fm. The second phrase (mm. 4–8) restates the same material as the first one, but now in A♭M. The new key in introduced by the new phrase, with no previous preparation.

Both of the above examples of direct modulation involve closely related keys and parallel phrases. Sometimes, however, the keys are not closely related and neither is the thematic material. Composers may wish to introduce a new key in an abrupt way, for tonal surprise, or to provide the music with a strong forward trust by means of tonal contrast. Example 19.20 illustrates this type of **abrupt modulation**, in this case from CM to E♭M, also introducing a new thematic idea along with the new key (m. 10).

Modulating Periods

A **modulating period** is a period which begins and ends in different keys. This type of period is most often found as the first section in binary forms, which we will study in the next chapter. The tonal function of a modulating period is to introduce

Cm:

B♭M:

V₆   I

Andante doloroso

Bm:

F♯m:

Example 19.20   J. Brahms, Symphony no. 4, III, mm. 1–14

and establish the tonic key, and then to move away from it, as part of a long-range formal tonal plan of departure from and return to the tonic key. The usual modulations are to the dominant key in major-mode compositions, and to the relative major in minor-mode pieces, although other modulations are also possible. Modulating periods are often parallel, and the modulation takes place in the second phrase. Such is the case in example 19.21, a period in the minor mode modulating to III. Where exactly does the modulation take place? What type of modulation is it? If it is a pivot chord modulation, identify a possible pivot chord and its double function. Beware that, because the texture is limited to two voices, you may have to imply the complete harmonies.

FURTHER ANALYSIS

Modulatory Processes

Most of the modulations we have seen in this chapter follow the "shortest possible path" between two keys: The modulation usually takes place by means of a single pivot chord or a chromatic alteration. Composers, on the other hand, often choose to modulate using more complex techniques or **modulatory processes**, even when the same modulation could be effected in shorter and easier ways. In this type of modulation several different techniques may be used, or several keys may be tonicized in the process of moving from one key to another. Consider, for instance, example 19.22. This is a modulation to the relative minor key, from DM to Bm, which, as you know, could be easily realized in no more than one measure. Mozart did not settle, however, for an easy solution, and therein lies the beauty of this modulation. The process of moving from DM to Bm takes us through secondary key areas in GM (IV), Em (ii), and DM again, before finally modulating to Bm. Identify each of these tonicizations on the score, and label a pivot chord for each of them.

Modulatory processes are usually found, within large formal types, in sections which have either a *transitional* or a *developmental* formal function (two concepts we studied in chapter 7). The Mozart passage in example 19.22 is, as a matter of fact, a transitional passage between two sections in a *rondo*. We will study modulation in transitional and developmental sections in the context of large formal types (sonata form and rondo) in chapter 26.

You will find several examples of modulating periods in the anthology, some of which we have already mentioned in this chapter, such as anthology, no. 32 (Beethoven, Sonata op. 2 no.1) and no. 11 (Bach, Minuet from French Suite no. 3). Anthology, no. 24 (Mozart, Sonata in DM, III, Tema) is a good example of a parallel period modulating to the dominant key. Analyze the modulation, finding and interpreting the pivot chord.

♪♪♪ Example 19.21   J. S. Bach, English Suite no. 3 in Gm, Gavotte I, mm. 1–8

PRACTICAL APPLICATION AND DISCUSSION

Modulation is one of the most essential harmonic processes in Western tonal music. It provides tonal variety necessary in complete compositions, it provides both a harmonic drive and tonal goals for long-range formal designs, and it contributes to creation of a tension between tonal definition and tonal instability, a basic element in formal generation of large movements. You have played many modulations in your life as a performer, and any of the compositions in your repertoire can illustrate modulating processes in one way or another. Find several of these modulations in pieces you perform, and bring them to class as examples. Specifically, try to find the following cases of modulation:

1. A modulation you especially like, perhaps because it leads from one key to another in an imperceptible, smooth way; or because it is very well crafted and perhaps you had always noticed how beautiful and effective the passage was; or because it is very surprising and you had always been struck by the boldness of harmonic motion in that passage; or for whatever other reason you may have to like it.

2. A modulating period. You may find these in the first section of a binary form (a minuet, a sarabande, or some other dance type).

3. A modulation from I to V or from i to III in the first movement of a sonata.

4. A developmental process based on a variety of modulatory processes.

Once you understand how modulations work, and what their formal function is, does this affect in any way your vision of music as a performer? How? Do modulations help you hear and transmit the principle of musical motion? Think of the tension that a modulatory process creates, and of the sense of arrival and the renewed musical impulse we feel when we reach the new tonic. Does the new tonic come along with new thematic material, further stressing the idea of renewal? How does the process of modulation contribute to the sense of instability and tonal motion in developmental sections? Does the developmental process lead to a return of the tonic key and of the original thematic material, and do we experience a release of tension when that happens?

HARMONIZING MODULATING MELODIES

Modulating melodies often provide sufficient information for a clear harmonization of the modulating passage. Sing the Haydn melody in example 19.23a. You will immediately realize three things: It begins in Cm, it ends in Gm, and m. 6 displays clear signs of the modulation when F♯ and A♮, two pitches from the Gm scale, are introduced. You will also notice that the melody appears to have two four-measure units, and that the end of the first unit can easily be harmonized with a V–i in Cm. In other words, you have followed the first steps in the process to harmonize modulating melodies, which can be summarized as follows:

Procedure to harmonize a modulating melody:

1. Sing and play through the melody. Identify the opening and closing keys. If they are the same, identify any possible inner fragments in a different key.

2. Identification of a new key will ideally be facilitated by some melodic features such as accidentals (perhaps the new LT).

3. Identify possible points of articulation that may indicate cadential gestures (in the original or new key). Write the bass for these cadences.

4. Identify the melodic area that clearly indicates the new key, and find a possible place for your pivot chord right before it.

5. Harmonize the rest of the melody according to the principles of good functional harmonization that you are familiar with.

♪♪♪ Example 19.22   W. A. Mozart, Piano Sonata in DM, K. 311, III, mm. 101–120

Example 19.23   J. Haydn, String Quartet op. 54, no. 2 in CM, II

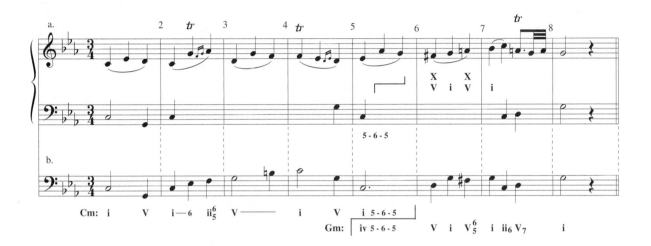

In our example, after we have identified the opening and closing keys, the accidentals that indicate Gm, and the cadential points, we can write the bass for the cadences in mm. 4–5 (on C) and 7–8 (on G). Next, we will harmonize the modulation. In m. 6, already in Gm, the F♯–G–A can be harmonized with some kind of V–i–V progression, and in m. 5 before it, a C in the bass can simply support a 5–6–5 figure. In Cm, m. 5 would then be i_{5-6-5}. Because the next measure is already in Gm, the pivot chord will need to be in m. 5. So the i_{5-6-5} in Cm becomes iv_{5-6-5} in Gm. All of this process is illustrated by the notes in example 19.23a. All that is left now is to complete the harmonization of the melody. A possible complete harmonization, using only bass line and Roman numerals, is shown in example 19.23b.

At times, *melodies do not indicate modulations clearly*, and then we need to use a bit more harmonic imagination to harmonize them. Sing or play the melody in example 19.24a. Our immediate reactions might be: It begins in BM, it cadences on B in m. 4, and the last two measures indicate a cadence in F♯M, so we must have modulated to the dominant key. We write down all of this information, as in example 19.24a. Knowing that it modulates to F♯M, let's go back to mm. 5–6, which in principle could simply be harmonized in BM. Can they also be heard in F♯M? Try it: Harmonize m. 5, beat 3, as a V_7 in F♯, and resolve it to I in m. 6. It works. Then we need a pivot chord. You could use the first chord in m. 5, as V in BM and I in F♯. An even better pivot could be the BM chord in m. 4. A complete harmonization appears in example 19.24b. Notice that the B♯ in m. 6 is interpreted as a chromatic PT, accompanied by another chromatic PT in the opposite direction in the bass.

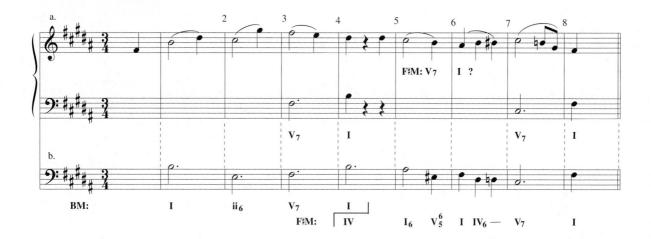

♩♪♪Example 19.24   J. Haydn, String Quartet op. 64, no. 2 in Bm, Trio

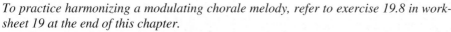

EXERCISES

To practice harmonizing a modulating chorale melody, refer to exercise 19.8 in worksheet 19 at the end of this chapter.

To practice harmonizing modulating periods, refer to exercise 19.10 in worksheet 19 at the end of this chapter.

Multiple Harmonizations of the Same Melody

Of course, there is not a single possible correct harmonization for any melody, let alone a modulating melody. We can verify this by comparing several different harmonizations of the same chorale tune by J. S. Bach. Three different harmonizations of the chorale "Freu' dich sehr, o meine Seele" appear in anthology, no. 10. Example 19.25 presents a summary of these three harmonizations, in the form of bass lines with harmonic beginnings and endings indicated with Roman numerals, and modulations indicated in circles. Play through each of these chorales, listening to the different harmonizations, and following them in example 19.25. Notice that the melody itself does not offer many (or rather, *any*) clear signs of modulations!

1. In Chorale 29, the melody is harmonized essentially in GM throughout, with a single instance of brief tonicization of V at the end of phrase 1.

2. More modulations appear in Chorale 64. The tonicization of V in phrase 1 is more extensive, phrase 5 features a modulation to the relative minor, Em, and phrase 6 tonicizes IV briefly.

♪♪♪ Example 19.25   J. S. Bach, Chorales 29, 64, and 76 ("Freu' dich sehr, o meine Seele")

3. In Chorale 76, on the other hand, Bach exploited all the modulating potential of this melody. Besides the usual modulation to V in phrase 1, phrase 3 now modulates to ii and ends on a half cadence (HC) in Am, and phrase 5 modulates to vi earlier than in Chorale 64. The tonicization in phrase 6 is here of ii rather than IV.

EXERCISES

To practice writing different harmonizations for the same modulating melody, refer to exercise 19.9 in worksheet 19 at the end of this chapter.

To practice analysis of musical fragments including modulations, refer to exercise 19.1 in worksheet 19 at the end of this chapter.

ASSIGNMENT AND KEYBOARD PROGRESSIONS

For analytical and written assignments and keyboard progressions based on the materials learned in this chapter, refer to chapter 19 in the workbook.

 Composers and Their Music 19

Biographies

Write a short biography of the following composer mentioned in this chapter: Duke Ellington.

Listening

Listen to the following compositions by composers mentioned in this chapter:

    Brahms, Symphony no. 2 in DM, op. 73.
    Haydn, String Quartets, op. 64.
    Ellington, "Ko-Ko," "Concerto for Cootie," "It Don't Mean a Thing (If It Ain't Got That Swing)."

Follow the score while you listen. Be able to place each of these compositions in one of the style periods and to comment on why and how it represents the musical characteristics of that period. Try to identify aurally as many modulations as possible. What is their function? Is a specific modulation you heard part of a transitional passage that leads to a new section in a new key, and perhaps also with new thematic material? Or is the modulation part of a developmental section in which a variety of modulations takes place? If so, does this development eventually lead to the return to the tonic key and perhaps also to the original thematic material for this movement?

PITCH PATTERNS

Sing the melodic pitch patterns in example 19.26, and as you sing listen to the modulation in each of the patterns, paying special attention to the "pivot pitch" or pitches, or to the chromatic motion that effects the modulation. Practice improvising similar pitch patterns modulating to different keys.

♪♪♪ Example 19.26

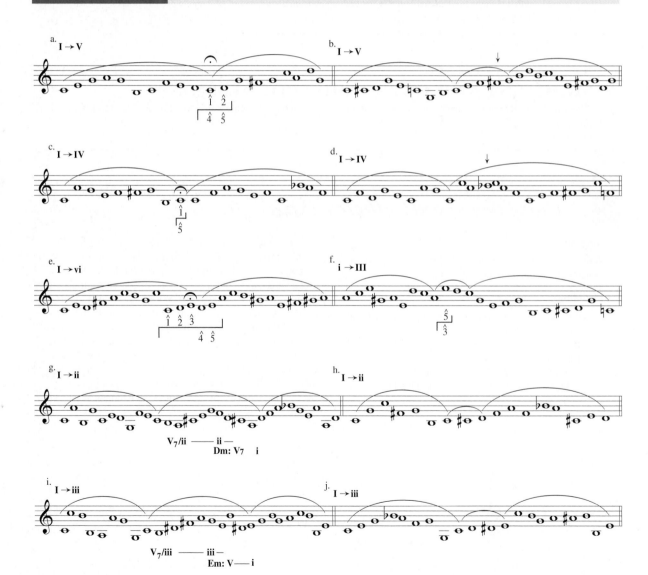

Terms for Review

Modulation
Change of mode
Closely related keys
Distantly related keys
Pivot chord modulation
Diatonic pivot chord
Fugue
Subject

Answer
Chromatic pivot chord
Chromatic modulation
Sequential modulation
Phrase (direct) modulation
Abrupt modulation
Modulating periods
Modulatory processes

Worksheet 19

EXERCISE 19.1   *Analysis.* Study and analyze the modulations in exercises 19.1.1 to 10, and follow the steps listed below for each of them.

1. Identify (and write in the space provided for each exercise) the keys involved in the modulation.

2. Identify (and write in the space provided for each exercise) the modulation procedure from among the following:

   a) Diatonic pivot chord

   b) Chromatic pivot chord

   c) Chromatic modulation

   d) Phrase modulation

   e) Abrupt modulation

   f) Sequential modulation or tonicizations

3. If it is a pivot chord modulation, identify the exact pivot or pivots, and label it or them on the score with the pivot chord bracket notation, indicating the function of the chord in both keys.

4. For a chromatic modulation, circle the exact passage where chromatic voice leading is used to modulate.

5. For phrase, abrupt, or sequential modulations, mark the exact spot or spots where modulation occurs.

Examples for Analysis:

1. Example 19.27.

2. Anthology, no. 32, Beethoven, Sonata in Fm, op. 2, no. 1, Trio, mm. 41–50.

3. Anthology, no. 32, Beethoven, Sonata in Fm, op. 2, no. 1, Trio, mm. 51–66.

4. Example 19.28.

Example 19.27   J. Haydn, String Quartet op. 77, no. 1, Minuet, mm. 1–12

♪♪♪ Example 19.28   C. Schumann, Trio in Gm, I, mm. 22–32

5. Anthology, no. 11, Bach, French Suite no. 3, Minuet, mm. 17–24.

6. Anthology, no. 34, Beethoven, Sonata in Cm, op. 13, III, mm. 16–25.

7. Anthology, no. 31, Paradis, *Sicilienne*, mm. 4–10.

8. Anthology, no. 20, Haydn, Piano Sonata in DM, II, mm. 1–12.

9. Example 19.29.

10. Anthology, no. 47, Schumann, "Ich grolle nicht," mm. 12–16.

♪♪♪ Example 19.29   F. Schubert, Sonata in B♭M, D. 960, I, mm. 113–119

EXERCISE 19.2   Make a list of all five keys closely related to each of the following keys.

1. DM:

2. B♭M:

3. F♯m:

4. Fm:

5. C♯m:

6. D♭M:

EXERCISE 19.3   The following statements refer to diatonic pivot chord relationships. Fill in the blank in each statement.

1. I in DM becomes _____ in AM.
2. _____ in Gm becomes IV in B♭M.
3. I in _____ becomes V in A♭M.
4. iv in Em becomes ii in _____.

EXERCISE 19.4   The following two progressions represent modulations by diatonic pivot chord.

Progression a. Provide RNs for the given bass, accounting for the modulation and indicating the pivot chord with the usual bracket. Use secondary dominants or diminished seventh chords where possible.

Progression b. Write a bass line for the given RNs. Be careful to modulate to the right key.

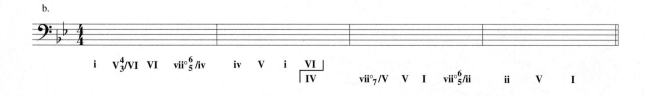

EXERCISE 19.5 The following progression represents a chromatic modulation. Provide RNs for the given bass, accounting for the modulation and indicating the pivot chord with the usual bracket. Use secondary dominants or diminished seventh chords where possible.

EXERCISE 19.6 After you are sure that your bass line for exercise 19.4b is correct, realize the progression in four voices on the staff below.

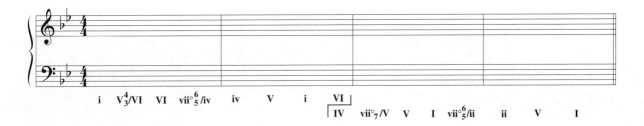

EXERCISE 19.7 Write the following modulations (bass and RNs). Choose an appropriate pivot chord for each of them, and indicate it with the customary bracket.

a. A modulation from AM to EM. Use the following chords somewhere in your progression, along with any other chords you wish: a series of successive secondary dominants, vii°$^6_5$/vi, and vii°$^4_2$/ii.

b. A modulation from Dm to FM. Use the following chords somewhere in your progression: vii°$^4_2$/V, vii°$^6_5$/IV, and an irregular resolution of V$^6_5$.

c. A chromatic modulation from B♭M to Dm, using secondary chords in various inversions in the process of establishing both keys.

EXERCISE 19.8   Harmonize the following chorale ("Warum betrübst du dich, mein Herz") with a bass line and RNs, accounting for possible modulations. After you are sure that your harmonization works, add the two inner voices.

EXERCISE 19.9   Provide two different harmonizations of the following chorale tune. Bass and RNs are sufficient, but as an additional exercise you can also fill in inner voices. The following suggestions will guide you through the different modulations.

Harmonization a

1. Mostly in GM.
2. Both phrases 1 and 2 end on authentic cadences (AC).
3. Phrase 3 modulates, and ends on an AC in the new key.
4. Phrase 4 modulates back to GM, and ends on a HC in a tonicized area (the same key area as phrase 3).
5. Phrase 5: back in GM.

Harmonization b

1. This harmonization will have more modulations than harmonization a.
2. Phrase 1 modulates to the relative minor, and ends on a HC in the new key.
3. Phrase 2 modulates back to GM.
4. Phrase 3 modulates, and ends on an AC in the new key.
5. Phrase 4 modulates back to GM, then modulates to the relative minor, and ends on a HC in the latter key.
6. Phrase 5: back in GM.

EXERCISE 19.10   Write simple keyboard accompaniments for the following modulating periods by Haydn. Provide RNs for your harmonizations, and indicate your pivot chord in each case.

b.   **Molto vivace**

Chapter 20

Small Forms: Binary and Ternary

In chapters 2, 5, and 6 we studied the elements of form. We defined *form* as the tonal, rhythmic, and thematic relationships among musical units or sections, and we saw that *cadences* are a harmonic element of formal articulation. The basic formal units are the *motive*, *phrase segment*, *phrase*, and *period*. We learned to use *form diagrams*, which we called *bubble diagrams*, to express form graphically. Phrase segment relationships in these diagrams are indicated by lowercase letters with subscripts, whereas capital letters indicate thematic relationships between larger formal units.

Throughout part 1 we have also used occasionally a type of graph in which a *bass reduction* illustrates long-range tonal motion (see, especially, chapters 2, 6, and the appendix to part 1). As we will see in this chapter, this type of bass reduction is most useful to diagram tonal motion in a formal context, and it can also be used in association with a bubble diagram to show both tonal motion and thematic relationships.

In this chapter we will study how all of these formal elements come together to shape independent, complete formal units. We will focus on the so-called small formal designs, binary and ternary, as opposed to such larger formal designs as sonata form and rondo, which we will study in chapter 26.

We should emphasize that, because composers have used musical design and formal growth in free and creative ways, the study of form is fraught with difficulties. Even within more or less preestablished formal designs, the possibilities of variations, transformations, or exceptions are multiple. As William Rothstein states after defining ternary form, "however, as so often with matters of form, there are endless complications" (*Phrase Rhythm in Tonal Music*, p. 108). Form being indeed an ambiguous matter, in textbooks dealing with this topic there is no consistency or agreement on the exact terminology and definitions applied to formal types. Having clarified this, we will now attempt to provide as clear a discussion as possible.

♪♪♪Example 20.1

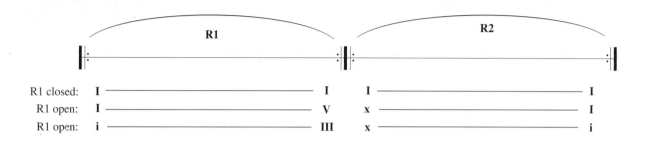

R1 closed:	I	————————————————————	I	I	———————————————————	I
R1 open:	I	————————————————————	V	x	———————————————————	I
R1 open:	i	————————————————————	III	x	———————————————————	i

THE BINARY PRINCIPLE

Binary pieces are structured in two parts, which we will call **reprises**. Binary is one of the most common formal designs in the baroque and Classical periods. In the baroque, the dance types that usually constitute a **suite** (such as **allemande**, **courante**, **minuet**, **bourrée**, **gavotte**, **sarabande**, **gigue**, etc.) were normally in binary form. In the Classical period, the most frequently found case of a piece in binary form is the minuet (and the trio) in sonatas or string quartets. You are quite likely to have performed numerous binary pieces in your musical life.

Each reprise in a binary design (which we will refer to as reprise 1 and reprise 2, abbreviated as R1 and R2) is usually, but not always, repeated. A reprise is **closed**, or harmonically complete, if it ends on the tonic of the main key, and it is **open**, or harmonically incomplete, if it does not. In binary, reprise 1 begins in the tonic key, and it may end on the tonic (closed), on a half cadence (HC) (open), or in a different key (open). Reprise 2 may begin and end in the tonic, or, more often, it begins on a key or harmony other than the tonic, and ends on the tonic. Example 20.1 summarizes all these possibilities for the binary principle, with the "harmony other than the tonic" at the beginning of reprise 2 expressed by means of an "x."

BINARY TONAL TYPES

Because binary pieces, like most tonal pieces, begin and end on the tonic, tonal types are mostly determined by the harmony that closes reprise 1. Refer to anthology, no. 6 (Minuet from *Notebook for Anna Magdalena Bach*). Reprise 1 closes with a perfect authentic cadence (PAC) in the tonic key. This is a binary piece of the **tonic type** (also called "sectional binary" by some authors). As in our minuet, the beginning of reprise 1 in this tonal type is usually a prolongation of the tonic, and the dominant is usually reached toward the middle of reprise 2, leading to a return of the tonic (see the cadence in m. 24 in the minuet, leading to the return of I in m. 25). This tonal type is represented by the bass reduction in example 20.2a.

 Example 20.2   Binary Tonal Types

The Haydn minuet in CM in anthology, no. 19 illustrates another binary tonal type, the **dominant type** (also called "continuous binary" in some texts). Reprise 1 ends on the dominant, in this case on a HC on V, without a modulation. A similar example of the same tonal type appears in anthology, no. 24 (Mozart, Sonata in DM, Tema), only in this case reprise 1 is a modulating period, that is, it ends with a PAC in the key of the dominant. The modulating dominant type does not differ, essentially, from the nonmodulating type. In both cases, reprise 1 is open-ended, and in both cases the beginning of reprise 2 usually prolongs the V which closes reprise 1. This prolongation is extended all the way to the cadence on V toward the middle of reprise 2, before the tonic returns. This tonal type is represented in example 20.2b.

In minor keys, the "dominant type" usually becomes the **relative major type**, that is, the modulation at the end of reprise 1 leads to III rather than V. An example of this type appears in example 20.10. At the end of reprise 1 we have reached the relative-major key, which is prolonged into reprise 2. The return of the tonic key in m. 19 (confirmed in m. 27) is preceded by an arrival on the dominant in m. 14, reiterated in m. 18. In other words, as in the dominant type, in the relative-major type we also reach V toward the middle of reprise 2, before moving back to the tonic. Both the V type and the III type are based on the familiar tonal paradigm, "tonic established/departure from tonic/return to tonic." See the bass reduction for the relative-major type in example 20.2c.

NOTE

As we learned in chapter 2, "white" notes in our bass reductions are used only for the most structurally significant tonal events: the initial tonic, the V that either closes reprise 1 (20.2b) or which leads to the return of the tonic in reprise 2 (examples 20.2a and c), the return of the tonic in reprise 2, and the final cadence; a stemmed "black" note is used in example 20.2c for the cadence on III which, although less significant in the tonal plan than the tonic and the dominant, closes reprise 1; and unstemmed black notes are used for cadences or beginning harmonies that simply prolong previously established tonal areas.

BINARY FORMAL DESIGNS

Different binary formal designs result from various possible thematic relationships between both reprises. In general, however, some formal traits are common to all binary designs:

1. Reprise 2 is often longer (sometimes as much as twice as long or more) than reprise 1.

2. Reprise 1 is usually divided into two phrases (constituting a period), and reprise 2 is itself divided into two sections, each of which can have several phrases. This sectional division is best expressed by the diagram in example 20.3a. We will use the abbreviations R1 and R2 to refer to reprise 1 and reprise 2, respectively, regardless of their thematic content. Lowercase letters will designate thematic relationship at the phrase level.

In our sample paradigms in example 20.3, we will assume that the two phrases in R1 are related thematically (a_1 and a_2), while the first phrase in R2 is contrasting (b), although various other thematic relationships are certainly possible. In general, the first phrase of R2 is the least stable harmonically, and it may have a developmental character both harmonically and thematically. The different binary formal designs are determined by the existence or nonexistence of a *return* of the main thematic material from reprise 1 in the tonic key toward the end of reprise 2, as we will discuss below.

Simple Binary

In the **simple binary** design, there is no return of the main thematic material from reprise 1, at the original tonic level, in the second section of reprise 2. Study example 20.4. This is a brief binary piece, with each reprise clearly delimited by repeat signs. The tonal and thematic structure of this minuet is summarized by the graph in example

Example 20.3 Binary Formal Designs

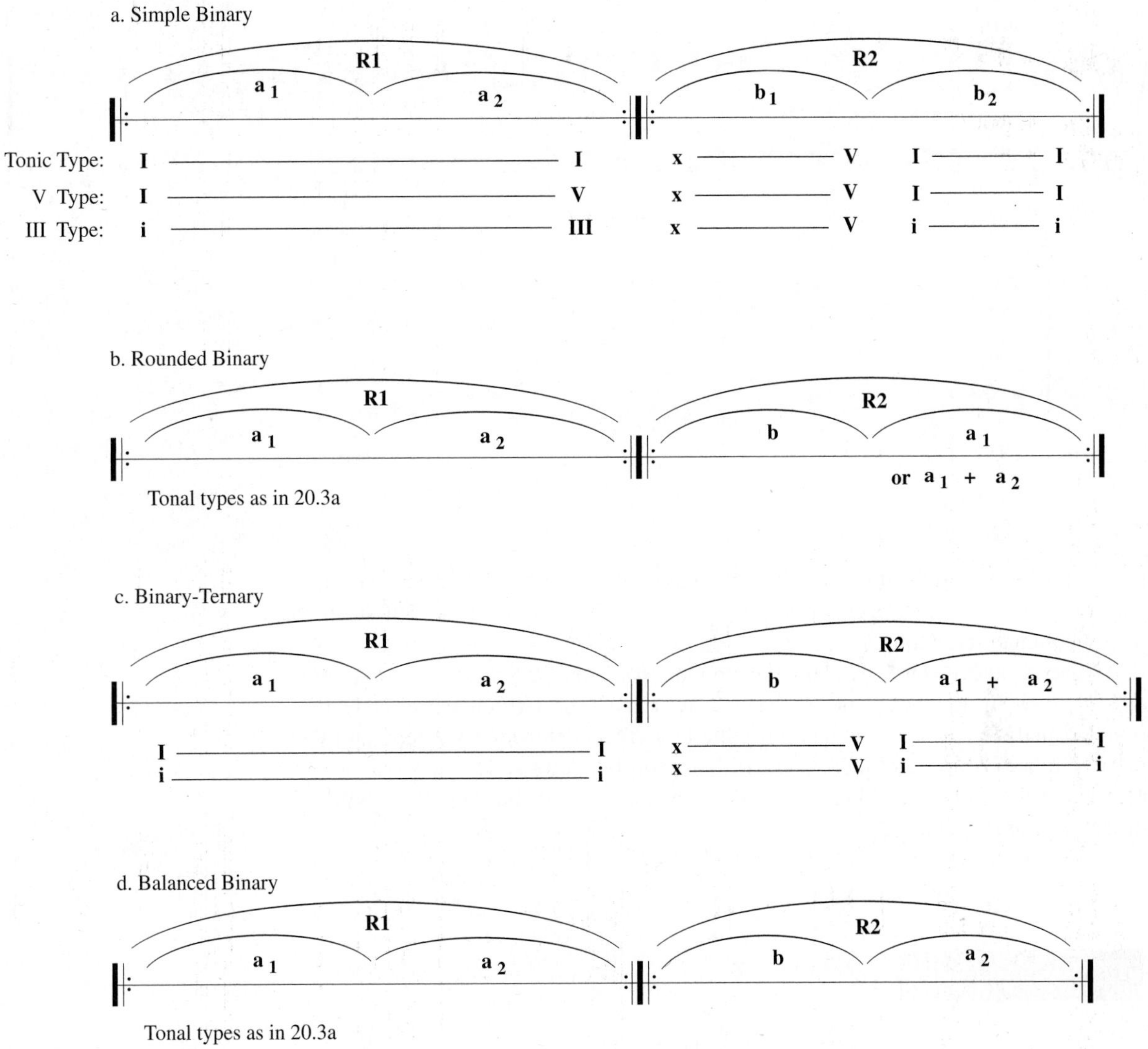

a. Simple Binary
R1
a 1
a 2
R2
b 1
b 2
Tonic Type: I — I x — V I — I
V Type: I — V x — V I — I
III Type: i — III x — V i — i
b. Rounded Binary
R1
a 1
a 2
R2
b
a 1
or a 1 + a 2
Tonal types as in 20.3a
c. Binary-Ternary
R1
a 1
a 2
R2
b
a 1 + a 2
I — I x — V I — I
i — i x — V i — i
d. Balanced Binary
R1
a 1
a 2
R2
b
a 2
Tonal types as in 20.3a

20.5. Because there is no return of thematic material from reprise 1 in the second section of reprise 2 (in m. 13, where the tonic returns), this is a simple binary design. Otherwise, we can observe that the two phrases in R1 are contrasting (designated as a_1 and b). In R2, the first phrase is a varied statement of a_1, but now at the dominant level, hence the designation a_2, whereas the second phrase is based on new, contrasting

♪♪♪Example 20.4   J. Haydn, Piano Sonata in AM, Hob. XVI:5, II, Minuet

material, labeled c in the diagram. From a tonal point of view, R1 moves from I to V. An extension of V in R2 leads to the return of I in m. 13. The piece is, then, in simple binary dominant-type form.

Analyze and discuss in class the minuet from the *Notebook for Anna Magdalena Bach* in anthology, no. 6. Review its tonal type (which we already mentioned), analyze the cadences and possible key areas, determine sections and their motivic relationships, and label them with appropriate letters. Then provide a complete formal graph (including bass reduction and bubble diagram) following the model in example 20.5.

♪♪♪Example 20.5

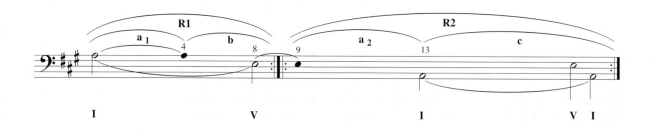

Rounded Binary

The formal design known as **rounded binary** features a return of the initial material from reprise 1 in the second section of reprise 2 (consult the formal diagram in example 20.3b).[1] The return, in the tonic key and at the same tonal level as the original statement, can be of two types. In the first type, the opening section of R1 (a_1 in our diagram) returns as the closing section of R2. In the second type, all of R1 ($a_1 + a_2$) returns as the final section of R2. Let us study two examples to clarify these two formal designs.

The binary piece in example 20.6a is of the dominant type. R1 is an eight-measure modulating period, divided into two phrases (mm. 1–4 and 5–8, featuring an a–b thematic relationship). Considering this relationship between the two phrases, is this a parallel or a contrasting period? R2 begins with a four-measure phrase (thematically contrasting or c) which prolongs the dominant key area established at the end of R1 and confirms it by means of a new cadence on the dominant in m. 12. After the cadence on V in m. 12, we can expect a return of the tonic key, for the second section of R2. What we get is not only the return of DM, but also the return of the opening phrase, a. After three measures of "return" (mm. 13–15), the phrase is extended sequentially and finally closes with a PAC in DM. Why is this second section of R2 ten measures long instead of eight? Where are the two added measures, and what harmonic and formal functions do they have? Study the formal graph in example 20.6b: compare it with the piece and understand the relationship between both.

Refer now to example 20.7. This binary trio has a similar tonal structure to the one we have just discussed. It begins with an eight-measure reprise 1 modulating to the dominant and is also divided into two four-measure phrases with an a–b thematic structure. The first phrase of R2 prolongs the dominant key area for eight measures by means of a contrasting four-measure phrase repeated twice (mm. 9–12 and 13–16), leading to the expected return of the tonic key in the second section of R2. The return brings not only the tonic key (m. 17), but also the complete R1, including both the a and b phrases. The only difference between this return of R1 and the original R1 is that, in the original, the second phrase (mm. 5–8) modulated to V, whereas in the return the equivalent phrase (mm. 21–24) stays in the tonic key to allow for the final PAC on I.

To practice your understanding of rounded binary, analyze two pieces from the anthology: no. 24 (Mozart, Sonata in DM, Tema) and no. 19 (Haydn, Minuet in CM). For each of these, discuss the tonal type (Is R1 a modulating period?), cadences and key areas, divisions into phrases, and relationships among phrases. What

---

[1] Some authors emphasize the ternary (that is, three-part) structure of this type of design, rather than its binary structure. From that point of view, the first reprise is an "exposition," the first section of R2 is a "contrasting middle," and the second section of R2 a "recapitulation." Although in this book we do not adopt this view, the interested student may find it articulated in detail in Caplin, *Classical Form*, pp. 71–86.

♪♪♪ Example 20.6a   J. Haydn, Piano Sonata in DM, Hob. XVI:4, Trio

♪♪♪ Example 20.6b

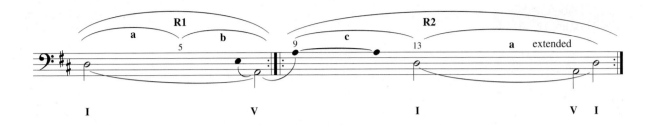

♪♪♪ Example 20.7   L. v. Beethoven, String Quartet op. 18, no. 5, Trio

♪♪♪Example 20.7   (Continued)

is the extent of the return? Does the complete R1 return, or only its first phrase? Finally, realize a complete formal graph for each of these pieces, including a bass reduction and indication of form and phrase relationships by means of a bubble diagram above the staff.

A Special Type of Rounded Binary: The Binary-Ternary Design

As we will see in the next section of this chapter, ternary form is structured in three sections. The most common formal design for ternary is A–B–A, in which the A section, which returns in complete form after the B section, is harmonically closed, and the B section is usually in a contrasting key and may be harmonically open. The formal design we are going to discuss now is unquestionably binary, and it has all the characteristics of a rounded binary design. However, this specific formal and tonal design is also a close approximation to ternary, as if it were "almost ternary, but not quite." We will refer to this design as **binary-ternary**, a hybrid term that reflects the fact that it is really binary, and yet it is made up of three distinct sections that approximate a ternary design.

Examine example 20.8a. You will immediately see that the piece is *tonic-type binary*. At the beginning of R2, a contrasting eight-measure b section leads to the usual cadence on V (m. 16), after which *the complete R1 returns*. These are exactly the conditions for binary-ternary design: *it is a rounded binary, tonic type, and the complete*

♩♪♪Example 20.8a   J. Haydn, Piano Sonata in FM, Hob. XVI:9, III, Scherzo

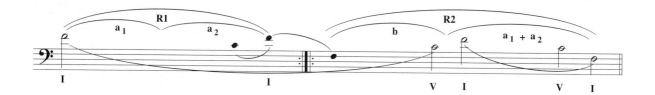

♪♪♪ Example 20.8b

reprise 1 returns. Compare example 20.8b (the formal and tonal graph for the Haydn scherzo) and example 20.3c (the general formal paradigm for binary-ternary) with example 20.10 (the formal and tonal paradigm for ternary) and understand the differences and similarities between binary-ternary and ternary.

Analyze, for an additional example, anthology, no. 19 (Haydn, Trio from Divertimento in CM). What makes this piece an example of binary-ternary form? Analyze cadences, tonal motion, phrases, and sections and their formal relationship, and explain the formal-tonal design.

NOTE

Binary-ternary is not really ternary. It is a special type of rounded binary. It is still in two parts which are repeated (reprises), and the tonal type is typically binary. It simply points toward the ternary characteristics, and that is why we study it as a special subdivision of the rounded binary principle.

The Balanced Binary

In this formal design, what returns in the second section of R2 is neither the opening phrase from R1 nor the complete R1, but rather only *the final phrase of R1*, as expressed in the formal diagram in example 20.3d. A well-known example of the tonic-type balanced binary appears in example 20.9. R1 is an eight-measure parallel period, including a tonicized HC in m. 4, and a PAC on I in m. 8. These two cadences close the two phrases of R1, respectively, which form a parallel period (a_2–a_2). R2 opens with a contrasting b phrase that includes tonicizations of vi and V. (What chords are used to tonicize these degrees, in mm. 9 and 11?) Finally, the closing phrase of R2 (mm. 13–16) turns out to be an almost literal return of a_2, the phrase that previously closed R1. The form is thus "balanced" by this ending phrase common to both R1 and R2, hence the name of this formal design. Notice that in a balanced binary of the dominant or relative major tonal types, in which the final phrase of R1 ends on V or III, the return of this second phrase of R1 at the end of R2 will lead to a cadence in the tonic key, rather than on V or III.

♪♪♪ Example 20.9   W. A. Mozart, *Eine kleine Nachtmusik*, K. 525, III (Menuetto)

FURTHER ANALYSIS

1. An example of extended simple binary

We will first study an example of simple binary more complex than the one we studied earlier in the chapter. Listen to example 20.10, and as you listen identify cadences, key areas, sections, and thematic relationships. After you do so, read the following analytical comments.

The key of this gavotte is Gm, with the first reprise ending on a PAC in B♭M. The piece thus represents the relative-major tonal type. Reprise 1 is eight measures long, whereas reprise 2, at twenty-six measures long, is more than three times longer.

Cadences and Key Areas. Let us now identify cadences and key areas. The opening phrase ends in m. 4 on a Gm cadence, while the second phrase modulates to B♭M. You already studied the pivot chord modulation to B♭M (m. 6) in chapter 19 (see example 19.21). Reprise 1 is thus a modulating parallel period (a_1–a_2), ending in the relative major key. The first section in reprise 2 leads from the initial B♭M to a PAC in Dm, the minor dominant key, in m. 18. The actual modulating process takes place in mm. 10–14. What key is briefly tonicized in mm. 11–12? After the cadence on v in m. 18, the home key, Gm, returns in the form of a section on a tonic pedal, mm. 19–26, ending on a HC in Gm in m. 26. A final section, mm. 27–end, reasserts Gm and creates a powerful drive toward the final cadence by means of a continuous flow of eighth notes and a highly chromatic ascending upper voice (circle the pitches, from m. 26 to m. 32, which lead linearly from G4 to C6). R2, in summary, contains four phrases, delimited by the cadences in mm. 14, 18, 26, and 34. Because all of these phrases are made up of the same thematic material presented in the initial phrase, we label them as a_3, a_4, a_5, and a_6, respectively.

Thematic Relationships. From a thematic point of view, the main motivic content of the piece is presented in m. 1 (see the motives labeled M_1 and M_2 on the score). The second phrase segment of a_1 (mm. 2–4), on the other hand, introduces a new motivic element which will be thoroughly developed later, the running eighth-note motives (M_3 and M_4) in the left hand. R2 begins with the initial motives M_1 and M_2, while the process modulating to Dm features a sequential development based on the running eighth-note material. Phrase a_5 also begins with a melodic development based on the initial motives, followed by a passage in eighth notes. Explain how fragmentation is the essential developmental procedure used in this phrase (mm. 19–26). The last phrase, mm. 27–end, presents an even more complex case of development based on fragmentation. Although the right hand spins out what seems to be a fairly free flow of eighth notes, it has a clearly developmental character because it is closely based on motive M_2 (see the "hidden" motive M_2 marked on the score in m. 27). Besides the ascending upper voice, notice, in mm. 26–32, the sequential pattern ascending by fourths (you can best identify it by looking at the bass line, mm. 26–32).

In summary, Bach's gavotte features strong motivic coherence and unity. Although two different thematic elements are used throughout the piece, both are clearly derived from the motives in the initial four measures, and there is not an area of definite thematic contrast (that is, a phrase in which new, contrasting material is introduced). The piece is in simple binary form because there is not a return of the exact original material in the original key (see formal design diagram in example 20.3a). This return could have been expected in phrases a_5 or a_6, after one of the cadences on D. Instead of a full thematic return, all we get is a varied reference to the opening motives (M_1–M_2 in mm. 26–27), not sufficient for us to think of this design as a rounded binary. *Characteristic baroque binary dances, as represented by this piece, are usually in simple binary form and feature a strong motivic unity.*

NOTE

What have we learned from this piece with this analysis? Listen to the gavotte again after you understand its form, or play it if you have keyboard skills. How does our discussion affect your listening or performance? Now you understand the formal design of the piece, its sections, and how they are related both motivically and tonally; you can also hear the key areas, the long-range harmonic motion, and how it all fits into a coherent tonal plan. Does all of it help you think more musically in any way? Discuss this matter in class with your peers and instructor.

2. A further example of balanced binary

A remarkable example of balanced binary appears in anthology, no. 27 (Mozart, Sonata in AM, I, Theme). You may have noticed that all the examples of rounded and balanced binary we have mentioned are from the Classical period. Unlike baroque composers, Classical composers (such as Haydn, Mozart, and Beethoven) favored binary designs that include a thematic return over the simple binary formal design. The Mozart example from the AM sonata is truly a "textbook example" of Classical binary form. In the first place, its phrase structure is strictly periodic. That is, it grows in additive units of equal length. Measure 1, for instance, is a clear thematic unit, repeated a step down in m. 2, to form a two-measure phrase member. Measure 3–4 also make up an obvious unit or phrase member, resulting into a 2 + 2 antecedent phrase ending on a HC. A repeat of the same process for the consequent, now ending on a PAC on I, turns reprise 1 into a typically Classical 2 + 2 + 2 + 2 = 4 + 4 phrase structure.

The first phrase of R2, which also breaks up into clear 2 + 2 units, ends on a tonicized HC, preparing the return of the tonic in m. 13. If we compare mm. 13–16 with mm. 5–8, we see that what actually returns is the second phrase of R1. Instead of closing, as he could have, in m. 16,

Mozart chose to add a two-measure cadential extension to confirm the final PAC on I. The complete phrase structure is thus ‖: 4 + 4 :‖: 4 + 4 + 2 :‖, supported by a standard tonic-type tonal scheme as represented in example 20.2a, and a balanced-binary formal plan as represented in example 20.3d. Discuss the motivic unity in this piece. The complete piece is motivically derived from m. 1. How? How many different motives are used?

Example 20.10 J. S. Bach, English Suite no. 3 in Gm, BWV 808, Gavotte I

♪♪♪ Example 20.10   (Continued)

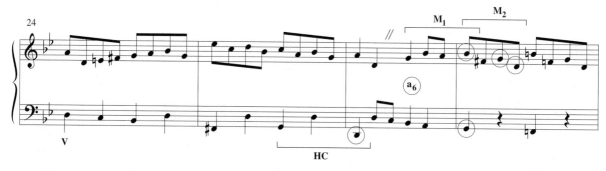

THE TERNARY PRINCIPLE

A piece in **ternary form** is any piece made up of three closed, independent parts. In principle, the formal and harmonic possibilities for this definition are many. The three parts may be related by a variety of formal designs, such as A–A–B, A–B–A, A–B–B, or A–B–C. We will focus here, however, on the most standard tonal and formal design of ternary. In this design, summarized as A–B–A, the initial section, A, returns after a contrasting section, B. Moreover, the A sections are tonally closed, and the B section, which may be open or closed, is often (but not necessarily) in the dominant or relative major key. Example 20.11 shows a standard tonal and formal paradigm for this ternary principle.

Turn now to anthology, no. 46 (Schumann, Kinder Sonate no. 1), a splendid example of ternary composition. Because this piece contains many of the harmonic and formal concepts that you already know well by now, it is worth studying and discussing it in some detail. First listen through it, and you will notice that the opening section, mm. 1–14, comes back at m. 35 in its entirety, with only a slight alteration toward the end to provide a brief cadential extension or *coda* (mm. 48–51). It is also immediately apparent that the first and last sections, the A sections, begin and end in GM, and that the middle B section begins and ends in Em. All three sections are then closed, and the middle section presents a contrasting tonal area, in the relative minor. We have thus identified our normative, standard ternary principle.

Next we can focus on each of the main sections separately. Identify all the phrases in the A section. Then, continue reading. You will probably have identified a first four-measure phrase, with two clear phrase members. This initial phrase establishes the tonic key and presents the main thematic material of the section. Beginning at m. 5, we start

♪♪♪ Example 20.11

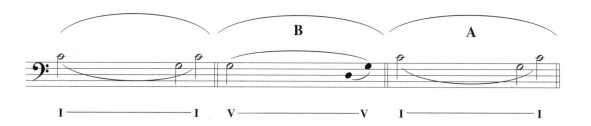

moving away from the tonic. Where are we moving to tonally? What is the first indication of this modulation? Where are we sure that we have modulated? (Do not keep reading until you have answered these questions!) The move is, clearly, to the dominant key, announced by the C♯ in m. 5, confirmed by the V–I progressions in DM in mm. 7–8, and further confirmed by the cadence in DM in m. 10. Now go back to m. 5. Here we are still in GM, but the next measure is in DM. Which chord is the pivot chord? And now go again to m. 10, where the cadence on DM takes place. In m. 11, the opening material comes back in GM. How did we modulate so fast from DM in m. 10 to GM in m. 11?

Now let's look at the B section (mm. 15–34). There is no question that it functions as a contrasting section, not only tonally, but also in several other ways. So let's ask the question: What changes between the A and the B sections? On the other hand, why do we feel that the unity of the piece is preserved? What is similar between the two sections? Answer these questions yourself. For contrast, discuss such elements as texture, rhythm, articulation, character, and type of melody. For unity and similarity, you may want to look at motivic content, and especially at the role of the perfect 4th as a motivic and melodic interval. Is the 4th an important interval in both the A and B sections? Moreover, look at the ascending eight-note motive in m. 2. Is it replicated in the B section?

The most interesting measures in the B section, from a harmonic point of view, are mm. 19–22. How are mm. 19–20 related to 21–22 melodically and harmonically? What are the secondary key areas in mm. 19–20 and 21–22, respectively? On the other hand, mm. 18–22 outline a circle-of-fifths progression. Identify each of the members of the circle (which is not complete).

Now that you have analyzed this interesting piece, listen to it again or play through it, and try to hear all the things you have discovered about it. Does your knowledge of form, tonal areas, tonal direction, and motivic and harmonic details make the listening or playing more enjoyable?

Compound Ternary

In the Classical period, one of the inner movements of sonatas and symphonies was often a *minuet* with its accompanying *trio*, after which you may have seen the familiar indication *Menuetto da capo*. The complete movement was, then, the minuet, the trio, and the complete minuet again. In this type of A–B–A design, which we call **compound ternary**, each of the three sections is a closed, independent piece in itself and,

1. *A challenging question.* This is indeed a question to challenge your understanding of binary formal designs. Both the A and B sections of the Schumann ternary piece we just analyzed can be considered binary forms, but in neither case is it obvious because Schumann did not provide the customary repeat signs. Explain both sections as binary forms, and determine where you would write the repeat signs if you wanted the reprises to be repeated. Note that in some cases the repetitions may actually have been written in by Schumann!

   To help you in the process, remember that reprise 1 will end on the tonic, the dominant, or possibly the relative major; that the first section of reprise 2 will have a developmental character, probably more unstable harmonically than the reprise 1; and finally, that the final section of R2 may be a return of thematic material from R1 in the tonic key. To help you even more if you need it, you may think of mm. 1–14 of the Schumann piece as a binary-ternary design, and of mm. 15–34 as dominant-type rounded binary.

2. *Songs in ternary form.* Numerous songs from the popular repertoire are in ternary form. The following are some suggestions for further analysis of ternary:

   Cole Porter, "Wunderbar," from *Kiss Me, Kate*!

   A. J. Lerner–F. Loewe, "On the Street Where You Live," from *My Fair Lady*.

   S. Sondheim–L. Bernstein, "Tonight," from *West Side Story*.

   Fred Ebb–John Kander, "Cabaret," from *Cabaret*.

   Hal David–Burt Bacharach, "I'll Never Fall in Love Again," from *Promises, Promises*.

moreover, each of the sections is in one of the binary forms. (Notice that, in spite of the fact that each of the three sections in the Schumann Kinder Sonate has a binary design, the piece is not in compound ternary because the three sections are not actually independent pieces. The binary design, moreover, was not even brought out by the composer by means of the customary repeat signs.)

Refer to anthology, no. 19 (Haydn, Minuet from Divertimento in CM). We have already discussed the minuet and the trio of this movement separately. The minuet is a V-type rounded binary in which all of reprise 1 returns in the second section of reprise 2, and the trio is a binary-ternary formal design. Now listen to the complete movement, including the *Menuet da capo* as a single formal unit. You will, of course, recognize the A–B–A design of ternary, but because each of the sections is an independent binary piece, this is a compound ternary. Can you think of any compound ternary in your performance repertoire? If not, find (and listen to) an example of this formal design in some symphony by Haydn or Mozart.

The *Da Capo* Aria

The major three vocal genres of the baroque period were the opera, the cantata, and the oratorio. Although the function of each of these genres was very different, by the late seventeenth century all three were made up of the same kind of compositional types: *choruses*, *recitatives*, and *arias*. The **recitatives** were sections in which a vocal soloist, with a very light accompaniment (often only the continuo section playing chords), delivered a musical recitation of some story or dramatic action, usually in a very free and speechlike melodic and rhythmic style. The *aria*, on the other hand, was the genre in which singers could display their vocal skills through highly melodic, lyrical lines, often with full accompaniment by the orchestra.

Although several different formal designs are found in baroque arias, perhaps the most frequent one is a ternary design know as ***da capo* aria**. This formal design fulfills the characteristics which we have studied for ternary designs: it is in three parts, the middle part is usually contrasting tonally and thematically, and the third part is a literal return of the first part. Because the return is literal, composers normally avoided copying it again, and simply wrote the indication *da capo* at the end of the B section. At the end of the A section you are likely to find the indication *Fine*, telling the performer that this is the real end of the composition. *Da capo* arias often include passages, especially in the A section, in which the orchestra plays alone. These passages are normally statements of the main thematic material and are called **ritornellos**.

An example of a *da capo* aria is provided in anthology, no. 16 (Handel, "Lascia ch'io pianga," from *Rinaldo*). First discuss the A section. Is it closed? What is its formal and tonal design? Does it include an orchestral *ritornello*? Now look at the B section. It is shorter, accompanied only by the continuo, and, in spite of its shorter length, it is more chromatic than the A section. This B section also shows a typical characteristic of B sections in *da capo* arias: They usually begin and end in different keys, rather than featuring a closed tonal motion. After the major-mode A section in our example, the B section begins in the relative minor key, vi, and ends in the key of iii. This is a frequent tonal plan for *da capo* arias in major mode. In minor-mode arias, the B section often begins in the relative major and ends in the dominant key. These tonal designs are summarized in example 20.12.

It is interesting to note that, in a way, binary is more complex than ternary, mostly because of the various possibilities of tonal motion within the reprises and because of the several different formal designs within the general binary paradigm. We should also point out that both binary and ternary generate larger, more complex forms, which we will study later in the book. Sonata form, an outgrowth of binary form, is a large binary design in which the first section of R2 becomes the development and the second section of R2

♪♪♪ Example 20.12

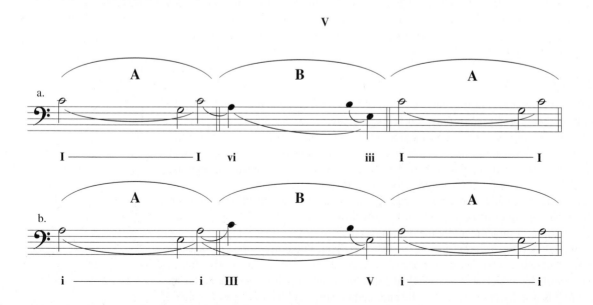

PRACTICAL APPLICATION AND DISCUSSION

Try to find at least one example each of binary and ternary forms in the pieces that you currently perform or have performed in the past. Bring them to class, perform them if time allows, and explain what formal and tonal type your chosen pieces represent. How does our study of these forms help you in performing and understanding these pieces?

Does your awareness of form and long-range tonal plan help you hear the pieces in "larger chunks"? That is, can you hear and perform the piece more as a coherent whole now, creating and hearing long-range tensions and directed motions that make performance (and hopefully listening to you perform it) more exciting?

becomes a complete recapitulation of the complete R1, but now without the modulation away from the tonic key. The rondo form, on the other hand, is also an outgrowth of ternary. Ternary has three parts, A–B–A. If you continue the pattern of alternating a return (the refrain) with a contrasting section, you will come up with such typical rondo schemes as A–B–A–C–A or A–B–A–C–A–D–A. The formal principles we have learned in this chapter, then, set the stage for some of the major formal designs in the music literature.

EXERCISES

To practice analyzing binary and ternary pieces, refer to exercise 20.1 in worksheet 20 at the end of this chapter.

   For an assignment of an analytical paper on a binary or ternary piece, refer to exercise 20.2 in worksheet 20 at the end of this chapter.

   For melody harmonizations and composition exercises, refer to exercises 20.3 to 20.5 in worksheet 20 at the end of this chapter.

ASSIGNMENT AND KEYBOARD PROGRESSIONS

For analytical and written assignments based on the materials learned in this and previous chapters, refer to chapter 20 in the workbook.

 Composers and Their Music 20

Listening

For your listening assignment in this chapter, two tasks are suggested.

1. Go back to three of the compositions you have already listened to in previous chapters: Mozart's Symphonies nos. 40 in Gm and 41 in CM, and Bach's Cantata no. 140 ("Wachet auf, ruft uns die Stimme"). In the two Mozart symphonies, verify that the minuets and trios are in binary form, and identify the tonal and formal designs. Then listen to both sets of minuet-trio, and hear them as a compound ternary. In the Bach cantata, identify the movement or movements in *da capo* aria form, and listen to it/them.

2. Listen to a complete keyboard suite or partita by J. S. Bach as assigned by your instructor, and identify as many of the formal designs as possible. As you listen, take notes and learn the main characteristics of each of the dances that make up the core of a baroque suite: allemande, courante, sarabande, and gigue. Notice particularly meter, tempo, and character. Other dance types in the suites may be minuet, gavotte, bourrée, rondeau. Take notes on these types too.

   Follow the score while you listen. Be able to place each of these compositions in one of the style periods and to comment on why and how it represents the musical characteristics of that period.

Terms for Review

Binary
Reprise
Suite:
    allemande, courante, sarabande,
    gigue, bourrée, gavotte, minuet-trio
Closed unit
Open unit
Binary tonal types:
    I type, V type, III type

Simple binary
Rounded binary
Binary-ternary
Balanced binary
Ternary
Compound ternary
Recitative
Da capo aria
Ritornello

Worksheet 20

EXERCISE 20.1 *Analysis.* For each of the pieces to be analyzed, determine and discuss the formal and tonal types, the key areas in the complete piece, and construct a bubble diagram using the given line. The diagram should show sections (labeled with letters) and tonal motion. As an additional exercise, provide bass reductions for some or all of the pieces, showing the tonal type, the long-range tonal motion, and the key areas. Use the various diagrams and reductions in this chapter as models.

In essence, the basic questions about this chapter's formal designs are as follows:

1. Binary or ternary?
2. If binary, does it feature a return in the tonic key?
   a) No return: Simple binary.
   b) Return:
      1) Of all of R1: rounded binary? binary-ternary?
      2) Of the beginning of R1: rounded binary.
      3) Of the end of R1: balanced binary.

Examples for Analysis:

1. Anthology, no. 11, Bach, French Suite no. 3, Minuet.
   a) Form and formal design:

   b) Key areas:

   c) Bubble diagram and bass reduction:

---

2. Anthology, no. 32, Beethoven, Sonata in Fm, op. 2, no. 1.

Menuetto

a) Form and formal design:

b) Key areas:

c) Bubble diagram and bass reduction:

Trio

a) Form and formal design:

b) Key areas:

c) Bubble diagram and bass reduction:

Menuetto

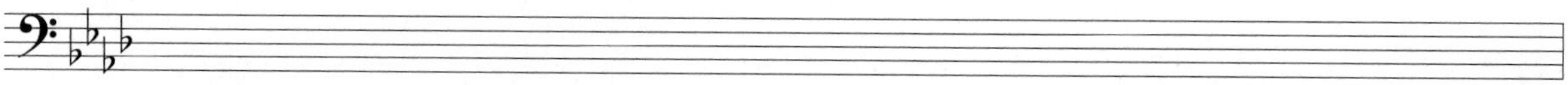

Trio

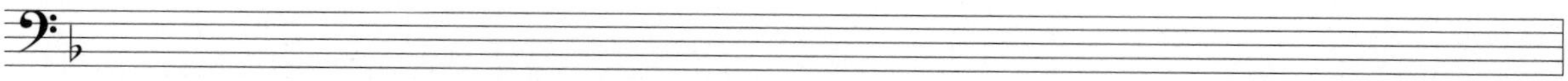

3. Example 20.13.

   a) Form and formal design:

   b) Key areas:

   c) Bubble diagram and bass reduction:

Example 20.13   J. Haydn, String Quartet no. 21, op. 9, no. 3, II

♪♪♪ Example 20.13   (Continued)

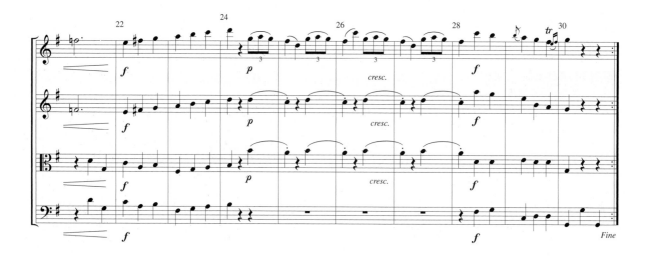

4. Example 20.14.

   a) Form and formal design:

   b) Key areas:

c) Bubble diagram and bass reduction:

Example 20.14   R. Schumann, "An Important Event," from *Scenes from Childhood*, op. 15, no. 6

♪♪♪Example 20.14   (Continued)

5. Anthology, no. 32, Beethoven, Sonata op. 2, no. 1.

   Menuetto and Trio (Complete Movement)

   a) Form and formal design:

   b) Key areas:

   c) Bubble diagram and bass reduction:

---

6. Anthology, no. 17, Handel, "Amaz'd to Find the Foe so Near," from *Belshazzar*.

   a) Form and formal design:

   b) Key areas:

   c) Bubble diagram and bass reduction:

EXERCISE 20.2 *Analytical paper.* Choose one of the pieces you have just studied in exercise 20.1, and write a brief analytical paper on it. Discuss, with good narrative prose, form, formal and tonal types, sections, key areas and tonal motion, and thematic/motivic relationships. Identify also special compositional techniques (such as imitation, sequence, textural inversion between hands), and discuss the techniques of motivic and thematic development used in the piece. Attach (and comment on) a bass reduction and a bubble diagram. You may use the various analytical discussions of pieces you have found in this chapter's text as possible models for your paper (and your narrative).

EXERCISE 20.3 Harmonize the following chorale ("Wer nur den lieben Gott lässt walten") with a bass line and RNs, accounting for possible modulations. As an additional exercise, you can also fill in inner voices.

EXERCISE 20.4   Harmonize the following two folk melodies and write realizations of your harmonizations in keyboard style.

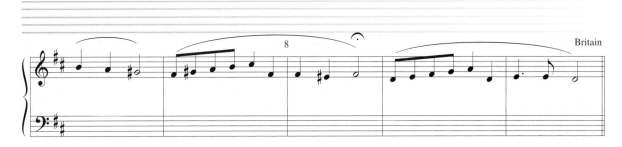

EXERCISE 20.5   Compose two modulating periods (melody and accompaniment in keyboard style) based on the given motives. The modulating periods by Haydn in the worksheet and workbook for chapter 19 may serve as models. You may compose the melody first and then write the accompaniment, or write both at the same time.

1. Modulate to the key of V. A possibility is to write an antecedent in CM, ending on a HC, and a parallel consequent that modulates to V (as in Mozart's familiar "Tema" from his DM sonata). Remember that the easiest way to modulate to V is to introduce $\sharp\hat{4}$, as in the example provided below.

2. Modulate to the relative major key (III). Remember: To modulate to III, cancel the leading-tone accidental in minor, and resolve either the new leading tone or the new $\hat{5}$ to the new $\hat{1}$. We do not need any new accidentals in this modulation (see the example provided below).

Chapter 21

Contrapuntal Genres

A variety of new genres and styles emerged and were developed during the Baroque period (approx. from 1600 to 1750). Two very different textural principles can be found in these genres. In the homophonic **thoroughbass texture**, on the one hand, a melodic line is supported by a harmonic bass (in which leaps are frequent) and the chordal realizations of the figures that accompany the bass. Polyphonic genres, on the other hand, receive an enormous impulse in this period, both in vocal and instrumental music. The polyphonic or contrapuntal style is often combined with the thoroughbass texture in what we know as **continuo polyphony**, found for instance in J. S. Bach's sacred music (such as his cantatas and Masses). In continuo polyphony a figured bass is added to an otherwise polyphonic texture. Baroque polyphony in general, whether the figured bass is present or not, is eminently *harmonic*, that is, it is a contrapuntal elaboration of underlying functional harmonic progressions. In this chapter we will study three characteristic contrapuntal genres of the baroque period: the *chorale prelude*, the *invention*, and the *fugue*. Because J. S. Bach brought each of these three genres to its highest level of development, we will focus especially on examples by this composer.

The importance of studying the genres that we will cover in this chapter goes much beyond their immediate historical significance. Contrapuntal techniques, as found in these genres, are essential to the compositional style of any historical period. Fugue and fugal techniques have been used by composers all the way to the twentieth century (and, presumably, they will continue to be used in the twenty-first century). Learning about these genres is learning about musical process in general, and although the literature we will study is centered on the keyboard, contrapuntal genres and the musical processes they embody can be found in the literature for any instrument, and hence should be a relevant component, at least from an analytical point of view, in the education of any musician.

THE CHORALE PRELUDE

In 1517, Martin Luther started a movement (the Reformation) first intended to address certain problems of corruption in the Roman Catholic Church and eventually leading to the foundation of an independent branch of Christianity, the Lutheran Church. The main musical genre in the services of the new, reformed church, was the chorale, a type of hymn sung by the congregation to simple, tuneful melodies, originally in monophonic style. Because early hymnbooks contained only text (and most people were not able to read music anyway), it was customary for the organist to perform (usually to improvise) a brief prelude based on the chorale melody as an introduction to the singing, with the function of reminding the congregation of the tune. The **chorale prelude** soon became an independent compositional type and eventually developed into one of the major contrapuntal genres of the mature baroque in Lutheran Germany. Among many outstanding composers of chorale preludes one may cite Franz Tunder, Johann Pachelbel, Friedrich Zachau, Dietrich Buxtehude, Johann Kuhnau, Johann Walther, and J. S. Bach.

The chorale prelude as a genre features a great variety of compositional types and techniques. In general, one can expect that the chorale tune will appear in one of the voices (frequently the treble or bass), either presented literally in longer note values than those in the accompanying voices or elaborated by means of melodic diminution and ornamentation. Chorale preludes are thus *cantus firmus* compositions. A *cantus firmus* is a preexistent melody used, literally or in ornamented form, as the basis for a polyphonic composition.

A Chorale Prelude by Zachau: Vorimitation

Refer to anthology, no. 4 (Zachau, "In dich hab ich gehoffet, Herr"). This is a piece in three voices, in which the chorale tune appears literally in the treble as a long-note *cantus firmus*, while the two accompanying voices feature more active figuration. The chorale melody has six phrases, and the structure of the prelude is determined by these six melodic sections. Identify the six phrases, and number them on the score, from 1 to 6. Then study the tonal scheme for the piece: Mark all the cadences, and determine the key areas. You will find a simple and standard long-range tonal plan: establishment of the tonic, digression to the dominant, return to the tonic, and further extension of the tonic by means of a subdominant key area. In terms of key areas, this is the familiar progression I–V–I–IV–I.

Let us examine the specific contrapuntal devices at the beginning of phrases. Phrases 1 and 2 begin with points of imitation (mm. 1–3 and 8–9). Where do the subjects used in these two imitative beginnings come from? In each case, the subject is a rhythmic diminution of the respective chorale phrase. In other words, each chorale phrase is used to generate an imitative beginning which marks the opening of each section (the end of both sections is clearly marked by cadences on I and V, respectively). Because the original melodic material, however, is the chorale tune in the treble, we cannot say that the tune "imitates" the initial diminuted subject, but rather that the initial diminuted subject is a "foreimitation" of the chorale tune which appears after it. The German term *Vorimitation* is normally used to refer to this compositional device. Does Zachau use *Vorimitation* clearly in any other phrase in this prelude?

A Chorale Prelude by Walther: Melodic Diminution of the Chorale Tune

Refer to anthology, no. 2 (Walther, "Ach Gott und Herr," verse 6). The original chorale tune is shown in example 21.1. How does the tune appear in this prelude? As in the Zachau example, it is presented in the upper voice. Here, however, it does not

♪♪♪Example 21.1   Chorale "Ach Gott und Herr"

appear as a bare *cantus firmus*, but rather it is elaborated with melodic diminution. Circle all the pitches of the original chorale melody in Walther's elaboration, and understand how his melodic diminution works.

From a contrapuntal and textural point of view, you will also see that here the upper voice blends in better with the other two voices, and as a matter of fact is often part of a **contrapuntal "give and take"** in which voices complement each other rhythmically (that is, when one voice is active the other one is not, and vice versa), as in mm. 9–10 and 14–16. Find other instances in this prelude of this type of "give and take" counterpoint involving the elaborated chorale tune. Finally, examine the beginning of each section. Are there any instances of *Vorimitation*?

Two Chorale Preludes by Bach: *Cantus firmus* and Canon

Bach's production of chorale preludes is monumental (over 150), and it is contained in several collections, including the early *Orgelbüchlein*, the "Schübler Chorales," the "Eighteen Chorales," and, later in his life, volume 3 of the *Clavierübung*. The openings of two preludes from the *Orgelbüchlein* are reproduced in examples 21.2 and 21.3. The texture of chorale 2, "Gott, durch deine Güte," is of the "continuous motion" type: The rhythmic relationship among the voices established in the initial measures is preserved throughout the piece. The upper voice presents the chorale tune in unornamented long-note *cantus firmus* style, while the manual bass (middle staff) carries a continuous "walking bass" in quarter notes, and the alto voice features a more active counterpoint in continuous eighth notes. The compositional challenge in this prelude is provided by the fourth voice, a tenor line played on the pedals. How is this fourth voice related to the upper-voice *cantus firmus*?

The compositional and contrapuntal challenge is compounded (to be exact, doubled!) in the prelude on "In dulci jubilo" (example 21.3). How are the four voices related? This is a **double canon**. Why?

EXERCISE

To practice analyzing a chorale prelude, refer to exercise 21.1 in worksheet 21 at the end of this chapter.

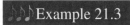

THE TWO-VOICE INVENTION

In 1723, J. S. Bach published a pedagogical collection of fifteen two-voice and fifteen three-voice keyboard pieces, entitled Inventions and Sinfonias, respectively. Although this is not a common genre in the Baroque period (there are hardly any precedents for it), Bach's inventions have become central pedagogical pieces both for the study of the keyboard and as compositional and contrapuntal models.

Although there is not a single standard type of tonal design and form in Bach's two-voice inventions, the following characteristics apply generally to the genre:

1. An **invention** is a *contrapuntal, imitative piece*, in which the two voices are totally independent and equally important.

2. Inventions are characterized by *strict motivic unity*. They are usually built on a single motive, which is found pervasively throughout the composition.

3. Pieces begin with an *imitative* **exposition** (imitation is mostly at the octave, but in some cases it is at the fifth). The subject reappears in various keys within the invention.

4. Motion from one key area to another key area is effected by means of sequential passages, called **episodes**, often based on a descending or ascending circle of fifths.

5. Secondary key areas normally involve *nearly related keys* such as the dominant, relative major or minor, and subdominant keys (sometimes also the supertonic key, the "dominant of the dominant").

6. The original key **returns** at the end of the invention, possibly along with a return of the initial point of imitation.

BACH: INVENTION NO. 3, IN DM

We will now analyze, as an example of the genre, Bach's Invention no. 3 in DM (anthology, no. 13).

1. *The Exposition*. This is the section in which the subject is presented by each voice in imitation. The exposition in our example comprises mm. 1–4 (to the downbeat of 5).

    a) Comment on the *subject*: what is its rhythmic characteristic? Notice the two halves (m. 1 and m. 2): how are they symmetrical (consider the grouping of notes)? How is the largest leap "strategically" placed? Comment on the progressive ascent from $\hat{1}$ to $\hat{5}$, and the subsequent descent from $\hat{5}$ to $\hat{1}$.

    b) What is the *interval of imitation*?

    c) Examine the *counterpoint to the subject* in mm. 3–4. As a general principle throughout the invention, when one voice is active (in sixteenth notes), the other voice is less active (in eighth notes). Few measures in the whole invention feature sixteenth notes throughout the measure in both voices.

2. *Episode 1*. This episode (mm. 5–12) leads to the cadence on V (AM) in m. 12. It is remarkable in its simplicity: It is based on an A pedal (which establishes the new key) and on repetition rather than sequence. Notice the cadential formula in mm. 10–12: You will later see that Bach uses the same formula in each of the subsequent cadences. Comment on the motive in mm. 5–6. It is obviously derived from the subject, but with some variation. Explain exactly how it is derived.

3. *Episode 2*. A new episode (mm. 12–24) leads to the cadence in Bm (the relative minor) in m. 24. The first section, mm. 12–18, moves through an ascending fifth progression: A–E–B–F♯ (identify each of the steps in this circle of fifths on the score). The circle stops on F♯, V in the new key of Bm.

   Notice the imitative interplay ("give and take") between voices in mm. 12–18. Have notes been added to the original subject to come up with the version used in these measures? How does the motive proceed melodically in mm. 19–21? Do you recognize the cadential formula in mm. 22–24?

4. *Episode 3*. This episode (mm. 24–38) is also based on a "give and take" texture, and in this case voices are totally complementary: When one moves, the other is sustained. The episode leads to the cadence in AM (V) in m. 38.

   a) The imitative passage in mm. 24–32 is built on a very familiar progression. What is it?

   b) The passage in mm. 32–35, on the other hand, features an interesting free development on the subject, with active motion in both voices creating a drive toward the important cadence on V in m. 38.

   c) The cadential gesture in mm. 36–38 is slightly varied with respect to the previous ones, but do you still recognize our basic cadential formula?

5. *The return*. An extension of the AM cadence (mm. 38–42) leads to the return of DM and to the recapitulation of the initial point of imitation (mm. 43–46). How does the motive proceed melodically in mm. 39–41?

6. *The final episode and the codetta*. Compare the episode in mm. 47–54 with episode 1 (mm. 5–12). How do they differ texturally? And how do they differ tonally?

   a) Whereas the original episode has the function of leading away from the original key, this new, final episode stays within the key of DM, and leads to what could be the closing cadence on D, in m. 54.

   b) Instead, Bach writes a deceptive cadence and a **codetta** (a brief coda), now taking us to the closing statement of the cadential formula and to the final cadence on D.

After discussing the complete invention in class, study the tonal/formal graph in example 21.4, and understand how it represents the design and structure of the piece. Comment on the long-range tonal plan provided by the key areas (the white notes). What familiar linear melodic figure is it based on? How is this plan replicated at a smaller scale in the return-codetta sections (mm. 44–59)?

♪♪♪Example 21.4

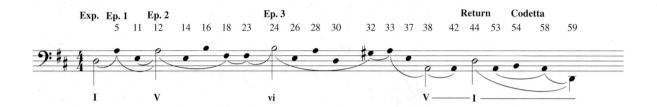

NOTE

For clarity of visual reference, in this and subsequent bass-line sketches showing the tonal/formal characteristics of extended compositions or sections, we will use white notes to signify the main key areas (rather than reserving white notes, as we have done so far, only for structural I–V–I progressions). In the DM invention, for example, the main key areas are I–V–vi–V–I, as you can easily verify by looking at the graph in example 21.4.

The chart in example 21.5, on the other hand, is what we call a "distributional graph," a comparative study of melodic segments. By placing related motives one on top of the other we can see exactly how they are derived from the initial subject. Comment on

♪♪♪Example 21.5

this graph and how it shows the thematic transformations undergone by the original subject.

EXERCISE

To practice analyzing an invention, refer to exercise 21.2 in worksheet 21 at the end of this chapter.

THE FUGUE

The contrapuntal genre *par excellence*, the **fugue**, developed throughout the sixteenth and seventeenth centuries to become one of the most elaborate and complex compositional types and a symbol of good contrapuntal and compositional craft. The genre reached its peak with J. S. Bach. As Robert Gauldin wrote in his counterpoint textbook, *A Practical Approach to Eighteenth-Century Counterpoint* (Englewood Cliffs, NJ: Prentice Hall, 1988), "despite the great accomplishments of the late Baroque masters, their efforts in the area of fugue pale against the achievements of J. S. Bach" (p. 210). Gauldin adds: "The fugal output of J. S. Bach is staggering. Aside from the collections (two volumes of the *WTC*, the seven Toccatas and Fugues for keyboard, and *Die Kunst der Fuge* [*The Art of Fugue*]), there are at least forty significant fugues for organ. These do not include the numerous choral movements cast in fugal style from cantatas or oratorios." The *WTC* is the *Well-Tempered Clavier*, a collection of forty-eight preludes and fugues in two volumes (24 + 24), each of which contains a prelude and a fugue in each of the twenty-four major and minor keys.

Just as with the invention, there is not a single formal or tonal type for the fugue. The fugue is a compositional procedure that can be adapted to numerous formal and tonal designs. In general, however, we can define the following characteristics for the genre:

1. A fugue begins with an imitative **exposition**, in which a **subject** presented by one voice is imitated by each of the other voices at the fifth (in the key of the dominant) or at the unison/octave (in the tonic key).

2. The remainder of the fugue is usually made up of alternating *middle entries*, statements of the *complete subject* in a variety of keys, and **episodes**, modulatory passages with a developmental character, usually sequential and based on the ascending or descending circle of fifths. After a modulating episode, the subject may be stated by a single voice (**middle entry**, ME), or by several voices in imitation (**middle entry group**, MEG).

3. Modulations are usually to closely related keys, although consecutive modulations may end up leading to keys distant from the original home key. At the end of the fugue there is a return to the tonic key, with or without a recapitulation of the subject in this key.

4. A variety of contrapuntal devices may be used throughout the fugue. Among these, the most common are the **stretto** (imitation of the subject at a closer metrical distance than the original imitation), augmentation or diminution, and inversion.

5. Fugues are often seamless formal entities, not clearly sectional, and we perceive them as a continuous flow of rhythmic and harmonic activity. They often create increasing and cumulating tension which may not be resolved until the final cadence.

The Exposition: Subject and Answer

Sing or play through the five subjects in example 21.6. In all of these examples you will notice some general traits of a good fugal subject: They all have definite, characteristic contours; they also have definite, characteristic rhythmic designs. Both traits together make these subjects clearly recognizable when they appear within the fugue. Moreover, a good subject usually has a strong rhythmic drive that propels it forward; it breaks easily into motives (thus allowing for fragmentation in developmental episodes), and it often has two contrasting halves (see subjects b, c, and d in example 21.6)

Now listen, following the score, to mm. 1–9 of Fugue no. 2 in Cm, from *The Well-Tempered Clavier*, I, anthology, no. 14). This fugue is in three voices, and this passage introduces all three, each beginning with a statement of the two-measure subject. In mm. 1–2, the alto states the *subject* in Cm, the tonic level. In mm. 3–4, the treble states the subject at the 5th, that is, at the dominant level. We will call this the **answer** (the subject transposed up a 5th). Finally, in mm. 7–8, the bass enters with the subject, again at the tonic level. Measures 1–9 are thus this fugue's *exposition*. The exposition ends as soon as the last voice completes its statement of the subject.

Real and Tonal Answers

You may have noticed that the answer of the Cm fugue (mm. 3–4) is not literally at the 5th: the initial interval C–G ($\hat{1}$–$\hat{5}$) in the subject is not answered with a G–D ($\hat{5}$–$\hat{2}$), but rather with a G–C ($\hat{5}$–$\hat{1}$). After this initial adjustment, however, the answer is not only a literal transposition of the subject at the upper 5th, but moreover it is in Gm, the key of the dominant. This type of answer, which includes a minor adjustment, usually at the beginning, is called **tonal answer**. Examine, on the other hand, the subject and answer in example 21.6a. Here the answer is literally at the 5th throughout. This is a **real answer**.

The following principles summarize the most frequent cases in which a subject will require a tonal answer:

1. If the subject begins on $\hat{5}$, the answer will usually begin on $\hat{1}$ (and *not* on $\hat{2}$).

2. If the subject begins with a motive based on $\hat{1}$–$\hat{5}$, the answer will respond with $\hat{5}$–$\hat{1}$ (and not $\hat{5}$–$\hat{2}$), as in example 21.6b. Similarly, a $\hat{5}$–$\hat{1}$ beginning will be imitated with $\hat{1}$–$\hat{5}$ (and not $\hat{2}$–$\hat{5}$), as in examples 21.6c and d.

3. A $\hat{1}$–$\hat{7}$ beginning will be imitated with a $\hat{5}$–$\hat{3}$ instead of $\hat{5}$–$\hat{4}$. See example 21.6e, where the initial $\hat{1}$–$\hat{7}$–$\hat{1}$ is answered with a $\hat{5}$–$\hat{3}$–$\hat{4}$, and not a literal $\hat{5}$–$\hat{4}$–$\hat{5}$.

The reason for each of these changes is that, although answers as a whole are in (or modulate to) the dominant key, it is customary that the opening motive (usually only two or three notes) is in the tonic key, in order to fit tonally with the end of the

♪♪♪ Example 21.6

subject on the tonic. Minor adjustments like the ones we have just discussed are sufficient to solve the problem. Example 21.6f illustrates a connection between a subject and its tonal answer, followed by the tonally impossible connection with a real answer.

EXERCISE

To practice writing fugal answers, refer to exercise 21.5 in worksheet 21 at the end of this chapter.

BACH: FUGUE NO. 2 IN Cm FROM THE WELL-TEMPERED CLAVIER, I

We will now study Bach's Cm fugue, reproduced in anthology, no. 14.

1. *The exposition.* We have already discussed the subject/answer entries in the exposition (mm. 1–9), and the tonal answer. When in a fugue the second voice comes in with the answer, the first voice provides a counterpoint to it (mm. 3–4). If the same counterpoint is repeated every time (or most of the time) the subject (S) appears in later entries, we call it a **countersubject** (CS). In this case, this is indeed a countersubject. Verify its appearance in mm. 7–8, 11–12, 15–16, 20–21, and 26–28, in all cases accompanying the subject. In mm. 7–8, the third voice comes in with S, the treble carries the CS, and the alto provides a further counterpoint, which, in this fugue, also appears every time S is stated subsequently. We will then call this second counterpoint CS2 (the previous CS then becomes CS1). Verify its appearance in all the statements of S listed above.

    The bridge. The answer, in m. 5, ends in Gm. But the new entry, the subject again, must begin in the tonic key. Before the subject comes in again, we need to modulate back to Cm. This modulation from the dominant to the tonic after the end of the answer is called the **bridge** (mm. 5–6). What techniques of melodic development do you recognize in this passage? Where are both voices derived from, and how? How do the motives proceed melodically?

    Double and triple counterpoint. Expositions are often written in **invertible counterpoint**: Voices may be texturally switched (top becomes bottom, and bottom becomes top) and the counterpoint still works. Invertible counterpoint in two voices is called **double counterpoint**; in three voices it is **triple counterpoint**. Compare mm. 17–18 with the bridge (mm. 5–6). Aside from the minimal addition of the treble in parallel 3rds with the bass motive, you will see that mm. 17–18 are basically built on the same two voices as mm. 5–6, only now they are inverted (and transposed). Measures 5–6 are thus written in invertible (double) counterpoint. Compare now mm. 20–21 with 7–8. The tonal level and pitch content are the same, but in mm. 20–21 all three voices have been switched around. Measures 7–8 are thus written in triple counterpoint.

2. *The middle entries (ME): tonal plan.* Middle entries are the complete statements of S throughout the fugue. Mark them on the score, and notice that they always appear in the form of S/CS1/CS2:

a) ME1, E♭M (III), mm. 11–12.

b) ME2, Gm (v), mm. 15–16 (the subject begins in Cm and modulates to Gm; it actually appears in the form of the answer, as in mm. 3–4).

c) ME3, Cm (i), mm. 20–21.

d) ME4, Cm (i), mm. 26–28.

The tonal plan for this fugue is straightforward: ME1 is in the relative major key, ME2 is in the minor dominant key, and ME3 is the return to i, and also a recapitulation, in Cm, of the complete three-voice statement of S/CS1/CS2 from mm. 7–8. ME4 is a final restatement of the three-voice complex, confirming the return to the tonic key, Cm.

The Pedal. Fugues often include a pedal point toward the end, on either the dominant or the tonic. The function of this **pedal** is to help release the accumulated harmonic and rhythmic tension created throughout the fugue. In our example, Bach wrote a pedal on $\hat{1}$ after the final perfect authentic cadence (PAC) in m. 29. Over the pedal, he wrote a final statement of S with a beautiful harmonization full of biting dissonances.

3. *The Episodes.* The above key areas and middle entries are connected by means of the following modulating episodes:

a) *Episode 1, mm. 9–10.* Modulates from Cm to E♭M by means of a four-step circle of 5ths: C–F–B♭–E♭ (verify each step on the score). Where is the thematic material in each voice derived from? How are the two upper voices related texturally and contrapuntally?

b) *Episode 2, mm. 13–14.* Moves from E♭M to Gm by means of an ascending circle of 5ths: E♭–B♭–F–C–G (identify each step on the score; several of these chords appear in first inversion). Comment on the melodic material: Is any of it derived from S?

c) *Episode 3, mm. 17–19.* Modulates from Gm back to Cm in two sequences up by steps (identify both sequences, each of which has three segments). We have already seen that this episode is directly related with the bridge through invertible counterpoint.

d) *Episode 4, mm. 22–26.* Does not modulate, but rather leads from Cm to Cm through a complete circle of 5ths. Identify each of the steps in the circle. Compare this episode with episode 1: They are both based on the same material, but whereas in Episode 1 the circle stopped at E♭, here it continues until it reaches C again. Comment on the texture: How do the voices function contrapuntally? Are there any examples of continuous motion and of "give and take" counterpoint?

After you have studied this fugue, examine the tonal/formal graph in example 21.7, and understand how it summarizes the design and structure of this piece. Then, listen to the fugue again and try to hear everything we have discussed.

FURTHER ANALYSIS

Apply your knowledge of fugue to the analysis in class of Bach's Fugue no. 11 in FM, from *The Well-Tempered Clavier*, I (anthology, no. 15). Besides the usual concepts and sections which we have already studied, in this fugue you will find the following additional elements:

1. *Counterexposition*. After the exposition (mm. 1–13) and a brief nonmodulating episode (mm. 13–17), you will see that all three voices come in again with the same subject-answer-subject statements as before, still in the tonic key (mm. 18, 22, and 26, respectively). This "repetition" of the exposition is called a **counterexposition**. It may be in the tonic key, as in this case, or it may be in a related key.

2. *Stretto*. Examine the middle entry groups in mm. 37–44 and 47–54. In both MEGs all three voices state

the subject. But if you compare the metric distance between statements here (ninety-two measures in each case) and in the exposition (four measures), you will see that in the MEGs entries are closer. Each of these MEGs is actually a *stretto*, a presentation of the subject in imitation at a closer distance than the original imitation.

Finally, study the exposition in example 21.8. This fugue is in three voices, but if you listen carefully you will hear "four" voices coming in in the exposition: alto (subject, m.1), treble (answer, m. 3), "tenor" (subject, m. 8), and "bass" (answer, m.12). That is, a full S–A–S–A cycle in four voices. The fourth entry is what we call an **extra entry**, and it allows the "faking" of a four-voice exposition in a three-voice fugue.

EXERCISE

To practice analyzing a fugue, refer to exercise 21.3 in worksheet 21 at the end of this chapter.

THE FUGATO

Composers sometimes use fugal techniques in the context of compositions other than fugues, such as variation forms. In such cases the fugal passages often take the form of a fugal exposition or perhaps the exposition and a developmental section (an episode), after which the texture changes back to a nonfugal, or even noncontrapuntal, style. Such a passage in the style of a fugal beginning in the context of larger formal types is called a **fugato**. You may listen to two fugatos in the last movement of Beethoven's Symphony no. 3, *Eroica*. The movement is a set of variations, and the large-scale middle section is both introduced and closed by fugatos. Listen to the opening fugato in mm. 117–175, and the closing fugato in mm. 277–348. To see where the subject of the first fugato comes from, listen to the opening of the movement. How is the subject of the second fugato related to the subject of the first fugato?

♪♪♪Example 21.7

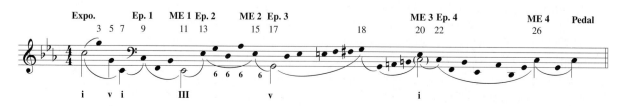

♪♪♪ Example 21.8   J. S. Bach, Fugue no. 8 in D♯m, from *The Well-Tempered Clavier*, I, mm. 1–14

Notice also that in the second fugato each entry of the subject in half notes is accompanied by a countersubject (or a second subject) in sixteenth notes. A fugue in which there are two subjects is called a **double fugue**. Beethoven's second fugato is, then, a double fugato. For an excellent example of double fugue, in which the main subject is always presented simultaneously with a countersubject, you may wish to listen to the "Kyrie" from Mozart's *Requiem*.

PRACTICAL APPLICATION AND DISCUSSION

1. What have you learned in this chapter that you would consider valuable as a musician?

2. What do you know now that you did not know before about formal and tonal processes in the baroque period, and about musical processes in general? What have you learned about compositional craft?

3. How does this affect your understanding of the music you play and listen to? For instance, how does it affect your perception or performance of the Cm fugue?

4. Do you think you will be able to apply any of this knowledge in the future when you study a chorale prelude, an invention, or a fugue?

5. Have you played any pieces in any of the genres we have studied in this chapter? Do you understand them better now? How? How does this understanding affect your performance? Can it give you a better sense of direction, of phrasing, of the role of sections as long-range formal and tonal units, of the piece as an organic whole made up of related parts?

6. Can you demonstrate any of the above by performing something in class?

EXERCISE

For an assignment of an anlytical paper on a fugue, refer to exercise 21.4 in worksheet 21 at the end of this chapter.

ASSIGNMENT AND KEYBOARD PROGRESSIONS

For analytical and written assignments based on the materials learned in this chapter, refer to chapter 21 in the workbook.

 Composers and Their Music 21

Biographies

Write short biographies of the following composers mentioned in this chapter: Friedrich Zachau, Johann Walther.

Listening

Listen to the following compositions by composers mentioned in this chapter:

　　Selected chorale preludes by Pachelbel, Zachau, Buxtehude, Kuhnau, and Walther.
　　J. S. Bach: the fifteen two-voice Inventions.
　　J. S. Bach: *The Art of Fugue*, fugues nos. 1–7.

At this point you would also enjoy (and benefit from) listening to J. S. Bach's Cantata no. 4, "Christ lag in Todesbanden," which you may have listened to after studying chapter E. This type of cantata is called "chorale cantata." Why? Before you listen to the complete work, listen first to the last movement, "Versus VII." As you listen to each movement, you will easily recognize some of the chorale prelude techniques we have studied in this chapter, here used by Bach in the context of a vocal-instrumental composition. What are some of the techniques that you recognize?

Follow the score while you listen. Be able to place these compositions in one of the style periods and to comment on why and how they represent the musical characteristics of that period.

Terms for Review

Thoroughbass texture
Continuo polyphony
Chorale prelude
Cantus firmus
Vorimitation
"Give and take" counterpoint
Double canon
Invention:
    Exposition, Episodes, Return,
    Codetta

Fugue:
    Exposition, Subject, Episodes,
    Middle entry, Middle entry group,
    Stretto, Answer, Real and tonal
    answers, Countersubject, Bridge,
    Invertible counterpoint, Double and
    triple counterpoint, Pedal,
    Counterexposition, Extra entry
Fugato
Double fugue

Worksheet 21

EXERCISE 21.1 Listen to and analyze Bach's chorale prelude on the chorale "Wer nur den lieben Gott lässt walten," BWV 647. You will find this prelude in the *Six Schübler Chorales*, and also in the Arlin anthology (*Music Sources*). You harmonized the original chorale tune (in a different key) in exercise 20.3. Note that the pedal part will sound one octave higher than notated because of the indication "4 Fuss." (4 feet). This line is thus really the tenor, while the left hand part is the real bass. Write a brief essay, on your own piece of paper, covering the following questions:

1. Where and how does the chorale tune appear in this prelude?

2. How would you describe the texture of this piece?

3. Mark, on the score, all the cadences and what degrees they are on. Then, based on the cadences and on the chorale phrases, determine the sectional divisions for the prelude.

4. Identify all the key areas in the complete piece. How are all the keys related among themselves? The piece, of course, is in Cm. Although the key signature may appear misleading, it is not if you think of it as a modal signature (actually an archaic practice by the time Bach wrote this prelude). What mode with a C tonic carries this signature?

5. Circle pitches 1–4 in the original chorale tune (tenor, mm. 5–6), and label this motive "a." Now circle pitches 5–8 (mm. 6–7) and label them motive "b." How do these two motives appear in mm. 1–2? What is their role in the rest of the prelude? Are there any other motives throughout the prelude that appear more or less consistently?

6. How are the two upper voices related in mm. 1–5?

7. Can we speak of *Vorimitation* in this prelude?

EXERCISE 21.2 Analyze Bach's Invention no. 6 in EM (the score and recording will be available at your music library). Turn in an annotated copy of the score, and answer the following questions.

1. Explain the characteristics of the exposition. How are the voices related in mm. 1–4 as compared to mm. 5–8? Provide the exact term for this type of counterpoint.

2. Measures 9–20. What is the harmonic function of this section? _____
   What is the best term to describe its formal function? _____
   What thematic/harmonic techniques are used (be very specific, and circle pitches or fragments on the score as needed to illustrate what you mean).

3. Measures 21–28. Describe this section formally and tonally.

4. Measures 29–42. What is the formal function of this section within the whole piece? What techniques are used? _____
What is the main key of this section? _____ What other secondary key areas are briefly touched on in mm. 33–36? _____

5. What is the formal and harmonic function of the section beginning at m. 43?

6. Measures 51–60 are equivalent to a previous section in the piece. Which section (mm. nos.)? _____ How do the two sections differ tonally and texturally?

7. What is the overall form of the piece? Provide a simple bubble diagram (use the line provided below) with clear indication of sections and keys. Is there a standard term to designate this characteristic tonal and formal type?

_____

EXERCISE 21.3   Analyze Bach's Fugue in B♭M, *WTC*, I, no. 21. The score and recording are available at your music library. On a copy of the score, provide a complete analysis of the fugue, indicating the usual, characteristic sections (including all appearances of the subject or answer) and contrapuntal or developmental techniques as they are found in this particular example. You may use some clear abbreviations such as S (subject), A (answer), ME (middle entry), Ep. (Episode). Be sure to mark on the score all appearances of such devices (if they are present in this fugue) as inversion, stretto, augmentation, and so on, and such techniques as fragmentation, sequence, circle of fifths, and so forth. Indicate also *all the main keys or key areas*.

Answer the following specific questions.

1. Is there a countersubject, or maybe more than one? If so, provide measure nos. and voice for its (their) first appearance.

2. Indicate two passages (provide two sets of measures) related by invertible counterpoint. Is it double or triple?

3. Is the answer real or tonal? Why is it as it is (real or tonal)?

4. Is there a bridge (provide mm. nos.)?
   What is the function of a bridge in a fugue?

5. Is there an extra entry (mm. nos.)?
6. Where does the exposition end?
7. Is there a counterexposition? What is a counterexposition?

8. Is there a stretto? What is a stretto?

9. Is there a return? Where?

10. Is there a pedal? Where?

EXERCISE 21.4   Write a brief analytical paper on Bach's Fugue in Gm, *WTC*, I, no. 16 (score and recording available at the library). You may use the discussion of the Cm fugue on pages 626–627 of the text as a model. The organization by sections used in that analysis is perfectly appropriate for your paper. Turn in an annotated score with clear indication of keys, tonal areas, cadences, sections, and compositonal or contrapuntal techniques. Make sure you discuss (and mark on the score) the following specific points:

1. Subject.
2. Answer: tonal or real? Why?
3. Countersubject and invertible counterpoint.
4. Bridge.

5. Length of exposition.

6. Counterexposition? In what key?

7. All episodes and middle entries.

8. Stretto.

9. Return, pedal.

10. Any instances of inversion, augmentation, or diminution of the subject?

EXERCISE 21.5   Determine whether the answer to each of the following fugal subjects should be real or tonal. Then, write the appropriate answer for each of them.

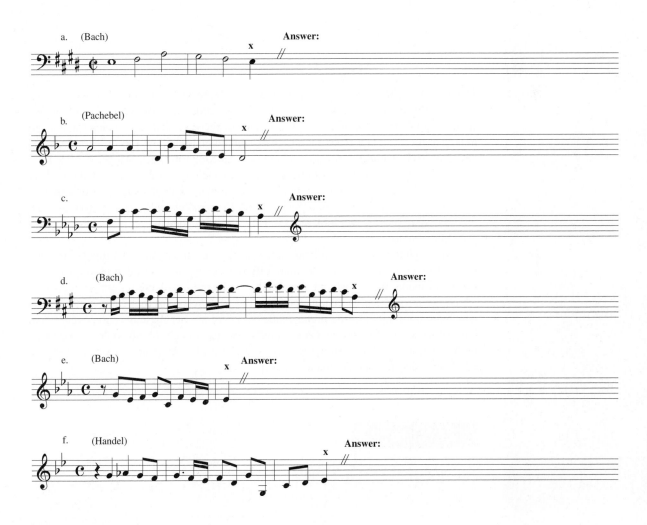

Chapter 22

Modal Mixture; Variation Forms

The harmonic chromaticism we have studied so far results from tonicization or modulation. In the first part of this chapter we will study **modal mixture**, a type of chromaticism resulting from the mixture of scales from the two different modes (major and minor) of the same key. Such mixture between the major and minor forms of the same key (that is, the parallel major/minor keys) can take the form of a change of mode for a fragment of music, or it can simply appear as a single chord from one mode used, or "borrowed," in the parallel mode. In all cases, the main scale in use, major or minor, is enriched chromatically by some pitches from the parallel scale. As a review of what these possible pitches are, look at example 22.1 for a comparison of scale degrees in each of the modes.

Although there are not so many different degrees, the chords that involve the different degrees are numerous. The main differences, of course, are the $\flat\hat{3}$, $\flat\hat{6}$, and $\flat\hat{7}$ in the minor mode. What, then, are the chords involving these degrees in the minor mode which are not present as major mode possibilities? What are the major mode chords which are not present in the minor mode? We will answer these questions very soon, but first try to make your own list of chords from each mode which could be borrowed in the other mode. Before studying borrowed chords, however, let us examine the case of change of mode for a complete segment.

♪♪♪ Example 22.1

M:	1	2		3	4	5		6		7		1
m:	1	2	$\flat$3		4	5	$\flat$6	$\natural$6	$\flat$7	$\natural$7		1

CHANGE OF MODE

Changes of mode from major to minor or from minor to major of the same key are frequently found in music. In purely instrumental music, modal change is normally used for tonal contrast and to introduce a factor of chromatic variety. Thus, a phrase that is first presented in a mode may be restated in the opposite mode rather than repeated in the same mode. Notice the element of surprise produced by the second phrase of Antonín Dvořák's period reproduced in example 22.2. The sense of forward motion that we feel because of the sudden change to GM could not have been matched by the simple repetition of the phrase in Gm.

In texted, vocal music, modal change often has an expressive purpose, reflecting musically some aspect of the text, while at the same time also providing a factor of tonal variety. Listen to the fragment in example 22.3. The initial key is Am, while the mill worker explains how much more he could do if he had a thousand arms. (How is the constant turning of the millstone represented by the music?) Then, in mm. 16–19, we find out why he wishes he could perform such feats at the mill: to impress "die schöne Müllerin," the lovely millermaid. At the mention of the millermaid, the heart of the miller boy brightens up, and so does the music. How? As an unrelated question, can you explain the chromaticism in mm. 11–15?

♪♪♪ **Example 22.2**   Antonín Dvořák, Slavonic Dance in Gm, op. 46, no. 8, mm. 1–8

BORROWED CHORDS

The term **borrowed chord** refers to a chord from one mode used in the other mode (that is, the borrowing takes place between parallel keys). We can borrow chords from major into minor, or from minor into major. In both cases, we use chords that, in the main key and mode of our fragment, are chromatic.

Borrowing Chords from the Major Mode in a Minor Key

Theoretically, the triads from major which are foreign to minor are I, ii, iii, IV, and vi (V and vii° are the same in both modes if we use the harmonic minor scale). Borrowing chords from the major mode in a minor key is less frequent than the other way around (borrowing from the minor mode in a major key). The only chords from major which are found in minor keys with some frequency are I, the major tonic chord, most often used in the context of a final tonic with Picardy third, and IV, used to harmonize ♯$\hat{6}$ in the melodic-minor ascending segment $\hat{5}$–♯$\hat{6}$–♯$\hat{7}$–$\hat{1}$. Because we have already studied both of these cases (review examples 3.5g and h, and example 13.4e), we need not discuss them all over again, other than commenting on the short illustration that appears in example 22.4. The passage begins in FM and modulates to Am. The actual move toward Am is effected by the bass line in m. 10, with a strong $\hat{5}$–♯$\hat{6}$–♯$\hat{7}$–$\hat{1}$ melodic figure. What is the harmonization of scale degrees ♯$\hat{6}$–♯$\hat{7}$ leading to Am? Does the passage actually end on an Am chord? Which of these chords are borrowed from the major mode? Now go back to m. 9. Are there any tonicizations in the short span leading from FM to Am? Bach truly could pack a lot of interesting harmony into only a couple of measures!

Borrowing Chords from the Minor Mode in a Major Key

The triads from the (harmonic) minor mode which are foreign to major are i, ii°, III, iv, and VI. Three of these, ii°, iv, and VI, *involve the degree* $\hat{6}$. The same degree, moreover, is also present in ii°$_7$ and its inversions. All of these chords may be effectively borrowed

♩♩♩Example 22.4   J. S. Bach, Chorale 96, "Jesu, meine Freude," mm. 9–11

in major modes, and among them the chords involving $\hat{6}$ (which in a major-mode context becomes $\flat\hat{6}$) are the most frequently borrowed. Another chord that properly belongs to the minor mode because of its inclusion of $\flat\hat{6}$, and which is often used in major keys, is vii°$_7$. Although this chord is indeed a borrowed chord when used in the major mode, we will not include it in this chapter because we already studied it in chapter 15.

iv and ii°$_7$ in the Major Mode

The minor subdominant ($\hat{4}$–$\flat\hat{6}$–$\hat{1}$) is used effectively in major keys as either a tonic prolongation (including plagal cadences) or as a predominant chord (see the sample progressions in examples 22.13a and b). A iv prolonging a major tonic appears in

♪♪♪Example 22.5a   Felix Mendelssohn, *Song without Words*, op. 102, no. 2, mm. 24–27

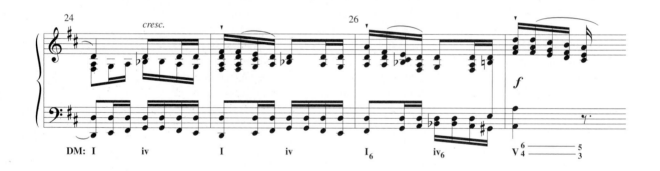

♪♪♪Example 22.5b   D. Ellington, "I Let a Song Go Out of My Heart" (Final Cadence)

example 22.5a. Notice how the simple use of ♭$\hat{6}$ instead of ♮$\hat{6}$ as an upper neighbor to $\hat{5}$ adds an element of chromatic and expressive interest to the passage. A similar plagal prolongation of I by means of iv can be observed in the plagal cadence which follows the perfect authentic cadence (PAC) in example 22.5b.

NOTE

The symbol iv$^{add\ 6}$ in example 22.5b refers to an "added sixth chord," a common sonority in popular music and jazz. An added sixth chord consists of a triad plus a sixth as in our example, A♭–C♭–E♭–F. We would think of this chord in the last measure of our example as iv$^{add\ 6}$ rather than ii$^6_5$ (although the pitch content of these two chords is the same) because it is part of a clear plagal cadential gesture (I–iv–I).

The minor-mode supertonic seventh chord, ii$^{ø}_7$, is used as a predominant chord in the major mode even more often than iv (see example 22.13c). In example 22.6, Bach approaches the cadential dominant in FM by means of a ii$^{ø6}_5$, the most frequent form of this chord. Notice that, here also, ♭$\hat{6}$ appears as an upper neighbor to $\hat{5}$. Other inversions of ii$^{ø}_7$, however, are also found in the literature. What inversion appears in example 22.7? How is it used in this example? Although in m. 27 it precedes a dominant chord which moves on to the tonic, do both supertonic seventh chords in m. 26 and m. 27 have any other linear function in this context? Examine also the rest of the example. Does it feature any tonicization?

In example 22.8, Beethoven takes advantage of the chromatic possibilities afforded by ♭$\hat{6}$ and ♮$\hat{6}$ by using both degrees in an interesting melodic interplay. The passage is in B♭M. What are the two inversions of the ii$^{ø}_7$ chord in mm. 35–36? What familiar voice-leading figure connects them? What chord does Beethoven use to harmonize the ♮$\hat{6}$ in m. 38? The ♭$\hat{6}$ in m. 39, on the other hand, has a linear function. What is it?

♪♪♪ Example 22.6   J. S. Bach, Chorale 6, "Christus, der ist mein Leben," mm. 7–8

♪♪♪ **Example 22.7**   Fanny Mendelssohn Hensel, "Du bist die Ruh," from *Six Songs*, op. 7, no. 4, mm. 26–32

♭VI and ♭III in the Major Mode

The notation "♭VI" and "♭III," that is, a Roman numeral preceded by a ♭ sign, refers to chords built on lowered scale degrees. Thus, the ♭ sign before the Roman numeral affects the root of the chord: ♭VI is a major chord built on ♭6̂, and ♭III is a major chord built on ♭3̂ (notice that the same two chords in the minor mode are diatonic, and hence labeled as VI and III).

♭VI is a beautiful chromatic chord, used with a variety of functions, all similar to the functions of the diatonic submediant, vi (see examples 22.13d to f). ♭VI includes two chromatic degrees, ♭6̂ as the root, and ♭3̂ as the fifth. Because of the strong half-step pull

♪♪♪ Example 22.8   L. v. Beethoven, Piano Sonata in E♭M, op. 81a, I, mm. 35–42

♪♪♪ Example 22.9   J. Haydn, Symphony no. 101 in DM, IV, mm. 13–16

of ♭6̂ toward 5̂, ♭VI can effectively function as a *predominant chord*. This is exactly how it is used by Haydn in example 22.9.

On the other hand, V may also resolve to ♭VI in a striking, chromatic *deceptive progression*. In example 22.10, the dominant of EM in m. 102 resolves deceptively to a CM chord, a ♭VI in EM. Observe, however, that this ♭VI is then tonicized, creating a brief ♭VI secondary key area (mm. 103–105). The resolution of ♭6̂ in the bass to 5̂ in mm. 106–107 takes us back to V in EM. (Notice the strong linear pull toward 5̂ created by the double half-step resolution of C *down* to B♮ and A♯ *up* to B♮; we will study the chord that results from this voice leading, an augmented sixth chord, in the next chapter.) The end of the passage is built on a pedal on 5̂. What chords does Beethoven write on this pedal?

♪♪♪ **Example 22.10**   L. v. Beethoven, Piano Sonata in EM, op. 14, no. 1, I, mm. 101–109

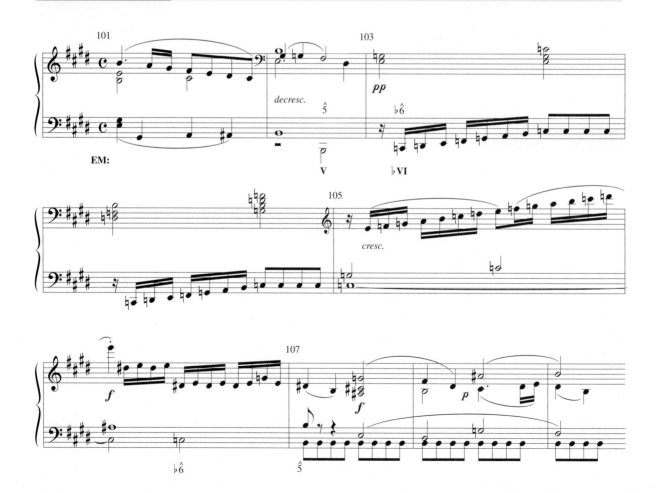

Typical Errors to Avoid

▶ Writing parallel 5ths and or 8ves in the ♭VI–V progression. The ♭VI–V₇ progression is easier to write from this point of view.

▶ Writing parallel 5ths in the V–♭VI deceptive progression. The standard voice-leading rules for the V–vi progression also apply to the "borrowed" deceptive progression.

♭VI may also function as a chord prolonging, or embellishing, the major tonic. Example 22.11 shows an instance of such a chromatic, prolonging progression, I–♭VI–I. The cadence also involves another borrowed chord. What is the chord, and what kind of cadence is this?

♭III is a relatively unusual chord. When it appears in the literature, it is often paired with ♭VI, and, as a matter of fact, it is often used as the secondary dominant of ♭VI (example 22.13g). In Modest Mussorgsky's phrase reproduced in example 22.12a, in E♭M, ♭III is indeed coupled with ♭VI in the progression ♭VI–♭III (or ♭VI–V/♭VI, although the secondary dominant progression never continues to its possible resolution, ♭VI). These chords here function as a surprising chromatic extension of the E♭M tonic triad which is prolonged in this passage. In example 22.12b, on the other hand, ♭III appears, in the context of a plagal cadential gesture, as part of a passing motion from IV to I (IV–♭III–P₄⁶–I).

EXERCISE

To practice spelling borrowed chords, refer to exercise 22.2 in worksheet 22 at the end of this chapter.

♩♩♩ Example 22.11   J. Brahms, Symphony no. 3, II, cadence (mm. 128–134)

Example 22.12a   Modest Mussorgsky, "The Great Gate of Kiev," from *Pictures at an Exhibition*, mm.156–162

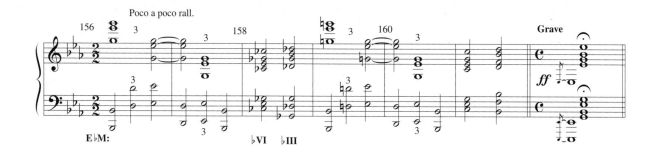

Example 22.12b   George Harrison, "Something," from the album *Abbey Road* (The Beatles)

The progressions discussed in this chapter are summarized in example 22.13. Study and understand their voice leading and the function of each of the borrowed chords in these examples.

The most characteristic melodic degree which may be harmonized with iv or ii$^{\varnothing 6}_5$ in major is, of course, ♭$\hat{6}$, although both chords also work well to harmonize $\hat{1}$ and $\hat{4}$, and ii$^{\varnothing 6}_5$ can also harmonize $\hat{2}$. ♭VI in major can be used to harmonize the melodic degrees ♭$\hat{6}$, $\hat{1}$, or ♭$\hat{3}$.

EXERCISES

To practice realizing progressions including modal mixture, refer to exercise 22.3 in worksheet 22 at the end of this chapter.

To practice harmonizing a melody including modal mixture, refer to exercise 22.4 in worksheet 22 at the end of this chapter.

For a summary of most of the borrowed chords we have just discussed, refer now to anthology, no. 53 (Verdi, *Il trovatore*, Act 2, no 11). In the first place, what is the progression in mm. 5–6? Now examine the progression in mm. 7–8. In m. 7 we see an example of ♭III functioning as the dominant of ♭VI, in the progression V/♭VI–♭VI. The latter chord acts here as a predominant, and the dominant prolongation in m. 8 seems to lead to a tonic in m. 9. Instead, the cadence is interrupted (or delayed) in m. 9 by a IV$_4^6$ which begins a new cadential process. What other predominant chords are present in mm. 9–10? Which one is tonicized? Which one is a borrowed chord? Notice that this second cadential process finally finds resolution in m. 11.

EXERCISE

To practice analysis of musical fragments including modal mixture, refer to exercise 22.1.1 in worksheet 22 at the end of this chapter.

VARIATION FORMS

The variation principle is a basic musical device often used in any type of composition. Composers frequently decide to repeat musical statements, and sometimes they do so literally (in what we call a **literal counterstatement**). At other times, however, the repetition is not literal, but varied (a **varied counterstatement**): The previous material may be altered or embellished in a number of ways, including addition of notes or figuration, simplification, rhythmic alteration, and so on. Examples of varied counterstatements

♪♪♪ Example 22.13

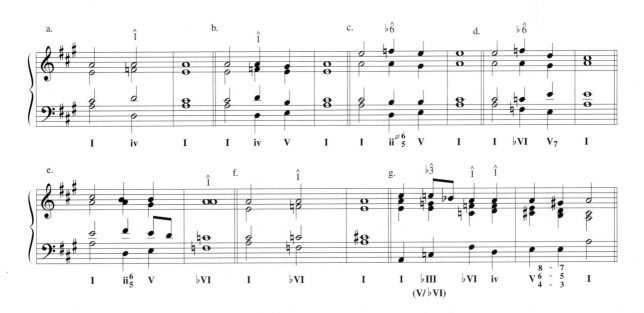

appear, for instance, in anthology, no. 35 (Beethoven, Piano Sonata no. 21 in CM, *Waldstein*, I), in the context of the first movement of a sonata. Compare the initial theme (mm. 1–4) with its varied repetition in mm. 14–17. What did Beethoven change in the counterstatement? Now compare the statement of the new theme in EM that appears in mm. 35–42 with the immediate varied counterstatement in mm. 43–49. The difference here is quite considerable: What stays the same, and what is varied in the counterstatement?

In the second part of this chapter we will study the variation principle as a form-building process applied to complete movements or compositions. The types of compositions totally built on the variation principle are usually called "variations" or "theme and variations." The variations as a genre allow for great freedom on the composer's part. In their most usual compositional type, variations begin with the statement of a theme, a phrase, or a short piece (perhaps in binary or ternary form) which is then restated in varied forms as many times as the composer wishes.

Types of Variations

The first question we ask for each variation should be, as above: What stays the same, and what is varied? The following are some of the elements we can examine for this purpose: *key, mode, form, length, melody* (*both pitch and rhythm*), *tonal structure, precise harmonic sequence, bass, tempo, texture.* Some types of variations result from standard procedures that recur in variation sets by different composers. Some of these specific variation types are listed below.

1. **Ornamental variation**: The melody is elaborated (diminuted) by means of added notes.
2. **Simplifying variation**: The melody is simplified (reduced).
3. **Figural variation**: Built on a particular motive or figure.
4. **Contrapuntal variation**: Uses some kind of contrapuntal technique, such as imitation, canon, fugato, or free counterpoint.
5. **Characteristic variation**: In the style of some characteristic compositional type such as march, dance form, adagio, or finale.
6. **Double variation**: The first and second statements of each reprise in a binary form are written out, and each constitutes a different variation (instead of the more frequent repetition, by the repeat signs, of the same material).

Shape and Form of Complete Sets

Sets of variations constitute musical wholes, and composers design their musical shape and form thinking of the complete movement as a unit. For long-range design of shape, then, we must examine grouping, contrast, and tempi. Is there a rhythmic *crescendo* that groups several variations? Is there a pattern of increasing complexity? Is one of the central variations an *adagio*, functioning as a "slow movement" within the movement? Is the last variation a characteristic *finale*, in fast tempo and with brilliant figurations? Is there a long-range tonal design (such as, perhaps, M–m–M) which groups several variations? Does the grouping reveal any kind of long-range formal design (say, some kind of ternary)?

CONTINUOUS VARIATIONS

If we take into consideration the formal type of each variation and the connection between adjacent variations, there are two types of variation forms: continuous and sectional. In **continuous variations** the theme and each variation are usually short (one or
two phrases) and there is no interruption between variations. In **sectional variations**,
on the other hand, the theme and each variation are usually self-sufficient formal units
(such as binary or rounded binary pieces), including a clear cadential pause at the end
of the theme and each variation.

The most common type of continuous variation is built on a **bass ostinato**
or **ground bass** (a melodic fragment repeated over and over again, and often associated with a harmonic progression). Study, for instance, Purcell's "Ah, Belinda," from
Dido and Aeneas (anthology, no. 3). You will see that the complete aria is composed
on a four-measure repeated bass phrase. Having said this, you can ask yourself the following questions regarding this (or any other) bass-ostinato piece:

1. Is the bass phrase repeated unaltered every time, or is it ornamented?
2. Is it transposed in some section? To what tonal level or key area?
3. Is the bass phrase harmonized with the same progression every time it appears, or
   does the harmony change?
4. How is the melody phrasing related to the bass phrasing? Do they correspond? Or
   do they overlap? Overlap of phrases (which takes place when beginnings and endings of phrases in different voices do not correspond) is a frequent means to
   achieve continuity and a sense of continuous flow in this type of variation. Is this
   the case in our example?
5. What is the long-range form or shape of the complete piece? In Purcell's example,
   factors to consider are first, the repeat signs marking off a section at the beginning,
   then, the motivic character of the melody associated with the words "Peace and
   I. . . . " Do these words, and the motive that goes with them, return? Another factor to consider is the statements of the bass phrase in a secondary key area. How
   does this key area fit into the formal scheme created by the statement and return of
   the words "Peace and I . . . "?
6. What kind of contrapuntal device do you recognize, in the "Peace and I . . . " passages, between melody and bass? How does it contribute to the sense of phrase
   overlap? How does this overlap (the phrases "do not go together") depict what the
   words are expressing?
7. If you sing or play the vocal line, you will notice that, other than the "Peace and
   I . . . " fragments, the melody grows quite freely, with hardly any motivic references or repetitions (as opposed to the strict bass ostinato). This type of freely
   growing melody is characteristic of the baroque period and results from the technique known in German as *Fortspinnung*, or "spinning out."

Some Characteristic Ground-Bass Types

Continuous variations are often based on characteristic bass types such as the chaconne
and folia. Characteristic bass formulas became popular in the Renaissance both as
grounds on which to improvise or as bass phrases on which to write variations. Three

bass types widely used in the sixteenth century are the *folia*, the *romanesca*, and the *passamezzo antico*, shown in examples 22.14a to c. As with any ground bass, these bass formulas are usually associated with standard harmonic progression. Refer to example 14.5c, where you can review the progressions commonly used to harmonize the *romanesca* and *folia* basses respectively.

The **chaconne** bass, on the other hand, is more typical of the baroque period, and it appears in various forms. The most common chaconne bass, however, is the **descending tetrachord** $\hat{1}-\hat{7}-\hat{6}-\hat{5}$ (or $\hat{1}-\flat\hat{7}-\flat\hat{6}-\hat{5}$ in minor), as shown in examples 22.14d and e (a *tetrachord* is a collection of four pitches, in this case outlining a descending P4). A chromatic elaboration of the descending tetrachord (of the type found, for instance, in "Dido's Lament," from Purcell's opera *Dido and Aeneas*) appears in exam-

♪♪♪Example 22.14

a.   **Folia**

b.   **Romanesca**

c.   **Passamezzo Antico**

d.   **Chaconne**   e.

f.

g.   **Bach, Passacaglia in Cm**

ple 22.14f. Because the descending tetrachord bass, in both its diatonic and chromatic forms, was often used in baroque operas as the basic structure for songs of sadness, loss, and mourning, it is often referred to as the **lament bass**. For examples of lament bass in popular music, listen to Percy Mayfield's song "Hit the Road, Jack" (as performed by Ray Charles) and Led Zeppelin's "Babe, I'm Gonna Leave You."

The term **passacaglia** also denotes a piece in continuous variation style on a ground bass, but composers have used this term to refer to a variety of different basses. Sometimes passacaglia simply means the same as chaconne, that is, a piece titled *passacaglia* may be built on the descending tetrachord bass. At other times, a passacaglia is built on an original bass phrase, as in the case of the well-known Passacaglia in Cm by J. S. Bach (example 22.14g).

To illustrate the type of ground-bass theme on which baroque composers built sets of *continuo* variations, three of the most famous among them appear in example 22.15. Corelli's Sonata "La Follia" is a set of variations on the popular folia bass (example 22.15a). Handel's Chaconne in GM (example 22.15b) is built on the major-mode, diatonic version of the chaconne bass. Bach's "Crucifixus," on the other hand, is built

Example 22.15a   Archangelo Corelli, Sonata *La Follia*, op. 5, no. 12, mm. 1–16

♪♪♪Example 22.15b   G. F. Handel, Chaconne in GM

♪♪♪Example 22.15c   J. S. Bach, "Crucifixus," from Mass in Bm, mm. 1–9 (Vocal Parts Omitted)

on the minor-mode chromatic version of the same bass. Why did Bach choose to use this bass for this particular section of his Mass? The example includes the first two statements of the bass phrase so that you can appreciate how Bach presents it with contrasting harmonizations from the very outset.

Ground basses are an important compositional technique in popular music. Besides the Ray Charles and Led Zeppelin songs mentioned above, other popular songs that include ground basses are Del Shannon's "Runaway" (by Charles Westover and Max Crook), The Beatles's "I'll Be Back" (by Lennon and McCartney, from the album

A Hard Day's Night), and The Lovin' Spoonful's "Summer in the City" (by John Sebastian, Mark Sebastian, and Steve Boone).

EXERCISE

To practice composing variations on a ground bass, refer to exercise 22.6 in worksheet 22 at the end of this chapter.

SECTIONAL VARIATIONS

As we saw above, in **sectional variations** (the traditional type of "theme and variations"), the theme and each variation are independent formal units, separated by a conclusive cadence and a break in the musical flow. This is the most common type of variation in the Classical and Romantic periods. The first movement of Mozart's Sonata in AM, K. 331, in "theme and variations" form, is reproduced in anthology, no. 27. Listen to the *complete set*, and then discuss the following points in class.

1. We have already studied the form of the theme. Review what exact formal design it represents, and note that it is a totally self-contained, conclusive formal unit.

2. Is the formal design of the theme preserved intact in each of the variations?

3. Variations I–IV can be considered both *ornamental* and *figural* variations. Review the definitions of these terms, and explain how each of these four variations can be seen to represent both types. Can you trace the melodic structure of the original theme in each of the six variations?

4. In variations I and II, Mozart was not content with simply writing the complete first reprise using the same variation material (the same figuration, texture, etc.). Compare phrase 1 and phrase 2 in each of these two opening periods, and explain how Mozart varied the second phrase with respect to the first one.

5. The theme and variations I–IV can be heard as a formal group. Why? What is the character and function of variation III within this group? And of variation IV?

6. Considering their character within the complete set, variations V and VI are *characteristic variations*. What "genres" do they represent? Could variation V itself be an independent movement within a sonata? How about variation VI? What is the formal function of the added mm. 18–26 in this last variation?

7. Provide some kind of a diagram showing the overall grouping and formal design for the complete movement.

EXERCISES

To practice analysis of variations, refer to exercise 22.1.2 in worksheet 22 at the end of this chapter.

To practice composing a binary piece for a melodic instrument, refer to exercise 22.5 in worksheet 22 at the end of this chapter.

PRACTICAL APPLICATION AND DISCUSSION

If you have a set of variations in your performance repertoire, bring it to class. Explain to the class what kind of variations they are (continuous or sectional). If they are continuous, what bass or harmonic progression are they built on? If they are sectional, what is the form of the theme? Give a brief presentation to the class explaining the variation techniques and the variation types used in your piece. What is the long-range design of the complete movement? Demonstrate your points by performing some of the variations.

ASSIGNMENT AND KEYBOARD PROGRESSIONS

For analytical and written assignments and keyboard progressions based on the materials learned in this chapter, refer to chapter 22 in the workbook.

PITCH PATTERNS

Sing the pitch patterns in example 22.16, and as you sing listen to the borrowed chord used in them. Then improvise similar pitch patterns using a variety of borrowed chords.

♪♪♪ Example 22.16

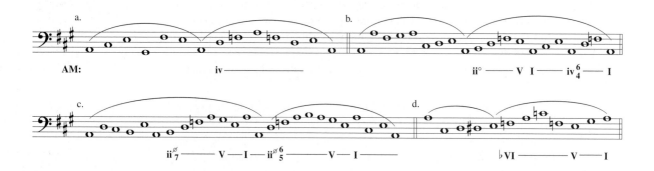

 Composers and Their Music 22

Biographies

Write short biographies of the following composers mentioned in this chapter: Antonín Dvořák, Fanny Mendelssohn Hensel, Modest Mussorgsky.

Listening

Listen to the following compositions by composers mentioned in this chapter:
Dvořák, *Slavonic Dances*.

Fanny Mendelssohn Hensel, *Six Songs*, op. 7.
Mussorgsky, *Pictures at an Exhibition*.

Follow the score while you listen. Be able to place each of these compositions in one of the style periods and to comment on why and how it represents the musical characteristics of that period.

Terms for Review

Modal mixture
Change of mode
Borrowed chords
Borrowing from M into m
Borrowing from m into M
iv and ii°₇ in the major mode
♭VI and ♭III in the major mode
Variation forms
Literal or varied counterstatement
Ornamental variation
Simplifying variation
Figural variation
Contrapuntal variation
Characteristic variation

Double variation
Shape and form of complete sets
Continuous variations
Sectional variations
Bass ostinato
Ground bass
Fortspinnung
Folia
Romanesca
Passamezzo antico
Chaconne
Descending tetrachord
Lament bass
Passacaglia

Worksheet 22

EXERCISE 22.1   Analysis.

1. Analyze and explain the type of modal mixture in the following examples. If borrowed chords are involved, be specific as to what they are.

    a) Example 22.17.

Example 22.17   F. Schubert, *Wanderers Nachtlied*, op. 96, no. 3, mm. 4–6

Ruh', in al - len Wip - feln spü - rest du   kaum   ei - nen Hauch;

    b) Example 22.18. In this example, some chromaticism results from tonicization, and some from borrowing. Explain all of it. Explain also the modulation.

    c) Anthology, no. 59, Beach, *Ecstasy*, mm. 27–31.

    d) Example 22.19.

Example 22.18   F. Chopin, Mazurka in GM, op. 67, no. 1, mm. 38–49

Example 22.19   J. S. Bach, Chorale 96, "Jesu, meine Freude," mm. 1–6

e) Example 22.20.

♪♪♪ Example 22.20   W. A. Mozart, Piano Sonata in B♭M, K. 333, I, mm. 86–95

f) Anthology, no. 48, Schumann, "Widmung," mm. 3–6 and 10–13.

g) Anthology, no. 31, Paradis, *Sicilienne*, mm. 1–6.

2. Listen to Beethoven's Symphony no. 3 in E♭M (*Eroica*), op. 55, IV, and follow the score while you listen. Think of this movement as a set of variations, and explain exactly what each of the following statements means.

a) These variations are on two elements: a bass (introduced in mm. 12–44), and a theme built on this bass.

b) Measures 76–107 constitute a double variation (variation 3).

c) The movement's first large section (part 1) is expository and ends in m. 107.

d) Measures 107–116 are transitional to the movement's second large section (part 2). Part 2 begins and ends with fugatos.

e) Variation 4 is a fugato.

f) Measures 175–210 constitute a double variation (var. 5).

g) A characteristic variation begins in m. 211 (var. 6).

h) The variation in mm. 258–277 (var. 7) contains an inversion of the theme, and it also features modal mixture.

i) The variation beginning in m. 277 (var. 8) is a double fugato which closes part 2. One of the subjects is related in some interesting way with the subject of the previous fugato.

j) Part 2 is a section of tonal and modal contrast within the overall tonal design of the movement.

k) The third large section of the movement (part 3) begins in m. 349.

l) Variation 9 is a double variation that features a tempo contrast.

m) Variation 10 presents a climactic "tempo augmentation" of the theme: Although it is written in the same values as usual, it sounds like an augmentation. Why, and where is it?

n) A long coda begins in m. 396. This coda has several distinct sections. What are they? What distinguishes each of them?

o) Provide a formal diagram of this movement, showing the long-range grouping of variations and the over-all tonal design.

EXERCISE 22.2   Spell the following borrowed chords in four voices in the given keys.

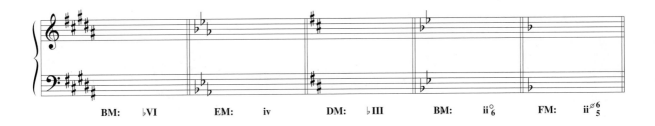

EXERCISE 22.3   Realize the following short progressions in four voices.

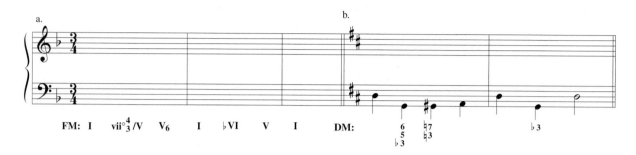

FM: I   vii°$^4_3$/V   V$_6$ I   ♭VI   V   I   DM: $^6_5$ ♮7   ♭3
                                                                              ♭3   ♮3

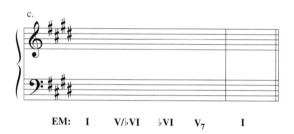

EM: I   V/♭VI   ♭VI   V$_7$ I

EXERCISE 22.4   Harmonize the melody in exercise 22.4 with a left-hand keyboard figuration, using borrowed chords where possible. Be sure to check your first-species outer-voice frame for correct voice leading.

GM:

EXERCISE 22.5   Write a brief binary piece for a single instrument (such as violin, flute, oboe, cello, etc.) using the theme provided below.

1. Begin by composing a modulating period, which will be your first reprise. The modulation should be to the relative major (III).

2. After you are satisfied with your initial period, continue writing the second reprise of the binary piece. First write a short developmental phrase on the given theme, perhaps used sequentially. This section will lead to V, which in turn will lead to a return of the tonic.

3. Then write again the initial phrase (the return), only now it should not modulate, but it should instead remain in the tonic key.

EXERCISE 22.6

1. On your own music paper, first write a harmonization for keyboard of one of the ground basses that appear in example 22.14.

2. Then, write a set of continuous variations on this harmonized bass. You can write for your own instrument or, if you are a keyboard player, for any melodic instrument you choose. Perform your variations in class or for some friends. Make sure that you like what you write, and that you write beautiful, musical phrases.

3. As an alternative to composing these variations, you may also improvise on one or more of the ground basses. You should "prepare" your improvisation before you present it to the class or to your friends. You are likely to find that improvising on these basses is a fun and musically rewarding activity, as musicians in the Renaissance and the baroque knew well.

Chapter 23

The Neapolitan and Augmented Sixth Chords

In this chapter we will study two types of chromatic chords that have a special expressive and dramatic power: the Neapolitan chord (♭II), and the augmented sixth chords. Both types are based on the strong voice-leading tendency created by half-step relationships above and below such fundamental scale degrees as $\hat{1}$ and $\hat{5}$. And both appear in a variety of harmonic contexts, although their most common function is as predominant chords.

THE NEAPOLITAN SIXTH

Study the passage by Paradis in example 23.1. The bass figure in the cadence is the familiar $\hat{4}$–$\hat{5}$–$\hat{1}$. The first chord in m. 9, however, on the bass $\hat{4}$, is not so familiar: It is an FM triad in the key of Em, that is, *a major triad on* ♭$\hat{2}$, here presented in first inversion. Because it was used widely (although not "invented") by seventeenth-century opera composers in the Italian city of Naples, it came to be known as the **Neapolitan chord**. More specifically, the chord appears most frequently in first inversion, with a predominant function, as in example 23.1. Hence its usual name of **Neapolitan sixth**, and its frequent label, N_6. In order to avoid confusion with the N we have used to label "neighbor chords," however, we will use the Roman numeral ♭II (♭II_6 in first inversion) to label the Neapolitan chord.

In the Paradis fragment we can observe some of the characteristics of this chord, which we summarize as follows:

1. Because the Neapolitan chord contains scale degrees ♭$\hat{2}$–$\hat{4}$–♭$\hat{6}$ (♭$\hat{2}$–$\hat{4}$–$\hat{6}$ in minor), it is chromatic in both major and minor modes (technically, these degrees are diatonic in a Phrygian scale, and for this reason this chord is sometimes called the *Phrygian II*). Because of the presence of the minor-mode 6th degree, however, it belongs more properly to (and is more common in) the minor mode. It may certainly also be used in major, in which case it is a borrowed chord (example 23.2b).

2. The chord is most often used in first inversion, with a *predominant function*. Compare the ♭II₆–V–i progression in example 23.2a with its very close relatives, iv–V–i and ii°₆–V–i. Notice that all three progressions feature the bass motion $\hat{4}$–$\hat{5}$ supporting the predominant-dominant harmonies. In four voices, it is best to *double the bass of ♭II₆ (the third of the chord, $\hat{4}$)*. Notice also how the reductive notation at the end of example 23.2a indicates the predominant function of ♭II₆.

3. II₆ is most effective when its characteristic degree, ♭$\hat{2}$, is in the upper voice. *The normative voice leading for ♭$\hat{2}$ is to descend to ♯$\hat{7}$* (through the melodic interval of a diminished 3rd), which then resolves to $\hat{1}$. The melodic figure ♭$\hat{2}$–♯$\hat{7}$–$\hat{1}$ creates a most dramatic tension toward the resolution, $\hat{1}$, by means of the upper leading tone, ♭$\hat{2}$, and the lower leading tone, ♯$\hat{7}$. This half-step voice leading toward $\hat{1}$ from both above and below is the characteristic trademark of this chord. In example 23.1, you can see the normative ♭$\hat{2}$–♯$\hat{7}$ in the piano's upper voice. Before resolving to $\hat{1}$, a change of voicing within the V₇ chord results in a move of ♯$\hat{7}$ to an inner voice.

4. The V chord after a ♭II₆ may be ornamented, as is usual at cadences, with a cadential $^6_4$. The progression then becomes ♭II₆–V$^{6-5}_{4-3}$–I, as in example 23.2c. Notice that the $^6_4$ chord provides a passing step between ♭$\hat{2}$ and ♯$\hat{7}$. The line now becomes ♭$\hat{2}$–$\hat{1}$–♯$\hat{7}$–$\hat{1}$.

NOTE

Beware that if ♭$\hat{2}$ is in an inner voice, the $^6_4$ chord may very easily produce parallel 5ths, as illustrated by example 23.2e. With ♭$\hat{2}$ in the upper voice, the 5ths become correct parallel 4ths.

♪♪♪ Example 23.1   Maria Theresia von Paradis, *Sicilienne*, mm. 7–10

♭II₆

♪♪♪ Example 23.2

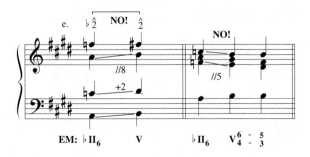

Typical Errors to Avoid

▶ Resolving ♭$\hat{2}$ to ♮$\hat{2}$ instead of ♯$\hat{7}$. Besides this being an unusual resolution, it also will easily produce parallel octaves and a faulty +2 voice leading in the major mode (see example 23.2e).

▶ Writing parallel 5ths if ♭$\hat{2}$ is in an inner voice and the resolution of ♭II$_6$ to V is done through a cadential $^6_4$ (see example 23.2e).

Study the progressions in example 23.2 for instances of the voice leading we have just explained. You may also see a "textbook" treatment of ♭II$_6$ in Beethoven's fragment reproduced in example 23.3.

EXERCISE

To practice spelling Neapolitan sixth chords, refer to exercise 23.2.1 in worksheet 23 at the end of this chapter.

Other Harmonic Contexts for ♭II$_6$

Example 23.2d illustrates a frequent progression with ♭II$_6$, in which *vii°$_7$/V is inserted between the Neapolitan and its resolution to V*. This progression, as well as the possible cadential $^6_4$ elaboration of V, does not affect the voice-leading principles we discussed, as you can verify in example 23.2d. Notice that the reductive notation at the end of this example shows how the vii°$_7$/V is a linear passing chord between ♭II$_6$ predominant chord and V.

♩♩♩**Example 23.3**   L. v. Beethoven, Piano Sonata in C♯m, op. 27, no. 2, *Moonlight*, I, mm. 49–51

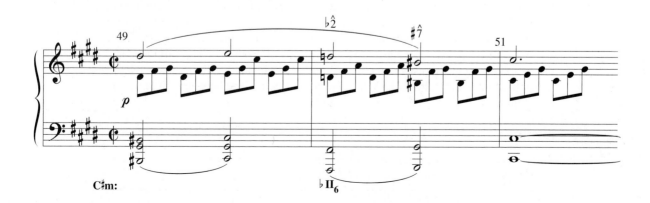

♪♪♪ Example 23.4   W. A. Mozart, Fantasia in Cm, K. 475, mm. 170–173

Now study the phrase in example 23.4. You will see in it a standard use of ♭II₆, with a passing vii°₇/V leading toward the cadential V. This dominant, however, is elaborated by a cadential $^6_4$, which is itself further elaborated or prolonged contrapuntally (m. 172). Discuss this interesting cadential gesture and how it works linearly.

♭II₆ may also appear in the context of a succession of parallel $^6_3$ chords. Analyze anthology, no. 24 (Mozart, Sonata in DM, III, variation 7), mm. 9–12, in Dm. First, notice the nice textural exchange between voices in mm. 9–10, and the compound melody which makes up one of the lines. Then, analyze the passage with Roman numerals (RNs). In m. 10 you will identify a short sequential fragment, made up of parallel $^6_3$ chords. Is there a ♭II₆ in the sequence?

Because in the major mode ♭II₆ is a borrowed chord, it sometimes appears along with other borrowed chords, usually for expressive purposes. The complete text for the passage of the song by Lang reproduced in example 23.5 is: "It is a wondrous feeling that forever cripples the heart, When we experience our first disappointment— A feeling that we never get over." Our example begins with the words "the heart," in the key of CM. Beginning in m. 63, to the word "disappointment," and continuing from there ("a feeling that we never get over"), the mode of the music changes to minor. The ♭II₆ in m. 66 is preceded by a prominent chord which, in the major-mode key of the complete passage, appears as a borrowed ♭VI. Both the change of mode and the Neapolitan help express the feeling of the heart crippled by disappointment. Examine the chords that follow ♭II₆. What chords are interpolated between the latter and its resolution to V?

EXERCISE

To practice realizing short progressions including Neapolitan chords, refer to exercises 23.3a to f in worksheet 23 at the end of this chapter.

TONICIZATION OF THE NEAPOLITAN

The Neapolitan chord, like any other consonant triad, may be tonicized. The dominant of the Neapolitan is, precisely, ♭VI in major (or VI in minor). Because the resolution of this secondary dominant will usually be to a triad in first inversion (♭II₆), the dominant appears often in $\frac{4}{2}$ position. In example 23.6, in Gm, we hear ♭II₆ in m. 11, but before it moves to V in Gm, in m. 12 we hear its own dominant in third inversion, V^4_2/♭II, followed again by ♭II₆. The Neapolitan is thus tonicized in m. 12. What are the remaining chords after m. 12? Here again, this passage with several ♭II₆ chords provides a musical setting to words of sadness and longing: "the sun moves in its course, like yours, my sorrows, deep in the heart, always to rise tomorrow." We see again how ♭II₆ is a chord suitable to add intensity to minor-mode expressivity.

 **Example 23.5**   J. Lang, "Ich gab dem Schicksal dich zurück," m. 59–68

Example 23.6   F. Schubert, "An Mignon," op. 19, no. 2, mm. 9–16

THE NEAPOLITAN IN ROOT POSITION

Although the Neapolitan appears most frequently in first inversion, instances of the ♭II chord in root position are also abundant in the literature. *Erlkönig* (anthology, no. 38) is one of Schubert's most famous songs, and perhaps his most touching one. It tells the story of a father riding late at night holding his child in his arm. Throughout the ride, and the song, the somber king of the elves, the Erlking, is trying to take the boy with him, by lure or by force, to the realm of the spirits. After a long, tense ride in which the poor, scared boy keeps warning his father about the danger, the song ends climactically with the following words: "[The father] reaches home with effort and toil: In his arms the child lay dead!"

Musically, these measures (138–148) are among the most moving in the literature. What chord does Schubert choose to harmonize the arrival to the house, and the subsequent realization that the boy is dead (in mm. 143–146; the key is Gm)? In what position is the chord presented in m. 143 and m. 145? What is the intervening chord in m. 144, and what is its function? Does the chord in m. 145 switch to a familiar position? How does it resolve? How does Schubert depict the horse's gallop, and what happens to this depiction once the rider arrives home? How does the texture express the extremely dramatic moment of the last sentence, when the child is found dead? (We will study this complete song in more detail in chapter 28.)

TRITONE SUBSTITUTION: THE NEAPOLITAN AS A SUBSTITUTE FOR V₇

In jazz and popular music, the Neapolitan most often functions as a dominant substitute rather than a predominant. This is indeed the case in example 23.7, where the final tonic chord ($I^{add\,6}$) is preceded by a Neapolitan (in this case a $♭II^{♭9}_{7}$ which substitutes for

| ♪♪♪Example 23.7 | D. Ellington–J. Mercer–B. Strayhorn, "Satin Doll" (Final Cadence) |

CM: $♭II^{♭9}_{7}$ $I^{add\,6}$

FURTHER ANALYSIS

A final example in this section on the Neapolitan will summarize a lot of what we have discussed. The passage in example 23.8 is in Dm. How is the Neapolitan used in m. 17? What chord does it move to? What is the progression in mm. 20–21? You will hear that mm. 20–22 create a strong directed forward motion toward the final resolution to the tonic in m. 23. Explain what the role of the half step is in creating such a powerful linear pull throughout these measures.

♪♪♪ Example 23.8   W. A. Mozart, *Don Giovanni*, Overture, mm. 17–23

a dominant seventh chord. Notice that ♭II$_7$ (in CM, D♭–F–A♭–C♭) and V$_7$ (G–B–D–F) have two common tones (B/C♭ and F), while ♭II$^{♭9}_7$ (D♭–F–A♭–C♭–E♭♭) and V$_7$ have three common tones (B/C♭, D/E♭♭, and F). Because the roots of V$_7$ (G) and ♭II$_7$ or ♭II$^{♭9}_7$ (D♭) are a tritone apart, this type of substitution (in which we replace a chord with another chord whose root is a tritone away from the root of the chord being replaced) is known as *tritone substitution*.

AUGMENTED SIXTH CHORDS WITH A PREDOMINANT FUNCTION

In the ♭II$_6$ chord, the upper and lower leading tones to î are presented melodically. Examine now the short passage by Chevalier de Saint–Georges in example 23.9. The basic harmonic content of mm. 69–70 is a subdominant chord in Cm, which is

Example 23.9   Chevalier de Saint–Georges, Sonata no. 3 for Violin and Piano, mm. 69–72

Cm: iv₆   V⁶₅/iv   iv   iv₆   +6

first tonicized and then prolonged by means of a passing $^6_4$ (including the customary voice exchange). In m. 71, beat 4, the $\hat{4}$ from iv₆ moves chromatically to a passing $\sharp\hat{4}$, which continues, of course, to $\hat{5}$ (F–F♯–G). This is happening over a bass $\hat{6}$, which moves down to $\hat{5}$ (A♭–G). Notice that what we have here are the two leading tones (upper and lower) to $\hat{5}$, presented simultaneously, or harmonically. The interval between them, from ♭$\hat{6}$ up to $\sharp\hat{4}$, is an augmented sixth, +6. Although the process which we have described is linear, this augmented 6th between the two leading tones to $\hat{5}$ generates a very striking family of chords, the **augmented-sixth chords**.

In this chapter we will focus on some types of +6 chords which display a *predominant function*. These are the types most frequently found in eighteenth- and early nineteenth-century music. +6 chords with either a dominant function or functioning as linear embellishments to the tonic can also often be found in nineteenth-century music. We will study these +6 types in chapter 25, in the context of more advanced chromatic harmony.

Like the Neapolitan, the +6 chords with a predominant function belong more properly to the minor mode, because they are constructed above a "minor" degree ($\hat{6}$ in minor, ♭$\hat{6}$ in major; in the following discussion we will refer to this degree as "♭$\hat{6}$" regardless of the mode). But, also like the Neapolitan, the +6 chords are used both in minor and major keys. In example 23.10 you can see an example of +6 chord in a major key, E♭M. Measure 38 begins with a IV₆. Two members of this chord move then chromatically toward $\hat{5}$: the bass, $\hat{6}$, moves to ♭$\hat{6}$, and on to $\hat{5}$. The middle voice, $\hat{4}$, moves up to $\sharp\hat{4}$ and on to $\hat{5}$. These are, again, our two leading tones to $\hat{5}$, both resolving by contrary motion to $\hat{5}$. Study also the rest of this example. What degrees are tonicized? If you consider only the diatonic chords in the phrase (that is, the degrees that are actually tonicized), what familiar progression do you recognize?

Example 23.10   Nicolò Paganini, Caprice op. 1, no. 14 for Solo Violin, mm. 35–39

In both examples 23.9 and 23.10 we can observe some common features of predominant +6 chords:

1. +6 chords may appear both *in major or in minor* keys.

2. The common framework for all predominant +6 chords is the *+6 interval* between ♭$\hat{6}$ and ♯$\hat{4}$. ♭$\hat{6}$ is normally in the bass.

3. The +6 chord includes at least one more pitch, and, as we can see in both of the above examples, this pitch is usually $\hat{1}$.

4. The +6 chord *resolves to V or V$_7$*. It may do so directly (as in example 23.9), or through the cadential $^6_4$ (as in example 23.10).

5. In either case, *both ♭$\hat{6}$ and ♯$\hat{4}$ resolve to $\hat{5}$* by contrary motion.

6. This simultaneous double leading-tone tendency toward $\hat{5}$ creates a strong tension in this chord, a directed motion toward V, which gives it its typical *predominant function*, as well as a highly dramatic character.

7. The +6 chord is often, although not always, approached, from IV$_6$ (or iv$_6$). In major, it is sometimes preceded by a borrowed chord such as iv$_6$ or ♭VI, both of which introduce ♭$\hat{6}$ in the bass.

Example 23.11 summarizes the standard voice leading and function for the type of +6 chord which we have illustrated so far. The +6 chord made up of only three different pitches (♭$\hat{6}$–$\hat{1}$–♯$\hat{4}$) is known as the *Italian +6* (It +6). In four voices, $\hat{1}$ should be doubled. Examples 23.11a to d show characteristic resolutions of the It +6 to V, V$^{6-5}_{4-3}$, and V$_7$. You will see that in the resolution of the +6 chord to V$_7$, ♯$\hat{4}$ does not move up to $\hat{5}$, but rather down to the seventh of V$_7$, $\hat{4}$. Example 23.11e shows the linear predominant function of the +6 chord by means of reductive notation.

There are, however, two other common types of +6 chords, conveniently (if arbitrarily) labeled *German* (Gr +6) and *French* (Fr +6). Both chords add a fourth pitch to the ♭$\hat{6}$–$\hat{1}$–♯$\hat{4}$ framework of the It +6. In the case of the German +6, the added pitch is a P5 above the bass ($\hat{3}$ in minor, ♭$\hat{3}$ in major; we will refer to this degree as ♭$\hat{3}$ for clarity, regardless of the mode). The complete chord is then ♭$\hat{6}$–$\hat{1}$–♭$\hat{3}$–♯$\hat{4}$. The added pitch in the French +6 is $\hat{2}$, resulting in a complete chord ♭$\hat{6}$–$\hat{1}$–$\hat{2}$–♯$\hat{4}$. Verify these degrees, and hear the sonority for each chord in example 23.11f. We will now study each of these three "national" varieties in some more detail.

♪♪♪Example 23.11

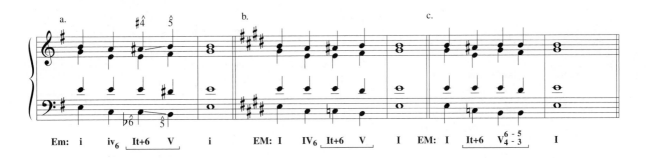

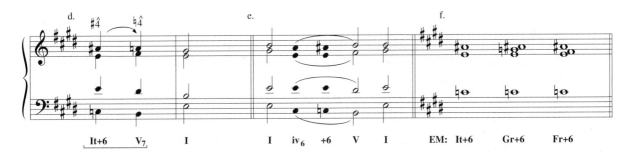

NOTE

In chapter 29, and in the context of our discussion of Wagner's Tristan *prelude, we will study a fourth type of predominant +6 chord which has been called the "dual German +6 chord."*

THE ITALIAN +6

Example 23.11 summarizes the characteristics of the **It +6** (figured bass: +6 or ♯6): It contains three different pitches ($\flat\hat{6}$–$\hat{1}$–$\sharp\hat{4}$), and $\hat{1}$ is doubled in four voices. We referred to the dramatic power of the +6. The chord has indeed often been used for two purposes: to signal the arrival of an important structural cadential point or a point of formal articulation, and, in vocal music, to mark dramatically intense moments when the text so requires. An illustration of the latter appears in example 23.12, from Mozart's opera *Don Giovanni*. Donna Elvira is still in love with Don Giovanni, even after being betrayed by this libertine womanizer. In our example, she is begging him to change his life, over an embellished I chord in FM which turns out to be a pivot for a modulation to B♭M. Notice that the pivot and the "change" of tonal center come not only at the word "cangi," ("change"), but moreover introduce a sharp change of tone in the dialogue

♪♪♪ Example 23.12   W. A. Mozart, *Don Giovanni*, Finale

between the two characters: Don Giovanni now responds, with cold sarcasm, "Brava!" (meaning, "Yes, sure!"), and Donna Elvira's painful answer to his coldness is "Cor perfido!," "wicked heart!" How is her cry of suffering and heartbreak stressed musically, in mm. 10–11 of our example, and twice again in the following measures? How is the harmonic and linear tension in m. 10 supported by such factors as texture and dynamics?

We find many examples of the +6 chord used as a *marker for formal articulation* in the music of Beethoven. Examples 23.13a and b reproduce two fragments from a rondo by this composer. As you will remember, the form of a rondo is based on the alternation of a refrain, which always returns in the tonic key, and episodes that may present new material or develop the material from the refrain (in a formal scheme such as A–B–A–C–A–D–A). In example 23.13a we see the measures leading from the end of the C section, a developmental episode, into the return of the A material at m. 132. The dominant chord in this passage (reached in m. 129, and anticipated in m. 127) has a structural function within the overall form: to take us back to the return of the home key. What chord does Beethoven use to precede the arrival of the dominant in both of these measures?

In example 23.13b, on the other hand, we see the end of the last A section (with the imperfect authentic cadence in mm. 247–248) and the subsequent beginning of the closing coda, which simply functions as a long cadential extension. What chords are used in the fragment of this cadential extension reproduced in our example? What chord is extended in mm. 252–255? In all of these examples by Mozart and Beethoven, can you verify the conventional voice leading for the +6 chord which we discussed?

EXERCISES

To practice spelling Italian +6 chords, refer to exercise 23.2.2 in worksheet 23 at the end of this chapter.

To practice realizing short progressions including Italian +6 chords, refer to exercises 23.3g to j in worksheet 23 at the end of this chapter.

Example 23.13a   L. v. Beethoven, Piano Sonata in GM, op. 31/1, III, mm. 126–134

THE GERMAN +6

As we saw in example 23.11f, the **German +6** chord (figured bass: $^{+6}_{5}$ or $^{\sharp 6}_{5}$) includes four different pitches, $\flat\hat{6}$–$\hat{1}$–$\flat\hat{3}$–$\sharp\hat{4}$. $\flat\hat{3}$ has thus been added to the basic core of the It +6. If you play or sing this chord, you will notice that its sonority is identical to a Mm_7 (that is, a V_7 type of sonority) on $\flat\hat{6}$, only that the seventh of the chord is spelled as an +6th. In example 23.14a we can see the Gr +6 in its conventional function as a predominant chord, in this case preceded by $\flat$VI. Notice also that the Gr +6 (mm. 35–36) leads directly to V, and that Mozart's voice leading includes clear parallel 5ths. As a matter of fact, *the parallel 5ths between the Gr +6 and V are not only permissible, but frequently found in the literature.* There are several reasons why these parallel 5ths are permissible. In the first place and as we can see in the Mozart example, the 5ths are not

♪♪♪Example 23.13b   L. v. Beethoven, Piano Sonata in GM, op. 31/1, III, mm. 247–256

so evident if they appear, as they most often do, in the context of arpeggiated chords (that is, not presented as harmonic intervals), rather than in block chords or chorale textures. Moreover, we hear the +6 chord as a dissonant chord, and our attention is drawn to the linear resolution of the +6 interval (the dissonance) rather than to the parallel 5ths, especially if the +6 is placed in the outer voices and the 5ths involve an inner voice. In any case, these are the only parallel fifths in tonal harmonic theory in which you can indulge and which you can enjoy without fear of being corrected!

Very often, however, composers "hide" the parallel 5ths by means of an intervening cadential $^6_4$. This is the case in another Mozart example from *Don Giovanni* (example 23.14b). Can you find the parallel 5ths Mozart avoids by moving the Gr +6 to V (mm. 10–11) through a cadential $^6_4$? The conventional voice-leading possibilities for the Gr +6 are summarized in examples 23.23a and b.

Don Giovanni also affords good examples of the dramatic use of the Gr +6. Early in the opera Don Giovanni kills the Commendatore in a fight, after having betrayed the latter's daughter, Donna Anna. Toward the end of the opera, in a defiant gesture, Don Giovanni invites the statue of the Commendatore to supper. As Donna Elvira, after her unsuccessful bid to change Don Giovanni's life, opens the door to leave, she runs into none other than . . . the statue coming for dinner! This passage in the opera, reproduced in example 23.15, illustrates the dramatic use of modulation, of the vii°$_7$ chord, and of the Gr +6 chord. The passage begins in B♭M, as Donna Elvira goes to the door. What chord marks her scream of terror ("Ah!") at finding the statue at the door? What modulation takes place to underscore the heightening tension of Don Giovanni's words, "A scream,

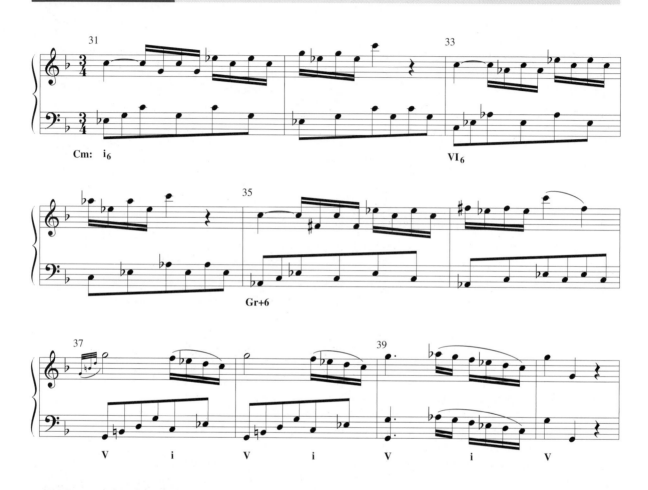

Example 23.14a   W. A. Mozart, Piano Sonata in FM, K. 332, I, mm. 31–40

Example 23.14b   W. A. Mozart, *Don Giovanni*, Overture, mm. 10–13

♪♪♪ Example 23.15   W. A. Mozart, *Don Giovanni*, Finale

what can have happened?" What chord is used in m. 10 of the passage, to stress even more the third statement of this questioning sentence? Notice that in this case Mozart moves this chord directly to a V chord. How does he avoid the usual parallel 5ths?

Because the Gr +6 contains three common tones with ♭VI, it is often approached from that chord. The Haydn passage in example 23.16 is in GM. In m. 239 we hear a powerful deceptive cadence to a borrowed ♭VI, which is prolonged and tonicized (how?) for eight measures, until it becomes a Gr +6 by the simple addition of #$\hat{4}$ to the ♭VI triad. Here again, Haydn avoids the parallel 5ths in the same way Mozart did in example 23.15. How?

EXERCISES

To practice spelling German +6 chords, refer to exercise 23.2.3 in worksheet 23 at the end of this chapter.

To practice realizing short progressions including German +6 chords, refer to exercises 23.3k to n in worksheet 23 at the end of this chapter.

♪♪♪Example 23.16   J. Haydn, Symphony no. 100, *Military*, I, mm. 236–249

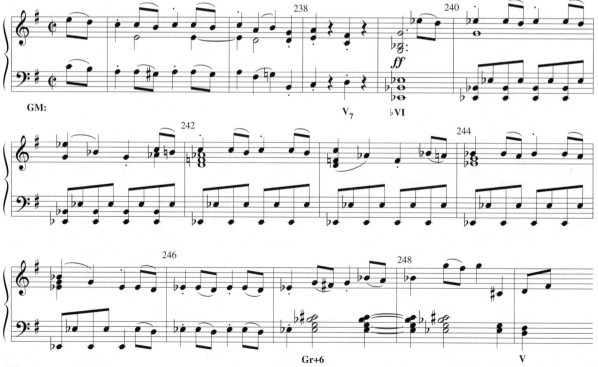

In chapter 19 we studied a case of chromatic modulation in anthology, no. 28 (Mozart, B♭M Sonata, III), mm. 56–65. We pointed out that the arrival on the tonic of the new key (Gm) is delayed in m. 63 by means of a deceptive cadence, and that, for the time being, we should consider the C♯ as a linear passing tone. It is indeed a linear passing tone (albeit producing a melodic +2!), but at the same time, what chord does it generate?

An interesting passage from the anthology which you can now analyze in full is the closing of Beethoven's Fm sonata, op. 2, no. 1, I (anthology, no. 32). Begin in mm. 139–140, with the perfect authentic cadence in Fm. What three chord progressions does Beethoven repeat in mm. 140–145? Analyze also the harmonic content of the final measures (145–152). Which degrees are tonicized and how? Is there an irregular resolution of a dominant seventh, and if so, does the voice leading follow the conventional principles for this type of resolution, which we studied in chapter 17?

Alternate Spelling of the Gr +6: The Doubly Augmented Fourth Chord

Example 23.17 shows the beginning measures of a song by Schumann, in B♭M. You will notice two unusual things. First, the song begins with a Gr +6 chord, an unconventional chord to begin a piece with, to be sure. Second, this chord is spelled ♭$\hat{6}$–$\hat{1}$–♯$\hat{2}$–♯$\hat{4}$ instead of the more familiar ♭$\hat{6}$–$\hat{1}$–♭$\hat{3}$–♯$\hat{4}$. In other words, ♭$\hat{3}$ has been replaced by its enharmonic spelling, ♯$\hat{2}$. The reason is mostly of visual voice-leading logic: in major keys, when the Gr +6 moves to a cadential $^6_4$, one voice carries the voice leading ♭$\hat{3}$–♮$\hat{3}$–$\hat{2}$. Sometimes composers use an alternative notation for this line, one that seems to reflect more logically the ascent from ♭$\hat{3}$ to ♮$\hat{3}$: ♯$\hat{2}$–♮$\hat{3}$; hence the enharmonic spelling of ♭$\hat{3}$ in example 23.17. Verify this same alternate spelling in example 23.23c. Because of the doubly augmented 4th interval that this enharmonic spelling creates (♭$\hat{6}$–♯$\hat{2}$), this chord is usually referred to as the **doubly augmented fourth chord**.

♪♪♪ Example 23.17   R. Schumann, "Am leuchtenden Sommermorgen," from *Dichterliebe*, op. 48, mm. 1–4

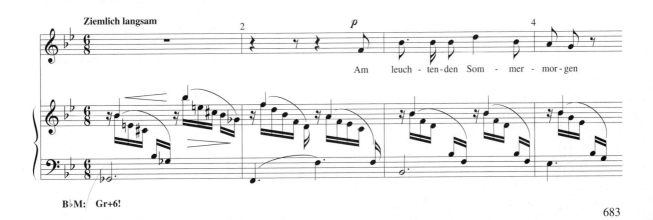

B♭M: Gr+6!

EXERCISES

To practice spelling doubly +4th chords, refer to exercise 23.2.4 in worksheet 23 at the end of this chapter.

To practice realizing short progressions including doubly +4th chords, refer to exercises 23.3o and p in worksheet 23 at the end of this chapter.

THE FRENCH +6

The most peculiar and dissonant of the +6 chords is the **French +6** (figured bass: $^{+6}_{\ 4}$ $_3$ or $^{\sharp 6}_{\ 4}$ $_3$. The fourth pitch in this chord, added to the basic frame of the It +6, is $\hat{2}$. The total sonority, $\flat\hat{6}$–$\hat{1}$–$\hat{2}$–$\sharp\hat{4}$, includes two overlapping tritones and a major 2nd, besides the +6th. The function of this chord, as well as its resolution to V or to the cadential $^6_5$, are the same as in the other two types of +6 chord. Example 23.18 illustrates Beethoven's

♪♪♪ **Example 23.18**   L. v. Beethoven, Symphony no. 3, op. 55 (*Eroica*), mm. 37–49

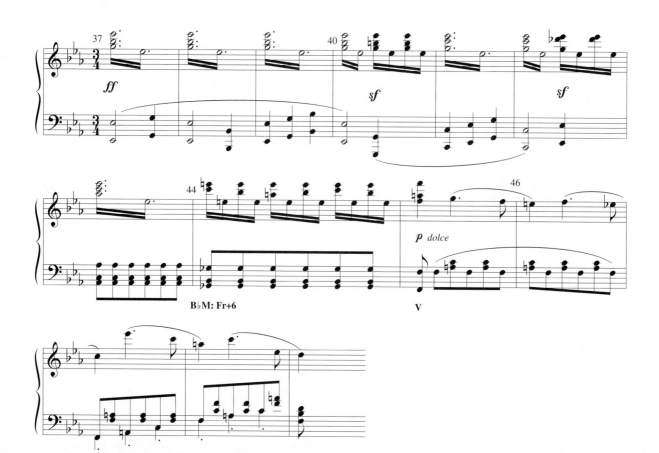

♪♪♪ Example 23.19a   Celeste Heckscher, *Valse Bohème*, mm. 77–84

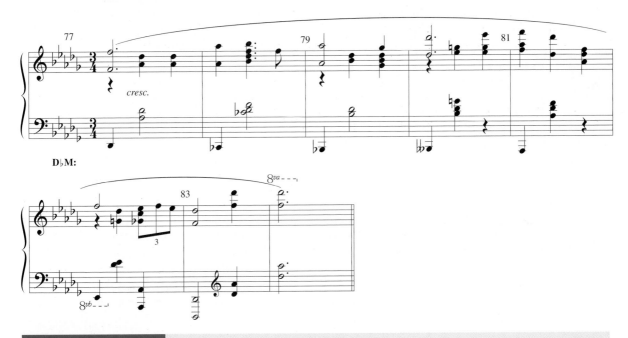

♪♪♪ Example 23.19b   F. Chopin, Prelude 20 in Cm, mm. 5–7

use of this chord at a point of great formal significance, the beginning of the second theme (and the secondary key area, in the dominant key) in the first movement of the *Eroica* Symphony. The secondary key area begins in m. 45 on V of the dominant key, B♭M, approached from a Fr +6 in m. 44. Verify the pitches and spelling of this chord, as well as its voice-leading resolution to V in B♭M. Hear the powerful tension created by this dissonant sonority, so well used by Beethoven as a formal marker in this passage.

The phrase by Celeste Heckscher in example 23.19a, on the other hand, illustrates the resolution of a Fr +6 to a cadential $^6_4$. Identify the chord, and double-check its spelling and voice leading. Whereas both this example and the Beethoven example above show the linear character of this chord, the Chopin fragment in example 23.19b features a Fr +6 in the context of a larger linear harmonic process. What is the essential bass motion that generates harmony in this passage? Which familiar diatonic linear technique do the first two chords illustrate? What chord does the A♮ in m. 6 produce? Explain the linear function of the Fr +6 in m. 6. Which of its pitches can be explained as passing tones, neighbor notes, anticipations, or some other linear concept?

EXERCISES

To practice spelling French +6 chords, refer to exercise 23.2.5 in Worksheet 23 at the end of this chapter.

To practice realizing short progressions including French +6 chords, refer to exercises 23.3q to t in worksheet 23 at the end of this chapter.

OTHER TYPES OF +6 CHORDS

Although the three characteristic types of +6 chords we discussed usually appear individually, at times all three types are lumped into a "**moving**" **+6** chord, such as the one shown in example 23.20. The chord in m. 41, beat 3, begins as a Gr +6. But because of the moving viola line (the sixteenth-note figure), it immediately becomes a Fr +6, and then an It +6, before it resolves to V in Fm. Because this type of moving +6 chord includes all three "nationalities," we could appropriately call it the "European Union +6 chord"!

♪♪♪Example 23.20   J. Haydn, Quartet in B♭M, op. 64, no. 3, I, mm. 39–42

The Diminished Third (°3) Chord

Inversions of the +6 chord are not frequent, because the chord is most effective when ♭6̂ is in the bass (and, possibly, ♯4̂ in the top voice). The inversion which places ♯4̂ in the bass, however, also produces a chord strongly directed toward V. This inversion is found occasionally in music of the Romantic period. Because this chord includes the inversion of an +6, a diminished 3rd, counted from the bass upward, we call it the **°3 chord**. In the Verdi fragment reproduced in example 23.21, the music is coming from the key of AM. The Gr +6 chord in AM is F♮–A–C♮–D♯. In mm. 2–4 of our example you can see this chord with the D♯ in the bass (first spelled enharmonically as E♭) and the F♮ in the upper voice, thus spelling out a °3rd interval, and a °3 chord. The resolution in m. 5 is to V in AM, with all the conventional voice leading.

♪♪♪ **Example 23.21**   G. Verdi, *Aida*, "Ritorna vincitor," mm. 1–6

EXERCISE

To practice spelling diminished 3rd chords, refer to exercise 23.2.6 in worksheet 23 at the end of this chapter.

Secondary +6 Chords

All the +6 chords we have seen so far function as a predominant chord to the primary dominant, V. Secondary dominants, however, may also be preceded by their own, **secondary +6 chord**, an event that is often part of a secondary key area. Example 23.22 is in D♭M, as indicated by the two initial chords, the cadence in m. 25, and the final cadence. In mm. 22–23 we see a brief secondary key area of vi, closing with a V/vi in m. 24. The two chords that precede this V/vi (m. 23, beats 2 and 3) are examples of secondary +6 chords (of which type?). Complete the Roman numeral analysis of m. 22 to m. 24, beat 1, using the secondary key area notation already started on the example. What other tonicizations can you identify in the example?

SUMMARY

In example 23.23 you will find a summary of spelling and voice leading for the Gr +6, Fr +6, and °3 chords. Study these carefully, and play these examples at the piano to learn the characteristic sound of these interesting chromatic chords.

> ♪♪♪ Example 23.22   R. Schumann, *Papillons*, op. 2, no. 8, mm. 21–32

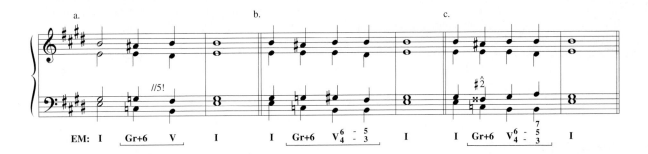

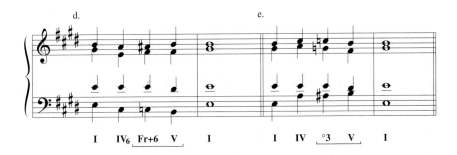

TONAL RELATIONSHIP BETWEEN THE NEAPOLITAN AND THE +6 CHORDS

As we saw above, the dominant of the Neapolitan chord is the ♭VI triad. We have also seen that the sonority of the Gr +6 chord is the same as a Mm_7 sonority on ♭$\hat{6}$. In other words, the dominant seventh of the Neapolitan, V_7/♭II, and the Gr +6 are the same sonority, although spelled differently. Example 23.24 shows the relationship between the two chords. As you can imagine, this opens up some interesting possibilities. If the Gr +6 and the ♭II chord are connected by a dominant/tonic relationship, couldn't we use the Gr +6 respelled as V_7/♭II, to modulate to such a distant key as the Neapolitan key (say, from Cm to C♯m or to C♯M)? This is indeed one of the distant modulations which we will study in the next chapter.

EXERCISES

To practice realizing progressions including Neapolitan and +6 chords, refer to exercise 23.4 in worksheet 23 at the end of this chapter.

   To practice harmonizing a melody including Neapolitan or +6 chords, refer to exercise 23.5 in worksheet 23 at the end of this chapter.

   To practice analyzing musical fragments including Neapolitan or +6 chords, refer to exercise 23.1 in worksheet 23 at the end of this chapter.

PRACTICAL APPLICATION AND DISCUSSION

Are there any ♭II₆ or +6 chords that you are aware of in any of the pieces you perform? If not, try to find some. If you find an +6 chord, bring it to class and explain its function. What is its expressive or formal context? If the music is vocal, does the +6 emphasize some aspect of the text? If the music is not vocal, is the +6 marking the arrival on an important cadence or perhaps an important point of formal articulation? Is this emphasis brought out in any other way with the use of dynamics, rhythm, articulation markings, and so forth? How does your awareness of this chord's character affect your performance of it? If you and your class peers do not find any of your own examples, this same discussion may be referred to one or more of the examples you have to analyze in this chapter's worksheet and workbook assignments.

♪♪♪ Example 23.24

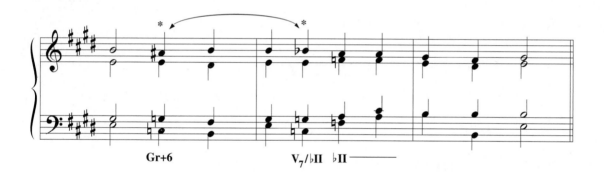

Gr+6   V₇/♭II ♭II ————

ASSIGNMENT AND KEYBOARD PROGRESSIONS

For analytical and written assignments and keyboard progressions based on the materials learned in this chapter, refer to chapter 23 in the workbook.

PITCH PATTERNS

Sing the pitch patterns in example 23.25, and as you sing listen to the Neapolitan or +6 chords and their resolution. Then, *improvise* similar pitch patterns using linearized ♭II₆ or +6 chords.

♪♪♪ Example 23.25

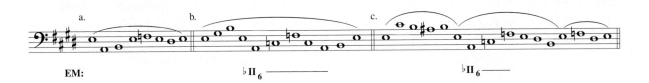

EM: ♭II₆ ————————   ♭II₆ ————

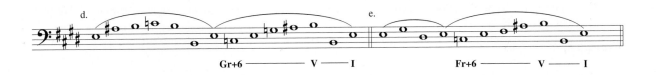

Gr+6 ——————— V — I   Fr+6 ——————— V — I

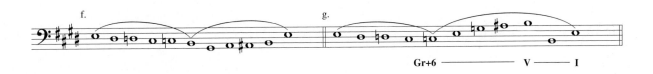

Gr+6 ——————————— V —— I

Composers and Their Music 23

Biographies

Write short biographies of the following composers mentioned in this chapter: Nicolò Paganini, Celeste Heckscher.

Listening

Listen to the following compositions by composers mentioned in this chapter:

Paganini, 24 Caprices, op. 1 (selected caprices).
Mozart, *Don Giovanni* (complete opera if possible).

Follow the score while you listen. Be able to place each of these compositions in one of the style periods, and to comment on why and how it represents the musical characteristics of that period.

Terms for Review

Neapolitan chord
Neapolitan sixth (♭II₆)
Tonicization of the ♭II chord
Augmented sixth (+6) chords
It +6
Gr +6

Alternate spelling of the Gr +6 (the
    doubly augmented fourth chord)
Fr +6
"moving" +6
°3 chord
Secondary +6 chords

Worksheet 23

EXERCISE 23.1   *Analysis.* For each of the following examples, identify possible Neapolitan or +6 chords.

1. For ♭II chords, verify and mark the voice leading of the voice with ♭$\hat{2}$. Is the ♭II chord in first inversion or root position?

2. For +6 chords, identify the type (nationality). If it is Gr +6, is it spelled with a ♭$\hat{3}$ or a ♯$\hat{2}$?

3. In all cases, provide RNs for the actual ♭II or +6 chord, and also for the chords that precede and follow it.

4. What chord precedes the ♭II or +6 chord? Is the ♭II chord tonicized?

5. Does the ♭II or +6 chord resolve directly to V? Does it resolve to V through some other harmonies? Are parallel 5ths avoided?

Examples for Analysis:

1. Example 23.26.

2. Anthology, no. 35, Beethoven, *Waldstein* Sonata, mm. 132–136.

Example 23.26   F. Chopin, Waltz op. 34, no. 2, mm. 145–152

3. Example 23.27.

Example 23.27   F. Chopin, Prelude in Cm, op. 28, no. 20, mm. 11–13

4. Example 23.28.

Example 23.28   F. Schubert, Symphony no. 9 in CM, II, mm. 255–259

5. Example 23.29.

♪♪♪ Example 23.29   W. A. Mozart, Sonata for Violin and Piano, K. 380, III, mm. 101–108

6. Example 23.30.

♪♪♪Example 23.30   J. Brahms, Symphony no. 1, II, mm. 1–4

7. Example 23.31.

♪♪♪Example 23.31   W. A. Mozart, Piano Sonata in FM, K. 280, II, mm. 9–14

8. Anthology, no. 24, Mozart, Sonata in DM, III, Var. 7, mm. 3–4, 5–8, and 14–17.

9. Anthology, no. 34, Beethoven, Sonata op. 13, *Pathétique*, III, mm. 6–7, 44–47, 131–135, and 182–186.

10. Example 23.32.

♪♪♪ Example 23.32   F. Chopin, Prelude in Em, op. 28, no. 4, mm. 20–25

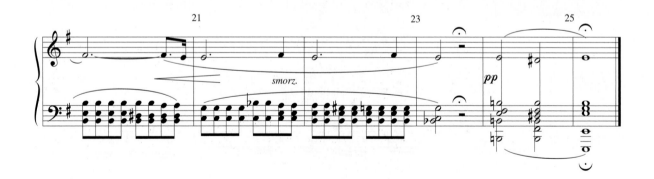

EXERCISE 23.2   Spell the following chords in four voices, in the required keys:

1. Neapolitan sixth chords

2. Italian +6 chords

3. German +6 chords

4. Doubly augmented 4th chords

5. French +6 chords

6. Diminished 3rd chords

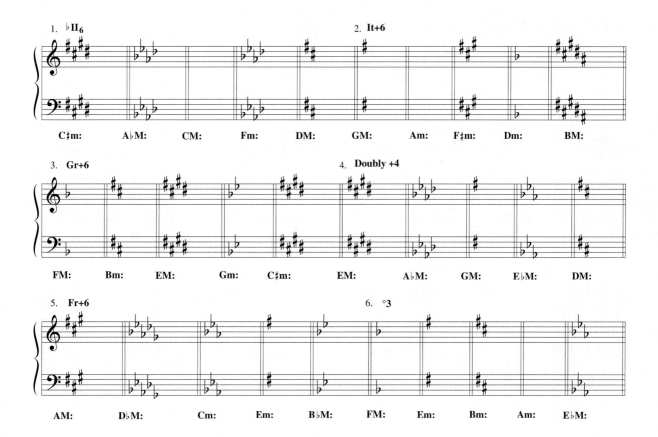

EXERCISE 23.3   Realize the following short progressions in four voices. Add RNs to the progressions with a figured bass. Be careful with your spelling and resolution of the numerous Neapolitan and +6 chords in these progressions.

EXERCISE 23.4   Realize the following progressions in four voices. Provide RN analyses for progressions b and d.

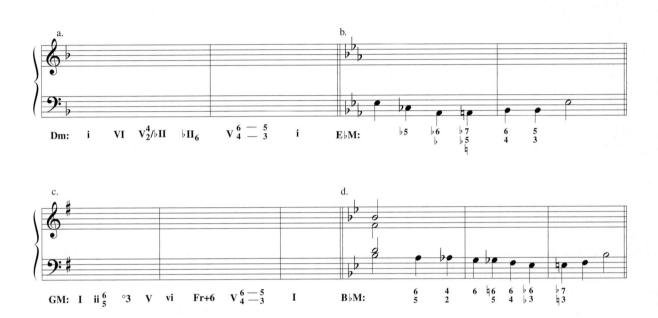

EXERCISE 23.5   Harmonize the melody in this exercise (adapted from Bach's Cantata BWV 21, no. 3) with a bass and RNs. In mm. 1–2, the harmonic rhythm is one chord per beat. In m. 3, you will have to adjust the harmonic rhythm to the needs of the melody.

The initial words of this aria's text are: "Seufzer, Tränen, Kummer, Not. Seufzer, Tränen, ängstlich's Sehnen." ("Sighing, tears, suffering, need. Sighing, tears, anguished yearning."). How do the melody and the harmony reflect the mood of the text? Would you say that Bach's use of dissonance in this phrase is also related with the character of the text? How? Can you comment on (and explain) the dissonances in m. 1, beats 1–2?

Chapter 24

Chromatic Modulatory Techniques: Modulation to Distantly Related Keys I

In this chapter we will continue our study of modulation, focusing on techniques that allow tonal motion to distantly related keys. **Distantly related keys** are keys whose signatures differ in more than one accidental. Any two keys that are not closely related are distantly related, although the distance can be smaller or greater (for instance, CM and DM, with a difference of only two sharps, are not as distantly related as CM and C♯M, with a difference of seven sharps, or CM and F♯M, with a difference of six sharps). In this chapter we will first study three types of modulation to distantly related keys: by *chromatic pivot chord*, by *enharmonic reinterpretation of the +6 chord*, and by *enharmonic reinterpretation of vii°₇*. We will close the chapter with further study of linear modulatory processes, with focus on chromatic sequences as a means of modulation.

CHROMATIC PIVOT CHORDS

In chapter 19 we studied modulation by means of diatonic pivot chords, which we defined as chords that have a diatonic function in both of the keys for which they act as a connection. We also introduced **chromatic pivot chords**, chords that are not diatonic in at least one of the keys involved in the modulation. In this section we will further our study of chromatic pivot relationships, including those that allow modulations to distantly related keys.

Example 24.1 illustrates a few possible **chromatic pivot relationships** from CM to several other keys. Notice that the second key in this type of modulation may be closely or distantly related. And notice also that the pivot chord may be of three types, depending on whether it is chromatic in the first key, in the second key, or in both:

1. In the first type, **diatonic-chromatic**, the chord is diatonic in the first key and chromatic in the second. Both examples for this type (example 24.1a) involve borrowed chords in the second key, including a ♭II₆.

2. The second type, **chromatic-diatonic**, features chords that are chromatic in the first key and diatonic in the second. A frequent example for this type features a secondary dominant in the first key, which becomes the diatonic dominant of the second key (example 24.1b). In our second example, ♭II₆ (a chromatic chord) becomes a diatonic IV₆ in the new key.

♪♪♪ Example 24.1

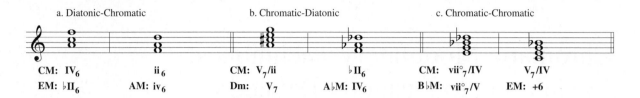

a. Diatonic-Chromatic

b. Chromatic-Diatonic

c. Chromatic-Chromatic

CM: IV₆   ii₆   CM: V₇/ii   ♭II₆   CM: vii°₇/IV   V₇/IV

EM: ♭II₆   AM: iv₆   Dm: V₇   A♭M: IV₆   B♭M: vii°₇/V   EM: +6

3. In the third type, **chromatic-chromatic**, the chord is chromatic in both keys. In example 24.1c, a secondary vii°₇ in the first key also becomes a secondary vii°₇ in the second key, and in the second example a secondary dominant in the first key becomes the Gr +6 chord in the second key. (This latter example takes advantage of

♪♪♪ Example 24.2   W. A. Mozart, *Die Entführung aus dem Serail*, Act III, no. 18, mm. 11–17

seufzt' Tag und Nacht und wein - te gar,   wollt' ge - rn er - lö - set

GM: V₇   I ————

F♯m: ♭II₆ V⁶₄ - ⁷₅₃   I₆

sein, ———— wollt' gern er - lö - set sein.

i ————

the fact that the Gr +6 sonority is the same as a Mm_7 sonority, but it involves an enharmonic respelling of the chord. Try it: How would you spell V_7/IV in CM, and how would you spell the same sonority but now functioning as the Gr +6 in EM? We will study enharmonic reinterpretation of the Gr +6 in more detail below.)

EXERCISE

To practice determining the chromatic pivot function of a chord between two keys, refer to exercise 24.2 in worksheet 24 at the end of this chapter.

The Diatonic-Chromatic Pivot Relationship

In example 24.2, taken from Mozart's *The Abduction from the Seraglio*, Pedrillo tells the story of the Spanish lady Kostanze, of whom he is a servant, and who has been the captive of a Moorish ruler. The beginning of our example, in which we learn that Kostanze has been sighing in despair day and night, is in GM. The second sentence refers to the lady's longing for freedom, and this allusion to the liberation that would allow her to return to her distant homeland comes with a modulation to the distantly related keys of F♯m/F♯M. Connecting both keys (G and F♯) is a chromatic pivot chord, the GM triad in first inversion which is diatonic in GM (I_6) and chromatic in F♯ ($♭II_6$). Two progressions illustrating the *diatonic-chromatic* pivot relationship appear in example 24.3. Play these

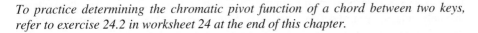

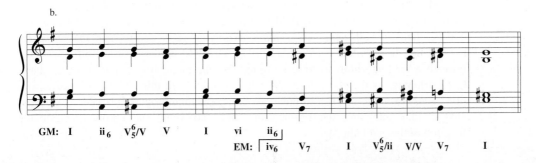

progressions, sing them in class, and hear the modulation and the pivot chord function in both keys.

The Chromatic-Diatonic Pivot Relationship

This chromatic pivot relationship between two keys is beautifully illustrated by the Brahms passage reproduced in example 24.4, although the keys involved here are not distantly related (Fm and D♭M, or i–VI). When you analyze the harmonies in mm. 25–32 you will see that the passage is based on a standard diatonic progression in Fm (i–VI–iv–V) which has been slightly elaborated: The V in m. 29 is extended by means of a deceptive resolution, and then it is tonicized before reaching the half cadence (HC) in m. 32. The predominant iv in m. 27 is itself prolonged by means of the ♭II₆ chord in m. 28. In Fm, ♭II₆ is, of course, chromatic. Now refer to the progression after the HC (mm. 33–38). It begins with the same chord that we just saw in m. 28 (♭II₆ in Fm), but now it moves on to the dominant of D♭M, which eventually resolves to the tonic of the new key (in first inversion, m. 38). In D♭M, the G♭M triad in m. 33 is a diatonic chord, IV₆. In other words, this is a *chromatic-diatonic* pivot that has taken us from Fm to D♭M.

Modulations are sometimes achieved by the introduction of the new dominant, which we first hear as a secondary dominant. The Beethoven passage in example 24.5 begins with a cadence in A♭M. In the context of this key, we hear mm. 29–30 as a tonicization of vi, that is, we hear the CM chord in m. 29 as a secondary dominant of vi (hence as a chromatic chord in A♭M). As the music goes on, we realize that we are modulating to Fm. The CM chord in m. 29 is, then, chromatic in A♭M and diatonic in Fm. This is a case of a chromatic-diatonic relationship in the form of the dominant of the new key first heard as a tonicizing secondary dominant in the old key.

The two progressions in example 24.6 summarize the two types of chromatic-diatonic pivot relationship we just studied.

The Chromatic-Chromatic Pivot Relationship

In this type of pivot relationship, the pivot chord is chromatic in both keys. A frequent type of chromatic-chromatic pivot features a chord with a secondary function in both keys. Refer to anthology, no. 32 (Beethoven, Sonata in Fm, op. 2 no. 1), mm 49–57. The passage begins in A♭M and ends in B♭m. The chord in m. 53 is a secondary vii°₅⁶/vi in A♭M, which actually leads not to vi (an Fm triad) but rather to V in B♭m (an FM triad) in m. 55. Our vii°₅⁶/vi in A♭M is thus also a vii°₅⁶/V in B♭m, hence it is a secondary chord in both keys, a *chromatic-chromatic* pivot chord. You may have remarked that the resolution from the vii°₅⁶/V in m. 53 to the V in m. 55 is effected through a passing chord in m. 54 (notice the chromatic linear motion in the bass, G–G♭–F). What is the chord in m. 54 which results from this chromatic passing motion? Study example 24.7a, a summary of the modulating progression we have just discussed. Play and sing the progression, and understand the chromatic-chromatic function of the pivot chord.

♪♪♪ Example 24.5   L. v. Beethoven, Piano Sonata op. 7 in E♭M, II, mm. 27–32

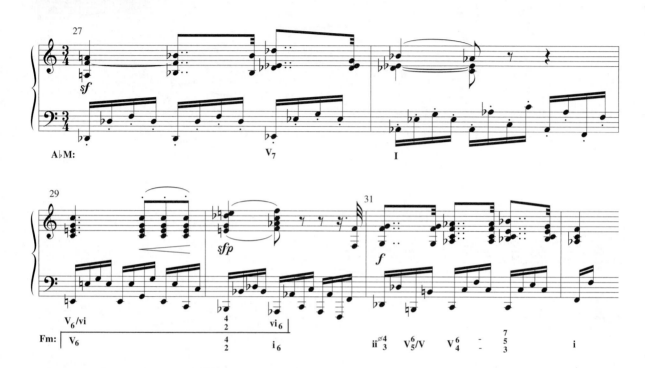

Example 24.7b illustrates the use of a chromatic-chromatic pivot chord to modulate between two closely related keys, CM and GM. Although one could argue that the dominant in this example's m. 4 could be interpreted as a diatonic pivot chord (I in GM), in this measure we do not hear this GM chord as a tonic at all, but only as V of CM. Then, we hear the following EM seventh chord as V_7/vi in CM. But by m. 6 we

♪♪♪ Example 24.6

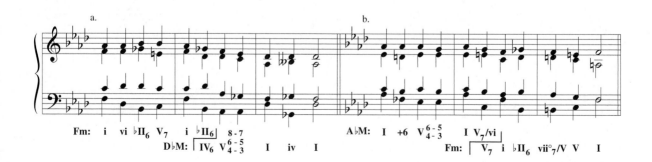

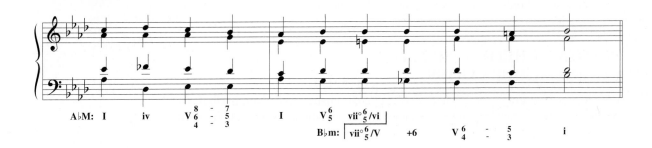

Example 24.7a

$A\flat M$: I   iv $V^{8-7}_{6-5}_{4-3}$ I V^6_5 $vii°^6_5/vi$

$B\flat m$: $vii°^6_5/V$ +6 V^{6-5}_{4-3} i

Example 24.7b   Mike Love–Brian Wilson (The Beach Boys), "The Warmth of the Sun"

the   sun - set   at   night,   or   liv - ing   this   way?

CM: I   vi $\flat$III i_7 ii

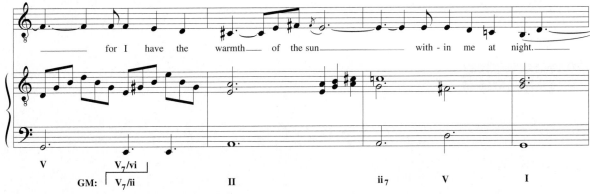

for I   have   the   warmth   of   the sun   with - in   me   at   night.

V V_7/vi

GM: V_7/ii II ii_7 V   I

realize that we are moving to GM, and that the V_7/vi was actually a V_7/ii tonicizing a predominant chord in GM. This secondary chord, chromatic in both keys, is then the actual pivot (a chromatic-chromatic pivot) between the two keys. Comment also on the use of borrowed chords in this passage. How many of them are there?

WRITING CHROMATIC PIVOT CHORD MODULATIONS

The process of writing a modulation involving a chromatic pivot chord is similar to the process we learned in chapter 19 of writing modulations using diatonic pivot chords.

1. You may first determine the keys you will use in your modulation, and then investigate possible chromatic pivot chords. For instance, if you want to modulate from FM to EM, you may take advantage of the fact that I in FM is the Neapolitan chord in EM, and thus you can use the diatonic-chromatic pivot FM: I_6/EM: $\flat II_6$.

2. Or you may wish to use a specific pivot relationship (say, $\flat II_6$ in the first key) to modulate to some other key. Then, you will investigate possible keys you can go to by means of that pivot. $\flat II_6$ in FM, for instance, can become IV_6 in $D\flat M$, I_6 in $G\flat M$, or V_6 in BM (try all of these possibilities at the piano or on paper).

3. We will now write several progressions using some of these procedures. First, let us write a *diatonic-chromatic* pivot modulation from FM to EM. We would like our pivot chord to be a borrowed chord in the second key, EM. What diatonic chords in FM can function as borrowed chords in EM? iii in F becomes iv in E, and V in F becomes $\flat VI$ in E. Because V of the old key is not the best possible pivot, we will choose iii/iv as a diatonic-chromatic pivot. Now we need to write a good progression in each of the keys, and connect the two progressions by means of our chosen pivot. Example 24.8 shows a possible realization of this modulation.

   Now try writing your own modulating progression using a diatonic-chromatic pivot. Choose your first key, and write a modulation in which some diatonic major triad in the first key becomes $\flat II_6$ in the second key.

♪♪♪ Example 24.8

FM: I   iii   IV   vii°$_7$/V   V$^6_4$ - $^5_3$ I   iii
                                                        EM: | iv   V$^6_4$ - $^5_3$ I   V$^4_2$/IV   IV$_6$ +6   V$^6_4$ - $^5_3$ I

♪♪♪Example 24.9

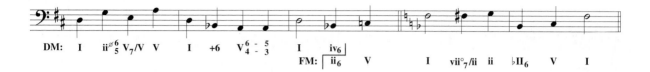

DM: I   ii⌀$^6_5$ V$_7$/V V   I   +6   V$^{6-5}_{4-3}$ I   iv$_6$⌐
                                                    FM: ⌐ ii$_6$ V   I   vii°$_7$/ii ii ♭II$_6$ V   I

4. Next, we will write some modulations using a chromatic-diatonic pivot. First, we want to write a modulation from DM using a borrowed chord in the first key, for instance, iv or iv$_6$, the Gm triad. The Gm triad can be found as a diatonic chord in quite a few keys (for instance, it is i in Gm, ii in FM, iii in E♭M, etc.). Because DM and FM are distantly related keys, and iv in DM is a predominant chord in FM (ii, a good pivot), we choose FM as our second key. Then we try to write two interesting progressions in DM and FM, and connect them with the iv$_6$/ii$_6$ chromatic-diatonic pivot that we previously determined. Example 24.9 shows a possible solution for this modulation.

   Write now two modulations with chromatic-diatonic pivots. In the first modulation, begin in CM, and use as the pivot ♭II$_6$ in CM, which will become V$_6$ in the new key. What key does this pivot take us to? Notice that this is an interesting distant modulation. What is the Roman numeral (RN) relationship between these two keys?

   For your second modulation, begin from a major key, and modulate to the ♭VII key using the dominant of the new key first as a secondary dominant in the old key.

5. Finally, write your own modulation using a chromatic-chromatic pivot. As a suggestion, try beginning in A♭M, and use vii°$_7$/iii in the first key as your pivot. How can you go to FM using this chord as a chromatic-chromatic pivot?

EXERCISES

To practice writing your own chromatic pivot chord modulations, refer to exercises 24.3 and 24.11 in worksheet 24 at the end of this chapter.

MODULATION BY ENHARMONIC REINTERPRETATION OF THE GR +6

This interesting chromatic modulation takes advantage of the fact that the Gr +6 features the same sonority as a Mm$_7$ chord. Hence, a Gr +6 may be reinterpreted as a V$_7$ chord in a different key or, vice versa, a V$_7$ chord may be reinterpreted as a Gr +6. In both cases, the chord needs to be respelled enharmonically, even if it's only mentally (composers do not provide both spellings in actual music, although we will in most of

♪♪♪Example 24.10

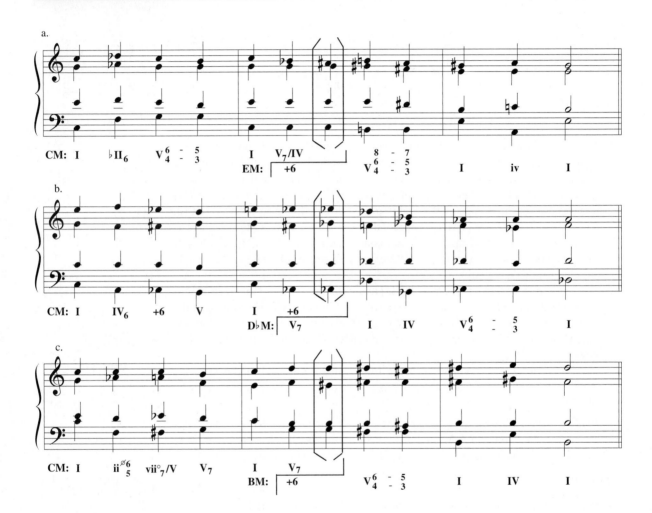

our examples and exercises, to clarify the process as much as possible; the spelling in the second key will always be provided in brackets after the spelling in the first key). Example 24.10 shows you the most frequent pivot and key relationships using this type of reinterpretation. Essentially, they can be reduced to two types:

1. In example 24.10a, a V_7/IV in a major key is reinterpreted as a Gr +6 of a key a M3 above the original key (iii or III) by respelling B♭ as A♯.

2. In example 24.10b, the Gr +6 is reinterpreted as V_7 of a key a half step above the original tonic (the key of ♯i or ♯I; or also ♭ii or ♭II, the "Neapolitan" key) by respelling F♯ as G♭. In the reverse process (example 24.10c), V_7 in the original key becomes the Gr +6 of a key a half step below the original tonic by respelling F as E♯.

Modulation to iii or III Using the +6

Listen to example 24.11. Measures 23–26 are in A♭M. The chord in mm. 27–28, functions as vii°$_7$/ii in A♭M, although here it does not resolve as such. Instead, it moves to the chord in m. 29, which, coming from A♭M, sounds like V$_7$/IV. As such, it would be spelled as A♭–C–E♭–G♭. Instead, it is spelled as A♭–C–E♭–F♯, that is, as an +6 in C (M or m). Its resolution, indeed, confirms this function: It resolves to V$_{4-3}^{6-5}$ in CM, which takes us to the next phrase in CM. We have modulated from a major key (I) to its mediant key (in this case the chromatic mediant, that is, major III, instead of the diatonic mediant, iii, or Cm) by enharmonically reinterpreting V$_7$/IV in the first key as an +6 chord in the second key.

 **Example 24.11**   L. v. Beethoven, Symphony no. 5 in Cm, II, mm. 23–33

Example 24.12

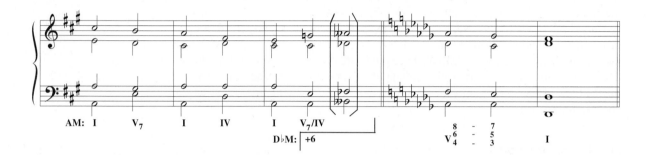

For another example of this modulation from I to the distantly related key of III, refer to anthology, no. 39 (Schubert, Waltz, op. 9, no. 14), mm. 17–24. The key of AM was established at the end of the previous section (mm. 15–16). Measures 17–20 continue in the same key, and at m. 21 we see that, by the addition of the seventh, the AM tonic chord becomes V_7/IV. Although the chord in m. 21, however, is spelled as a V_7/IV in AM, it does not resolve as such, but is rather followed by a perfect authentic cadence (PAC) in D♭M. Play the progression in mm. 21–24, hearing the chord in m. 21 in D♭M. You will hear that it functions as a Gr +6 in this key, and in this way it provides a pivot in the modulation between the two distantly related keys. What is the correct spelling for the Gr +6 in D♭M? After you figure it out (and realize that it is a cumbersome spelling to be sure!), study the summary for this modulation as it appears in example 24.12.

Modulation Up or Down a Half Step Using the +6

Although a half step is the closest distance among pitches in the chromatic scale, it can also be the greatest tonal distance between two keys (for instance, CM and C♯M, with a difference of seven sharps). The modulation up or down a half step, however, can easily be effected with an enharmonic reinterpretation of the +6 chord. Consider, for instance, example 24.13. The key of AM is first established in the passage, and in m. 117 we hear a chord which, in AM, *sounds* like the Gr +6. The +6 interval (F–D♯), however, has been respelled enharmonically as a m7, F–E♭. Thus, the chord *looks* like a Mm_7, specifically like V_7 in B♭M. Its resolution to I in B♭M indeed confirms the modulation to the key a half step above AM, the "Neapolitan key," ♭II. The Gr +6 in AM has been reinterpreted as V_7/♭II.

An instance of the reverse process (down a half step) appears in example 24.14. This song is in Fm, and our example begins with a passage in the secondary key area of G♭M, the Neapolitan key (mm. 45–47, on a G♭M dominant pedal). V_7 in G♭, which appears several times in these measures spelled as D♭–F–A♭–C♭, is enharmonically respelled, in the last beat of m. 47, as D♭–F–A♭–B♮, that is, as the Gr +6 in Fm. The resolution of this chord in m. 48 confirms the modulation to Fm, a half step down.

♪♪♪ Example 24.13   Louise Farrenc, Trio in Em, op. 45, I, mm. 113–121

♪♪♪Example 24.13   Continued

EXERCISE

To practice enharmonic spellings of V₇ and +6 chords, refer to exercise 24.4 in work-sheet 24 at the end of this chapter.

WRITING MODULATIONS WITH +6 CHORDS

As an exercise, first write summaries in four voices of the modulations we have studied in examples 24.11, 24.13, and 24.14. The process of writing modulations similar to these is really quite simple:

1. To modulate from a major key to a key a M3 above its tonic (iii or III), after you write a complete progression establishing the first key, write a V₇/IV in this first key, and respell it as an +6 chord in the second key. Resolve this +6 to the dominant of the new key, and continue writing a complete progression in the new key.

2. To modulate from any M or m key to a key a half step above it, write the Gr +6 chord in the first key, and respell it as a V₇ in the new key. Then, resolve this V₇ to the new tonic chord, a half step above the original tonic.

3. To modulate from any M or m key to a key a half step below it, write V₇ in the original key, and respell it as the Gr +6 chord in the new key. Then, resolve this +6 to a dominant-tonic progression in the new key, a half step below the original key.

Try these three techniques with several keys of your choice.

Example 24.14   F. Schubert, "Gefror'ne Thränen," from *Winterreise*, no. 3, mm. 45–51

EXERCISES

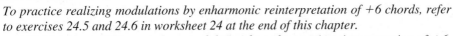

To practice realizing modulations by enharmonic reinterpretation of +6 chords, refer to exercises 24.5 and 24.6 in worksheet 24 at the end of this chapter.

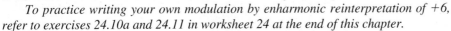

To practice writing your own modulation by enharmonic reinterpretation of +6, refer to exercises 24.10a and 24.11 in worksheet 24 at the end of this chapter.

THE NEAPOLITAN AS A KEY AREA

Modulations to the Neapolitan key, as well as *Neapolitan secondary key areas*, are frequent in the nineteenth-century repertoire. Although sometimes the new ♭II key area is approached directly, most often the modulation is effected by means of the +6, using

Example 24.15   L.v. Beethoven, Piano Sonata in Cm, op. 10, no. 1, III, mm. 99–117

one of the processes we have just studied. As we already discussed above, the fragment by Schubert reproduced in example 24.14, for instance, includes a Neapolitan secondary key area.

A very deliberate case of tonal motion to the Neapolitan as a key area can also be observed in example 24.15. The movement is in Cm, and the passage from our example takes place toward the end of the last movement, long after the tonic key has been reestablished, and at a point where the listener does not expect much more than motion to the final cadence. All of a sudden, the Neapolitan key is introduced in a very direct way: mm. 100–101 confirm Cm, and mm. 102–103 introduce us to D♭M, the ♭II key, by direct statement of V_7 of the new key in m. 102. Of course, V_7 of the new key does not sound abrupt to us because not only does it have two common tones with the Cm tonic triad, but moreover it is the same chord as the Cm +6. Notice how this common chord between the two distant keys is emphasized in mm. 104–106 in the form of a HC in D♭M. Next comes the last complete statement, in D♭M, of one of the two main themes in the movement (which is in sonata form), functioning formally as a coda (mm. 107–112). Now comment on the return to Cm. What is the *double function*, in D♭M and Cm, of the chord in m. 112? We can consider that this chord resolves two measures later, in m. 114. To what harmony? What chord has been *inserted* in m. 113? Is this a chord you have seen before as "inserted" harmony? This example shows Beethoven's ability to provide a final, surprising tonal impulse to a movement toward its end, by introducing a striking tonal diversion (such as the distant key of ♭II) before leading us to the final, closing cadence.

MODULATION BY ENHARMONIC REINTERPRETATION OF vii°$_7$

Let us examine the "inserted chord" in example 24.15 (m. 113) a little closer. If you think of the chord in m. 112 as the Gr +6 in Cm, you will have thought, correctly, that the chord in m. 113 is a vii°$^6_5$/V in Cm, inserted between the +6 and its resolution to the cadential $^6_4$ in m. 114. This vii°$^6_5$, however, can also be interpreted with a different function. If you think of the chord in m. 112 as V_7 in D♭M, the chord in m. 113 can be, with a different spelling, vii°$^4_2$ in D♭M. Try resolving it to I in this key, and you will see that it works just fine. As a matter of fact, we don't know that it is going to move on to Cm until we actually hear the following cadential $^6_4$ in Cm. In other words, the same vii°$_7$ sonority, spelled differently, can take us in this case to two different keys. In our specific example, both chords in mm. 112–113 can be respelled in either D♭M or Cm and can lead to either key depending on the interpretation (and resolution) we give them. Beethoven has just introduced us to the possible *enharmonic reinterpretation of vii°$_7$* as a means to modulate. Let us look at this procedure more carefully.

As you will remember, there are only three different fully diminished seventh sonorities. All the vii°$_7$ chords in all keys, including all the secondary vii°$_7$s, are thus drawn from a very limited pool of only three sonorities! Obviously, this means that each of these sonorities has a great variety of possible spellings, functions, and resolutions. Take, for instance, the vii°$_7$ on F♯, with F♯ as the leading tone. The same sonority can be built on A, C, or D♯, using each of these pitches as a leading tone. And each of these sonorities can be resolved to its tonic (G, B♭, D♭, or E, respectively). Example 24.16a

♪♪♪ Example 24.16

a.

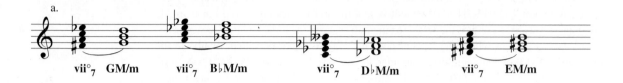

vii°₇   GM/m   vii°₇   B♭M/m   vii°₇   D♭M/m   vii°₇   EM/m

b.

G: vii°₇   B♭: vii°$^4_2$ D♭: vii°$^4_3$ E: vii°$^6_5$

c.

CM: vii°₇/V   FM: vii°₇/ii   A♭M: vii°$^4_2$/ii   F♯m: vii°$^4_3$/V   BM: vii°$^6_5$/IV

shows each of these spellings in root position and its resolution to the corresponding tonic. Example 24.16b demonstrates how the same position can be reinterpreted to represent different inversions in different keys. Examples 24.16a and b assume only "primary" resolutions. Of course, the same sonority can also have numerous secondary functions in a great variety of keys. Example 24.16c shows just a few of these possibilities.

So we now see that the two possible functions of this sonority which we discussed with respect to example 24.15 (vii°₇/V in Cm, or vii°₇ in D♭, regardless of the particular inversion in which it appears) were only two among many. In other words, *by respelling and reinterpreting the function of vii°₇, we could conceivably modulate from any key to any other possible key!* This is truly one of the most powerful techniques of chromatic modulation we have discussed so far. As an exercise, try to determine how you would modulate from CM (or Cm) to each of the other eleven M/m pairs of keys using vii°₇ chords as pivots (identify the specific vii°₇ you would use for each of the modulations).

Let us examine some examples from the literature using this procedure. In example 24.17 we find a modulation from G♭M to the distant key of Cm. After the V$^6_5$ in G♭M in m. 94, the chord in m. 95 first sounds like vii°₇ in this same key. Its spelling, however, is not F–A♭–C♭–E♭♭, as it would be if it were functioning in G♭M, but rather

♪♪♪Example 24.17   L. v. Beethoven, Piano Sonata in E♭M, op. 81a, I, mm. 91–98

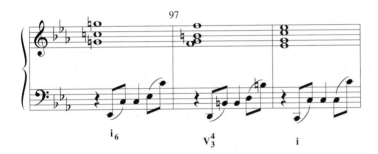

F–A♭–B♮–D, suggesting a vii°$^{o4}_{3}$ in Cm. The resolution of the chord to i$_6$ in Cm, and the subsequent confirmation of this key, prove that the chord in m. 95 is indeed reinterpreted enharmonically as a means to effect this distant modulation.

The vii°$_7$ chord used as a pivot in the previous example functions as a "primary" chord in both keys. Look now at example 24.18. The modulation here is from CM to E♭M, also a distant modulation. How would you interpret the last chord in m. 15 in CM (think of the exact function and inversion)? Obviously, although it is spelled according to this function, it does not resolve to the expected chord in CM. Instead, we move to E♭M. Go back to the last chord in m. 15, and reinterpret it in this new key (providing its exact position). Does it need any enharmonic respelling? If you do this right, you will find that the chord functions as a secondary vii°$_7$/V in each of the keys (in first inversion for CM, in root position for E♭M). These two examples provide a brief but sufficient illustration of the manifold modulating possibilities afforded by the fully diminished seventh sonority.

EXERCISES

To practice enharmonic spellings of vii°$_7$ chords, refer to exercise 24.7 in worksheet 24 at the end of this chapter.

To practice realizing modulations by enharmonic reinterpretation of vii°$_7$ chords, refer to exercises 24.8 and 24.9 in worksheet 24 at the end of this chapter.

Example 24.18   F. Schubert, Piano Sonata in Am, op. 164, I, mm. 10–17

WRITING MODULATIONS WITH vii°₇ CHORDS

If you want to modulate from any key to any other key, you can certainly find some enharmonic reinterpretation of some vii°₇ which will take you there. Say that we want to go from E♭M to BM. The following procedure will help us find the right pivot to do so.

1. First, examine the "primary" vii°₇ chord in E♭M: D–F–A♭–C♭. (If you were not to find any good pivot relationship using this chord, you could follow the same process with any secondary vii°₇, until you found a pivot that suited you.)

2. Can this chord be used as either the primary vii°₇ in BM, or perhaps as a secondary one? We see that although it cannot function as the primary chord, this is the same sonority as the one for vii°₇/V in BM (E♯–G♯–B–D). So we have a good pivot relationship on which to build our modulation.

3. Finally, it's all a matter of writing a good, musical realization of this modulation in the form of a modulating progression. Example 24.19 provides a sample realization of our modulation from E♭M to BM.

♪♪♪ Example 24.19

E♭M: I   vii°$^6_5$ I$_6$ ♭II$_6$ V$^6_4$ – $^5_3$ I   vii°$^6_5$

BM: vii°$_7$/V   V$^6_4$ – $^5_3$ I   vii°$^6_5$/V   +6   V   I

EXERCISES

To practice writing your own modulation by enharmonic reinterpretation of vii°$_7$, refer to exercises 24.10b and 24.11 in worksheet 24 at the end of this chapter.

To practice analysis of musical fragments including the types of modulation we have studied in this chapter, refer to exercise 24.1 in worksheet 24 at the end of this chapter.

FURTHER ANALYSIS

Chromatic Linear Modulatory Processes

Before studying this section, you may want to review two sections from chapter 19: "Sequential Modulation," and "Further Analysis: Modulatory Processes." In these two sections we were introduced to the circle of 5ths as a sequential modulatory process, and to the fact that sometimes modulations do not follow the shortest possible path. Quite to the contrary, composers often choose to extend the modulatory process, especially in developmental sections. In this section we will further our study of modulatory processes, with stress on chromatic sequential patterns.

The Circle of 5ths as a Modulatory Process: The *Fonte*

The descending circle of 5ths, as we already know, is a standard modulatory technique usually associated with a melodic sequence descending by steps. The eighteenth-century theorist Anton Riepel referred to this process as **fonte**, fountain, re-

flecting the fact that both the harmonic and the melodic sequences fall like water in a fountain. The *fonte* can often be found at the beginning of reprise 2 in binary pieces (b₁ section), and also in sonata form development sections.

As an example, consult anthology, no. 32 (Beethoven, Sonata in Fm, op. 2, no. 1), mm. 63–74. We begin in Cm, established by a G (5) pedal. In m. 68, a sequential process begins, and each of the sequence segments represents a tonicization following a pattern of keys descending by steps: Cm, B♭M, and A♭M. The bass follows a descending circle-of-5ths pattern: G–C–F–B♭–E♭–(A♭). Identify each of these sequential segments on the score, mark the exact area for each tonicization, and circle the bass pitches for the circle of 5ths. Notice that the last tonicized chord, A♭, does not appear in root position, but rather in first inversion, because the sequential pattern changes at this point (mm. 73–74). And even though the circle of "keys" stops in A♭M, notice also that the *fonte* continues as a diatonic circle of 5ths (A♭–D♭–G–C–F, in chords alternating $\frac{5}{3}$ and $\frac{6}{3}$ positions) leading all the way to the goal of this complete modulatory process, the key of Fm (reached in m. 78). Identify all the members of this diatonic circle, and then study the bass reduction for the complete passage reproduced in example 24.20. In the graph the tonicized areas are interpreted as secondary key areas in the home key of Fm (v, IV, and III), and the overall descending linear pattern from G (V/v) to C (V) which unifies the whole passage is indicated by upward stems.

The *fonte* appears frequently in the form of a $\frac{4-6}{2-3}$ sequential pattern which results from alternating the tonicizing V_7 in third inversion (V_2^4) with the corresponding resolution to a $\frac{6}{3}$ chord. The passage by Antonio Soler reproduced in example 24.21a is based on such a pattern. Play or listen to the excerpt, and analyze its harmonic content. Then examine the hypermetric reduction in example 24.21b. The reduction is based on two-bar hypermeasures. The grouping of measures in pairs seems obvious in this case because of the two-measure melodic and harmonic sequential segments.

In the reduction you will observe that the *fonte* passage is indeed based on a two-measure descending sequential segment, and that the underlying harmonic pattern is a $\frac{4-6}{2-3}$ sequence. Make sure you understand that this is still a circle-of-5ths pattern (what are the roots of the chords that make up this *fonte*?). Notice also that the excerpt as a whole does not really modulate, but rather stays within Dm, although with numerous tonicizations. This passage is developmental, and the *fonte* contributes to its developmental character (including the unstable harmonic content). The *fonte* leads to a tonicization of Gm, which functions as iv in the main key of the fragment, Dm, and which ultimately takes us to the concluding HC on V of D.

An ascending Sequential Pattern: The *Monte*

Along with the *fonte*, Riepel discusses the *monte*, mountain, an "uphill" sequential pattern. The passage by Domenico Scarlatti that appears in example 24.22a features a modulation from A♭M to Fm through a sequential process that illustrates the *monte*. Typically, the melodic sequence in this design ascends by half steps, whereas the bass line ascends in a pattern alternating a fourth up and a third down. The pattern can be continued for as many segments as wished. In the Scarlatti example, three segments of the sequence take us to the relative minor key, where the composer was aiming his modulation. The reduction of the passage which appears in example 24.22b shows the standard harmonic progression for this linear pattern: V_7/IV–IV–V_7/V–V, and so on. Listen to the example, play through the reduction, and then write and play your own *monte* in several keys of your choice.

An interesting ascending modulatory process is used by Brahms in the passage from *Im Herbst* reproduced in example 24.23. Here again, the passage begins and ends in the same key (it even begins and ends on the same harmony, V in CM). In the linear process, however, several tonicizations take place. What keys are tonicized? What are the chords used in each of the sequential segments for each key? Play or sing through the passage (notice that the tenor part should be read an octave lower than notated), and answer these questions before you continue reading.

The passage features sequential tonicizations ascending by whole steps (C–D–E–F♯). Each of the tonicized areas consists of a linear pattern that begins with an incomplete tonic and continues with a Gr +6 followed by a V with a cadential $^6_4$. Instead of a resolution of this dominant, two altered passing tones in the inner voices provide the harmonic connection with the next sequential segment and the next tonicized area. The sequence is stopped in F♯m (m. 26), a chord which is then reinterpreted as iii in DM (m. 27; this direct tonal motion from F♯m to DM is based on the two common tones between the two tonics). The DM tonic itself turns into V_7/V of CM (m. 28), and finally leads to the HC, which concludes the example. Although the large-scale function of this passage is simply to extend the V harmony in CM, its highly chromatic nature is indicated by the fact that all twelve pitches from the chromatic scale appear in the short span of three measures (24–26). Study the voice-leading reduction provided in example 24.24, and understand both the harmonic and linear processes displayed in this modulating passage.

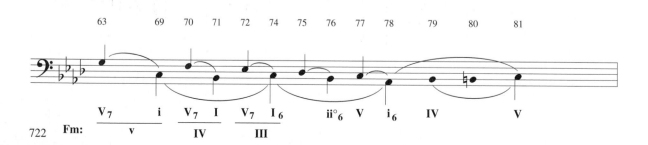

Example 24.20

Fm:

♪♪♪Example 24.21a   Antonio Soler, Sonata no. 84 in DM, mm. 59–78

Example 24.21b   Metric Reduction of Example 24.21a

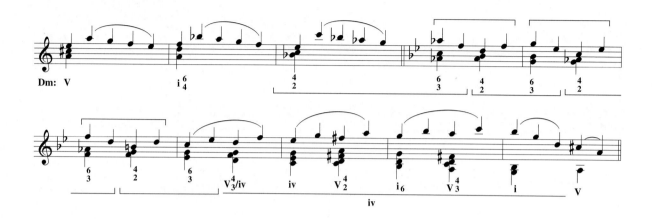

Example 24.22a   Domenico Scarlatti, Sonata K. 296 in FM, mm. 99–107

V

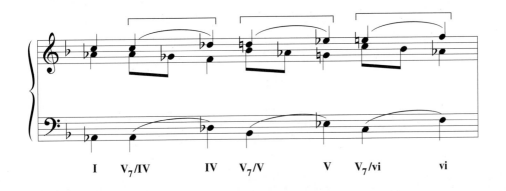

♪♪♪ Example 24.22b   Reduction of mm. 99–102

I   V₇/IV   IV   V₇/V   V   V₇/vi   vi

♪♪♪ Example 24.23   J. Brahms, *Im Herbst*, op. 104, no. 5, mm. 23–29

CM: V

♪♪♪ Example 24.23   Continued

♪♪♪ Example 24.24   Reduction of Example 24.23

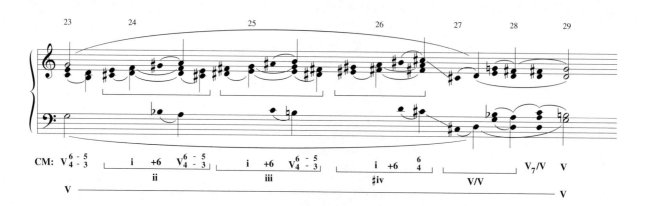

ASSIGNMENT AND KEYBOARD PROGRESSIONS

For analytical and written assignments and keyboard progressions based on the materials learned in this chapter, refer to chapter 24 in the workbook.

PRACTICAL APPLICATION AND DISCUSSION

The exact types of modulations we have studied in this chapter are not as easy to find in literature as diatonic pivot chord modulations to closely related keys. You should be able to find some of them, however, including some distant modulations, in the Romantic pieces you perform or know well, or in developmental sections of classical compositions, especially sonatas and concertos. Try to identify at least one of these modulations in your repertoire, understand its procedure, its function within a possible modulatory process, and the formal role of the section where it takes place. Bring your findings to class, and explain them to your teacher and classmates.

Find also a complete passage that is based on a modulatory process (probably in a development section in a sonata form movement). Where does the passage come from tonally, and where does it lead? How does the knowledge of the tonal and formal function of such a passage affect your hearing of it or your rendition of it if you perform it? Does this knowledge help you hear and transmit its forward motion, its unstable nature, probably leading toward a resolution to a more stable key or passage?

PITCH PATTERNS

Sing the following melodic pitch patterns in example 24.25, and as you sing listen to the modulation in each of the patterns, paying special attention to the chromatic pivot or to the enharmonic reinterpretation that effects the modulation. Practice *improvising* similar pitch patterns modulating to different keys.

♪♪♪ Example 24.25

Example 24.25   Continued

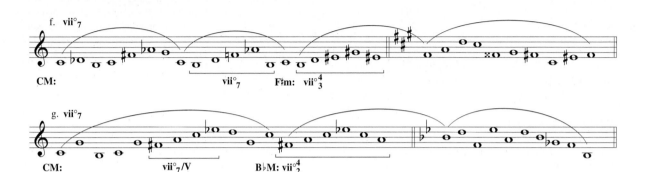

Composers and Their Music 24

Biographies

Write short biographies of the following composers mentioned in this chapter: Louise Farrenc, Domenico Scarlatti, Antonio Soler.

Listening

Listen to the following compositions by composers mentioned in this chapter:

Farrenc, Trio in Em, op. 45 (or any other composition available at your library).
Scarlatti, selected keyboard sonatas.
Soler, selected keyboard sonatas.

Follow the score while you listen. Be able to place each of these compositions in one of the style periods and to comment on why and how it represents the musical characteristics of that period. As you listen to these compositions, try to identify aurally sections in which modulation and modulatory processes play an essential role, perhaps as part of transitional or developmental processes. Do these passages display a sense of tonal instability and motion? Where do they lead to?

Terms for Review

Distantly related keys
Chromatic pivot chord
Chromatic pivot relationships:
    diatonic-chromatic, chromatic-
    diatonic, chromatic-chromatic
Modulation by enharmonic
    reinterpretation of the +6 chord
Modulation to iii or III using the +6

Modulation up or down a half step using
    the +6
Neapolitan as a key area
Enharmonic reinterpretation of vii°$_7$
Chromatic linear modulatory processes
Fonte
$^4_2$–$^6_3$ sequence
Monte

Worksheet 24

EXERCISE 24.1   Analysis.

1. The modulation in example 24.26 features a chromatic pivot chord. Analyze the complete passage with RNs, and explain the modulation and the pivot chord.

♪♪♪ Example 24.26   Chevalier de Saint–Georges, Aria "O Clemangis, lis dans mon âme," from *Ernestine*, mm. 90–101

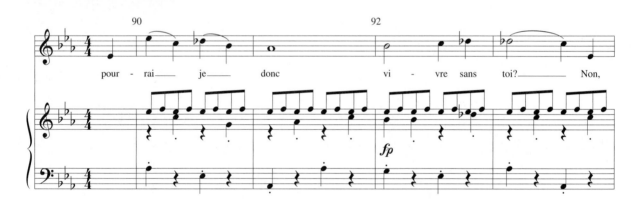

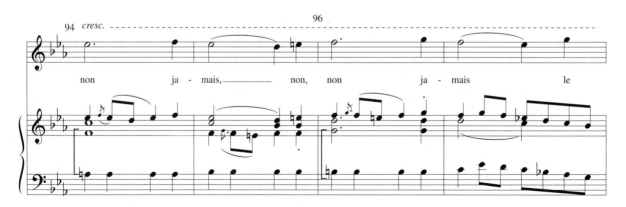

2. The following examples feature the ♭II key area and/or modulations by enharmonic reinterpretation of +6. Analyze each of them, identify the modulations or the ♭II key area, the keys involved, and the exact function of the pivot chord in each of the keys.

   a) Example 24.27.

♪♪♪ Example 24.27   F. Schubert, "Mein," from *Die schöne Müllerin*, mm. 58–65

♪♪♪ Example 24.27   Continued

Bäch - lein,   laß   dein   Rau - schen   sein,

b) Anthology, no. 34, Beethoven, Sonata op. 13, *Pathétique*, III, mm. 193–210.
   1) Explain the modulation from Cm to A♭M in mm. 197–203.

   2) Then, explain the return to Cm in mm. 206–210.

c) Example 24.28.

d) Anthology, no. 38, Schubert, *Erlkönig*.
   1) Explain the modulation in mm. 105–112.

   2) Measures 116–123 are in Dm. What secondary key area of Dm is included in these measures?

   3) Analyze mm. 131–148. What secondary key areas can you identify?

♪♪♪ Example 24.28   J. Brahms, *Im Herbst*, mm. 1–5

e) Anthology, no. 36, Beethoven, Sonata in E♭M, op. 7, II, mm. 33–51.

   1) This movement is in CM. What is the key in m. 33?

   2) Explain the modulation back to C, which actually takes place in mm. 36–37.

   3) How does Beethoven "postpone" the arrival on the C tonic (especially in mm. 38–44)?

3. The following examples feature modulation by enharmonic reinterpretation of vii°₇ chords. Analyze each of them, identify the modulations, the keys involved, and the exact function of the pivot chord in each of the keys.

   a) Example 24.29.

   b) Anthology, no. 51, Liszt, *Consolation* no. 4, mm. 23–25.

♪♪♪ Example 24.29   F. Schubert, "Gefror'ne Thränen," from *Winterreise*, no. 3, mm. 30–37

Und dringt doch aus der Quel - le der Brust so glü-hend heiss, als

woll - tet ihr   zer - schmel - zen des   gan - zen   Win - ters   Eis,

4. After you go over the "Further Analysis" section of this chapter, analyze the following examples of chromatic linear modulation processes, and identify in them *fonte* or *monte* patterns.

   a) Anthology, no. 35, Beethoven, *Waldstein* Sonata, I, mm. 104–109. Before you analyze this passage, make sure you study and understand the fragment from Soler's Sonata no. 84 which we analyzed above in examples 24.21a and b.

   b) Anthology, no. 14, Bach, Fugue no. 2 in Cm, *WTC* I, mm. 17–20.

EXERCISE 24.2   The statements below refer to chromatic pivot chord relationships. Fill in the blank in each statement.

Diatonic-Chromatic

1. IV$_6$ in _____ becomes ♭II$_6$ in C♯m.

2. VI in F♯m becomes V/V in _____.

3. _____ in Gm becomes ♭II$_6$ in AM.

4. iii in E♭m becomes _____ in DM.

Chromatic-Diatonic

1. $\flat\text{II}_6$ in Bm becomes V_6 in _____.
2. V_7/ii in _____ becomes V_7 in DM.
3. iv in EM becomes _____ in GM.
4. _____ in FM becomes IV_6 in D$\flat$M.

Chromatic-Chromatic

1. V^4_3/vi in FM becomes V^4_3/V in _____.
2. $\text{vii}°_7/\text{iv}$ in _____ becomes $\text{vii}°_7/\text{V}$ in Gm.
3. _____ in C$\sharp$m becomes $\text{vii}°_7/\text{iv}$ in Bm.
4. $\text{vii}°_7/\text{ii}$ in B$\flat$M becomes _____ in GM.

EXERCISE 24.3 Write the following chromatic pivot chord modulations (bass and RNs, with indication of the pivot chord).

a. From DM to C$\sharp$m using $\flat\text{II}_6$ of C$\sharp$m as a pivot.
b. From GM to E$\flat$M using a borrowed chord in GM as pivot.
c. From CM to AM using a $\text{vii}°_7$ chord with a secondary function in both keys (for instance, $\text{vii}°_7/\text{ii}$ in CM).

a.

DM:

b.

GM:

c.

CM:

EXERCISE 24.4 In each of the spaces in this exercise, spell the first chord in the required key. Then respell the chord to function as required by the second Roman numeral, and indicate in which key it would have this second function. An example is provided for each of the three types of required respelling.

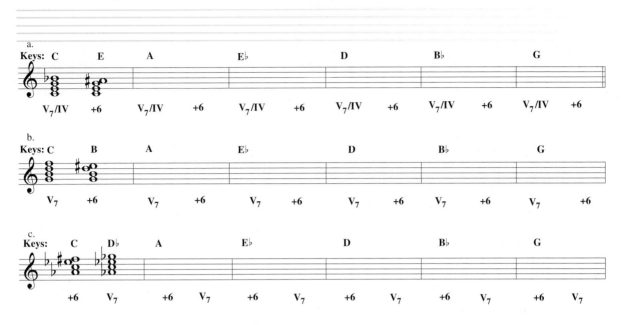

EXERCISE 24.5   The following RNs represent modulations by enharmonic reinterpretation of the Gr +6 chord. Write the bass line for each progression, and indicate what key we have modulated to in each case.

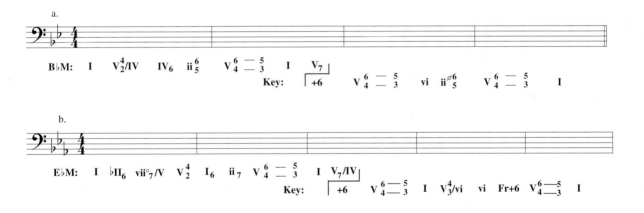

EXERCISE 24.6   Write the modulating progression in exercise 24.6 in four voices. Provide both enharmonic spellings for the pivot chord. Write the key signature for the new key after the double bar (in the space marked with an asterisk).

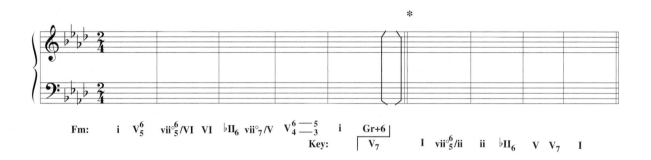

Fm: i V_5^6 $vii^{\circ6}_5$/VI   VI $\flat II_6$ vii°_7/V $V_4^{6\ -\ 5}_{\ -\ 3}$ i   Gr+6 |

Key: V_7 I $vii^{\circ6}_5$/ii   ii $\flat II_6$ V V_7 I

EXERCISE 24.7

a.   Write and resolve vii°_7 in Fm. This chord may be used to modulate to three other minor keys by respelling it enharmonically. Indicate the keys, and provide the spelling (leaving the chord in the same position), the correct RN, and the correct resolution to the corresponding tonic in each of the new keys. For a reference of what you are doing exactly, see example 24.16b in this chapter (although in that example the chords are not resolved).

b.   Follow the same process as above, but now show how vii°_7 in B♭M functions in three other major keys.

c.   The following statements refer to enharmonically respelled vii°_7 chords. Fill in the blank in each statement.

   1. vii°_7 in B♭ becomes _____ in G.

   2. _____ in G becomes $vii^{\circ4}_3$ in D♭.

   3. $vii^{\circ6}_5$ in _____ becomes vii°_7 in E♭.

   4. $vii^{\circ4}_2$ in F becomes $vii^{\circ6}_5$ in _____.

a.   **Key 1: Fm**   **Key 2:**   **Key 3:**   **Key 4:**   b. **Key 1: B♭M**   **Key 2:**   **Key 3:**   **Key 4:**

EXERCISE 24.8   The RNs in this exercise represent a modulation by enharmonic reinterpretation of vii°$_7$. Write the bass line, and indicate what key we have modulated to.

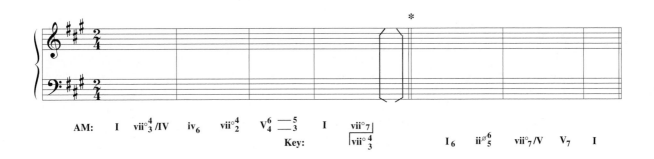

E♭M: I   vii°$_7$/ii   ii   vii°$_7$ I   vii°$_7$|
                                            Key: ⌐vii°$^4_2$ V$^6_4$ — $^5_3$ i   Gr+6   V$^6_4$ — $^5_3$ i

EXERCISE 24.9   Write the following modulating progression in four voices. Provide both enharmonic spellings for the pivot chord. Write the key signature for the new key after the double bar (in the space marked with an asterisk).

AM: I   vii°$^4_3$/IV   iv$_6$ vii°$^4_2$ V$^6_4$ — $^5_3$ I   vii°$_7$|
                                                              Key: ⌐vii°$^4_3$ I$_6$ ii$^{ø6}_5$ vii°$_7$/V   V$_7$ I

EXERCISE 24.10   Write your own modulating progressions (bass and RNs) using Gr +6 and vii°$_7$ chords as pivots.

a.   A modulation from DM to its Neapolitan key using an enharmonic reinterpretation of the Gr +6.

b.   A modulation from Gm to E♭M using an enharmonic reinterpretation of vii°$_7$ in Gm.

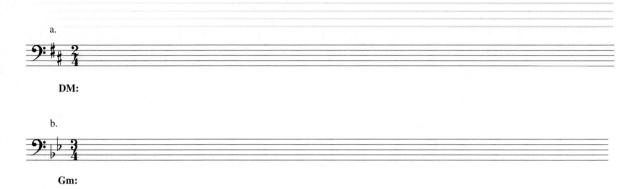

EXERCISE 24.11   Choose one of the modulating progressions you have written in exercise 24.3 and one from exercise 24.10, and, using your own music paper, write two phrases based on your progressions for a melodic instrument with keyboard accompaniment.

Chapter 25

Modulation to Distantly Related Keys II; Linear Chromaticism I

In this chapter we will first continue our study of modulation to distantly related keys. We will focus specifically on chromatic third–related keys and on the technique of common-tone modulation. In the second part of the chapter we will study several types of chords usually generated by means of linear chromaticism.

CHROMATIC THIRD RELATIONSHIPS

Two triads are related by **chromatic third** if their *roots are a M or m 3rd apart*, and their members belong to *different diatonic scales*. Example 25.1 presents a chart of all triads related by third with both a M and a m triad. The triads in parentheses (vi and iii in M, VI and III in m) have a *diatonic third* relationship with the tonic triad because their members belong to the *same diatonic scale* as the members of the tonic triad (vi: A–C–E and iii: E–G–B belong to the same diatonic scale as I: C–E–G, the CM "white-key" scale). The rest of the triads, on the other hand, display members belonging to different diatonic scales than the members of the tonic triad (both ♭VI: A♭–C–E♭ and III: E–G♯–B belong to different diatonic scales than I: C–E–G).

There are, then, six triads related by chromatic third to any M triad, and six more related to any m triad. These triads are also called **chromatic mediants** because they are altered mediant and submediant chords. Four of the set of six chromatic third–related triads have a *common tone* with I or i, and two of the triads do not. The triads that do not have common tones with I or i are indicated in brackets in our example. Verify what the common tone with I is for each of the following triads: VI, ♭VI, III, and ♭III; and with i for triads vi, ♯vi, iii, and ♯iii.

EXERCISE

To practice determining the set of triads related to a given triad by chromatic third, refer to exercise 25.2 in worksheet 25 at the end of this chapter.

♪♪♪Example 25.1

(vi), VI
Am, AM

(iii), III
Em, EM

I
CM

♭VI, [♭vi]
A♭M, A♭m

III, [♭iii]
E♭M, E♭m

(VI), vi
A♭M, A♭m

(III), iii
E♭M, E♭m

i
Cm

♯vi, [♯VI]
Am, AM

♯iii, [♯III]
Em, EM

TRIADS RELATED BY CHROMATIC THIRD

Chromatic third relationships can exist between triads or between keys. We will first examine third–related triads. Consider for instance the beginning of Franz Liszt's "Il pensieroso" (example 25.2a). The end of the phrase establishes the key of C♯m. The first two chords, on the other hand, are not related functionally within this key: The C♯m–Am triads do not belong to the same diatonic scale, and their relationship, i–vi, is not functional, but rather linear: The Am triad is a chromatic neighbor chord that prolongs i, as indicated by the reduction in example 25.2b. The phrase, however, is strongly tied together tonally by the reiterated E in the right hand, the pitch that connects the C♯m and Am triads by common tone and by the bass in descending 3rds (C♯–A–F♯) leading to the $\hat{5}$–$\hat{1}$ cadential motion. The third chord is an altered predominant, a iv$_7$ with a lowered fifth (iv$^{\emptyset}_7$). We will study altered chords (chords with a raised or lowered fifth) later in this chapter.

Because they do not belong to the same diatonic scale, and because, hence, they are not harmonically related according to the tenets of functional progression, chromatic third triads can suspend the sense of functional tonality momentarily. An interesting use of chromatic third–related triads can be found in the recitative introducing Verdi's famous aria, "Celeste Aida" (anthology, no. 55). Example 25.3 presents a harmonic reduction of the passage, in which the Egyptian general, Radames, expresses his ambition to be the leader in the upcoming war campaign against the Ethiopians, and to be able to dedicate his victory to his beloved Aida (a captive Ethiopian princess, none other than the daughter of the Ethiopian king Radames hopes to defeat!). The military trumpet calls reflect the mood of the occasion, and the seemingly erratic tonal content of the passage reflects the sense of brewing conflict. The path from the initial GM to

♪♪♪Example 25.2a   Franz Liszt, "Il pensieroso," from *Années de Pèlerinage*, mm. 1–4

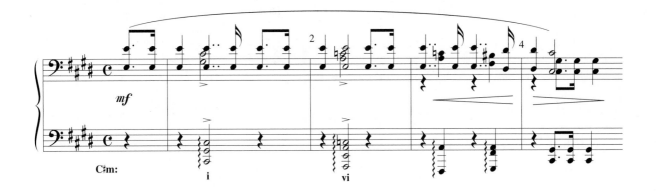

♪♪♪Example 25.2b

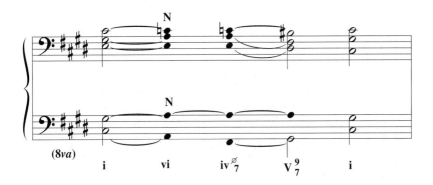

the final B♭M (two keys related by chromatic third) takes us through the distant tonal areas of E♭M, DM, G♭M, and E♭m. Play through the reduction, and notice that some of the key areas are barely suggested (E♭M and G♭M, for instance).

The connection between several of the key areas is effected by direct motion between chromatic third–related triads (marked with brackets over the graph). In mm. 3–4, we move directly from a GM triad to an E♭M triad (I–♭VI in GM). In mm. 8–11, the motion is from a B♭M triad to a DM triad (♭VI–I in DM). In mm. 14–17, the motion is from a DM triad to a G♭M $^6_4$ sonority (I–III in DM, with III spelled enharmonically). And, finally, in mm. 21–22 we hear a nonfunctional connection between an A♭M triad (IV in E♭m, or ♭VII in B♭M) and an FM triad (V in B♭M). These nonfunctional triadic connections that are used to move from one key area to the next further weaken both the sense of functional tonality and the overall sense of tonal unity in this passage.

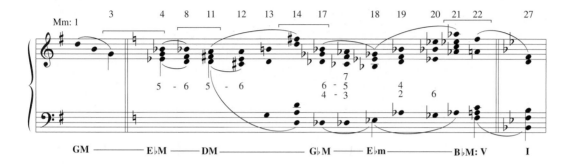

Example 25.3   Harmonic Reduction of Verdi's Recitative to "Celeste Aida," *Aida*, Act I

EXERCISE

To practice spelling triads related by chromatic third, refer to exercise 25.3 in worksheet 25 at the end of this chapter.

KEYS RELATED BY CHROMATIC THIRD: COMMON-TONE MODULATION

The chromatic third relationship among keys is a distant one (as illustrated by such key area relationships, in the Verdi example above, as GM–E♭M or DM–G♭M—an enharmonic spelling of the 3rd relationship DM–F♯M). The modulation between chromatic third–related keys, however, can be a very direct one, because of the common tone some of them share. In the most direct type of **common-tone modulation**, the pitch common to the tonic chords of two keys is reinterpreted as the new degree in the second key and used as a **pivot pitch** to modulate. Common-tone (CT) modulation directly connecting tonic chords is possible only between tonics that do have a common tone (the keys in brackets in example 25.1 are thus excluded). That leaves four possible chromatic third–related keys from any M or m key. Example 25.4 shows the common-tone connection from both CM and Cm to each of these possible keys. (Of course, common-tone modulation is also possible between diatonic third–related keys, and in these cases there are even two possible common tones between tonics.)

Third-related keys in general, and chromatic third–related keys in particular, were often favored by nineteenth-century composers, beginning with Beethoven, and continuing with such composers as Schubert, Schumann, Brahms, Liszt, and Verdi. The fragment by Louise Farrenc in example 25.5 illustrates a direct modulation from BM to ♭VI, GM, using the common-tone B as the only connecting device. Notice how the BM tonic in m. 140 gives prominence to the pitch B in both hands, and how the GM tonic in m. 141 also begins with B in both piano lines.

The CT in common-tone modulations need not be only between tonic chords. In example 25.6 you can see a fragment of a song in FM by Beethoven. The fragment begins with a phrase on V_7 in FM, and moves directly to I_6 in the new key, A♭M (♭III), taking advantage of the common tone C between V_7 in FM and I in A♭M, in both cases placed in the bass. Although this modulation uses a CT between V of the old key and I

♪♪♪ Example 25.5   L. Farrenc, Trio in Em. op. 45, I, mm. 133–148

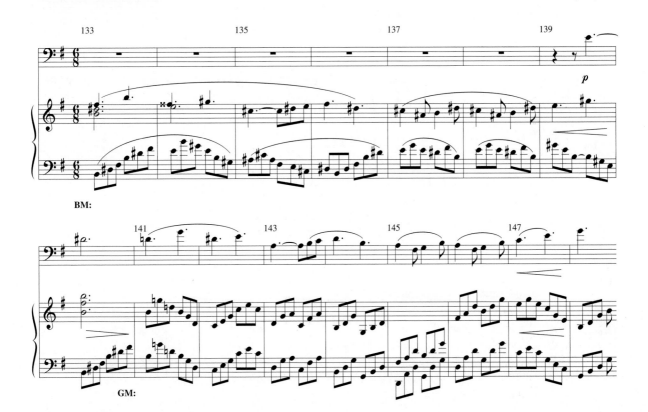

Example 25.6   L. v. Beethoven, "Hoffnung," from *Four Ariettas and a Duet*, op. 82, no. 1, mm. 9–15

♪♪♪ Example 25.7   W. A. Mozart, Fantasia in Cm, K. 475, mm. 24–27

of the new key, the tone, C, happens to be the same that would have been used to modulate directly from tonic to tonic of the same keys. A similar case appears in the excerpt reproduced in example 25.7. The passage begins in Bm, and moves to DM by CT. Does the CT connect the two tonics, or two chords other than the two tonics? Could the same CT have connected the two tonics? Are the two keys involved in this modulation related by chromatic third?

♭VI as a Key Area

Among the chromatic third–related keys displayed in example 25.1, ♭VI in M is the most frequently encountered in the repertoire. In long-range key schemes, the ♭VI key or secondary key area has a similar function as the ♭VI chord: It results from modal mixture, and it is really a key "borrowed" from minor. The modulation in example 25.8a illustrates the fact that the pivot pitch in this motion from I to ♭VI is Î. The tonic cadence in m. 24 stresses Î as the bass and as the top pitch in both hands. The next measure, I in A♭M, includes the same pitch in the same register in both hands, now with a $\hat{3}$ function. Consult this complete passage in anthology, no. 36, as an example of long-range mixture. The movement is in CM, and the key areas in mm. 22–51 are CM–A♭M–Fm–D♭M–Cm–CM, that is, I–♭VI–iv–♭II–i–I. In other words, the overall

♪♪♪Example 25.8a   L. v. Beethoven, Piano Sonata op. 7 in E♭M, II, mm. 22–28

♪♪♪Example 25.8b   Large-Scale Bass Reduction of mm. 22–37

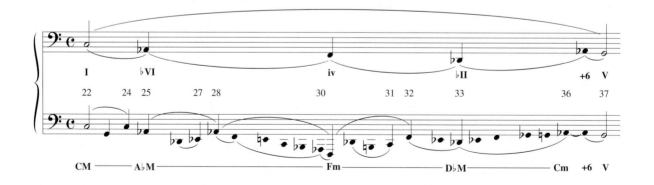

Chromatic Third Relationships in Modulatory Processes

Listen or play through example 25.9a. This passage is from the beginning of a sonata form development. The movement as a whole is in E♭M, and the development begins with a dominant of Cm which does not resolve to Cm, but directly into the key of A♭M (as in a deceptive V₇–VI progression). The modulatory process that follows takes us through A♭M, EM, and CM (that is, down by M3s; because M3s divide the octave into three equal segments, after two M3 modulations we are back in C, in a circle C–A♭–E–C). Play the harmonic reduction in example 25.9b, and then the reduction at a higher level in example 25.9c. How are the three keys related? How is the modulatory process effected?

The key sequence A♭M–EM–CM spells out two successive ♭VI modulations, if we consider the adjacent keys with respect to one another (that is, EM is ♭VI of A♭M, and CM is ♭VI of EM). Both of these modulations would allow for CT connections between tonics. Instead, Mozart first moves to the minor tonic in each case, and then takes advantage of the two common tones between the minor tonic and the dominant of the next key to achieve an extremely smooth modulation. Example 25.9b demonstrates the whole harmonic process in detail, and example 25.9c shows the

essence of the process: the motion from I to i in each key, and the double CT connection between i and V₃⁴ of the next key (♭VI). Notice also the stepwise bass that supports the complete process linearly.

For another interesting example of modulatory process involving CT modulation to distant keys, refer to anthology, no. 35 (Beethoven, *Waldstein* Sonata, I), mm. 123–132. This is a segment of the development, reduced in example 25.10. In the first modulation, the keys are related by chromatic third (E♭m–Bm, or i–vi spelled enharmonically). How is this modulation similar to the ones we have just discussed by Mozart? How many common tones are used, between what chords? The next modulation, Bm–Cm, is also a CT modulation, but in this case not to a third-related key, but up a half step. The process, however, is almost exactly the same (by means of two common tones between the tonic chord and the dominant of the next key). How does the same process take us to two different key relationships (down a M3 in the first case, up a m2 in the second)? For an answer, examine the members of the tonic triad that are used as CTs in each case, and you will see the slight difference between the two modulations.

design is of descending thirds, and all the areas between the two C major tonic areas are borrowed from C minor. This large-scale progression of keys resulting from modal mixture is summarized in the form of a bass reduction in example 25.8b. The lower staff in this reductive graph shows the bass motion in sufficient detail to illustrate how each key area is established and how motion from one key area to the next is effected. The upper staff, on the other hand, consists of a further reduction in which only the tonic pitches for each of the key areas are shown, thus illustrating the long-range tonal motion for the complete passage.

An example from the anthology (anthology, no. 39, Schubert, Waltz, op. 9, no. 14) will demonstrate the possible enharmonic spelling of ♭VI. The key scheme of this short waltz is D♭M–AM–D♭M. You will remember that in the previous chapter we discussed the second modulation, from AM back to D♭M by means of enharmonic reinterpretation of V₇/IV in AM, which becomes the +6 in D♭M. We can now look at the first modulation, in mm. 12–16, from D♭M to AM. This is really a modulation to ♭VI, which, however, has been respelled as AM to avoid the cumbersome key of B♭♭M. What is the common tone between these two keys? How is it spelled in each of the keys in our example?

EXERCISE

To practice writing a common-tone modulation, refer to exercise 25.4 in worksheet 25 at the end of this chapter.

Example 25.9a   W. A. Mozart, Symphony no. 39 in E♭M, K. 543, IV, mm. 105–125

Example 25.9b and c

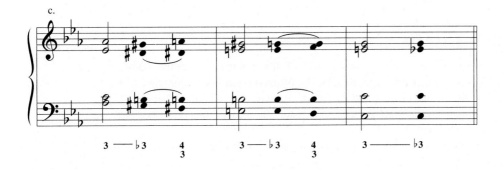

Example 25.10

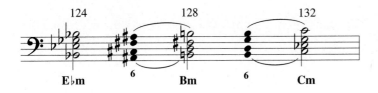

EXERCISE

To practice analyzing musical fragments including triads related by chromatic third or common-tone modulations, refer to exercises 25.1.1 and 25.1.2 in worksheet 25 at the end of this chapter.

LINEAR CHROMATICISM I: LINEAR CHROMATIC CHORDS

Throughout our study of harmony in previous chapters we have stressed that some chords are generated linearly, that is, they result from melodic processes rather than vertical chord generation. In the sections that follow we will continue our study of linear harmony, focusing on some chromatic chords that result from linear processes.

ALTERED TRIADS

Romantic composers (especially in the second half of the nineteenth century) often *altered the fifth of a major triad* chromatically. An **altered triad** is a major triad with an augmented or diminished fifth. Most commonly, triads are altered to become augmented, and among all the diatonic triads, V is the one most often presented with a sharpened fifth, to become V^+.

Altered triads are sometimes generated by chromatic linear motion. In example 25.11, a passing C♯, part of the linear gesture C–C♯–D in mm. 1–5, turns the initial I into an augmented triad, I^+.

<table>
<tr><td>♩♩♩ Example 25.11</td><td>C. Schumann, "Notturno," from Vier Stücke aus Soirées Musicales, op. 2, no. 2, mm. 1–6</td></tr>
</table>

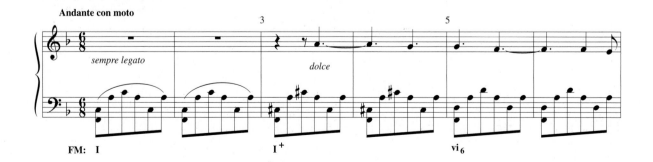

♪♪♪Example 25.12   Alma Mahler, "Ekstase," from *Five Songs,* no. 2, mm. 15–23

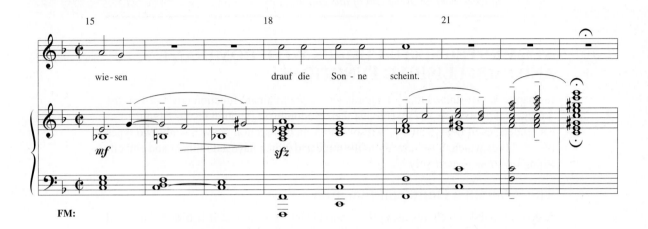

Not all altered triads, however, result from such linear motions. Romantic composers also altered triads for dramatic, expressive, or simply coloristic purposes, to create a richer, more chromatic (and also less stable) harmonic vocabulary. In example 25.12, the dominant of FM appears both in its unaltered form (as V and V_7) and with a sharpened fifth, as V^+ and V^+_7. Identify each of the dominant chords in the passage and determine whether it is an altered chord.

Examine the spelling and voice leading for the V^+ and V^+_7 chords in examples 25.13a to c. In four voices, the altered fifth should not be doubled and should moreover resolve upward to $\hat{3}$ (notice that resolving it down to $\hat{1}$ would create a melodic $+2$).

♪♪♪Example 25.13

EXERCISE

To practice realizing short progressions including altered triads, refer to exercises 25.5a to c in worksheet 25 at the end of this chapter.

AUGMENTED SIXTH CHORDS WITH DOMINANT AND EMBELLISHING FUNCTIONS

In chapter 23 we studied that +6 chords with a predominant function are based on the +6 interval between ♭$\hat{6}$ and ♯$\hat{4}$, and that their predominant function results from the linear tendencies of both ♭$\hat{6}$ and ♯$\hat{4}$ to resolve to $\hat{5}$. In this section we will study two types of +6 chords which move directly to the tonic and which have a dominant and embellishing function, respectively.[1]

The +6 with a Dominant Function

Just as we build +6 chords using the predominant ♭$\hat{6}$–♯$\hat{4}$ frame, it is possible to build +6 chords using the +6 frame provided by ♭$\hat{2}$ and $\hat{7}$ (♯$\hat{7}$ in minor), two degrees that have a linear tendency to resolve to $\hat{1}$. Because such +6 chords move indeed directly to the tonic, and because they include the leading tone, they have a dominant function. Most often, this type of +6 appears in the form of a Fr +6 on ♭$\hat{2}$ (♭$\hat{2}$–$\hat{4}$–$\hat{5}$–$\hat{7}$), as you can see in example 25.14b.

The dominant function of this type of Fr +6 becomes even more evident if we think of it as an altered V$^4_3$ chord. Example 25.14a illustrates a V$_7$ in E♭M with a diminished fifth, V°$_7$ (notice, in this example, that lowering the fifth of a major triad

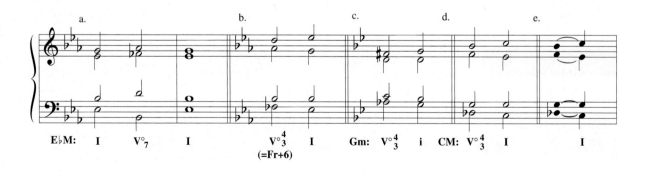

Example 25.14

E♭M: I   V°$_7$ I   V°$^4_3$ I   Gm: V°$^4_3$ i   CM: V°$^4_3$ I   I
(=Fr+6)

---

[1] For a study of the different +6 functional types, with a detailed discussion of +6 chords that do not have a predominant function, see Daniel Harrison, "Supplement to the Theory of Augmented-Sixth Chords," *Music Theory Spectrum* 17 (1995): 170–95.

produces a sonority that is *not* a diminished triad, for instance, C–E–G♭, or B♭–D–F♭ in our example). This interesting sonority appears most often in second inversion, in the form of V°$^4_3$. If you play example 25.14b, you will recognize that this sonority is the same as the Fr +6 built on ♭$\hat{2}$. We can best think of this chord as a **Fr +6 on ♭$\hat{2}$, with a V°$^4_3$ function**, and resolving directly to the tonic. To avoid confusion with the label for the predominant Fr +6 on ♭$\hat{6}$, we will refer to the Fr +6 on ♭$\hat{2}$ as V°$^4_3$. Examples 25.14c and d show the spelling and resolution of this chord in Gm and CM, respectively. In all cases, notice the linear motion to $\hat{1}$ of the upper and lower leading tones, $\hat{7}$ and ♭$\hat{2}$, as indicated by the notation in example 25.14e.

NOTE

To write a Fr +6 as an altered dominant, start from ♭$\hat{2}$. Build your Fr +6 sonority on this degree: ♭$\hat{2}$–$\hat{4}$–$\hat{5}$–$\hat{7}$. In other words, you have written a dominant seventh chord with a lowered fifth ($\hat{5}$–$\hat{7}$–♭$\hat{2}$–$\hat{4}$), but in second inversion.

The expressive power of this chord is dramatically realized in the passage reproduced in example 25.15, taken from one of Schubert's most intense songs. In Heine's poem, a man goes back, after many years, to the house where his "dear one once dwelt." In front of the house, he finds a man "wringing his hands in overwhelming grief." The grief, "Schmerzensgewalt" in mm. 31–33, is musically depicted by our chord (m. 32). Does register play any role in this depiction? Explain the linear function of our V°$^4_3$ as it connects III and i in these measures. Incidentally, the next appearance of the V°$^4_3$ chord comes a few bars later, in m. 42, when the poet realizes that the man wringing his hands in pain is none other than . . . himself! (The title of the song is "Der Doppelgänger," "The Phantom Double"!)

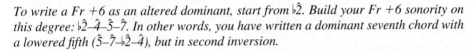

♪♪♪ Example 25.15   F. Schubert, "Der Doppelgänger," from *Schwanengesang,* no. 13, mm. 29–34

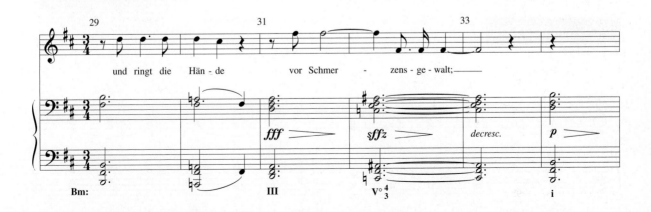

EXERCISE

To practice realizing short progressions including the Fr +6 as an altered dominant, refer to exercises 25.5d to f in worksheet 25 at the end of this chapter.

The Embellishing (or Common-Tone) Gr +6 Chord

Because the Gr +6 chord on ♭$\hat{6}$ has two common tones with the minor tonic chord ($\hat{1}$ and ♭$\hat{3}$) and one common tone with the major tonic ($\hat{1}$), it can be used as a chord prolonging the tonic, with a voice leading that takes advantage of the common tone or tones. Example 25.16a demonstrates the voice leading with both i and the +6 in root position and with the root doubled in i: Two voices feature common tones, the bass moves by an arpeggiation of a third, and the third voice is a neighbor note. Example 25.16b shows the same chord, but with the prolonged (and common) $\hat{1}$ in the bass and the fifth doubled in i. The +6 chord is now in first inversion, and the voice leading features two neighbor notes (NNs).

   Examples 25.16c and d present the same chords in a major key, with only one CT. The root-position example (with the root doubled in I) features two NNs, whereas the example with the +6 in first inversion and the fifth doubled in I features three NNs. (Notice, in the examples in the major mode, the enharmonic spelling of the fifth in the +6 chord, F♯ instead of G♭, to stress the NN function of this pitch.)

   In other words, this is an +6 that functions linearly by means of CTs and NNs, and whose function is to prolong and embellish the tonic triad as a *neighbor chord*. We will then call it the *embellishing +6* (or *common-tone +6*). Notice the similarities in both voice leading and function between this progression and the familiar embellishing N$_4^6$ progression (I–N$_4^6$–I).

NOTE

To write an embellishing +6 chord, think first of the spelling of the Gr +6 chord on ♭$\hat{6}$ in the given key. Leave the CT or CTs in the same voice, and take each of the remaining pitches of the tonic triad to the closest pitch in the +6 chord.

♪♪♪ **Example 25.16**

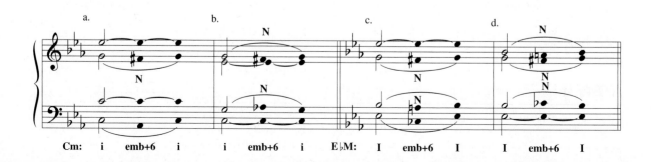

Cm: i   emb+6   i   i   emb+6   i   E♭M: I   emb+6   I   I   emb+6   I

♪♪♪Example 25.17   César Franck, Sonata for Violin and Piano, I, mm. 5–13

In the fragment by César Franck reproduced in example 25.17, the Gr +6 chord in AM is first introduced as a linear prolongation of the tonic chord, an embellishing +6, in m. 9. Compare this measure with example 25.16c, and verify the CT and NN functions. How could Franck have spelled this chord to clarify the NN role of the pitch C♮? When the chord appears again in m. 10, does it resolve as an emb. +6?

EXERCISE

To practice realizing short progressions including embellishing Gr +6 chords, refer to exercises 25.5g and h in worksheet 25 at the end of this chapter.

FURTHER ANALYSIS

As an additional challenge, study the modulation from AM to C#M in example 25.17, mm. 11–13. Notice that although the two keys are related by chromatic third, this is not a CT modulation. Rather, it is a slightly disguised modulation of a type you studied in the previous chapter. What kind of modulation is it, and how does it work exactly? Some hints: When the V₇ of AM in m. 11 resolves to what would be an AM tonic in beat 3, the tonic actually sounds like a sec-ondary dominant, which is spelled and resolved as an +6 of the new key. The harmonic activity in m. 12, which is simply an elaboration of the dominant of C#M, may seem especially confusing. Interpret the A in the bass as a nonchord tone (an appoggiatura to the following G). How about the fifth of this chord? Is this an example of an altered dominant chord? What kind of alteration?

F. Schubert, "Frühlingstraum," from *Die Winterreise,* no. 11, mm. 15–22

♪♪♪Example 25.18b

Em: i₆ emb+6   i₆ Dm: Gm: Am:

As we saw in example 25.16, the embellishing +6 can appear in any inversion. Play through, or listen to, example 25.18a. Then, play through example 25.18b. This reduction represents the key areas in the Schubert example. Considering that Am is the main key of the passage, these areas are v–iv–vii–i. Each of these areas closes with a tonic embellished by an +6 chord, as indicated in the reduction. What type ("nationality") of +6 chord is it? In what inversion does it appear in the first three key areas? And in the last key area? Identify all the NN motions in this linear connection. Now examine the common tone between the +6 and the tonic in each key area. Where is it placed in each case? Is it stressed rhythmically or texturally in any way?

PRACTICAL APPLICATION AND DISCUSSION

1. Study and understand each of the modulations between the key areas in example 25.18a.

2. The text of this passage is as follows: "And as the cocks are crowing, I rise and look without; the day is cold and dreary, the ravens are screaming about." The title of the song is "Spring Dream," and the poem (by Wilhelm Müller) tells of a dream of spring, beauty, and love the poet just had. Upon awakening, he is confronted again by his reality: He is lonely, it is cold, gloomy, and the ravens are shrieking. How is this re-flected by the music? The song is in AM. What is the mode of each of the key areas in this passage? Is this a tonally stable passage? How is the poet's dreary reality reflected by the tonality of this fragment? Are the crowings of cocks and the screams of ravens depicted musically in any way?

3. Discuss in class how your analyses of text and harmony would affect your performance of this passage. What moods and feelings would you try to transmit through your performance, and how?

THE COMMON-TONE DIMINISHED SEVENTH CHORD

The **common-tone diminished seventh chord (CT °7)** is another linear chord which, like the emb. +6, is based on common tone and NN voice leading. This is a °7 chord which prolongs or embellishes any chord, provided that the root of the prolonged chord be a note of the °7 chord. Look at example 25.19 for clarification: The root of the E♭M chord is a pitch also present in the following embellishing °7 chord, which spelled from its own root is F♯–A–C–E♭. This is a nonfunctional chromatic chord that prolongs the original triad by means of a CT, two NNs, and a leap of a

♪♪♪Example 25.19

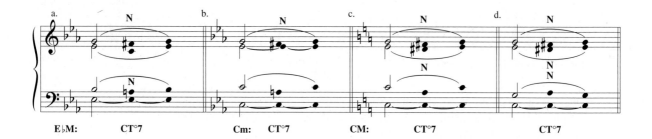

 third (or just a CT and three NNs if you doubled the fifth in the original chord, as in example 25.19d). If the prolonged chord is minor, then the °7 chord has two common tones (example 25.19b).

NOTE

To write a CT °7, find the °7 chord that contains the root of the given chord; leave this CT in the bass, and then take each of the pitches in the original chord to the closest possible pitch in the °7 chord. If you doubled the root in the original chord, your voice leading to the °7 chord will include two NN figures (only one for a minor chord) and a downward third arpeggiation in the upper voices. With a doubled fifth, you will have three NNs.

The CT °7 often appears at the beginning of a piece or phrase, providing an opening tonic prolongation in the form of a *neighbor chord*. This is exactly how it is used by Mendelssohn in example 25.20, where the chord returns to the tonic, completing the

♪♪♪Example 25.20   Felix Mendelssohn, *Rondo Capriccioso,* op. 14, mm. 4–8

Example 25.21   Nathaniel Dett, "Magnolias," from *Magnolia Suite,* no. 1, mm. 1–4

NN figures. In example 25.21, however, the chord does not return to the tonic, but is rather followed by a predominant-dominant progression. The CT °7 functions here as a *passing chord* rather than a neighbor chord. Can you explain exactly how? Can you identify a borrowed chord in this passage?

Refer back to Franck's excerpt in example 25.17. What is the chord that precedes the emb. +6? Notice the similarity of both chords, in pitch content and function. Example 25.22, on the other hand, presents a slightly different type of CT °7. It connects I with V_5^6, and, as it turns out, the root of I is not a CT with the °7 chord but, rather, the root of V_7 (G) is. On the other hand, both the third and fifth of I (E and G) are common tones with the °7 chord. In other words, our °7 has two CTs with I and one CT with V_7. If you consider the basic melodic motion that these three chords harmonize (the C–C♯–D figure in the voice), what is the linear function of this CT °7?

Example 25.22   G. Donizetti, *Don Pasquale,* Act III, no. 9

EXERCISES

To practice realizing short progressions including CT°7 chords, refer to exercises 25.5i and j in worksheet 25 at the end of this chapter.

To practice realizing a progression including chromatic chords of the types we studied, refer to exercise 25.6 in worksheet 25 at the end of this chapter.

To practice analyzing musical fragments including chromatic chords of the types we studied, refer to exercise 25.1.3 in worksheet 25 at the end of this chapter.

ASSIGNMENT AND KEYBOARD PROGRESSIONS

For analytical and written assignments and keyboard progressions based on the materials learned in this chapter, refer to chapter 25 in the workbook.

PITCH PATTERNS

Sing the melodic pitch patterns in example 25.23, and as you sing listen to the modulation to a chromatic third–related key in the patterns which include one. In the CT modulations, take time at the fermata to hear the new tonic as it relates to the common tone.

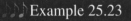 Example 25.23

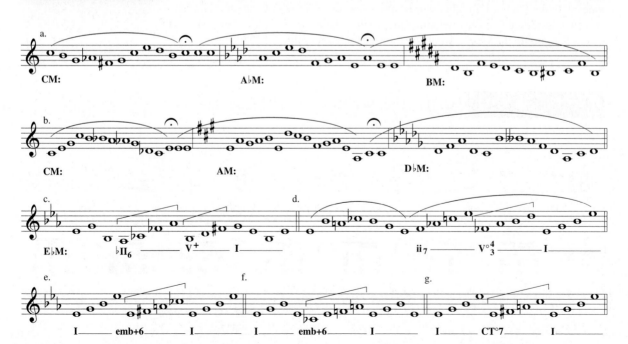

Practice *improvising* similar pitch patterns modulating to different chromatic third–related keys. For the patterns which do not modulate, hear the linear chromatic chord featured in each of them.

 Composers and Their Music 25

Biographies

Write short biographies of the following composers mentioned in this chapter: Alma Mahler, César Franck, Nathaniel Dett.

Listening

Listen to the following compositions by composers mentioned in this chapter:

Alma Mahler, *Fünf Lieder.*
Franck, Sonata for Violin and Piano.
Dett, *Magnolia Suite.*
Follow the score while you listen. Be able to place each of these compositions in one of the style periods and to comment on why and how it represents the musical characteristics of that period.

Terms for Review

Chromatic third relationships
Chromatic mediants
Triads related by chromatic third
Keys related by chromatic third with a given key
Common-tone modulation
Pivot pitch

♭VI as a key area
Altered triads
+6 with a dominant function
Fr +6 on ♭$\hat{2}$ as V^{o4}_3
Embellishing (common-tone) +6
Common-tone °7 chord

Worksheet 25

EXERCISE 25.1 Analysis.

1. Study the chordal relationships in example 25.24. Provide Roman numerals (RNs), and explain with the correct term how the chords are related.

♪♪♪ Example 25.24 Gabriel Fauré, "Les Roses d'Ispahan," op. 39, no. 4, mm. 47–51

2. Study the modulations that follow. For each of them, determine these points:
   1. What keys are involved?
   2. How are the keys related (diatonic third, chromatic third, half step, etc.)
   3. What is the RN relationship between the keys? (Be aware of possible enharmonic spellings of keys.)
   4. What type of modulation is it?
   5. If it is a CT modulation, what is the CT? Or is there, perhaps, more than one CT?
   6. What are the functions of the triads used in the CT modulation?

Following are the modulations to be analyzed:

a) Example 25.25.

♪♪♪ Example 25.25   F. Chopin, Étude in A♭M, from *Trois Nouvelles Études,* mm. 14–18

b) Anthology, no. 51, Liszt, *Consolation,* no. 4, mm. 15–18.

3. The following passages include examples of altered triads, Fr +6 as V$^{o4}_3$, embellishing +6, or CT^{o}7 chords. Identify and label the particular chord illustrated in each example, and determine its exact linear function (passing, neighbor/embellishing, etc.).

a) Example 25.26.

♪♪♪ Example 25.26   J. Brahms, Piano Concerto no. 2, op. 83, III, mm. 16–18

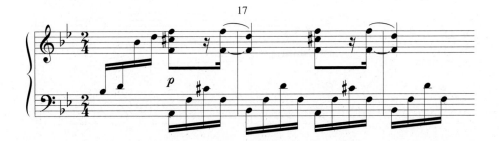

b) Anthology, no. 43, Fanny Mendelssohn, "Bitte," mm. 15–19.

c) Example 25.27. This example features an embellishing +6 chord, which, however, is not in root position. What is the exact label for this chord?

Example 25.27   F. Chopin, Mazurka 45 in Am, op. posth. 67, no. 4, mm. 1–8

d) Example 25.28.

Example 25.28   N. Dett, "Song of the Shrine," from *Enchantment*, II, mm. 1–4

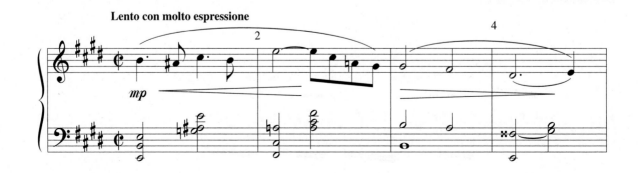

EXERCISE 25.2

1. List the six triads (or keys) related by chromatic third to each of the following triads (or keys). Write down both the triad name and the RN that indicates its relationship with the original triad.

2. Then, circle the four triads that have a CT with the original triad.

   EM:

   B♭M:

   F♯m:

   Dm:

EXERCISE 25.3   Write each of the following triads (chromatic mediants) in the required keys.

FM: III   Dm: vi   GM: VI   Am: iii   DM: ♭VI   E♭M: ♭III   C♯m: ♯vi   Em: ♯iii

B♭M: ♭vi   EM: ♭iii   Bm: ♯VI   Gm: ♯III   F♯m: vi   AM: ♭VI   Fm: iii   A♭M: III

EXERCISE 25.4   Write a CT modulation in four voices, from GM to a key of your choice, related to GM by chromatic third. In the first key area (GM), use a tonicized ♭VI and a secondary vii°₇. In the second key area, use a Gr +6.

GM:

EXERCISE 25.5   Realize the following short progressions in four voices. Pay attention to the RN quality (uppercase or lowercase), which may denote a chromatic-third relationship (for instance, I–III is not the same, of course, as I–iii).

a.

EM: I   Fr+6   V⁺   I

b.

Dm: i   ♯vi   vii°₇/V   V⁺   i

c.

B♭M: I   III   V⁺₇   I

d.

FM: I   IV   ii⌀₇   V°⁴₃   I

e.

DM: I   ♭II₆   V°⁴₃   I

f.

Gm: i   V⁴₂   i₆   V°⁴₃   i

g.

AM: I   emb+6   I

h.

Fm: i   emb+6   i

i.

GM: I   CT°7   I

j.

Em: i   CT°7   i

EXERCISE 25.6   Realize the following progression in four voices.

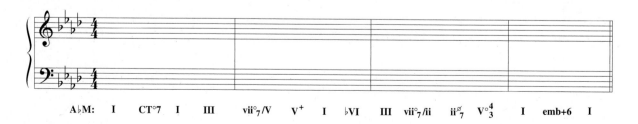

A♭M: I   CT°7   I   III   vii°₇/V   V⁺   I   ♭VI   III   vii°₇/ii   ii⌀₇   V°⁴₃   I   emb+6   I

Chapter 26

Introduction to Large Forms

Large formal designs fall into several categories. Among these, the most standard types are sonata form and rondo, besides variation forms, which we already discussed in chapter 22. In this chapter we will introduce the fundamental concepts involving sonata form and rondo, and we will study several examples of these formal types in some detail. Because of the wealth of possibilities they afford, however (and because different composers often treat them in different, idiosyncratic ways), a thorough discussion of these two large designs would require several chapters and is beyond the scope of this book. Students interested in furthering their study of large forms beyond the present introductory chapter should refer to any of the various available books devoted to the study of form.[1]

Sonata form and rondo as standard formal designs were particularly favored by composers in the Classical period, especially for the first and last movements of sonatas, symphonies, and concertos. Both of these formal designs are derived from smaller forms we have already studied (binary and ternary, respectively), and both merge in a formal type that we will see at the end of this chapter, the sonata-rondo.

SONATA FORM

This formal type is most frequently found in the opening *allegro* movement of Classical and Romantic sonatas and symphonies, and also sometimes in the slow movement and the closing fast movement of the same genres. **Sonata form** *is an outgrowth of the*

---

[1] I particularly recommend Douglass Green's *Form in Tonal Music* for a study of large forms in general. For studies that focus more specifically on formal designs in the Classical period, you may consult William Caplin's *Classical Form*, Charles Rosen's *Sonata Forms* (New York: Norton, 1988), and Leonard Ratner's *Classic Music: Expression, Form, and Style* (New York: Schirmer, 1980).

♪♪♪ Example 26.1a   A Rounded Binary Formal Design

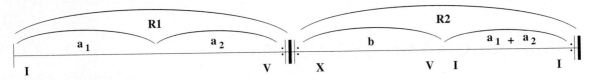

♪♪♪ Example 26.1b   A Sonata Form Design

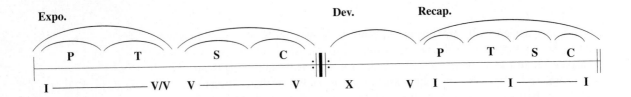

familiar rounded binary form, dominant type, as illustrated by example 26.1 (we are referring here to the type of rounded binary in which the complete first reprise comes back at the end of the second reprise). In both cases, the harmonic process consists of (1) establishment of the tonic key, (2) movement away from the tonic key and establishment of a secondary key area, (3) an area of harmonic instability which leads to (4) a return of the tonic key.

1. *The first reprise of binary* now becomes the **exposition**. As a general principle, the exposition contains *two key areas* (in the classical sonata form usually I and V, or i and III), which we will label **P** (for **primary**) and **S** (for **secondary**). P and S may each include a characteristic theme or a group of themes (which we will label P_1, P_2, etc., and S_1, S_2, etc.). Although the motion to a secondary key area is an essential element in the exposition the existence of an independent S theme is not (although the S theme is most frequently independent from the P theme). In what we know as a *monothematic sonata form* (frequently favored by Haydn), the S key area is based on a transposition of the P theme.

2. Between P and S there is usually a *modulating transition,* which we will label T. T may include its own theme (**independent transition**), or may use thematic material from P (**dependent transition**). T usually (although not always) ends with a half cadence (HC) in the secondary key. The frequently active rhythmic character of the transition as well as its modulating harmonic content create a drive toward this cadence around the middle of the exposition. The cadence

itself has the double function of marking the end of the first part of the exposition, while at the same time opening the tonal space for the second part, the S area.[2]

3. The S area closes with a perfect authentic cadence (PAC) in the secondary key, V or III. This cadence may itself be followed by a **closing section** (possibly with its own theme) which confirms the secondary key area. Our label for the closing section will be C. A closing section comes after a clearly articulated cadence closing the last theme of the S area, and its function is to reinforce the important cadence at the end of the exposition, often by means of a chain of cadential gestures.

4. *The second reprise of binary* becomes, in sonata form, a large unit with two harmonic areas: (1) the **development** (corresponding with the first section of reprise 2 [R2] in rounded binary), a modulating, harmonically unstable area in which thematic material from the exposition may be developed (and new thematic material may be introduced); and (2) the **recapitulation**, usually (but not always!) a return of the complete exposition, only that now it is in the tonic key throughout (that is, T and S stay in the primary key, although here we must also say "usually but not always"!).

5. A great variety of developmental techniques may be found in developmental sections. Some of these may include fragmentation, sequence (on a circle of 5ths), thematic expansion or compression (either intervallically or rhythmically), variation, contrapuntal combination of different motives, textural changes, reharmonization, and so forth. You may want to review our study of developmental procedures in chapter 7. Before the recapitulation, and leading into it, there is usually a dominant prolongation which we call **retransition**.

6. The motion to the secondary key area in the exposition and the harmonically unstable development create an extended area of dramatic tension which is resolved in the recapitulation. Although in the recapitulation there may be various tonicized areas (in particular, the subdominant is sometimes tonicized in the transition section of the recapitulation), this final large section in a sonata form is an area of tonal stability, which essentially stays in the tonic key. From a tonal point of view, the recapitulation provides a sense of balance and symmetrical proportions to the complete movement, following the familiar scheme "establishment of tonic (stability)-departure from tonic (instability)-return to tonic (stability)."

7. At the end of the recapitulation there may be a **coda**, which either extends the final cadence or, at times, becomes a **second development**, including modulations to new key areas, before finally reaching a closing cadence on the tonic.

We should emphasize that the criteria we have just provided are no more than generalizations. Exceptions to almost everything stated in these criteria do abound, as can be expected in a musical design as complex and rich in possibilities as sonata form.

---

[2] For a study of different types of midexposition cadences and their role within the complete exposition, see James Hepokoski and Warren Darcy, "The Medial Caesura and its Role in the Eighteenth-Century Sonata Exposition," *Music Theory Spectrum* 19 (Fall 1997): 155–83.

Any analysis of movements following this formal design thus requires some creative interpretation and a lot of flexibility, as we will soon realize. We will now study several specific sonata form movements in some detail.

MOZART, PIANO SONATA IN CM, K. 309, I (ANTHOLOGY, NO. 25)

1. *The Exposition (mm. 1–58).* First, listen to the complete movement. Then listen to the exposition again, marking the key areas as you listen. You will hear clearly that the secondary key area in GM (V) begins in m. 35, and that the section in mm. 21–32 is the modulating area, T.

    a) *Primary key area (P).* The tonic area extends from m. 1 to the cadence on C in m. 21. How many different themes can you identify? The opening theme, P_1 (mm. 1–8), clearly establishes the tonic key in the first two measures and is restated in mm. 8–14 (in a **counterstatement**, or repeated statement of a theme). Notice that m. 8 functions both as end of the first statement and beginning of the second (an *elision*). A second theme (still in CM, but now beginning on vi), P_2, starts in m. 15, and leads to the PAC in mm. 20–21. Discuss the phrase structure for the complete P area (mm. 1–21).

    b) *Transition (T).* A new theme, and a new accompaniment figure, mark the beginning of the modulating and independent transition, T (mm. 21–32). Where exactly does the modulation from CM to GM take place, and how? The transition closes on a HC in GM (that is, on V/V), which leads to the beginning of the secondary key area in GM. Notice the dramatic pause in m. 32, after the strong HC in G, which prepares and emphasizes the coming of the new theme. Hepokoski and Darcy have studied this type of transition (which results in what they call a **two-part exposition**) at length. They write: "The two-part exposition is characterized by a strong mid-expositional punctuation break, the *medial caesura*—most often articulating a half cadence—followed (almost invariably) by a rhetorical drop to *piano* marking the onset of a gentle, usually contrasting *secondary-theme zone* in the second key-area."[3] As you can easily verify, this narrative applies fully to the sonata we are analyzing.

    c) *Secondary key area (S).* Two measures extending V/V (mm. 33–34) introduce us to the S area, in m. 35. Two open statements of an initial GM theme (S_1) appear in mm. 35–42. As is often the case with S themes, S_1 is here contrasting with respect to P_1. Whereas the latter is characterized by a loud, energetic, and angular beginning gesture, S_1 is softer and more lyrical, as characterized in the definition of a two-part exposition we just quoted above. A new theme (S_2) is introduced in m. 43 and restated with variation in mm. 46–47. A cadential process that begins in m. 48 eventually leads to the extended cadential gesture of mm. 51–54.

    d) *Closing theme (C).* Following the cadence in m. 54 (which could certainly close the exposition) a final, closing theme (C) functions as a codetta or

---

[3] Hepokoski and Darcy, "The Medial Caesura," p. 117.

cadential extension. C also has a parallel structure, including a second state-ment (mm. 56–57) which varies the first statement. How exactly does it do so?

e) *Thematic relationships.* If you look closely at the various themes in this exposi-tion, you will notice a motive that recurs in most of them: a step in one direction followed by a 3rd leap in the opposite direction or the other way around. Using a 2 or a 3 to designate a second or a third, and + or − signs for up or down, the possibilities are +2−3, −2+3, +3−2, or −3+2. The most prominent occur-rences of this motive, including motives from the P, S, T, and C areas, are illus-trated in example 26.2. The motive provides a connection among all of them. Notice also the connections between the S themes, illustrated in example 26.3. How is the motive in m. 45 (example 26.3c) related to m. 35 (example 26.3a)?

2. *The development (mm. 59–93).* Listen to the development section. Identify the key areas and the origin of the thematic material used in this section. What develop-mental techniques are used? When does the recapitulation really begin?

a) Measures 59–62 are in Gm, and state P_1.

b) Measures 63–66 move toward Dm. What is the origin of this theme? Is it a new theme? Or could it be derived from mm. 3–4?

c) P_1 is stated in Dm in mm. 67–68, after which we move toward Am.

Example 26.2

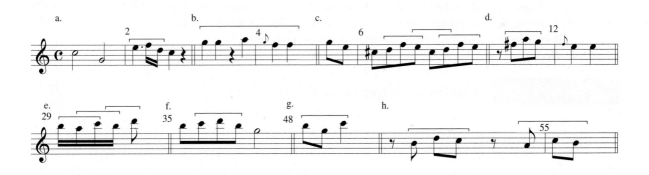

Example 26.3

    d) A new section, beginning in m. 73, treats P_1 sequentially. What key areas are touched in mm. 73–82? Can you identify an example of thematic fragmentation in these measures?

    e) The C section (closing theme) is stated in complete form, but now in Am, in mm. 82–85, leading to an apparent recapitulation (return of the first theme) in m. 86. This is, however, what is known as a **false recapitulation**, a return of the "right theme" but in the "wrong key," in this case Am.

    f) Measures 90–93, a statement of P_1 outlining V_7 of CM, function as a *retransition*, a dominant prolongation leading to the return of the tonic key.

    g) The true recapitulation comes in m. 94, the return of P_1 in CM.

3. *The recapitulation (mm. 94–155).* Listen to the complete second reprise (development and recapitulation). Compare the recapitulation with the exposition, and determine what is the same and what is different. You will find the following discrepancies between these two sections:

    a) Mozart varies the counterstatement of P_1 in the recapitulation (mm. 101–108). How? Analyze this passage harmonically if you have not done so yet.

    b) Unlike many T sections in recapitulations, the T section here does modulate to the key of the dominant. The difference with the original T section, however, is that now it does not lead to a HC in GM, as it did in m. 32, but rather to a cadence on the tonicized G. How does this change in the cadential pitch at the end of T affect the S area in the recapitulation?

    c) What is the key of the S area now? How does Mozart vary the S_1 theme?

    As a conclusion of your analysis, study the bass reduction for the exposition and the development provided in example 26.4. Discuss how this reduction represents the tonal and formal design of this movement in particular and of sonata form in general.

Example 26.4   Bass Reduction for Mozart, K. 309, I

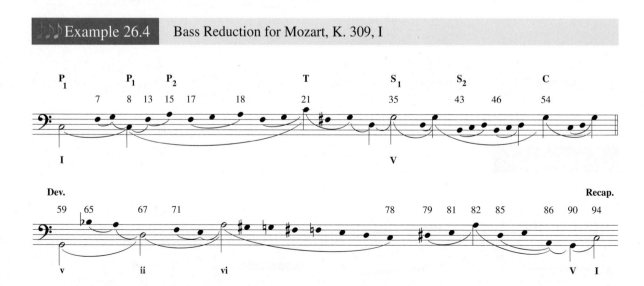

Guided Studies of Sonata Form

The following are guided analyses of two compositions in sonata form included in the anthology: Beethoven's Fm Sonata, op. 2, no. 1, I, and his celebrated *Waldstein* Sonata, I. Their most significant formal and tonal features are pointed out to help you work through these fascinating movements.

Beethoven, Piano Sonata No. 1 in Fm, op. 2, No. 1, I (anthology, no. 32)

1. Identify the modulating T area. Is it based on an independent theme? What sets apart the P area from T?

2. The S area begins in m. 20 with the S_1 theme. As usual in a classical sonata of the standard minor key type, S is in the key of III. What is unusual about the harmonization of S_1? When is the first time we hear III unequivocally in root position?

3. Compare the P theme with the S_1 theme. How are they similar, contrasting, or complementary? Think in terms of shape and contour.

4. We may call the theme in mm. 33–41 the S_2 theme, and the new theme after the PAC on III (m. 41) the C theme.

5. Study the development (mm. 49–101). What are its sections, and what themes are they based on? What are the various key areas? We have studied some of the tonal features of this development in previous chapters as examples of modulation. Review and discuss these features again, focusing especially on the following points:
   a) Explain the modulation from A♭M to Fm in mm. 52–55.
   b) What familiar modulating/developmental process takes place in mm. 63–74?

6. By m. 78 we are back in Fm, and in m. 81 we reach V in this key. For how long is this V prolonged? What is the function and name of this extended dominant prolongation? Where does it lead to?

7. How do you explain harmonically the interesting seconds in the bass, mm. 94–100?

8. Are there any discrepancies between the recapitulation and the exposition?

9. The final cadence could be in mm. 145–146. How is it delayed? What chords are tonicized in these final measures?

Beethoven, Piano Sonata No. 21 in CM, *Waldstein,* op. 53, I (anthology, no. 35)

The *Waldstein* Sonata is one of the masterpieces of Beethoven's middle period. The following comments will guide you through the analysis of its monumental first movement in sonata form.

1. *The exposition.*
   a) Analyze phrase 1 harmonically (mm. 1–4). What is unusual about this harmonic beginning? How is CM established? Does phrase 2 (mm. 5–8) confirm the tonic key? (What secondary key areas do phrase 1 and phrase 2 actually represent? What are the chords within each of these two areas?) Where is the first V–I progression in CM?
   b) In mm. 7–11 notice the fluctuation between the FM (as V of B♭) and Fm chords (and hence between A♮ and A♭, $\hat 6$ and $\flat\hat 6$). In mm. 12–14 you will also see the juxtaposition of Cm and CM. More of these M/m complexes will appear later in the movement.
   c) What is the formal function of mm. 14–21? What secondary key areas are represented here, and what are the chords within each area?
   d) Explain (or review) the modulation in mm. 21–23. Measures 23–34 function as the T section. What harmony is prolonged here?
   e) S_1 begins in m. 35. We have already seen that in his middle and late periods, Beethoven, like the Romantic composers after him, often preferred third-related keys over the functionally stronger fifth relationships favored in the Classical period. Explain how this applies to the S area in this sonata.
   f) Explain mm. 43–50 from a formal/thematic point of view.
   g) A new theme, S_2, appears in mm. 50–53. Brilliant keyboard figuration beginning in m. 58 leads to an extended cadential gesture in mm. 66–74.
   h) The brief section that follows functions as a codetta, C.
   i) Comment on the many counterstatements in this exposition. Are they literal or varied? What effect do they have on the length and scope of the exposition?
   j) Focus now on *thematic relationships*.
      1) The contour of P, in mm. 1–3, features two intervals: the 3rd, and the P5. How is it balanced by the motive in m. 4?
      2) The T area has two clear sections: mm. 23–30 and 31–34. How are they related thematically to P?

3) How is S_1 related to P, and how does it balance the contour of mm. 1–3?

4) The thematic relationship of S_2 with the previous themes is more obscure. Consider, however, the notes on beats 1 and 3 in mm. 50–51, along with the B in m. 52. How does the resulting line balance S_1?

5) Finally, comment on the C theme (mm. 74–77).

2. *The development.* The development can be broken up into several harmonic areas, as suggested by the following points:

a) Explain the modulating process that leads from the closing C section in EM to FM in m. 90.

b) FM/m is an important key complex throughout the development (Remember the $\hat{6}/\flat\hat{6}$, as well as CM/m juxtapositions in the opening measures!). You can think of mm. 90–104 as being in F and of the two other key areas in this section as secondary key areas of F. Which are these key areas, and how do they relate to F? Explain the thematic development in these measures. Where do the two motives in mm. 96–103 come from?

c) A fast-moving harmonic and linear process which we have already studied (as an assignment in chapter 24) takes place in mm. 104–112. Because it leads from i in Fm (m. 104) to V in FM (m. 112), this is also an extension of the F complex of keys. Review the linear process in mm. 105–109, and understand how it functions harmonically (a circle of 5ths) and linearly (a $^4_2 - ^6_3$ *fonte* sequence similar to the one by Soler which we studied in example 24.21). What is the chord that precedes the arrival on V of F in m. 112?

d) We have also studied the modulating process that follows in mm. 116–136 (see the comments to example 25.10). Review and understand the role of common-tone modulation in this area. What theme is this section based on?

e) What harmony is reached in m. 136? What is the formal/harmonic function of mm. 136–155? What happens in m. 156?

3. *The recapitulation.* In the first place, notice the length of what is left after this point: We are in m. 156, and we have 146 more measures to go! Comment on everything that is different between the recapitulation and the exposition.

a) What is the function of the newly added mm. 169–173?

b) We would now expect the S area to be in CM, and T to be nonmodulating. What do we find instead? How does the present key of S_1 provide a tonal balance to the key of S_1 in the exposition (with respect to the tonic key, CM)?

c) Comment on the key of S_2 and C.

d) A surprising series of events takes place after m. 245. After the C theme cadences in CM, we could expect some kind of conclusive gesture to end the movement. What we get is fifty-seven measures of coda!

4. *The coda as a second development*

a) First, the C theme is extended through a modulation to Fm, as it did at the beginning of the development.

b) In mm. 247–248, V_7 of Fm resolves deceptively to a statement of P in D♭M (the Neapolitan key as a "coda key," a function we have already seen in example 24.15).

c) We soon realize that Beethoven launched into an unexpected second development in the place of the coda. Notice, however, that this new development does not stray very far from CM, and that, as a matter of fact, it has a "cadential character" if we consider its long-range tonal motion. Let us examine some of its details:

1) What key areas are touched upon in the first section of the development (mm. 249–259)? What familiar linear technique can you identify in the left hand of mm. 255–256? This first section, which started in the Neapolitan key (a "predominant function"), leads to the half cadence on V of CM in m. 259. (What chord does Beethoven use, in m. 258, to approach this important HC?)

2) What part of P which was not used in the first development is developed now, in mm. 259 and following? The development in mm. 261–275 is largely based on sequences. Examine mm. 261–267, then 267–270, then 270–271, and finally 272–274, and explain the use of sequential techniques in these passages. From a harmonic point of view, this whole area (from m. 259 to 278) is a long motion from V in CM to, again, V in CM (mm. 278–283).

3) A possible final cadence is set up again in mm. 282–283. The new surprise is a final statement of S_1, now in the tonic key which we were expecting in the recapitulation!

4) We pointed out, in the opening measures and in the development section, the fluctuation between FM and Fm (resulting in a fluctuation between A♮ and A♭). How does this fluctuation between $\hat{6}$ and $\flat\hat{6}$ reappear in the extended half cadence in mm. 290–294?

5) A final statement of P, which recalls the very beginning of the exposition, finally closes this astonishing example of sonata form. Here,

again, notice the final tonicization of the sub-dominant, and its appearance, once more, as an FM/m complex stressing the $\hat{6}$/$\flat\hat{6}$ fluctuation!

This discussion closes our study of sonata form. What is your impression of this movement? How does Beethoven achieve its monumental scope? How does it conform to, and how does it depart from, the standard sonata form design? What makes this movement so interesting and unpredictable? Do you understand the movement and its complexities better after this analysis?

EXERCISE

To practice analyzing a movement in sonata form, refer to exercise 26.1 in worksheet 26 at the end of this chapter.

THE RONDO

Listen to Haydn's Piano Sonata in DM, Hob. XVI:37, III (anthology, no. 21), an example of rondo form. You will recognize its character as typical of last movements in classical sonatas, concertos, and symphonies: It has a fast tempo, and its mood is light and playful. From a formal point of view, the **rondo** is usually simpler than the sonata form. The basic principle of a rondo is the recurrence of a **refrain**, which alternates with contrasting **episodes**. The contrast may be thematic, and also tonal: Whereas the refrain in a rondo *is always in the tonic key,* the episodes may be in different keys. Some authors prefer the term **couplets** for these contrasting areas, to avoid confusion with fugal episodes.

The simplest formal type that fits this definition is, of course, the familiar *ternary* form (or *aria* form), with an ABA design. Rondo form is indeed an outgrowth of ternary. Haydn's rondo is what we know as a five-part rondo, which, in its most frequent form, can be summarized as ABACA. Refrains in a rondo are closed harmonically and are often in *binary form.* The second episode (the C section), which tends to be larger, sometimes includes changes of tempo and meter and may have a developmental character. We may find a *modulating* **transition** (T) to connect the refrain with an episode, and a **retransition** (RT) to return to the refrain. Possible formal and tonal schemes for a five-part rondo appear in example 26.5.

♪♪♪ Example 26.5   Five-Part Rondo Designs

A		B		A		C	RT	A	
I————	I	V————	V	I————	I	i———i	V——I	————	I
I————	I	i————	i	I————	I	IV———IV	V——I	————	I
i————	i	III————	III	i————	i	iv———iv	V——i	————	i

A FIVE-PART RONDO: HAYDN, PIANO SONATA IN DM, HOB. XVI:37, III (ANTHOLOGY, NO. 21)

1. *The refrain.* When you listened to this piece you may have realized that mm. 1–20 constitute a closed formal unit, which returns later in a literal form (mm. 41–60) and in a slightly varied form (mm. 94–134). This is the recurring A section of this **five-part rondo,** its *refrain.* You may also have realized that this refrain is in rounded binary form, dominant type. Explain exactly what makes it so. Review, if necessary, the chapter on binary and ternary forms, and make sure you are familiar with all the types of binary before you continue the study of rondo. Explain exactly how the last return of A is varied (mm. 94–134).

2. *Episode 1.* The first contrasting episode, the B section (mm. 21–40), is in the parallel minor key, Dm. What is the form of this episode (be exact as to the specific formal design)? Explain how the thematic material in this section is contrasting with respect to the refrain. On the other hand, do the themes have anything in common (such as contour, important pitches, characteristic leaps, etc.)?

3. *Episode 2.* After the literal return of the refrain, the second episode (the C section, mm. 61–80), introduces the contrasting (but close) key of GM, the subdominant key. Notice the formal type of this section: It is a rounded binary, tonic type, in which the complete first reprise returns at the end of the second reprise. What do we call this formal type? What is the harmonic and formal function of the section in mm. 81–93, and what term do we use for such a section?

A bass reduction showing formal relationships and key areas for this rondo appears in example 26.6. Study it and understand how it represents the form of the piece we have just analyzed.

Example 26.6   Bass Reduction for Haydn, Hob. XVI:37, III

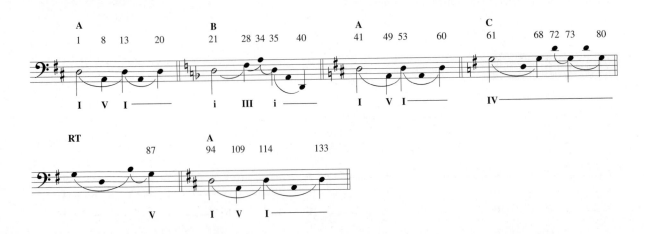

Guided Studies of Rondo Forms

Haydn's five-part rondo is a simple example of this formal type. We will now study two more complex instances: a seven-part rondo by Beethoven and a sonata-rondo by Mozart. The format for these studies will be the same that we used in our "Further Analysis" of sonata form: These may be done as class discussions, following the analytical guidelines provided by the following comments and questions.

I. A Seven-Part Rondo: Beethoven, Piano Sonata in Cm, op. 13 ("Pathétique"), III (anthology, no. 34)

In a **seven-part rondo**, one more episode and refrain are added to the five parts we are already familiar with. A hypothetical formal design would be ABACADA. More often, however, the last three sections mirror the first three, in a design such as ABACAB′A, where the third episode is a return, perhaps varied, of the first episode. Example 26.7 shows some possible designs for this formal type.

In example 26.7 we see that the first three and last three parts are often grouped tonally, whereas the second episode (the middle part) is the one that is likely to feature the greatest tonal contrast, and the one that allows for the largest variety of choices. We will now see how this general formal type is represented by Beethoven's *Pathétique* rondo.

1. *The refrain (mm. 1–17).* Study and discuss the phrase structure for the opening section of this movement, the refrain (mm. 1–17). How many phrases are there in this section? How are they related thematically? We have already studied the subsequent modulating transition to E♭M, III, through the secondary key area of iv, and leading to the B section, the first episode in E♭M (review this discussion in chapter 17, in the section, "Secondary Key Areas").

2. *Episode 1 (mm. 25–61).* This is a rich episode from a thematic point of view. Where have we seen, earlier in this movement, the characteristic rhythm for its initial theme (mm. 25 and following)? The second theme of this episode, in m. 37, features the motive Î–2̂–3̂–2̂–Î (in triplets). Is this contour derived in any way from the opening theme (see mm. 1–2, including the initial anacrusic motive)? The third theme, on the other hand, presents a truly contrasting character (mm. 44–50). Comment on aspects of this theme. Notice also how many times Beethoven has already used a certain chord to approach an important dominant harmony: What are the chords in mm. 6 (beat 2), 32 (beat 1), and 46 (beat 2)?

   The theme in triplets returns in m. 51, now in a section with a transitional function (to modulate back to Cm), leading to the literal return of the refrain (mm. 62–78).

3. *Episode 2 (mm. 79–120).* In essence, this episode is a set of variations on a four-measure theme in two voices (mm. 79–82). Explain what these variations are exactly, and how many of them there are. Notice also the contrapuntal character of this C section, and the abrupt change of key from Cm to A♭M in mm. 78–79. What common element between these two keys allows for such a direct (and yet smooth) modulation? On the surface, the theme of this episode seems new and contrasting. How is it derived, however, from the opening theme? Refer specifically to mm. 5–6.

   The last variation (mm. 103–106) leads into a long prolongation of the Cm dominant (mm. 107–120). How do we call this type of prolongation, and where does it take us?

4. *Episode 3 (mm. 134–170).* The refrain that begins in m. 121 is not stated in its complete original form. How is its "third phrase" varied (mm. 129–133)? One might think that it functions as a modulating transi-

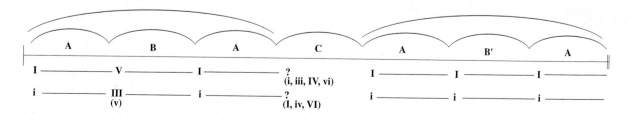

♪♪♪ Example 26.7   Seven-Part Rondo Designs

tion; actually, there is no "modulation," because the third episode is in the parallel major key, CM (beginning in m. 134). What is the chord leading to the new episode in m. 133 (beat 2)? Now compare episode 3 with episode 1. Other than the keys, is there any difference between them? Is episode 3 a D section, or rather a B′ section? Is there any reminiscence of the key from episode 1 (E♭M) in mm. 158–166?

5. *The final refrain and the coda.* The final return of the refrain takes place in mm. 171–182. In what form does the third phrase of the refrain appear (mm. 179–182)? Are the original pitches there?

    The cadence of this return is reached in m. 182. The additional section is a coda extending this Cm cadence. On what theme are mm. 182–193 based? And mm. 193–198 (notice the overlapping P4s, G–D/F–C)? The coda concludes with a surprising return of the initial theme in a last-minute recall of the key from episode 2, A♭M (VI). Review this interesting modulation which we already studied: What is the pivot chord function of the chord in m. 198? What kind of enharmonic reinterpretation takes place in m. 206, introducing the return of Cm only for the striking final cadence?

Study the formal/tonal diagram in example 26.8. How does it reflect the design of this movement? Does it conform to the standard designs of seven-part rondo that appear in example 26.7?

II. A Sonata-Rondo: Mozart, Piano Sonata in B♭M, K. 333, III (anthology, no. 28)

Listen to, and analyze, Mozart's B♭M rondo. It represents a formal type in which sonata form and seven-part rondo merge: **the sonata-rondo.** Go back to example 26.7, the diagram for the seven-part rondo formal types. The sonata-rondo is a logical consequence of this design: If the initial A and B sections are the primary and secondary key areas (P and S) in a sonata form exposition (with an added return of A in the tonic key), if the C section becomes a development, and if the final A–B′–A sections, all in the tonic key, function as the recapitulation, you will easily see how the two formal types (sonata and rondo) come together in this hybrid which we call sonata-rondo form (see example 26.9).

1. *The exposition.* In Mozart's B♭M rondo, the exposition comprises the sections from m. 1 to m. 64. The refrain (mm. 1–16) is followed by a modulating, transitional theme (T, mm. 16–24), leading to the secondary key area (the B section or first episode) in FM (V), mm. 24–36. A brief retransition (mm. 36–40) takes us to the return of the complete refrain in B♭M, mm. 41–56. The transitional theme now modulates to Gm (the relative minor) in mm. 56–64.

2. *The development.* The second episode, the C section, begins in m. 65, with its own new theme in Gm. After a new modulation to E♭M (IV), the section in mm. 76–105 has a clear developmental character. Why? What are the secondary key areas in this section? What previous themes are developed? What is the harmonic function of mm. 105–111? What do these measures lead to?

3. *The recapitulation.* The complete refrain returns, in B♭M, in mm. 112–127. The extended T section (mm. 127–148) now does not lead to FM, but rather to the prolonged B♭M dominant in mm. 144–148, which launches the return of the B section, now in the tonic key (mm. 148–171). After the brief cadenzalike passage in mm. 171–172 (a **lead-in** or *Eingang*, an improvisational passage used, especially in concertos, to introduce or lead into a solo passage or a return of an important theme), the refrain seems to return, for what should be the last appearance of the A section. Instead, we soon hear a new modulation to V (mm. 177–179), which begins an unexpected second development (the supposed return was, then a **false return**)! What theme or motive is this development based on? Could you think of this second development as an extended prolongation of FM, the dominant of B♭M? If so, what is its tonal function in the long-range design of the movement?

    A new, longer lead-in on V finally takes us to the true return of the refrain in m. 200, followed by a cadential section (mm. 207–214) and by a closing coda (which briefly tonicizes the subdomimant key) in mm. 215–225.

Can you provide a formal-tonal diagram for this movement? If possible, provide also a bass reduction showing all the main and secondary key areas and how they correspond with major formal divisions.

PRACTICAL APPLICATION AND DISCUSSION

Because the formal types we have studied in this chapter are essential in the Classical period, and to a certain extent also in the Romantic period, you will encounter them very often (and must certainly have come across them already) in your career as a performer, composer, or scholar.

What do you think is the significance of what you have learned in this chapter? How will it affect your understanding of complete movements? Do you think understanding the form, tonal plan, and thematic relationships of a large movement is important to you as a musician and performer? How? Will your knowledge of form affect the way you approach a large movement from now on, whether to listen to it or to perform it? The type of analysis we have demonstrated in this chapter tells us not only about sectional divisions and thematic connections, but also about long-range harmonic motion, directed harmonic tension, and tonal design. This allows you to hear large movements as single formal and tonal units, held together by underlying tonal structures that provide their coherence and forward drive. Are these concepts important to a performer? Discuss why and how (or why not and how not).

If anyone in the class is currently performing a movement in either sonata or rondo form, he or she may wish to perform it for the class and perhaps explain its formal and tonal characteristics. In any case, if you are a performer you can find a movement in either sonata or rondo form and play through it yourself. What has your new knowledge of form added to your understanding of this movement? How has it affected your performance of it or the way you hear it?

The following are some of the specific questions relating to sonata form which you may want to address in your discussion:

1. How can you enhance the transitional character of the T section to contribute to the urgency toward the S key area and theme?

2. How are the P and S themes different and contrasting in character, and how can you best emphasize the differences?

3. Can you contribute through your performance to the sense of instability and tonal motion of the development? What can you do to make sure that the tension and the sense of direction are kept throughout the development until they reach their goal (the return of the tonic key at the beginning of the recapitulation)?

4. How can you try to convince listeners that a "false recapitulation" is the real one, so that the effect of the real recapitulation is heightened?

5. The tension accumulated throughout the secondary key area and the development is resolved with the return of the tonic key and the opening theme at the beginning of the recapitulation. How can you enhance the structural significance of this important moment in a sonata form movement?

6. On the other hand, the rest of the recapitulation may be a long area of tonal stability. How can you make sure that you keep the level of musical motion and interest high now that you don't have the support of thematic development and unstable harmonic activity to create tension and excitement?

♪♪♪ Example 26.8   Bass Reduction for Beethoven, op. 13, III

♪♪♪ Example 26.9   Sonata-Rondo Designs

	Expo.			Dev.		Recap.		
A	B	A	C		A	B'		A
I	V	I	X		I	I		I
i	III	i	X		i	i		i

EXERCISE

For an assignment of an analytical paper on a movement in sonata-rondo form, refer to exercise 26.2 in worksheet 26 at the end of this chapter.

ASSIGNMENT

For analytical assignments based on the materials learned in this chapter, refer to chapter 26 in the workbook.

Composers and Their Music 26

Listening

Listen to the following compositions by composers mentioned in this chapter. Listen to these pieces following the score, and as you listen, try to identify the formal design for each of the movements. Within each formal type, identify the main sections and key areas and their function within the overall design.

Haydn, Symphony no. 97 in CM.
Mozart, Sonata in FM, K. 332.
Beethoven, Sonata in CM, op. 2 no. 3.

Terms for Review

Sonata form
Exposition
Primary key area
Secondary key area

P and S themes
Transition:
   dependent, independent
Closing section

Development
Recapitulation
Retransition
Coda
Second development
Counterstatement
Two-part exposition
False recapitulation
Rondo
Refrain

Episodes
Couplets
Transition
Retransition
Five-part rondo
Seven-part rondo
Sonata-rondo
Lead-in *(Eingang)*
False return

Worksheet 26

EXERCISE 26.1 Analyze Beethoven's Piano Sonata op. 10, no. 1, I, in sonata form. Turn in an annotated copy of the score (the score and the recording will be available at your music library). You should indicate the thematic/sectional content of the complete movement using the letter symbols we have learned in this chapter (P, T, S, C, etc.), and all keys and key areas for the complete movement.

Provide some kind of formal diagram and/or long-range bass reduction for the complete movement, and answer the following questions:

1. Exposition
   a) Measures 1–30, according to their formal and thematic function, are best described as:

      Explain the thematic content of these measures (which constitute a period) by phrases (how many phrases? how are they related?).

   b) Measures 32–56 are best described as:

      If we divide this section into five harmonic units, the key areas defined by the four first units are as follows: mm. 32–36, _____; mm. 37–40, _____; mm. 41–44, _____; mm. 45–48, _____. The harmonic function of mm. 48–55 is _____, leading into a new section in m. 56, in the key of _____.

      What is typical of Beethoven in the way the key areas in this section are related?

   c) Briefly explain the sectional/thematic/harmonic content of the rest of the exposition. Is it all one section, or does it break up into several subsections?

2. Development
   a) Explain the thematic content of the complete development (use the letter D to indicate any possible new theme in the development).

   b) Indicate, with measure numbers, the five key areas clearly established in mm. 106–142, including m. 142. (Be careful: Dominants are not keys, they are only dominants! Keys are defined by the resolution of the dominant to the tonic.)

c) Indicate the key areas at mm. 142–156, and explain their relationship.

d) The harmonic/formal function of mm. 158–167 is (explain and provide the exact *term*):

3. Recapitulation. Compare the recapitulation with the exposition. What is the same in both sections? What are the differences?

EXERCISE 26.2   Write a short analytical paper on Beethoven's Piano Sonata in GM, op. 31, no. 1, III, in sonata-rondo form. The score and a recording will be available at your music library. The score can also be found in the Arlin anthology *(Music Sources)*. You can use the guided analyses of Beethoven's and Mozart's rondos in this chapter as models for the organization of your paper. Turn in an annotated copy of the score.

The following are some specific questions about this particular movement by Beethoven which you should address in your paper.

1. What is interesting harmonically about the beginning?

2. Is there a T section between the tonic and dominant key areas in the exposition?

3. What contrapuntal technique is used in mm. 86–90? Where does this section lead?

4. What is the formal function of the C section (the second episode)? Discuss the harmonic processes in this section (mm. 98–129), with mention of all the specific key areas.

5. Is there a retransition after the C section? What chord does Beethoven use to approach this important point of formal articulation?

6. Is there a coda?

7. Beethoven uses variation techniques in several sections of this movement. Explain how this statement applies in mm. 1–32, 66–82, and 132–164. Compare also mm. 140–147 with 156–164.

8. Provide some kind of formal diagram and/or long-range bass reduction for the complete movement.

Chapter 27

Expanding Functional Tonality: Extended Tertian Chords; Linear Chromaticism II

Composers throughout the common practice period expanded the basic harmonic vocabulary in a variety of ways. In this chapter we will examine two of the means used for this expansion of tonality. First, we will focus on extended tertian chords, which allow for both diatonic and chromatic expansions of functional sonorities and which introduce, in either case, strong elements of dissonance. In the second part of the chapter we will further our study of linear chromaticism, and we will see that diatonic frames can be expanded through both sequential and nonsequential chromaticism.

EXPANDING CHORDAL SONORITIES: EXTENDED TERTIAN CHORDS

The harmonic event illustrated in example 27.2a is familiar enough to you: The ninth of a 9–8 suspension over a V_7 chord resolves, as expected, before the bass has moved on to the next chord. In example 27.2b, on the other hand, the same ninth does not resolve before the bass moves, but rather resolves along with the bass into the next chord. In this latter case, we can say that the ninth is part of the chord, which thus becomes a **ninth chord** on V, or V_7^9. The origin of this chord is linear, as shown by example 27.2a. As an independent chordal sonority (example 27.2b) it still often functions as a linear chord. Occasionally, however, the ninth chord is used as an independent, nonlinear chord, which results from adding one more third on top of a seventh chord, as shown in example 27.1. If we add one more third on top of the ninth chord, we will have an **eleventh chord**, and yet one more third will produce a **thirteenth chord**, both shown in example 27.1. These chords as a family are normally called **extended tertian chords**.

All of these chords have several things in common:

1. In the first place, they are highly dissonant and, most often, they are treated as such (the dissonance is resolved in some conventional manner, and sometimes, but not always, is also prepared).

2. They are most often used with a dominant function, although they can also appear, as we will see, on any degree of the scale besides $\hat{5}$.

3. In musical practice we do not always find these chords in their complete form. Although they are often written in more than four voices (usually five, or at times

♪♪♪ Example 27.1

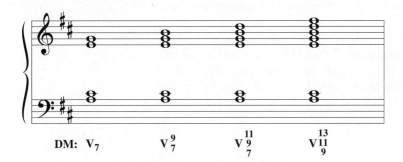

DM: V_7 V_7^9 $V_{\ 7}^{\ 11\ 9}$ $V_{\ 9}^{\ 13\ 11}$

more), in four-voice textures some pitches need to be left out. The seventh, however, is usually not left out in any of these chords.

We will now examine these characteristics as they apply to each of the specific extended tertian chords.

Ninth Chords

The dominant ninth is the most frequent of all extended tertian chords. The characteristics of the dominant ninth are as follows:

1. In a four-voice texture, the *fifth of the chord is omitted,* and the seventh is included.

2. The ninth (as well as the seventh) *resolves down by step.*

3. In the diatonic form of this chord, the ninth is major in major keys ($\hat{6}$) and minor in minor keys ($\flat\hat{6}$). The M9th chord V_7^9 is indeed normally found only in major keys. The m9th chord, on the other hand ($V_7^{\flat 9}$), can actually be used in both minor and major keys. In major keys, this is properly a "borrowed" chord, because of the use of $\flat\hat{6}$.

4. The ninth of the chord should at least be *at the distance of a 9th above the bass* (that is, it should not be a second above the bass).

Verify all the above points in example 27.2. Play or sing through these examples, and hear the dissonance of the 9th, its resolution, and whether the 9th is major or minor.

♪♪♪ Example 27.2

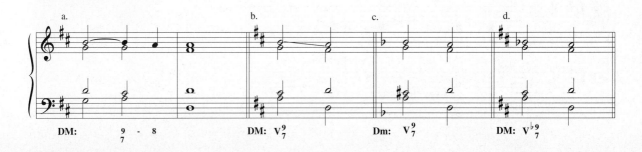

DM: $\begin{smallmatrix}9\\7\end{smallmatrix}$ - 8   DM: V_7^9 Dm: V_7^9 DM: $V_7^{\flat 9}$

Franck began his sonata for violin and piano with a V_7^9 in AM, as illustrated in example 27.3. Identify all the members of this chord in the example. Is the chord complete? What actual pitch is the ninth? The chord is extended through m. 5. How? What kind of harmonic gesture takes place in mm. 6–8? Where is the V_7^9 actually resolved? Comment on the resolution of the ninth.

In the Franck example the ninth is major, which in a major key is a diatonic pitch. Now listen to the Hugo Wolf fragment in example 27.4, in C♭M. Focus first on the cadence, beginning with the G♭ chord in m. 16. The upper voice in the piano (E♭–D♭) is a simple 6–5 motion over the bass. You can see the actual dominant chord in the last eighth note of m. 16 and the first beat of m. 17. What kind of a ninth chord is this? What scale degree is A♭♭ in C♭M?

♪♪♪ Example 27.3   C. Franck, Sonata for Violin and Piano, I, mm. 1–8

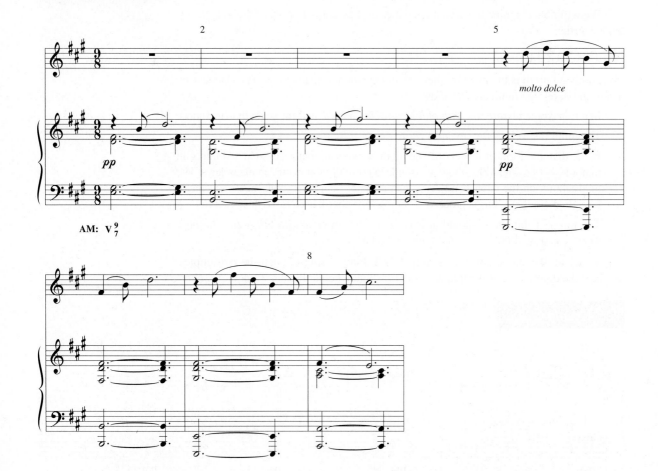

Example 27.4   Hugo Wolf, "Der Mond hat eine schwere Klag' erhoben," from *Italienisches Liederbuch,* mm. 15–18

Now study the progression in mm. 15–16, leading to the $V^{\flat 9}_7$ which we just analyzed. You will recognize a circle-of-5ths bass (D♭–G♭–C♭–F♭) supporting a progression made up of three consecutive dominants leading to the predominant on F♭. One of these chords is a secondary V^9_7 chord. Which one, and what is the exact Roman numeral (RN) for it?

Eleventh and Thirteenth Chords

Listen now to example 27.5. The only two chords in this excerpt are a DM tonic chord and a linear chord that functions as a neighbor chord to the DM tonic. If you try to organize this chord in thirds over the bass note A ($\hat{5}$), you will find out that it can indeed be interpreted as a linear dominant chord. As a dominant harmony, the chord is missing the third (the C♯), and it includes instead a seventh, a ninth, and an eleventh (think of the interval of 11th as a compound 4th). By this functional interpretation, this is a $V^{11}_{9\ 7}$ chord.

Dominant eleventh chords are normally spelled according to the following conventions, especially in four voices:

1. The 11th in an eleventh chord should be an 11th (not a 4th) above the bass.

2. Because the pitch an 11th above $\hat{5}$ in V_{11} is actually $\hat{1}$, the third ($\hat{7}$) is usually omitted in this chord in order to avoid the harsh clash between the leading tone ($\hat{7}$) and $\hat{1}$.

3. In four voices, one more pitch must also be omitted. The two possibilities for the eleventh chord are root-fifth-seventh-eleventh (V^{11}_7, as in example 27.6a) or root-seventh-ninth-eleventh ($V^{11}_{9\ 7}$ chord, as in example 27.6b).

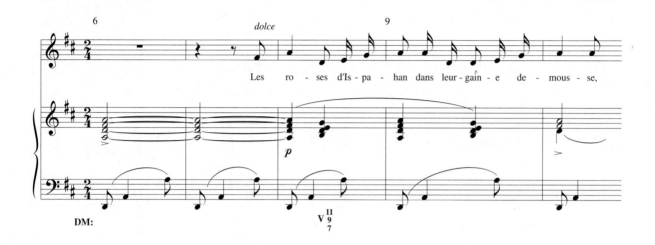

♪♪♪ Example 27.5   G. Fauré, *Les roses d'Ispahan,* op. 39, no. 4, mm. 6–10

4. In the resolution of the V_{11} chord to the tonic chord, the eleventh stays in the same voice as a common tone with the tonic ($\hat{1}$).

In examples 27.6c and d we see yet another type of extended tertian chord, the *dominant thirteenth chord.* Examine the use of this chord by Chopin in example 27.7a. Then, read the following basic principles for writing the dominant thirteenth chord:

1. In this chord, neither the third nor the seventh is left out. Its most frequent form in four voices is, then, V_7^{13}.

2. The thirteenth (think of it as a compound sixth) may be major ($\hat{3}$) or minor ($\flat\hat{3}$), and it should always be a 13th (not a 6th) above the bass.

♪♪♪ Example 27.6

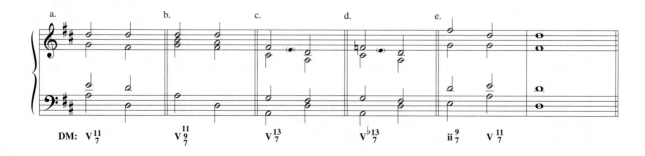

3. The thirteenth usually resolves by leaping down a third to $\hat{1}$. This leap is often bridged by a passing tone, as suggested in examples 27.6c and d. Occasionally, the thirteenth may also stay in the same voice as a common tone with the tonic, as you can see in example 27.7c.

Study the cadence in example 27.7b (mm. 127–129) by Alma Mahler. Identify the exact type of dominant chord (don't forget to take into account the voice part), and comment on its resolution. (We will study the first measure of this example later in this chapter.) The cadence in example 27.7c also includes a V^{13}_7, and in this case the

♩♪♪Example 27.7a   F. Chopin, Prelude, op. 28, no. 13, mm. 18–20

♩♪♪Example 27.7b   A. Mahler, "In meines Vaters Garten," from *Five Songs*, no. 2, mm. 126–129

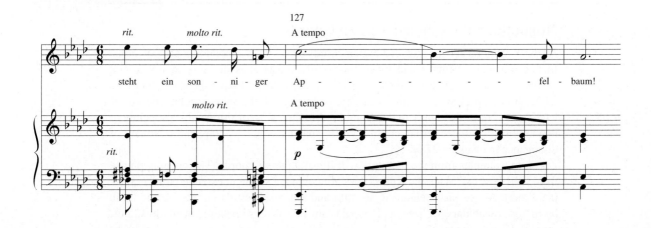

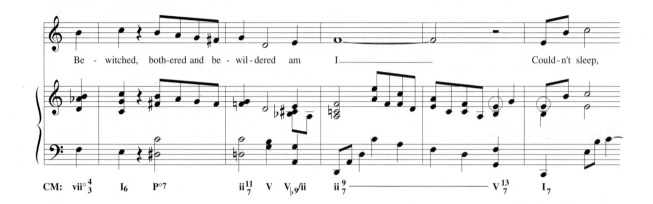

♪♪♪Example 27.7c   Lorenz Hart–Richard Rodgers, "Bewitched," from *Pal Joey* (Cadence in Chorus)

thirteenth stays in the same voice as a common tone with the tonic. What other extended dominant chord can you find in this passage? This phrase also illustrates how, in jazz and popular music, extended tertian sonorities are an essential component of harmony. Notice how many dominant and nondominant extended chords (which we will study in the next section) are featured in this example. As a final observation on this passage, comment on the passing °7 chord (P°7) in m. 1. In chapter 25 we studied another linear °7 chord, the CT °7 chord. Explain the linear nature of the P°7 in this example and specifically how it functions as a passing chord.

EXERCISE

To practice spelling and resolving dominant ninth, eleventh, and thirteenth chords, refer to exercise 27.2 in worksheet 27 at the end of this chapter.

Nondominant Extended Tertian Chords

As we mentioned above, extended tertian chords can also have nondominant functions. In late nineteenth-century and twentieth-century music it is not rare to find ninth, eleventh, or thirteenth chords on any degree of the scale, including the tonic. Example 27.6e shows a progression using such chords. In general, the same spacing and voice-leading principles that apply to dominant ninths, elevenths, or thirteenths also apply to nondominant extended tertian chords. Verify spacing, voice leading, and treatment of dissonance in example 27.6e.

Two examples from the literature will illustrate these chords. The opening phrase from Kurt Weill's "Mack the Knife" does not contain a single unextended triad (example 27.8a). As we just mentioned, seventh and extended tertian chords are the basic harmonic vocabulary of jazz and popular music, as this example well illustrates.

Example 27.8a   Marc Blitzstein–Bertolt Brecht–Kurt Weill, "Mack the Knife," from *The Threepenny Opera* (Opening Phrase)

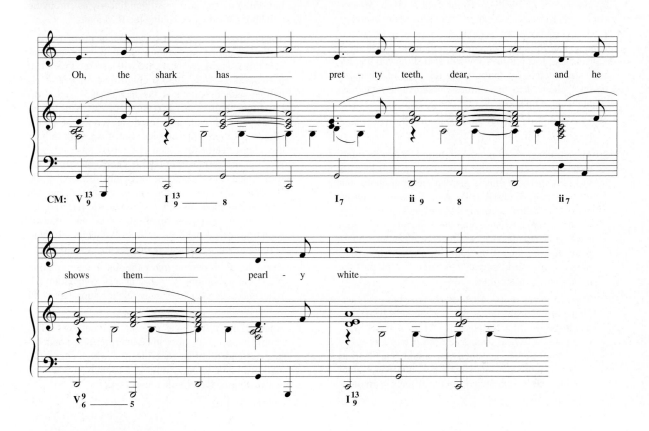

Example 27.8b   Mary Lou Williams, *Nite Life,* mm. 5–9

FURTHER ANALYSIS

A Fragment by William Grant Still

The passage from William Grant Still's opera *Minette Fontaine* reproduced in example 27.9a illustrates several of the harmonic idioms we have studied in this and previous chapters. The following comments will help you through the analysis of this music. They will also show you the difficulties of interpreting music using this type of advanced harmonic idioms and the various possible interpretations you might come up with.

1. The example is in B♭M. In what form is the tonic chord presented in m. 139?

2. The dominant chord in m. 139, beat 4, is doubly interesting. What kind of triad is it based on (consider the fifth!)? Otherwise, this is also an eleventh chord, but the eleventh is raised (B♮). A chord with a raised eleventh is called an augmented eleventh chord (V^{+11}). In our example, because both the fifth and the eleventh are augmented, the label would be V_+^{+11}. From a linear point of view, notice the two half-step neighbor motions in the inner voices, two "sighs" depicting the mourning character of the song.

3. The harmonies in m. 140, beats 3–4 are not easily explained from a functional point of view. In B♭M, they would be ♭II₇ (the Neapolitan) and an unusual ♭vii₇⁹. One could also hear them as a brief detour into a key area of G♭M (♭VI), and then you would hear them as IV_7-ii_7^9, two predominant chords that, however, do not continue into the expected dominant-tonic harmonies

in G♭M. You can also hear them linearly as chromatic neighbor chords embellishing the B♭M tonic.

4. The chord in m. 141, beat 4, can also be heard as a linear embellishment of the tonic chord. If we try to organize this sonority by thirds, we will also see that it can be read as F–A–(C)–E♭–G♭ chord, that is, a $V_7^{♭9}$, although with the ninth in the bass, that is, a fourth-inversion ninth chord! Inversions of extended tertian chords are unusual, and fourth inversions of ninths chords are even more unusual. But if we want to hear this chord "vertically," that is the best interpretation. In a linear interpretation of this chord, of course, we would hear it as a common-tone embellishment of the B♭ tonic, in which the top voice is retained and the other voices move by step (neighbor note [NN]) or by third. In any case, this highly dissonant and somber-sounding chord perhaps tells us something about Diron's mood, as Minette notices in the next line!

5. Example 27.9b demonstrates the linear interpretation of the chords in mm. 139–142 as a prolongation of I. Read and understand the linear relationships expressed in this graph.

6. Analyze the rest of the excerpt on your own. The chords in mm. 142–143 can be interpreted as nondominant extended tertian sonorities (on which degrees?), and the chords in mm. 144–146 as dominant extended tertian chords. Identify their exact types.

Notice that although the functional content of this phrase is quite simple (in essence, V–I–ii–V–I), the progression is greatly enriched by means of tertian dissonance applied to each of the three basic functions (tonic, predominant, and dominant). Mary Lou Williams's fragment in example 27.8b, on the other hand, includes an area of tonicization in which both the secondary dominant and the tonicized chord (V/VI and VI) are extended tertian sonorities. Identify both the secondary dominant and the tonicized chord and what kind of sonorities they constitute. Then examine example 27.7c again, and discuss the nondominant tertian chords in that phrase.

EXERCISES

To practice realizing progressions including a variety of extended tertian chords, refer to exercises 27.3 and 27.4 in worksheet 27 at the end of this chapter.

To practice analysis of musical fragments including extended tertian chords, refer to exercise 27.1.1 in worksheet 27 at the end of this chapter.

🎵🎵🎵 Example 27.9a   William Grant Still, *Minette Fontaine,* mm. 139–147

♪♪♪ Example 27.9a   Continued

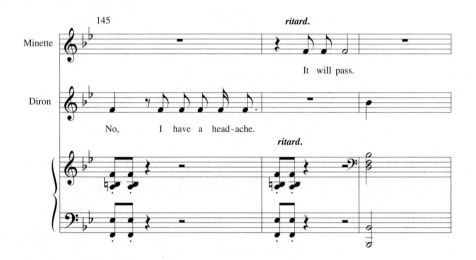

♪♪♪ Example 27.9b   Reduction, mm. 139–142

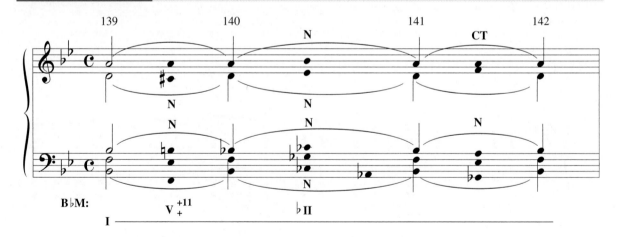

LINEAR CHROMATICISM II: LINEAR EXPANSIONS OF TONALITY

In chapter 25 we discussed a category of chromatic chords that result from linear motion (see section "Linear Chromaticism I: Linear Chromatic Chords"). We will now continue our study of linear chromaticism, focusing mainly on extended sequential and nonsequential processes that have the effect of expanding tonality.

APPOGGIATURA CHORDS

A factor that often contributes to the expansion of tonality in the late nineteenth century is the extensive use of nonchord tones (NCTs), especially appoggiaturas, which in turn create linear, nonfunctional sonorities. **Appoggiatura chords** are dissonant sonorities, often placed on downbeats, generated by melodic appoggiaturas. We can see illustrations of appoggiatura chords in some of the preceding examples in this chapter.

Look, for instance, at Alma Mahler's phrase in example 27.7b. The harmony in the first measure, m. 126, seems highly complex and chromatic. Now play the reduction in example 27.10. In A♭M, it turns out to be a simple tonicization of ii followed by a ♭II₆ predominant chord. What is it that makes this measure so chromatic and complex? Basically, all the appoggiaturas that, as a matter of fact, create two appoggiatura chords (marked "Ap." on the graph). Notice also the spelling of ♭II₆ on the score. How is it spelled? Now refer to the Wolf fragment in example 27.4. The last two measures contain only two functional chords: a dominant and a tonic. Can you explain the role of appoggiaturas and appoggiatura chords in this cadence?

Appoggiatura chords do not necessarily have to fall on the downbeats. The harmonization of the phrase by Dett reproduced in example 27.11 is strongly based on the principle of appoggiatura chords, and all of them are placed on a weak fraction of the beat (unaccented appoggiaturas). Play through the example, and notice how a simple functional progression is enriched by all the linear dissonance produced by the appoggiatura chords.

Now play through the short passage by Richard Wagner in example 27.12a. Think of it in EM. What is the role of nonchord tones, and specifically appoggiaturas, in this passage? Circle all of them on the score, and then try to reduce this texture to a functional chordal progression in block chords (a metric reduction). You will end up with a fairly simple progression, which you can verify in example 27.12b. You can see that most of the wonderful dissonant tension in this phrase is produced melodically by

♩♪♪ **Example 27.10**   Reduction of Example 27.7b

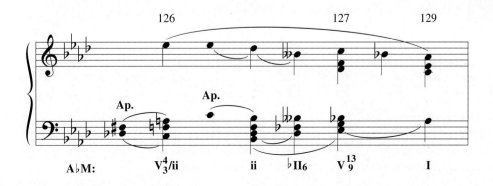

🎵🎵🎵 Example 27.11   N. Dett, Barcarolle, from *In the Bottoms,* mm. 1–8

chromatic nonchord tones, one of the salient characteristics in the music of Richard Wagner. In m. 27 you can interpret the B♮ as a long 4–3 suspension resolving to the A♯. You can also think of it, however, as a chord tone creating an extended tertian dominant harmony. Which chord would this be exactly? Notice also that the G♯ in the top voice at the end of this measure is an anticipation, although it does not actually anticipate a chord tone in the next chord, but rather an appoggiatura.

🎵🎵🎵 Example 27.12a   R. Wagner, *Tristan und Isolde,* Prelude to Act I, mm. 25–28

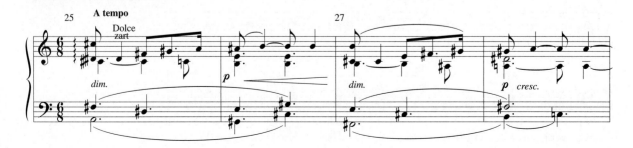

♪♪♪ Example 27.12b | Metric Reduction

CHROMATIC SEQUENCES

In previous chapters we already studied the most usual types of **chromatic sequences**. You may want to review the section of chapter 17, "Consecutive Secondary Dominants: Chromatic Sequences," and "Further Analysis: Chromatic Linear Modulatory Processes" in chapter 24, which discuss the sequences we have called the *fonte* and the *monte*. Because chromatic sequences can suspend tonality momentarily, they are often used by Romantic and post-Romantic composers to enrich and expand their tonal structures. We will now review some of the most characteristic types of chromatic sequences.

The Descending Circle-of-5ths Sequence: The *Fonte*

As we studied in chapter 24, the **fonte**, or "fountain," is a sequence that results from a descending circle of 5ths. If the successive chords are all secondary dominants, the sequence is chromatic, and two of the voices feature descending chromatic lines. You can find this type of progression in examples 17.13b, d, e, and f. For a review of this sequence, refer to examples 27.13a and b. In example 27.13a, the succession of secondary dominants is in root position. Notice the two chromatic lines that result. If one of the two chromatic lines is placed in the bass, as in example 27.13b, the progression takes the form of alternating $^4_2$ and $^6_5$ chords.

Study mm. 32–37 from anthology, no. 45 (Chopin, Mazurka no. 49 in Fm). These measures are the continuation of a phrase in Cm which begins in m. 27. After the half cadence in m. 31, we hear a chromatic sequence that takes us through successive tonicizations of G, C, F, B♭, and E♭. A metric reduction of this passage appears in example 27.13c. Play through the reduction, and then discuss how the *fonte* is enriched by extensive use of chromatic nonchord tones.

♪♪♪Example 27.13

The Ascending 5–6 (or 6–5) Sequence: The *Monte*

The ascending chromatic sequence known as **monte**, mountain, has already appeared in examples 17.13h and 24.22b. This pattern consists of an alternation of secondary dominants and their resolutions, with a resulting bass line that alternates a 4th up and a 3rd down (example 27.14a). If the secondary chords are in first inversion, then we have a chromatic line in the bass, above which $^6_3$ (or $^6_5$) and $^5_3$ chords alternate, as in example 27.14b. A simple case of this sequential pattern appears in example 27.14c, where the

♪♪♪ Example 27.14a and b

a.

b.

♪♪♪ Example 27.14c   Paul Vance–Lee Pockriss (The Cuff Links), "Tracy" (Refrain)

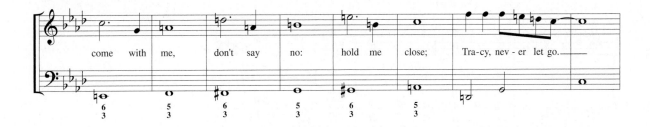

come with me,   don't say   no: hold me close;   Tra-cy, nev - er let go.

♪♪♪ Example 27.15a   F. Chopin, Mazurka no. 37 in A♭M, op. 59, no. 2, mm. 81–89

♪♪♪ Example 27.15b, c, and d

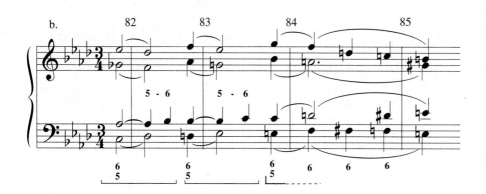

c.   Chopin

d.

FM: **V₇**

sequence involves only triads ($\frac{6}{3}$–$\frac{5}{3}$) rather than seventh chords. The same pattern (now in $\frac{6}{5}$–$\frac{5}{3}$ form) can also be found underlying another fragment by Chopin reproduced in example 27.15a. First, identify in mm. 81–84 the basic $\frac{6}{5}$–$\frac{5}{3}$ pattern in this sequence. Then notice how this linear pattern is embellished in a variety of ways. In the first place, the $\frac{5}{3}$ chords (the resolutions of the secondary dominants) are themselves elaborated by means of 5–6 figures. Moreover, the complete texture is ornamented with chromatic nonchord tones. Study the reduction in example 27.15b, and identify all the NCTs in the actual music.

Chromatic Voice Leading by Contrary Motion: The Omnibus

Look again at example 27.15a, mm. 85–88. You will see a sequence in which the upper voice descends chromatically, while the lower voice ascends chromatically in one-measure-long segments. If you take each of these segments in isolation, you will observe that the basic contrapuntal principle here is chromatic voice leading by contrary motion. In example 27.15c we see a reduction of these measures. Needless to say, this passage is not ruled by the principles of functional harmony. If you look at the sequential segments from the point of view of vertical sonorities, you will notice that they are made up of a Mm₇ sonority and a °7th sonority (whose roots are a whole step apart) connected chromatically by a passing $\frac{6}{5}$ sonority. The fourth sonority in each case is a triad on which the °7th resolves. Play the example, and understand how this is basically a chromatic contrary-motion passage in which the resulting sonorities function as described above.

The Chopin progression is actually a slight variation of a standard chromatic progression known as the **omnibus**. This interesting linear pattern is reproduced in example 27.15d. In the Chopin example, the omnibus harmonizes a descending chromatic line in the soprano. Here it takes the form of an ascending chromatic line in the bass, and instead of a passing chord connecting a Mm_7 and a °7th as in Chopin, in example 27.15d we have a passing $^6_4$ connecting a °7th and a Mm_7. That is, the order of the seventh chords has been reversed because here the chromatic scale ascends instead of descending. For a descending chromatic line in the bass, just read example 27.15d backward. Notice the chromatic voice exchanges marked in each of the sequence segments. Observe also that the omnibus in example 27.15d is simply a chromatic linear prolongation of an FM V_7 chord.

The Descending 5–6 Sequence

Whereas the basic voice leading in the *monte* involves a descending 5–6 or 6–5 sequential pattern, the equivalent descending 5–6 pattern over a chromatic bass is also very effective musically, as shown by the well-known excerpt in example 27.16a. As in the *monte,* the sequence may involve only triads, and then the pattern results from alternating $^5_3$ and $^6_5$ chords over a chromatic bass (as in example 27.16b), or it may instead alternate $^5_3$ and $^6_5$ chords (as in both examples 27.16a and c).

The $^{7-6}_{5-3}$ Sequence

In example 27.17a you can recognize a standard 7–6 sequential pattern. While the 7th is sounding (the suspension), the only other pitch other than the bass is the third above it. In example 27.17b, you will see a slight change to this sequence: While the 7th is sounding, you also have a 3rd and a 5th above the bass; that is, you hear a complete $^7_{5\atop3}$ "suspension" chord. Now look at the resolution of the 7th to the 6th: To avoid the clash of the 6th with the 5th which was sounding before it, this 5th "gets out of the way," while the 3rd is sustained. The result is a $^{7-6}_{5-\;3\atop3}$ sequential pattern, which makes for an interesting and rich linear passage. Play through or listen to the Mozart passage in example 27.18a, and note that example 27.17b is simply a metric reduction of the Mozart example. Explain how the progression is elaborated in the music by means of NCTs.

Now play through example 27.17c. What in Mozart was a mostly diatonic sequential pattern, here becomes a highly chromatic linear phrase. But in essence the pattern is the same: a $^{7-6}_{5-3\atop3}$ sequence. The only real difference is that the bass moves chromatically at the same time as the 7th resolves to the 6th. Understand how this linear pattern works. Then, play through Wagner's phrase in example 27.18b, and verify that example 27.17c is its metric reduction. As you did with the Mozart example, explain the role of chromatic NCTs to enrich and elaborate this progression (in this case, quite extensively so!).

♪♪♪Example 27.16a   Don Feldes–Don Henley–Glenn Frey (The Eagles), "Hotel California"
(Final Verse)

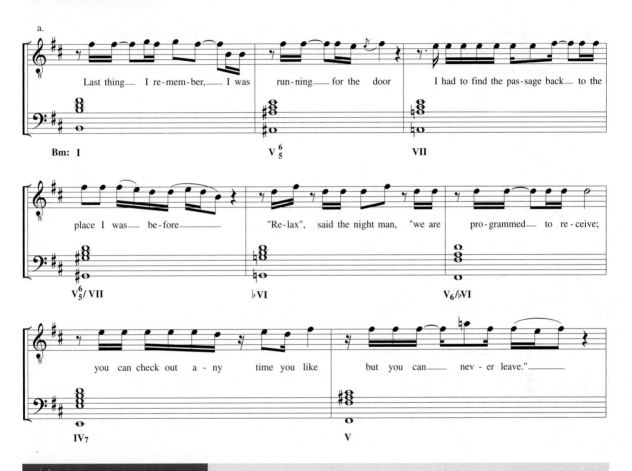

a.

Last thing— I re-mem-ber,— I was   run-ning— for the   door   I had to find the pas-sage back— to the

Bm: I   **V$^6_5$**   **VII**

place I was— be-fore————   "Re-lax", said the night man, "we are   pro-grammed— to re-ceive;

V$^6_5$/ VII   **♭VI**   **V$_6$/♭VI**

you can check out a-ny   time you like   but you can— nev-er leave."————

IV$_7$ **V**

♪♪♪Example 27.16b and c

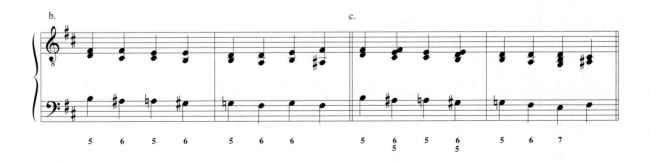

b.   c.

5   6   5   6   5   6   6   5   6   5   6   5   5   6   7
                                      5   5

Example 27.17

a.

Cm: 5 - 6   7 - 6   7 - 6   +6   V

b. Mozart

Cm: 5 ——— 6   7 ——— 6   7 ——— 6   6   +6   V
                 5   5
                 3 ————   3 ————

c. Wagner

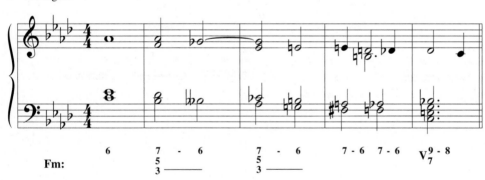

Fm: 6   7 - 6   7 - 6   7 - 6 7 - 6   V$^{9\ -\ 8}_7$
                  5   5
                  3 ——   3 ——

d. Chopin

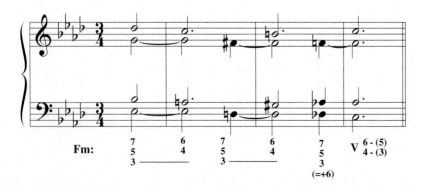

Fm: 7   6   7   6   7   V $^{6\ -\ (5)}_{4\ -\ (3)}$
       5   4   5   4   5
       3 ——   3 ——   3
                              (=+6)

♪♪♪ Example 27.18a   W. A. Mozart, Symphony no. 39, I, mm. 160–168

♪♪♪ Example 27.18b   R. Wagner, *Tristan und Isolde,* Prelude to Act III, mm. 11–15

Finally, look at example 27.17d. The pattern here is essentially the same, but the 5th of the $^7_5$ sonority now moves to a 4th above the same bass. The result is a $^{7\ 6}_{5-4}$ sequential pattern, in which both sonorities involved are seventh chords. Play this example, and then study how it represents a metric reduction of anthology, no. 45 (Chopin, Mazurka no. 49, in Fm), mm. 37–40. The Chopin phrase enriches this sequence in a variety of ways: It contains numerous chromatic NCTs, as well as voice exchanges in every measure, involving the soprano and tenor voices. Discuss these aspects of this example carefully. Observe also that the last "$^{7}_{5}$" is actually spelled, and functions, as an +6th chord in Fm. It is interesting to realize that all three passages we just studied (the Mozart, Wagner, and Chopin phrases) consist of linear passages leading to dominant harmonies.

EXERCISES

To practice realizing sequential progressions, refer to exercises 27.5 and 27.6 in worksheet 27 at the end of this chapter.

To practice analysis of musical fragments including chromatic sequences, refer to exercise 27.1.2 in worksheet 27 at the end of this chapter.

NONSEQUENTIAL LINEAR PROCESSES

We will now study a type of linear/harmonic process often used by Chopin and other composers in the second half of the nineteenth century. Listen to example 27.19, and pay attention to its harmonic content. Does it sound functional to you? How are chords connected? The piece is in Em, but what are the clear signs of an Em tonality? What is it that tells us clearly that we are in Em?

After you listen to the excerpt, play through example 27.20a. Does the piece begin with a clear Em chord? Is Em clearly defined by a dominant-tonic progression? The following comments and concepts will help you understand the harmonic processes involved in this composition.

1. The basic frame for the phrase is provided by the outer voices. The melodic line is based on a NN motive, which outlines either a half step (B–C–B) or a whole step (A–B–A). In any case, and especially in its half-step form, this "sigh" motive gives the melody a character of mourning and grief. This character is confirmed by the bass line, which first outlines a chromatic descending tetrachord (G down to D), that is, a "lament bass," followed by several statements of the C–B half-step sigh.[1]

2. *Implied tonality.* The piece begins with a tonic chord in first inversion, a weak form of the tonic. There is not any other Em triad in the complete passage, and there is not a clear dominant of Em until the half cadence in m.12. In other words, although we hear the phrase as being in Em, the key is **implied** rather than established.

3. *Tonal parenthesis.* Tonally, this phrase moves from the beginning i_6 to the ending V_7, and these two harmonies are connected through a succession of nonfunctional chords. This process illustrates the principle of **tonal parenthesis**: Although the beginning and end of the phrase tell us we are in Em, the harmonies within the phrase do not define the key in any clear way from a functional point of view. The tonal motion for this passage can thus be expressed as i_6–( )–V_7.

---

[1] For an analysis of this piece which includes interesting discussions of its affective characteristics and of the linear design underlying its structure, see Carl Schachter, "The Triad as Place and Action," *Music Theory Spectrum* 17 (Fall 1995): 149–69.

♪♪♪ Example 27.19   F. Chopin, Prelude no. 4 in Em, mm. 1–13

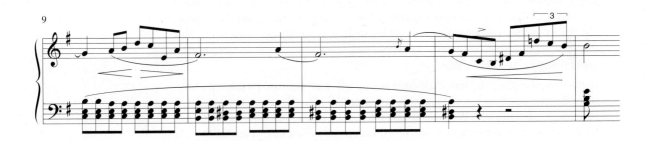

4. *Linear chromaticism.* What we find filling in the parenthesis, instead of a functional progression, is an area of *linear chromaticism* which actually provides tonal coherence to the passage by prolonging the initial tonic chord linearly. Looking at example 27.20a, how would you define the constructive principle of this type of linear chromaticism? In this example, the pitch or pitches that move from one chord to the next are represented as black note heads, and the pitches that remain are notated as white notes. The figures between the two staves refer to half-step voice leading: a 1 means motion by half step (1 semitone), a 2 means motion by step (2 semitones). We will think of the motivic neighbor figure in the melody (right hand, B–C–B) as a melodic NN, except where it is clearly part of the voice leading for a vertical sonority, as in m. 3.

Example 27.20

5. *Voice leading as a constructive principle.* At a glance, we see that chord connections are based on *stepwise motion* in one or two voices at a time, and the remaining voices sustain *common tones.* Stepwise motion is mostly by descending half step, although in some cases also by whole step. *Chromatic voice leading* is thus the defining feature in this passage.

6. *Implied tonal regions.* As was mentioned above, a Roman numeral functional analysis of this passage does not yield any kind of logical result. Chords are not connected functionally, but linearly. We have an initial harmony (i_6), a final harmony (V_7), and we travel the space between them through linear, mostly chromatic voice leading. At some points, however, we can hear momentary tonal points of reference, especially when we fall on a Mm_7 sonority which seems to want to resolve to a tonicized degree. The first chord in m. 4, for instance, can be heard as a V_7/iv, and the chord in m. 7 similarly appears as a V_7/III. In both cases, however, the tonicizing tendency is not confirmed or resolved, and the chords proceed linearly. These would be cases of *implied tonal regions.* Tonal regions are implied or suggested *by means of their dominants,* but they are not confirmed by a resolution to the tonic.

7. *Underlying structure.* Example 27.20b shows a reduction of this passage, charting a linear path through a possible underlying progression of implied tonal areas. The graph allows us to make several interesting observations. In the first place we notice that, after all, we do find an underlying linear sequential pattern in this passage, the series of 7–6 suspensions indicated by the figures under the graph. We see, moreover, that the root motion of the stemmed chords in mm. 2–7 (F♯–B–E–A–D) is the familiar circle of 5ths. The graph also shows how the underlying sequential structure

is elaborated chromatically by means of anticipations, NNs, and PTs (passing tones), and that these linear elaborations are not sequential themselves. From a different perspective, if we group the $^6_4$–7 patterns in mm. 3–7, we see that each of these patterns can be interpreted as implying a secondary key area (indicated as iv? and III? under the graph). Similarly, the final $^6_3$–7 pattern in mm. 9–10 represents the goal chords for the phrase, a predominant-dominant progression in Em.

Example 27.21 shows an interesting case of harmonization that brings together the linear principles we have just discussed with elements of functional tonality. The chordal voice leading is strictly linear, and very much in the style of the Chopin example. The bass, however, provides a strong functional anchoring: It is based on a circle

♪♪♪ **Example 27.21**   G. Fauré, "Après un rêve," mm. 1–9

of 5ths. In Fauré we often find this type of extended linear procedure over a functional bass, as in this case. First, play through the passage or listen to it. Then, discuss the voice leading in the piano's right hand. Then, analyze the passage functionally (with Roman numerals), with the understanding that each of the bass notes is the root of the chord above it. What key area is tonicized in mm. 3–4? What extended tertian sonorities can you identify in mm. 3–5? What is the triad on G in m. 6? How is the dominant chord in mm. 7–8 embellished linearly?

EXERCISES

To practice writing a passage using nonsequential linear chromaticism, refer to exercise 27.7 in worksheet 27 at the end of this chapter.

To practice analysis of a musical fragment based on nonsequential linear chromaticism, refer to exercise 27.1.3 in worksheet 27 at the end of this chapter.

ASSIGNMENT AND KEYBOARD PROGRESSIONS

For analytical and written assignments and keyboard progressions based on the materials learned in this chapter, refer to chapter 27 in the workbook.

PITCH PATTERNS

Sing the pitch patterns in example 27.22, hearing their harmonic content. Pitch pattern a illustrates a variety of extended tertian sonorities. Pitch pattern c features a descending chromatic sequence (the *fonte*) and pattern d an ascending chromatic sequence (the *monte*). Finally, pattern e provides a summary of the nonsequential linear process found in Chopin's Em prelude.

♪♪♪ Example 27.22

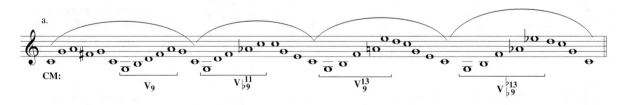

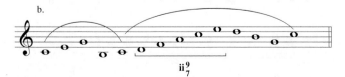

c.

DM: I ——— 6 ——— $\frac{4}{2}$ ——— 6 ——— $\frac{4}{2}$ ——— 6 ——— $\frac{4}{2}$ ——— 6 ——— +6 ——— V ——— I

d.

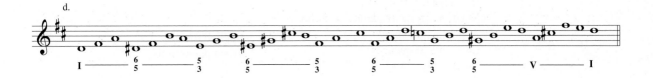

I ——— $\frac{6}{5}$ ——— $\frac{5}{3}$ ——— $\frac{6}{5}$ ——— $\frac{5}{3}$ ——— $\frac{6}{5}$ ——— $\frac{5}{3}$ ——— $\frac{6}{5}$ ——— V ——— I

e. Chopin

Em:

Composers and Their Music 27

Biographies

Write short biographies of the following composers mentioned in this chapter: Gabriel Fauré, William Grant Still, Mary Lou Williams, Kurt Weill.

Listening

Listen to the following compositions by composers mentioned in this chapter:

Chopin, Mazurkas, op. 59, and op. posth. 67; Ballade no. 1, op. 23.

Still, Symphony no. 1, *Afro-American.*
Fauré: *Requiem.*
Weill, *The Threepenny Opera* (selections).

Follow the score while you listen. Be able to place each of these compositions in one of the style periods and to comment on why and how it represents the musical characteristics of that period. As you listen, can you identify passages of linear chromaticism, either sequential or nonsequential? Do any of these compositions feature numerous extended tertian chords?

Terms for Review

Ninth chord
Eleventh chord
Thirteenth chord
Extended tertian chords
Nondominant extended tertian chords
Appoggiatura chords
Chromatic sequences
Fonte

Monte
Omnibus
Descending 5–6 sequence

$\frac{7}{5}$–$\frac{6}{3}$ sequence

Implied tonality
Tonal parenthesis

Worksheet 27

EXERCISE 27.1   Analysis.

1. The following passages include examples of extended tertian chords. Identify and label these chords, and verify the resolution of the dissonant chord members.

   a) Refer back to worksheet 22, example 22.18 (Chopin, Mazurka in GM, op. 67, no. 1). What extended tertian chord can you identify in m. 43?

   b) Example 27.23.

♪♪♪ Example 27.23   L. v. Beethoven, Piano Sonata in Em, op. 90, I, mm. 67–71

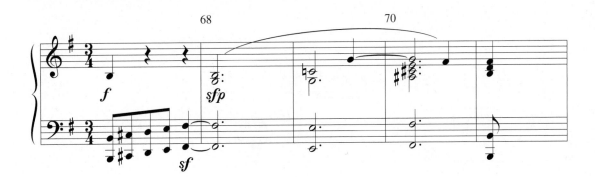

   c) Example 27.24. Comment on the use of melodic chromaticism and appoggiaturas in this passage. Discuss whether the passage is in CM or GM. What is the function of, and exact label for, the chord in m. 78?

♪♪♪ **Example 27.24**   R. Wagner, *Tristan und Isolde,* Act I, Scene 5, mm. 76–82

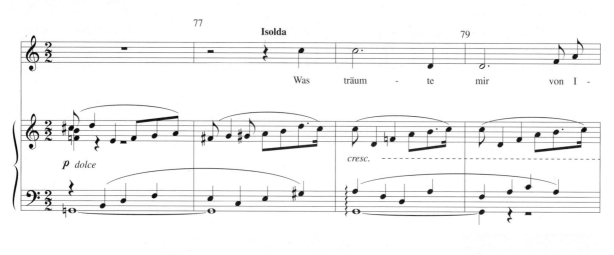

d) Analyze each of the parallel phrase beginnings in example 27.25 and determine their harmonic differences.

e) Analyze mm. 13–21 of Amy Beach's *Ecstasy* (anthology, no. 59). The complete passage is in E♭M. You will find several interesting examples of tonicization, extended tertian chords, and appoggiatura chords in this fragment.

Example 27.25   R. Schumann, "Träumerei," from *Kinderszenen,* op. 15, no. 7

♪♪♪ Example 27.25   Continued

2. Analyze the following examples of chromatic sequences. Name the exact type of sequence, and provide the necessary figures to identify the sequential pattern.

   a) Anthology, no. 14, Bach, Fugue in Cm, *WTC,* I, mm. 17–20.

   b) Example 27.26

      1) Measures 11–16 can be analyzed as an extended $^{7\ 6}_{5\ 4}_{3\ 3}$ sequence. The beginning of the sequence is labeled for you on the example. Analyze the rest of it. The sequence is not always straightforward: In some cases the third is delayed by a 4–3 suspension, and in some other cases one or more linear chords are introduced between the $^{7}_{5}_{3}$ and its resolution to $^{6}_{4}_{3}$. But the resolution actually takes place in all cases.

      2) What extended tertian chords appear in m. 16, beats 3–4?

3. Study anthology, no. 45, Chopin, Mazurka 49 in Fm, mm. 1–15.

   a) On a separate sheet, explain the linear process in mm. 1–8 using the same concepts we applied to the analysis of Chopin's Prelude no. 4 in Em. Provide a diagram for these measures similar to the graph in example 27.20a.

   b) What is the main melodic difference between mm. 9–15 and mm. 1–8?

   c) Explain the modulation to AM. How are the two keys related?

♪♪♪ Example 27.26   A. Beach, *Sous les étoiles,* op. 65, no. 4, mm. 11–18

EXERCISE 27.2   Write and resolve the following extended tertian chords in four voices.

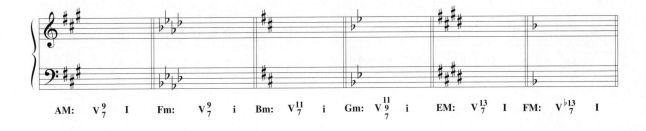

EXERCISE 27.3   Realize the short progressions in this exercise in four voices.

B♭M: I   vi$^9_7$ IV$_9$ V$^9_7$ I   DM: I   V$^9_7$/ii   V$^{♭13}_7$/V   V$^9_7$ I

EXERCISE 27.4   Realize the following progression in four voices.

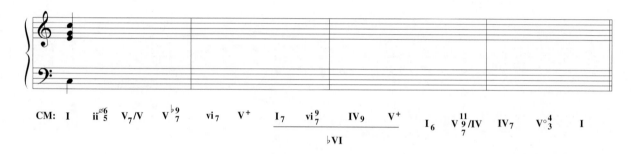

CM: I   ii$^{⌀6}_5$ V$_7$/V   V$^{♭9}_7$ vi$_7$ V$^+$ I$_7$ vi$^9_7$ IV$_9$ V$^+$ I$_6$ V$^{11}_{9\ 7}$/IV   IV$_7$ V$^{○4}_3$ I

$$♭VI$$

EXERCISE 27.5   Realize the sequential progression in exercise 27.5 in four voices. Although accidentals have not been indicated in the figured bass, all chords should be inverted Mm$_7$ sonorities.

E♭M: $^6_5$ $^4_2$ $^6_5$ $^4_2$ $^6_5$ $^4_2$ $^6_5$ $^4_2$ $^6_5$ $^4_2$ $^6_5$ $^4_2$ $^6_5$

EXERCISE 27.6   Realize the following sequential progression in four voices. This is a diatonic sequence and all necessary accidentals are indicated in the figured bass.

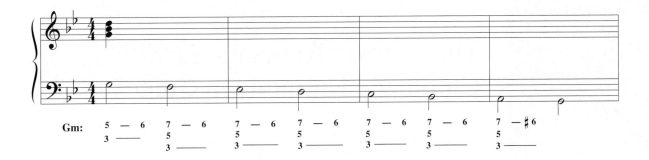

EXERCISE 27.7   Write a progression in four voices using the same linear techniques we studied in Chopin's Prelude no. 4 in Em. Your progression will be in Gm, and although it will be similar to Chopin's, it should be different. Cover the path from i or i$_6$ to a final V or V$_7$ by means of stepwise voice leading (mostly by chromatic motion) and common tones. In this exercise you are illustrating the use of implied tonality, tonal parenthesis, linear chromaticism, and implied tonal regions. If possible, determine which underlying progression your linear chromaticism is elaborating (see example 27.20b for a model).

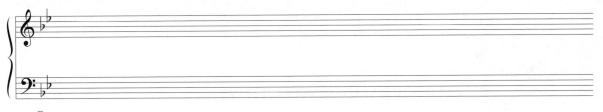

Chapter 28

The German Romantic *Lied*: Chromatic Harmony in Context

In this chapter we will study representative examples of German ***Lieder*** (singular: ***Lied***, "song"), the songs that constitute one of the most characteristic genres of the Romantic period. We will first focus in detail on two *Lieder* by Schubert and Schumann, and then we will analyze a song by Hugo Wolf to demonstrate modulation by enharmonic reinterpretation of the augmented triad. Many of the harmonic concepts we have learned in part 2 of this book, including various types of modulation to distantly related keys, will appear in the songs that we will study. For this reason, this chapter will also serve as a review of chromatic harmony in context.

THE GERMAN ROMANTIC *LIED*

Composers in the Classical period (such as Haydn, Mozart, and Beethoven) favored large formal structures driven by long-range tonal plans and extensive developmental processes, such as the ones we studied in chapter 26. Romantic composers, on the other hand, had an introspective interest in the soul, the passions, and the inner world of the individual. They often strove for *lyrical, intense poetic expression* through music. Some of the means they used for these expressive purposes were *lyrical melody, chromatic harmony,* and *harmonic color to depict mood.* The best vehicles for this intimate and subjective expression of emotions and moods were the "character piece" for piano (the typical Romantic short piano piece) and the song, the *Lied.*

The German *Lied* arose as a musical response and counterpart to the short lyrical poems by such major Romantic poets as Goethe and Schiller. Important composers of German Romantic *Lieder* are Franz Schubert (who composed over 600 songs), Fanny Mendelssohn, Robert and Clara Schumann, Josephine Lang, Pauline Viardot-García, Johannes Brahms, Hugo Wolf, Gustav and Alma Mahler, and Richard Strauss.

In principle, Romantic songs are a *musical expression of a poetic text*. This does not mean that the music necessarily follows the text in any particular way. A composer may choose, among other options, to depict the text musically in some detail (**text painting**), to depict or evoke only the general mood of the text, to give a personal interpretation of the text through music by means of distortion or exaggeration, or simply to ignore the text and its poetic meaning. In any case, because text and music are two essential components that come together in song, and because the music is usually built around the words in one way or another, the structure and content of the song's text should as a principle be considered carefully before examining the music. Some frequent themes one finds in Romantic poetry, and hence in Romantic songs, are death or loss, unrequited love, melancholy, yearning for the impossible, the irrational, contradictory, or complex aspects of the soul, and the psychic, mysterious aspects of nature.

Formally, *Lieder* can be of many types. **Formal types** are usually small and non-developmental. Among the most frequent types are the **strophic form** (each stanza of text is set to the same music), **ternary** (usually ABA), **binary** (AB, with a possible repetition of both sections, ABAB), and **through-composed** (which does not include any clear return or repetitions of material).

We recommend the following *general methodology* in the analysis of songs:

1. *The text*. What is the meaning of the poem? What moods, situations, emotions, does it depict? How many characters are there? Who is speaking, and in which tone? What is the form of the poem? How many verses are there, and how are they grouped into stanzas?

2. *The musical setting*. In general terms, what are the musical characteristics of the song? What are the textures, meter and rhythm, character, tempo, dynamics, of the setting? What are the melodic style and features (such as motives and phrase structure) of the vocal part? Do any of these musical traits seem to reflect any elements from the text? If there are different characters in the text, are they depicted musically in any particular way?

3. *The tonal and formal plan*. What is the formal design of the song? What is its long-range tonal plan? Do both the formal design and the tonal plan correspond in any way with the poem's structure and form?

4. *The harmonic detail*. Are there any modulations, fragments, or particular progressions we want to examine in detail because they seem to be especially interesting or because they seem to depict or reflect some specific elements of the text?[1]

We will first apply this methodology to a well-known song by Schubert, *Erlkönig*.

---

[1] For an extensive introduction to all relevant aspects of *Lied* analysis, see Deborah Stein and Robert Spillman, *Poetry in Song: Performance and Analysis of Lieder* (New York: Oxford University Press, 1996).

ANALYSIS 1: SCHUBERT, *ERLKÖNIG*

Listen carefully to this song, following the score (anthology, no. 38) and the translation of the text. *Erlkönig*, probably one of the most moving songs in the whole Romantic song literature, was written by Schubert on a text by Goethe in 1815, when he was only 18.

1. *The text and the story.* First, determine how many stanzas the poem has, how many characters are involved in it, and whether it has any recurring material (a refrain?). Does the poem have a form determined by its dramatic content and its characters? How do you think this is a characteristically Romantic text?

   The poem has eight stanzas, of which the first and the last are spoken by a narrator (N). Three more characters are involved in the story: the father (F), the son (S), and the Erlking (E) (in German folklore, a spirit who does mischief and evil, especially to children). Stanzas 2, 4, and 6 are dialogues between the son and the father, alternating with stanzas 3 and 5, where the Erlking speaks, and stanza 7, where both the Erlking and the son speak. The text is thus dramatic and narrative, including fast dialogue and a total of four characters.

   This is the story of a father and child riding a horse late on a cold night. The evil Erlking constantly tries to seduce the poor, scared boy with charms and promises. In a three-way dialogue, the boy responds to the Erlking's approaches by desperate calls of fear to his father, who tries to reassure the son as well as he can, despite his own mounting tension. Song, dialogue, and tension keep spiraling until the riders reach home and the galloping rhythm stops. And then comes the chilling, final line: "In seinen Armen das Kind war todt" ("In his arms the child lay dead"). Characteristically Romantic features in this poem are its expression of powerful emotions (tension, fear), the proximity and presence of death, and the presence of a mysterious character from the psychic underworld (the Erlking).

2. *The musical setting.* The challenge of setting such a poem to music comes from having to characterize four different dramatic persons. Listen to the song again, and now focus on how Schubert deals with the challenge: How does the single singer differentiate between characters? How does Schubert achieve unity in a song with so much dialogue between so many characters? What is the general character (mood) of the song, and what musical elements contribute to it?

   The action of the song takes place on a galloping horse. The first element that unifies the song is, of course, the galloping triplets in the piano, including the "galloping motive," in the piano's left hand, mm. 1–2. The song projects a mood of tension, which increases with the fear of the child. The ostinato triplet rhythm contributes to the increasing tension, and so does the quickening of the dialogue and the faster tempo, both toward the end. Most of all, tension and dramatic progression are determined by harmonic and tonal progression, as we will discuss below.

   Register and harmony are the essential elements in the characterization of the four persons. The father, trying to be reassuring, sings in a low, deep register, but the chromaticism in his melodies suggests his underlying tension. The son, more and more scared, sings his chromatic melodies in a high register, becoming progressively higher. The sections of dialogue between father and son are tonally unstable, modulating sections. The Erlking tries to be charming and seducing (except toward

♪♪♪ Example 28.1

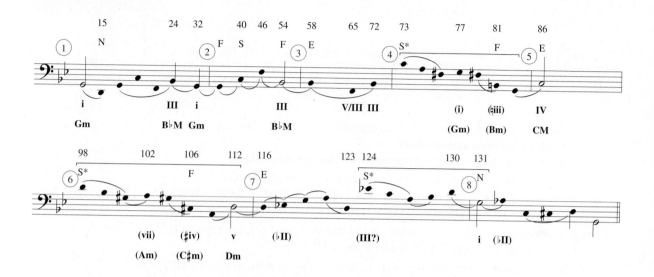

the end, when he becomes threatening), and although he also sings in a high register, his melodies are diatonic, and his speeches are in the major mode, nonmodulating, and perfectly stable and closed tonally. Is the accompaniment for father and son different texturally than the accompaniment for the Erlking? Notice also the grouping of the persons in each of the stanzas. Stanzas 1, 4, and 6 are shared by father and son, while the Erlking sings his solo stanzas 3 and 5. By stanza 7, however, we have the Erlking and the son grouped together in the same stanza, representing the final victory of the Erlking in his attempt to take the child away from the father.

3. *The tonal and formal plan.* Examine the score again, and now identify the key areas in the complete song. Make a simple graph showing how these key areas correspond with the eight stanzas/musical sections. After you do this, study the tonal and formal graphs in examples 28.1 and 28.2, comparing them with both the score and your own graph.

   The bass line reduction in example 28.1 shows sections and their correspondence with text stanzas (in circled numbers), underlying tonal motion in the form of tonal areas and some other important tonal events, and speaking characters for each of the sections/stanzas (N, F, S, and E, above the staff). Example 28.2 presents a further reduction of the formal/tonal scheme, including stanzas, characters, and tonal motion. The grouping of the stanzas as represented in example 28.2 shows the initial and final sections spoken by the narrator and three large formal areas that group two stanzas each (2–3, 4–5, and 6–7). In each of these groups, the first stanza is a F–S dialogue, and the second stanza is an E monologue, except for stanza 7, which toward the end incorporates the last phrase by S. The three

♪♪♪ Example 28.2

1		2		3	4		5	6		7		8	
N		F S	F	E	S*	F	E	S*	F	E	S*	N	
i	III i	i	→ III	III	(i)	(♮iii)	IV	(vii)	(♯iv)	v	v	i	i

asterisked phrases by S (S*) are the recurring call of the child, "Mein Vater, mein Vater!" which functions as a refrain of sorts.

Several things become immediately apparent through these graphs:

a) Sections 1 and 8 frame the song, not only narratively, but also tonally. They are harmonically closed, in the tonic Gm, and section 1 prefigures the first large-scale tonal motion (to III, in sections 2–3) with a i–III–i motion.

b) E's monologues (3, 5, 7) are tonally closed and in major keys, except for the last one in the minor dominant key (the keys are III, IV, and v).

c) The F–S sections are modulating, and unstable tonally. In sections 4 and 6 key areas are touched on (the keys in parentheses on the graph), but only as stepping stones toward the following, stable sections. Sections 2, 4, and 6 are thus transitional.

d) The music rises by steps (see E monologues, in III, IV, and v), and we hear that especially in the son's calls of distress to his father (sections S*), which are one step higher each time, rising along with the tension.

e) The overall tonal plan, then, is i–III–IV–v–i. We can notice here two harmonic elaborations of this general tonal plan: the neighbor ♭II area in Dm, which ornaments v in mm. 117–119, and the implied III area in mm. 124–127. Taking these two secondary areas into consideration, we could think of the tonal plan as i–III–IV–v–(♭II/v)–v–(III)–i. We will comment more on this tonal design below.

4. *Harmonic detail*. Two aspects of this song deserve more detailed attention: first, the use of vii°$_7$ sonorities on pedals, and second, sections 4, 6, and the end of 7, all of which begin with the S* refrain (that is, the unstable sections).

a) Schubert uses the beautiful, but tense, sonority of a vii°$_7$ chord against a pedal in association with the son. First, in m. 25–27, vii°$_7$ of B♭ against the B♭ pedal accompanies the first mention of the child. The next two appearances of this sonority take place during the child's first phrase, stressing the fear and tension of his words (mm. 42 and 47, against C and F pedals).

b) All three beginnings of the S* sections also feature the same sonority. First, in mm. 73–76, the same chord which, in mm. 25–27 was functioning as vii°$_7$ of B♭ (A–C–E♭–G♭) now appears as F♯–A–C–E♭, vii°$_7$ of G, over a D pedal, and now leading to Gm. In mm. 98–101, vii°$_7$ of A over an E pedal takes us to Am. Following the sequence up by steps of the "Mein Vater" cry (Gm–Am–B♭M), the next S* section begins in m. 124 with vii°$_7$ of B♭, spelled as if going to B♭. This is, again, the same chord which in mm. 25–27 took us to B♭, and in mm. 73–76 took us to Gm. The ambiguity is renewed here, where instead of the expected B♭, the chord takes us back to the home key, Gm (and hence B♭ is only implied).

c) Now go back to the beginning of section 4, m. 73, and let us study the modulating process in the S* phrase. After the vii°$_7$ takes us to Gm, the music moves on immediately to Bm. How is this modulation realized? Gm to Bm is a chromatic third–related motion (i to ♯iii). There are two modulating techniques at work in these measures. One is the chromatic bass from G to B. The other one is the one you would expect in a chromatic third modulation. What is it?

d) We do not stay in Bm for long, either (this is the unstable, modulating section). Instead, the music moves to CM by way of G. Bm to CM is a modulation from i to ♭II, the Neapolitan key. What is the role of G in both keys? You can see this even better in the next S* section, stanza 6, where the whole process is a step up from stanza 4. The vii°$_7$ took us to Am, and we move, by chromatic bass and common tone, to ♯iii, C♯m. In m. 106 we reach i in C♯m, and we move immediately to the minor Neapolitan key, Dm. How? What is the function of the modulating chord, the AM$_7$ chord in m. 108, in both keys?

e) Finally, let us examine further the role of the Neapolitan in the song. Besides the modulations to Neapolitan areas we just discussed, a ♭II relationship appears prominently, as a brief key area, in mm. 117–119. This is the phrase where the Erlking goes from charm to threat: "Listen, I love you, but if you don't want to come, I'll take you by force!" We are in Dm, and we go directly to E♭M. We hear, again, the vii°$_7$ on a pedal, this time vii°$_7$/♭II in Dm (m. 118). The final, and most dramatic Neapolitan area, however, comes at m. 140, when the father reaches "home with effort and toil," only to find that his child is dead in his arms. Here again we hear, one last time, not only ♭II, but also the vii°$_7$/♭II on the ♭$\hat{2}$ pedal.

As a conclusion of our analysis, examine example 28.3a. This example shows a reduction of the complete tonal structure of the song: beginning in Gm, motion through the areas of B♭M, CM, and Dm, the E♭ Neapolitan area as a neighbor note (NN) to D, then the implied B♭ area, and the return to Gm. As we saw above, this design can be

♪♪♪Example 28.3

Our study of *Erlkönig* serves as an introduction to the analysis of song. We have taken into account the text, its divisions and meaning, and its characters. We have seen how the music reflects the sections, meaning, and mood of the text. We have demonstrated that tonal motion, modulations, tonal stability and instability, rhythmic figuration, texture, and register, all serve the dramatic and textual purpose of the poem. After listening again to the song, discuss in class how the analysis and in-depth knowledge of the structure of the song can help you listen to it or perform it. Would you rather perform the song without having any of these insights on how it works and why? How could the insights affect and improve your performance?

For instance, how could you make sure that your performance contributed to the enhanced tension provided by the tonal plan as it rises by steps toward a higher register? How can you emphasize the sense of distress and instability in the S* sections? Stanza 8 features two important dramatic characteristics. First, the return of the narrator, instead of the expected response of the father to the last cry of his son, is a signal to the listener to expect the worst. Finally, when the riders reach home we learn the tragic outcome of the story, punctuated by the ♭II harmony and the closing recitative passage. What would you do to enhance the drama and horror of this section?

summarized as i–III–IV–v–(♭II/v)–v–(III)–i. Now compare this sketch with example 28.3b, the "galloping motive" in the piano's left hand: $\hat{1}-\hat{2}-\hat{3}-\hat{4}-\hat{5}-\hat{6}-\hat{5}-\hat{3}-\hat{1}$. This is an instance of *replication of a melodic motive at the deeper level of tonal structure*. One can only admire Schubert's amazing compositional craft at age 18![2]

ANALYSIS 2: SCHUMANN, "WIDMUNG"

This song (anthology, no. 48), on a text by Friedrich Rückert, is from a collection entitled *Myrthen*. It was composed in 1840, Schumann's "year of song," in which he composed a total of 127 songs. This was the same year in which he married Clara Wieck (to become Clara Schumann), after winning a court suit against her father to obtain his permission to get married. Fittingly enough, "Widmung," ("Dedication") is a love song. Listen to it following the score and words, and determine whether there is more than one character or mood represented by the text and music.

1. *The text and the song's meaning.* The poem has three sections: verses 1–6 display a clearly passionate character, verses 7–12 show the more contemplative, mystical aspect of love, and finally verses 13–17 are a return to the initial verses and passionate character. The tripartite form of the poem, of course, provides the structure for a song in ternary form, as the one Schumann wrote.

   One could see the text merely as a simple, if passionate, love poem. There is more to it, however. Schumann, who had a very active private world of inner fantasy, saw himself as divided into two personalities, represented by the imaginary characters *Florestan* and *Eusebius*. Florestan was the impetuous, passionate, and revolutionary Schumann. Eusebius, on the other hand, was the contemplative,

---

[2] This motivic parallelism between the galloping motive and the song's tonal plan was first noted by Charles Burkhart in "Schenker's 'Motivic Parallelisms,'" *Journal of Music Theory* 22 (Fall 1978): 145–76. For a more extensive study of motivic parallelisms in this song, as well as an interesting discussion of textual and poetic images and their correspondence with musical structure, see Deborah Stein, "Schubert's *Erlkönig*: Motivic Parallelism and Motivic Transformation," *19th-Century Music* 13 (Fall 1989): 145–58.

introspective dreamer. (A third personality would join these two in later years, *Master Raro*, the wise and judicious moderator of the two contradictory personalities of Florestan and Eusebius.)

"Widmung" thus has a self-referential quality: It contains expressions of love coming from both of Schumann's personalities. The A sections (first and third) represent the impetuous Florestan, whereas the calmer B section represents Eusebius. This is a good example of a Romantic "character piece," a piece that expresses one or more emotional or psychological "moods."

2. *The musical setting*. How are the two characters represented musically? First, examine the melody in both sections. How do the following melodic aspects help define Schumann's personalities: range, register, melodic contour (leaps or steps), and rhythmic values. Then look at the accompaniment. How does it represent the two different characters? Other factors that contribute to psychological depiction in the song are dynamics (how?) and tempo. You will have noticed that, even though there is no quantitative tempo change between sections (the beat remains the same), we perceive section B as being slower. Why?

3. *The tonal and formal plan*. We have already determined that both the text and the song are in ternary form. The key of the A section is A♭M. The key of the B section is EM. How are these two keys related? How are the modulations into and out of EM effected?

   The A♭M–EM relationship is an enharmonically spelled ♭VI relationship (as in A♭M–F♭M). This is, thus, a chromatic third relationship. The modulation in mm. 13–14 is a direct common-tone modulation between tonic chords, using the common A♭/G♯ as a connection. The return is a little more complex. In mm. 23–25, the secondary key area of AM (IV in EM) is established. The chord before the change of key signature (m. 25) is IV in EM (the AM triad), with several nonchord tones (NCTs) (identify and label them). From there we move directly to V_7 in A♭M, followed by a long pedal on $\hat{5}$ of A♭, leading to the return in m. 30.

   What made the motion between IV in EM (the AM triad) and V_7 in A♭ so effective? First, function: What is the AM triad in A♭M, and why does V_7 follow so naturally? Second, melodic connection: Is there a common tone between the two chords Schumann uses as a melodic pivot?

   What is significant about this long-range relationship? Romantic composers definitely preferred third relationships over fifth relationships in their structural plans, and both *Erlkönig* and "Widmung" are examples of this preference. (Examine, as a confirmation, how many adjacent keys are third-related in *Erlkönig*'s tonal plan.) Schumann, in particular, was especially fond of chromatic third relationships, as this song illustrates.

4. *Harmonic detail and text painting*. The harmony of "Widmung" is not especially venturesome. In the A section, the most notable harmonic event is the occasional presence of the pitch F♭, which not only introduces modal borrowing at the chordal level, but also prefigures the ♭VI modulation in section B. Does the F♭ have any textual significance? It first appears in m. 5 (What borrowed chord results from this F♭?), coloring the word *Schmerz* ("grief"). Its next appearance is in m. 10

How is this song Romantic? How does the above analysis help you as a listener or performer of the song? Is there anything in particular, in the above discussion, that you would want to project in a performance? How would you do so? Can you help depict, with your performance, the two different characters represented in the song? If you happen to have this song in your repertoire, you may want to perform it in class in light of this discussion.

(What is the borrowed chord here?), to the word *Grab* ("grave"). The association thus seems to be quite obvious! Notice also another touch of text painting in the A section: What is the highest vocal pitch in the whole song? What textual concept is it associated with? The pitch is G♭ in mm. 8–9, and the words are "You my heaven, into which I soar"! Now, after soaring into heaven, the next phrase of text is "O you my grave." How does the melody move from heaven to the grave?

The harmony in the B section is also quite straightforward. What familiar linear chord appears in m. 15? What key area is tonicized in mm. 18–19? What is the NCT in m. 19, beat 1? And in m. 23, beat 1? How is the phrase "Du bist die Ruh' " depicted musically (Think, for instance, of the bass!)? How does texture depict the word *Frieden* ("peace")?

Notice now the interesting textual role of secondary key areas in the song. In both the A section (mm. 7–9) and the B section (mm. 18–19), the word *Himmel* ("Heaven"), is represented by secondary key areas: heaven and earth, of course, are not in the same "tonal levels"! The only other secondary key area is, in the B section, the AM key area in mm. 23–25. And here the words are "Your glance has transfigured me." Once the poet is transfigured, he is no more in the same "tonal level" either!

MODULATION BY ENHARMONIC REINTERPRETATION OF V⁺

The augmented triad, like the °7 chord, is a symmetrical chord that divides the octave into equal segments. Whereas the °7 chord divides it into four segments (minor thirds), the augmented triad divides it into three major thirds. Just as there are only three different °7 chords, there are only four different augmented triads. If you begin from C, you will have different augmented triads on C, C♯, D, and D♯. The next triad, on E, contains the same pitches as the triad on C. This means that one sonority, with three different spellings, can function as V⁺ in three different pairs of M/m keys. Example 28.4 demonstrates the three different spellings and resolutions of a single augmented triad, functioning as V⁺ first in A♭M/m, then in CM/m, and finally in EM/m.

♪♪♪Example 28.4

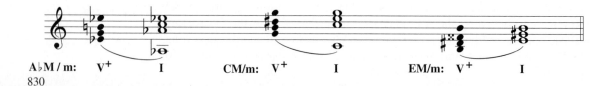

A♭M / m: V⁺   I   CM/m: V⁺   I   EM/m: V⁺   I

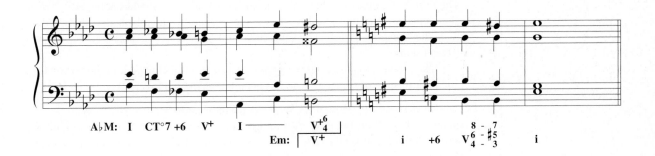

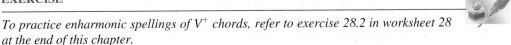

AbM: I   CT°7 +6   V⁺   I ——————   V⁺⁺⁶₄

                              Em: V⁺   i   +6   V⁶₄ ⁻ #⁵₃   i

EXERCISE

To practice enharmonic spellings of V⁺ chords, refer to exercise 28.2 in worksheet 28 at the end of this chapter.

This capacity of the augmented triad to function as V⁺ in three different pairs of keys allows us to reinterpret it enharmonically in modulations to distantly related keys. Keys connected by this type of modulation are a M3rd apart. Example 28.5 illustrates one of the possible modulations using the triad from example 28.4. The modulation shown here, from AbM to Em, is between two chromatic third–related keys whose tonics do not share a common tone (that is, one of the chromatic third modulations that cannot be effected by common tone). Play and study this modulation, and understand how it works, before moving on to the following analysis of the Wolf song.

EXERCISE

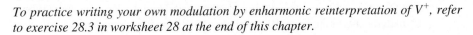

To practice writing your own modulation by enharmonic reinterpretation of V⁺, refer to exercise 28.3 in worksheet 28 at the end of this chapter.

ANALYSIS 3: WOLF, "DAS VERLASSENE MÄGDLEIN"

This song ("The Forlorn Maiden," from *Gedichte von Mörike*, anthology, no. 57), one of the best-known *Lieder* by Hugo Wolf, is based on a poem by Mörike, and it again contains many of the characteristic elements of Romantic poetry and song. Read the poem, and think about its structure, its character and moods, and its sections.

1. *The text and the story*. These are the reflections of a forlorn servant girl as she gets up in the early morning to start the fire and faces the prospect of one more sad and lonesome day. The setup is, thus, purely Romantic. In the first stanza we find out about the time of the day and the immediate circumstances (it is very early, cold,

and she has to get up to light the fire). There is also a moment of certain joy (second stanza), when the fire catches up and for a moment she gets carried away by the beauty of the flames and the sparks. Next, we find that she is in deep sorrow. The third stanza tells us about the reason for her sorrow: She has apparently been abandoned by the boy she loves, and she suddenly remembers that during the night she dreamed of him. The song ends with more tearful expressions of sorrow (fourth stanza).

The moods suggested by the poem are sadness, loneliness, and the sorrowful and painful state of someone who has been forsaken by a lover.

2. *The musical setting.* How does Wolf depict these moods musically? Try to determine the key of the song by examining its beginning and end. The beginning is very ambiguous: It is all dyads (not triads), and although we feel the presence of A as a tonal center, there is no A triad until m. 13. And then it is a major triad, although we were hearing Am as the implied tonality. The end does not clarify the problem completely: The last measures also feature dyads, this time open fifths on A, avoiding the major/minor definition. Both beginning and end transmit a sense of emptiness and ambiguity (the dyads, the undefined tonal center, the unclear mode of the song). Does this correspond with the young woman's state of mind? Could the missing root in the dyads, or the unclear tonal center and mode, reflect that something is missing from the maiden's life and her resulting feeling of emptiness?

The melodic structure of the beginning also contributes to the sad mood. The melody is grouped into two-measure units, and each unit is made up of a descending fifth, E–A, D–G♯, C–F, and B–E. If you take the first pitch of each segment of the sequence, you also come up with a descending line, E–D–C–B. The melody drags our mood downward. Notice then what happens in mm. 13–18: For a brief moment, when the fire catches up, her mood lightens up. The key is clarified for the first time, and now it is in the major mode: AM. Moreover, look at the melody: It is ascending, like the flames, and the rhythms become more lively. Not for long, though. In mm. 19–22 we learn about her sorrow: The key goes down a half step (to A♭M), and the melody repeats the half step C–B. Of course, the half step is the traditional musical "sigh," the symbol of sorrow and lament. Here we have it both in the melody and in the keys! The melodic structure of these measures is summarized in example 28.6.

With the remembrance of her dream, the music becomes more agitated and tonally complex, and the melody reaches its highest pitches (mm. 27–34). Then we return to the original mood of sorrow, and to the initial, ambiguous musical materials (mm. 38–end).

The rhythm should also be mentioned as contributing to the character of the song: The obsessive, repeated rhythmic figure reflects the one thought she cannot get out of her mind and the one feeling she cannot ban from her heart.

3. *The tonal and formal plan.* How do you think the form of the song is determined by the poem? We have already seen that there is an initial section which returns, and that these sections correspond with stanzas 1 and 4. These two sections stay within what we could call the "ambiguous Am" key. The two middle sections,

♪♪♪ Example 28.6

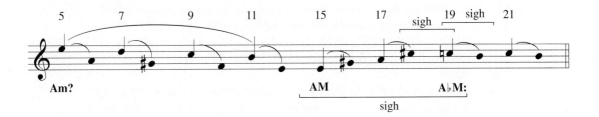

stanzas 2 and 3, can be grouped into one section. The main tonal characteristic of this middle section is its modulating character, and the tonal ambiguity provided by the use of the augmented triad, as we will see below. We have already seen that at m. 13 the mode changes to AM, and that the stanza ends with the A♭M section (mm. 19–22). In m. 23 we move to B♭M, until m. 31 where the "sigh" motive comes back, again in A♭M (compare mm. 31–34 with mm. 19–23). A modulating passage (mm. 33–37) takes us back to the return of the initial material in Am. The form can then be summarized as A–B–A. And the two secondary key areas in the B section (A♭M and B♭M) are chromatic neighbors to the two main keys, the Am/M pair. This formal/tonal plan is summarized graphically in example 28.7.

4. *Harmonic detail*. The most interesting harmonic feature of this song is the use of augmented triads, both to create tonal ambiguity and unrest within phrases and as a means to modulate. Before we look at this aspect of the song, however, notice the two chords in mm. 13–18. The chords alternated in these measures are the AM tonic, and a Mm$_7$ in third inversion, C♯–E♯–G♯–B, that is, the dominant seventh of F♯, V$^4_2$/vi in AM. Because it does not resolve to vi, however, this Mm$_7$ chord does not function as a secondary dominant. In other words, it is not a functional chord. What kind of chord relationship is this, between AM and C♯Mm$_7$? (As a hint, you studied this chord relationship in chapter 25.)

♪♪♪ Example 28.7

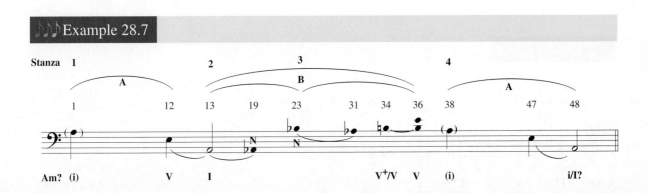

Let us examine the role of augmented triads in this song.

a) The augmented triad first appears in m. 20. What is its function here? Think of it as spelled from E♭ (E♭–G–B♮), and resolving to A♭M: V⁺ of A♭.

b) Measures 23–26, the beginning of the B♭M area, is all based on augmented triads: I⁺–V⁺. Notice the connection between A♭M and B♭M (mm. 22–23): From V⁺ in A♭M (E♭–G–B♮) to I⁺₆ in B♭ (D–G♭–B♭, as Wolf spells it), all voices move down by half step. This motion from A♭M to B♭M again stresses the "sigh" motive.

c) In m. 31, we return to the A♭M area, with a I⁺ on A♭. The chord in m. 32 is the same sonority as the V⁺ in m. 20, but now its spelling is not E♭–G–B♮, but B–D♯–G. Think of it as B–D♯–F𝄪, and you will recognize V⁺ in E. We realize its new function in mm. 34–36, when it goes first to Em, then to EM, the V of Am which takes us back to Am in m. 38. Look again at mm. 32–33. In A♭M, you would read these chords as V⁺–I⁺. In Am, you would read them as V⁺/V–V⁺. This second reading is confirmed in mm. 34–36.

d) What makes this modulation possible is the enharmonic reinterpretation of the augmented triads. Notice that the reinterpretation of V⁺ in A♭M as V⁺/V of A is the same as that you already studied in examples 28.4 and 28.5. Example 28.8 provides a summary of this modulation, showing how these chords are interpreted in both keys.

The passage in mm. 23–26, all based on augmented triads, represents an important juncture in the narrative. In the previous section the girl had been in an early morning dreamlike state, and suddenly reality dawns on her, with the remembrance, in the phrase beginning in m. 27, of her unfortunate state. Augmented triads are introduced precisely in the passage that takes us from the dreamy moments by the fire to the remembrance of reality and the anxiety that comes with it.

EXERCISE

To practice analyzing a Lied, *refer to exercise 28.1 in worksheet 28 at the end of this chapter.*

♩♪♪ Example 28.8

PRACTICAL APPLICATION AND DISCUSSION

To summarize, discuss in class how tonality, harmony, modulations, melody, rhythm, and texture contribute to the depiction of what our forlorn maiden felt that early morning when she got up to light the fire. Discuss also how this discussion of the song affects your hearing of it (listen to it again after finishing its analysis), and how it would affect your performance if you were to perform it.

From a more general point of view, what are your impressions of the expressive power of musical elements as displayed in these German *Lieder*? We are all aware that music in itself is expressive. In these songs, however, we can see in detail why it is expressive, what makes it so, and we see that it is not expressive by chance: Romantic composers knew very well how to use musical elements such as melody, harmony, rhythm, to express very specific feelings and moods or to depict situations. In these songs, composers achieved the artistic and expressive unity of poetry and music. These songs are truly "musical poems."

A SUMMARY OF CHROMATIC FUNCTIONS

In the appendix to part 1 we summarized and reviewed the main diatonic chords and functions. We will now review, in a similar way, the main chromatic chords and functions we have studied in part 2 of this book. These are summarized, in graphic form, in examples 28.9 and 28.10. Realize at the keyboard the harmonic paradigms represented in these examples in the form of bass lines and Roman numerals (RNs).

> ♪♪♪ Example 28.9   A Summary of Chromatic Chordal Functions

♪♪♪ Example 28.10   A Summary of Modulation Types

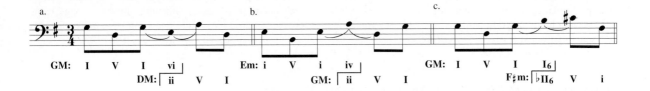

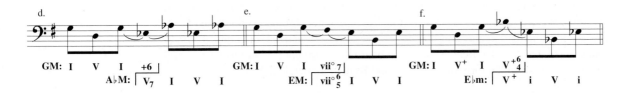

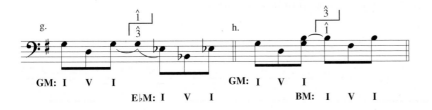

We can think of harmonic chromaticism as resulting from one of two general processes. The first type of chromaticism takes place within a single key, and we can refer to it as "chordal" chromaticism. Chordal chromaticism often results from chromatic linear processes that elaborate or embellish an otherwise diatonic framework. Various examples of chordal chromaticism appear in example 28.9. In this example, chromatic chords are presented in the context of a I–V–I fundamental progression, and they function as elaborations of either the opening tonic, or the cadential dominant, or also the cadential predominant. We also have studied chordal chromaticism resulting from different sequential processes. This type of chromaticism is not represented in example 28.9 (you may review various types of chromatic sequences in chapters 17, 24, and 27). The second type of chromaticism results from a change of key or tonal center, that is, as a result of modulation. Different types of modulation are represented in example 28.10.

1. We will first comment briefly on example 28.9. In essence, we can group chordal chromaticism into the following categories:

   a) *Tonicization.* Examples 28.9a to e illustrate some common paradigms involving tonicization (of course, many other models are possible, including various other inversions of secondary chords and the tonicization of other degrees). In examples 28.9a to c, V or IV is tonicized by means of secondary dominants. In examples 28.9d and e, ii and vi are tonicized by means of secondary diminished seventh chords.

b) *Modal mixture (modal borrowing).* Examples 28.9f to h illustrate some cases of modal borrowing of chords from the minor mode into a major key. Modal mixture also includes changes of mode in more extended passages.

c) *The Neapolitan and +6 chords.* These two characteristic chords, built on $\flat\hat{2}$ and $\flat\hat{6}$, respectively, are represented in examples 28.9i–j.

d) *Triads related by chromatic third.* Triads related to the tonic by chromatic 3rd appear in example 28.9k.

e) *Altered chords (augmented and diminished).* The most common type of altered triads, V^+, appears in example 28.9l, and the Fr +6 chord on $\flat\hat{2}$ functioning as an altered dominant is represented in example 28.9m.

f) *Linear chords.* Although many types of linear chords are possible, two types of chromatic neighbor chords, the emb. +6 and the CT°7, are represented in examples 28.9n and o.

g) *Extended tertian chords.* Extended tertian chords are not necessarily chromatic. In any case, they provide expansions of functional sonorities, as well as an element of dissonance, whether it be diatonic or chromatic. These chords are represented by examples 28.9p and q.

2. In example 28.10 you can review the basic types of modulation we have studied in this book, which can be summarized by the following categories (two other types of modulation we also studied, phrase modulation and sequential modulation, are not represented in this example):

a) *Modulation by diatonic pivot chord.* Examples 28.10a and b show two cases of diatonic pivot modulation, both to closely related keys (the key of the dominant and the relative major key).

b) *Modulation by chromatic pivot chord.* Example 28.10c shows a modulation by chromatic pivot chord to a distantly related key.

c) *Modulation by enharmonic reinterpretation of +6, °7, or V+.* These three types of modulation by enharmonic reinterpretation are represented by examples 28.10d, e, and f, respectively.

d) *Common-tone modulation.* Examples 28.10g and h illustrate two cases of common-tone modulation to keys related to the original tonic by chromatic third.

ASSIGNMENT AND KEYBOARD PROGRESSIONS

For analytical and written assignments and keyboard progressions based on the materials learned in this chapter, refer to chapter 28 in the workbook.

PITCH PATTERNS

Sing the pitch patterns in example 28.11, and as you sing listen to the modulation by enharmonic reinterpretation of an augmented triad.

♪♪♪ Example 28.11

a.

CM: V$^+_6$——I$^+$ V$^+$ I$^+$ V$^+_6$——I

b.

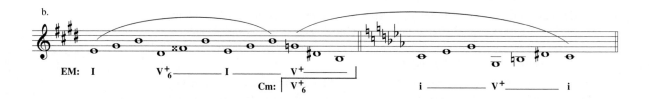

EM: I   V$^+_6$——I——V$^+$——|
Cm: | V$^+_6$ i ——— V$^+$——— i

c.

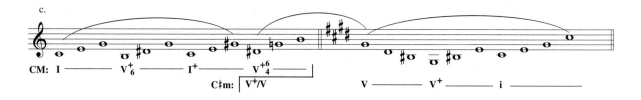

CM: I ——— V$^+_6$ ——— I$^+$——— V$^{+6}_4$——|
C#m: | V$^+$/V   V ——— V$^+$ ——— i ———

Composers and Their Music 28

Biographies

Write short biographies of the following composers mentioned in this chapter: Hugo Wolf, Richard Strauss, Gustav Mahler.

Listening

Listen to the following compositions by composers mentioned in this chapter:

Schumann, *Dichterliebe*, op. 48 (complete).
Wolf, *Gedichte von Mörike* (selected songs).
Richard Strauss, *Till Eulenspiegel*.

Follow the score while you listen. Be able to place each of these compositions in one of the style periods and to comment on why and how it represents the musical characteristics of that period.

Terms for Review

Lied (*Lieder*)
Text painting
Formal types:
    strophic form, ternary, binary,
    through-composed

Schubert: *Erlkönig*
Schumann: "Widmung"
Modulation by enharmonic
    reinterpretation of V^+
Wolf: "Das verlassene Mägdlein"

Worksheet 28

EXERCISE 28.1 *Analysis*. Analyze anthology, no. 49, Schumann, "Am leuchtenden Sommermorgen," from *Dichterliebe*, op. 48. Answer the following questions with as much detail as possible.

1. Does the poem establish two contrasting moods? What moods?

2. What is the initial chord? Explain its spelling. What is unusual about this beginning?

3. Both in m. 1 and m. 6 this chord functions as _____ in the key of _____, and as such it resolves to _____.

4. How is the second chord in m. 8 related to the above chord? How does it function here, and in what key?

5. Focus now on mm. 8–13. The first chord in m. 9 is a linear chord leading to the second chord. Explain how the first chord works linearly, and what the function of the second chord is. What key area is suggested in mm. 8–9? How is this key area related (by RN) to the original key?

6. Thinking of the key area suggested in mm. 8–9, how does the second chord in m. 9 resolve? What is the exact RN and function of the first chord in m. 10 with respect to the key area of m. 9?

7. On the other hand, the first chord in m. 10 is also part of a harmonic pattern that follows (mm. 10–11), and which leads back to the original key. Explain clearly, and using all the correct harmonic terms, how mm. 8–13 function harmonically, and what pivot chords are used between key areas.

8. Now look at the text for these measures (mm. 8–12). Does the tonal ambiguity reflect the mood of the text? Could we also say, now, that the opening chord itself also reflects and announces the ambiguous moods of the text.

9. Who is speaking beginning in m. 17? What is the secondary key area in mm. 17–19? How is the secondary tonic in m. 17 related to the main key? What words of the text does this relationship emphasize?

10. Explain the linear chord in m. 16, beat 2. Can you also explain this chord functionally with respect to the key of m. 17? What kind of an altered chord is it from a functional point of view?

11. Write a concluding paragraph explaining how this song reflects the content of the poem it is based on.

EXERCISE 28.2   Write V$^+$, and resolve it to I, in EM. This chord may be used to modulate to two other major keys by respelling it enharmonically. Indicate the keys, and provide the spelling (leaving the chord in the same position) and the correct resolution to the tonic in each of the new keys.

Key 1: EM	Key 2:	Key 3:

EXERCISE 28.3   Write a modulation in four voices by enharmonic reinterpretation of V$^+$, from C♯m to a key of your choice.

C♯m:

Chapter 29

Toward (and Beyond) the Limits of Functional Tonality

In the last two chapters of this book we will study a variety of harmonic techniques and musical processes used by composers in the latter part of the nineteenth century and the beginning of the twentieth century. Some of the procedures we will see have the effect of weakening functional tonality; others suspend tonality, create a sense of tonal ambiguity, or provide the means to organize triadic (or in some cases nontriadic) sonorities in alternative ways to functional tonality. The weakening and eventual dissolution of tonality in the late Romantic harmonic language which we will study in the present chapter is one of the determinant factors that eventually led to the search, on the part of composers in the early twentieth century, for alternative systems to organize their pitch structures.

TONAL AMBIGUITY AND IMPLIED TONALITY

In our study of Chopin's Prelude no. 4 in chapter 27 we introduced the concept of implied tonality. Because tonal ambiguity and implied tonality are harmonic concepts essential to our understanding of much music from the late-Romantic period, we will devote some time to them now, focusing on a piece that demonstrates these ideas extensively: the Prelude to Wagner's *Tristan und Isolde*. The opera, one of Wagner's great masterpieces, is based on a medieval story of Celtic origin, which at the same time contains all the ingredients for a fervently Romantic drama. Tristan, a knight, has been sent to fetch the bride who has been chosen for his king in a mostly political arrangement. The mother of the bride prepares a love potion to help her win the love of the king but, by a fateful mistake, Tristan and Isolde end up drinking the love potion themselves. The rest of the story is best summarized by Wagner himself in his program notes to the performance of the Prelude, in the following sentences which amount to a Romantic manifesto on life, love, and death:

> Fired by [the love potion's] draught, their love leaps suddenly to vivid flame, and they have to acknowledge that they belong only to each other. Henceforth no end to the yearning, longing, rapture, and misery of love: world, power, fame, honor, chivalry, loyalty,

and friendship scattered like an insubstantial dream; one thing alone left living: longing, longing unquenchable, desire forever renewing itself, craving and languishing; one sole redemption: death, surcease of being, the sleep that knows no waking!

The *Tristan* Prelude

Example 29.1 is an annotated piano reduction of mm. 1–46 of the ***Tristan* prelude**, slightly less than half its complete length. This limited fragment will suffice to illustrate the characteristics of Wagner's harmonic and formal style in his later works (best represented by *Tristan und Isolde* and *Parsifal*). Listen to the example, or if possible to the whole prelude, and play through it if you have sufficient keyboard skills. How do you think this music grows formally? What are the fundamental compositional blocks and elements? Is it periodic? Are there clear cadences? How is tonality defined? What "key" is the prelude in? How are keys defined? Are chords clearly identifiable? If not, why not? What is the dramatic and expressive result of all these musical traits? After you have tried to answer at least some of these questions, read the following comments.

1. You will have heard that this music moves in a *continuous flow*. It is *nonperiodic*, and phrases are open-ended. Cadences are systematically avoided or resolved deceptively, so that clear arrivals on any kind of tonic chord or tonicized degree are avoided.

2. The music is *highly motivic*. The prelude contains a number of characteristic motives which will become prominent throughout the opera. These are called **Leitmotifs**, musical ideas that are associated with a particular person, idea, or situation in the drama. Several of these motives are labeled in our example according to generally accepted designations.

3. Formal growth results from the *spinning out of motives*. This music is based on *continuous development* and on an unending flow of melody. *Sequences* are often used as a developmental technique.

4. *Tonality is obscured* by the avoidance of cadences and of arrivals on a tonic. Moreover, there is not a single clear tonal center (**tonal ambiguity**), and tonal centers are not clearly defined. Key areas are more often defined by unresolved dominants than by arrivals on a tonic (**implied tonality**). The resulting effect is of constant **tonal fluctuation**.

5. Chords and harmony are further obscured by the extensive use of *chromatic nonchord tones* (NCTs) (especially suspensions, appoggiaturas, and passing tones).

6. Each of the above elements contributes to the dramatic purpose of this music. Wagner achieves an unparalleled constant buildup of tension, unresolved and continuous tension, which provides a suitable musical setting for the "longing, longing unquenchable, desire forever renewing itself, craving and languishing." The tension does not really find resolution until the very end of the opera, when Tristan and Isolde find the fulfillment of their tragic love only in death, and the music finally reaches a resting point on a long BM tonic chord.

Example 29.1   R. Wagner, Prelude to *Tristan und Isolde*, mm. 1–46

♪♪♪ **Example 29.1**   Continued

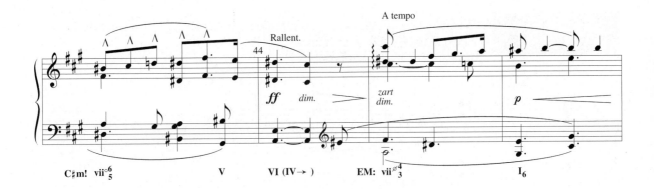

C#m! vii°$^{6}_{5}$ V   VI (IV→)   EM: vii$^{4}_{3}$ I$_6$

We will now study some of these particular musical characteristics as they appear in our excerpt.[1]

The opening unit (mm. 1–17).   *The "Tristan chord."* The principles of tonal ambiguity and implied tonality are present from the very outset of the prelude. The initial idea (mm. 1–3) includes two motivic units: the "love" motive (mm. 1–2), with its descending chromatic gesture, and the desire motive (mm. 2–3), chromatically ascending. The key signature indicates Am or CM. This opening gesture ends on a chord that appears to be V$_7$ of A, so we'll think of this opening as being in Am. The prelude opens with one of the most mysterious, and certainly one of the most famous, chords in tonal literature, widely known as the **Tristan chord**. The sonority sounds like a half-diminished seventh chord on F (in ascending thirds, F–A♭–C♭–E♭, spelled as F–G♯–B–D♯). In itself, this is an extremely ambiguous chord which, as is very often the case with late-Romantic harmony, allows for several possible interpretations. Let us see some of these possible interpretations:

1. Because in Am this chord seems to be totally nonfunctional, some authors have interpreted the G♯ as being an appoggiatura, and then the A in m. 2 becomes the real chord tone. This has allowed for two interpretations: as B–D♯–F♮–A, it is an altered form of V$_7$/V in Am (with a lowered fifth). As F–A–B–D♯ it is the Fr +6 chord in Am. A possible criticism to either interpretation is that the G♯ takes most of the measure and is five times as long as the brief A. Shouldn't one perhaps think of the G♯ as the "real tone," and the A as a passing tone?

---

[1] An interesting collection of historical and analytical studies on the prelude, along with the orchestral score, can be found in the Norton Critical Score, Richard Wagner, *Prelude and Transfiguration from Tristan and Isolde*, ed. Robert Bailey (New York: Norton, 1985). Especially interesting from an analytical point of view are the contributions to the collection by Robert Bailey ("An Analytical Study of the Sketches and Drafts," pp. 113–46), and William Mitchell ("The *Tristan* Prelude: Techniques and Structure," pp. 242–67). Some of the ideas in the following discussion of the Prelude are borrowed from these two sources. Piano reductions of the complete Prelude can be found in the music anthologies by Charles Burkhart (*Anthology for Musical Analysis*, Fort Worth: Harcourt Brace, 1994) and Mary Wennerstrom (*Anthology of Musical Structure and Style*, Englewood Cliffs, NJ: Prentice Hall, 1982).

♪♪♪Example 29.2   Wagner, *Tristan*, Prelude, m. 82; Prelude to Act III, mm. 1–2; and the "Tristan chord" (Prelude, mm. 2–3)

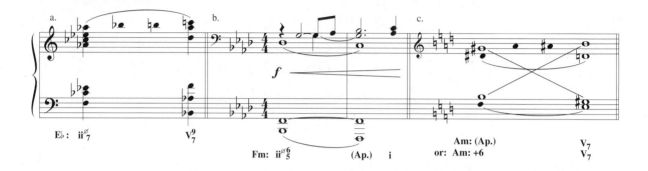

2. The chord appears numerous times later in the opera, in a variety of other tonal contexts which stress the ambiguous quality of this sonority, but which also show its use by Wagner as a more functional $^{\varnothing}7$ chord. Examples 29.2a and b, for instance, show appearances of this same sonority as $ii^{\varnothing}{}_7$ in E♭ and (transposed up a step and inverted) as $ii^{\varnothing 6}_{5}$ in Fm.

3. If we consider, then, the G♯ in the first chord of the prelude as the "real" chord tone, a linear interpretation of this chord, as presented in example 29.2c, seems to be plausible. *The chord has two common tones with V$_7$, the B and the G♯, which undergo a voice exchange, whereas the other two tones move by chromatic voice leading to tones in V$_7$.* According to this interpretation, we can think of the Tristan chord as an *appoggiatura chord* of the same type we studied in chapter 28.

4. Considering the G♯ as the chord tone, however, also allows for yet another interpretation which is not contradictory with the one we have just discussed. If you organize the sonority F–B–D♯–G♯ as F–G♯–B–D♯, you can verify that it is actually a type of +6 chord, framed by the +6 interval F–G♯. Although the standard "nationalities" for +6 chords are indeed the most commonly found types, we should not just dismiss the possibility of other intervallic arrangements for the two inner pitches that fill in the +6 framework in an +6 chord. The Tristan chord, from this perspective, is then an +6 chord in Am which resolves, as expected, to V$_7$, as shown in the alternative interpretation under example 29.2c.[2]

The double-tonic complex. In mm. 5–7 a second statement of the initial idea leads to a Mm$_7$ chord on G, V$_7$ of CM. And yet a third statement leads to V$_7$ of EM (or V$_7$/V in Am). Within the first twelve measures of the piece, Wagner has already established

---

[2] The linear interpretation of the Tristan chord was proposed by Mitchell in the article cited in footnote 1. The interpretation as an F–G♯–B–D♯ +6 chord, on the other hand, is proposed by Daniel Harrison in his article "Supplement to the Theory of Augmented-Sixth Chords," cited in chapter 25. Harrison calls this type of +6 chord the "dual German-sixth chord."

the tonal conflict that will prevail for the rest of the prelude. The music fluctuates between Am and CM (along with some other key areas), and EM is stressed throughout, both as a chord and as a key area, as the dominant of A. The prelude concludes on a dominant of C, leading to the beginning of act I in Cm. Moreover, modal definition is far from clear in *Tristan*, and thus both Am/AM and CM/Cm are present in the music. This fluctuating aspect of the prelude's tonal center (between Am/M and CM/m) is well expressed by the term **double-tonic complex**.

The opening unit concludes with a deceptive resolution of V_7 in Am (to the F chord in m. 17). Notice that this resolution completes the full-octave chromatic ascent that started in m. 2 in the top voice (from G♯ to the G♯–A, an octave above it).

The second unit (mm. 18–24).   The theme that begins in m. 17, beat 2, is known as the "glance" motive. The FM chord in m. 17, which functioned as a deceptive resolution of V_7 in Am, is immediately reinterpreted as IV in CM, and in mm. 18–20 we are back in the CM key area. Not for long, though: In mm. 21–22 Dm is implied (What is the chord in m. 21, beat 2, in Dm?), and in m. 24 we hear again V of EM (that is, V/V in Am). If we think of this section in Am throughout, the key areas are then III–iv–V (or CM–Dm–EM), all in fast succession. In m. 24 we reach some kind of a cadence on A (bass E–A), embellished by an appoggiatura chord. Could it be our first arrival on A as a tonic? As a matter of fact, it is the clearest arrival on A in the whole prelude, only it is AM, not Am; and as the music continues into mm. 25–26, clearly in EM, we hear the AM chord, retrospectively, as IV in E!

The third unit (mm. 25–36).   In mm. 25–29 we hear the "love potion" motive, in a sequential passage in which EM is again implied. The bass motive in mm. 28–29 is known as the "death" motive (B–C–D♯). In the measures that follow, several key areas are implied in fast succession: CM in mm. 32–33 (the glance motive again), and then FM and Dm (both briefly tonicized in mm. 35–36).

The fourth unit (mm. 36–44).   Notice the harmonization of the theme that begins in m. 36, beat 2 (the "magic casket" motive). We hear the two chords (on D♭ and C) as +6–V_7 in FM, then repeated an octave higher. What comes after is a sequence on this same motive, up by steps: we hear +6–V_7 in GM, and then what would have been another sequence segment in A (mm. 40–41) turns into a return of the glance motive and of the EM key area. You will have observed that in all these "key areas" (F, G, E) we have not encountered a tonic chord. All three have been "established" (or implied) by their respective dominants.

Look at the second chord in m. 42 (F♯ in the bass). It sounds like vii^{o6}_{5} of E, that is, vii^{o6}_{5}/V in A. And the new key signature, three sharps, seems indeed to announce AM. Now listen to m. 43. The first chord is the same sonority we just heard as vii^{o6}_{5}/V in A, now reinterpreted as vii^{o6}_{5} in C♯m! And by the time we get to the AM chord in m. 44, it comes as a deceptive resolution of V_7 in C♯m, that is, as VI in C♯. Or does it? Our excerpt really ends in m. 44, but we have included two more measures to show that actually the music goes on to EM, so we can also hear the AM in m. 44 as IV in EM! In other words, in spite of the "AM" key signature, we hear our AM chord in m. 45 in either C♯m or EM, but certainly not in AM!

So why this long discussion of a fragment from the *Tristan* prelude? Because it illustrates, perhaps better than any other work of the period, a stage in the history of tonality. In this stage, tonal ambiguity and instability become the norm, rather than tonal definition and stability. The music is in a state of constant tonal fluctuation, key areas are implied rather than established, chords often allow for several possible interpretations, and key areas are defined more by dominant than by tonic chords. Formally, the music is highly motivic, and melodic, motivic cells become the essential building blocks.

Tristan und Isolde has often been seen as a turning point in music history. Because of the enormous impact it had on composers, it represents an important step in the process toward the breakup of tonality. Composers who were directly influenced by Wagner's harmonic and melodic idioms in this opera include, among many others, Anton Bruckner, Max Reger, Hugo Wolf, Gustav Mahler, Richard Strauss, and Arnold Schoenberg in Germany and Austria, and César Franck, Gabriel Fauré, and Claude Debussy in France.

EXERCISE

To practice analysis of musical fragments featuring tonal ambiguity, implied tonality, or the double-tonic complex, refer to exercises 29.1.1 and 29.1.2 in worksheet 29 at the end of this chapter.

EQUAL DIVISIONS OF THE OCTAVE

The diatonic scale divides the octave unequally into some combination of tones and semitones. Functional harmonic root motions are based on unequal divisions of the octave that result from the diatonic scale, such as major and minor thirds and perfect fifths and fourths. There are, however, five possible divisions of the octave into equal segments. Each of these divisions requires the use of tones foreign to the diatonic scale. These *symmetrical divisions* are as follows:

1. The **chromatic scale** divides the octave into twelve semitones. There is only one chromatic scale.

2. The **whole-tone scale** divides the octave into six whole tones (example 29.3a). There are only two possible whole-tone scales using different pitches.

3. A **cycle of minor thirds** (the fully diminished seventh chord) divides the octave into four minor-third segments (example 29.3b). There are only three possible different °7 chords.

4. A **cycle of major thirds** (the augmented triad) divides the octave into three major-third segments (example 29.3c). There are only four possible different augmented triad chords.

5. The **tritone** divides the octave into two tritone segments (example 29.3d). There are six possible different tritones.

Because all of these equal divisions of the octave produce nondiatonic pitch relationships, using them as roots on which chords are built or as key areas will produce chromatic, nonfunctional tonal relationships. This feature of equally divided octaves

♪♪♪ Example 29.3

was used by composers in the late-Romantic period (and certainly also in the twentieth century) to expand (or to suspend) functional tonality. The examples we will now study illustrate some of these harmonic relationships.

First, examine example 29.4, which begins in E♭M. The passage moves sequentially up by whole steps: FM is tonicized in m. 151, GM in m. 152, and then AM and BM in m. 153, leading to a $^6_4$ chord on C♯ in m. 154. This progression by whole steps has obviously taken us away from E♭M very quickly! Although the music returns to E♭M shortly after this passage, the whole-tone scale allowed Chopin to create a moment of "tonal parenthesis."

♪♪♪ Example 29.4   F. Chopin, Ballade no. 1, op. 23, mm. 150–154

♪♪♪Example 29.5   R. Wagner, *Parsifal*, Act I, scene 2, mm. 30–41

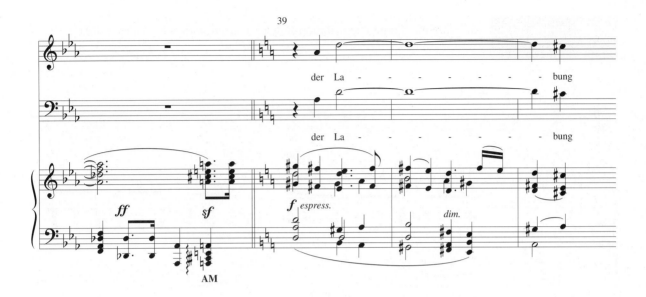

The keys tonicized in the Wagner fragment in example 29.5 also quickly take us away from the initial CM. As the Knights of the Grail assemble for a banquet, this solemn processional music moves through the distant keys of CM, E♭M, G♭M, and AM. Identify each of these keys on the score. How has the octave been divided by these key areas?

The Brahms phrase in example 29.6, on the other hand, takes us through the key areas of Cm, G♯m, Em, back to Cm, and again to G♯m, all in the space of five measures. Identify each of the tonicized chords in these key areas. How are they related intervalli-cally? The chords on the downbeats of mm. 24 and 26 are particularly dissonant against the bass, and obviously do not resolve until beat 2. What kind of chords are they?

The following example by Maurice Ravel will illustrate the close relationship be-tween two of the symmetrical divisions of the octave: the tritone and the whole-tone scale. The roots of the chord pairs in mm. 45–48 of example 29.7 are related by tritone: F–B, E♭–A. Now look at mm. 49–50, where you will see a bass motion in which as-cending tritones alternate with descending major 3rds. Put all the pitches of this bass together as a scale, and you will come up with a whole-tone scale. Notice that this scale contains two symmetrical halves of three notes each, and that the two halves are at the distance of a tritone (F–G–A//B–C♯–D♯). Ravel is here taking advantage not only of the symmetrical division of the octave, but also of the symmetrical division of the whole-tone scale!

EXERCISES

To practice writing progressions using equal divisions of the octave, refer to exercise 29.2 in worksheet 29 at the end of this chapter.

To practice analysis of musical fragments featuring equal divisions of the octave, refer to exercise 29.1.3 in worksheet 29 at the end of this chapter.

♪♪♪ Example 29.6   J. Brahms, "Treue Liebe dauert lange," from *Romanzen aus Magelone*, op. 33, mm. 23–27

BEYOND THE CONFINES OF FUNCTIONAL TONALITY

The types of harmonic processes we studied above (implied tonality, double-tonic complex, equal division of the octave, etc.) obviously resulted in a weakening of functional tonality. In some cases, however, similar processes lead not only to the weakening of tonality but, beyond that, to passages or pieces in which tonality is altogether absent. We will now examine two such passages, by Franz Liszt and Richard Strauss, respectively.

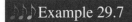 Example 29.7   Maurice Ravel, Waltz no. 1, from *Valses nobles et sentimentales*, mm. 45–51

An Example by Franz Liszt

The opening section of Liszt's *Faust* Symphony (example 29.8) is an excellent illustration of avoidance of tonal definition through the use of augmented triads and of long-range equal division of the octave. Some of the salient aspects of pitch organization in this passage can be outlined as follows:[3]

1. The lack of tonal definition becomes clear at the very outset of the movement. After the initial fortissimo A♭, mm. 1–2 feature a series of four arpeggiated augmented triads with roots descending by half steps, which not only do not create any sense of functional tonality, but moreover introduce the twelve pitches of the chromatic scale within two measures. The thematic material for the rest of the passage is also based to a great extent on augmented triads. Notice the descending scalar passage in mm. 9–10, based on two overlapping augmented triads (the two descending triads D♭–A–F and C–A♭–E).

2. Looking at the long-range design for this passage, we see that the bass in mm. 1–2 unfolds a chromatic scale from A♭ to E, and that E is again reached in m. 11 after

---

[3] An analysis of this passage, on which the present discussion is based, can be found in R. Larry Todd, "Franz Liszt, Carl Friedrich Weitzmann, and the Augmented Triad," in *The Second Practice of Nineteenth-Century Tonality*, ed. by William Kinderman and Harald Krebs (Lincoln: University of Nebraska Press, 1996), pp. 153–77.

Lento assai

the descending scalar passage in mm. 9–10. After the fermata, the initial thematic material is repeated beginning on E, now unfolding a chromatic motion from E to C. C is also the high point we reach in m. 15, and an octave lower in m. 17. The descending scalar passage in mm. 20–21 now leads to A♭, providing a sense of circularity to the complete section (which, of course, also started on an A♭).

3. In summary, we notice that no particular key is defined or established throughout this opening section. The pitches that stand out as points of formal articulation are A♭–E–C–A♭. Here again, the long-range design of the passage outlines an augmented triad, which divides the tonal space into equal segments.

4. Moreover, these same pitches constitute the main tonalities for the complete composition. The first movement is in Cm (with an important section in EM). The second movement is in A♭M, with a final passage that oscillates between A♭ and E. The third and final movement oscillates between the tonal centers C and E, and includes a final section that begins in A♭M and ends in CM. The equal division of the octave is here applied to the tonal design of a complete symphony.

5. We should remember that this opening is a musical evocation of the opening of Goethe's *Faust*, a monologue in which Faust expresses his disenchantment with life, philosophy, and religion, his desire to extend the limits of his knowledge, and his willingness to turn to magic to attain his goals. Liszt uses the augmented triad in a nontonal context, both as a chord and as a long-range framework, for his musical depiction of Faust's psychology and state of mind. Because of its ambiguous character and tonal implications, the augmented triad was indeed used in association with magic and mystery by composers before and after Liszt.

An Example by Richard Strauss

Example 29.9 shows a reduction of mm. 1–20 from Richard Strauss's 1894 song, "Ruhe, meine Seele!" (anthology, no. 58). Play through the reduction (or through this passage in the song), and try to hear tonal references (to a key or to key areas). You will discover that there are not any clear ones. The first two chords are built on an E pedal, and the voice leading is by half steps in all voices. Although the end of the song (and the key signature)

♪♪♪ **Example 29.9**   Richard Strauss, "Ruhe, meine Seele," mm. 1–20 (Reduction)

PRACTICAL AND CLASS DISCUSSION

In this chapter we have studied various harmonic techniques that contribute to the weakening of functional tonality. In some cases, functional tonality disappears altogether. How is tonal and harmonic coherence achieved in this type of composition in which functional relationships are missing? From our discussions, you will have noticed that linear relationships and stepwise voice leading are frequent elements of coherence in this type of nonfunctional harmonic language. Another possible factor of coherence is the symmetrical division of the octave into equal segments.

Discuss how melody and harmony are intertwined in the *Tristan* prelude. What has priority in Wagner's example, melody or harmony? The sense of forward motion (quite overwhelming!) in Wagner is created by numerous elements that constantly pile up tension. What are these elements? Although the music moves by itself, performances of the prelude vary enormously. Whereas some of them stress and play up the tension, others fall short of communicating and expressing the emotional and dramatic conflicts this music contains. If you were a conductor, how would you try to convey the dramatic power of this music? What elements would you use to your advantage to keep the music alive and moving forward? Would our above discussion of the piece help you in any way for this purpose?

indicates a CM key, these opening chords hardly function in CM: If you consider the roots, you come up with a Mm$_7$ chord on C, followed by a mm$_7$ chord on F♯ (roots a tritone apart). Considered as a whole, mm. 1–6 can be heard as chords built on a linear bass (E–D–C♯) and in which all other voice leading is by half step or common tone.

In mm. 6–13 we have a succession of Mm$_7$ chords built on an ascending-fourth bass pattern (that is, the circle-of-fifths fragment C♯–F♯–B) which, again, is hardly related to a possible CM key area. Finally, in mm. 14–20 the descending linear bass returns, but now it leads all the way to C (E–D–C♯–C). This is the first appearance of the "tonic" pitch, C, in the bass. Over it, however, we find the most ambiguous of all sonorities, a vii°$_7$ chord. You can see that eventually, at the end of the song, the same harmonic phrase (mm. 31–34) ends up leading to the functional progression in CM that closes the song. But what signs have you seen or heard of the CM tonality, or any other tonal center for that matter, in mm. 1–20?

PITCH PATTERNS

Sing the pitch patterns in example 29.10, which feature equal divisions of the octave.

> ♩♪♪ Example 29.10

a. WT   b. m3

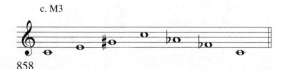

c. M3

858

ASSIGNMENT AND KEYBOARD PROGRESSIONS

For analytical and written assignments and keyboard progressions based on the materials learned in this chapter, refer to chapter 29 in the workbook.

 Composers and Their Music 29

Biographies

Write short biographies of the following composers mentioned in this chapter: Franz Liszt, Richard Wagner, Maurice Ravel.

Listening

Listen to the following compositions by composers mentioned in this chapter:

    Wagner, *Tristan und Isolde* (Act I).

Liszt, *Faust* Symphony.

Ravel, Concerto for piano and orchestra.

Follow the score while you listen. Be able to place each of these compositions in one of the style periods and to comment on why and how it represents the musical characteristics of that period. To what extent are each of these pieces ruled by the principles of functional tonality? Can you identify some particular passages in which tonality is clearly weakened or absent?

Terms for Review

Tristan prelude
Leitmotif
Tonal ambiguity
Implied tonality
Tonal fluctuation
"Tristan chord"

Double-tonic complex
Equal divisions of the octave:
    chromatic scale, whole-tone scale,
    cycle of minor thirds, cycle of major
    thirds, tritone

Worksheet 29

EXERCISE 29.1   Analysis.

1. Example 29.11. On a separate sheet, write a brief essay explaining the tonal ambiguity of this passage (which reflects the tonal ambiguity of the complete song). Does the term *double tonic complex* apply to this phrase? A translation of Goethe's poem on which the song is based is provided. How do the tonal characteristics of this phrase (and of the song) reflect the meaning of the poem?

> ♪♪♪ **Example 29.11**   F. Schubert, "Erster Verlust," mm. 17–22

First Loss

Oh, who will bring back the fair days,
Those days of first love,
Oh, who will bring back but one hour
Of that sweet time!

Lonely I feed my wound,
And with ever-renewed lament
I mourn the lost happiness.

Oh, who will bring back the fair days,
That sweet time!

2. Example 29.12. On a separate sheet, write a brief essay on this example, discussing the following matters:
   a) Explain the tonality of this excerpt. What are the keys? How are they established? What are the elements of tonal ambiguity?
   b) How does melody obscure harmony in this example?
   c) Explain the following specific passages from a harmonic point of view: mm. 1–4, 5–8, 10–12 (What key is implied in these measures?), and 13–15.
   d) This collection of songs dates from 1901–1904. What specific influences from Wagner and *Tristan* can you identify in this fragment?

Gustav Mahler, "Nun seh' ich wohl, warum so dunkle Flammen," from *Kindertotenlieder*, mm. 1–15

3. Comment on root and triad relationships in the following examples.
   a) Example 29.13.

Example 29.13   C. Franck, "Choral no. 1 Pour Grand Orgue," mm. 19–23

b) Example 29.14. In this example, focus on the relationship among tonicized triads.

Example 29.14   F. Chopin, Nocturne in GM, op. 37, no. 2, mm. 129–132

EXERCISE 29.2   On your own music paper, write four different progressions using equal divisions of the octave, in the following keys, respectively: EM, DbM, Am, and Fm.

Chapter 30

Nonfunctional Pitch Centricity

In chapter 29 we studied a number of harmonic and compositional techniques used by composers in the late Romantic period. A common trait of these techniques is their tendency to create tonal ambiguity and to avoid a clear definition of tonality or tonal areas. In some cases, moreover, the sense of tonic and functional tonality is completely lost. Music, however, does not necessarily have to be organized according to the principles of functional tonality in order to feature **pitch centricity** (that is, the organization of pitches around one or more tonal centers). In other words, the concept of "tonality" is not only limited to "functional tonality." In a broader sense, all music that features pitch centricity can be thought of as being "tonal" (although not necessarily "functionally tonal"). Multiple approaches to nonfunctional tonality can be found in the music of the nineteenth and twentieth centuries. In this chapter we will provide an introduction to nonfunctional pitch centricity of several types often found in the music of the late nineteenth and early twentieth centuries.

PARSIMONIOUS VOICE LEADING: THE PLR MODEL

Although the music of late nineteenth century composers such as Liszt, Wagner, Franck, Richard Strauss, and others is triadic, we have already seen that their triadic progressions often do not follow the functional model based on the circle of 5ths and on tonic-predominant-dominant relationships. We have already studied several alternative techniques of chordal organization (sequential and nonsequential linear progressions, symmetrical divisions of the octave, etc.). Now we will study another alternative model that accounts for many of the triadic relationships in the music by composers in the Romantic period, and which we will refer to as the **PLR model**, or also as **parsimonious voice leading**.[1]

---

[1] This section is a pedagogical adaptation of recent work by David Lewin, Brian Hyer, and Richard Cohn. I am especially indebted to the following articles by Cohn: "Maximally-Smooth Cycles, Hexatonic Systems, and the Analysis of Late-Romantic Triadic Progressions," *Music Analysis* 15 (1996): 9–40, and "Neo-Riemannian Operations, Parsimonious Trichords, and Their *Tonnetz* Representations," *Journal of Music Theory* 41 (1997): 1–66.

♪♪♪Example 30.1

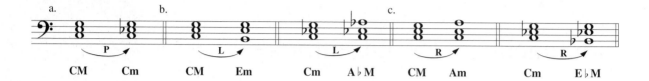

Examine example 30.1. In example 30.1a, the two triads form a parallel major-minor pair, defining a P (parallel) relationship. In example 30.1b, the fifth of one triad is the same pitch as the leading tone for the other triad (for instance, the fifth of the Em triad, B, is the same pitch as the leading tone for the C triad; and the fifth of the Cm triad, G, is the same pitch as the leading tone for the A♭M triad), hence the label L (for "leading-tone exchange"). In example 30.1c, the triads form a relative major-minor pair, and they define the R (relative) relationship. In all three cases, note that:

1. Each of the pairs includes a major and a minor triad. PLR transformations are always between a M and a m triad.

2. In all cases, the voice leading includes two common tones, while a single tone moves by half step (in P and L) or whole step (in R). Hence the term *parsimonious voice leading* (*parsimonious* means "frugal, stingy").

3. In L and R transformations, triad roots are third-related, although root relationships are not the main issue in this type of linear transformation, essentially based on common-tone and stepwise voice leading.

4. It is interesting to note that, although these transformations are usually associated with nonfunctional, highly chromatic music, the only chromatic triadic relationship in example 30.1 results from the P transformation (CM and Cm are chromatically related). You can verify that both L and R transformations, on the other hand, are effected between diatonically related triads. In other words, whereas P involves chromatic voice leading, the voice leading in both L and R simply involves a diatonic step.

The *Tonnetz*

A useful graphic tool to understand these three types of triadic transformations, their interaction, and the type of progressions they can generate, is a two-dimensional matrix of tones, or harmonic network, usually known by the German term ***Tonnetz***. Although several types of *Tonnetze* can be designed, each showing different tonal relationships, the type which we will introduce here, the *parsimonious Tonnetz*, is best represented by a matrix in which tones are related by minor thirds in horizontal lines and by major thirds in vertical lines. Examine the *Tonnetz* in example 30.2, and

♪♪♪ Example 30.2

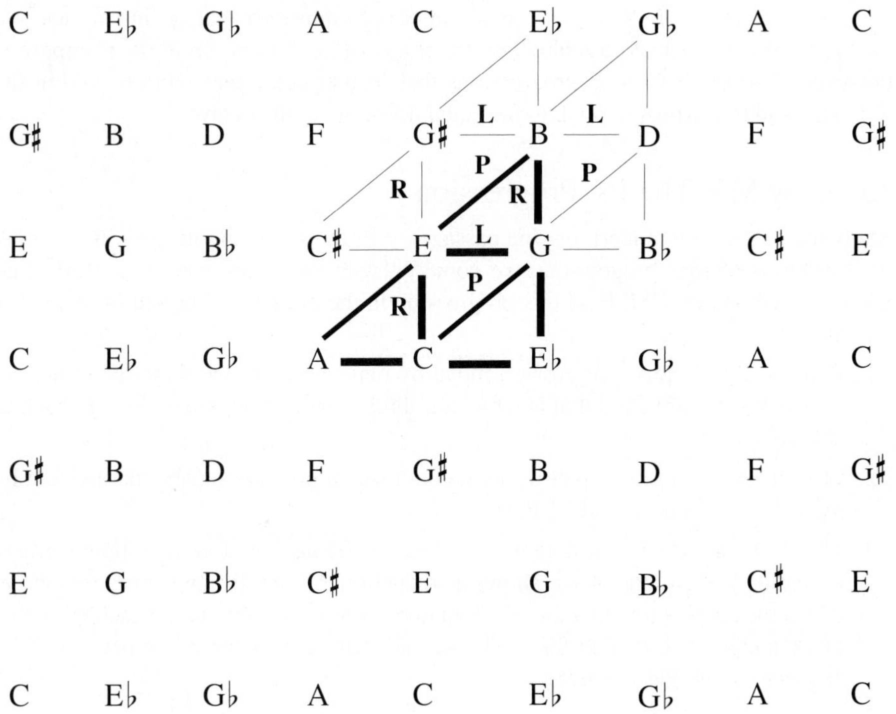

C	E♭	G♭	A	C	E♭	G♭	A	C
G♯	B	D	F	G♯ —L— B —L— D	F	G♯		
E	G	B♭	C♯ —E—L— G — B♭	C♯	E			
C	E♭	G♭	A — C — E♭	G♭	A	C		
G♯	B	D	F	G♯	B	D	F	G♯
E	G	B♭	C♯	E	G	B♭	C♯	E
C	E♭	G♭	A	C	E♭	G♭	A	C

(diagram labels: L, P, R transformations around center pitches)

understand how it works. Begin, for instance, from the center pitch, C, and see the intervallic increments of m3 to its right and left, and of M3 above and below. Now let us see how PLR transformations work within this *Tonnetz*.

1. A triad is represented by a triangle of adjacent pitches. Find, for instance, the CM triad, C–E–G.

2. Pairs of triads represented by adjacent triangles are related by PLR operations, and hence feature parsimonious voice leading. The three triads that share an edge with the CM triad, for instance, form the collection of triads related to CM by PLR (these triads are indicated by boldface lines in example 30.2).

3. In all cases, P-related triads share a hypotenuse; L-related triads share a horizontal edge; and R-related triads share a vertical edge. Identify these relationships on the *Tonnetz*, first from the CM triad, then from other triads.

4. As it is obvious from the *Tonnetz*, it is not possible to have two of the same operations in a row (PP, RR, or LL), unless you wish to go back to the same triad you started with (as in CM–Cm–CM). Thus, after P you must have L or R; and

after L you must have P or R. Before we go on, try to experiment playing several progressions using the *Tonnetz* as a guide (in other words, try "navigating the *Tonnetz*").

You will have found out that because after each move you can go in two possible directions, the number of possible different progressions is quite limitless. Composers, however, have often favored progressions that feature consistent motions within the *Tonnetz*. And this brings us back to the equal divisions of the octave.

Roots by M3: The PL Progression

Study the progression underlying the passage by Brahms in example 30.3. If we think of it in terms of root progression, we come up with the triads A♭M–G♯m–EM–Em–CM–Cm–A♭M–G♯m–EM. Find this progression in the *Tonnetz*. You will observe several things:

1. Roots in the Brahms progression move by major 3rds, hence they divide the octave symmetrically, and that is why after three pairs of M/m triads, we are back to the original pair.

2. The *binary operation* (a pair of operations) which produces this equal division by M3 is PL (or its retrograde, LP).

3. The PL binary operation is represented in the *Tonnetz* by a vertical line of transformations. Example 30.4a shows a reduction of the Brahms progression, in which the single pitch that moves from one chord to the next is represented with a black notehead. Example 30.4b shows the vertical path for this binary cycle as abstracted from the *Tonnetz*.

Roots by m3: The PR Progression

Refer to anthology, no. 51 (Liszt, *Consolation*, no. 4), mm. 18–26. Play through the passage, and identify the key areas that are tonicized. You will see that beginning in m. 18, beat 3, we are in D♭M, followed by D♭m in m. 21, EM and Em in m. 22, Gm in 23, and back in D♭M in m. 26. Find the beginning of this progression, D♭M–D♭m–EM–Em–Gm in the *Tonnetz*. You will see that:

1. Roots in this progression move by minor thirds, producing another equal division of the octave.

2. The *binary operation* which produces this equal division by m3 is PR (or its retrograde, RP).

3. The PR binary operation is represented in the *Tonnetz* by a horizontal line of transformations.

4. Liszt skips one step in the parsimonious progression by moving directly from Em to Gm, instead of Em–GM–Gm. Then he leaps a tritone by going directly from Gm back to D♭M. He nevertheless stays within the same horizontal path of transformations. How many steps in the process does he skip to leap from Gm to D♭M?

♪♪♪ Example 30.3 J. Brahms, Concerto for Violin and Cello, I, mm. 270–278

Example 30.4a

P   L   P   L   P   L   P   (L)

Example 30.4b

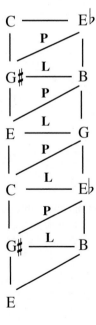

5. Example 30.5a is a reduction of Liszt's progression, followed in example 30.5b by a PLR reduction of the complete parsimonious progression on which it is based (with the steps skipped by Liszt indicated in parenthesis). Example 30.5c shows the horizontal path for this binary cycle as abstracted from the *Tonnetz*.

♪♪♪ Example 30.5

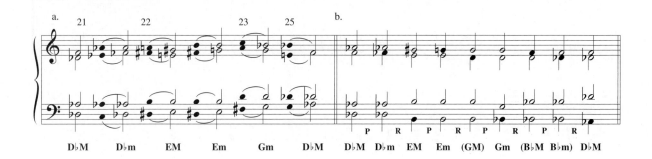

Roots Alternating M3 and m3: The LR Progression

We will now look at what is perhaps one of the most spectacular examples of parsimonious voice leading in the whole music literature: Beethoven's 9th Symphony, II, mm. 143–167, reproduced in piano reduction in example 30.6. Beginning in CM, the passage travels through the following triads: CM–Am–FM–Dm–B♭M–Gm–E♭M–Cm–A♭M–Fm–D♭M–B♭m–G♭M–E♭m–BM–G♯m–EM–C♯m–AM. That is, nineteen different triads in fast succession. Considering that there is a combined total of twenty-four major and minor triads, Beethoven gets close to (but falls short of) going through all of them! Of course, we would need to extend our *Tonnetz* from example 30.2 in order to see it represented in its totality. You can easily find, however, at least fragments of this progression in the *Tonnetz*, and you can verify the following observations:

1. Roots in this progression move by alternating major and minor thirds. This is not, then, a case of equal division of the octave.

2. The *binary operation* which produces the alternating M3s and m3s is LR (or its retrograde, RL).

3. The LR binary operation is represented in the *Tonnetz* by a diagonal line of transformations.

4. Example 30.7a is a reduction of a portion of Beethoven's LR progression, and example 30.7b shows the diagonal path for this binary cycle as abstracted from the *Tonnetz*.

Example 30.7a

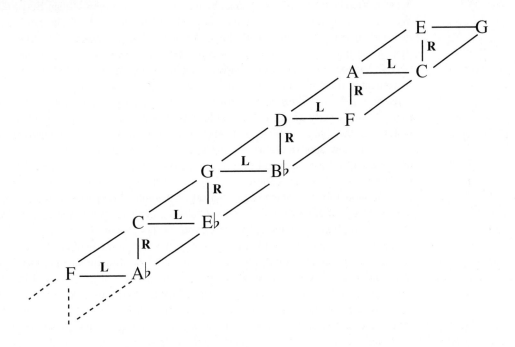

Example 30.7b

EXERCISES

To practice writing parsimonious progressions, refer to exercises 30.2 and 30.3 in worksheet 30 at the end of this chapter.

To practice analysis of PLR progressions, refer to exercise 30.1.1 in worksheet 30 at the end of this chapter.

ALTERNATIVES TO CHROMATICISM: NONFUNCTIONAL DIATONIC COLLECTIONS

By the end of the nineteenth century and the beginning of the twentieth century some composers were finding that functional tonality was no longer a satisfactory or viable system for the organization of their pitch structures. Various alternative systems of pitch organization appeared in these decades. In general, in the early stages of post-tonal composition we find two major trends with respect to the organization of pitch and harmonic materials. On the one hand, some composers, mostly in France and in eastern European countries, reacted to late Romantic extreme chromaticism by turning often to nonfunctional diatonic pitch collections (such as the pentatonic scale and the old Church modes) or to nonfunctional, nondiatonic symmetrical scales such as the whole-tone and octatonic scales. Composers in this group include Maurice Ravel, Claude Debussy, Igor Stravinsky, and Béla Bartók, and their music features, with few exceptions, some type of pitch centricity.

In the German-speaking world, on the other hand, the focus of post-tonal composition became Vienna, where Arnold Schoenberg and two of his pupils, Alban Berg and Anton Webern (a group usually referred to as the **Second Viennese School**), became heirs to the German chromatic tradition of Brahms, Wagner, Wolf, Bruckner, and Mahler. But although chromaticism remained an essential element in the music by the composers of the Second Viennese School, in their early-twentieth-century music we find a progressive replacement of tonal structures with such compositional elements as intervallic and motivic cells, nontriadic sonorities, and nontonal linear relationships. In general, we refer to their music from the early decades of the century as *atonal*, and by this we mean that it usually features neither pitch centricity nor other types of tonal structures as characteristic elements. The new approaches to musical syntax and composition these composers introduced would have a deep and lasting impact on twentieth-century music. The study of twentieth-century art music, however, is beyond the scope of this text. This applies especially to atonal music, which requires a set of theoretical principles and analytical techniques totally different from the ones we have learned and applied throughout this book. We will limit our discussion, in the remainder of this chapter, to some of the alternative means of pitch centricity found in composers of the first group mentioned above.

As we explained, some composers turned to nonfunctional diatonic scales and other diatonic collections as an alternative to the intense chromaticism of late Romantic composers. Excerpts from a single piece by Claude Debussy will suffice to demonstrate several of these diatonic techniques. But before doing so, you may want to review the scales for the Medieval and Renaissance modes which we studied in chapter C, as well as the section "Other Modes and Scales" in the same chapter.

An Example by Debussy

Listen now to example 30.8a. Although the term most often used to label the music of Debussy is *impressionism*, his style parallels in many ways the poetic style of Stéphane Mallarmé, known as *symbolism*, in which poetry loses its intensity by the explicit naming of an object. Instead, suggestion and subtle allusion are practiced in symbolism. The title of this prelude for piano by Debussy is "The Sunken Cathedral" (1910).

♪♪♪ Example 30.8a   Claude Debussy, "La cathédrale engloutie," from *Preludes*, Book I, mm. 1–15

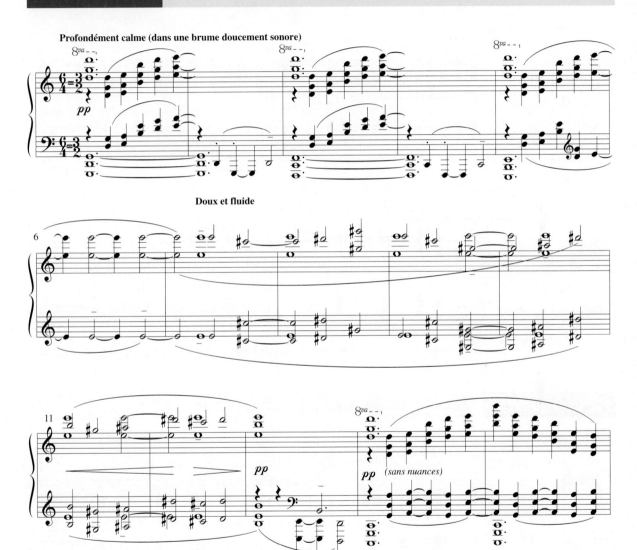

♩♪♪Example 30.8b   Debussy, "La cathédrale engloutie," mm. 28–40

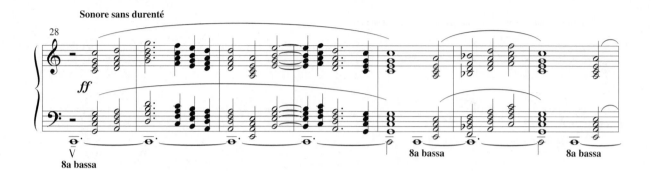

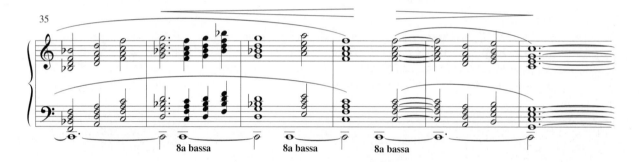

♪♪♪Example 30.8c   Debussy, "La cathédrale engloutie," mm. 62–66

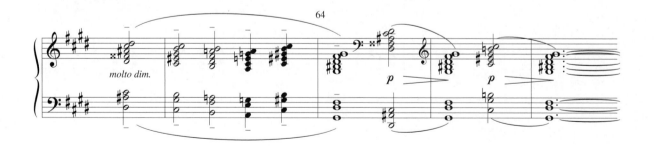

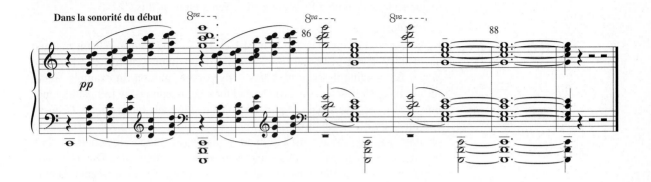

♪♪♪Example 30.8d   Debussy, "La cathédrale engloutie," mm. 84–89

How is the idea of a submerged cathedral suggested and evoked in this music? For instance, can you hear the distant, underwater bells? Now study the following musical characteristics:

1. *Pitch collections*

   a) What notes, and how many of them, are used in mm. 1–2? You will see that if we organize them as a scale, such as, say, G–A–B–D–E, we come up with only five notes. This is one of the many possible **pentatonic scales**, specifically one that contains no semitones. Because there are no half-step tendencies in this scale, it is tonally ambiguous: Any of its pitches can function as a tonal center.

   b) What kind of sonorities constitute the "chords" in the ascending motive in mm. 1, 3, and 5? Actually, these are not chords, but simply open fifths, evoking both the sounds of bells and of an archaic, ancient world.

   c) Examine mm. 14–15, where we see a complete phrase based on our pentatonic theme. What are the chords here? These are indeed chords, and they are *not* made up of thirds, but rather of stacked *fifths*. These are **quintal chords**, chords by fifths.

   d) Now look at example 30.8d, the phrase that closes the prelude. What chords are used here to harmonize our theme? Notice that the intervals stacked up here are *fourths*. These are **quartal chords**, chords by fourths.

   e) Let us find out more about pitch organization in this example. After the initial motive, a second theme appears in mm. 7–13. What we have here is simply a pedal on E and a melody doubled in three octaves. If you construct a scale based on E and using the pitches of the melody, what scale do you come up with? You will notice that it is a major scale on E with an A♯, a raised 4̂. What mode is this?

f) Later in the piece, the main theme appears again in a climactic *ff* in full sonorities, on a C pedal (example 30.8b). Consider the melody of this passage (the top voice only), and construct a C scale using its pitches. You come up with a major scale on C with a B♭, a lowered $\hat{7}$. What mode is this?

2. *Voice leading*

a) Comment on the voice leading in mm. 1–5, 14–15, and 28–40. What is unusual about it? Whether the sonorities are open fifths, quintal chords, or triads, the only voice leading in these passages is by parallel motion. In example 30.8b, for instance, all sonorities are triads, and their connection is by full parallel motion in all cases. This type of parallel voice leading, characteristic of Debussy and other French composers of this period, is called *planing*. Observe that in planing, parallel 5ths are not a problem in the least. Quite to the contrary, they become very much part of the sound wanted by the composer. This is a good example of how parallel 5ths and other voice-leading conventions are bound to specific styles. Although they would be avoided (and "wrong") in eighteenth-century common practice, here they are highly desirable!

b) In mm. 28–40 the planing follows the diatonic scale: We begin with a triad, and we move in parallel voice leading following the content of the diatonic scale. This will create, of course, triads of different qualities (M, m, or even diminished). We call this type of voice leading **diatonic planing**. Now look at example 30.8c (mm. 62–64). We begin with a Mm₇ sonority and we move in parallel voice leading in such a way that all subsequent sonorities are still Mm₇ chords. Accidentals foreign to the diatonic scale are immediately introduced. This is **chromatic planing**.

3. *Tonality*

a) To close this discussion of Debussy's piece, we will explore tonality in our excerpt. There is no question that this music features pitch centricity (that is, it has a tonal center). The piece as a whole is "in C." But we should not speak of CM or Cm, because we have not seen any instances of major-minor tonality and scales. How would you say tonality is established? Certainly not by functional progressions involving dominant resolutions. Rather, Debussy establishes his tonal centers in this piece (and elsewhere) with the use of pedal tones. We see this in mm. 14–15, 28–40, and 84–89 (all "in C"), and in mm. 5–13, "in E." On a larger scale, you can see a linear bass beginning on G (m. 1), then F (m. 3), then E (m. 5), down to D (m. 13), finally leading to the tonal center of the piece, C (m. 14).

Why do you think Debussy's harmonic language is so significant? We see that although in most of his music Debussy preserved the sense of tonal centers, his unconventional harmonic resources (such as the use of the diatonic modes, pentatonic and whole-tone scales, the avoidance of functional progressions, the use of parallel voice-leading techniques, etc.) create a musical language that breaks away from both functional major-minor tonality and from the German tradition of Romantic and post-Romantic chromaticism (including the pervading influence of Wagner). It is not for nothing that on his visiting cards Debussy identified himself as "Claude Debussy, Compositeur Français."

EXERCISE

To practice writing musical fragments using the types of scales and techniques we have just studied, refer to exercises 30.4 and 30.5 in worksheet 30 at the end of this chapter.

SYMMETRICAL SCALES

In the last chapter we studied the symmetrical divisions of the octave from a harmonic point of view. Among the several scales that divide the scale symmetrically, two of them, the *whole-tone scale* and the *octatonic scale*, were especially favored by some composers in the first half of the twentieth century.

The Whole-Tone Scale

We have already studied the **whole-tone** (WT) **scale**: it has only six different pitches, it divides symmetrically in two halves a tritone apart, and there are only two different whole-tone scales. Verify all of these characteristics at the piano, and experiment by playing with the two possible scales. You will hear that, because of its symmetry and because of the intervallic uniformity of this scale, any pitch can function as a "center," although the scale immediately takes us away from any references to functional harmony or to the major-minor system.

An interesting piece by Debussy is almost totally built on a single WT scale, the prelude "Voiles" (1909). Here again, notice what the title suggests: "veils," which evoke images of half-hidden, somewhat blurred forms, as in a symbolist poetic world. The music also moves in that same type of space, and a lot of it is due to the WT scale. Example 30.9a features the main theme of the prelude, in the right hand. Notice the chords in the left hand, built with members of the same WT scale as the theme. What kind of chords (or triads) are they?

In example 30.9b, on the other hand (the end of the prelude), we hear the theme again, now accompanied by two other types of chords. One type appears in the right hand, mm. 58 and 60, beat 1; the other type, in the left hand, mm. 58–61. Both types of chords are nontertian (that is, the intervals used to build them are not thirds, or not only thirds), and both types can be called *whole-tone chords*, because they are built with members of the WT scale. Analyze each of the types, and describe the exact interval combination used in constructing each type. What kind of voice leading is featured in both chord groups? As a final observation, these two excerpts reflect the rest of the piece from the point of view of tonal centricity. What do you think the tonal center is in the piece, and how does Debussy establish it? Could he have chosen a different tonal center with the same scale?

EXERCISE

To practice writing a musical fragment using WT scales, refer to exercise 30.6 in worksheet 30 at the end of this chapter.

Example 30.9a   C. Debussy, "Voiles," from *Preludes*, Book I, mm. 15–22

Example 30.9b   Debussy, "Voiles," mm. 58–64

The Octatonic Scale

The **octatonic scale** is an eight-note scale in which semitones (S) and tones (T) alternate. Study the scale in example 30.10a. Several interesting features become immediately apparent. This scale can be divided into two halves related by tritone. It is, then, another symmetrical scale. Play this scale (alternating S and T) transposed a half step up. You will come up with a transposition of the initial scale. Another ascending half-step transposition will give you a third scale, but if you transpose it again up a halfstep (beginning, by now, on E♭), you will see that the scale now contains exactly the same pitches as your original scale. Thus, there are only three possible different transpositions of this form of the octatonic scale.

There is, however, another form of the scale, shown in example 30.10b. In this case, also beginning from C, the pattern is **T–S–T–S** rather than **S–T–S–T**. As much as this shows you two apparently different forms for the scale beginning from a single pitch, there are still only three possible different octatonic scales in no matter what form. The scale in example 30.10b, then, has the same pitch content as one of the three possible transpositions of the scale in example 30.10a. Which one? Verify this point at the piano. You might enjoy spending a few minutes experimenting at the piano with this interesting scale and its transpositions. And you can notice, too, that the scale is also the result of overlapping two adjacent diminished seventh chords, as indicated in example 30.10c.

Now listen to example 30.11, an excerpt from Béla Bartók's *Mikrokosmos* (1926–1937), "Diminished Fifth." Play through mm. 1–5, and identify the scale Bartók uses in this passage. Of course, it is an octatonic scale. Write it in ascending order beginning on E♭. Is this a S–T–S–T or T–S–T–S type of scale? Notice how Bartók takes advantage of the two tritone-related symmetrical halves by placing one of them in each hand and presenting each of them as a motive. How are the motives related in mm. 1–2? What happens in mm. 6–11? The scale is the same, but how has it been texturally altered? At what interval is there imitation between the two hands in mm. 6–9? There is one single pitch, in m. 10, which does not belong to this scale. Which one? Could it be interpreted as functioning as a nonchord tone?

The new thematic material we hear in mm. 12–19 indicates that this is a contrasting phrase. Is it also contrasting tonally? What scale is it built on? After m. 19, the music goes back to the initial thematic material and the initial scale. Could we think of

♪♪♪ Example 30.10

Example 30.11   Béla Bartók, "Diminished Fifth," from *Mikrokosmos*, vol. IV, mm. 1–19

the change of scale in mm. 12–19, the contrasting phrase, as creating an octatonic "secondary key area" similar to the type of dominant-key secondary key area we have seen so many times in tonal music?

What does the octatonic scale do to the concept of "tonal center"? Consider, for instance, mm. 1–11. Is the tonal center E♭ or A? Or could we say that this scale creates a "double-center complex" such as, in this case, E♭/A, in which the two centers are a tritone apart? Do you think the title of this piece ("Diminished Fifth") is appropriate?

It is also interesting to see how another of the major composers of the twentieth century, Igor Stravinsky, broke away from Romantic chromatic harmony while at the same time preserving in his music a sense of pitch centricity. In anthology, no. 60, you will find a fragment from *The Rite of Spring*, one of the century's masterpieces, first performed in 1913. This is an eminently rhythmic dance (as is the case

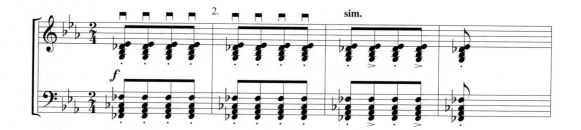

Example 30.12a   Igor Stravinsky, "Danses des adolescentes," from *The Rite of Spring*, mm. 1–4

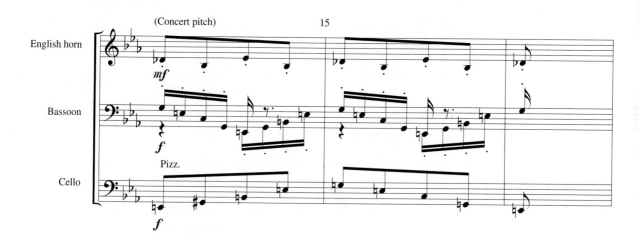

Example 30.12b   Stravinsky, "Danses des adolescentes," mm. 14–16

with most of the *Rite*), which features a chord hammered out in the strings in continuous eighth notes, some of them accented in an irregular pattern punctuated by the horns. Example 30.12a shows a piano reduction of the chordal texture in the initial measures. The chord is really a **polychord** (a chord made up of more than one chord), built from two different chords whose roots are a half step apart: In the left hand of the reduction (double basses and cellos) you can see an EM triad, enharmonically spelled as F♭M, and in the right hand (violas and violins) you have an E♭ Mm₇ chord in first inversion, that is, E♭$^6_5$. Does the pitch content of the complete sonority approximate an octatonic scale? Try to build an octatonic scale from these pitches (begin from E♭), and you will see that all but one of the pitches are part of the same scale.

The second musical idea in this movement is shown in example 30.12b. Here we have three layers of ostinato lines, each of them with a different harmonic content: The cellos arpeggiate two triads, EM and CM, in eighth notes. The bassoons arpeggiate CM and Em in sixteenth notes. And the English horn (written here in concert pitch) plays an intervallic ostinato pattern (alternating a m3 and a P4) with pitches from the E♭ Mm$_7$ sonority. The total pitch content for this passage includes all the pitches from the F♭M/E♭$^6_5$ polychord, plus the pitch C♮. How does this collection compare to the octatonic scale on E♭ you just built? In essence, in this example Stravinsky has dispensed with Romantic chromatic harmony by disposing of harmonic progression altogether, and replacing it with the repetition of a polychord and with layers of ostinato pitch cells.

Could we speak of some type of pitch centricity in this passage? First, notice that the two chords that make up the polychord are built on E♭ and E (or F♭), respectively, and that these two pitches are actually the lowest (F♭) and highest (E♭) pitches in the actual voicing of the chord in example 30.12a. They are also the highest and lowest pitches in the ostinato layers in example 30.12b. The English horn, moreover, seems to stress the centricity of E♭ by repeating the melodic turn D♭–B♭–E♭, which we hear as directed toward E♭. Considering all these factors, we could consider that the passage also features a "double-center complex," in this case made up by the pitches E♭/E.[2]

EXERCISES

To practice writing a composition using octatonic scales, refer to exercise 30.7 in worksheet 30 at the end of this chapter.

To practice analysis of musical fragments based on various scales and pitch collections, refer to exercises 30.1.2 and 30.1.3 in worksheet 30 at the end of this chapter.

CONCLUSIONS

In this chapter we have learned that music can be organized around one or more tonal centers without recourse to the principles of functional tonality. Late nineteenth- and twentieth-century composers have used a variety of techniques to create some kind of pitch centricity by nonfunctional means. In many other cases, however, pitch centricity has not been a concern of twentieth-century composers. Quite to the contrary, twentieth-century music has often been composed using techniques that explicitly avoid any reference to a tonal center of any type. Radically new approaches to composition and pitch organization were already fully operative early in the century. The old tonal methodologies we used effectively throughout this book are not appropriate to analyze this type of post-tonal music. New compositional approaches require new theoretical formulations and analytical means, and their study, beyond the scope of this book, will most likely be the next step in your music theory education.

---

[2] For a more thorough study of pitch centricity in post-tonal music, see Joseph Straus, *Introduction to Post-Tonal Theory* (Englewood Cliffs, NJ; Prentice Hall, 1990), chapter 4, "Centricity and Some Important Referential Collections." For discussions of pitch centricity in the music of Stravinsky and Bartók, see Robert P. Morgan, *Twentieth-Cen...* (New York: Norton, 1991), chapters 4 ("New Tonalities") and 8 ("Neo-Classicism").

ASSIGNMENT AND KEYBOARD PROGRESSIONS

For analytical and written assignments and keyboard progressions based on the materials learned in this chapter, refer to chapter 30 in the workbook.

PITCH PATTERNS

Practice and be able to sing scales in all of the Church modes, as well as the pentatonic and whole-tone scales. Then, sing the pitch patterns in example 30.13, which include quintal and quartal sonorities and octatonic scales.

♪♪♪Example 30.13

a. A PL cycle

b. A PR cycle

c. An RL cycle

d.   e.   f.

g.

Composers and Their Music 30

Biographies

Write short biographies of the following composers mentioned in this chapter: Claude Debussy, Igor Stravinsky, Béla Bartók.

Listening

Listen to the following compositions by composers mentioned in this chapter, *following the score while you listen*:

   Debussy, *Ibéria*.

Stravinsky, *The Rite of Spring*.
Bartók, *Music for Strings, Percussion, and Celesta*.

As you listen to these compositions, focus on pitch organization and tonality. Would you say that most of this music sounds like it features some kind of pitch centricity? Can you hear areas of functional tonality, or are you hearing mostly nonfunctional pitch centricity? What role do scales (modal, symmetrical, or otherwise) seem to play in this music?

Terms for Review

Pitch centricity
PLR model
Parsimonious voice leading
Tonnetz
PLR binary operations:
   PL, PR, and LR
Second Viennese School
Pentatonic scale

Quintal chords
Quartal chords
Diatonic planing
Chromatic planing
Whole-tone scale
Octatonic scale:
   T–S–T–S and S–T–S–T types
Polychords

Worksheet 30

EXERCISE 30.1 Analysis.

1. Refer to anthology, no. 51, Liszt, *Consolation*, no. 4. Determine the key areas in mm. 6–9 and 10–17. Explain exactly how these keys are related by PLR transformations. For this purpose, it will be useful to consider the modulation in m. 14 as passing through AM before moving on to F♯m.

2. Determine the scale or pitch collection on which each of the following melodies is based.

♪♪♪ Example 30.14

3. Determine the scale or pitch collection on which each of the following passages is based. In some cases the collection may not be complete, but all the pitches in the passage are clearly derived from it. In the examples of octatonic collections, determine whether the scale belongs to the S–T–S–T or the T–S–T–S type.

Example 30.15   B. Bartók, "Song of the Harvest," from *Forty-four Violin Duets*, no. 33, mm. 1–5

Example 30.16   Olivier Messiaen, "Danse de la fureur, pour les sept trompettes," from *Quatuor pour la fin du temps*, VI, reh. M

🎵🎵🎵Example 30.17   I. Stravinsky, *Symphony of Psalms*, I, mm. 1–4

EXERCISE 30.2   Write the following parsimonious progressions in four voices: (1) a PL progression, (2) a PR progression, and (3) an LR progression. Begin each of the progressions on a B♭m triad. (Use your own music paper for this and the following exercises.)

EXERCISE 30.3   Write a phrase for piano (melody and accompaniment) based on a PR parsimonious progression, beginning on an Fm triad.

EXERCISE 30.4   Write three melodies using the following scales: (1) pentatonic, (2) Phrygian, and (3) Lydian. Craft the motivic and periodic structures of your melodies carefully (refer to the melodies in example 30.13 as models).

EXERCISE 30.5   Write two phrases (melody and harmonic accompaniment) using the following harmonic techniques: (1) diatonic planing and (2) quartal chords.

EXERCISE 30.6   Write a phrase (melody and harmony) using whole-tone scale(s). Your chords should be derived from the WT scale (see examples 30.9a and b for models).

EXERCISE 30.7   Write a brief composition for piano or for two melodic instruments of your choice, using one or more octatonic scales. You can model your piece on Bartók's fragment in example 30.11.

Subject Index

Z

Musical Example Index